STUDENT TESTED, FACULTY APPROVED

W9-BZC-359

THE  SOLUTION

Every 4LTR Press solution includes:

Visually Engaging Textbook + **Online Study Tools** + **Tear-out Review Cards** + **Interactive eBook**

STUDENT RESOURCES:

- Interactive eBook
- Auto-Graded Quizzes
- Flashcards
- Media Quizzing
- KnowNOW!
- Career Transitions
- Games: Crossword Puzzles, Beat the Clock, & Quiz Bowl
- PowerPoint® Slides
- Videos
- Part and Chapter Cases
- Review Cards

Students sign in at **www.cengagebrain.com**

INSTRUCTOR RESOURCES:

- All Student Resources
- Engagement Tracker
- First Day of Class Instructions
- LMS Integration
- Instructor's Manual
- Test Bank
- PowerPoint® Slides
- Instructor Prep Cards

Instructors sign in at **www.cengage.com/login**

> "MKTG was a great way to help study for quizzes and tests. There were lots of different ways to challenge your mind and help you remember information.
>
> – **Jenna Rigdon**, Student, *Minnesota State University*

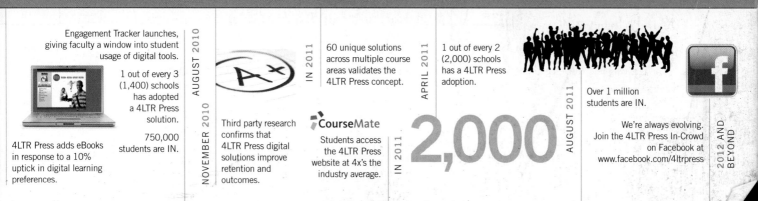

Engagement Tracker launches, giving faculty a window into student usage of digital tools.

JULY 2010

4LTR Press adds eBooks in response to a 10% uptick in digital learning preferences.

AUGUST 2010

1 out of every 3 (1,400) schools has adopted a 4LTR Press solution.

750,000 students are IN.

NOVEMBER 2010

Third party research confirms that 4LTR Press digital solutions improve retention and outcomes.

IN 2011

60 unique solutions across multiple course areas validates the 4LTR Press concept.

CourseMate
Students access the 4LTR Press website at 4x's the industry average.

IN 2011

APRIL 2011

1 out of every 2 (2,000) schools has a 4LTR Press adoption.

2,000

AUGUST 2011

Over 1 million students are IN.

We're always evolving. Join the 4LTR Press In-Crowd on Facebook at www.facebook.com/4ltrpress

2012 AND BEYOND

MKTG6

Charles W. Lamb
Texas Christian University

Joseph F. Hair, Jr.
Kennesaw State University

Carl McDaniel
University of Texas–Arlington

SVP, Learning Acquisitions & Solutions
Planning: Jack W. Calhoun

Vice President, 4LTR Press: Neil Marquardt

Publisher: Erin Joyner

Sr. Acquisitions Editor: Michael Roche

Developmental Editor: Laura Rush,
B-books, Ltd.

Editorial Assistant: Megan Fischer

Product Development Manager,
4LTR Press: Steven E. Joos

Associate Project Manager, 4LTR Press:
Pierce Denny

Marketing Manager, 4LTR Press:
Courtney Sheldon

Marketing Manager: Gretchen Swann

Sr. Marketing Communications Manager:
Jim Overly

Production Director: Amy McGuire,
B-books, Ltd.

Sr. Content Project Manager:
Tamborah Moore

Media Editor: John Rich

Manufacturing Planner: Ron Montgomery

Production Service: B-books, Ltd.

Sr. Rights Acquisitions Specialist:
Deanna Ettinger

Photo Researcher: Terri Miller/E-Visual
Communications, Inc.

Text Permissions Researcher: Ganesh
Kumar Alagiri, PreMediaGlobal

Sr. Art Director: Stacy Jenkins Shirley

Internal Designer: KeDesign, Mason, OH

Cover Designer: KeDesign, Mason, OH

© 2013, 2012 South-Western, Cengage Learning

ALL RIGHTS RESERVED. No part of this work covered by the copyright herein may be reproduced, transmitted, stored or used in any form or by any means graphic, electronic, or mechanical, including but not limited to photocopying, recording, scanning, digitizing, taping, Web distribution, information networks, or information storage and retrieval systems, except as permitted under Section 107 or 108 of the 1976 United States Copyright Act, without the prior written permission of the publisher.

For product information and technology assistance, contact us at
Cengage Learning Customer & Sales Support, 1-800-354-9706.

For permission to use material from this text or product,
submit all requests online at **www.cengage.com/permissions**.
Further permissions questions can be emailed to
permissionrequest@cengage.com.

Library of Congress Control Number: 2011943940

Student Edition ISBN-13: 978-1-133-19011-0
Student Edition ISBN-10: 1-133-19011-1

South-Western
5191 Natorp Boulevard
Mason, OH 45040
USA

Cengage Learning products are represented in Canada by
Nelson Education, Ltd.

For your course and learning solutions, visit **www.cengage.com**.
Purchase any of our products at your local college store or at our
preferred online store **www.CengageBrain.com**.

Cover and Page i Photography Credits:
Front Cover: © iStockphoto.com/Kenneth C. Zirkel, © iStockphoto.com/
1 design, © iStockphoto.com/charity myers, © iStockphoto.com/quavondo,
© iStockphoto.com/Christopher Futcher, © iStockphoto.com/Daniel
Laflor, © iStockphoto.com/Andy Dean, © iStockphoto.com/Les Cunliffe,
© iStockphoto.com/mustafahacalaki+B38; Inside Front Cover: © iStockphoto.
com/sdominick, © iStockphoto.com/alexsl, © iStockphoto.com/A-Digit;
Page i: © iStockphoto.com/CostinT, © iStockphoto.com/photovideostock,
© iStockphoto.com/Leontura; Back Cover: © iStockphoto.com/René Mansi

Printed in the United States of America
1 2 3 4 5 6 7 15 14 13 12

USE THE TOOLS.

- Rip out the Review Cards in the back of your book to study.

Or Visit CourseMate to:

- Read, search, highlight, and take notes in the Interactive eBook
- Review Flashcards (Print or Online) to master key terms
- Test yourself with Auto-Graded Quizzes
- Bring concepts to life with Games, Videos, and Animations!

Go to CourseMate for MKTG to begin using these tools.
Access at **www.cengagebrain.com**

Complete the Speak Up
survey in CourseMate at
www.cengagebrain.com

f Follow us at
www.facebook.com/4ltrpress

Stockphoto.com/A-Digit | © Cengage Learning 2013

ONE APPROACH.
70 UNIQUE SOLUTIONS.

www.cengage.com/4ltrpress

© Cengage Learning 2013

Brief Contents

© JURIAH MOSIN\SHUTTERSTOCK.COM / © THOMAS NORTHCUT/GETTY IMAGES / © ISTOCKPHOTO.COM\ELENA POPIC / © ISTOCKPHOTO.COM/PRILL MEDIENDESIGN & FOTOGRAFIE

Contents

3 Ethics and Social Responsibility 34

© ISTOCKPHOTO.COM/STEVE CADY

© ISTOCKPHOTO.COM/LEV DOLGATSHJOV

© ISTOCKPHOTO.COM/ROYDEE

© ISTOCKPHOTO.COM/DNY59

© ISTOCKPHOTO.COM/MILOS LUZANIN

© ISTOCKPHOTO.COM/VALERIE LOISELEUX

© FENG YU/SHUTTERSTOCK.COM

© SAD/SHUTTERSTOCK.COM

11 Developing and Managing Products 178

12 Services and Nonprofit Organization Marketing 194

© ISTOCKPHOTO.COM/CHRIS GRAMLY

© IVONNE WIERINK/SHUTTERSTOCK.COM

PART 4
DISTRIBUTION DECISIONS 208

© JOANNA ZOPOTH-LIPIEJKO/SHUTTERSTOCK.COM

© ISTOCKPHOTO.COM/KYOSHINO

PART 5
PROMOTION AND COMMUNICATION STRATEGIES 256

16 Promotional Planning for Competitive Advantage 256

17 Advertising and Public Relations 274

18 Sales Promotion and Personal Selling 294

© TACAR/SHUTTERSTOCK.COM

PART 6
PRICING DECISIONS 310

© ISTOCKPHOTO.COM/JEAN GILL

© LANA LANGLOIS/SHUTTERSTOCK.COM

© ISTOCKPHOTO.COM/JACOB WACKERHAUSEN

© ISTOCKPHOTO.COM/STEPHEN STRATHDEE

© ISTOCKPHOTO.COM/NICOLAS LORAN

© MICHAELJUNG/SHUTTERSTOCK.COM

PART 7
TECHNOLOGY-DRIVEN MARKETING 346

21 Customer Relationship Management (CRM) 346

© ISTOCKPHOTO.COM/LISE GAGNE

© ISTOCKPHOTO.COM/ED SWEETMAN

© ISTOCKPHOTO.COM/SAD444

WHY CHOOSE?

Every 4LTR Press solution comes complete with a visually engaging textbook in addition to an interactive eBook. Go to CourseMate for MKTG to begin using the eBook. Access at **www.cengagebrain.com**

Complete the Speak Up
survey in CourseMate at
www.cengagebrain.com

 Follow us at
www.facebook.com/4ltrpress

©iStockphoto.com/A-Digit | © Cengage Learning 2013

MARKETING

> "Marketing is too important to be left only to the marketing department."
> —David Packard

AFTER YOU FINISH THIS CHAPTER, GO TO PAGE 14 FOR STUDY TOOLS

LO1 What Is Marketing?

What does the term *marketing* mean to you? Many people think it means personal selling. Others think marketing means advertising. Still others believe marketing has to do with making products available in stores, arranging displays, and maintaining inventories of products for future sales. Actually, marketing includes all of these activities and more.

Marketing has two facets. First, it is a philosophy, an attitude, a perspective, or a management orientation that stresses customer satisfaction. Second, marketing is an organization function and a set of processes used to implement this philosophy.

The American Marketing Association's definition of marketing focuses on the second facet. **Marketing** is the activity, set of institutions, and processes for creating, communicating, delivering, and exchanging offerings that have value for customers, clients, partners, and society at large.[1]

Marketing involves more than just activities performed by a group of people in a defined area or department. In the often-quoted words of David Packard, co-founder of Hewlett-Packard, "Marketing is too important to be left only to the marketing department." Marketing entails processes that focus on delivering value and benefits to customers, not just selling goods, services, and/or ideas. It uses communication, distribution, and pricing strategies to provide customers and other stakeholders with the goods, services, ideas, values, and benefits they desire when and where they want them. It involves building long-term, mutually rewarding relationships when these benefit all parties concerned. Marketing also entails an

marketing the activity, set of institutions, and processes for creating, communicating, delivering, and exchanging offerings that have value for customers, clients, partners, and society at large

What do you think?

Marketing is selling.

1	2	3	4	5	6	7
STRONGLY DISAGREE				STRONGLY AGREE		

Find out what others think at the CourseMate for MKTG. Log in at cengagebrain.com.

3

© ISTOCKPHOTO.COM/SAN NGUYEN

exchange people giving up something in order to receive something they would rather have

production orientation a philosophy that focuses on the internal capabilities of the firm rather than on the desires and needs of the marketplace

understanding that organizations have many connected stakeholder "partners," including employees, suppliers, stockholders, distributors, and others.

Research shows that companies that reward employees with incentives and recognition on a consistent basis are those that perform best.[2] SAS, a business and analytics software solutions company, was voted *Fortune*'s Best Company to Work For in 2010. Employees at SAS enjoy perks such as a gym, on-site day care, massage therapists, classes focusing on health-related issues, and the ability for employees to set their own schedules. CEO Jim Goodnight says, "My chief assets drive out the gate every night. My job is to make sure they come back."[3]

One desired outcome of marketing is an **exchange**, people giving up something in order to receive something they would rather have. Normally, we think of money as the medium of exchange. We "give up" money to "get" the goods and services we want. Exchange does not require money, however. Two (or more) people may barter or trade such items as baseball cards or oil paintings. An exchange can take place only if the following five conditions exist:

1. There must be at least two parties.
2. Each party has something that might be of value to the other party.
3. Each party is capable of communication and delivery.
4. Each party is free to accept or reject the exchange offer.
5. Each party believes it is appropriate or desirable to deal with the other party.[4]

Exchange will not necessarily take place even if all these conditions exist. They are, however, necessary for exchange to be possible. For example, you may place an advertisement in your local newspaper stating that your used automobile is for sale at a certain price. Several people may call you to ask about the car, some may test-drive it,

and one or more may even make you an offer. All five conditions are necessary for an exchange to exist. But unless you reach an agreement with a buyer and actually sell the car, an exchange will not take place. Notice that marketing can occur even if an exchange does not occur. In the example just discussed, you would have engaged in marketing by advertising in the local newspaper even if no one bought your used automobile.

LO 2 Marketing Management Philosophies

Four competing philosophies strongly influence an organization's marketing processes. These philosophies are commonly referred to as production, sales, market, and societal marketing orientations.

Production Orientation

A **production orientation** is a philosophy that focuses on the internal capabilities of the firm rather than on the desires and needs of the marketplace. A production orientation means that management assesses its resources and asks these questions: "What can we do best?" "What can our engineers design?" "What is easy to produce, given our equipment?" In the case of a service organization, managers ask, "What services are most convenient for the firm to offer?" and "Where do our talents lie?" Some have referred to this orientation as a *Field of Dreams* orientation, from the well-known movie line, "If we build it, they will come." The furniture industry is infamous for its disregard of customers and for its slow cycle times. This has always been a production-oriented industry.

There is nothing wrong with assessing a firm's capabilities; in fact, such assessments are major considerations in strategic marketing planning (see Chapter 2). A production orientation falls short because it does not consider whether the goods and services that the firm produces most efficiently also meet the needs of the marketplace. Sometimes what a firm can best produce is exactly what the market wants. Apple has a history of production orientation, creating computers, operating systems, and other gadgetry because it can and hoping to sell the result. Some items have found a waiting market (early computers, iPod, iPhone). Other products, like the Newton, one of the first versions

© ISTOCKPHOTO.COM/DMITRY OSHCHEPKOV

of a PDA, were simply flops. In other situations, as when competition is weak or demand exceeds supply, a production-oriented firm can survive and even prosper. More often, however, firms that succeed in competitive markets have a clear understanding that they must first determine what customers want and then produce it, rather than focusing on what company management thinks should be produced and hoping that product is something customers want.

Sales Orientation

A **sales orientation** is based on the ideas that people will buy more goods and services if aggressive sales techniques are used and that high sales result in high profits. Not only are sales to the final buyer emphasized, but intermediaries are also encouraged to push manufacturers' products more aggressively. To sales-oriented firms, marketing means selling things and collecting money.

The fundamental problem with a sales orientation, as with a production orientation, is a lack of understanding of the needs and wants of the marketplace. Sales-oriented companies often find that, despite the quality of their sales force, they cannot convince people to buy goods or services that are neither wanted nor needed.

One of the dangers of a sales orientation is failing to understand what is important to the firm's customers.

When that occurs, sales-oriented firms sometimes use aggressive incentives to drive sales. For example, after Toyota recalled millions of vehicles due to acceleration problems and other safety concerns, the company implemented aggressive incentives to bring customers back. Zero percent financing, increased cash back, and free maintenance packages, as well as other incentives, enabled some customers to lease new Rav 4s for $169 a month, whereas before the recalls they would have paid $279 a month.[5]

Market Orientation

The **marketing concept** is a simple and intuitively appealing philosophy that articulates a market orientation. It states that the social and economic justification for an organization's existence is the satisfaction of customer wants and needs while meeting organizational objectives. What a business thinks it produces is not of primary importance to its success. Instead, what customers think they are buying—the perceived value—defines a business. The marketing concept includes the following:

▸▸ Focusing on customer wants and needs so that the organization can distinguish its product(s) from competitors' offerings

▸▸ Integrating all the organization's activities, including production, to satisfy customer wants

▸▸ Achieving long-term goals for the organization by satisfying customer wants and needs legally and responsibly

The recipe for success is to develop a thorough understanding of your customers and your competition, your distinctive capabilities that enable your company to execute plans on the basis of this customer understanding, and delivering the desired experience using and integrating all of the resources of the firm.[6]

Firms that adopt and implement the marketing concept are said to be **market oriented**, meaning they assume that a sale does not depend on an aggressive sales force but rather on a customer's decision to purchase a product. Achieving a market orientation involves obtaining information about customers, competitors, and markets; examining the information from a total business perspective; determining how to deliver superior customer value; and implementing actions to provide value to customers.

sales orientation the ideas that people will buy more goods and services if aggressive sales techniques are used and that high sales result in high profits

marketing concept the idea that the social and economic justification for an organization's existence is the satisfaction of customer wants and needs while meeting organizational objectives

market orientation a philosophy that assumes that a sale does not depend on an aggressive sales force but rather on a customer's decision to purchase a product; it is synonymous with the marketing concept

© ISTOCKPHOTO.COM/BOB INGELHART

THE ESSENCE OF MARKETING

A theme that you will find running throughout this text is the critical importance of providing a **good customer experience**. When one strips away all of the functions, plans, and strategies of marketing and asks the simple question, "What is this all about?" the answer is the customer experience. Think about it—whether you buy something a second or third time or become loyal to a brand depends on the experience that you had while purchasing and consuming the product or service. Most products need to be sold to a customer more than once in order for the company to start making money. Your favorite places rely on repeat business: a favorite grocery store, the local record shop/bookstore, the best stand in the food court. By considering the product, convenience, prices, and customer service, those places give you a good customer experience, all so you will come back.

Some firms are known for delivering superior customer value and satisfaction. The 2011 National Retail Federation/American Express Customer Service Survey listed Zappos.com, Amazon.com, L.L.Bean, Overstock.com, and Land's End as the top five U.S. retailers for customer service.[7] *Bloomberg Businessweek* listed L.L. Bean, USAA, Apple, Four Seasons Hotels and Resorts, and Publix Super Markets as its top five best-in-class Customer Service Champs.[8]

Understanding your competitive arena and competitors' strengths and weaknesses is a critical component of a market orientation. This includes assessing what existing or potential competitors might be intending to do tomorrow and what they are doing today. Western Union failed to define its competitive arena as telecommunications, concentrating instead on telegraph services, and was eventually outflanked by fax technology. Had Western Union been a market-oriented company, its management might have better understood the changes taking place, seen the competitive threat, and developed strategies to counter the threat.

© ISTOCKPHOTO.COM/SAI CHAN

Societal Marketing Orientation

societal marketing orientation the idea that an organization exists not only to satisfy customer wants and needs and to meet organizational objectives but also to preserve or enhance individuals' and society's long-term best interests

The **societal marketing orientation** extends the marketing concept by acknowledging that some products that customers want may not really be in their best interests or the best interests of society as a whole. This philosophy states that an organization exists not only to satisfy customer wants and needs and to meet organizational objectives but also to preserve or enhance individuals' and society's long-term best interests. Marketing products and containers that are less toxic than normal, are more durable, contain reusable materials, or are made of recyclable materials is consistent with a societal marketing orientation. The American Marketing Association's definition of marketing recognizes the importance of a societal marketing orientation by including "society at large" as one of the constituencies for which marketing seeks to provide value.

Although the societal marketing concept has been discussed for more than 30 years, it did not receive widespread support until the early 2000s. Concerns such as climate change, the depleting ozone layer, fuel shortages, pollution, and health concerns have caused consumers and legislators to be more aware of the need for companies and consumers to adopt measures that conserve resources and cause less damage to the environment.

Studies reporting consumers' attitudes toward, and intentions to buy, environmentally friendly products show widely varying results. Procter & Gamble has found that consumers want to buy environmentally friendly products, but not if they cost more or don't meet their needs.[9] On the other hand, market-research firm Packaged Facts found that sales of products promoted as environmentally friendly held up well during the recession, despite their premium prices. From 2004 to 2009, sales of "ethical" household products nearly tripled, reaching an estimated $1.6 billion in 2009.[10]

Many marketers have made substantial commitments to either producing products using more environmentally friendly processes or making more environmentally friendly products. Best Buy responded to the environmental concerns raised by its customers and workers by offering free recycling of large and small gadgets. This initiative fits well with the company's overall focus of helping customers get better use out of technology, whether they are buying, installing, fixing, or disposing of their hardware.[11] Burt's Bees, Whole Foods, Google, and Microsoft are also among the business leaders in the "eco-friendly" movement.[12]

What will the future bring? The current trends indicate that more customers are becoming concerned about the environment each year, more customers are trying to buy environmentally friendly products and support more environmentally friendly companies,

and more companies are joining the movement by developing processes and products that do less damage to the environment than in the past. A 2009 Cone Consumer Environmental Survey found that 35 percent of Americans continue to have high expectations for companies to produce and sell environmentally friendly products and services.[13] Adopting a societal marketing orientation and clearly communicating this decision and the actions that support it help firms differentiate themselves from competitors and strengthen their positioning.

© AP IMAGES/PRNEWSFOTO/BURT'S BEES

Burt's Bees is among the leading eco-friendly brands and uses ads like this to emphasize its "commitment to the Greater Good."

HOW DO YOU GET ALL THE MOISTURE
WITHOUT THE MUCK?

BEESWAX   VS.   PETROLATUM

Naturally replenishing moisturizer made by bees. / Non-renewable hydrocarbon made from crude oil.

Hydrating barrier that keeps lips moisturized. / Greasy film that could contain contaminants.

With pomegranate oil, keeps lips smooth & supple. / Sometimes used to stop corrosion on car batteries.

HAVE YOU READ YOUR LIP BALM LABEL LATELY?

beeswax · pomegranate oil · sunflower seed oil · coconut oil
BURT'S BEES REPLENISHING LIP BALM
Your well-being is important to us. It's our commitment to The Greater Good.

| customer value | the relationship between benefits and the sacrifice necessary to obtain those benefits |

LO3   Differences between Sales and Market Orientations

The differences between sales and market orientations are substantial. The two orientations can be compared in terms of five characteristics: the organization's focus, the firm's business, those to whom the product is directed, the firm's primary goal, and the tools used to achieve those goals.

The Organization's Focus

Personnel in sales-oriented firms tend to be "inward looking," focusing on selling what the organization makes rather than making what the market wants. Many of the historic sources of competitive advantage—technology, innovation, economies of scale—allowed companies to focus their efforts internally and prosper. But that same inward focus characteristic of the sales orientation has also led to the demise of firms like 3D Realm, Steve and Barry's, and SeeqPod.

Today, many successful firms derive their competitive advantage from an external, market-oriented focus. A market orientation has helped companies such as Zappos.com and Bob's Red Mill Natural Foods outperform their competitors. These companies put customers at the center of their business in ways most companies do poorly or not at all.

Customer Value The relationship between benefits and the sacrifice necessary to obtain those benefits is known as **customer value**. Customer value is not simply a matter of high quality. A high-quality product that is available only at a high price will not be perceived as a good value, nor will bare-bones service or low-quality goods selling for a low price. Instead, customers value goods and services that are of the quality they expect and that are sold at prices they are willing to pay. Value can be used to sell a Mercedes-Benz as well as a Tyson frozen chicken dinner.

Lower-income consumers are price sensitive, but they will pay for products if they deliver a benefit that is worth the money.[14]

The expanding and fiercely competitive luxury mattress market has prompted mattress companies to develop ultra-luxe mattress sets that sell for tens of thousands of dollars. California-based mattress firm E.S. Kluft incorporates luxurious fibers such as cashmere and silk into its products to entice customers to purchase its $33,000 mattress sets, which take roughly 20 days apiece to make by hand. Hästens, a Swedish company, offers to flip your mattress every month to add value to its $27,500 price tag. Department stores, such as Bloomingdale's, are even supporting the trend by offering a low-pressure environment where prospective buyers can test an assortment of luxury mattresses and well-informed staff are available to answer questions.[15]

Value is not about pricing alone, however. Barnes & Noble has relied on its comfortable, upscale bookstores to add more value to its book offerings than its competitors offer. For example, Barnes & Noble stores have sample Nook e-readers that customers can test out before purchasing. In addition, customers who bring their own Nooks to the store can take advantage of "browsing" services and read selected e-books for an hour at a time.

Old Logo

Marketers interested in customer value:

▸▸ *Offer products that perform:* This is the bare minimum requirement. After grappling with the problems associated with its Vista operating system, Microsoft listened to its customers and made drastic changes for Windows 7, which has been receiving greatly improved reviews.

▸▸ *Earn trust:* A stable base of loyal customers can help a firm grow and prosper. Residents in Brooklyn are fiercely loyal to their neighborhood's businesses. So, as part of their product introductions, Sixpoint Craft Ales brewery and Crop to Cup coffee did extensive sidewalk

New Logo

brand introduction in Brooklyn, offering passersby samples and personally developing relationships with local retailers to get their products on shelves and in restaurants. Both have made a huge market impact in Brooklyn through their constant presence, and Crop to Cup has opened its first store.[16]

▸▸ *Avoid unrealistic pricing:* E-marketers are leveraging Internet technology to redefine how prices are set and negotiated. With lower costs, e-marketers can often offer lower prices than their brick-and-mortar counterparts. The enormous popularity of auction sites such as eBay and the customer-bid model used by Priceline and uBid illustrates that online customers are interested in bargain prices. Many are not willing to pay a premium for the convenience of examining the merchandise and taking it home with them. Others will gladly pay a premium for an experience that is not only functionally rewarding, but emotionally rewarding as well. The superior coffee drinking experience and knowledgeable staff help explain why people pay $3 and up for a cup of coffee at Intelligentsia coffee locations in Chicago.

▸▸ *Give the buyer facts:* Today's sophisticated consumer wants informative advertising and knowledgeable salespeople. It is becoming very difficult for business marketers to differentiate themselves from competitors. Rather than trying to sell products, salespeople need to find out what the customer needs, which is usually a combination of products, services, and thought leadership.[17] In other words, salespeople need to start with the needs of the customer and work toward the solution.

▸▸ *Offer organization-wide commitment in service and after-sales support:* The Arizona Cardinals realized that their competitors were not only other NFL teams, but every organization that competes for the customers' entertainment dollars. The team hired Disney Institute, the professional development unit of the Walt Disney Company that helps other companies learn how to adopt Disney best practices and transform how they approach business. The Cardinals wanted Disney Institute to show them how to keep everyone in the organization focused on great customer service and help them draw in more customers.[18]

▸▸ *Co-creation:* Some companies and products allow customers to help create their own experience. For example, Case-Mate, a firm that makes form-fitting cases for cell phones, laptops, and other personal devices, allows customers to design their own cases by uploading their own photos. Customers who don't have designs of their own can manipulate art from designers using the "design with" feature at case-mate.com. Either way, customers produce completely unique covers for their devices.

© AP IMAGES/ARIZONA CARDINALS

Customer Satisfaction **Customer satisfaction** is the customers' evaluation of a good or service in terms of whether that good or service has met their needs and expectations. Failure to meet needs and expectations results in dissatisfaction with the good or service. Some companies, in their passion to drive down costs, have damaged their relationships with customers. Comcast, Dish Network, and Sprint Nextel are examples of companies where executives lost track of the delicate balance between efficiency and service.[19] Firms that have a reputation for delivering high levels of customer satisfaction do things differently from their competitors. Top management is obsessed with customer satisfaction, and employees throughout the organization understand the link between their job and satisfied customers. The culture of the organization is to focus on delighting customers rather than on selling products.

Coming back from customer dissatisfaction can be tough—particularly for enormous firms like Walmart. In 2008, the retail giant had a 45.5 percent customer satisfaction rating in the MSN *Money* survey. By 2010, however, customers' satisfaction with Walmart had climbed to 56.9 percent, the largest gain in the survey. How did Walmart improve so dramatically? The company targeted recession customers by re-vamping its stores to offer a more enjoyable shopping experience, and it increased its offering of upscale products at low prices. Even Walmart's new slogan reflects its focus on customer satisfaction: "Save money, live better."[20]

Building Relationships Attracting new customers to a business is only the beginning. The best companies view new-customer attraction as the launching point for developing and enhancing a long-term relationship. Companies can expand market share in three ways: attracting new customers, increasing business with existing customers, and retaining current customers. Building relationships with existing customers directly addresses two of the three possibilities and indirectly addresses the other.

Relationship marketing is a strategy that focuses on keeping and improving relationships with current customers. It assumes that many consumers and business customers prefer to have an ongoing relationship with one organization rather than switch continually among providers in their search for value. USAA is a

customer satisfaction customers' evaluation of a good or service in terms of whether it has met their needs and expectations

relationship marketing a strategy that focuses on keeping and improving relationships with current customers

YOUR MIRROR AND YOUR BILLBOARD ARE WATCHING YOU

Technology is allowing marketers to build more personalized relationships with customers in shorter amounts of time, but new technology is in the works that can customize advertisements in the blink of an eye. This type of motion recognition software can recognize gestures and facial expressions. One company, Barbarian, has introduced billboards that can tell when customers are paying attention and show them more of the text or imagery that caught their eye in the first place. Some use mirrors that scan an outfit the customer is trying on and recommend accessories to complement it. As this recognition technology develops, marketers may even use cameras to capture customers' faces and link to their shopping history—making in-person retail shopping more like online shopping. Motion recognition technology is taking relationship building to the next level and helping marketers step into the future—just don't roll your eyes, or you might offend your billboard.[21]

SOURCE: Emily Steel, "The Billboard that Knows," *Wall Street Journal*, February 28, 2011.

© CANDYBOXPHOTO/SHUTTERSTOCK.COM

empowerment
delegation of authority to solve customers' problems quickly—usually by the first person the customer notifies regarding a problem

teamwork collaborative efforts of people to accomplish common objectives

good example of a company focused on building long-term relationships with customers. In an annual Customer Service Champs survey conducted by *Bloomberg Businessweek* and J.D. Power and Associates, USAA has been the only company to be ranked in the top two for four years running. Not only does USAA have an incredible 97.8 percent client retention rate, but 87 percent of the respondents in the survey said they would purchase from USAA again. Clearly, USAA provides services to its customers that make their lives easier, and the customers respond very positively.[22]

Most successful relationship marketing strategies depend on customer-oriented personnel, effective training programs, employees with authority to make decisions and solve problems, and teamwork.

Customer-Oriented Personnel

For an organization to be focused on building relationships with customers, employees' attitudes and actions must be customer oriented. An employee may be the only contact a particular customer has with the firm. In that customer's eyes, the employee is the firm. Any person, department, or division that is not customer oriented weakens the positive image of the entire organization. For example, a potential customer who is greeted discourteously may well assume that the employee's attitude represents the whole firm.

Customer-oriented personnel come from an organizational culture that supports its people. American Express goes by the theory that "happy employees make happy customers." When giving its global customer-service division a makeover, it asked employees what they wanted, and then delivered. For example, employees received better pay, flexible schedules, and more career development. It also changed from the practice of keeping calls short and transaction oriented to engaging customers in longer conversations. The results of the changes have improved service margins by 10 percent.[23]

Some companies, such as Coca-Cola, Delta Air Lines, Hershey, Kellogg, Nautilus, and Sears, have appointed chief customer officers (CCOs). These customer advocates provide an executive voice for customers and report directly to the CEO. Their responsibilities include ensuring that the company maintains a customer-centric culture and that all company employees remain focused on delivering customer value.

The Role of Training

Leading marketers recognize the role of employee training in customer service and relationship building. Sales staff at The Container Store receive over 240 hours of training and generous benefits compared to an industry average of 8 hours of training and modest benefits.

Empowerment

In addition to training, many market-oriented firms are giving employees more authority to solve customer problems on the spot. The term used to describe this delegation of authority is **empowerment**. Employees develop ownership attitudes when they are treated like part-owners of the business and are expected to act the part. These employees manage themselves, are more likely to work hard, account for their own performance and that of the company and take prudent risks to build a stronger business and sustain the company's success. In an attempt to change Cadillac's image, General Motors is looking to wow its customers with excellent, fast, and reliable service. Emulating Ritz-Carlton hotels, Cadillac service chiefs are given $300 to $500 to spend on individual customers. A chief can reduce rates, give free maintenance, or reduce service fees for unhappy customers—all at his or her discretion.[24]

Empowerment gives customers the feeling that their concerns are being addressed and gives employees the feeling that their expertise matters. The result is greater satisfaction for both customers and employees.

Teamwork

Many organizations that are frequently noted for delivering superior customer value and providing high levels of customer satisfaction, such as Southwest Airlines and Walt Disney World, assign employees to teams and teach them team-building skills. **Teamwork** entails collaborative efforts of people to accomplish common objectives. Job performance, company performance, product value, and customer satisfaction all improve when people in the same department or work group begin supporting and assisting each other and emphasize cooperation instead of competition. Performance is also enhanced when cross-functional teams align their jobs with customer needs. For example, if a team of telecommunications service representatives is working to improve interaction with customers, back-office people such as computer technicians or training personnel can become part of the team with the ultimate goal of delivering superior customer value and satisfaction.

The Firm's Business

A sales-oriented firm defines its business (or mission) in terms of goods and services. A market-oriented firm defines its business in terms of the benefits its customers seek. People who spend their money, time, and energy expect to receive benefits, not just goods and services. This distinction has enormous implications. As a senior executive of Coca-Cola noted, Coke is in the hydration business.[25]

Because of the limited way it defines its business, a sales-oriented firm often misses opportunities to serve customers whose wants can be met through a wide range of product offerings instead of specific products. For example, in 1989, 220-year-old Britannica had estimated revenues of $650 million and a worldwide sales force of 7,500. Just five years later, after three consecutive years of losses, the sales force had collapsed to as few as 280 representatives. How did this respected company sink so low? Britannica managers saw that competitors were beginning to use CD-ROMs to store huge masses of information but chose to ignore the new computer technology as well as an offer to team up with Microsoft.

Having a market orientation and a focus on customer wants does not mean offering customers everything they want. It is not possible, for example, to profitably manufacture and market automobile tires that will last for 100,000 miles for $25. Furthermore, customers' preferences must be mediated by sound professional judgment as to how to deliver the benefits they seek. As Henry Ford once said, "If I had listened to the marketplace, I would have built a faster, cheaper horse."[26] Consumers have a limited set of experiences. They are unlikely to request anything beyond those experiences because they are not aware of benefits they may gain from other potential offerings. For example, before the Internet, many people thought that shopping for some products was boring and time-consuming but could not express their need for electronic shopping.

WHAT IS THIS FIRM'S BUSINESS?

Answering the question "What is this firm's business?" in terms of the benefits customers seek, instead of goods and services, offers at least three important advantages:

▸▸ It ensures that the firm keeps focusing on customers and avoids becoming preoccupied with goods, services, or the organization's internal needs.

▸▸ It encourages innovation and creativity by reminding people that there are many ways to satisfy customer wants.

▸▸ It stimulates an awareness of changes in customer desires and preferences so that product offerings are more likely to remain relevant.

Those to Whom the Product Is Directed

A sales-oriented organization targets its products at "everybody" or "the average customer." A market-oriented organization aims at specific groups of people. The fallacy of developing products directed at the average user is that relatively few average users actually exist. Typically, populations are characterized by diversity. An average is simply a midpoint in some set of characteristics. Because most potential customers are not "average," they are not likely to be attracted to an average product marketed to the average customer. Consider the market for shampoo as one simple example. There are shampoos for oily hair, dry hair, and dandruff. Some shampoos remove the gray or color hair. Special shampoos are marketed for infants and elderly people. There are even shampoos for people with average or normal hair (whatever that is), but this is a fairly small portion of the total market for shampoo.

A market-oriented organization recognizes that different

© AP IMAGES/PRNEWSFOTO/ENCYCLOPAEDIA BRITANNICA, INC.

IMAGE COURTESY OF THE ADVERTISING ARCHIVES

Most potential customers are not "average" and are not likely to be attracted to an "average" product marketed to an "average" customer. Shampoo ads like this one are aimed at the customer with a special hair care need, such as dandruff control or split ends.

customer groups want different features or benefits. It may therefore need to develop different goods, services, and promotional appeals. A market-oriented organization carefully analyzes the market and divides it into groups of people who are fairly similar in terms of selected characteristics. Then the organization develops marketing programs that will bring about mutually satisfying exchanges with one or more of those groups. Chapter 8 thoroughly explores the topic of analyzing markets and selecting those that appear to be most promising to the firm.

The Firm's Primary Goal

A sales-oriented organization seeks to achieve profitability through sales volume and tries to convince potential customers to buy, even if the seller knows that the customer and product are mismatched. Sales-oriented organizations place a higher premium on making a sale than on developing a long-term relationship with a customer. In contrast, the ultimate goal of most market-oriented organizations is to make a profit by creating customer value, providing customer satisfaction, and building long-term relationships with customers. The exception is so-called nonprofit organizations that exist to achieve goals other than profits. Nonprofit organizations can and should adopt a market orientation. Nonprofit organization marketing is explored further in Chapter 12.

Tools the Organization Uses to Achieve Its Goals

Sales-oriented organizations seek to generate sales volume through intensive promotional activities, mainly personal selling and advertising. In contrast, market-oriented organizations recognize that promotion decisions are only one of four basic marketing mix decisions that have to be made: product decisions, place (or distribution) decisions, promotion decisions, and pricing decisions. A market-oriented organization recognizes that each of these four components is important. Furthermore, market-oriented organizations recognize that marketing is not just a responsibility of the marketing department. Interfunctional coordination means that skills and resources throughout the organization are needed to create, communicate, and deliver superior customer service and value.

Word of Caution

This comparison of sales and market orientations is not meant to belittle the role of promotion, especially personal selling, in the marketing mix. Promotion is the means by which organizations communicate with present and prospective customers about the merits and characteristics of their organization and products. Effective promotion is an essential part of effective marketing. Salespeople who work for market-oriented organizations are generally perceived by their customers to be problem solvers and important links to supply sources and new products. Chapter 18 examines the nature of personal selling in more detail.

© ISTOCKPHOTO.COM/P-WEI

MARKETING POTENTIAL IN TWITTER

© ISTOCKPHOTO.COM/MATT JEACOCK

Ninety percent of the more than 300 million people in the United States are aware of the social networking site Twitter, but only 17 million Americans actually *use* it. With the huge potential for user growth, companies are looking for ways to use Twitter to increase brand awareness. The report *Twitter Usage in America* by Edison Research and Arbitron found that more than 40 percent of users locate and review product and service information on their accounts. Getting the word out to these users could be a potential boon for marketers, as long as marketers are offering fun information that doesn't seem like spam. The companies with the most successful Twitter accounts update them regularly and respond specifically to tweets to and about them. Check out @GrayWolfPress—it has more than 105,000 followers and focuses on fun, cheeky content that doesn't even necessarily relate to its books but keeps attention on the company.[27]

SOURCES: Courtney Rubin, "The Truth about Who's Using Twitter," *Inc.*, May 10, 2010; Jessie Kunhardt, "The Best Publisher on Twitter and Facebook," *Huffington Post*, June 24, 2010.

LO4 Why Study Marketing?

Now that you understand the meaning of the term *marketing,* why it is important to adopt a marketing orientation, and how organizations implement this philosophy, you may be asking, "What's in it for me?" or "Why should I study marketing?" These are important questions whether you are majoring in a business field other than marketing (such as accounting, finance, or management information systems) or a nonbusiness field (such as journalism, education, or agriculture). There are several important reasons to study marketing: Marketing plays an important role in society, marketing is important to businesses, marketing offers outstanding career opportunities, and marketing affects your life every day.

Marketing Plays an Important Role in Society

The total population of the United States exceeds 310 million people.[28] Think about how many transactions are needed each day to feed, clothe, and shelter a population of this size. The number is huge. And yet it all works quite well, partly because the well-developed U.S. economic system efficiently distributes the output of farms and factories. A typical U.S. family, for example, consumes 2.5 tons of food a year. Marketing makes food available when we want it, in desired quantities, at accessible locations, and in sanitary and convenient packages and forms (such as instant and frozen foods).

Marketing Is Important to Businesses

The fundamental objectives of most businesses are survival, profits, and growth. Marketing contributes directly to achieving these objectives. Marketing includes the following activities, which are vital to business organizations: assessing the wants and satisfactions of present and potential customers, designing and managing product offerings, determining prices and pricing policies, developing distribution strategies, and communicating with present and potential customers.

All businesspeople, regardless of specialization or area of responsibility, need to be familiar with the terminology and fundamentals of accounting, finance, management, and marketing. People in all business areas need to be able to communicate with specialists in other areas. Furthermore, marketing is not just a job done by people in a marketing department. Marketing is a part of the job of everyone in the organization. Therefore, a basic understanding of marketing is important to all businesspeople.

Marketing Offers Outstanding Career Opportunities

Between one-fourth and one-third of the entire civilian workforce in the United States performs marketing activities. Marketing offers great career opportunities in such areas as professional selling, marketing research, advertising, retail buying, distribution management, product management, product development, and wholesaling. Marketing career opportunities also exist in a variety of nonbusiness organizations, including hospitals, museums, universities, the armed forces, and various government and social service agencies.

Marketing in Everyday Life

Marketing plays a major role in your everyday life. You participate in the marketing process as a consumer of goods and services. About half of every dollar you spend pays for marketing costs, such as marketing research, product development, packaging, transportation, storage, advertising, and sales expenses. By developing a better understanding of marketing, you will become a better-informed consumer. You will better understand the buying process and be able to negotiate more effectively with sellers. Moreover, you will be better prepared to demand satisfaction when the goods and services you buy do not meet the standards promised by the manufacturer or the marketer.

STUDY TOOLS CHAPTER 1

Flip to the back of your textbook to:

❑ **Rip out Chapter Review Card**

Log in to the CourseMate for MKTG at cengagebrain.com to:

❑ **Review Key Terms Flash Cards (Print or Online)**

❑ **Review Audio and Visual Summaries**

❑ **Complete both Practice Quizzes to prepare for tests**

❑ **Play "Beat the Clock" and "Quizbowl" to master concepts**

❑ **Complete "Crossword Puzzle" to review key terms**

❑ **Watch the video on "Method" for a real company example on Marketing**

4LTR Press solutions are designed for today's learners through the continuous feedback of students like you. Tell us what you think about MKTG and help us improve the learning experience for future students.

YOUR FEEDBACK MATTERS.

© iStockphoto.com/mustafahacalak | © Cengage Learning 2013

Complete the Speak Up survey in CourseMate at www.cengagebrain.com

 Follow us at www.facebook.com/4ltrpress

Strategic Planning for Competitive Advantage

A good strategic plan can help protect and grow the firm's resources.

LO 1 The Nature of Strategic Planning

AFTER YOU FINISH THIS CHAPTER, GO TO PAGE 32 FOR STUDY TOOLS

Strategic planning is the managerial process of creating and maintaining a fit between the organization's objectives and resources and the evolving market opportunities. The goal of strategic planning is long-run profitability and growth. Thus, strategic decisions require long-term commitments of resources.

A strategic error can threaten a firm's survival. On the other hand, a good strategic plan can help protect and grow the firm's resources. For instance, if the March of Dimes had decided to focus only on fighting polio, the organization would no longer exist because polio is widely viewed as a conquered disease. The March of Dimes survived by making the strategic decision to switch to fighting birth defects.

Strategic marketing management addresses two questions: What is the organization's main activity at a particular time? How will it reach its goals? The next page has some examples of strategic decisions.

strategic planning
the managerial process of creating and maintaining a fit between the organization's objectives and resources and the evolving market opportunities

What do you think?

The marketing plan is only as good as the information it contains and the effort, creativity, and thought that went into it.

1 2 3 4 5 6 7
STRONGLY DISAGREE   STRONGLY AGREE

Find out what others think at the CourseMate for MKTG. Log in at cengagebrain.com. | 17

© ISTOCKPHOTO.COM/DEM10

strategic business unit (SBU) a subgroup of a single business or collection of related businesses within the larger organization

▸▸ Macy's is implementing an additional beauty sales approach to more niche markets. Impulse Beauty showcases a variety of smaller brands and allows shoppers to browse by themselves. If customers prefer assistance, the Impulse Beauty advisers are well versed in multiple lines. The idea is to provide access to additional items that are unique to that store's area and shopper. Macy's has already implemented a similar strategy in apparel.[1]

▸▸ Saab, the struggling Swedish automobile nameplate, had been owned by General Motors for nearly 20 years before the debt-ridden company sold Saab to a boutique carmaker called Spyker Cars in 2010. Despite the hope for reinvention, Spyker struggled to revitalize the brand. In order for the once popular brand to survive, Saab was sold once more in October 2011 to two Chinese carmakers who also purchased Volvo from Ford in 2010. [2]

▸▸ PepsiCo has decided to grow its portfolio of "healthy fare" business from $10 billion to $30 billion over the next decade. In order to reach this goal, the company has hired physicians and PhDs who have researched diabetes and heart disease to help in developing healthier snack-food options.[3]

All these decisions have affected or will affect each organization's long-run course, its allocation of resources, and ultimately its financial success. In contrast, an operating decision, such as changing the package design for Post Toasties or altering the sweetness of a Kraft salad dressing, probably won't have a big impact on the long-run profitability of the company.

COURTESY DAISY BRAND LLC.

This ad for Daisy cottage cheese shows five different ways to use the product. Daisy is hoping to increase market share among existing customers by encouraging its use as an ingredient in various meals.

LO 2 Strategic Business Units

Large companies may manage a number of very different businesses, called **strategic business units (SBUs)**. Each SBU has its own rate of return on investment, growth potential, and associated risks, and requires its own strategies and funding. When properly created, an SBU has the following characterisstics:

▸▸ A distinct mission and a specific target market

▸▸ Control over its resources

▸▸ Its own competitors

▸▸ A single business or a collection of related businesses

▸▸ Plans independent of the other SBUs in the total organization.

In theory, an SBU should have its own resources for handling basic business functions: accounting, engineering, manufacturing, and marketing. In practice, however, because of company tradition, management philosophy, and production and distribution economies, SBUs sometimes share manufacturing facilities, distribution channels, and even top managers.

LO 3 Strategic Alternatives

There are several tools available that a company, or SBU, can use to manage the strategic direction of its portfolio of businesses. Three of the most commonly used tools are Ansoff's strategic opportunity matrix, the Boston Consulting Group model, and the General Electric model. Selecting which strategic alternative to pursue depends on which of two philosophies a company maintains about when to expect profits—right away or after increasing market share. In the long run, market share and profitability are compatible goals. For example, Michelin, the tire producer, consistently sacrifices short-term profits to achieve market share. On the other hand, IBM stresses profitability and stock valuation over market share, quality, and customer service. As you can see, the same strategic alternative may be viewed entirely differently by different firms.

Ansoff's Opportunity Matrix

One method for developing alternatives is Ansoff's strategic opportunity matrix (see Exhibit 2.1), which matches products with markets. Firms can explore these four options:

▶▶ *Market penetration:* A firm using the **market penetration** alternative would try to increase market share among existing customers. Kraft Foods introduced an advertising campaign to try and get consumers of its Philadelphia brand cream cheese to think about using it on more than just bagels for breakfast. For example, one ad shows a female accountant eating a cracker topped with Philadelphia cream cheese to refuel during an afternoon break.[4] Customer databases, discussed in Chapters 9 and 21, would help managers implement this strategy.

▶▶ *Market development:* **Market development** means attracting new customers to existing products. Ideally, new uses for old products stimulate additional sales among existing customers while also bringing in new buyers. McDonald's, for example, has opened restaurants in Russia, China, and Italy and is eagerly expanding into Eastern European countries. In the nonprofit arena, the growing emphasis on continuing education and executive development by colleges and universities is a market development strategy.

▶▶ *Product development:* A **product development** strategy entails the creation of new products for present markets. McDonald's introduced yogurt parfaits, entrée salads, and fruit to offer its current customers more healthy options. Managers following the product development strategy can rely on their extensive knowledge of the target audience. They usually have a good feel for what customers like and dislike about current products and what existing needs are not being met. In addition, managers can rely on established distribution channels.

▶▶ *Diversification:* **Diversification** is a strategy of increasing sales by introducing new products into new markets. For example, CVS, which has always stocked cosmetics, launched adjacent Beauty 360 stores that stock premium cosmetic lines. Forty percent of shoppers at Beauty 360 are new customers looking for great customer service and premium cosmetic lines.[5] C. Dean Metropoulos, a private equity investor, has traditionally made its living off pantry staples such as Bumble Bee Tuna and Vlasic pickles, but the company purchased Pabst Brewing Company, and is diversifying into adult beverages.[6] A diversification strategy can be risky when a firm is entering unfamiliar markets. On the other hand, it can be very profitable when a firm is entering markets with little or no competition.

The Boston Consulting Group Model

Management must find a balance among the SBUs that yields the overall organization's desired growth and profits with an acceptable level of risk. Some SBUs generate large amounts of cash, and others need cash to foster growth. The challenge is to balance the organization's "portfolio" of SBUs for the best long-term performance.

To determine the future cash contributions and cash requirements expected for each SBU, managers

market penetration a marketing strategy that tries to increase market share among existing customers

market development a marketing strategy that entails attracting new customers to existing products

product development a marketing strategy that entails the creation of new products for present markets

diversification a strategy of increasing sales by introducing new products into new markets

---

EXHIBIT 2.1
Ansoff's Strategic Opportunity Matrix

	Present Product	**New Product**
Present Market	*Market Penetration* Starbucks sells more coffee to customers who register their reloadable Starbucks cards.	*Product Development* Starbucks develops powdered instant coffee called Via.
New Market	*Market Development* Starbucks opens stores in Brazil and Chile.	*Diversification* Starbucks launches Hear Music and buys Ethos Water.

© CENGAGE LEARNING 2013

portfolio matrix a tool for allocating resources among products or strategic business units on the basis of relative market share and market growth rate

star in the portfolio matrix, a business unit that is a fast-growing market leader

cash cow in the portfolio matrix, a business unit that generates more cash than it needs to maintain its market share

problem child (question mark) in the portfolio matrix, a business unit that shows rapid growth but poor profit margins

dog in the portfolio matrix, a business unit that has low growth potential and a small market share

can use the Boston Consulting Group's portfolio matrix. The **portfolio matrix** classifies each SBU by its present or forecast growth and market share. The underlying assumption is that market share and profitability are strongly linked. The measure of market share used in the portfolio approach is *relative market share*, the ratio between the company's share and the share of the largest competitor. For example, if a firm has a 50 percent share and the competitor has 5 percent, the ratio is 10 to 1. If a firm has a 10 percent market share and the largest competitor has 20 percent, the ratio is 0.5 to 1.

Exhibit 2.2 is a hypothetical portfolio matrix for a computer manufacturer. The size of the circle in each cell of the matrix represents dollar sales of the SBU relative to dollar sales of the company's other SBUs. The portfolio matrix breaks SBUs into four categories:

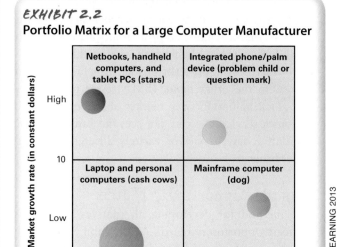

EXHIBIT 2.2
Portfolio Matrix for a Large Computer Manufacturer

Market growth rate (in constant dollars) — High / 10 / Low

- Netbooks, handheld computers, and tablet PCs (stars)
- Integrated phone/palm device (problem child or question mark)
- Laptop and personal computers (cash cows)
- Mainframe computer (dog)

Market share dominance (share relative to largest competitor): 10x / High / 1x / Low / 0.1x

© CENGAGE LEARNING 2013

▸▸ *Stars:* A **star** is a fast-growing market leader. For example, the iPad is Apple's current star. Star SBUs usually have large profits but need lots of cash to finance rapid growth. The best marketing tactic is to protect existing market share by reinvesting earnings in product improvement, better distribution, more promotion, and production efficiency. Management must capture new users as they enter the market.

▸▸ *Cash cows:* A **cash cow** is an SBU that generates more cash than it needs to maintain its market share. It is in a low-growth market, but the product has a dominant market share. Personal computers and laptops are categorized as cash cows in Exhibit 2.2. The basic strategy for a cash cow is to maintain market dominance by being the price leader and making technological improvements in the product. Managers should resist pressure to extend the basic line unless they can dramatically increase demand. Instead, they should allocate excess cash to the product categories where growth prospects are the greatest. The Macintosh line is Apple's cash cow. Despite ending its "I'm a Mac" ad campaign, Apple sold more than 3.36 million Macs in the first quarter of 2010. (It sold 3.29 million in all of 2004.)[7] Another example is Heinz, which has two cash cows: ketchup and Weight Watchers frozen dinners.

▸▸ *Problem children:* A **problem child**, also called a **question mark**, shows rapid growth but poor profit margins. It has a low market share in a high-growth industry. Problem children need a great deal of cash. Without cash support, they eventually become dogs. The strategy options are to invest heavily to gain better market share, acquire competitors to get the necessary market share, or drop the SBU. Sometimes a firm can reposition the products of the SBU to move them into the star category. Elixir guitar strings, made by W.L. Gore & Associates, maker of Gore-Tex and Glide floss, were originally tested and marketed to Walt Disney theme parks to control puppets. After trial and failure, Gore repositioned and marketed heavily to musicians, who have loved the strings ever since.

▸▸ *Dogs:* A **dog** has low growth potential and a small market share. Most dogs eventually leave the marketplace. In the computer manufacturer example, the mainframe

© AIMVBAENR/SHUTTERSTOCK.COM

computer has become a dog. Other examples include Warner-Lambert's Reef mouthwash and Campbell's Red Kettle soups. Microsoft stopped developing its Kin phone series after only two months on the market because it failed to connect with buyers in a market flooded with iPhones and Androids.[8] The strategy options for dogs are to harvest or divest.

After classifying the company's SBUs in the matrix, the next step is to allocate future resources for each. The four basic strategies are to:

▶▶ *Build:* If an organization has an SBU that it believes has the potential to be a star (probably a problem child at present), building would be an appropriate goal. The organization may decide to give up short-term profits and use its financial resources to achieve this goal. In the case of the Elixir guitar strings by W.L. Gore & Associates, the company had already invested in research and development of the high-tech puppet cables. Rather than abandon the product, managers decided to build on the research by redeveloping the cables as guitar strings.

▶▶ *Hold:* If an SBU is a very successful cash cow, a key goal would surely be to hold or preserve market share so that the organization can take advantage of the very positive cash flow. Apple plans to add some features, such as built-in projectors, to its Macintosh line to keep its market share growing.[9]

▶▶ *Harvest:* This strategy is appropriate for all SBUs except those classified as stars. The basic goal is to increase the short-term cash return without too much concern for the long-run impact. It is especially worthwhile when more cash is needed from a cash cow with long-run prospects that are unfavorable because of a low market growth rate. For instance, Lever Brothers has been harvesting Lifebuoy soap for a number of years with little promotional backing.

▶▶ *Divest:* Getting rid of SBUs with low shares of low-growth markets is often appropriate. Problem children and dogs are most suitable for this strategy. Procter & Gamble dropped Cincaprin, a coated aspirin, because of its low growth potential.

The General Electric Model

The third model for selecting strategic alternatives was originally developed by General Electric. The dimensions used in this model—market attractiveness and company strength—are richer and more complex than those used in the BCG model, but are harder to quantify.

Exhibit 2.3 presents the GE model. The horizontal axis, Business Position, refers to how well positioned the organization is to take advantage of market opportunities. Business position answers questions such as: Does the firm have the technology it needs to effectively penetrate the market? Are its financial resources adequate? Can manufacturing costs be held down below those of the competition? Can the firm cope with change? The vertical axis measures the attractiveness of a market, which is expressed both quantitatively and qualitatively. Some attributes of an attractive market are high profitability, rapid growth, a lack of government regulation, consumer insensitivity to a price increase, a lack of competition, and availability of technology. The grid is divided into three overall attractiveness zones for each dimension: high, medium, and low.

Those SBUs (or markets) that have low overall attractiveness (indicated by the red cells in Exhibit 2.3) should be avoided if the organization is not already serving them. If the firm is in these markets, it should either harvest or divest those SBUs. The organization should selectively maintain markets with medium attractiveness (indicated by the yellow cells in Exhibit 2.3). If attractiveness begins to slip, then the organization should withdraw from the market.

Conditions that are highly attractive—an attractive market plus a strong business position (the green

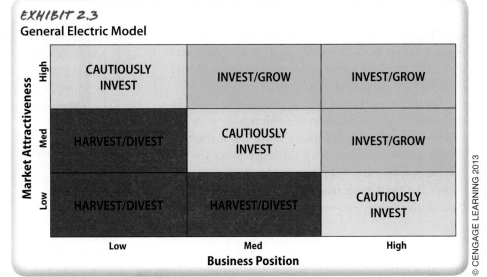

EXHIBIT 2.3
General Electric Model

	Low	Med	High
High	CAUTIOUSLY INVEST	INVEST/GROW	INVEST/GROW
Med	HARVEST/DIVEST	CAUTIOUSLY INVEST	INVEST/GROW
Low	HARVEST/DIVEST	HARVEST/DIVEST	CAUTIOUSLY INVEST

Market Attractiveness (vertical axis) — Business Position (horizontal axis)

© CENGAGE LEARNING 2013

planning the process of anticipating future events and determining strategies to achieve organizational objectives in the future

marketing planning designing activities relating to marketing objectives and the changing marketing environment

marketing plan a written document that acts as a guidebook of marketing activities for the marketing manager

cells in Exhibit 2.3)—are the best candidates for investment. For instance, Black & Decker used marketing research to uncover a market for the "serious do-it-yourselfer." These people were willing to pay a premium price for quality home tools. Black & Decker responded with a line called Quantum, which sold over $40 million in its first year.

The Marketing Plan

Based on the company's or SBU's overall strategy, marketing managers can create a marketing plan for individual products, brands, lines or customer groups. **Planning** is the process of anticipating future events and determining strategies to achieve organizational objectives in the future. **Marketing planning** involves designing activities relating to marketing objectives and the changing marketing environment. Marketing planning is the basis for all marketing strategies and decisions. Issues such as product lines, distribution channels, marketing communications, and pricing are all delineated in the **marketing plan**. The marketing plan is a written document that acts as a guidebook of marketing activities for the marketing manager. In this chapter, you will learn the importance of writing a marketing plan and the types of information contained in a marketing plan.

Why Write a Marketing Plan?

By specifying objectives and defining the actions required to attain them, you can provide in a marketing plan the basis by which actual and expected performance can be compared. Marketing can be one of the most expensive and complicated business activities, but it is also one of the most important. The written marketing plan provides clearly stated activities that help employees and managers understand and work toward common goals.

Writing a marketing plan allows you to examine the marketing environment in conjunction with the inner workings of the business. Once the marketing plan is written, it serves as a reference point for the success of future activities. Finally, the marketing plan allows the marketing manager to enter the marketplace with an awareness of possibilities and problems.

Marketing Plan Elements

Marketing plans can be presented in many different ways. Most businesses need a written marketing plan because a marketing plan is large and can be complex. Details about tasks and activity assignments may be lost if communicated orally. Regardless of the way a marketing plan is presented, some elements are common to all marketing plans. Exhibit 2.4 shows these elements, which include defining the business mission, performing a situation analysis, defining objectives, delineating a target market, and establishing components of the marketing mix. Other elements that may be included in a plan are budgets, implementation timetables, required marketing research

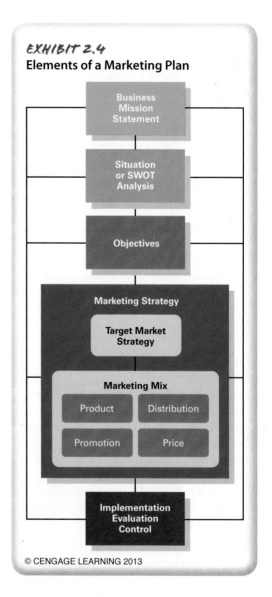

EXHIBIT 2.4
Elements of a Marketing Plan

Business Mission Statement

Situation or SWOT Analysis

Objectives

Marketing Strategy
- Target Market Strategy
- Marketing Mix
  - Product
  - Distribution
  - Promotion
  - Price

Implementation Evaluation Control

© CENGAGE LEARNING 2013

efforts, or elements of advanced strategic planning. Log in to the CourseMate for MKTG at cengagebrain.com for a marketing planning outline and an example of a marketing plan.

Writing the Marketing Plan

The creation and implementation of a complete marketing plan will allow the organization to achieve marketing objectives and succeed. However, the marketing plan is only as good as the information it contains and the effort, creativity, and thought that went into its creation. Having a good marketing information system and a wealth of competitive intelligence (covered in Chapter 9) is critical to a thorough and accurate situation analysis. The role of managerial intuition is also important in the creation and selection of marketing strategies. Managers must weigh any information against its accuracy and their own judgment when making a marketing decision.

Note that the overall structure of the marketing plan (Exhibit 2.4) should not be viewed as a series of sequential planning steps. Many of the marketing plan elements are decided on simultaneously and in conjunction with one another. Further, every marketing plan has different content, depending on the organization, its mission, objectives, targets, and marketing mix components. There is not one single correct format for a marketing plan. Many organizations have their own distinctive format or terminology for creating a marketing plan. Every marketing plan should be unique to the firm for which it was created. Remember, however, that although the format and order of presentation should be flexible, the same types of questions and topic areas should be covered in any marketing plan.

LO 4 Defining the Business Mission

The foundation of any marketing plan is the firm's **mission statement**, which answers the question, "What business are we in?" The way a firm defines its business mission profoundly affects the firm's long-run resource allocation, profitability, and survival. The mission statement is based on a careful analysis of benefits sought by present and potential customers and an analysis of existing and anticipated environmental conditions. The firm's mission statement establishes boundaries for all subsequent decisions, objectives, and strategies.

A mission statement should focus on the market or markets the organization is attempting to serve rather than on the good or service offered. Otherwise, a new technology may quickly make the good or service obsolete and the mission statement irrelevant to company functions. Business mission statements that are stated too narrowly suffer from **marketing myopia**—defining a business in terms of goods and services rather than in terms of the benefits customers seek. In this context, *myopia* means narrow, short-term thinking. For example, Frito-Lay defines its mission as being in the snack-food business rather than in the corn chip business. The mission of sports teams is not just to play games but to serve the interests of the fans.

Alternatively, business missions may be stated too broadly. "To provide products of superior quality and value that improve the lives of the world's consumers" is probably too broad a mission statement for any firm except Procter & Gamble. Care must be taken when stating what business a firm is in. For example, the mission of Ben & Jerry's centers on three important aspects of its ice cream business: (1) Product: "To make, distribute and sell the finest quality all natural ice cream and euphoric concoctions with a continued commitment to incorporating wholesome, natural ingredients and promoting business practices that respect the Earth and the Environment"; (2) Economic: "To operate the Company on a sustainable financial basis of profitable growth, increasing value for our stakeholders and expanding opportunities for development and career growth for our employees"; and (3) Social: "To operate the Company in a way that actively recognizes the central role that business plays in society by initiating innovative ways to improve the quality of life locally, nationally, and internationally."[10] By correctly stating the business mission in terms of the benefits that customers seek, the foundation for the marketing plan is set. Many companies are focusing on designing more appropriate mission statements because these statements are frequently displayed on the companys' Web sites.

mission statement a statement of the firm's business based on a careful analysis of benefits sought by present and potential customers and an analysis of existing and anticipated environmental conditions

marketing myopia defining a business in terms of goods and services rather than in terms of the benefits customers seek

LO 5 Conducting a Situation Analysis

Marketers must understand the current and potential environment in which the product or service will be marketed. A situation analysis is sometimes referred to as a **SWOT analysis**—that is, the firm should identify its internal strengths (**S**) and weaknesses (**W**) and also examine external opportunities (**O**) and threats (**T**).

When examining internal strengths and weaknesses, the marketing manager should focus on organizational resources such as production costs, marketing skills, financial resources, company or brand image, employee capabilities, and available technology. For example, Dell's stock has fallen 42 percent since January 2007, so management needs to examine strengths and weakness in the company and its competition. Dell has a $6 billion server business (strength), but the shrinking PC market accounts for a significant 24 percent of sales (weakness). Competitors like IBM and Hewlett-Packard (HP) are moving heavily into software and consulting, so to avoid them, Dell might instead consider the $7.1 billion networking equipment market.[11] Another issue to consider in this section of the marketing plan is the historical background of the firm—its sales and profit history.

When examining external opportunities and threats, marketing managers must analyze aspects of the marketing environment. This process is called **environmental scanning**—the collection and interpretation of information about forces, events, and relationships in the external environment that may affect the future of the organization or the implementation of the marketing plan. Environmental scanning helps identify market opportunities and threats and provides guidelines for the design of marketing strategy. The six most often studied macroenvironmental forces are social, demographic, economic, technological, political and legal, and competitive. These forces are examined in detail in Chapter 4. PepsiCo has been trying to increase SoBe Lifewater's market share since 2001, but when Coca-Cola purchased **vitamin**water in 2007, urgency skyrocketed. With the help of Tom Silk, a Web-savvy marketer who oversaw the marketing for the *Call of Duty* and *Guitar Hero* video game series, Lifewater has refocused on the market that made SoBe popular: millenials. Understanding youth's love of viral marketing, SoBe tests television ads on YouTube before airing them. To drive sales, SoBe dropped the price per bottle by four cents as competitor **vitamin**water raised prices by four cents. The changes are working. Understanding who buys Lifewater, and making marketing changes to address the environment, has doubled the market share of Lifewater this year.[12]

SWOT analysis identifying internal strengths (S) and weaknesses (W) and also examining external opportunities (O) and threats (T)

environmental scanning collection and interpretation of information about forces, events, and relationships in the external environment that may affect the future of the organization or the implementation of the marketing plan

competitive advantage a set of unique features of a company and its products that are perceived by the target market as significant and superior to those of the competition

LO 6 Competitive Advantage

Performing a SWOT analysis allows firms to identify their competitive advantage. A competitive advantage is a set of unique features of a company and its products that are perceived by the target market as significant and superior to those of the competition. It is the factor or factors that cause customers to patronize a firm and not the competition. There are three types of competitive advantage: cost, product/service differentiation, and niche.

Cost Competitive Advantage

Cost leadership can result from obtaining inexpensive raw materials, creating an efficient scale of plant operations, designing products for ease of manufacture,

© AP IMAGES/PRNEWSFOTO/PEPSICO

controlling overhead costs, and avoiding marginal customers. For example, many modern furniture design and production companies, like IKEA, consider creativity their unique competitive advantage. IKEA, however, also derives a significant cost competitive advantage by focusing on pricing. When developing a new product, the first decision IKEA designers make is how much the end product will cost in the store. Then they develop the design according to that number. The result is a fun, functional, high-quality product for much less than any of IKEA's competitors can match.[13] Having a **cost competitive advantage** means being the low-cost competitor in an industry while maintaining satisfactory profit margins.

A cost competitive advantage enables a firm to deliver superior customer value. Walmart, the world's leading low-cost general merchandise store, offers good value to customers because it focuses on providing a large selection of merchandise at low prices and good customer service. Walmart is able to keep its prices down because it has strong buying power in its relationships with suppliers. Costs can be reduced in a variety of ways:

▸▸ *Experience curves:* **Experience curves** tell us that costs decline at a predictable rate as experience with a product increases. The experience curve effect encompasses a broad range of manufacturing, marketing, and administrative costs. Experience curves reflect learning by doing, technological advances, and economies of scale. Firms like Boeing use historical experience curves as a basis for predicting and setting prices. Experience curves allow management to forecast costs and set prices based on anticipated costs as opposed to current costs.

▸▸ *Efficient labor:* Labor costs can be an important component of total costs in low-skill, labor-intensive industries such as product assembly and apparel manufacturing. Many U.S. publishers and software developers send data entry, design, and formatting tasks to India, where skilled engineers are available at lower overall cost.

▸▸ *No-frills goods and services:* Marketers can lower costs by removing frills and options from a product or service. Southwest Airlines, for example, offers low fares but no seat assignments or meals. Low costs give Southwest a higher load factor and greater economies of scale, which, in turn, mean lower prices.

▸▸ *Government subsidies:* Governments can provide grants and interest-free loans to target industries. Such government assistance enabled Japanese semiconductor manufacturers to become global leaders.

▸▸ *Product design:* Cutting-edge design technology can help offset high labor costs. BMW is a world leader in

designing cars for ease of manufacture and assembly. Reverse engineering—the process of disassembling a product piece by piece to learn its components and obtain clues as to the manufacturing process—can also mean savings. Reverse engineering a low-cost competitor's product can save research and design costs. Japanese engineers have reversed many products, such as computer chips from Silicon Valley.

▸▸ *Reengineering:* Reengineering entails fundamental rethinking and redesign of business processes to achieve dramatic improvements in critical measures of performance. It often involves reorganizing functional departments such as sales, engineering, and production, into cross-disciplinary teams.

▸▸ *Production innovations:* Production innovations such as new technology and simplified production techniques help lower the average cost of production. Technologies such as computer-aided design (CAD) and computer-aided manufacturing (CAM) and increasingly sophisticated robots help companies such as Boeing, Ford, and General Electric reduce their manufacturing costs.

▸▸ *New methods of service delivery:* Medical expenses have been substantially lowered by the use of outpatient surgery and walk-in clinics. Online-only magazines deliver great savings, and even some print magazines are exploring ways to go online to save material and shipping costs.

Product/Service Differentiation Competitive Advantage

Because cost competitive advantages are subject to continual erosion, product/service differentiation tends to provide a longer lasting competitive advantage. The durability of this strategy tends to make it more attractive to many top managers. A **product/service differentiation competitive advantage** exists when a firm provides something that is unique and valuable to buyers beyond simply offering a lower price than that of the competition. Examples include brand names (Lexus), a strong dealer network (Caterpillar for construction work), product reliability (Maytag appliances), image (Neiman Marcus in retailing), or service (FedEx).

© FRANK RUMPENHORST/DPA/LANDOV

cost competitive advantage being the low-cost competitor in an industry while maintaining satisfactory profit margins

experience curves curves that show costs declining at a predictable rate as experience with a product increases

product/service differentiation competitive advantage the provision of something that is unique and valuable to buyers beyond simply offering a lower price than that of the competition

niche competitive advantage the advantage achieved when a firm seeks to target and effectively serve a small segment of the market

sustainable competitive advantage an advantage that cannot be copied by the competition

Many organic farms and local farmers markets are very common, but there aren't many such businesses that deliver right to your house. Green B.E.A.N. Delivery in Ohio uses its network of local organic and artisan farmers to deliver fresh produce directly to homes. Instead of bringing customers to the produce, Green B.E.A.N. Delivery brings produce to the customers.[14]

Niche Competitive Advantage

A **niche competitive advantage** seeks to target and effectively serve a single segment of the market (see Chapter 8). For small companies with limited resources that potentially face giant competitors, niche targeting may be the only viable option. A market segment that has good growth potential but is not crucial to the success of major competitors is a good candidate for developing a niche strategy.

Many companies using a niche strategy serve only a limited geographic market. Buddy Freddy's is a very successful restaurant chain, but it is found only in Florida. Migros is the dominant grocery chain in Switzerland. It has no stores outside that small country.

Chef's Garden, a 225-acre Ohio farm, specializes in growing and shipping rare artisan vegetables directly to its customers. Chefs from all over the world call to order or request a unique item, which is grown and shipped by Chef's Garden. The farm provides personal services and specialized premium vegetables that aren't available anywhere else and relies on its customers to supply it with ideas for what they would like to be able to offer in their restaurants. The excellent service and feeling of contribution keep chefs coming back.[15]

Building Sustainable Competitive Advantage

The key to having a competitive advantage is the ability to sustain that advantage. A **sustainable competitive advantage** is one that cannot be copied by the competition. For example, Netflix, the online movie subscription service, has a steady hold over the movie rental market. No company has come close to the incomparable depth of titles available to be sent directly to homes or to be streamed online. Blockbuster tried to set up a similar online subscription service tied to new releases, but so far it has

not been able to compete with the convenience and selection offered by Netflix. Netflix's 14 million subscribers have a 28-day delay on most of the latest movies, but Netflix says that only a couple hundred customers have complained about the delay. Up-and-comer Hulu just released a new subscription service, and Netflix is hoping to maintain its advantage with its iPhone app that lets you carry Netflix in your pocket.[16] In contrast, when Datril was introduced into the pain-reliever market, it was touted as being exactly like Tylenol, only cheaper. Tylenol responded by lowering its price, thus destroying Datril's competitive advantage and ability to remain on the market. In this case, low price was not a sustainable competitive advantage. Without a competitive advantage, target customers don't perceive any reason to patronize an organization instead of its competitors.

The notion of competitive advantage means that a successful firm will stake out a position unique in some manner from its rivals. Imitation by competitors indicates a lack of competitive advantage and almost ensures mediocre performance. Moreover, competitors rarely stand still, so it is not surprising that imitation causes managers to feel trapped in a seemingly endless game of catch-up. They are regularly surprised by the new accomplishments of their rivals.

Rather than copy competitors, companies need to build their own competitive advantages. The sources

© THOMAS NORTHCUT/GETTY IMAGES

of tomorrow's competitive advantages are the skills and assets of the organization. Assets include patents, copyrights, locations, equipment, and technology that are superior to those of the competition. Skills are functions such as customer service and promotion that the firm performs better than its competitors. Marketing managers should continually focus the firm's skills and assets on sustaining and creating competitive advantages.

Remember, a sustainable competitive advantage is a function of the speed with which competitors can imitate a leading company's strategy and plans. Imitation requires a competitor to identify the leader's competitive advantage, determine how it is achieved, and then learn how to duplicate it.

LO 7 Setting Marketing Plan Objectives

Before the details of a marketing plan can be developed, objectives for the plan must be stated. Without objectives, there is no basis for measuring the success of marketing plan activities.

A **marketing objective** is a statement of what is to be accomplished through marketing activities. To be useful, stated objectives should be:

▸▸ *Realistic:* Managers should develop objectives that have a chance of being met. For example, it may be unrealistic for start-up firms or new products to command dominant market share, given other competitors in the marketplace.

▸▸ *Measurable:* Managers need to be able to quantitatively measure whether or not an objective has been met. For example, it would be difficult to determine success for an objective that states, "To increase sales of cat food." If the company sells 1 percent more cat food, does that mean the objective was met? Instead, a specific number should be stated, "To increase sales of Purina brand cat food from $300 million to $345 million."

▸▸ *Time specific:* By what time should the objective be met? "To increase sales of Purina brand cat food between January 1, 2013, and December 31, 2013."

▸▸ *Compared to a benchmark:* If the objective is to increase sales by 15 percent, it is important to know the baseline against which the objective will be measured. Will it be current sales? Last year's sales? For example, "To increase sales of Purina brand cat food by 15 percent over 2012 sales of $300 million."

Objectives must also be consistent with and indicate the priorities of the organization. Specifically, objectives flow from the business mission statement to the rest of the marketing plan.

Carefully specified objectives serve several functions. First, they communicate marketing management philosophies and provide direction for lower-level marketing managers so that marketing efforts are integrated and pointed in a consistent direction. Objectives also serve as motivators by creating something for employees to strive for. When objectives are attainable and challenging, they motivate those charged with achieving the objectives. Additionally, the process of writing specific objectives forces executives to clarify their thinking. Finally, objectives form a basis for control; the effectiveness of a plan can be gauged in light of the stated objectives.

marketing objective a statement of what is to be accomplished through marketing activities

marketing strategy the activities of selecting and describing one or more target markets and developing and maintaining a marketing mix that will produce mutually satisfying exchanges with target markets

LO 8 Describing the Target Market

Marketing strategy involves the activities of selecting and describing one or more target markets and developing and maintaining a marketing mix that will produce mutually satisfying exchanges with target markets.

Target Market Strategy

A market segment is a group of individuals or organizations who share one or more characteristics. They therefore may have relatively similar product needs. For example, parents of newborn babies need formula, diapers, and special foods.

© ANIAD/SHUTTERSTOCK.COM

market opportunity analysis (MOA) the description and estimation of the size and sales potential of market segments that are of interest to the firm and the assessment of key competitors in these market segments

marketing mix a unique blend of product, place (distribution), promotion, and pricing strategies designed to produce mutually satisfying exchanges with a target market

four Ps product, place, promotion, and price, which together make up the marketing mix

The target market strategy identifies the market segment or segments on which to focus. This process begins with a **market opportunity analysis (MOA)**—the description and estimation of the size and sales potential of market segments that are of interest to the firm and the assessment of key competitors in these market segments. After the firm describes the market segments, it may target one or more of them. There are three general strategies for selecting target markets.

Target market(s) can be selected by appealing to the entire market with one marketing mix, concentrating on one segment, or appealing to multiple market segments using multiple marketing mixes. The characteristics, advantages, and disadvantages of each strategic option are examined in Chapter 8. Target markets could be 18- to 25-year-old females who are interested in fashion (Nintendo DS and Wii game developers), people concerned about sugar and calories in their soft drinks (Diet Pepsi), or parents without the time to potty train their children (Booty Camp, classes where kids are potty trained).

Any market segment that is targeted must be fully described. Demographics, psychographics, and buyer behavior should be assessed. Buyer behavior is covered in Chapters 6 and 7. If segments are differentiated by ethnicity, multicultural aspects of the marketing mix should be examined. If the target market is international, it is especially important to describe differences in culture, economic and technological development, and political structure that may affect the marketing plan. Global marketing is covered in more detail in Chapter 5.

LO 9 The Marketing Mix

The term **marketing mix** refers to a unique blend of product, place (distribution), promotion, and pricing strategies (often referred to as the **four Ps**) designed to produce mutually satisfying exchanges with a target market. The marketing manager can control each component of the marketing mix, but the strategies for all four components must be blended to achieve optimal results. Any marketing mix is only as good as its weakest component. For example, the first pump toothpastes were distributed over cosmetic counters and failed. Not

KICKIN' UP THE COLT 45 BRAND

Colt 45 is introducing a new family member— Blast by Colt 45—and hoping to attract a new, younger market. Colt 45 is a malt liquor beverage that has seen steady decline in the past decade. Blast hopes to invigorate the staid brand with a fruit-infused drink that has a high alcohol content and a long-term sponsorship by Snoop Dog. Rather than targeting the typical Colt 45 drinker (an urban, African American male), Blast is targeting the people drinking other adult progressive beverages such as Mike's Hard Lemonade, Four Loko, and Tilt—women and younger drinkers. However, the makers of these beverages are at the center of increasing controversy over the safety of their highly alcoholic, candy-flavored, caffeinated beverages. The company

releasing Blast has made it clear that the beverage is targeted to of-age drinkers and that it does not encourage underage drinking. The beverage comes in a colorful 23.5-ounce can, is very sweet, and contains the same amount of alcohol as four 12-ounce beers. It is a far cry from the 5.6 percent alcohol by volume found in Colt 45.[17]

SOURCE: David Kesmodel, "Pabst's Horse of a Different Color: Colt 45 Enters Controversial Ring," *Wall Street Journal*, March 18, 2011.

© ARNOLD TURNER/WIREIMAGE/GETTY IMAGES

until pump toothpastes were distributed the same way as tube toothpastes did the products succeed. The best promotion and the lowest price cannot save a poor product. Similarly, excellent products with poor placing, pricing, or promotion will likely fail.

Successful marketing mixes have been carefully designed to satisfy target markets. At first glance, McDonald's and Wendy's may appear to have roughly identical marketing mixes because they are both in the fast-food hamburger business. However, McDonald's has been most successful at targeting parents with young children for lunchtime meals, whereas Wendy's targets the adult crowd for lunches and dinner. McDonald's has playgrounds, Ronald McDonald the clown, and children's Happy Meals. Wendy's has salad bars, carpeted restaurants, and no playgrounds.

Variations in marketing mixes do not occur by chance. Astute marketing managers devise marketing strategies to gain advantages over competitors and best serve the needs and wants of a particular target market segment. By manipulating elements of the marketing mix, marketing managers can fine-tune the customer offering and achieve competitive success.

Product Strategies

Of the four Ps, the marketing mix typically starts with the product. The heart of the marketing mix, the starting point, is the product offering and product strategy. It is hard to design a place strategy, decide on a promotion campaign, or set a price without knowing the product to be marketed.

The product includes not only the physical unit but also its package, warranty, after-sale service, brand name, company image, value, and many other factors. A Godiva chocolate has many product elements: the chocolate itself, a fancy gold wrapper, a customer satisfaction guarantee, and the prestige of the Godiva brand name. We buy things not only for what they do (benefits) but also for what they mean to us (status, quality, or reputation).

Products can be tangible goods such as computers, ideas like those offered by a consultant, or services such as medical care. Products should also offer customer value. Product decisions are covered in Chapters 10 and 11, and services marketing is detailed in Chapter 12.

Place (Distribution) Strategies

Place, or distribution, strategies are concerned with making products available when and where customers want them. Would you rather buy a kiwi fruit at the

24-hour grocery store within walking distance or fly to Australia to pick your own? A part of this P—place—is physical distribution, which involves all the business activities concerned with storing and transporting raw materials or finished products. The goal is to make sure products arrive in usable condition at designated places when needed. Place strategies are covered in Chapters 13 and 15.

Promotion Strategies

Promotion includes advertising, public relations, sales promotion, and personal selling. Promotion's role in the marketing mix is to bring about mutually satisfying exchanges with target markets by informing, educating, persuading, and reminding them of the benefits of an organization or a product. A good promotion strategy, like using a loved cartoon character such as SpongeBob SquarePants to sell gummy snacks, can dramatically increase sales. Each element of this P—promotion—is coordinated and managed with the others to create a promotional blend or mix. These integrated marketing communications activities are described in Chapters 16, 17, and 18. Technology-driven aspects of promotional marketing are covered in Chapter 21. The social media aspect of promotion is covered extensively in Chapter 22.

Pricing Strategies

Price is what a buyer must give up in order to obtain a product. It is often the most flexible of the four Ps—the quickest element to change. Marketers can raise or lower prices more frequently and easily than they can change other marketing mix variables. Price is an important competitive weapon and is very important to the organization because price multiplied by the number of units sold equals total revenue for the firm. Pricing decisions are covered in Chapters 19 and 20.

LO 10 Following Up on the Marketing Plan

Implementation

Implementation is the process that turns a marketing plan into action assignments and ensures that these assignments are executed in a way that accomplishes the plan's objectives. Implementation activities may involve detailed job assignments, activity descriptions,

implementation
the process that turns a marketing plan into action assignments and ensures that these assignments are executed in a way that accomplishes the plan's objectives

evaluation gauging the extent to which the marketing objectives have been achieved during the specified time period

control provides the mechanisms for evaluating marketing results in light of the plan's objectives and for correcting actions that do not help the organization reach those objectives within budget guidelines

time lines, budgets, and lots of communication. Implementation requires delegating authority and responsibility, determining a time frame for completing tasks, and allocating resources. Sometimes a strategic plan also requires task force management. A *task force* is a tightly organized unit under the direction of a manager who, usually, has broad authority. A task force is established to accomplish a single goal or mission and thus works against a deadline. AT&T assigned a task force to develop marketing plans that would protect its long-distance market from MCI and Sprint.

Implementing a plan has another dimension: gaining acceptance. New plans mean change, and change creates resistance. One reason people resist change is that they fear they will lose something. For example, when new-product research is taken away from marketing research and given to a new-product department, the director of marketing research will naturally resist this loss of part of his or her domain. Misunderstanding and lack of trust also create opposition to change, but effective communication through open discussion and teamwork can be one way of overcoming resistance to change.

Although implementation is essentially "doing what you said you were going to do," many organizations repeatedly experience failures in strategy implementation. Brilliant marketing plans are doomed to fail if they are not properly implemented. These detailed communications may or may not be part of the written marketing plan. If they are not part of the plan, they should be specified elsewhere as soon as the plan has been communicated. Strong, forward-thinking leadership can overcome resistance to change, even in large, highly integrated companies where change seems very unlikely.

Evaluation and Control

After a marketing plan is implemented, it should be evaluated. **Evaluation** entails gauging the extent to which marketing objectives have been achieved during the specified time period. Four common reasons for failing to achieve a marketing objective are unrealistic marketing objectives, inappropriate marketing strategies in the plan, poor implementation, and changes in the environment after the objective was specified and the strategy was implemented.

Once a plan is chosen and implemented, its effectiveness must be monitored. **Control** provides the mechanisms for evaluating marketing results in light of the plan's objectives and for correcting actions that do not help the organization reach those objectives

Best coverage worldwide.

More phones that work in more than 200 countries, like Costa Rica.   att.com/global

© AP IMAGES/PRNEWSFOTO/AT&T INC.

within budget guidelines. Firms need to establish formal and informal control programs to make the entire operation more efficient.

Perhaps the broadest control device available to marketing managers is the **marketing audit**—a thorough, systematic, periodic evaluation of the objectives, strategies, structure, and performance of the marketing organization. A marketing audit helps management allocate marketing resources efficiently.

Although the main purpose of the marketing audit is to develop a full profile of the organization's marketing effort and to provide a basis for developing and revising the marketing plan, it is also an excellent way to improve communication and raise the level of marketing consciousness within the organization. It is a useful vehicle for selling the philosophy and techniques of strategic marketing to other members of the organization.

Postaudit Tasks

After the audit has been completed, three tasks remain. First, the audit should profile existing weaknesses and inhibiting factors, as well as the firm's strengths and the new opportunities available to it. Recommendations have to be judged and prioritized so that those with the potential to contribute most to improved marketing performance can be implemented first. The usefulness of the data also depends on the auditor's skill in interpreting and presenting the data so decision makers can quickly grasp the major points.

The second task is to ensure that the role of the audit has been clearly communicated. It is unlikely that the suggestions will require radical change in the way the firm operates. The audit's main role is to address the question "Where are we now?" and to suggest ways to improve what the firm already does.

The final postaudit task is to make someone accountable for implementing recommendations. All too often, reports are presented, applauded, and filed away to gather dust. The person made accountable should be someone who is committed to the project and who has the managerial power to make things happen.

LO 11 Effective Strategic Planning

Effective strategic planning requires continual attention, creativity, and management commitment. Strategic planning should not be an annual exercise in which managers go through the motions and forget about strategic planning until the next year. It should be an ongoing process because the environment is continually changing and the firm's resources and capabilities are continually evolving.

Sound strategic planning is based on creativity. Managers should challenge assumptions about the firm and the environment and establish new strategies. For example, major oil companies developed the concept of the gasoline service station in an age when cars needed frequent and rather elaborate servicing. These major companies held on to the full-service approach, but independents were quick to respond to new realities

marketing audit a thorough, systematic, periodic evaluation of the objectives, strategies, structure, and performance of the marketing organization

FOUR CHARACTERISTICS OF A MARKETING AUDIT:

▸▸ *Comprehensive:* The marketing audit covers all the major marketing issues facing an organization—not just trouble spots.

▸▸ *Systematic:* The marketing audit takes place in an orderly sequence and covers the organization's marketing environment, internal marketing system, and specific marketing activities. The diagnosis is followed by an action plan with both short-run and long-run proposals for improving overall marketing effectiveness.

▸▸ *Independent:* The marketing audit is normally conducted by an inside or outside party who is independent enough to have top management's confidence and has the ability to be objective.

▸▸ *Periodic:* The marketing audit should be carried out on a regular schedule instead of only in a crisis. Whether it seems successful or is in deep trouble, any organization can benefit greatly from such an audit.

and moved to lower-cost self-service and convenience-store operations. Major companies took several decades to catch up.

Perhaps the most critical element in successful strategic planning is top management's support and participation. For example, when Michael Anthony was CEO of Brookstone, Inc., he and the Brookstone buying team earned hundreds of thousands of frequent flyer miles searching the world for manufacturers and inventors of unique products that could be carried in its retail stores, catalogs, and Web site. Anthony co-developed some of these products and also was active in remodeling efforts for Brookstone's 250 permanent and seasonal stores.

© ISTOCKPHOTO.COM/PRILL MEDIENDESIGN & FOTOGRAFIE

STUDY TOOLS
CHAPTER 2

Flip to the back of your textbook to:

❑ **Rip out Chapter Review Card**

Log in to the CourseMate for MKTG at cengagebrain.com to:

❑ **Review Key Terms Flash Cards (Print or Online)**

❑ **Review Audio and Visual Summaries**

❑ **Complete both Practice Quizzes to prepare for tests**

❑ **Play "Beat the Clock" and "Quizbowl" to master concepts**

❑ **Complete "Crossword Puzzle" to review key terms**

❑ **Watch the video on "Recycline" for a real company example on Strategic Planning for Competitive Advantage**

THE **IN-** CROWD

Share your 4LTR Press story on Facebook at
www.facebook.com/4ltrpress for a chance to win.

To learn more about the
In-Crowd opportunity 'like'
us on Facebook.

© Go Media I © Cengage Learning 2013

> If you have ever resented a line-cutter, then you understand ethics and have applied ethical standards in life.

LO 1 The Concept of Ethical Behavior

AFTER YOU FINISH THIS CHAPTER, GO TO PAGE 43 FOR STUDY TOOLS

It has been said that ethics is something everyone likes to talk about but nobody can define. Others have noted that "defining ethics is like trying to nail Jello to the wall. You begin to think that you understand it, but that's when it starts squirting out between your fingers."

ethics the moral principles or values that generally govern the conduct of an individual or a group

Ethics refers to the moral principles or values that generally govern the conduct of an individual or a group. Ethics also can be viewed as the standard of behavior by which conduct is judged. Standards that are legal may not always be ethical, and vice versa. Laws are the values and standards enforceable by the courts. Ethics, then, consists of personal moral principles. For example, there is no legal statute that makes it a crime for someone to "cut in line." Yet, if someone doesn't want to wait in line and cuts to the front, it often makes others very angry.

If you have ever resented a line-cutter, then you understand ethics and have applied ethical standards in life. Waiting your turn in line is a social expectation that exists because lines ensure order and allocate the space and time needed to complete transactions. Waiting your turn is an expected but unwritten behavior that plays a critical role in an orderly society.[1]

So it is with ethics. Ethics consists of those unwritten rules we have developed for our interactions with one another. These unwritten rules govern us when we are sharing resources or honoring contracts. "Waiting your turn" is a higher standard than the laws that are passed to maintain order. Those laws apply when physical force

What do you think?

Businesses need to focus on helping people.

1   2   3   4   5   6   7
STRONGLY DISAGREE   STRONGLY AGREE

© QUAYSIDE/SHUTTERSTOCK.COM

morals the rules people develop as a result of cultural values and norms

or threats are used to push to the front of the line. Assault, battery, and threats are forms of criminal conduct for which the offender can be prosecuted. But the law does not apply to the stealthy line-cutter who simply sneaks to the front, perhaps using a friend and a conversation as a decoy. No laws are broken, but the notions of fairness and justice are offended by one individual putting himself or herself above others and taking advantage of others' time and position.

Ethical questions range from practical, narrowly defined issues, such as a businessperson's obligation to be honest with customers, to broader social and philosophical questions, such as whether a company is responsible for preserving the environment and

Some beauty companies sell products using exaggerated language, claiming to hide lack of sleep or erase age lines with creams or powders.

recover or reactivate.

reactivate with twice the power. regenerist

Olay Regenerist transforms tired skin into skin that looks beautifully regenerated. What better way to reactivate your skin. And your life. Without the drastic measures.

OLAY
love the skin you're in™

protecting employee rights. Many ethical conflicts develop from conflicts between the differing interests of company owners and their workers, customers, and surrounding community. Managers must balance the ideal against the practical—that is, the need to produce a reasonable profit for the company's shareholders against honesty in business practices and concern for environmental and social issues.

LO 2 Ethical Behavior in Business

Morals are the rules people develop as a result of cultural values and norms. Culture is a socializing force that dictates what is right and wrong. Moral standards may also reflect the laws and regulations that affect social and economic behavior. Thus, morals can be considered a foundation of ethical behavior.

Morals are usually characterized as good or bad. "Good" and "bad" have different connotations, including "effective" and "ineffective." A good salesperson makes or exceeds the assigned quota. If the salesperson sells a new stereo or television set to a disadvantaged consumer—knowing full well that the person can't keep up the monthly payments—is the salesperson still a good one? What if the sale enables the salesperson to exceed his or her quota?

"Good" and "bad" can also refer to "conforming" and "deviant" behaviors. A doctor who runs large ads offering discounts on open-heart surgery would be considered bad, or unprofessional, in the sense of not conforming to the norms of the medical profession. "Bad" and "good" are also used to express the distinction between criminal and law-abiding behavior. And finally, different religions define "good" and "bad" in markedly different ways. A Muslim who eats pork would be considered bad, as would a fundamentalist Christian who drinks whiskey.

Morality and Business Ethics

Today's business ethics actually consist of a subset of major life values learned since birth. The values businesspeople use to make decisions have been acquired through family, educational, and religious institutions.

Ethical values are situation specific and time oriented. Everyone must have an ethical base that applies to conduct in the business world and in personal life. One approach to developing a personal set of ethics is to examine the consequences of a particular act. Who

IMAGE COURTESY OF THE ADVERTISING ARCHIVES

is helped or hurt? How long do the consequences last? What actions produce the greatest good for the greatest number of people? A second approach stresses the importance of rules. Rules come in the form of customs, laws, professional standards, and common sense. "Always treat others as you would like to be treated" is an example of a rule.

Another approach emphasizes the development of moral character within individuals. Ethical development can be thought of as having three levels:[2]

▸▸ *Preconventional morality,* the most basic level, is childlike. It is calculating, self-centered, and even selfish, based on what will be immediately punished or rewarded. Fortunately, most businesspeople have progressed beyond the self-centered and manipulative actions of preconventional morality.

▸▸ *Conventional morality* moves from an egocentric viewpoint toward the expectations of society. Loyalty and obedience to the organization (or society) become paramount. A marketing decision maker would be concerned only with whether the proposed action is legal and how it will be viewed by others.

▸▸ *Postconventional morality* represents the morality of the mature adult. At this level, people are less concerned about how others might see them and more concerned about how they see and judge themselves over the long run. A marketing decision maker who has attained a post-conventional level of morality might ask, "Even though it is legal and will increase company profits, is it right in the long run? Might it do more harm than good in the end?"

Ethical Decision Making

There is rarely a cut-and-dried answer to ethical questions. Studies show that the following factors tend to influence ethical decision making and judgments:[3]

▸▸ *Extent of ethical problems within the organization:* Marketing professionals who perceive fewer ethical problems in their organizations tend to disapprove more strongly of "unethical" or questionable practices than those who perceive more ethical problems. Apparently, the healthier the ethical environment, the more likely it is that marketers will take a strong stand against questionable practices.

▸▸ *Top management's actions on ethics:* Top managers can influence the behavior of marketing professionals by encouraging ethical behavior and discouraging unethical behavior. Research found that when top managers develop a strong ethical culture, there is reduced pressure to perform unethical acts, fewer unethical acts are performed, and unethical behavior is reported more frequently.[4]

▸▸ *Potential magnitude of the consequences:* The greater the harm done to victims, the more likely it is that

marketing professionals will recognize a problem as unethical.

▸▸ *Social consensus:* The greater the degree of agreement among managerial peers that an action is harmful, the more likely it is that marketers will recognize a problem as unethical. Research found that a strong ethical culture among co-workers decreases observations of ethical misconduct. In companies with strong ethical cultures, 8 percent of employees observed misconduct, compared with 31 percent in companies with weaker cultures.[5]

▸▸ *Probability of a harmful outcome:* The greater the likelihood that an action will result in a harmful outcome, the more likely it is that marketers will recognize a problem as unethical.

▸▸ *Length of time between the decision and the onset of consequences:* The shorter the length of time between the action and the onset of negative consequences, the more likely it is that marketers will perceive a problem as unethical.

▸▸ *Number of people to be affected:* The greater the number of persons affected by a negative outcome, the more likely it is that marketers will recognize a problem as unethical.

As you can see, many factors determine the nature of an ethical decision. Kellogg's is the world's largest cereal maker with sales over $13 billion. In 2010, the Federal Trade Commission said the company had over-stepped by claiming that its Rice Krispies cereal bolstered immunity. As a result, Kellogg's agreed to abide by the same restrictions regarding health claims that the company had accepted earlier for its Frosted Mini-Wheats cereal. Jon Leibowitz, chairman of the FTC, said, "We expect more from a great American company than making dubious claims—not once but twice—that its cereals improve children's health."[6]

On packages, Kellogg's had claimed Rice Krispies "now helps support your child's immunity" with "25% daily value of antioxidants and nutrients—vitamins A, B, C and E." The back of the boxes had stated that Rice Krispies "has been improved to

© TRIPPLAAR KRISTOFFER/SIPA/NEWSCOM

code of ethics a guideline to help marketing managers and other employees make better decisions

include antioxidants and nutrients that your family needs to help them stay healthy."

Another agency, the Food and Drug Administration, warned General Mills about its Cheerios cereal, saying the box's claims about heart benefits contained "serious violations" of federal law. The FDA said statements such as Cheerios "is clinically proven to help lower cholesterol" make the cereal a drug under federal law.[7]

Ethical Guidelines

Many organizations have become more interested in ethical issues. One sign of this interest is the increase in the number of large companies that appoint ethics officers—from virtually none several years ago to almost 33 percent of large corporations today. In addition, many companies of various sizes have developed a **code of ethics** as a guideline to help marketing managers and other employees make better decisions. Creating ethics guidelines has several advantages:

» The guidelines help employees identify what their firm recognizes as acceptable business practices.

» A code of ethics can be an effective internal control on behavior, which is more desirable than external controls such as government regulation.

» A written code helps employees avoid confusion when determining whether their decisions are ethical.

» The process of formulating the code of ethics facilitates discussion among employees about what is right and wrong and ultimately leads to better decisions.

PepsiCo, like virtually all major corporations, has a code of ethics, sometimes referred to as a "code of conduct." PepsiCo has a single code of conduct for Pepsi and all of its subsidiaries around the world. Major topics include respect for employees, global relations, health and safety, the environment, and a number of other factors.

Businesses, however, must be careful not to make their code of ethics too vague or too detailed. Codes that are too vague give little or no guidance to employees in their day-to-day activities. Codes that are too detailed encourage employees to substitute rules for judgment. For instance, if employees are involved in questionable behavior, they may use the absence of a written rule as a reason to continue behaving that way, even though their conscience may be telling them to stop. Following a set of ethical guidelines will not guarantee the "rightness" of a decision, but it will improve the chances that the decision will be ethical.

Although many companies have issued policies on ethical behavior, marketing managers must still put

the policies into effect. They must address the classic "matter of degree" issue. For example, marketing researchers must often resort to deception to obtain unbiased answers to their research questions. Asking for a few minutes of a respondent's time is dishonest if the researcher knows the interview will last 45 minutes. Not only must management post a code of ethics, but it must also give examples of what is ethical and unethical for each item in the code. Moreover, top management must stress to all employees the importance of adhering to the company's code of ethics. Without a detailed code of ethics and top management's support, creating ethical guidelines becomes an empty exercise.

Ethics training is a good way to help employees put good ethics into practice. Because of various scandals, such as Bernard Madoff's financial trickery that cost investors billions, more and more companies are offering ethics training to their employees. Today, about 70 percent of all large employers (over 500 employees) provide ethics training.[8] Simply giving employees a long list of "dos and don'ts" is a start, but it doesn't really help employees navigate the gray areas. What is needed is a more contextual approach to ethics training.

Do ethics training programs work? The National Business Ethics survey found that in companies with ethics training, fewer employees said that they had witnessed misconduct on the job; the measure fell from 56 percent in 2007 to 49 percent in 2009. Sixty-three percent said that they had reported misconduct when they had seen it (up from 58 percent). Only 8 percent of employees said they had felt pressure to commit an

© ISTOCKPHOTO.COM/STEVE CADY

ethics violation—to cut corners or worse.[9] Not only do employees seem to be becoming more ethical, but they also believe in the value of ethics training programs. Ninety percent of the workers surveyed said that ethics training is useful or somewhat useful to them.[10] Senior managers were most likely to find ethics training very valuable.

Ethics in Other Countries

Studies suggest that ethical beliefs vary little from culture to culture. Certain practices, however, such as the use of illegal payments and bribes, are far more acceptable in some places than in others, though increasingly enforced laws are making the practice less accepted. One such law, the **Foreign Corrupt Practices Act (FCPA)**, was enacted because Congress was concerned about U.S. corporations' use of illegal payments and bribes in international business dealings. This act prohibits U.S. corporations from making illegal payments to public officials of foreign governments to obtain business rights or to enhance their business dealings in those countries. The act has been criticized for putting U.S. businesses at a competitive disadvantage. Many contend that bribery is an unpleasant but necessary part of international business, especially in countries such as China, where business gift giving is widely accepted and expected. But, as prosecutions under

the FCPA have increased worldwide, some countries are implementing their own anti-bribery laws. For example, even though China is among the three countries with the most international corruption cases prosecuted under the FCPA, the country is working to develop its own anti-bribery laws. In 2010, Chinese courts sentenced four employees of Rio Tinto, a mining company with headquarters in London, to prison for taking bribes.[11]

> **Foreign Corrupt Practices Act (FCPA)** a law that prohibits U.S. corporations from making illegal payments to public officials of foreign governments to obtain business rights or to enhance their business dealings in those countries
>
> **corporate social responsibility (CSR)** a business's concern for society's welfare

LO 3 Corporate Social Responsibility

Corporate social responsibility (CSR) is a business's concern for society's welfare. This concern is demonstrated by managers who consider both the long-range best interests of the company and the company's relationship to the society within which it operates.

CSR can be a divisive issue. Some analysts believe that business should focus on making a profit and leave social and environmental problems to nonprofit organizations and government. Economist Milton Friedman

DODGE WON'T DODGE CSR

PETA (People for the Ethical Treatment of Animals) is infamous for its shock tactics and its efforts to persuade companies to stop using products that harm animals or whose production destroys habitats. PETA expects companies to operate at a highly ethical level. Dodge was one recent recipient of PETA's demands for sustainability and responsibility. In one TV spot, Dodge used a chimpanzee actor to shoot off some confetti. PETA sent the company videos of chimps being maltreated, hit, and torn from their mothers to demonstrate the unethical and violent lives many of these chimps lead before starring in TV commercials. Dodge pleaded no knowledge and took the chimp out of the ad—replacing it with an "invisible monkey."[12]

SOURCE: Jeanne Moos, "Dodge vs. PETA," *CNN*, August 16, 2010.

© ERIC ISSELÉE/SHUTTERSTOCK.COM

pyramid of corporate social responsibility a model that suggests corporate social responsibility is composed of economic, legal, ethical, and philanthropic responsibilities and that the firm's economic performance supports the entire structure

sustainability the idea that socially responsible companies will outperform their peers by focusing on the world's social problems and viewing them as opportunities to build profits and help the world at the same time

believed that the free market, and not companies, should decide what is best for the world.[13] Friedman argued that to the degree that business executives spend more money than necessary—to purchase delivery vehicles with hybrid engines, pay higher wages in developing countries, or even donate company funds to charity—they are spending shareholders' money to further their own agendas. Better to pay dividends and let the shareholders give the money away, if they choose.

On the other hand, CSR has an increasing number of supporters based on several compelling factors. One is that it is simply the right thing to do. Some societal problems have been brought about by corporations' actions such as pollution and poverty-level wages; it is the responsibility of business to right these wrongs. Business also has the resources, so business should be given the chance to solve social problems. For example, business can provide a fair work environment, safe products, and informative advertising.

Another, more pragmatic, reason for being socially responsible is that if business doesn't act responsibly then government will create new regulations and perhaps levy fines against corporations.

Finally, social responsibility can be a profitable undertaking. Smart companies can prosper and build value by tackling global problems. General Electric is committed to upholding its reputation as a responsible company. When it comes to philanthropy, supply chain audits designed to keep GE from being linked to sweatshops, or decisions about granting domestic-partner benefits, the business makes decisions based on maintaining its reputation and its desire to attract and engage great people. For example, GE decided not to sell low-end ultrasound machines in China (and to put warning labels on the high-end machines it did sell) because it did not want the machines to be used for gender screening that could lead to abortions. The potential harm to GE's image was too great for it to take the risk.

Total CSR has four components: economic, legal, ethical, and philanthropic.[14] The **pyramid of corporate social responsibility**, as shown in Exhibit 3.1, portrays economic performance as the foundation for the other three responsibilities. At the same time that it pursues profits (economic responsibility), however, a business is expected to obey the law (legal responsibility); to do what is right, just, and fair (ethical responsibility); and to be a good corporate citizen (philanthropic responsibility). These four components are distinct but together constitute the whole. Still, if the company doesn't make a profit, then the other three responsibilities are moot.

Sustainability

The newest theory in social responsibility is called **sustainability**. This refers to the idea that socially responsible companies will outperform their peers by focusing on the world's social problems and viewing them as opportunities to build profits and help the world at the same time.

When an organization focuses on sustainability, it is acting with long-term consequences in mind and managing its business in such a way that its processes or overall state can be maintained indefinitely. A company that believes in sustainability will integrate long-term economic, environmental, and social factors into its business strategies while maintaining its competitiveness and brand reputation. To do so, a company must have effective planning for long-run economic growth. This requires focusing on product and service innovation and building customer loyalty. It also means having the highest ethical standards and a meaningful code of conduct. Sustainability also demands that human resources be managed in a way that maintains workforce capabilities and employee satisfaction. Some com-

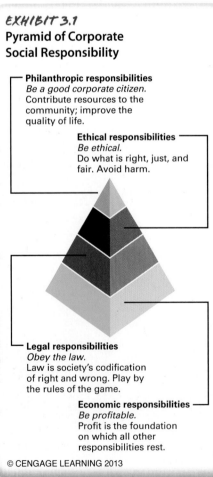

EXHIBIT 3.1
Pyramid of Corporate Social Responsibility

Philanthropic responsibilities
Be a good corporate citizen.
Contribute resources to the community; improve the quality of life.

Ethical responsibilities
Be ethical.
Do what is right, just, and fair. Avoid harm.

Legal responsibilities
Obey the law.
Law is society's codification of right and wrong. Play by the rules of the game.

Economic responsibilities
Be profitable.
Profit is the foundation on which all other responsibilities rest.

© CENGAGE LEARNING 2013

panies that excel in their sustainability philosophies are Adidas, BMW, King Fisher, Nokia, and Unilever.[15]

Sustainability is not simply "green marketing," though environmental sustainability is an important component of the sustainability philosophy. An environmentally sustainable process contributes to keeping the environment healthy by using renewable resources and by avoiding actions that depreciate the environment.

Growth of Social Responsibility

Social responsibility of businesses is growing around the world. A recent study of social responsibility in selected countries asked the following: "Does your company consider social responsibility factors when making business decisions?" The percentage of firms that said yes in each country were as follows: Brazil, 62 percent; Canada, 54 percent; Australia, 52 percent; the United States, 47 percent; India, 38 percent; China, 35 percent; and Mexico, 26 percent.[16] Another survey found that companies around the globe are coming under increasing pressure from governments, advocacy groups, investors, prospective employees, employees, and consumers to make their organizations more socially responsible. In turn, firms are seeing social responsibility as an opportunity. Eighty-seven percent of the respondents believed that social responsibility can aid in improving operational efficiency, and 69 percent felt that it will lead to new revenue opportunities.[17]

COURTESY OF BEN & JERRY'S HOMEMADE, INC.

Ben & Jerry's fun flavors are paired with a commitment to social responsibility that gives the company a highly unique selling point.

FAMILY FARMS

Our dense, rich ice cream uses only the freshest dairy from local family-owned farms that pledge not to treat their cows with rBGH. It's another way that Ben & Jerry's works to make the best possible ice cream in the best way possible. Go to benjerry.com to learn more about responsible sourcing.

It's what's inside that counts.

The FDA has said no significant difference has been shown and no test can now distinguish between milk from rBGH treated & untreated cows. Not all the suppliers of our other ingredients can promise that the milk they use comes from untreated cows.

green marketing
the development and marketing of products designed to minimize negative effects on the physical environment or to improve the environment

United Nations Global Compact One way that U.S. firms can do more is by joining the United Nations Global Compact (UNGC). The UNGC, the world's largest global corporate citizenship initiative, has seen its ranks swell over the past few years. In 2001—the first full year after its launch—just 67 companies joined, agreeing to abide by ten principles covering, among other things, human rights, labor practices, and the environment. In its tenth-anniversary Annual Review, the UNGC boasts more than 8,000 participants in 135 countries.[18]

Firms are realizing that CSR isn't easy or quick. It doesn't work without a long-term strategy, effort, and coordination throughout the enterprise. It doesn't always come cheap, either. And the payoff, both to society and to the business itself, isn't always immediate. Businesses say they want to be responsible citizens, but that's often not their only reason for taking action. In a recent survey, the UNGC asked members why they had joined. "Networking opportunities" was the second most popular reason; "addressing humanitarian concerns" was third. The first was to "increase trust in the company."[19]

Green Marketing

An outgrowth of the social responsibility movement is green marketing. **Green marketing** is the development and marketing of products designed to minimize negative effects on the physical environment or to improve the environment.[20] A study by Pricewaterhouse Coopers states that in 25 years the earth will run out of raw materials, assuming the top 500 global companies grow at 4 to 5 percent annually.[21]

cause-related marketing the cooperative marketing efforts between a for-profit firm and a nonprofit organization

Not only can a company aid the environment through green marketing, but it can often help its bottom line as well. Environmentally aware consumers tend to earn more and are willing to pay more for green products. However, only a very small percentage of customers make their buying decisions based primarily on the environmentally friendly qualities of a product.[22] Also, marketers may have to educate the consumer about the green product if its environmental benefit is not readily apparent. To make the sale, the green marketer may even use a traditional nongreen benefit. For example, General Electric's energy-efficient CFL floodlights are better for the environment than incandescent lightbulbs. The promotion theme is "Long life for hard to reach places."

GE is selling convenience because the floodlight doesn't need to be replaced as often.[23]

Some green products have practical consumer benefits that are readily apparent to consumers. A few examples are energy-efficient appliances (cut electric bills), heat-reflective windows (cut air-conditioning costs), and organic foods (no pesticides poisoning the food or planet). Each Dole organic banana has a sticker with a number. If you enter that number at www.doleorganic.com, a Google Earth application will show you the exact place the fruit was grown.[24]

Recent surveys have found that both consumers and many firms are still not motivated by the green movement. One survey of 1,500 consumers found that while 75 percent said that buying energy-efficient products is important to them, less than half have bought a green electronic product. Thirty-five percent said they are unwilling to pay any premium for green products.[25] On the business side, a separate survey of 270 corporate communications professionals found that 43 percent expect to increase their marketing of their sustainability programs. However, only 36 percent said that their businesses embraced recycling, and only 20 percent were actively pursuing more efficient electric energy usage.[26]

LO4 Cause-Related Marketing

A sometimes controversial subset of social responsibility is **cause-related marketing.** Sometimes referred to as simply "cause marketing," it is the cooperative efforts of a for-profit firm and a nonprofit organization for mutual benefit. Any marketing effort for social or other charitable causes is sometimes referred to as cause-related marketing. Cause marketing differs from corporate giving (philanthropy) as the latter generally involves a specific donation that is tax deductible, whereas cause marketing is a marketing relationship not based on a straight donation.

Cause-related marketing is very popular and is estimated to generate about $7 billion a year in revenue. It creates good public relations for the firm and will often stimulate sales of the brand. Nevertheless, the huge growth of cause-related marketing can lead to a case of consumer cause fatigue. Researchers have found that businesses need to guard against being perceived as cause exploitative, or using a cause simply to sell more of a product.[27]

IMAGE COURTESY OF THE ADVERTISING ARCHIVES

Bourjois advertises a natural makeup that filters pollution to detoxify skin.

Examples of cause-related marketing are abundant. Arby's asked customers for a $1 donation to help Big Brothers Big Sisters. In turn, the customer received a coupon for a dollar. (RED), an organization that helps fight AIDS, has partnered with the Gap, Emporio Armani, American Express, Apple, and Nike to provide AIDS education and medicine. At Christmas, Macy's makes a $1 donation to the Make A Wish Foundation when a letter is dropped off to Santa Claus. Whirlpool donated a range and refrigerator to every home built by Habitat for Humanity for a year. Nike and the Lance Armstrong Foundation have sold over $70 million Livestrong bracelets for cancer research.

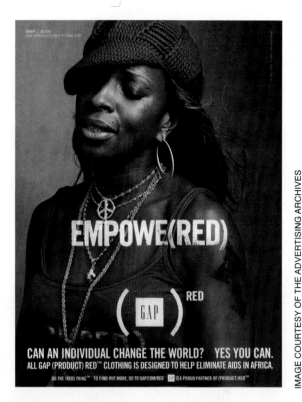

EMPOWE(RED)

(**GAP**) RED

CAN AN INDIVIDUAL CHANGE THE WORLD? YES YOU CAN.
ALL GAP (PRODUCT) RED™ CLOTHING IS DESIGNED TO HELP ELIMINATE AIDS IN AFRICA.

DO THE (RED) THING™ TO FIND OUT MORE, GO TO GAP.COM/RED GAP IS A PROUD PARTNER OF (PRODUCT) RED™

IMAGE COURTESY OF THE ADVERTISING ARCHIVES

STUDY TOOLS
CHAPTER 3

Flip to the back of your textbook to:

❑ **Rip out Chapter Review Card**

Log in to the CourseMate for MKTG at cengagebrain.com to:

❑ **Review Key Terms Flash Cards (Print or Online)**

❑ **Review Audio and Visual Summaries**

❑ **Complete both Practice Quizzes to prepare for tests**

❑ **Play "Beat the Clock" and "Quizbowl" to master concepts**

❑ **Complete "Crossword Puzzle" to review key terms**

❑ **Watch the video on "Method" for a real company example on Social Responsibility and Ethics**

Although managers can control the marketing mix, they cannot control elements in the external environment.

LO 1 The External Marketing Environment

AFTER YOU FINISH THIS CHAPTER, GO TO PAGE 60 FOR STUDY TOOLS

Perhaps the most important decisions a marketing manager must make relate to the creation of the marketing mix. Recall from Chapters 1 and 2 that a marketing mix is the unique combination of product, place (distribution), promotion, and price strategies. The marketing mix is, of course, under the firm's control and is designed to appeal to a specific group of potential buyers or target market. A **target market** is a group of people or organizations for which an organization designs, implements, and maintains a marketing mix intended to meet the need of that group, resulting in mutually satisfying exchanges.

target market a group of people or organizations for which an organization designs, implements, and maintains a marketing mix intended to meet the need of that group, resulting in mutually satisfying exchanges

Managers must alter the marketing mix because of changes in the environment in which consumers live, work, and make purchasing decisions. Also, as markets mature, some new consumers become part of the target market; others drop out. Those who remain may have different tastes, needs, incomes, lifestyles, and buying habits than the original target consumers. Zippo lighters, including customized and collectable lighters, have been known as windproof wonders for 78 years. However, yearly lighter sales overall have seen a decline from the peak of 18 million in 1998 to 12 million in 2010.[1] With increasing laws and government warnings against smoking, those numbers are

What do you think?

Marketing has to change according to what people care about, or it doesn't work.

| 1 | 2 | 3 | 4 | 5 | 6 | 7 |
STRONGLY DISAGREE · · · · · · · STRONGLY AGREE

Find out what others think at the CourseMate for MKTG. Log in at cengagebrain.com.

© ISTOCKPHOTO.COM/SINIŠA BOTAŠ

environmental management when a company implements strategies that attempt to shape the external environment within which it operates

unlikely to rebound. To counter the slipping demand for lighters, Zippo is focusing on expanding into other lighter-friendly areas, such as camping stoves, handwarmers, and grill lighters, as well as encouraging increased customization of the collectable lighters.

Although managers can control the marketing mix, they cannot control elements in the external environment that continually mold and reshape the target market. Controllable and uncontrollable variables affect the target market, whether it consists of consumers or business purchasers. The uncontrollable elements in the center of the environment continually evolve and create changes in the target market. In contrast, managers can shape and reshape the marketing mix to influence the target market. That is, managers react to changes in the external environment and attempt to create a more effective marketing mix.

Understanding the External Environment

Unless marketing managers understand the external environment, the firm cannot intelligently plan for the future. Thus, many organizations assemble a team of specialists to continually collect and evaluate environmental information, a process called environmental scanning. The goal in gathering the environmental data is to identify future market opportunities and threats.

Environmental Management

No single business is large or powerful enough to create major change in the external environment. Thus, marketing managers are basically adapters rather than agents of change. For example, despite the huge size of firms like General Electric, Walmart, Apple, and Caterpillar, they don't control social change, demographics, or other factors in the external environment.

Just because a firm cannot fully control the external environment, however, doesn't mean that it is helpless. Sometimes a firm can influence external events. For example, extensive lobbying by FedEx has enabled it to acquire virtually all the Japanese routes it has sought. When a company implements strategies that attempt to shape the external environment within which it operates, it is engaging in **environmental management**.

The factors within the external environment that are important to marketing managers can be classified as social, demographic, economic, technological, political and legal, and competitive.

LO2 Social Factors

Social change is perhaps the most difficult external variable for marketing managers to forecast, influence, or integrate into marketing plans. Social factors include our attitudes, values, and lifestyles. Social factors influence the products people buy; the prices paid for products; the effectiveness of specific promotions; and how, where, and when people expect to purchase products.

American Values

A *value* is a strongly held and enduring belief. During the United States' first 200 years, four basic values strongly influenced attitudes and lifestyles:

» *Self-sufficiency:* Every person should stand on his or her own two feet.

» *Upward mobility:* Success would come to anyone who got an education, worked hard, and played by the rules.

» *Work ethic:* Hard work, dedication to family, and frugality were moral and right.

» *Conformity:* No one should expect to be treated differently from everybody else.

IMAGE COURTESY THE ADVERTISING ARCHIVES

This ad targets upwardly mobile customers by suggesting that owning the Baby Phat product offers upward mobility and a reward for hard work.

The Natural Marketing Institute has marked some burgeoning **trends** that are apparently becoming American **values.** Some of them are:

▸▸ *Getting off the grid:* Consumers are pursuing ways to become more self-sufficient, including household-generated energy, water conservation and purification, and private gardens.

▸▸ *Meaningful green:* Green initiatives must be distinctive, memorable, and measurable to have an impact on environmental, social, and economic dimensions.

▸▸ *EcoTechMed:* New economic realities are motivating many to take greater steps toward proactive health care rather than sick care and to take greater responsibility for their own health and wellness.[2]

SOURCE: Partial list of trends projected by the Natural Marketing Institute, "Healthy, Green, Simple—Trends to Watch in the Next Ten Years," *Quirk's Marketing Research Review,* May 2010, 6.

These core values still hold for a majority of Americans today. A person's values are key determinants of what is important and not important, what actions to take or not to take, and how one behaves in social situations.

People typically form values through interaction with family, friends, and other influencers such as teachers, religious leaders, and politicians. The changing environment can also play a key role in shaping one's values.

Values influence our buying habits. Today's consumers are demanding, inquisitive, and discriminating. No longer willing to tolerate products that break down, they are insisting on high-quality goods that save time, energy, and often calories. U.S. consumers rank the characteristics of product quality as (1) reliability, (2) durability, (3) easy maintenance, (4) ease of use, (5) a trusted brand name, and (6) a low price. Shoppers are also concerned about nutrition and want to know what's in their food, and many have environmental concerns.

The Growth of Component Lifestyles

People in the United States today are piecing together **component lifestyles**. A lifestyle is a mode of living; it is the way people decide to live their lives. With component lifestyles, people are choosing products and services that meet diverse needs and interests

rather than conforming to traditional stereotypes.

In the past, a person's profession—for instance, banker—defined his or her lifestyle. Today, a person can be a banker and also a gourmet, fitness enthusiast, dedicated single parent, and Internet guru. Each of these lifestyles is associated with different goods and services and represents a target audience. Component lifestyles increase the complexity of consumers' buying habits. Each consumer's unique lifestyle can require a different marketing mix.

The Changing Role of Families and Working Women

Component lifestyles have evolved because consumers can choose from a growing number of goods and services, and most have the money to exercise more options. The growth of dual-income families has resulted in increased purchasing power. Approximately 59 percent of all females between

component lifestyles the practice of choosing goods and services that meet one's diverse needs and interests rather than conforming to a single, traditional lifestyle

Atkins is targeting people with component lifestyles by linking one component (winter adventure sports) to another (health food/nutrition).

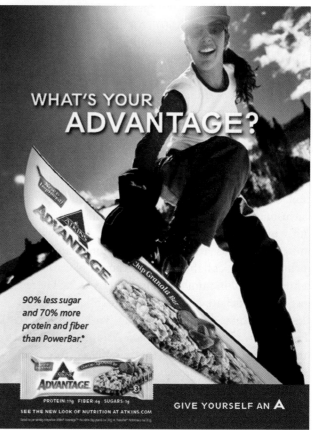

© AP IMAGES/PRNEWSFOTO/D2P MARKETING COMMUNICATIONS

demography the study of people's vital statistics, such as age, race and ethnicity, and location

16 and 65 years of age are now in the workforce. Working wives bring in 45 percent of the total family earnings.[3] The phenomenon of working women has probably had a greater effect on marketing than any other social change.

As women's earnings grow, so do their levels of expertise, experience, and authority. Working-age women are not the same group businesses targeted 30 years ago. They expect different things in life—from their jobs, from their spouses, and from the products and services they buy. For example, more women are purchasing personal guns and the accessories to go with them. The National Sporting Goods Association reported that 6.4 million women took up arms in 2009—up from 5.35 million in 2008. These women not only are looking for guns that fit their smaller body types (women's guns have smaller grips and tend to be lighter), but they are also looking to buy accessories for them. Cabela's, a sporting-goods chain, carries pink pistol cases and bedazzled camouflage hats to appeal to the female hunter.[4]

Technology and Time Use Today

The increase in available technology and the proliferation of screen-based technological devices is having an impact on how Americans spend their time and on how long their attention span for activities may be. In addition to the average 7.5-hour workday, 85 percent of women and 67 percent of men spend some time doing household activities such as housework, cooking, lawn care, or financial and other household management. Leisure time accounts for less than six hours a day, with at least an hour of that time devoted to computer use or gaming.[5]

Increasingly, however, our leisure time is punctuated by work. Researchers found that 40 percent of people check work messages at home or on vacation.[6] A New York sociologist calls our emerging work-life culture "weisure time."[7] It means that more Americans are using Smartphones and other technology to collaborate with business associates while engaged in family or leisure activities.[8] There is less time to deflate and truly engage in leisure activities when we are always mingling work and leisure. There is no time to decompress. Also, new research has shown that being constantly tethered to e-mail, Smartphones, tablets, and other digital media can take a toll on a person's life and ability to focus. Such immersion in a digital life can cause multitaskers to have more fractured thinking and to have trouble shutting out irrelevant information—even when they are offline.[9]

LO 3 Demographic Factors

Another uncontrollable variable in the external environment—also extremely important to marketing managers—is **demography**, the study of people's vital statistics, such as age, race and ethnicity, and location. Demographics are significant because the basis for any market is people. Demographic characteristics are strongly related to consumer buyer behavior in the marketplace.

Population

People are directly or indirectly the basis of all markets, making population the most basic statistic in marketing. The U.S. population is now slightly more than 300 million and is expected to reach 400 million in 30 to 35 years. Those additional 100 million people, many of them immigrants, will replace aging baby boomers in the workforce, fill the Social Security coffers, and, in all likelihood, keep the economy vital and life interesting. But they also will further crowd cities and highways, put new strains on natural resources, end the majority status of whites, and probably widen the gulf between society's haves and have-nots.

The United States has about 86 people per square mile nationwide, and even after the next 100 million people are added, the United States still will have one-sixth the density of Germany. But the majority of the population increase is happening in the western, southwestern, and southeastern states. Many midwestern and northeastern states have decreasing populations.[10] Those who are able to move despite the difficult housing market and economic slowdown tend to downsize and relocate from the suburbs back to cities where there are more job openings.[11] This trend is likely to result in megacities of 25 million or more as the population increases and jobs become available.

Population is a broad statistic that is particularly useful when broken into smaller increments. Age groups present opportunities to focus on a section of the population and offer opportunities for marketers. These groups are called tweens, teens, Generation Y, Generation X, and baby boomers. You will find that each cohort group has its own needs, values, and consumption patterns.

Tweens

America's tweens (ages 8 to 12) are a population of more than 20 million. With attitudes, access to information, sophistication well beyond their years, and purchasing power to match, these young consumers spend over $200 billion annually. Tweens directly spend about $50 billion per year, and the remainder is spent by parents and family members for them.[12] For example, the average family budget for back-to-school clothes is $225.[13]

With such spending power, many markets are striving to attract this age group. One of the fastest growing tween markets is home décor. Both boys and girls want their rooms to be more than just rooms, and retailers such as Pottery Barn, Pier 1 Imports, and other homegoods retailers sell bedding, furniture, and wall art designed specifically for tweens. By introducing tweens to home furnishings at a younger age, these businesses hope to keep their business as they change their fashion sense and need to furnish dorms or apartments for college.[14]

Walmart uses colorful swirls and cool, youthful models to advertise OP for Walmart.

© AP IMAGES/PRNEWSFOTO/ICONIX BRAND GROUP, INC.

Only at **Walmart**

Teens

Generation Y people
born between 1979 and 1994

There are approximately 25 million teens in the United States. They spend approximately 72 hours per week tuned in electronically. This includes television, Internet, music, video games, and cell phones. About 93 percent of U.S. teens are on the Internet, 75 percent own a cell phone, and 66 percent say they text. Seventy-three percent of teens in the United States are into social networking, and 50 million teens worldwide post their profiles on Facebook. Only 14 percent of American teens blog, but about half post comments on blogs. Only 8 percent of teens use Twitter.[15]

For teens, shopping has become a social sport whether online or at the mall, though most teens prefer to shop in stores instead of online.[16] The average teen spends about $45 per week (25 percent report working part time, and 70 percent work odd jobs).[17] Thirty-one percent of teen spending went toward clothing, shoes, and accessories in 2011, and the biggest purchase influence came from friends.[18]

Two keys to effectively market to teens are:

▸ *Make the product modern and convenient:* Apple's compact, easy-to-use iPod holds a large library of sounds and has been a hit with teens.

▸ *Engage teens through promotion that gets them involved:* It is important to engage teens with interactive contests and voting challenges and to empower the teen audience with the opportunity to help a company with new ideas, commercials, and brand names.[19]

General Electric recently worked to engage teens and tweens with its "Tag Your Green" YouTube campaign. Hoping to get its typically businesspeople-directed brand into a younger generation's mind, GE worked with 15 YouTube celebrities to make videos telling their followers about GE's commitment to the environment. By using YouTube celebrities and asking them to encourage their young followers to come up with inventive ways to work in the environment without harming it, GE's campaign shot to the top of the viral chart and into teen and tween awareness.[20]

Generation Y

Generation Y, also called the millennial generation, is made up of people born between 1979 and 1994. Initially, Generation Y was a smaller cohort than baby boomers (discussed on the next page). However, due to immigration and the aging of the boomer generation, Gen Y passed the boomers in total population in 2010. Millennials are currently in two different

Generation X people born between 1965 and 1978
baby boomers people born between 1946 and 1964

stages of the life cycle. The youngest members of Gen Y, born in 1994, are in their late teens and fit the cohort group above. In contrast, the oldest Gen Yers, born in 1979, were 32 years old in 2011. They have started their careers, and many have become parents for the first time, leading to dramatic lifestyle changes. They care for their babies rather than go out, and they spend money on baby products. Gen Yers already spend more than $200 billion annually and over their lifetimes will likely spend about $10 trillion. Many have already started their careers and are making major purchasing decisions such as cars and homes; at the very least, they are buying computers, MP3 players, cell phones, tablet computers, and sneakers.

Researchers have found Gen Yers to be:

▸▸ *Inquisitive:* Gen Yers want to know why things happen, how things work, and what they can do next.

▸▸ *Opinionated:* Gen Yers have been encouraged by their parents, teachers, and other authority figures to share their opinions. As a result, this group feels that their opinions are always needed and welcomed.

▸▸ *Diverse:* This is the most ethnically diverse generation the nation has ever seen, making the group more accepting overall of people who are different from themselves.

▸▸ *Time managers:* Their entire lives have been scheduled— from playgroups to soccer camp to Little League—so it's no surprise that they've picked up a knack for planning along the way.

▸▸ *Quick shoppers:* Millennials favor mass supercenters and mass merchandisers like Walmart and Target over more traditional formats like grocery or drug stores. Gen Yers are more likely to use shopping lists and coupons than other cohort groups.[21]

▸▸ *Want fulfillment:* Gen Yers realize that if they are going to work hard for a lifetime, they should find something that is meaningful to them. They want to make a difference.[22]

▸▸ *Multitaskers:* Millennials have grown up in a digital, social, mobile-technology-heavy world. They can socialize with friends, access news, do research, and be entertained at the same time. Some Gen Yers find media multitasking addictive—that is, they have a constant desire to "stay in touch" or "be in the know."[23]

▸▸ *Brand besotted:* Gen Yers love to be involved in what their favorite brands are doing. They talk about the Old Spice Guy and share their favorite clips. Two-thirds of Gen Yers follow brands, and nearly 80 percent of women interact with their favorite brands on social media.[24]

Vera Wang's Lavender line, targeted at Gen Y and Gen X, is hoping to tap into Gen Y's love of brands.

Generation X

Generation X—people born between 1965 and 1978—consists of 40 million consumers. It was the first generation of latchkey children—products of dual-career households or, in roughly half of the cases, of divorced or separated parents. Gen Xers often spent more time without adult support and guidance than any other age cohort. This experience made them independent, resilient, adaptable, cautious, and skeptical.[25]

Marketing to Gen Xers has often been described as difficult. Yet understanding their needs, wants, and attitudes can make the task much easier. Gen Xers, now in their 30s and 40s, are reaching the age when they are planning to send their kids off to college. Seventy-one percent of Gen Xers still have children under the age of 18.[26] Gen Xers tend to be more protective and involved with their kids than the baby boomer generation was. Gen Xers tend to feel deadline pressures, and want things that will make shopping less work—particularly places that will distract their kids. More than 80 percent of Gen Xers use social media such as Facebook to check prices and reviews. Marketers should offer speedy information and promotions via new media to sell to this group.[27]

Gen Xers are the biggest spenders at mass merchandisers such as Walmart and at drugstores. Likely because many still have young families, Gen Xers spend the most money on baby food, cereal, and laundry detergent of all the cohorts.[28]

Baby Boomers

In 2010, there were approximately 75 million **baby boomers** (persons born between 1946 and 1964). Today, their ages range from the late 40s to the mid-60s. With average life expectancy at an all-time high

© RENATA ESPINOSA/NEWSCOM

of 77.4 years, more and more Americans over 50 consider middle age a new start on life. Boomers purchase iPads, redecorate, go on vacation, and postpone retirement.[29] They control about 80 percent of personal wealth in the United States and spend about $50 billion on their grandchildren alone.[30] Boomers spend $1.8 trillion annually on food, cars, personal care, and other personal products. In addition, they are willing to change brands and try new things, making them an ideal group—affluent, experienced, and flexible.[31] Clearly, boomers and seniors are still a huge market with significant needs. In fact, many advertisers are homing in on the boomer market. For example, Procter & Gamble teamed up with NBC Universal to launch a group of Web sites targeted at boomers using the phrase "life goes strong." The sites cover topics such as technology and health, and hope to catch boomers' fancy as well as some of their $1 trillion in spending power.[32] The array of other businesses targeting boomers is staggering—as is the range of services they offer. For example, Florence Henderson created a technology hotline for seniors called FloH Club, where there is no such thing as a stupid question. There are fitness franchises (Nifty after Fifty), driving services (SilverRide), and even street fashion blogs (GranPaparazzi) for seniors.[33]

LO4 Growing Ethnic Markets

In 2015, it is estimated that Hispanics will wield $1.5 trillion in purchasing power. In the same year, African Americans will have $1.2 trillion, followed by Asian Americans at $775 billion. Native American spending is expected to increase more than 30 percent to $90.4 billion.[34]

The minority population of the United States reached 110 million in 2011. About one in three U.S. residents is a member of a minority group. By 2050, about one in three U.S. residents will be Hispanic. Currently, nonwhite minorities account for 49 percent of the children born in the United States.[35] Hawaii (75 percent), the District of Columbia (68 percent), New Mexico (58 percent), California (58 percent), and Texas (53 percent) are all majority-minority areas in the United States.[36] Counties around Denver, Las Vegas, and Orlando became majority-minority districts in 2010.

In addition to the increase in minority population, more people are identifying themselves as multiracial. U.S. Census data from 2005 to 2006 revealed that 5 percent of American children consider themselves multiracial. This number is expected to increase in the 2010 census. Both the increase in minority populations and the increase in people who are multiracial indicate a move towards breaking down racial barriers and unifying cultural and consumer interests.[37]

Despite the blurring of cultural interests, there is also a rising interest in preserving native heritage and identity. As you'll see in the following sections, minority populations embrace other cultures while continuing to patronize companies that understand their native cultural preferences.[38] Smart marketers are reaching out and tapping these dynamic, growing markets with a wide range of products and targeted advertising. For example, JCPenney's spent 16.4 percent of its media advertising budget on the Hispanic market.[39]

McDonald's conducts research on tastes preferred in minority communities and then introduces them to the general public, as it has done with many of its smoothies.

© TERRI MILLER/ E-VISUAL COMMUNICATIONS, INC.

Marketing to Hispanic Americans

The term *Hispanic* encompasses people of many different backgrounds. Nearly 60 percent of Hispanic Americans are of Mexican descent. Puerto Ricans, the next largest group, make up just under 10 percent of Hispanics. Other groups, including Central Americans, Dominicans, South Americans, and Cubans, each account for less than 5 percent of all Hispanics.

The diversity of the Hispanic population and the language differences create many challenges for those trying to target this market. Hispanics, especially recent immigrants, often prefer products from their native country. Therefore, many retailers along the southern U.S. border import goods from Mexico. If the brands found in their homeland are not available, Hispanics will choose brands that reflect their native values and culture.

In addition to the immigrant population, the second- and third-generation Hispanic American population aged 20–34 has increased to 12 million nationwide. People in this group are comfortably bi-national, viewing themselves as equally American and Hispanic and speaking English and Spanish. Nearly all of them have Internet access at home (94 percent) and are in constant contact via their cell phones. This group is particularly valuable to marketers looking to connect with Hispanic Americans over new media.[40] Marketers have also found that third-generation Hispanic American women speak English when discussing financial issues and Spanish when discussing topics related to womanhood. Ads reflecting this difference have had marked success.[41]

Marketing to African Americans

African Americans are nearly six years younger on average than all consumers; 47 percent are between 18 and 49 years old, which is considered the top-spending age demographic by marketers. Although their population is smaller, there are more African American households in the United States than Hispanic households because the latter tend to have larger families.[42] Nearly 30 percent of African American households are headed by a single women.[43]

Several companies owned by African Americans—such as SoftSheen-Culver and Pro-Line—target the African American market for health and beauty aids. Huge corporations like Revlon, Gillette, and Alberto-Culver have either divisions or major product lines for this market as well. The promotional dollars spent on African Americans continue to rise, as does the number of black media choices. BET, the black cable television network, has over 80 million viewers. The 45-year-old *Essence* magazine reaches one-third of all black females aged 18 to 49. African Americans spend considerable time with radio (an astounding 4 hours a day versus 2.8 hours for other groups), and urban audiences have an intensely personal relationship with the medium. ABC Radio Networks' Tom Joyner reaches an audience of more than 8 million in 115 markets, and Doug Banks is heard by 1.5 million listeners in 36 markets.

The election of President Obama has given hope and motivation to several generations of African Americans. Young people are realizing that hard work and good education can lead to opportunities once thought impossible. Recent research shows that more African Americans than ever before are achieving the American dream. In 2011, there were 2.8 million African Americans earning more than $75,000 annually.[44]

Marketing to Asian Americans

Asian Americans, who represent only 5 percent of the U.S. population, have the highest average family income of all groups. At $68,780, it exceeds the average U.S. household income by roughly $15,000. Fifty percent of all Asian Americans have at least a bachelor's degree.[45] Because Asian Americans are younger (the average age is 34), better educated, and have higher incomes than average, they are sometimes called a "marketer's dream." Asian Americans are

IMAGE COURTESY OF THE ADVERTISING ARCHIVES

heavy users of technology. Moreover, they are early adopters of the latest digital gadgets. A staggering 95 percent of Asian Americans own PCs.[46]

A number of products have been developed specifically for the Asian American market. For example, the Kayla Beverly Hills salon draws Asian American consumers because the firm offers cosmetics formulated for them. Cultural diversity within the Asian American market complicates promotional efforts, however, and marketers must understand the differences among the Chinese, Filipino, Japanese, Vietnamese, Korean, Indian, and Pakistani markets.

LO 5 Economic Factors

In addition to social and demographic factors, marketing managers must understand and react to the economic environment. The three economic areas of greatest concern to most marketers are consumers' incomes, inflation, and recession.

Consumers' Incomes

As disposable (or after-tax) incomes rise, more families and individuals can afford the "good life." In recent years, however, U.S. incomes have risen at a rather slow pace. The annual median household income in the United States in 2010 was approximately $50,000, though the median household income varies widely from state to state. This means half of all U.S. households earned less and the other half earned more.[47] Two percent of the U.S. population earns $250,000 a year or more.[48]

Education is the primary determinant of a person's earning potential. For example, only 1 percent of those with only a high school education earn over $100,000 annually. By comparison, 13 percent of college-educated workers earn six figures or more. People with a bachelor's degree take home an average of 38 percent more than those with just a high school diploma. Over a lifetime, an individual with a bachelor's degree will earn twice as much total income as a nondegree holder.[49] Along with "willingness to buy," or "ability to buy," income is a key determinant of target markets. A marketer who knows where the money is knows where the markets are. If you are seeking a new store location for Dollar General, a retail chain that caters to lower-income consumers,

you would probably concentrate on the South and Midwest because most households with annual incomes of less than $45,000 are concentrated in these areas.

Purchasing Power

Rising incomes don't necessarily mean a higher standard of living. Increased standards of living are a function of purchasing power. **Purchasing power** is measured by comparing income to the relative cost of a standard set of goods and services in different geographic areas, usually referred to as the cost of living. Another way to think of purchasing power is income minus the cost of living (i.e., expenses). In general, a cost of living index takes into account housing, food and groceries, transportation, utilities, health care, and miscellaneous expenses such as clothing, services, and entertainment. Homefair's salary calculator uses these metrics when it figures that the cost of living in New York City is almost three times the cost of living in Youngstown, Ohio. This means that a worker living in New York must earn nearly $279,500 to have the same standard of living as someone making $100,000 in Youngstown.

When income is high relative to the cost of living, people have more discretionary income. That means they have more money to spend on nonessential items (in other words, on wants rather than needs). This information is important to marketers for obvious reasons. Consumers with high purchasing power can afford to spend more money without jeopardizing their budget for necessities like food, housing, and utilities. They also have the ability to purchase higher-priced necessities—for example, a more expensive car, a home in a more expensive neighborhood, or a designer handbag versus a purse from a discount store.

Inflation

Inflation is a measure of the decrease in the value of money, generally expressed as the percentage reduction in value since the previous year, which is the rate of inflation. Thus, in simple terms, an inflation rate of 5 percent means you will need 5 percent more units of money than you would have needed last year to buy the same basket of products. If inflation is 5 percent, you can expect that, on average, prices have risen by about 5 percent since the previous year. Of course,

purchasing power a comparison of income versus the relative cost of a standard set of goods and services in different geographic areas

inflation a measure of the decrease in the value of money, expressed as the percentage reduction in value since the previous year

© ISTOCKPHOTO.COM/JAMES STEIDL

recession a period of economic activity characterized by negative growth, which reduces demand for goods and services

if pay raises are matching the rate of inflation, then employees will be no worse off in terms of the immediate purchasing power of their salaries.

In times of low inflation, businesses seeking to increase their profit margins can do so only by increasing their efficiency. If they significantly increase prices, no one will purchase their goods or services. The recent recession brought inflation rates to almost zero.

In creating marketing strategies to cope with inflation, managers must realize that, regardless of what happens to the seller's cost, the buyer is not going to pay more for a product than the subjective value he or she places on it. No matter how compelling the justification might be for a 10 percent price increase, marketers must always examine its impact on demand. Many marketers try to hold prices level for as long as is practical.

Recession

A **recession** is a period of economic activity characterized by negative growth. More precisely, a recession is defined as occurring when the gross domestic product falls for two consecutive quarters. Gross domestic product is the total market value of all final goods and services produced during a period of time. The official beginning of the 2007–2009 recession was December 2007. While the causes of the recession are very complex, this one began with the collapse of inflated housing prices. Those high prices led people to take out mortgages they couldn't afford from banks that should have known the money would not be repaid. By 2008, the recession had spread around the globe. A very slow economic recovery began in July 2009.

The 2007–2009 recession, called "the Great Recession" by some, was the largest economic downturn since the Great Depression of 1929 to 1939. Unemployment rose from slightly over 4 percent to over 10 percent.[50] The unemployment rate has been slowly falling since mid-2010 due to job creation and people leaving the workforce entirely. Uncertain economic times have caused many consumers to shift to store brands—60 percent of shoppers buy only private label bread or baked goods![51] Procter & Gamble has seen sales of its bargain-priced Gain detergent rise rapidly. More consumers than ever before are using coupons. Researchers found that during the recession, consumers were sticking very close to shopping lists and doing their best to completely empty their pantries before restocking. Also, consumers were going to fewer stores but selecting stores where they could get the widest array of products at the best value. Many people, for the first time, prepared their lunches to take to work.[52]

LO 6 Technological Factors

The recent economic downturn and slow recovery have had an impact on research and development (R&D) spending. In order to cut costs and boost short-term profits, many companies, particularly in the auto and drug industries, slashed R&D, product design, and

Kool-Aid reinvented itself as a low-cost alternative to soda during the recession.

© TERRI MILLER/E-VISUAL COMMUNICATIONS, INC.

laboratory spending. Other firms have taken a different tack and either increased or held R&D spending steady, hoping that they will be able to compete more effectively when the economy improves. Companies such as 3M, Microsoft, Google, Intel, and Cisco Systems have followed this strategy. Without investment in R&D, the United States cannot compete in a knowledge-based global economy.

Research

The United States, historically, has excelled at both basic and applied research. **Basic research** (or *pure research*) attempts to expand the frontiers of knowledge but is not aimed at a specific, pragmatic problem. Basic research aims to confirm an existing theory or to learn more about a concept or phenomenon. For example, basic research might focus on high-energy physics. **Applied research**, in contrast, attempts to develop new or improved products. The United States has dramatically improved its track record in applied research. For example, the United States leads the world in applying basic research to aircraft design and propulsion systems. In 2009, however, non-Americans were granted more U.S. patents than resident inventors.[53] This was partially the result of U.S. companies sending R&D offshore. One reason R&D has moved offshore is that the United States once had the most generous tax credits for R&D. Now it ranks 17th among developed countries.

Stimulating Innovation

Companies attempting to innovate often limit their searches to areas they are already familiar with. This can help lead to incremental progress but rarely leads to a dramatic breakthrough. Companies are now using several approaches to keeping innovation strong. These include:

▸▸ *Build scenarios:* Some firms use teams of writers to imagine detailed opportunities and threats for their companies, partners, and collaborators in future markets.

▸▸ *Enlist the Web:* A few companies have created Web sites that act as literal marketplaces of ideas where they can go to look for help with scientific and business challenges.

▸▸ *Talk to early adopters:* Early adopters tend to be innovators themselves. They are risk takers and look for new things or wish for something better to help in daily tasks at home and work.

▸▸ *Use marketing research:* Find out what customers like and dislike about your products and competitors' products.

▸▸ *Create an innovative environment:* Let employees know that they have the "freedom to fail." Create intranets to encourage sharing ideas. Most importantly, top management must lead by example to create an atmosphere where innovation is encouraged and rewarded.

basic research pure research that aims to confirm an existing theory or to learn more about a concept or phenomenon

applied research research that attempts to develop new or improved products

STRIKE A POSE FOR FASHION

One small start-up company in Santa Monica, California, is bringing innovation to its new app, Pose. Pose allows users to share shopping experiences with friends by photographing clothes and uploading the images into the app. While advice may be forthcoming, the main goal of the app is have quick access to the newest fashion trends while shopping. If you see a one-piece neon yellow lace top that you think is hip, you can check Pose and see that, when paired with a high-waisted black skirt, you'll be modeling one of the most to-the-minute runway looks. Pose has even enlisted top designers and stylists to post their favorites under a "Posers" tab so that everyday users can easily see what the top fashionistas are loving.[54]

SOURCE: Cate Corcoran, "New App Encourages Users to Strike a Pose," *Women's Wear Daily,* January 11, 2011, 10.

© ISTOCKPHOTO.COM/LEV DOLGATSHJOV

TOP TEN MOST INNOVATIVE COMPANIES[55]

1. Apple (U.S.)
2. Google (U.S.)
3. Microsoft (U.S.)
4. IBM (U.S.)
5. Toyota Motor (Japan)
6. Amazon.com (U.S.)
7. LG Electronics (South Korea)
8. BYD (China)
9. General Electric (U.S.)
10. Sony (Japan)

SOURCE: "The 50 Most Innovative Companies 2010," *Bloomberg Businessweek*, April 15, 2010, www.businessweek.com/interactive_reports/innovative_companies_2010.html.

▶▶ *Cater to entrepreneurs:* Policies that reserve blocks of time for scientists or engineers to explore their own ideas have worked well at some companies. At 3M, scientists can spend 15 percent of their time on projects they dream up themselves, and the company has set procedures for taking bright ideas forward, including grants and venture funding.[56]

Although developing new technology internally is a key to creating and maintaining a long-term competitive advantage, external technology is also important to managers for two reasons. First, by acquiring the technology, the firm may be able to operate more efficiently or create a better product. Second, a new technology may render existing products obsolete.

Innovation Carries to the Bottom Line Innovation pays off big for creative organizations and those who are willing to pursue calculated risk. During the recession, Intel built three new chip manufacturing plants, enabling the company to produce faster, lower-cost chips. Intel also pursued the Atom chip, used in netbooks and Smartphones despite warnings that the chip could negatively affect its business. Once the economy was on the rebound, Intel reported an astounding increase in revenue—up 28 percent in the fourth quarter—and the largest gross profit margin in its history.[57]

LO7 Political and Legal Factors

Business needs government regulation to protect innovators of new technology, the interests of society in general, one business from another, and consumers. In turn, government needs business because the marketplace generates taxes that support public efforts to educate our youth, pave our roads, protect our shores, and the like.

Every aspect of the marketing mix is subject to laws and restrictions. It is the duty of marketing managers or their legal assistants to understand these laws and conform to them, because failure to comply with regulations can have major consequences for a firm. Sometimes just sensing trends and taking corrective action before a government agency acts can help avoid regulation.

The challenge is not simply to keep the marketing department out of trouble, however, but to help it implement creative new programs to accomplish marketing objectives. It is all too easy for a marketing manager or sometimes a lawyer to say "no" to a marketing innovation that actually entails little risk. For example, an overly cautious lawyer could hold up sales of a desirable new product by warning that the package design could prompt a copyright infringement suit. Thus, it is important to have a thorough understanding of the laws established by the federal government, state governments, and regulatory agencies to govern marketing-related issues.

Federal Legislation

Federal laws that affect marketing fall into several categories of regulatory activity: competitive environment, pricing, advertising and promotion, and consumer privacy. The key pieces of legislation in these areas are summarized in Exhibit 4.1. The primary federal laws that protect consumers are shown in Exhibit 4.2 on page 58.

In 2010, Congress passed the Restoring American Financial Stability Act that brought sweeping changes to bank and financial market regulations. The legislation created the Consumer Financial Protection Bureau to oversee checking accounts, private student loans, mortgages, and other financial products. The agency deals with unfair, abusive, and deceptive practices.

State Laws

Legislation that affects marketing varies state by state. Oregon, for example, limits utility advertising to 0.5

percent of the company's net income. California has forced industry to improve consumer products and has enacted legislation to lower the energy consumption of refrigerators, freezers, and air conditioners. Several states, including California and North Carolina, are considering levying a tax on all in-state commercial advertising.

Many states and cities are attempting to fight obesity by regulating fast-food chains and other restaurants. For example, California has passed a law banning trans fats in restaurants and bakeries, New York City chain restaurants must now display calorie counts on menus, and Boston has banned trans fats in restaurants.

Regulatory Agencies

Although some state regulatory bodies actively pursue violators of their marketing statutes, federal regulators generally have the greatest clout. The Consumer Product Safety Commission, the Federal Trade Commission, and the Food and Drug Administration are the three federal agencies most directly and actively involved in marketing affairs. These agencies, plus others, are discussed throughout the book, but a brief introduction is in order at this point.

The sole purpose of the **Consumer Product Safety Commission (CPSC)** is to protect the health and safety of consumers in and around their homes. The CPSC has the power to set mandatory safety standards for almost all products consumers use (about 15,000 items) and can fine offending firms up to $500,000 and sentence their officers to up to a year in prison. It can also ban dangerous products from the marketplace. The CPSC oversees about 400 recalls per year. In 2008, Congress passed the Consumer Product Safety Improvement Act. The law is aimed primarily at children's products, which are defined as those used by individuals 12 years old or younger. The law addresses items such as cribs, electronics and video games, school supplies, science kits, toys, and pacifiers. The law requires mandatory testing and labeling and increases fines and prison time for violators.

The **Food and Drug Administration (FDA)**, another powerful agency, is charged with enforcing regulations against selling and distributing adulterated, misbranded, or hazardous food and drug products. In

Consumer Product Safety Commission (CPSC) a federal agency established to protect the health and safety of consumers in and around their homes

Food and Drug Administration (FDA) a federal agency charged with enforcing regulations against selling and distributing adulterated, misbranded, or hazardous food and drug products

---

EXHIBIT 4.1
Primary U.S. Laws That Affect Marketing

Legislation	Impact on Marketing
Sherman Act of 1890	Makes trusts and conspiracies in restraint of trade illegal; makes monopolies and attempts to monopolize misdemeanors.
Clayton Act of 1914	Outlaws discrimination in prices to different buyers; prohibits tying contracts (which require the buyer of one product to also buy another item in the line); makes illegal the combining of two or more competing corporations by pooling ownership of stock.
Federal Trade Commission Act of 1914	Created the Federal Trade Commission to deal with antitrust matters; outlaws unfair methods of competition.
Robinson-Patman Act of 1936	Prohibits charging different prices to different buyers of merchandise of like grade and quantity; requires sellers to make any supplementary services or allowances available to all purchasers on a proportionately equal basis.
Wheeler-Lea Amendments to FTC Act of 1938	Broadens the Federal Trade Commission's power to prohibit practices that might injure the public without affecting competition; outlaws false and deceptive advertising.
Lanham Act of 1946	Establishes protection for trademarks.
Celler-Kefauver Antimerger Act of 1950	Strengthens the Clayton Act to prevent corporate acquisitions that reduce competition.
Hart-Scott-Rodino Act of 1976	Requires large companies to notify the government of their intent to merge.
Foreign Corrupt Practices Act of 1977	Prohibits bribery of foreign officials to obtain business.

© CENGAGE LEARNING 2013

Federal Trade Commission (FTC) a federal agency empowered to prevent persons or corporations from using unfair methods of competition in commerce

2009, the Tobacco Control Act was passed. This act gave the FDA authority to regulate tobacco products, with a special emphasis on preventing their use by children and young people and reducing the impact of tobacco on public health. Another recent FDA action is the "Bad Ad" program. It is geared toward health care providers to help them recognize misleading prescription drug promotions and gives them an easy way to report the activity to the FDA.

The **Federal Trade Commission (FTC)** consists of five members, each holding office for seven years. Over the years, Congress has greatly expanded the powers of the FTC. Its responsibilities have grown so large that the FTC has created several bureaus to better organize its operations. One of the most important is the Bureau of Competition, which promotes and protects competition. The Bureau:

▶▶ reviews mergers and acquisitions, and challenges those that would likely lead to higher prices, fewer choices, or less innovation;

EXHIBIT 4.2
Primary U.S. Laws Protecting Consumers

Legislation	Impact on Marketing
Federal Food and Drug Act of 1906	Prohibits adulteration and misbranding of foods and drugs involved in interstate commerce; strengthened by the Food, Drug, and Cosmetic Act (1938) and the Kefauver-Harris Drug Amendment (1962).
Federal Hazardous Substances Act of 1960	Requires warning labels on hazardous household chemicals.
Kefauver-Harris Drug Amendment of 1962	Requires that manufacturers conduct tests to prove drug effectiveness and safety.
Consumer Credit Protection Act of 1968	Requires that lenders fully disclose true interest rates and all other charges to credit customers for loans and installment purchases.
Child Protection and Toy Safety Act of 1969	Prevents marketing of products so dangerous that adequate safety warnings cannot be given.
Public Health Smoking Act of 1970	Prohibits cigarette advertising on television and radio and revises the health hazard warning on cigarette packages.
Poison Prevention Labeling Act of 1970	Requires safety packaging for products that may be harmful to children.
National Environmental Policy Act of 1970	Established the Environmental Protection Agency to deal with various types of pollution and organizations that create pollution.
Public Health Cigarette Smoking Act of 1971	Prohibits tobacco advertising on radio and television.
Consumer Product Safety Act of 1972	Created the Consumer Product Safety Commission, which has authority to specify safety standards for most products.
Child Protection Act of 1990	Regulates the number of minutes of advertising on children's television.
Children's Online Privacy Protection Act of 1998	Empowers the FTC to set rules regarding how and when marketers must obtain parental permission before asking children marketing research questions.
Aviation Security Act of 2001	Requires airlines to take extra security measures to protect passengers, including the installation of stronger cockpit doors, improved baggage screening, and increased security training for airport personnel.
Homeland Security Act of 2002	Protects consumers against terrorist acts; created the Department of Homeland Security.
Do Not Call Law of 2003	Protects consumers against unwanted telemarketing calls.
CAN-SPAM Act of 2003	Protects consumers against unwanted e-mail, or spam.
Credit Card Act of 2009	Provides many credit card protections.
Restoring American Financial Stability Act of 2010	Created the Consumer Financial Protection Bureau to protect consumers against unfair, abusive, and deceptive financial practices.

© CENGAGE LEARNING 2013

- seeks out and challenges anti-competitive conduct in the marketplace, including monopolization and agreements between competitors;

- promotes competition in industries where consumer impact is high, such as health care, real estate, oil and gas, technology, and consumer goods; and

- provides information and holds conferences and work-shops for consumers, businesses, and policy makers on competition issues for market analysis.[58]

The FTC's Bureau of Consumer Protection works for the consumer to prevent fraud, deception, and unfair business practices in the marketplace. The Bureau claims that it:

- enhances consumer confidence by enforcing federal laws that protect consumers,

- empowers consumers with free information to help them exercise their rights and spot and avoid fraud and deception, and

- wants to hear from consumers who want to get information or file a complaint about fraud or identity theft.[59]

Another important FTC Bureau is the Bureau of Economics. It provides economic analysis and support to antitrust and consumer protection investigations. Many consumer protection issues today involve the Internet.

Consumer Privacy The popularity of the Internet for direct marketing, for collecting consumer data, and as a repository for sensitive consumer data has alarmed privacy-minded consumers. The U.S. Congress passed the CAN-SPAM Act in an attempt to regulate unsolicited e-mail advertising. The act prohibits commercial e-mailers from using false addresses and presenting false or misleading information, among other restrictions.

Internet users who once felt fairly anonymous when using the Web are now disturbed by the amount of information marketers collect about them and their children as they visit various sites in cyberspace. The FTC, with jurisdiction under the Children's Online Privacy Protection Act Rule, requires Web site operators to post a privacy policy on the home page and a link to the policy on every page where personal information is collected. An area of growing concern to privacy advocates is called behavioral targeting, which is discussed in more detail in Chapters 9 and 22.

LO 8 Competitive Factors

The competitive environment encompasses the number of competitors a firm must face, the relative size of the competitors, and the degree of interdependence within the industry. Management has little control over the competitive environment confronting a firm.

Competition for Market Share and Profits

As U.S. population growth slows, global competition increases, costs rise, and available resources tighten, firms find that they must work harder to maintain their profits and market share regardless of the form of the competitive market. Sometimes technology advances can usher in a whole new set of competitors that can change a firm's business model. In the single-serve coffee brewing market, Keurig and Green Mountain have the lion's share of the market, but Starbucks is hoping to cash in on some of that market share by working with Green Mountain to package its super-premium coffee into the single-serve pods used in the Keurig machines. Dunkin' Donuts coffee is also offered by Green Mountain, but Starbucks would represent the only super-premium coffee offered by the company. This is one of several moves Starbucks is making to add profit growth by selling in consumer goods markets beyond its retail coffee shops.[60]

Global Competition

Boeing is a very savvy international business competitor. Many foreign competitors also consider the United States to be a ripe target market. Thus, a U.S. marketing manager can no longer focus only on domestic competitors. In automobiles, textiles, watches, televisions, steel, and many other areas, foreign competition has been strong. In the past, foreign firms penetrated U.S. markets by concentrating on price, but today the emphasis has switched to product quality. Nestlé, Sony, Rolls-Royce, and Sandoz Pharmaceuticals are noted for quality, not cheap prices. Global competition is discussed in much more detail in Chapter 5.

LOCATION, LOCATION, We HAVE YOUR LOCATION

As Smartphones and mobile devices with Internet access have proliferated, so has the software available to consumers. Many apps provide information about your immediate area, restaurants, and even traffic conditions. Some software can calculate your location to within 60 feet and then sell your location to nearby companies to advertise to you. Using consumer locations to sell advertisements has recently raised alarm bells and spurred Rep. Rick Boucher (D-Virginia) to draft legislation. He, and most legislation-wary marketers, want consumers to know what kind of data is being collected about them, how long the information is kept, and what it's used for. Developers may not intend the software to be harmful, but hackers and accidents may pose threats, depending on the information the developer has collected.[61]

SOURCE: Emily Steel and Justin Scheck, "Smartphone Trackers Raise Privacy Worries," *Wall Street Journal*, June 14, 2010, http://online.wsj.com/article/SB10001424052748704067504575304643134531922.html.

© ISTOCKPHOTO.COM/JELENA POPIC

STUDY TOOLS
CHAPTER 4

Flip to the back of your textbook to:

❑ **Rip out Chapter Review Card**

Log in to the CourseMate for MKTG at cengagebrain.com to:

❑ **Review Key Terms Flash Cards (Print or Online)**

❑ **Review Audio and Visual Summaries**

❑ **Complete both Practice Quizzes to prepare for tests**

❑ **Play "Beat the Clock" and "Quizbowl" to master concepts**

❑ **Complete "Crossword Puzzle" to review key terms**

❑ **Watch the video on "Scholfield Honda" for a real company example about the marketing environment**

USE THE TOOLS.

- Rip out the Review Cards in the back of your book to study.

Or Visit CourseMate to:

- Read, search, highlight, and take notes in the Interactive eBook
- Review Flashcards (Print or Online) to master key terms
- Test yourself with Auto-Graded Quizzes
- Bring concepts to life with Games, Videos, and Animations!

Go to CourseMate for MKTG to begin using these tools.
Access at **www.cengagebrain.com**

Complete the Speak Up
survey in CourseMate at
www.cengagebrain.com

f **Follow us at
www.facebook.com/4ltrpress**

© iStockphoto.com/A-Digit | © Cengage Learning 2013

> Over the past two decades, world trade has climbed from $200 billion a year to over $13 trillion.

LO 1 Rewards of Global Marketing

AFTER YOU FINISH THIS CHAPTER, GO TO PAGE 80 FOR STUDY TOOLS

Today, global revolutions are under way in many areas of our lives: management, politics, communications, and technology. The word *global* has assumed a new meaning, referring to a boundless mobility and competition in social, business, and intellectual arenas. **Global marketing**—marketing that targets markets throughout the world—has become an imperative for business.

U.S. managers must develop a global vision not only to recognize and react to international marketing opportunities but also to remain competitive at home. Often a U.S. firm's toughest domestic competition comes from foreign companies. Moreover, a global vision enables a manager to understand that customer and distribution networks operate worldwide, blurring geographic and political barriers and making them increasingly irrelevant to business decisions. In summary, having a **global vision** means recognizing and reacting to international marketing opportunities, using effective global marketing strategies, and being aware of threats from foreign competitors in all markets.

Over the past two decades, world trade climbed from $200 billion a year to over $12.5 trillion in 2009. This was a 12 percent contraction from 2008 sparked by the global economic crisis. As the world slowly began to emerge from the Great Recession, world trade grew by 9.5 percent in 2010.[1]

global marketing
marketing that targets markets throughout the world

global vision
recognizing and reacting to international marketing opportunities, using effective global marketing strategies, and being aware of threats from foreign competitors in all markets

What do you think?

What a business decides to do overseas doesn't affect me.

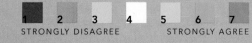

| 1 | 2 | 3 | 4 | 5 | 6 | 7 |

STRONGLY DISAGREE   STRONGLY AGREE

© PHIL ASHLEY/LIFESIZE/GETTY IMAGES

Find out what others think at the CourseMate for MKTG. Log in at cengagebrain.com.

gross domestic product (GDP) the total market value of all final goods and services produced in a country for a given time period

job outsourcing sending U.S. jobs abroad

Today's marketers face many challenges to their customary practices. Product development costs are rising, the life of products is getting shorter, and new technology is spreading around the world faster than ever. But marketing winners relish the pace of change instead of fearing it.

Adopting a global vision can be very lucrative for a company. Caterpillar, one of the world's largest manufacturers of construction and mining equipment, diesel and natural gas engines, and industrial turbines has sales of over $33 billion annually. Almost $21 billion comes from sales outside the United States.[2]

Despite the increasing availability of foreign customers, small businesses still account for only approximately 30 percent of U.S. exporting volume. Whether global business is daunting because of the various trade laws or tariffs, or because the markets are unfamiliar, small businesses are taking only slow, hesitant steps into the global market.[3]

Global marketing is not a one-way street whereby only U.S. companies sell their wares and services throughout the world. Foreign competition in the domestic market was once relatively rare but now is found in almost every industry. In fact, in many industries, U.S. businesses have lost significant market share to imported products. In electronics, cameras, automobiles, fine china, tractors, leather goods, and a host of other consumer and industrial products, U.S. companies have struggled at home to maintain their market shares against foreign competitors.

Importance of Global Marketing to the United States

Many countries depend more on international commerce than the United States does. For example, France, Britain, and Germany all derive more than 19 percent of their gross domestic product from world trade, which is considerably more than the United States does. **Gross domestic product (GDP)** is the total market value of all final goods and services produced in a country for a given time period (usually a year or a quarter of a year). *Final* in the definition refers to final products that are sold, not to intermediate products used in the assembly of a final product. For example, if the value of a brake (an intermediate product) and that of a car (the final product) were both counted, the brake would be counted twice. Therefore, GDP counts only the final goods and services to get the true value of a country's production.

Nevertheless, the impact of international business on the U.S. economy is still impressive:

» The United States exports about a fifth of its industrial production.

» More than 10 million Americans hold jobs that are supported by exports, accounting for 7 percent of employment.

» Exports represent approximately 13 percent of our GDP.[4]

» Every U.S. state has realized net employment gains directly attributed to foreign trade.

» The United States exports over $1.7 trillion in goods and services each year.[5]

About 85 percent of all U.S. exports of manufactured goods are shipped by 250 companies, and less than 10 percent of all manufacturing businesses, or around 25,000 companies, export their goods on a regular basis. Most small- and medium-sized firms are essentially nonparticipants in global trade and marketing. Only the very large multinational companies have seriously attempted to compete worldwide. Fortunately, more small companies are now aggressively pursuing international markets. To increase U.S. exports, in March 2010 President Barack Obama created the National Export Initiative (NEI). The NEI's goal is to double U.S. exports over the next five years and support 2 million U.S. jobs.

The Impact of Trade and Globalization

The protests during meetings of the World Trade Organization, the World Bank, and the International Monetary Fund (the three organizations are discussed later in the chapter) show that many people fear world trade and globalization. What do they fear? The negatives of global trade are as follows:

» Millions of Americans have lost jobs due to imports, production shifts abroad, or outsourcing of tech jobs. Some find new jobs, but they often pay less.

» Millions of others fear losing their jobs, especially at those companies operating under competitive pressure.

» Employers often threaten to outsource jobs if workers do not accept pay cuts.

» Service and white-collar jobs are increasingly vulnerable to operations moving offshore.

Job Outsourcing The notion of **job outsourcing** (sending U.S. jobs abroad) has been highly controversial for the past several years. Many executives

© MAX EAREY/SHUTTERSTOCK.COM

say that it leads to corporate growth, efficiency, productivity, and revenue growth. Most companies see cost savings as a key driver in outsourcing. Detroit has suffered as many factories in the auto industry have been shut down and relocated around the world. For example, Ford's newly reintroduced line of compact sedans and hatchbacks, called the Fiesta, is being built in several countries, including Mexico.

Benefits of Globalization Traditional economic theory says that globalization relies on competition to drive down prices and increase product and service quality. Business goes to the countries that operate most efficiently and/or have the technology to produce what is needed. In summary, globalization expands economic freedom, spurs competition, and raises the productivity and living standards of people in countries that open themselves to the global marketplace. For less developed countries, globalization also offers access to foreign capital, global export markets, and advanced technology while breaking the monopoly of inefficient and protected domestic producers. Faster growth, in turn, reduces poverty, encourages democratization, and promotes higher labor and environmental standards. Though government officials may face more difficult choices as a result of globalization, their citizens enjoy greater individual freedom. In this sense, globalization acts as a check on governmental power by making it more difficult for governments to abuse the freedom and property of their citizens.

Globalization deserves credit for helping lift many millions out of poverty and for improving standards of living of low-wage families. In developing countries around the world, globalization has created a vibrant middle class that has elevated the standard of living for hundreds of millions of people. In many developing countries around the world, life expectancies and health care have improved, as have educational opportunities.[6]

LO 2 Multinational Firms

The United States has a number of large companies that are global marketers. Many of them have been very successful. A company that is heavily engaged in international trade, beyond exporting and importing, is called a **multinational corporation**. A multinational corporation moves resources, goods, services, and skills across national boundaries without regard to the country in which its headquarters is located.

Multinationals often develop their global business in stages. In the first stage, companies operate in one country and sell into others. Second-stage multinationals set up foreign subsidiaries to handle sales in one country. In the third stage, multinationals operate an entire line of business in another country. The fourth stage has evolved primarily due to the Internet and involves mostly high-tech companies. For these firms, the executive suite is virtual. Their top executives and core corporate functions are in different countries, wherever the firms can gain a competitive edge through the availability of talent or capital, low costs, or proximity to their most important customers.

> **multinational corporation** a company that is heavily engaged in international trade, beyond exporting and importing

A multinational company may have several worldwide headquarters, depending on where certain markets or technologies are. Britain's APV, a maker of food-processing equipment, has a different headquarters for each of its worldwide businesses.

Many U.S.-based multinationals earn a large percentage of their total revenue abroad. Exhibit 5.1 shows revenue abroad for some industrial companies. Caterpillar, the construction-equipment company, receives 67 percent of its revenue from overseas, and General Electric earns 54 percent of its revenue abroad.

Are Multinationals Beneficial?

Although multinationals comprise far less than 1 percent of U.S. companies, they account for about 19 percent of all private jobs, 25 percent of all private wages, 48 percent of total exports of goods, and a remarkable 74 percent of nonpublic R&D spending. For decades, U.S. multinationals have driven an outsized share of U.S. productivity growth, the foundation of

EXHIBIT 5.1
Industrial Companies with the Largest Overseas Revenue

Company	Percent Foreign Revenue	Percent Growth of International Exposure (April 2008–April 2009)
Caterpillar	67	120
General Electric	54	64
United Technologies	46	59
Deere	35	57
Honeywell	39	58

SOURCE: David MacDougall, "Caterpillar Makes the Case for Going Abroad," *TheStreet*, April 27, 2010.

capital intensive
using more capital than labor in the production process
global marketing standardization
production of uniform products that can be sold the same way all over the world

rising standards of living for everyone. They are responsible for 41 percent of the increase in private labor productivity since 1990. More investment and employment abroad have tended to create more American investment and jobs as well. From 1988 to 2007, employment in foreign affiliates rose to 10 million from 4.8 million. During that same period, employment in U.S. parent companies rose to 22 million from 17.7 million.[7] Some multinationals have shifted income to low-tax countries, which has reduced corporate income tax payments in America. The multinationals claim that this was necessary because the United States has a very complicated tax structure with one of the highest corporate income tax rates among industrialized nations.

The role of multinational corporations in developing nations is a subject of controversy. The ability of multinationals to tap financial, physical, and human resources from all over the world and combine them economically and profitably can be of benefit to any country. They also often possess and can transfer the most up-to-date technology. Critics, however, claim that often the wrong kind of technology is transferred to developing nations. Usually, it is **capital intensive** (requiring a greater expenditure for equipment than for labor) and thus does not substantially increase employment. A "modern sector" then emerges in the nation, employing a small proportion of the labor force with relatively high productivity and income levels and with increasingly capital-intensive technologies. In addition, multinationals sometimes support reactionary and oppressive regimes if it is in their best interests to do so. Other critics say that the firms take more wealth out of developing nations than they bring in, thus widening the gap between rich and poor nations. The petroleum industry in particular has been heavily criticized in the past for its actions in some developing countries.

To counter such criticism, more and more multinationals are taking a proactive role in being good global citizens. Sometimes companies are spurred to action by government regulation, and in other cases multinationals are attempting to protect their good brand names.

Global Marketing Standardization

Traditionally, marketing-oriented multinational corporations have operated somewhat differently in each country. They use a strategy of providing different product features, packaging, advertising, and so on. However, Ted Levitt, a former Harvard professor, described a trend toward what he referred to as "global marketing," with a slightly different meaning.[9] He contended that communication and technology have made the world smaller so that almost all consumers everywhere want all the things they have heard about, seen, or experienced. Thus, he saw the emergence of global markets for standardized consumer products on a huge scale, as opposed to segmented foreign markets with different products. In this book, global marketing is defined as individuals and organizations using a global vision to effectively market goods and services across national boundaries. To make the distinction, we can refer to Levitt's notion as **global marketing standardization**.

Global marketing standardization presumes that the markets throughout the world are becoming more alike. Firms practicing global marketing standardization produce "globally standardized products" to be sold the same way all over the world. Uniform production should enable companies to lower production and marketing costs and increase profits. Levitt cited Coca-Cola, Colgate-Palmolive, and McDonald's as successful global marketers. His critics point out, however, that the success of these three companies is really based on variation, not on offering the same product everywhere. McDonald's, for example, changes its salad dressings and provides self-serve espresso for French tastes. It sells bulgogi burgers in South Korea and falafel burgers in

REVLON—A WORLD CLASS MAKEUP ARTIST

Revlon is a well-known brand in the United States and made its most successful mascara launch in 2010 with its Grow Luscious Mascara. But Revlon is also a huge (and growing) presence globally. Revlon is sold in 121 countries, which generate 50 percent of the company's business. This includes Asia—an area with particularly high economic growth.[8]

SOURCE: Andrea Nagel and Rachel Brown, "Gains Expected for Makeup," *Women's Wear Daily*, February 4, 2011, 3.

© ISTOCKPHOTO.COM/KONSTANTIN32

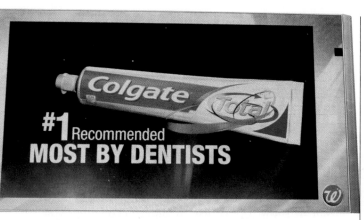

Colgate is marketing its toothpaste the same way globally, using global marketing standardization.

© RICHARD LEVINE/ALAMY

Egypt. Further, the fact that Coca-Cola and Colgate-Palmolive sell some of their products in more than 160 countries does not signify that they have adopted a high degree of standardization for all their products globally. Only three Coca-Cola brands are standardized, and one of them, Sprite, has a different formulation in Japan.

Companies with separate subsidiaries in other countries can be said to operate using a multidomestic strategy. A **multidomestic strategy** occurs when multinational firms enable individual subsidiaries to compete independently in domestic markets. Simply put, multidomestic strategy is how multinational firms use strategic business units (see Chapter 2). Colgate-Palmolive uses both strategies: Axion paste dishwashing detergent, for example, was formulated for developing countries, and La Croix Plus detergent was custom made for the French market—examples of multidomestic strategies. Colgate toothpaste is marketed the same way globally, using global marketing standardization.

Nevertheless, some multinational corporations are moving toward a degree of global marketing standardization. Alan Mulally, CEO of Ford, claims that his company is moving toward global marketing standardization with its new Focus. The new Focus is Ford's first truly global car—a single vehicle designed and engineered for customers in every region of the world and sold under one name. It is small, fuel efficient, and packed with technology and safety features that Mulally believes will appeal to consumers in Europe, Asia, and the Americas. "Why are we doing it this way?" he asked. "Because we believe the customer requirements are going to be more the same around the world than they are different."[10]

LO 3 External Environment Faced by Global Marketers

A global marketer or a firm considering global marketing must consider the external environment. Many of the same environmental factors that operate in the domestic market also exist internationally. These factors include culture, economic and technological development, political structure and actions, demographic makeup, and natural resources.

Culture

Central to any society is the common set of values shared by its citizens that determines what is socially acceptable. Culture underlies the family, the educational system, religion, and the social class system. The network of social organizations generates overlapping roles and status positions. These values and roles have a tremendous effect on people's preferences and thus on marketers' options. A company that does not understand a country's culture is doomed to failure in that country. Cultural blunders lead to misunderstandings and often perceptions of rudeness or even incompetence. For example, when people in India shake hands, they sometimes do so rather limply. This isn't a sign of weakness or disinterest; instead, a soft handshake conveys respect. Avoiding eye contact is also a sign of deference in India.

The rights to reproduce Broadway plays are increasingly being sold overseas, but the plays encounter some difficulty in translating cultural idioms and humor into the native languages. Performers in Seoul, South Korea, are producing the first non-English performance of *Billy Elliot the Musical*, but they are experiencing some cultural roadblocks. There is no Korean wordplay to mimic Billy's misinterpretation of "Billy Elliot Esquire" for "Billy Elliot is queer," so the translation uses some Korean profanity that requires parental permission to say. Some of the characters are very straightforward and cannot be "translated" into Korean culture, but the company is hopeful that the overall similarities in the plot will resonate with the audiences.[11]

> **multidomestic strategy** when multinational firms enable individual subsidiaries to compete independently in domestic markets

Singer and Model Daniela Katzenberger attends the premiere of the musical *Grease* at Admiralspalast in Berlin, Germany.

Language is another important aspect of culture that can create problems for marketers. Marketers must take care in translating product names, slogans, instructions, and promotional messages so as not to convey the wrong meaning. Free translation software, such as babelfish.com or Google Translate, allows users to input text in one language and output in another language. But marketers must take care using the software, as it can have unintended results—the best being unintelligible, the worst being insulting.

Each country has its own customs and traditions that determine business practices and influence negotiations with foreign customers. In many countries, personal relationships are more important than financial considerations. For instance, skipping social engagements in Mexico may lead to lost sales. Negotiations in Japan often include long evenings of dining, drinking, and entertaining, and only after a close personal relationship has been formed do business negotiations begin.

Making successful sales presentations abroad requires a thorough understanding of the country's culture. Germans, for example, don't like risk and need strong reassurance. A successful presentation to a German client will emphasize three points: the bottom-line benefits of the product or service, that there will be strong service support, and that the product is guaranteed. In southern Europe, it is an insult to show a price list. Without negotiating, you will not close the sale. The English want plenty of documentation for product claims and are less likely to simply accept the word of the sales representative. Scandinavian and Dutch companies are more likely to approach business transactions as Americans do than are companies in any other country.

Economic Factors

A second major factor in the external environment facing the global marketer is the level of economic development in the countries where it operates. In general, complex and sophisticated industries are found in developed countries, and more basic industries are found in less developed nations. Average family incomes are higher in the more developed countries compared to the less developed countries. Larger incomes mean greater purchasing power and demand not only for consumer goods and services but also for the machinery and workers required to produce consumer goods.

According to the World Bank, the average *gross national income (GNI)* per capita for the world is $10,341.[12] GNI is a country's GDP (defined earlier) together with its income received from other countries (mainly interest and dividends) less similar payments made to other countries. The United States' GNI per capita is $46,790 but it is not the world's highest. That honor goes to Luxembourg at $52,770. Of course, there are many very poor countries: Guinea, $970; Malawi, $810; Mozambique, $771; Sierra Leone, $770; Niger, $680; and Eritrea, $640.[13] GNI per capita is one measure of a country's citizens' ability to buy various goods and services. A marketer with a global vision can use these

© F84/F84/ZUMA PRESS/NEWSCOM

data to aid in measuring market potential in countries around the globe.

Not only is per capita income a consideration when going abroad, but so is the cost of doing business in a country. Although it is not the same as the cost of doing business, we can gain insights into expenses by examining the cost of living in various cities. The most expensive cities in the world are Paris, Tokyo, and Oslo. Other cities (with their rank out of 132 cities), are Frankfurt (5), Sydney (12), London (16), Chicago (36), Moscow (45), Beijing (57), Mexico City (84), and Mumbai (131). [14]

The Global Economy

A global marketer today must be fully aware of the intertwined nature of the global economy. In the past, the size of the U.S. economy was so large that global markets tended to move up or down depending on its health. It was said that "If America sneezes, then the rest of the world catches a cold." This is still true today. The U.S. housing market collapse and speculative financing led to a major global recession in 2008. It was, in fact, America's deepest decline in economic activity since the Great Depression. As the world slowly pulled itself out of the recession, the possibility of Greece defaulting on its national debt nearly stifled global economic recovery. The Greek crisis was followed by concern about other debt crises in Spain and Portugal. Moreover, the world now looks to other economies such as China, India, and Brazil to help jump-start economic growth. The lesson for the global marketer is clear: forecasting global demand and economic growth requires an understanding of what is happening economically in countries around the globe.

Doing Business in China and India

The two countries of growing interest to many multinationals are India and China because of their huge economic potential. They have some of the highest growth rates in the world and are emerging as megamarkets. China and India also have the world's two largest populations, two of the world's largest geographic areas, greater linguistic and sociocultural diversity than any other country, and among the highest levels of income

disparity in the world—some people are extremely poor whereas others are very rich. Given this scale and variety, there is no "average Chinese customer" or "average Indian customer."

Both India and China have exploded in spending power, particularly in the upper classes. By 2020, China will likely be the largest luxury market in the world, with sales exceeding $100 billion. [15] Driving this growth are Chinese below the age of 45, a demographic that constitutes 73 percent of China's luxury buyers. One market research firm reported a staggering 95 percent increase in online sales in China during 2010, marking another avenue for companies to reach shoppers. [16] Starbucks is hoping to mimic its success in China (where it plans to triple its stores) in India. The more affluent Indians often have experienced Starbucks outside of India and would welcome the coffee giant. It is a burgeoning market: coffee consumption increased roughly 90 percent from 1998 to 2008 because the Indian consumer enjoys the casual café atmosphere. Starbucks hopes to increase the distribution of its Indian coffee beans and to open premium locations in Tata's superluxurious Taj hotels. [17]

Relations between the United States and China have not always been smooth, however. China is committed to protecting its businesses and asserting new global strength, which has resulted in several legislative stalemates with the United States. China has the power and draw of a country with steadily increasing consumption and high growth potential, making it particularly attractive to U.S. firms. China is the fastest-growing importer of U.S. goods—up 330 percent since 2000. The rest of the world increased imports from the United States by only 29 percent. If trade fails, China loses significant U.S. imports, and the United States loses a rapid growth market. [18]

Political Structure and Actions

Political structure is a third important variable facing global marketers. Government policies run the gamut from no private ownership and minimal individual freedom to little central government and maximum personal freedom. As rights of private property increase, government-owned industries and centralized planning tend to decrease. But a political environment is rarely at one extreme or the other. India, for instance, is a republic with elements of socialism, monopoly capitalism, and competitive capitalism in its political ideology.

A recent World Bank study found that the least amount of business regulation fosters the strongest

© ISTOCKPHOTO.COM/ROYDEE

Mercosur the largest Latin American trade agreement; includes Argentina, Bolivia, Brazil, Chile, Colombia, Ecuador, Paraguay, Peru, and Uruguay

Uruguay Round an agreement to dramatically lower trade barriers worldwide; created the World Trade Organization

economies.[19] The least regulated and most efficient economies are concentrated among countries with well-established common-law traditions, including Australia, Canada, New Zealand, the United Kingdom, and the United States. On a par with the best performers are Singapore and Hong Kong. Not far behind are Denmark, Norway, and Sweden, social democracies that recently streamlined their business regulation. Vietnam has decentralized and begun eliminating red tape that had previously turned investors away. The country is also benefiting from political and labor strife in neighboring countries. Intel is opening a $1 billion plant in Vietnam, and the Vietnamese government hopes that others will follow.[20]

Legal Considerations Closely related to and often intertwined with the political environment are legal considerations. In France, nationalistic sentiments led to a law that requires pop music stations to play at least 40 percent of their songs in French (even though French teenagers love American and English rock and roll).

Many legal structures are designed to either encourage or limit trade:

▸▸ *Tariff:* a tax levied on the goods entering a country. Because a tariff is a tax, it will either reduce the profits of the firms paying the tariff or raise prices to buyers, or both. Normally, a tariff raises prices of the imported goods and makes it easier for domestic firms to compete. The United States maintains tariffs as high as 27 percent on Canadian softwood lumber because the Canadian government allegedly subsidizes the industry.

▸▸ *Quota:* a limit on the amount of a specific product that can enter a country. Several U.S. companies have sought quotas as a means of protection from foreign competition.

▸▸ *Boycott:* the exclusion of all products from certain countries or companies. Governments use boycotts to exclude companies from countries with which they have a political dispute. Several Arab nations boycotted Coca-Cola because it maintained distributors in Israel.

▸▸ *Exchange control:* a law compelling a company earning foreign exchange from its exports to sell it to a control agency, usually a central bank. A company wishing to buy goods abroad must first obtain a foreign currency exchange from the control agency. For instance, Avon Products drastically cut back new production lines and products in the Philippines because exchange controls prevented the company from converting pesos to dollars to ship back to the home office. The pesos had to be used in the Philippines.

▸▸ *Market grouping (also known as a common trade alliance):* occurs when several countries agree to work together to form a common trade area that enhances trade opportunities. The best-known market grouping is the European Union (EU).

▸▸ *Trade agreement:* an agreement to stimulate international trade. Not all government efforts are meant to stifle imports or investment by foreign corporations. The largest Latin American trade agreement is **Mercosur**, which includes Argentina, Bolivia, Brazil, Chile, Colombia, Ecuador, Paraguay, Peru, and Uruguay. The elimination of most tariffs among the trading partners has resulted in trade revenues of more than $16 billion annually. The economic boom created by Mercosur will undoubtedly cause other nations to seek trade agreements on their own or to enter Mercosur.

The Uruguay Round, the Failed Doha Round, and Bilateral Agreements The **Uruguay Round** is an agreement that has dramatically lowered trade barriers worldwide. Adopted in 1994, the agreement has been signed by 151 nations. It is the most ambitious global trade agreement ever negotiated. The agreement has reduced tariffs by one-third worldwide—a move that has raised global income by $235 billion annually. Perhaps most notable is the recognition of new global realities. For the first time, an agreement covers services, intellectual property rights, and trade-related investment measures such as exchange controls.

The Uruguay Round made several major changes in world trading practices.

▸▸ *Entertainment, pharmaceuticals, integrated circuits, and software:* The rules protect patents, copyrights, and trademarks for 20 years. Computer programs receive 50 years of protection and semiconductor chips receive 10 years of protection. But many developing nations were given a decade to phase in patent protection for drugs. France, which limits the number of U.S. movies and television shows that can be shown, refused to liberalize market access for the U.S. entertainment industry.

© ISTOCKPHOTO.COM/DANNY DE BRUYNE

- *Financial, legal, and accounting services:* Services came under international trading rules for the first time, creating a vast opportunity for these competitive U.S. industries. Now it is easier for managers and key personnel to be admitted to a country. Licensing standards for professionals, such as doctors, cannot discriminate against foreign applicants. That is, foreign applicants cannot be held to higher standards than domestic practitioners.

- *Agriculture:* Europe is gradually reducing farm subsidies, opening new opportunities for such U.S. farm exports as wheat and corn. Japan and Korea are beginning to import rice. But U.S. growers of sugar and citrus fruit have had their subsidies trimmed.

- *Textiles and apparel:* Strict quotas limiting imports from developing countries are being phased out, causing further job losses in the U.S. clothing trade. But retailers and consumers are the big winners, because past quotas have added $15 billion a year to clothing prices.

- *A new trade organization:* The **World Trade Organization (WTO)** replaced the old **General Agreement on Tariffs and Trade (GATT)**, which was created in 1948. The WTO eliminated the extensive loopholes of which GATT members took advantage. Today, all WTO members must fully comply with all agreements under the Uruguay Round. The WTO also has an effective dispute settlement procedure with strict time limits to resolve disputes.

The latest round of WTO trade talks began in Doha, Qatar, in 2001. For the most part, the periodic meetings of WTO members under the Doha Round have been very contentious. One of the most contentious goals of the round was for the major developing countries, known collectively as BRIC (Brazil, Russia, India, and China), to lower tariffs on industrial goods in exchange for European and American tariff and subsidy cuts on farm products. Concerned that lowering tariffs would result in an economically damaging influx of foreign cotton, sugar, and rice, China and India demanded a safeguard clause that would allow them to raise tariffs on those crops if imports surged. Unable to agree on what percentage increase constituted a surge in imports, the countries remain at an impasse.[21]

In addition to the slow progress of the Doha Round, many countries have moved toward protectionism after the global recession of 2008–2009. This movement discourages new trade agreements, which are designed to encourage international trade. Ecuador, for instance, has hiked tariffs on more than 600 categories of imports. Chinese companies have made several allegations that the United States is engaging in protectionism and blocking companies from participating in bids for work or companies for sale.[22]

However, the move toward protectionism has not reversed the agreements and organizations that arose from the period of increased globalization before the economic crisis in 2008: the North American Free Trade Agreement, the Central America Free Trade Agreement, the European Union, the World Bank, and the International Monetary Fund.

North American Free Trade Agreement At the time it was instituted, the **North American Free Trade Agreement (NAFTA)** created the world's largest free trade zone. Ratified by the U.S. Congress in 1993, the agreement includes Canada, the United States, and Mexico, with a combined population of 441 million and an economy of $17 trillion.

The main impact of NAFTA was to open the Mexican market to U.S. companies. When the treaty went into effect, tariffs on about half the items traded across the Rio Grande disappeared. The pact removed a web of Mexican licensing requirements, quotas, and tariffs that limited transactions in U.S. goods and services. For instance, the pact allowed U.S. and Canadian financial-services companies to own subsidiaries in Mexico.

In August 2007, the three member countries met in Canada to tweak NAFTA, but not make substantial changes. For example, the members agreed to further remove trade barriers on hogs, steel, consumer electronics, and chemicals. They also directed the North American Steel Trade Committee, which represents the three governments, to focus on subsidized steel from China.

The real question is whether NAFTA can continue to deliver rising prosperity in all three countries. America has certainly benefited from cheaper imports and more investment opportunities abroad. Exports to Mexico still account for only 1.1 percent of the economy, and imports from Mexico are less than 1.7 percent of the economy. Trade between Canada and the United States reached $740 billion in 2008, and U.S. capital invested in Canadian securities reached $41.7 billion in 2009—the largest annual American investment since 1977.[23]

World Trade Organization (WTO) a trade organization that replaced the old General Agreement on Tariffs and Trade (GATT)

General Agreement on Tariffs and Trade (GATT) a trade agreement that contained loopholes enabling countries to avoid trade-barrier reduction agreements

North American Free Trade Agreement (NAFTA) an agreement between Canada, the United States, and Mexico that created the world's then-largest free trade zone

Central America Free Trade Agreement (CAFTA) a trade agreement, instituted in 2005, that includes Costa Rica, the Dominican Republic, El Salvador, Guatemala, Honduras, Nicaragua, and the United States

European Union (EU) a free trade zone encompassing 27 European countries

NAFTA has also created millions of jobs for all three nations. It is estimated that Canada has gained almost 5 million jobs, the United States has picked up 25 million jobs, and Mexico has created nearly 10 million jobs.[24]

Central America Free Trade Agreement The **Central America Free Trade Agreement (CAFTA)** was instituted in 2005. Besides the United States, the agreement includes Costa Rica, the Dominican Republic, El Salvador, Guatemala, Honduras, and Nicaragua.

Between 2005 and 2007, trade between the United States and CAFTA countries grew 18 percent. The United States exported $23 billion of goods and services to CAFTA nations in 2007, up 33 percent since 2005. The United States imported $19 billion of goods and services from CAFTA nations, up 4 percent since 2005.[25] CAFTA has been an unqualified success. It has created new commercial opportunities for its members, has promoted regional stability, and is an impetus for economic development for an important group of U.S. neighbors.

European Union The **European Union (EU)** is one of the world's most important free trade zones and now encompasses most of Europe. More than a free trade zone, it is also a political and economic community. As a free trade zone, it guarantees the freedom of movement of people, goods, services, and capital between member states. It also maintains a common trade policy with outside nations and a regional development policy. The EU represents member nations in the WTO. Recently, the EU also began venturing into foreign policy as well, getting involved in issues such as Iran's refining of uranium.

The European Union currently has 27 member states: Austria, Belgium, Bulgaria, Cyprus, the Czech Republic, Denmark, Estonia, Finland, France, Germany, Greece, Hungary, Ireland, Italy, Latvia, Lithuania, Luxembourg, Malta, the Netherlands, Poland, Portugal, Romania, Slovakia, Slovenia, Spain, Sweden, and the United Kingdom. There are currently five official candidate countries: Croatia, Iceland, the Republic of Macedonia, Montenegro, and Turkey. In addition, the western Balkan countries of Albania, Bosnia and Herzegovina, and Serbia are officially recognized as potential candidates.[26]

In early 2010, Greece entered a financial crisis that highlighted the challenges of a large currency union where member nations maintain responsibility for their own fiscal policies. Unable to devalue its currency to boost sales of products without injuring other member nations, Greece turned to member states for a bailout. The crisis has highlighted debt problems in other EU nations such as Hungary, Italy, Portugal, and Spain. After failing to meet strict budget-cutting measures imposed by the EU and the International Monetary Fund, Hungary did not receive the next installment of financial aid, indicating how serious lenders are about implementing long-term fixes to irresponsible debt.[27]

The European Union Commission and the courts have not always been kind to multinationals. For example, the EU fined Procter & Gamble, Unilever, and Henkel for running a cartel that fixed laundry detergent prices. The EU investigated the three companies and found that they formed the cartel after joining in efforts to reduce packaging materials for Ariel and Tide (P&G), OMO and Radiant (Unilever), and Persil (Henkel). In that meeting, the three companies agreed on pricing and respective market share, which the EU determined unfairly limited competition and forced consumers to pay higher prices. All three companies agreed to cooperate with the investigation and are paying the fine.[28]

The EU is the largest economy in the world. The EU is also a huge market, with a population of nearly 500 million and a GDP of $18 trillion. The United States and the EU have the largest bilateral trade and investment relationship in world history. Together, they account for more than half of the global economy, while bilateral trade accounts for 7 percent of

© SINISA BOTAS/SHUTTERSTOCK.COM

the world total. U.S. and EU companies have invested an estimated $2 trillion in each other's economies, employing directly and indirectly as many as 14 million workers. Nearly every U.S. state is involved with exporting to, importing from, or working for European firms.[29]

The EU is an attractive market, with purchasing power almost equal to that of the United States. But the EU presents marketing challenges because, even with standardized regulations, marketers will not be able to produce a single European product for a generic European consumer. With more than 15 different languages and individual national customs, Europe will always be far more diverse than the United States. Thus, product differences will continue to be necessary.

An entirely different type of problem facing global marketers is the possibility of a protectionist movement by the EU against outsiders. For example, European automakers have proposed holding Japanese imports at roughly their current 10 percent market share. The Irish, Danes, and Dutch don't make cars and have unrestricted home markets; they would be unhappy about limited imports of Toyotas and Nissans. But France has a strict quota on Japanese cars to protect Renault and Peugeot. These local carmakers could be hurt if the quota is raised at all.

The World Bank, the International Monetary Fund, and the G-20 Two international financial organizations are instrumental in fostering global trade. The **World Bank** offers low-interest loans to developing nations. Originally, the purpose of the loans was to help these nations build infrastructure such as roads, power plants, schools, drainage projects, and hospitals. Now the World Bank offers loans to help developing nations relieve their debt burdens. To receive the loans, countries must pledge to lower trade barriers and aid private enterprise. In addition to making loans, the World Bank is a major source of advice and information for developing nations. The **International Monetary Fund (IMF)** was founded in 1945, one year after the creation of the World Bank, to promote trade through financial cooperation and eliminate trade barriers in the process. The IMF makes short-term loans to member nations that are unable to meet their budgetary expenses. It operates as a lender of last resort for troubled nations. In exchange for these emergency loans, IMF lenders frequently extract significant commitments from the borrowing nations to address the problems that led to the crises. These steps may include curtailing imports or even devaluing the currency.

The **Group of Twenty (G-20)** Finance Ministers and Central Bank Governors was established in 1999 to bring together industrialized and developing economies to discuss key issues in the global economy. The G-20 is a forum for international economic development that promotes discussion between industrial and emerging-market countries on key issues related to global economic stability. By contributing to the strengthening of the international financial system and providing opportunities for discussion on national policies, international cooperation, and international financial institutions, the G-20 helps to support growth and development across the globe. The members of the G-20 are shown in Exhibit 5.2.

In 2009, the G-20 met in Pittsburgh, Pennsylvania, where it adopted President Obama's proposed *Framework for Strong, Sustainable and Balanced Growth*. The document outlined a process to help avoid other financial crises such as the one that started in the financial markets in the United States in 2007. It also provided recommendations for long-term global growth.

Demographic Makeup

The three most densely populated nations in the world are China, India, and Indonesia. But that fact alone is not particularly useful to marketers. They also need to know whether the population is mostly urban or rural, because marketers may not have easy access to rural consumers. Belgium, with about 90 percent of the population living in urban settings, is an attractive market.

World Bank an international bank that offers low-interest loans, advice, and information to developing nations

International Monetary Fund (IMF) an international organization that acts as a lender of last resort, providing loans to troubled nations, and also works to promote trade through financial cooperation

Group of Twenty (G-20) a forum for international economic development that promotes discussion between industrial and emerging-market countries on key issues related to global economic stability

EXHIBIT 5.2
Members of the G-20

Argentina	European Union	Italy	South Africa
Australia	France	Japan	Republic of Korea
Brazil	Germany	Mexico	Turkey
Canada	India	Russia	United Kingdom
China	Indonesia	Saudi Arabia	United States

© CENGAGE LEARNING 2013

Another key demographic consideration is age. There is a wide gap between the older populations of the industrialized countries and the vast working-age populations of developing countries. This gap has enormous implications for economies, businesses, and the competitiveness of individual countries. It means that while Europe and Japan struggle with pension schemes and the rising cost of health care, countries like Brazil, China, and Mexico can reap the fruits of a demographic dividend: falling labor costs, a healthier and more educated population, and the entry of millions of women into the workforce. The demographic dividend is a gift of falling birthrates, and it causes a temporary bulge in the number of working-age people. Population experts have estimated that one-third of East Asia's economic miracle can be attributed to a beneficial age structure. But the miracle occurred only because the governments had policies in place to educate their people, create jobs, and improve health.

Natural Resources

A final factor in the external environment that has become more evident in the past decade is the shortage of natural resources. For example, petroleum shortages have created huge amounts of wealth for oil-producing countries such as Norway, Saudi Arabia, and the United Arab Emirates. Both consumer and industrial markets have blossomed in these countries. Other countries—such as Indonesia, Mexico, and Venezuela—were able to borrow heavily against oil reserves in order to develop more rapidly. On the other hand, industrial countries such as Japan, the United States, and much of western Europe experienced an enormous transfer of wealth to the petroleum-rich nations. The high price of oil has created inflationary pressures in petroleum-importing nations. It also created major problems for airlines and other petroleum-dependent industries. Petroleum is not the only natural resource that affects international marketing. Warm climate and lack of water mean that many of Africa's countries will remain importers of foodstuffs. The United States, on the other hand, must rely on Africa for many precious metals. Vast differences in natural resources create international dependencies, huge shifts of wealth, inflation and recession, export

opportunities for countries with abundant resources, and even a stimulus for military intervention.

LO 4 Global Marketing by the Individual Firm

A company should consider entering the global marketplace only after its management has a solid grasp of the global environment.

Companies decide to "go global" for a number of reasons. Perhaps the most important is to earn additional profits. Managers may feel that international sales will result in higher profit margins or more added-on profits. A second stimulus is that a firm may have a unique product or technological advantage not available to other international competitors. Such advantages should result in major business successes abroad. In other situations, management may have exclusive market information about foreign customers, marketplaces, or market situations not known to others. While exclusivity can provide an initial motivation for international marketing, managers must realize that competitors can be expected to catch up with the firm's information advantage. Finally, saturated domestic markets, excess capacity, and potential for economies of scale can also be motivators to "go global." Economies of scale mean that average per-unit production costs fall as output is increased.

© YAKOBCHUK VASYL/SHUTTERSTOCK.COM

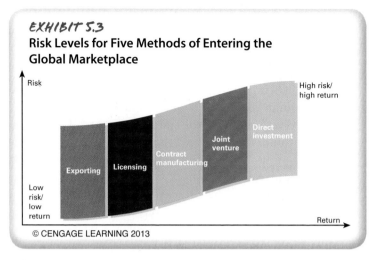

EXHIBIT 5.3
Risk Levels for Five Methods of Entering the Global Marketplace

© CENGAGE LEARNING 2013

Many firms form multinational partnerships—called strategic alliances—to assist them in penetrating global markets; strategic alliances are examined in Chapter 7. Five other methods of entering the global marketplace are, in order of risk, exporting, licensing and franchising, contract manufacturing, joint venture, and direct investment (see Exhibit 5.3).

Exporting

When a company decides to enter the global market, exporting is usually the least complicated and least risky alternative. **Exporting** is selling domestically produced products to buyers in other countries. A company can sell directly to foreign importers or buyers. The United States is the world's largest exporter.

Instead of selling directly to foreign buyers, a company may decide to sell to intermediaries located in its domestic market. The most common intermediary is the export merchant, also known as a **buyer for export**, which is usually treated like a domestic customer by the domestic manufacturer. The buyer for export assumes all risks and sells internationally for its own account. The domestic firm is involved only to the extent that its products are bought in foreign markets.

A second type of intermediary is the **export broker**, who plays the traditional broker's role by bringing buyer and seller together. The manufacturer still retains title and assumes all the risks. Export brokers operate primarily in agricultural products and raw materials.

Export agents, a third type of intermediary, are foreign sales agents/distributors who live in the foreign country and perform the same functions as domestic manufacturers' agents, helping with international financing, shipping, and so on. The U.S. Department of Commerce has an agent/distributor service that helps about 5,000 U.S. companies each year find an agent or distributor in virtually any country of the world. A second category of agents resides in the manufacturer's country but represents foreign buyers. This type of agent acts as a hired purchasing agent for foreign customers operating in the exporter's home market.

Licensing and Franchising

Another effective way for a firm to move into the global arena with relatively little risk is to sell a license to manufacture its product to someone in a foreign country. **Licensing** is the legal process whereby a licensor allows another firm to use its manufacturing process, trademarks, patents, trade secrets, or other proprietary knowledge. The licensee, in turn, pays the licensor a royalty or fee agreed on by both parties.

For example, the owners of the rights to Broadway plays, such as Disney's *The Lion King*, have seen increasing revenue from foreign markets through licensing. The rights to produce the plays internationally have different price points, but foreign presenters begin by

exporting selling domestically produced products to buyers in other countries

buyer for export an intermediary in the global market who assumes all ownership risks and sells globally for its own account

export broker an intermediary who plays the traditional broker's role by bringing buyer and seller together

export agent an intermediary who acts like a manufacturer's agent for the exporter; the export agent lives in the foreign market

licensing the legal process whereby a licensor allows another firm to use its manufacturing process, trademarks, patents, trade secrets, or other proprietary knowledge

© ADAM TAYLOR/DIGITAL VISION/GETTY IMAGES

DISNEY'S THE LION KING HAS BROUGHT IN MORE THAN $2 BILLION OVERSEAS ALONE.

contract manufacturing private label manufacturing by a foreign company

joint venture when a domestic firm buys part of a foreign company or joins with a foreign company to create a new entity

direct foreign investment active ownership of a foreign company or of overseas manufacturing or marketing facilities

paying $200,000 in advance to stage a U.S. production. Replica shows, using licensed sets and costumes, cost the most; and nonreplica shows, which pay for the rights to the play but not sets or costuming, cost less. Foreign revenue for licensing nonreplica shows grew more than 10 percent in the last two years.[30]

A licensor must make sure it can exercise sufficient control over the licensee's activities to ensure proper quality, pricing, distribution, and so on. Licensing may also create a new competitor in the long run, if the licensee decides to void the license agreement. International law is often ineffective in stopping such actions. Two common ways of maintaining effective control over licensees are shipping one or more critical components from the United States or locally registering patents and trademarks to the U.S. firm, not to the licensee. Garment companies maintain control by delivering only so many labels per day; they also supply their own fabric, collect the scraps, and do accurate unit counts.

Franchising is a form of licensing that has grown rapidly in recent years. More than 400 U.S. franchisors operate more than 40,000 outlets in foreign countries, bringing in sales of over $9 billion.[31] Over half of the international franchises are for fast-food restaurants and business services.

Contract Manufacturing Firms that do not want to become involved in licensing or to become heavily involved in global marketing may engage in **contract manufacturing**, which is private label manufacturing by a foreign company. The foreign company produces a certain volume of products to specification, with the domestic firm's brand name on the goods. The domestic company usually handles the marketing. Thus, the domestic firm can broaden its global marketing base without investing in overseas plants and equipment. After establishing a solid base, the domestic firm may switch to a joint venture or direct investment.

Joint Venture

Joint ventures are somewhat similar to licensing agreements. In an international **joint venture**, the domestic firm buys part of a foreign company or joins with a foreign company to create a new entity. A joint venture is a quick and relatively inexpensive way to go global and to gain needed expertise. Chronicle Books joined the existing Abrams marketing and sales team in the United Kingdom in a joint venture called Abrams & Chronicle Books to expand its presence in the UK market.[32]

Joint ventures can be very risky, however. Many fail; others fall victim to a takeover in which one partner buys out the other. Sometimes joint venture partners simply can't agree on management strategies and policies.

Direct Investment

Active ownership of a foreign company or of overseas manufacturing or marketing facilities is called **direct foreign investment**. Direct foreign investment by U.S. firms is currently about $2.1 trillion. Direct investors have either a controlling interest or a large minority interest in the firm. Thus, they have the greatest potential reward and the greatest potential risk. Because of problems with contract manufacturing and joint ventures in China, multinationals are going it alone. Today, nearly five times as much foreign direct investment comes into China in the form of stand-alone efforts as comes in for joint ventures.

A firm may make a direct foreign investment by acquiring an interest in an existing company or by building new facilities. It might do so because it has trouble transferring some resource to a foreign operation or getting that resource locally. One important resource is personnel, especially managers. If the local labor market is tight, the firm may buy an entire foreign firm and retain all its employees instead of paying higher salaries than competitors.

The United States is a popular place for direct investment by foreign companies. In 2008, the value of foreign-owned businesses in the United States was more than $650 billion. For

© MIKE KEMP/RUBBERBALL/JUPITERIMAGES

example, in 2007, Taiwan-based Aur bought U.S. computer maker Gateway.

LO5 The Global Marketing Mix

To succeed, firms seeking to enter into foreign trade must still adhere to the principles of the marketing mix. Information gathered on foreign markets through research is the basis for the four Ps of global marketing strategy: product, place (distribution), promotion, and price. Marketing managers who understand the advantages and disadvantages of different ways of entering the global market and the effect of the external environment on the firm's marketing mix have a better chance of reaching their goals.

The first step in creating a marketing mix is developing a thorough understanding of the global target market. Often this knowledge can be obtained through the same types of marketing research used in the domestic market (see Chapter 9). However, global marketing research is conducted in vastly different environments. Conducting a survey can be difficult in developing countries, where telephone ownership is growing but is not always common and mail delivery is slow or sporadic. Drawing samples based on known population parameters is often difficult because of the lack of data. In some cities in Africa, Asia, Mexico, and South America, street maps are unavailable, streets are unidentified, and houses are unnumbered. Moreover, the questions a marketer can ask may differ in other cultures. In some cultures, people tend to be more private than in the United States and will not respond to personal questions on surveys. For instance, in France, questions about one's age and income are considered especially rude.

Product and Promotion

With the proper information, a good marketing mix can be developed. One important decision is whether to alter the product or the promotion for the global marketplace. Other options are to radically change the product or to adjust either the promotional message or the product to suit local conditions.

One Product, One Message The strategy of global marketing standardization, which was discussed earlier, means developing a single product for all markets and promoting it the same way all over the world.

For instance, Procter & Gamble uses the same product and promotional themes for Head & Shoulders in China as it does in the United States. The advertising draws attention to a person's dandruff problem, which stands out in a nation of black-haired people. Head & Shoulders is now the best-selling shampoo in China despite costing over 300 percent more than local brands. Buoyed by its success with Head & Shoulders, P&G is using the same product and same promotion strategy with Tide detergent in China. It also used another common promotion tactic that has been successful in the United States. The company spent half a million dollars to reach agreements with local washing machine manufacturers, which now include a free box of Tide with every new washer.

Global media—especially satellite and cable television networks such as CNN International, MTV Networks, and British Sky Broadcasting—make it possible to beam advertising to audiences unreachable a few years ago. Eighteen-year-olds in Paris often have more in common with 18-year-olds in New York than with their own parents. Almost all of MTV's advertisers run unified, English-language campaigns in the 28 nations the firm reaches. The audiences buy the same products, go to the same movies, listen to the same music, and sip the same colas. Global advertising merely works on that premise. Although teens throughout the world prefer movies above all other forms of television programming, they are closely followed by music videos, stand-up comedy, and then sports.

Global marketing standardization can sometimes backfire. Unchanged products may fail simply because of cultural factors. Any type of war game tends to do very poorly in Germany, even though Germany is by far the world's biggest game-playing nation. A successful game in Germany is highly detailed and has a thick rulebook.

Sometimes the desire for absolute standardization must give way to practical considerations and local market dynamics. For example, because of the feminine connotations of the word *diet*, the European version of Diet Coke is Coca-Cola Light. Even if the brand name differs by market—as with Lay's potato chips, which are called Sabritas in Mexico—a strong visual relationship may be created by uniform application of the brandmark and graphic elements on packaging.

Product Invention In the context of global marketing, product invention can be taken to mean either creating a new product for a market or drastically changing an existing product. For example, Dunkin' Donuts offers American-style doughnuts in Korea, but the firm created a number of new items for Korean tastes. The company offers sweet potato donuts, glutinous rice donuts, and several varieties of tofu donuts.[33]

McDonald's was once vilified for pushing its American-created fast food on the world. Now it is taking a different approach and selling more than ever in the global marketplace.

© MICHAEL NEELON/ALAMY

Product Adaptation Another alternative for global marketers is to slightly alter a basic product to meet local conditions. Unilever's Rexona brand deodorant sticks sell for 16 cents and up. They are big hits in Bolivia, India, Peru, and the Philippines—where Unilever has grabbed 60 percent of the deodorant market.

Fast-food restaurants often adapt products to fit the needs of their foreign customers. In India, Dominos sells a pizza called the "Peppy Paneer," which features the popular Indian cheese Paneer and spicy red peppers. McDonald's, known for its foreign adaptations, sells Chicken Maharaja Macs instead of Big Macs, out of respect for the cow's sacred status for Hindus.[34]

Promotion Adaptation

Another global marketing strategy is to maintain the same basic product but alter the promotional strategy. Bicycles are mainly pleasure vehicles in the United States. In many parts of the world, however, they are a family's main mode of transportation. Thus, promotion in these countries should stress durability and efficiency. In contrast, U.S. advertising may emphasize escaping and having fun.

Language barriers, translation problems, and cultural differences have generated numerous headaches for international marketing managers. For example, a toothpaste claiming to give users white teeth was especially inappropriate in many areas of Southeast Asia, where the well-to-do chew betel nuts and black teeth are a sign of higher social status.

Place (Distribution)

Solving promotional and product problems does not guarantee global marketing success. The product still has to get adequate distribution. For example, Europeans don't play sports as much as Americans do, so they don't visit sporting-goods stores as often. Realizing this, Reebok started selling its shoes in about 800 traditional shoe stores in France. In one year, the company doubled its French sales.

To combat distribution problems, companies are using creative strategies. A small company in India is setting up a unique distribution system that will allow large and small companies to distribute their goods to very small retailers in villages of 5,000 people or less. The company, Universal Village, uses a large sales staff, often from the villages they work with, to take orders from the small retailers. The staff then sends the orders through a mobile application to a warehouse. The warehouse packs the order into small boxes, and those boxes are delivered to each retailer. Not only does the system help distribute a wider range of products, but it also allows these small retailers to operate more efficiently by not having to leave their shop to travel large distances to restock the store.[35]

In many developing nations, channels of distribution and the physical infrastructure are inadequate. In Africa, the continent's GDP is growing rapidly, and African businesses want to expand. Unfortunately, they face high tariffs, weak infrastructure, and severely impoverished populations. To expand into neighboring countries, Notore Chemicals Ltd., a Nigerian fertilizer company, appealed directly to the governments to develop a distribution chain across 20 African nations. Some East African countries are even developing a regional trade zone to encourage growth.[36]

American companies importing goods from overseas facilities to the United States are facing other problems. Logistics has been a growing challenge for U.S. companies seeking to cut costs by shifting more production to countries where manufacturing is cheaper. Now, however, the rising costs for shipping goods are adding to their profit pressures. The surge in global trade in recent years has added to strains and charges for all forms of transport. As a result, some manufacturers are developing costly buffer stocks—which can mean setting up days' or weeks' worth of extra components—to avoid shutting down production lines and failing to make timely deliveries. Others are shifting to more expensive but more reliable modes of transport, such as air freight, which is faster and less prone to delays than ocean shipping.

Pricing

Once marketing managers have determined a global product and promotion strategy, they can select the remainder of the marketing mix. Pricing presents some unique problems in the global sphere. Exporters must not only cover their production costs but also consider transportation costs, insurance, taxes, and tariffs. When deciding on a final price, marketers must also determine how much customers are willing to spend on a particular product. Marketers also need to ensure that their foreign buyers will pay the price. Because developing nations lack mass purchasing power, selling to them often poses special pricing problems. Sometimes a product can be simplified in order to lower the price. The firm must not assume low-income countries are willing to accept lower quality, however. L'Oréal was unsuccessful selling cheap shampoo in India, so the company targets the rising class. It now sells a $17 Paris face powder and a $25 Vichy sunscreen. Both products are very popular.

Exchange Rates The exchange rate is the price of one country's currency in terms of another country's currency. If a country's currency *appreciates*, less of that country's currency is needed to buy another country's currency. If a country's currency *depreciates*, more of that currency will be needed to buy another country's currency.

How do appreciation and depreciation affect the prices of a country's goods? If, say, the U.S. dollar depreciates relative to the Japanese yen, U.S. residents will have to pay more dollars to buy Japanese goods. To illustrate, suppose the dollar price of a yen is $0.012 and that a Toyota is priced at 2 million yen. At this exchange rate, a U.S. resident pays $24,000 for a Toyota ($0.012 × 2 million yen = $24,000). If the dollar depreciates to $0.018 to 1 yen, then the U.S.

resident will have to pay $36,000 for the same Toyota.

As the dollar depreciates, the prices of Japanese goods rise for U.S. residents, so they buy fewer Japanese goods—thus, U.S. imports may decline. At the same time, as the dollar depreciates relative to the yen, the yen appreciates relative to the dollar. This means prices of U.S. goods fall for the Japanese, so they buy more U.S. goods—and U.S. exports rise.

Currency markets operate under a system of **floating exchange rates**. Prices of different currencies "float" up and down based on the demand for and the supply of each currency. Global currency traders create the supply of and demand for a particular country's currency based on that country's investment, trade potential, and economic strength.

Dumping **Dumping** is the sale of an exported product at a price lower than that charged for the same or a like product in the "home" market of the exporter. This practice is regarded as a form of price discrimination that can potentially harm the importing nation's competing industries. Dumping may occur as a result of exporter business strategies that include (1) trying to increase an overseas market share, (2) temporarily distributing products in overseas markets to offset slack demand in the home market, (3) lowering unit costs by exploiting large-scale production, and (4) attempting to maintain stable prices during periods of exchange rate fluctuations.

Historically, the dumping of goods has presented serious problems in international trade. As a result, dumping has led to significant disagreements among countries and diverse views about its harmfulness. Some trade economists view dumping as harmful only when it involves the use of "predatory" practices that intentionally try to eliminate competition and gain monopoly power in a market. They believe that predatory dumping rarely occurs and that antidumping rules are a protectionist tool whose cost to consumers and import-using industries exceeds the benefits to the industries receiving protection.

Countertrade Global trade does not always involve cash. Countertrade is a fast-growing way to conduct global business. In **countertrade**, all or part of the payment for goods or services is in the form of other

floating exchange rates a system in which prices of different currencies move up and down based on the demand for and the supply of each currency

dumping the sale of an exported product at a price lower than that charged for the same or a like product in the "home" market of the exporter

countertrade a form of trade in which all or part of the payment for goods or services is in the form of other goods or services goods or services. Countertrade is thus a form of barter (swapping goods for goods), an age-old practice whose origins have been traced back to cave dwellers. The U.S. Department of Commerce says that roughly 30 percent of all global trade is countertrade. In fact, both India and China have made billion-dollar government purchasing lists, with most of the goods to be paid for by countertrade.

One common type of countertrade is straight barter. For example, PepsiCo sends Pepsi syrup to Russian bottling plants and in payment gets Stolichnaya vodka, which is then marketed in the West. Another form of countertrade is the compensation agreement. Typically, a company provides technology and equipment for a plant in a developing nation and agrees to take full or partial payment in goods produced by that plant. For example, General Tire Company supplied equipment and know-how for a Romanian truck tire plant. In turn, General Tire sold the tires it received from the plant in the United States under the Victoria brand name. Both sides benefit even though they don't use cash.

LO 6 The Impact of the Internet

In many respects, "going global" is easier than it has ever been before. Opening an e-commerce site on the Internet immediately puts a company in the international marketplace. Sophisticated language translation software can make any site accessible to people around the world. Global shippers such as UPS, FedEx, and DHL help solve international e-commerce distribution complexities. E4X, Inc. offers software to ease currency conversions by allowing customers to pay in the currency of their choice. E4X collects the payment from the customer and then pays the site in U.S. dollars. Nevertheless, the promise of "borderless commerce" and the global "Internet economy" are still being restrained by the old brick-and-mortar rules, regulations, and habits. For example, Lands' End is not allowed to mention its unconditional refund policy on its e-commerce site in Germany because German retailers, which normally do not allow returns after 14 days, sued and won a court ruling blocking mention of it.

STUDY TOOLS
CHAPTER 5

Flip to the end of your textbook to:

❏ **Rip out Chapter Review Card**

Log in to the CourseMate for MKTG at cengagebrain.com to:

❏ **Review Key Terms Flash Cards (Print or Online)**

❏ **Review Audio and Visual Summaries**

❏ **Complete both Practice Quizzes to prepare for tests**

❏ **Play "Beat the Clock" and "Quizbowl" to master concepts**

❏ **Complete "Crossword Puzzle" to review key terms**

❏ **Watch the video on "Evo" for a real company example on Developing a Global Vision**

ANATOMY OF a Multinational Company: Starbucks

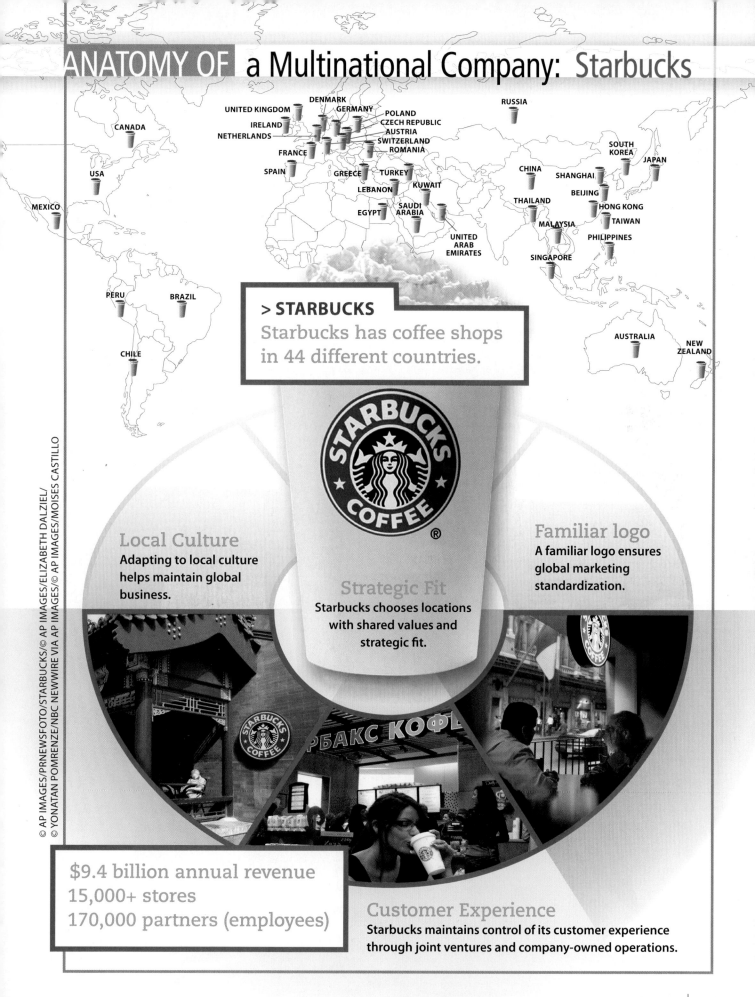

> **STARBUCKS**

Starbucks has coffee shops in 44 different countries.

Local Culture
Adapting to local culture helps maintain global business.

Strategic Fit
Starbucks chooses locations with shared values and strategic fit.

Familiar logo
A familiar logo ensures global marketing standardization.

$9.4 billion annual revenue
15,000+ stores
170,000 partners (employees)

Customer Experience
Starbucks maintains control of its customer experience through joint ventures and company-owned operations.

© AP IMAGES/PRNEWSFOTO/STARBUCKS/© AP IMAGES/ELIZABETH DALZIEL/
© YONATAN POMRENZE/NBC NEWWIRE VIA AP IMAGES/© AP IMAGES/MOISES CASTILLO

CHAPTER 6 Consumer Decision Making

Consumers' product and service preferences are constantly changing.

LO1 The Importance of Understanding Consumer Behavior

AFTER YOU FINISH THIS CHAPTER, GO TO PAGE 109 FOR STUDY TOOLS

Consumers' product and service preferences are constantly changing. Marketing managers must understand these desires in order to create a proper marketing mix for a well-defined market. So it is critical that marketing managers have a thorough knowledge of consumer behavior. **Consumer behavior** describes how consumers make purchase decisions and how they use and dispose of the purchased goods or services. The study of consumer behavior also includes factors that influence purchase decisions and product use.

Understanding how consumers make purchase decisions can help marketing managers in several ways. For example, if a manager knows through research that gas mileage is the most important attribute for a certain target market, the manufacturer can redesign a car to meet that criterion. If the firm cannot change the design in the short run, it can use promotion in an effort to change consumers' decision-making criteria, for example, by promoting style, durability, and cargo capacity.

consumer behavior processes a consumer uses to make purchase decisions, as well as to use and dispose of purchased goods or services; also includes factors that influence purchase decisions and product use

What do you think?

Shopping just boils down to "buy" or "don't buy."

| 1 | 2 | 3 | 4 | 5 | 6 | 7 |

STRONGLY DISAGREE   STRONGLY AGREE

© ISTOCKPHOTO.COM/ISTOCK INHOUSE

consumer decision-making process a five-step process used by consumers when buying goods or services

need recognition result of an imbalance between actual and desired states

want recognition of an unfulfilled need and a product that will satisfy it

stimulus any unit of input affecting one or more of the five senses: sight, smell, taste, touch, hearing

Shaping Public Policy and Educating Consumers

Understanding consumer behavior can also help the government make better public decisions and aid in educating consumers against buying and using goods and services that may injure their health or hurt society. Research on childhood obesity has led to public service advertising campaigns targeted toward parents to help them plan healthy diets for their children. Some states have passed laws regarding the types of meals that can be served at schools. Recent research on the use of tanning beds has found that it dramatically increases the risk of deadly skin cancers. In light of this research, the U.S. federal government instituted a 10 percent tax on indoor tanning sessions, which will increase the cost of a session by approximately $1.70.[1]

LO2 The Consumer Decision-Making Process

When buying products, particularly new or expensive items, consumers generally follow the **consumer decision-making process** shown in Exhibit 6.1:

YOU JUST ATE 16 PACKS OF SUGAR.

All those extra calories can bring on obesity, diabetes and heart disease.

(20oz. soda)

Are you pouring on the pounds?
Find out at nyc.gov/health/drinkingfat

Become a fan at facebook.com/drinkingfat

NYC Health

Michael R. Bloomberg, Mayor
Thomas Farley, M.D., M.P.H., Commissioner

(1) need recognition, (2) information search, (3) evaluation of alternatives, (4) purchase, and (5) postpurchase behavior. These five steps represent a general process that can be used as a guide for studying how consumers make decisions. It is important to note, though, that consumers' decisions do not always proceed in order through all of these steps. In fact, the consumer may end the process at any time or may not even make a purchase. The section on the types of consumer buying decisions later in the chapter discusses why a consumer's progression through these steps may vary. We begin, however, by examining the basic purchase process in greater detail.

Need Recognition

The first stage in the consumer decision-making process is need recognition. **Need recognition** occurs when consumers are faced with an imbalance between actual and desired states that arouses and activates the consumer decision-making process. A **want** is the new way that a consumer goes about addressing a need. For example, have you ever gotten blisters from an old running shoe? Or maybe you have seen a television commercial for a new sports car and wanted to buy it. Need recognition is triggered when a consumer is exposed to either an internal or an external **stimulus**. *Internal stimuli* are occurrences you experience, such as hunger or thirst. For example, you may hear your stomach growl and then realize you are hungry. *External stimuli* are influences from an outside source such as someone's recommendation of a new restaurant, the color of an automobile, the design of a package, a brand name mentioned by a friend, or an advertisement on television or radio.

The imbalance between actual and desired states is sometimes referred to as the "want-got gap." That is, there is a difference between what a customer has and what he or she would like to have. This gap doesn't always trigger consumer action. The gap must be large enough to drive the consumer to do something. Just because your stomach growls once doesn't mean that you necessarily will stop what you are doing and go eat.

A marketing manager's objective is to get consumers to recognize this want-got gap. Advertising and sales promotion often provide this stimulus. Surveying buyer preferences provides marketers with information about consumer needs and wants that can be used to tailor products and services. Marketing managers can create wants on the part of the consumer. For example, when college students move into their own apartment or dorm room, they often need

COURTESY OF NEW YORK CITY HEALTH DEPARTMENT

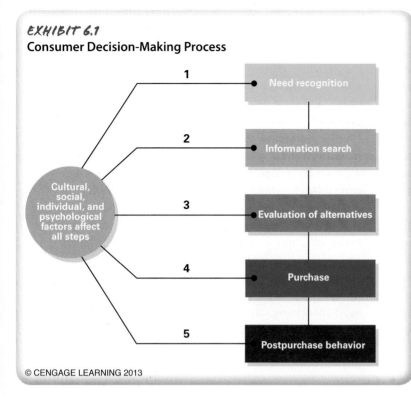

EXHIBIT 6.1
Consumer Decision-Making Process

Cultural, social, individual, and psychological factors affect all steps

1. Need recognition
2. Information search
3. Evaluation of alternatives
4. Purchase
5. Postpurchase behavior

© CENGAGE LEARNING 2013

to furnish them and want new furniture rather than hand-me-downs from their parents. A want can be for a specific product, or it can be for a certain attribute or feature of a product. In this example, the college students not only need home furnishings but also want items that reflect their personal sense of style. Similarly, consumers may want ready-to-eat meals, drive-through dry-cleaning service, and Internet shopping to fill their need for convenience.

Understanding Needs and Wants If marketers don't properly understand the target market's needs, the chances are good that the right good or service may not be produced. An excellent way to understand needs is to view them as job statements or outcome statements.[2] A job is a fundamental goal that consumers are trying to accomplish or a problem they are trying to resolve. Examples include: prevent mildew in a shower, hang a picture, or prepare income taxes. Desired outcome statements help marketers understand what consumers are seeking from a job. A desired outcome might be to minimize the time it takes to file an accurate income tax form that finds all possible legitimate deductions. People then can solve this problem several different ways: do the work themselves using government-provided information, do it themselves using software such as TurboTax, or hire a CPA to do it.

If you live in California and decide to go to college in Florida, the job is to get your furniture and stuff to Florida. The desired outcome is to get it there when needed, with the least hassle, and at the lowest cost. U-Haul understands the job and desired outcome. The firm is a one-stop shop for moving supplies; U-Haul offers customers prepackaged moving kits that reduce the time it takes to gather the various boxes and supplies required for a move. In addition, an online partnership with eMove helps customers quickly locate a variety of inputs in the form of human helpers such as packers, babysitters, cleaners, and painters.

Marketers selling their products in global markets must carefully observe the needs and wants of consumers in various regions. LG Electronics, a Korean company, is anticipating rising demand for education among India's rural population. Increased levels of education often precede growth in purchasing power, so LG is targeting India's rural population by developing durable appliances for little cost. Brightly colored appliances are designed with surge stabilizers (to handle sporadic electric supply) and more durable plastic parts (to withstand harsher environments). Consumers in rural villages have responded well to the appliances—LG has seen a 30 percent growth in its rural sales.[3]

Information Search

After recognizing a need or want, consumers search for information about the various alternatives available to satisfy it. For example, you see a great price on a bottle of wine, but you haven't heard of the brand or the type of wine, so you go to http://secondglass.com to get a realistic, jargon-free look at just what the wine tastes like. An information search can occur internally, externally, or both. In an **internal information search**, the person recalls information stored in the memory. This stored information stems largely from previous experience with a product. For example, while traveling with your family, you encounter a hotel where you stayed during spring break earlier that year. By searching your memory, you can probably remember whether the hotel had clean rooms and friendly service.

In contrast, an **external information search** seeks information in the outside environment. There are

internal information search the process of recalling past information stored in the memory

external information search the process of seeking information in the outside environment

nonmarketing-controlled information source a product information source that is not associated with advertising or promotion

marketing-controlled information source a product information source that originates with marketers promoting the product

two basic types of external information sources: nonmarketing-controlled and marketing-controlled. A **nonmarketing-controlled information source** is not associated with marketers promoting a product. These information sources include personal experiences (trying or observing a new product), personal sources (family, friends, acquaintances, and co-workers who may recommend a product or service), and public sources (such as Underwriters Laboratories, *Consumer Reports*, and other rating organizations that comment on products and services). For example, if you are in the mood to go to the movies, you may search your memory for past experiences at various cinemas when determining which one to go to (personal experiences). To choose which movie you will see, you may rely on the recommendations of friends and family (personal sources). Alternatively, you may read the critical reviews in the newspaper or online (public sources). Marketers gather information on how these information sources work and use it to attract customers. For example, car manufacturers know that younger customers are likely to get information from friends and family, so they try to develop enthusiasm for their products via word of mouth.

Living in the digital age has changed the way consumers get nonmarketing-controlled information. It can be from blogs, bulletin boards, activists, Web sites, Web forums, or consumer opinion sites such as www.consumerreview.com, www.tripadvisor.com, or www.epinions.com. Nearly 94 percent of U.S. consumers regularly or occasionally research products online before making an offline purchase, and nearly half of those consumers then share the information and advice they gleaned online with other consumers.[4] To give you an idea of the number of searches this implies, in the United States alone there were 23.7 billion searches in April 2010.[5]

The latest research has examined how consumers use information picked up on the Internet. For example, in Web forums, the information seeker has normally never met the information provider or ever interacted with the person before. Hui Chen found that online reviewers presenting full accounts of their entire online shopping experience influenced other shoppers to promote the company through word of mouth the most. Reviews about pricing and quality of product influenced other shoppers the sec-

ond most, and reviews discussing customer service by the company affected new consumers the least. Essentially, if other information seekers had found the provider trustworthy and kind, then the current seeker tended to believe the information, make a purchase, and then promote the company through other reviews.[6]

A **marketing-controlled information source** is biased toward a specific product because it originates with marketers promoting that product. Marketing-controlled information sources include mass media advertising (radio, newspaper, television, and magazine advertising), sales promotion (contests, displays, premiums, and so forth), salespeople, product labels and packaging, and the Internet. Many consumers, however, are wary of the information they receive from marketing-controlled sources, believing that most marketing campaigns stress the product's positive attributes and ignore its faults. These sentiments tend to be stronger among better-educated and higher-income consumers. Some marketing-controlled information sources can shift out of marketers' control,

Consumer Reports is a nonmarketing-controlled information source where consumers can find objective reviews of products. *Consumer Reports* magazines are available with a specific focus, in this case, car reviews.

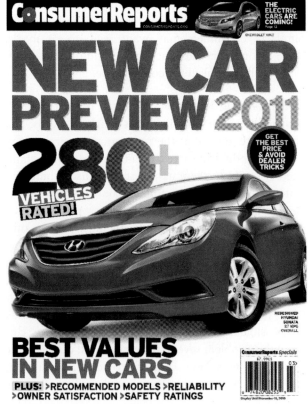

© YONHAP NEWS/YNA/NEWSCOM

however, when there is bad news to report. When news media blanketed the airwaves with coverage of Toyota's braking and acceleration problems, the carmaker responded with a series of television ads featuring customers talking about their loyalty to the brand and discussing Toyota's commitment to safety. The bottom line of the Toyota ads stressed the company's commitment to safety and continued investment in safety research for its vehicles.

The extent to which an individual conducts an external search depends on his or her perceived risk, knowledge, prior experience, and level of interest in the good or service. Generally, as the perceived risk of the purchase increases, the consumer enlarges the search and considers more alternative brands. For example, suppose that you want to purchase a surround sound system for your home stereo. The decision is relatively risky because of the expense and technical nature of the stereo system, so you are motivated to search for information about models, prices, options, compatibility with existing entertainment products, and capabilities. You may decide to compare attributes of many speaker systems because the value of the time expended finding the "right" stereo will be less than the cost of buying the wrong system.

A consumer's knowledge about the product or service will also affect the extent of an external information search. A consumer who is knowledgeable and well informed about a potential purchase is less likely to search for additional information. In addition, the more knowledgeable consumers are, the more efficiently they will conduct the search process, thereby requiring less time to search. For example, many consumers know that AirTran and other discount airlines have much lower fares, so they generally use the discounters and do not even check fares at other airlines.

The extent of a consumer's external search is also affected by confidence in one's decision-making ability. A confident consumer not only has sufficient stored information about the product but also

© TAVI/SHUTTERSTOCK.COM

feels self-assured about making the right decision. People lacking this confidence will continue an information search even when they know a great deal about the product. Consumers with prior experience in buying a certain product will have less perceived risk than inexperienced consumers. Therefore, they will spend less time searching and limit the number of products they consider.

A third factor influencing the external information search is product experience. Consumers who have had a positive prior experience with a product are more likely to limit their search to items related to the positive experience. For example, when flying, consumers are likely to choose airlines with which they have had positive experiences, such as consistent on-time arrivals, and avoid airlines with which they had a negative experience, such as lost luggage.

Finally, the extent of the search is positively related to the amount of interest a consumer has in a product. A consumer who is more interested in a product will spend more time searching for information and alternatives. For example, suppose you are a dedicated runner who reads jogging and fitness magazines and catalogs. In searching for a new pair of running shoes, you may enjoy reading about the new brands available and spend more time and effort than other buyers in deciding on the right shoe.

The consumer's information search should yield a group of brands, sometimes called the buyer's **evoked set** (or **consideration set**), which are the consumer's most preferred alternatives. From this set, the buyer will further evaluate the alternatives and make a choice. Consumers do not consider all brands available in a product category, but they do seriously consider a much smaller set. For example, from the many brands of pizza available, consumers are likely to consider only the alternatives that fit their price range, location, take-out/delivery needs, and taste preferences. Having too many choices can,

evoked set (consideration set) a group of brands, resulting from an information search, from which a buyer can choose

in fact, confuse consumers and cause them to delay the decision to buy or, in some instances, cause them not to buy at all.

Evaluation of Alternatives and Purchase

After getting information and constructing an evoked set of alternative products, the consumer is ready to make a decision. A consumer will use the information stored in memory and obtained from outside sources to develop a set of criteria. Recent research has shown that exposure to certain cues in your everyday environment can affect decision criteria and purchase. For example, when NASA landed the *Pathfinder* spacecraft on Mars, it captured media attention worldwide. The candy maker Mars also noted a rather unusual increase in sales. Although the Mars bar takes its name from the company's founder and not the planet, consumers apparently responded to news about the planet Mars by purchasing more Mars bars. Further research also suggests that consumer reviews are influenced by existing reviews—if there are existing one-star ratings, even positive consumer reviews will have fewer stars. Additionally, if consumers see large variations in consumer reviews, they are more likely to purchase the item and make a postpurchase evaluation on that site.[7]

The environment, internal information, and external information help consumers evaluate and compare alternatives. One way to begin narrowing the number of choices in the evoked set is to pick a product attribute and then exclude all products in the set that don't have that attribute. For example, assume Jane and Jill, both college sophomores, are looking for their first apartment. They need a two-bedroom apartment, reasonably priced and located near campus. They want the apartment to have a swimming pool, washer and dryer, and covered parking. Jane and Jill begin their search with all apartments in the area and then systematically eliminate possibilities that lack the features they need. Hence, if there are 50 alternatives in the area, they may reduce their list to just ten apartments that possess all of the desired attributes. Another way to narrow the number of choices is to use cutoffs. Cutoffs are either minimum or maximum levels of an attribute that an alternative must pass to be considered. Suppose Jane and Jill set a maximum of $1,000 per month to spend on combined rent. Then all apartments with rent higher than $1,000 will be eliminated, further reducing the list of apartments from ten to eight. A final way to narrow the choices is to rank the attributes under consideration in order of importance and evaluate the products based on how well each performs on the most important attributes. To reach a final decision on one of the remaining eight apartments, Jane and Jill may decide proximity to campus is the most important attribute. As a result, they will choose to rent the apartment closest to campus.

If new brands are added to an evoked set, the consumer's evaluation of the existing brands in that set changes. As a result, certain brands in the original set may become more desirable. Suppose Jane and Jill find two apartments located equal distance from campus, one priced at $800 and the other at $750. Faced with this choice, they may decide that the $800 apartment is too expensive given that a comparable apartment is cheaper. If they add a $900 apartment to the list, however, then they may perceive the $800 apartment as more reasonable and decide to rent it.

The purchase decision process described above is a piecemeal process. That is, the evaluation is made by examining alternative advantages and disadvantages along important product attributes. A different way consumers can evaluate a product is according to a categorization process. The evaluation of an alternative depends upon the particular category to which it is assigned. Categories can be very general (motorized forms of transportation), or they can be very specific (Harley-Davidson motorcycles). Typically, these categories are associated with some degree of liking or disliking. To the extent that the product can be assigned membership in a particular category, it will receive an evaluation similar to that attached to the category. If you go to the grocery store and see a new organic food on the shelf, you may evaluate it on your liking and opinions of organic food.

So, when consumers rely on a categorization process, a product's evaluation depends on the particular category to which it is perceived as belonging. Given this, companies need to understand whether consumers are using categories that evoke the desired evaluations. Indeed, how a product is categorized can strongly influence consumer demand. For example, what products come to mind when you think about the "morning beverages" category? To the soft drink industry's dismay, far too few consumers include sodas in this category. Several attempts have been made at getting soft drinks on the breakfast table, but with little success.

Brand extensions, in which a well-known and respected brand name from one product category is extended into other product categories, is one way companies employ categorization to their advantage. Brand extensions are a common business practice. J.Crew and Urban Outfitters are both extending the aesthetic of their clothing brands into bridal by launching wedding stores that sell wedding dresses, bridal accessories, and other bridal needs. Similarly, Collective Brands, which owns Payless ShoeSource, has teamed with Maesa Group, a cosmetics company that designs and manufactures products for retailers and beauty brands, to offer beauty and body care products at Payless stores.[8]

To Buy or Not to Buy Ultimately, the consumer has to decide whether to buy or not buy. Specifically, consumers must decide:

1. Whether to buy
2. When to buy
3. What to buy (product type and brand)
4. Where to buy (type of retailer, specific retailer, online or in store)
5. How to pay

When a person is buying an expensive or complex item, it is often a *fully planned purchase* based upon a lot of information. People rarely buy a new home simply on impulse. Often consumers will make a *partially planned purchase* when they know the product category they want to buy (shirts, pants, reading lamp, car floor mats) but wait until they get to the store to choose a specific style or brand. Finally, there is the *unplanned purchase*, which people buy on impulse. Research has found that up to 68 percent of the items bought during major shopping trips and 54 percent on smaller shopping trips are unplanned.[9]

LO3 Postpurchase Behavior

When buying products, consumers expect certain outcomes from the purchase. How well these expectations are met determines whether the consumer is satisfied or dissatisfied with the purchase. For example, if a person bids on a used car stereo from eBay and wins, he may have fairly low expectations regarding performance. If the stereo's performance turns out to be of superior quality, then the person's satisfaction will be high because his expectations were exceeded. Conversely, if the person bid on a new car stereo expect-

ing superior quality and performance, but the stereo broke within one month, he would be very dissatisfied because his expectations were not met. Price often influences the level of expectations for a product or service.

For the marketer, an important element of any postpurchase evaluation is reducing any lingering doubts that the decision was sound. When people recognize inconsistency between their values or opinions and their behavior, they tend to feel an inner tension called **cognitive dissonance**. For example, say someone is looking to upgrade her cell phone to a new Android Smartphone. For $299, she can get a Samsung Galaxy S II with a two-year contract, a dual core processor, and all the up-to-date features. Or, for $249 she can buy the Thunderbolt by HTC, which runs Flash and has two cameras and one well-above-average processor. Prior to choosing the Samsung Galaxy S II, the shopper may experience inner tension or anxiety because she is worried that the current top-of-the-line technology, which costs much more than the middle-of-the-line technology, will be obsolete in a couple of months. That feeling of dissonance arises as her worries over obsolescence battle her practical nature, which is focused on the lower cost of the Thunderbolt and its adequate—but less fancy—technology.

Consumers try to reduce dissonance by justifying their decision. They may seek new information that reinforces positive ideas about the purchase, avoid information that contradicts their decision, or revoke the original decision by returning the product. To ensure satisfaction, thereby reducing dissonance, the customer buying the Samsung Galaxy S II may talk to people who have the phone, read online reviews, and talk to her provider to obtain additional information. In some instances, people deliberately seek contrary information in order to refute it and reduce dissonance. Dissatisfied customers sometimes rely on word of mouth to reduce cognitive dissonance by letting friends and family know they are displeased.

Marketing managers can help reduce dissonance through effective communication with purchasers. For example, a customer service manager may slip a note inside the package congratulating the buyer on making a wise

cognitive dissonance inner tension that a consumer experiences after recognizing an inconsistency between behavior and values or opinions

© ISTOCKPHOTO.COM/DNY59

involvement the amount of time and effort a buyer invests in the search, evaluation, and decision processes of consumer behavior

routine response behavior the type of decision making exhibited by consumers buying frequently purchased, low-cost goods and services; requires little search and decision time

limited decision making the type of decision making that requires a moderate amount of time for gathering information and deliberating about an unfamiliar brand in a familiar product category

decision. Postpurchase letters sent by manufacturers and dissonance-reducing statements in instruction booklets may help customers feel at ease with their purchase. Advertising that displays the product's superiority over competing brands or guarantees can also help relieve the possible dissonance of someone who has already bought the product. In the case of the cell phone, Samsung's Web site, www.samsung.com/us/guide-page/galaxy-s, offers in-depth technology specifications about the different Samsung phones in the Galaxy line. Because the decision to purchase the top-of-the-line technology suggests the customer is influenced by technology, a Web site with detailed specifications is likely to reduce dissonance and exceed her expectations.

LO 4 Types of Consumer Buying Decisions and Consumer Involvement

All consumer buying decisions generally fall along a continuum of three broad categories: routine response behavior, limited decision making, and extensive

decision making (see Exhibit 6.2). Goods and services in these three categories can best be described in terms of five factors: level of consumer involvement, length of time to make a decision, cost of the good or service, degree of information search, and the number of alternatives considered. The level of consumer involvement is perhaps the most significant determinant in classifying buying decisions. **Involvement** is the amount of time and effort a buyer invests in the search, evaluation, and decision processes of consumer behavior.

Frequently purchased, low-cost goods and services are generally associated with **routine response behavior**. These goods and services can also be called low-involvement products because consumers spend little time on search and decision before making the purchase. Usually, buyers are familiar with several different brands in the product category but stick with one brand. For example, a person may routinely buy Tropicana orange juice. Consumers engaged in routine response behavior normally don't experience need recognition until they are exposed to advertising or see the product displayed on a store shelf. Consumers buy first and evaluate later, whereas the reverse is true for extensive decision making. A consumer who has previously purchased a whitening toothpaste and was satisfied with it will probably walk to the toothpaste aisle and select that same brand without spending 20 minutes examining all other alternatives.

Limited decision making typically occurs when a consumer has previous product experience but is unfamiliar with the current brands available. Limited decision making is also associated with lower levels of involvement (although higher than

© ANDREW HARRER/BLOOMBERG VIA GETTY IMAGES

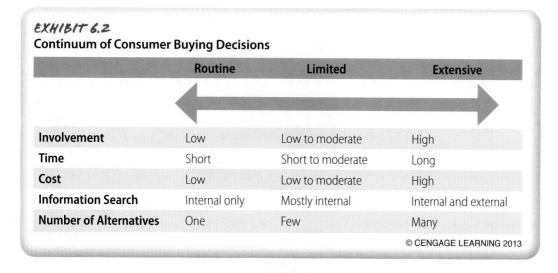

EXHIBIT 6.2
Continuum of Consumer Buying Decisions

	Routine	Limited	Extensive
Involvement	Low	Low to moderate	High
Time	Short	Short to moderate	Long
Cost	Low	Low to moderate	High
Information Search	Internal only	Mostly internal	Internal and external
Number of Alternatives	One	Few	Many

© CENGAGE LEARNING 2013

extensive decision making the most complex type of consumer decision making, used when buying an unfamiliar, expensive product or an infrequently bought item; requires use of several criteria for evaluating options and much time for seeking information

routine decisions) because consumers expend only moderate effort in searching for information or in considering various alternatives. But what happens if the consumer's usual brand of whitening toothpaste is sold out? Assuming that toothpaste is needed, the consumer will be forced to choose another brand. Before making a final decision, the consumer will likely evaluate several other brands based on their active ingredients, their promotional claims, and the consumer's prior experiences.

Consumers practice **extensive decision making** when buying an unfamiliar, expensive product or an infrequently bought item. This process is the most complex type of consumer buying decision and is associated with high involvement on the part of the consumer. This process resembles the model outlined in Exhibit 6.1. These consumers want to make the right decision, so they want to know as much as they can about the product category and available brands. People usually experience the most cognitive dissonance when buying high-involvement products. Buyers use several criteria for evaluating their options and spend much time seeking information. Buying a home or a car, for example, requires extensive decision making.

The type of decision making that consumers use to purchase a product does not necessarily remain constant. For instance, if a routinely purchased product no longer satisfies, consumers may practice limited or extensive decision making to switch to another brand. And people who first use extensive decision making may then use limited or routine decision making for future purchases. For example, when a family gets a new puppy, they will spend a lot of time and energy trying out different toys to determine which one the dog prefers. Once the new owners learn that the dog prefers a bone to a ball, however, the purchase no longer requires extensive evaluation and will become routine.

Factors Determining the Level of Consumer Involvement

The level of involvement in the purchase depends on the following factors:

▶▶ *Previous experience:* When consumers have had previous experience with a good or service, the level of involvement typically decreases. After repeated product trials, consumers learn to make quick choices. Because consumers are familiar with the product and know whether it will satisfy their needs, they become less involved in the purchase. For example, a consumer purchasing cereal has many brands to choose from—just think of any grocery store cereal aisle. If the consumer always buys the same brand because it satisfies his hunger, then he has a low level of involvement. When a consumer purchases cereal for the first time, however, it likely will be a much more involved purchase.

▶▶ *Interest:* Involvement is directly related to consumer interests, as in cars, music, movies, bicycling, or electronics. Naturally, these areas of interest vary from one individual to another. A person highly involved in bike racing will be more interested in the type of bike she owns and will spend quite a bit of time evaluating different bikes. If a person wants a bike only for recreation, however, he may be fairly uninvolved in the purchase and just look for a bike from the most convenient location.

▶▶ *Perceived risk of negative consequences:* As the perceived risk in purchasing a product increases, so does a consumer's level of involvement. The types of risks that concern consumers include financial risk, social risk, and psychological risk.

- *Financial risk* is exposure to loss of wealth or purchasing power. Because high risk is associated with high-priced purchases, consumers tend to become extremely involved. Therefore, price and involvement are usually directly related: As price increases, so does the level of involvement. For example, someone who is purchasing a new car for the first time (higher perceived risk) will spend a lot of time and effort making this purchase. Financial risk may carry greater weight today because of the Great Recession of 2008–2009. The loss of jobs and potential loss of jobs meant that prices did not necessarily have to be high to have high involvement. One study found that consumers are not only buying less but want brands to offer proof of value—73 percent of consumers would rather have a few, high-quality items. The recession has created more value-driven shoppers—more than 90 percent of consumers use coupons, shop at discount stores, and buy store brands.[10]

- *Social risks* occur when consumers buy products that can affect people's social opinions of them (for example, driving an old, beat-up car or wearing unstylish clothes).

- *Psychological risks* occur if consumers feel that making the wrong decision might cause some concern or anxiety. For example, some consumers feel guilty about eating foods that are not healthy, such as regular ice cream rather than fat-free frozen yogurt.

▸▸ *Social visibility:* Involvement also increases as the social visibility of a product increases. Products often on social display include clothing (especially designer labels), jewelry, cars, and furniture. All these items make a statement about the purchaser and, therefore, carry a social risk.

Not All Involvement Is the Same High involvement means that the consumer cares about a product category or a specific good or service. The product or service is relevant and important, and means something to the buyer. High involvement can take a number of different forms. The most important types are discussed below:

▸▸ *Product involvement* means that a product category has high personal relevance. Product enthusiasts are consumers with high involvement in a product category. The fashion industry has a large segment of product enthusiasts. These people are seeking the latest fashion trends and want to wear the latest clothes.

▸▸ *Situational involvement* means that the circumstances of a purchase may temporarily transform a low-involvement decision into a high-involvement one. High involvement comes into play when the consumer

Walmart seeks to provide products with low financial risk through its Great Value brand.

perceives risk in a specific situation. For example, an individual might routinely buy low-priced brands of liquor and wine. When the boss visits, however, the consumer might make a high-involvement decision and buy more prestigious brands.

▸▸ *Shopping involvement* represents the personal relevance of the process of shopping. Some people simply love shopping whether they buy anything or not. These highly involved shoppers are more likely to process information about deals and more likely to react to price reductions and limited offers. They are also more likely to leave slack in their budgets to make unplanned purchases when on a shopping excursion.[11]

▸▸ *Enduring involvement* represents an ongoing interest in some product or activity. The consumer is always searching for opportunities to consume the product or participate in the activity. Enduring involvement typically gives personal gratification to consumers as they continue to learn about, shop for, and consume these goods and services. Therefore, there is often linkage between enduring involvement and shopping and product involvement.

▸▸ *Emotional involvement* represents how emotional a consumer gets during some specific consumption activity. Emotional involvement is closely related to enduring involvement because the things that consumers care most about will eventually create high emotional involvement. Sports fans typify consumers with high emotional involvement. Recall the outpouring of emotion at the recent World Cup Soccer Tournament in South Africa.[12]

© TERRI MILLER/ E-VISUAL COMMUNICATIONS, INC.

Marketing Implications of Involvement

Marketing strategy varies according to the level of involvement associated with the product. For high-involvement product purchases, marketing managers have several responsibilities. First, promotion to the target market should be extensive and informative. A good ad gives consumers the information they need for making the purchase decision and specifies the benefits and unique advantages of owning the product. For example, Ford has a vehicle with many custom options that is marketed to small business owners. One example of a recent print ad appears on this page, showing how one entrepreneur customized his Ford Transit Connect to help him have better efficiency for his home theater and electronics installation business. Ford highlights the fact that unique businesses need unique and customizable transportation. This ad not only demonstrates the customer's satisfaction, but also shows the hauling capacity of the vehicle.

For low-involvement product purchases, consumers may not recognize their wants until they are in the store. Therefore, in-store promotion is an important tool when promoting low-involvement products. Marketing managers focus on package design so the product will be eye-catching and easily recognized on the shelf. Examples of products that take this approach are Campbell's soups, Tide detergent,

Velveeta cheese, and Heinz ketchup. In-store displays also stimulate sales of low-involvement products. A good display can explain the product's purpose and prompt recognition of a want. Displays of health and beauty aid items in supermarkets have been known to increase sales many times above normal. Coupons, cents-off deals, and two-for-one offers also effectively promote low-involvement items.

Linking a product to a higher-involvement issue is another tactic that marketing managers can use to increase the sales or positive publicity of a low-involvement product. PepsiCo channeled the money usually spent on Super Bowl ads ($3 million for 30 seconds) into the Pepsi Refresh Project, a grant program designed to fund people's ideas to improve their communities. To participate, people pitch their ideas on www.refresheverything.com, where site visitors vote on the proposals. The projects that receive the most votes each month are each awarded a grant of $5,000 to $250,000. Funded projects range from pajamas for babies to self-defense classes for women.[13]

LO 5–LO 8 Factors Influencing Consumer Buying Decisions

The consumer decision-making process does not occur in a vacuum. On the contrary, underlying cultural, social, individual, and psychological factors strongly influence the decision process. These factors have an effect from the time a consumer perceives a stimulus through postpurchase behavior. Cultural factors, which include culture and values, subculture, and social class, exert a broad influence over consumer decision making. Social factors sum up the social interactions between a consumer and influential groups of people, such as reference groups, opinion leaders, and family members. Individual factors, which include gender, age, family life cycle stage, personality, self-concept, and lifestyle, are unique to each individual and play a major role in the type of products and services consumers want. Psychological factors determine how consumers perceive and interact with their environments and influence the ultimate decisions consumers make. They include perception, motivation, learning, beliefs, and attitudes. Exhibit 6.3 on the next page summarizes these influences.

© FORD MOTOR COMPANY/PHOTOGRAPHY BY RON STRONG

© PHOTODISC/GETTY IMAGES

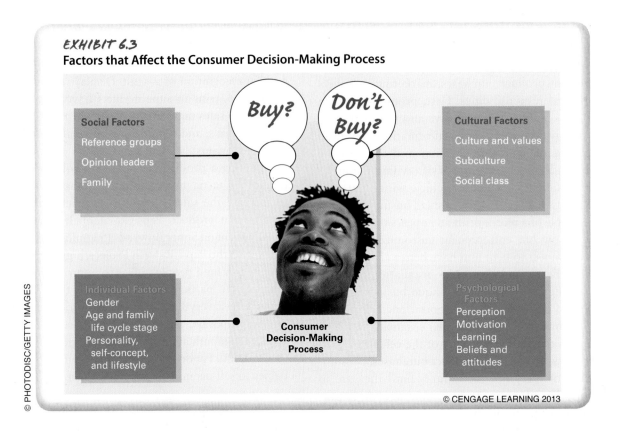

EXHIBIT 6.3
Factors that Affect the Consumer Decision-Making Process

LO 5 Cultural Influences on Consumer Buying Decisions

Of all the factors that affect consumer decision making, cultural factors exert the broadest and deepest influence. Marketers must understand the way people's culture and its accompanying values, as well as their subculture and social class, influence their buying behavior.

Culture and Values

Culture is the essential character of a society that distinguishes it from other cultural groups. The underlying elements of every culture are the values, language, myths, customs, rituals, and laws that shape the behavior of the people, as well as the material artifacts, or products, of that behavior as they are transmitted from one generation to the next.

culture the set of values, norms, attitudes, and other meaningful symbols that shape human behavior and the artifacts, or products, of that behavior as they are transmitted from one generation to the next

Culture is pervasive. Cultural values and influences are the ocean in which individuals swim, and yet most are completely unaware that it is there. What people eat, how they dress, what they think and feel, and what language they speak are all dimensions of culture. It encompasses all the things consumers do without conscious choice because their culture's values, customs, and rituals are ingrained in their daily habits.

Culture is functional. Human interaction creates values and prescribes acceptable behavior for each culture. By establishing common expectations, culture gives order to society. Sometimes these expectations are enacted into laws. For example, drivers in our culture must stop at a red light. Other times these expectations are taken for granted: Grocery stores and hospitals are open 24 hours, whereas banks are open only during bankers' hours.

Culture is learned. Consumers are not born knowing the values and norms of their society. Instead, they must learn what is acceptable from family and friends. Children learn the values that will govern their behavior from parents, teachers, and peers. As members of our society, they learn to shake hands when they greet someone, to drive on the right-hand side of the road, and to eat pizza and drink Coca-Cola.

THE ELEMENT OF SURPRISE... OUTINGS?

New Yorkers are known for their penchant for the secret, underground, surprise bars, taco trucks, and pop-up shops. Seeing an opening for a business built on their love of the unknown, **Surprise Industries** offers its customers a surprise activity ranging from $25 to $10,000. Customers sign up for a surprise, receive the date, the meeting place, and clothing suggestions. Upon arrival, their surprise activity leader greets them for the unknown activity. The surprises range from pottery making and kayaking to firing ranges and tango classes. The most expensive surprise package offers customers a weeklong series of surprises, ensuring a shocking week.[14]

SOURCE: Joe Piazza, "Booking Spontaneity, at a Price," *Wall Street Journal*, June 7, 2011.

© R. GINO SANTA MARIA/SHUTTERSTOCK.COM

Culture is dynamic. It adapts to changing needs and an evolving environment. The rapid growth of technology in today's world has accelerated the rate of cultural change. Television has changed entertainment patterns and family communication and has heightened public awareness of political and other news events. Automation has increased the amount of leisure time we have and, in some ways, has changed the traditional work ethic. Cultural norms will continue to evolve because of our need for social patterns that solve problems.

The most defining element of a culture is its values. A **value** is an enduring belief shared by a society that a specific mode of conduct is personally or socially preferable to another mode of conduct. People's value systems have a great effect on their consumer behavior. Consumers with similar value systems tend to react alike to prices and other marketing-related inducements. Values also correspond to consumption patterns. For example, Americans place a high value on convenience. This value has created lucrative markets for products such as breakfast bars, energy bars, and nutrition bars that allow consumers to eat on the go. Values can also influence consumers' television viewing habits or the magazines they read. For instance, people who strongly object to violence avoid crime shows, and those who oppose pornography do not buy *Hustler*.

Understanding Cultural Differences

As more companies expand their operations globally, the need to understand the cultures of foreign countries becomes more important. A firm has little chance of selling products in a culture that it does not understand. Like people, products have cultural values and rules that influence their perception and use. Culture, therefore, must be understood before the behavior of individuals within the cultural context can be understood. Colors, for example, may have different meanings in global markets than they do at home. In China, white is the color of mourning and brides wear red. In the United States, black is for mourning and brides wear white.

Language is another important aspect of culture that global marketers must consider. When translating product names, slogans, and promotional messages into foreign languages, they must be careful not to convey the wrong message. General Motors discovered too late that Nova (the name of an economical car) literally means "doesn't go" in Spanish; Coors encouraged its English-speaking customers to "Turn it loose," but the phrase in Spanish means "Suffer from diarrhea."

Although marketers expanding into global markets generally adapt their products and business

value the enduring belief that a specific mode of conduct is personally or socially preferable to another mode of conduct

subculture a homogeneous group of people who share elements of the overall culture as well as unique elements of their own group

social class a group of people in a society who are considered nearly equal in status or community esteem, who regularly socialize among themselves both formally and informally, and who share behavioral norms

formats to the local culture, some fear that increasing globalization, as well as the proliferation of the Internet, will result in a homogeneous world culture of the future. U.S. companies in particular, they fear, are Americanizing the world by exporting bastions of American culture, such as McDonald's fast-food restaurants, Starbucks coffeehouses, Microsoft software, and American movies and entertainment.

Subculture

A culture can be divided into subcultures on the basis of demographic characteristics, geographic regions, national and ethnic background, political beliefs, and religious beliefs. A **subculture** is a homogeneous group of people who share elements of the overall culture as well as cultural elements unique to their own group. Within subcultures, people's attitudes, values, and purchase decisions are even more similar than they are within the broader culture. Subcultural differences may result in considerable variation within a culture in what, how, when, and where people buy goods and services.

In the United States alone, countless subcultures can be identified. Many are concentrated geographically. People who belong to the Church of Jesus Christ of Latter-Day Saints, for example, are clustered mainly in Utah; Cajuns are located in the bayou regions of southern Louisiana. Many Hispanics live in states bordering Mexico, whereas the majority of Chinese, Japanese, and Korean Americans are found on the West Coast. Other subcultures are geographically dispersed. Computer hackers, people who are hearing or visually impaired, Harley-Davidson bikers, military families, university professors, and gays may be found throughout the country. Yet they have identifiable attitudes, values, and needs that distinguish them from the larger culture.

Once marketers identify subcultures, they can design special marketing to serve their needs. Some companies launch simultaneous campaigns to reach different subcultures. According to the U.S. Census Bureau, the Hispanic population is the largest and fastest-growing subculture, increasing four times as fast as the general population. To tap into this large and growing segment, marketers have been forming partnerships with broadcasters that have an established Latino audience. The Univision Radio network covers approximately 73 percent of the U.S. Hispanic popula-

tion and has over ten million listeners weekly. MocoSpace is a youthful multicultural social networking tool developed for people without traditional Internet access who have a feature phone, which is a cell phone with less connectivity than a Smartphone. The phone-only approach appeals to the 87 percent of African Americans and Latinos who own cell phones. MocoSpace is projected to earn $10 million this year, mainly from advertising directed at Latinos and African Americans. It has had successful campaigns with Kmart back-to-school, Spike TV, and the U.S. Census.[15]

Social Class

The United States, like other societies, has a social class system. A **social class** is a group of people who are considered nearly equal in status or community esteem, who regularly socialize among themselves both formally and informally, and who share behavioral norms.

A number of techniques have been used to measure social class, and a number of criteria have been used to define it. One view of contemporary U.S. status structure is shown in Exhibit 6.4.

As you can see from Exhibit 6.4, the upper and upper middle classes comprise the small segment of affluent and wealthy Americans. In terms of consumer buying patterns, the affluent are more likely to own their own home and purchase new cars and trucks and are less likely to smoke. The very rich flex their financial muscles by spending more on vacation homes, vacations and cruises, and housekeeping and gardening services. The most affluent consumers are more likely to attend art auctions and galleries, dance performances, operas, the theater, museums, concerts, and sporting events. Marketers often pay attention to the superwealthy. The luxury book market is targeting superwealthy collectors with books sporting price tags that rival original artwork. For example, ten limited edition copies of an autobiography by Indian cricket star Sachin Tendulkar feature a page with his blood mixed into the paper pulp. Even though a copy of the book cost $75,000, all ten sold! Taschen, another novelty publisher, sold pieces of the moon with 12 copies of its photography book of the lunar landing. One sold for $112,500.[16]

The majority of Americans today define themselves as middle class, regardless of their actual income or educational attainment. This phenomenon most likely occurs because working-class Americans tend to aspire to the middle-class lifestyle, while some of those who do achieve affluence may downwardly

EXHIBIT 6.4
U.S. Social Classes

Upper Classes		
Capitalist class	1%	People whose investment decisions shape the national economy; income mostly from assets, earned or inherited; university connections
Upper middle class	14%	Upper-level managers, professionals, owners of medium-sized businesses; well-to-do, stay-at-home homemakers who decline occupational work by choice; college educated; family income well above national average
Middle Classes		
Middle class	33%	Middle-level white-collar, top-level blue-collar; education past high school typical; income somewhat above national average; loss of manufacturing jobs has reduced the population of this class
Working class	32%	Middle-level blue-collar, lower-level white-collar; income below national average; largely working in skilled or semi-skilled service jobs
Lower Classes		
Working poor	11–12%	Low-paid service workers and operatives; some high school education; below mainstream in living standard; crime and hunger are daily threats
Underclass	8–9%	People who are not regularly employed and who depend primarily on the welfare system for sustenance; little schooling; living standard below poverty line

SOURCES: Adapted from Richard P. Coleman, "The Continuing Significance of Social Class to Marketing," *Journal of Consumer Research*, December 1983, 267; Dennis Gilbert and Joseph A. Kahl, *The American Class Structure: A Synthesis* (Homewood, IL: Dorsey Press, 1982), ch. 11.

aspire to respectable middle-class status as a matter of principle.

The working class is a distinct subset of the middle class. Interest in organized labor is one of the most common attributes among the working class. This group often rates job security as the most important reason for taking a job. The working-class person depends heavily on relatives and the community for economic and emotional support.

Lifestyle distinctions between the social classes are greater than the distinctions within a given class. The most significant difference between the classes occurs between the middle and lower classes, where there is a major shift in lifestyles. Members of the lower class have incomes at or below the poverty level.

Social class is typically measured as a combination of occupation, income, education, wealth, and other variables. For instance, affluent upper-class consumers are more likely to be salaried executives or self-employed professionals with at least an undergraduate degree. Working-class or middle-class consumers are more likely to be hourly service workers or blue-collar employees with only a high school education. Educational attainment, however, seems to be the most reliable indicator of a person's social and economic status. Those with college degrees or graduate degrees are more likely to fall into the upper classes, while those people with some college experience fall closest to traditional concepts of the middle class.

Marketers are interested in social class for two main reasons. First, social class often indicates which medium to use for advertising. Suppose an insurance company seeks to sell its policies to middle-class families. It might advertise during the local evening news because middle-class families tend to watch more television than other classes do. If the company wanted to sell more policies to upscale individuals, it might place an ad in a business publication like the *Wall Street Journal*. The Internet, long the domain of more educated and affluent families, is becoming an increasingly important advertising outlet for advertisers hoping to reach blue-collar workers and homemakers. As the middle class rapidly adopts the medium, marketers have to do more research to find out which Web sites will reach their audience.

Second, knowing what products appeal to which social classes can help marketers determine where to best distribute their products. Affluent Americans, a fifth of the U.S. population, have changed their buying habits since the recession. They now are willing

reference group a group in society that influences an individual's purchasing behavior

primary membership group a reference group with which people interact regularly in an informal, face-to-face manner, such as family, friends, and co-workers

secondary membership group a reference group with which people associate less consistently and more formally than a primary membership group, such as a club, professional group, or religious group

aspirational reference group a group that someone would like to join

norm a value or attitude deemed acceptable by a group

to spend more of their discretionary income on travel, but want to pay a large price only for unique one-of-a-kind items. They also don't think less of a brand that puts items on sale—a major shift in a group of consumers who have traditionally viewed items that don't go on sale as an indication of quality.[17]

For the first time in a long while, however, industry analysts are seeing discount chains faring better than their full-priced and upscale counterparts. These days, analysts say, the big-box and discount retailers' greatest challenge has been courting consumers who fall in the middle-income level. The result is a fiercely competitive retail environment where discount retailers have focused less on their core—low-income consumers, who are most affected by rising housing and gas costs. Overall, however, discount chains fared better during the Great Recession because more affluent customers traded down to obtain more value for their money. Harrison Group researchers discovered that Target and CostCo were wealthy consumers' favorite stores.[18]

LO6 Social Influences on Consumer Buying Decisions

Many consumers seek out the opinions of others to reduce their search and evaluation effort or uncertainty, especially as the perceived risk of the decision increases. Consumers may also seek out others' opinions for guidance on new products or services, products with image-related attributes, or products for which attribute information is lacking or uninformative. Specifically, consumers interact socially with reference groups, opinion leaders, and family members to obtain product information and decision approval.

Reference Groups

People interact with many reference groups. A **reference group** consists of all the formal and informal groups that influence the buying behavior of an individual. Consumers may use products or brands to identify with or become a member of a group. They learn from observing how members of their reference groups consume, and they use the same criteria to make their own consumer decisions.

Reference groups can be categorized very broadly as either direct or indirect (see Exhibit 6.5). Direct reference groups are face-to-face membership groups that touch people's lives directly. They can be either primary or secondary. A **primary membership group** includes all groups with which people interact regularly in an informal, face-to-face manner, such as family, friends, and co-workers. Today, they may also communicate by mail, text messages, Facebook, Skype, or other electronic means. In contrast, people associate with a **secondary membership group** less consistently and more formally. These groups might include clubs, professional groups, and religious groups.

Consumers also are influenced by many indirect, nonmembership reference groups to which they do not belong. An **aspirational reference group** is a group a person would like to join. To join an aspirational group, a person must at least conform to the norms of that group. (A **norm** consists of the values and attitudes deemed acceptable by the group.) Thus, a person who wants to be elected to public office may begin to dress more conservatively, as other politicians do. He or she may go to many of the restaurants and social engage-

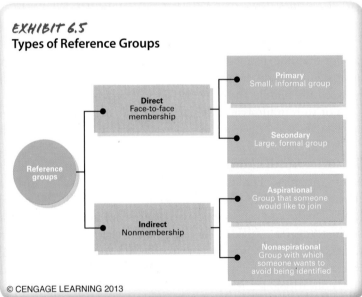

EXHIBIT 6.5
Types of Reference Groups

Reference groups

Direct
Face-to-face membership

Primary
Small, informal group

Secondary
Large, formal group

Indirect
Nonmembership

Aspirational
Group that someone would like to join

Nonaspirational
Group with which someone wants to avoid being identified

© CENGAGE LEARNING 2013

ments that city and business leaders attend and try to play a role that is acceptable to voters and other influential people. Similarly, teenagers today may dye their hair and experiment with body piercing and tattoos. Athletes are an aspirational group for several market segments. To appeal to the younger market, Coca-Cola signed basketball star LeBron James to be the spokesperson for its Sprite and Powerade brands, and Nike signed a sneaker deal with him reportedly worth $90 million. Coca-Cola and Nike assumed James would encourage consumers to drink Coke brands and buy Nike shoes because they would like to identify with him.

Nonaspirational reference groups, or dissociative groups, influence our behavior when we try to maintain distance from them. A consumer may avoid buying some types of clothing or cars, going to certain restaurants or stores, or even buying a home in a certain neighborhood in order to avoid being associated with a particular group.

The activities, values, and goals of reference groups directly influence consumer behavior. For marketers, reference groups have three important implications: (1) They serve as information sources and influence perceptions; (2) they affect an individual's aspiration levels; and (3) their norms either constrain or stimulate consumer behavior. For example, research firms devoted to uncovering what's cool in the teen market have identified a couple of influential groups among today's teens based on their interests in clothes, music, and activities. Tracking these groups reveals how products become cool and how groups influence the adoption of cool products by other groups. A trend or fad often starts with teens who have the most innovative tastes. These teens are on the cutting edge of fashion and music, and they wear their attitude all over their bodies in the form of tattoos, body piercings, studded jewelry, or colored tresses. Certain fads embraced by these "Edgers" will spark an interest in the small group of teens researchers call "Influencers," who project the look other teens covet. Influencers also create their own trends in music and clothing choices. Once a fad is embraced and adopted by Influencers, the look becomes cool and desirable. The remaining groups that comprise the majority of the teen population will not embrace a fad until it gets its seal of approval from the Influencers.

Research has shown that reference groups are particularly powerful in influencing purchases of fragrances, wine, snack food, candy, clothing, and sodas.[19] LG Electronics and General Electric are using the sustainable green living movement as a reference group to encourage green homeowners to functionally and stylistically "keep up with the Joneses." Once hidden away, boilers and water heaters are now designed to be aesthetically pleasing as well as energy efficient. After purchasing an expensive solar-powered water heater, homeowners want to show it off, so it must be stylish. In-room air conditioners look like sculptures, and the Everun water heater has a shelf that hides wires and holds decorative objects. Some consumers even consider the mechanical room to be like a wine cellar or library—a place to demonstrate how you fit in with your peers and the eco-friendly movement.[20] People with well-formed networks of somewhat overlapping reference groups and those with strong personal values are less susceptible to reference group influences.[21]

Opinion Leaders

Reference groups frequently include an individual known as a group leader, or **opinion leader**—a person who influences others. Obviously, it is important for marketing managers to persuade such people to purchase their goods or services. Many products and services that are integral parts of Americans' lives today got their initial boost from opinion leaders. For example, Kindles and iPads were purchased by opinion leaders well ahead of the general public.

Opinion leaders are often the first to try new products and services out of pure curiosity. They tend to possess more accurate knowledge and to be more innovative.[22] Technology companies have found that teenagers, because of their willingness to experiment, are key opinion leaders for the success of new technologies.

Opinion leadership is a casual phenomenon and is usually inconspicuous, so locating opinion leaders can be a challenge. Thus, marketers often try to create opinion leaders. They may use high school cheerleaders to model new fall fashions or civic leaders to promote insurance, new cars, and other merchandise. On a national level, companies sometimes use movie stars, sports figures, and other celebrities to promote products, hoping they are appropriate opinion leaders. The effectiveness of celebrity endorsements varies, though, depending largely on how credible and attractive the spokesperson is and how familiar people are with him or her. Endorsements are most likely to succeed if a reasonable association between the spokesperson and the product can be established.

> **nonaspirational reference group** a group with which an individual does not want to associate
>
> **opinion leader** an individual who influences the opinions of others

socialization process how cultural values and norms are passed down to children

Respected organizations such as the American Heart Association and the American Cancer Society may also serve as opinion leaders. Marketers may seek endorsements from them as well as from schools, churches, cities, the military, and fraternal organizations as a form of group opinion leadership. Salespeople often ask to use opinion leaders' names as a means of achieving greater personal influence in a sales presentation.

Increasingly, marketers are looking to blogs to find opinion leaders, but the sheer volume of blogs makes determining true opinion leaders challenging. So, marketers are focusing their attention on teen blogs because those blogs better identify the social trends that are shaping consumer behavior. With their unprecedented ability to network and communicate with each other, young people rely on each others' opinions more than marketing messages when making purchase decisions. And blogs are becoming a key way that teens communicate their opinions. Consequently, today's marketers are reading teen blogs, developing products that meet the very specific needs that teens express there, and learning unique and creative

ways to put key influencers in charge of marketing their brands for them. Marketers are also using other social networking and online media to determine and attract opinion leaders, which will be discussed in Chapter 22.

Family

The family is the most important social institution for many consumers, strongly influencing values, attitudes, self-concept, and buying behavior. For example, a family that strongly values good health will have a grocery list distinctly different from that of a family that views every dinner as a gourmet event. Moreover, the family is responsible for the **socialization process**, the passing down of cultural values and norms to children. Children learn by observing their parents' consumption patterns, so they tend to shop in similar patterns.

Decision-making roles among family members tend to vary significantly, depending on the type of item purchased. Family members assume a variety of roles in the purchase process. *Initiators* suggest, initiate, or plant the seed for the purchase process. The initiator can be any member of the family. For example, Sister might initiate the product search by asking for a new bicycle as a birthday present. *Influencers* are those members of the family whose opinions are valued. In our example, Mom might function as a price-range watchdog, an influencer whose main role is to veto or approve price ranges. Brother may give his opinion on certain makes of bicycles. The *decision maker* is the family member who actually makes the decision to buy or not to buy. For example, Dad or Mom is likely to choose the final brand and model of bicycle to buy after seeking further information from Sister about cosmetic features such as color and then imposing additional criteria of his or her own, such as durability and safety. The *purchaser* (probably Dad or Mom) is the one who actually exchanges money for the product. Finally, the *consumer* is the actual user—Sister, in the case of the bicycle.

Marketers should consider family purchase situations along with the distribution of consumer and decision-maker roles among family members. Ordinary marketing views the individual as both decision maker and consumer. Family marketing adds several other possibilities: Sometimes more than one family member or all family members are involved in the decision, sometimes only children are involved in the decision, sometimes more than one consumer is involved, and sometimes the decision maker and the

Yes. She checks herself out in the mirror.

1 in 5 Americans will develop skin cancer in their lifetime. That's why Jennifer Garner made a promise to herself to examine her skin every month and see her dermatologist for a screening every year.

The Neutrogena Partnership for Skin Health, working with the American Academy of Dermatology (AAD), invites you to join them in their mission to stop skin cancer before it strikes. Empower their cause by wearing broad-spectrum sun protection, covering up and seeking shade between 10:00 am and 4:00 pm. Perform self-examinations regularly and report any changes in existing moles or birthmarks to your doctor. Because with early detection, skin cancer is 99% curable. And that's a statistic we love to share.

Protect yourself starting today.
The AAD and the Neutrogena Partnership for Skin Health encourage you to **get a free skin cancer screening** in May, June or July. Find one in your area by visiting aad.org or neutrogenaskinhealth.com. Mark the date of your screening on this slip as a healthy reminder.
©2008 Neutrogena Corp.

Neutrogena®
PARTNERSHIP FOR SKIN HEALTH

© AP IMAGES/PRNEWSFOTO/NEUTROGENA

Kids should drink bananas, not go bananas.

When we sat down to make some kids' smoothies, we kept it natural. The only ingredients we use are the finest crushed whole fruit and pure juice. That's it. 100% fruit, with none of those weird additives or added sugar that will have your little ones running riot. Just a full portion of fruit in every little carton, and a whole seven portions in every big carton.

innocent smoothies for kids. nothing but nothing but fruit.

IMAGE COURTESY OF THE ADVERTISING ARCHIVES

Because children influence buying decisions, some companies have begun targeting children for adult purchases.

consumer are different people. In most households, when parental joint decisions are being made, spouses consider their partner's needs and perceptions to maintain decision fairness and harmony. This tends to minimize family conflict. Research also shows that in harmonious households, the spouse who has "won" a previous decision is less likely to use strong influence in a subsequent decision.[23] This balancing factor is key in maintaining long-term family harmony.

Children can have great influence over the purchase decisions of their parents. In many families, with both parents working and short on time, children are encouraged to participate. In addition, children in single-parent households become more involved in family decisions at an earlier age. Children influence purchase decisions for many products and services. They are most influential in purchase decisions for products with which they will be directly involved or will be the primary user. Among the products about which children exhibit greatest influence are breakfast cereal, juice, mobile phones, and soft drinks.[24] Children also often participate in decisions about many other products, including toys, clothes, vacations, rec-

reation, and automobiles, even though they usually are not the actual purchasers of such items. What if those children happen to be teenagers? There are 20 million U.S. teens, and half of them receive as much as $39 a week. Teen spending power amounts to more than $200 billion, a significant amount of money for a group that is willing to spend.[25]

Traditionally, children learned about consumption from their parents. In today's technologically overloaded world, that trend is reversing. Teenagers and adult children often contribute information and influence the purchase of parents' technology products.[26] Often they even help with installation and show the parents how to use the product!

LO 7 Individual Influences on Consumer Buying Decisions

A person's buying decisions are also influenced by personal characteristics that are unique to each individual, such as gender; age and life cycle stage; and personality, self-concept, and lifestyle. Individual characteristics are generally stable over the course of one's life. For instance, most people do not change their gender, and the act of changing personality or lifestyle requires a complete reorientation of one's life. In the case of age and life cycle stage, these changes occur gradually over time.

Gender

Physiological differences between men and women result in different needs, such as health and beauty products. Just as important are the distinct cultural, social, and economic roles played by men and women and the effects that these have on their decision-making processes. For example, the wedding industry is overwhelmingly focused on brides and what they want. But Chris Easter and Bob Horner thought that the groom should be able to register for gifts he would like as well. So they began The Man Registry (www.themanregistry.com), a Web site with thousands of guy-friendly gifts for which grooms can register. The Man Registry also offers advice to grooms about groomsmen gifts and local vendors.[27]

Trends in gender marketing are influenced by the changing roles of men and women in society. For example, men used to rely on the women in their lives to shop for them. Today, however, more men are shopping for themselves. Fifty-seven percent of men shopped online in 2007, up from 38 percent in 2006. In 2009, 7.4 percent of fathers with children younger than 18 years stayed at home while their wives worked. That is the highest recorded percentage, up 2 percentage points from 2008.[28] Whether because of the advent of online shopping or retailers becoming aware of the way men like to shop, today more men are comfortable shopping for themselves. A study commissioned by *GQ* found that 84 percent of men said they purchased their own clothes, up from 65 percent four years earlier.[29] On the other hand, technology companies are working to develop new high-tech products that resonate with women. For example, Barnes & Noble's Nook was rated more highly by women than Apple's iPad. A campaign featuring women's magazines and greater availability of titles loved by women on the Nook (not to mention the purse-friendly size) have given Barnes & Noble the edge on the coveted female tech market.[30]

Age and Family Life Cycle Stage

The age and family life cycle stage of a consumer can have a significant impact on consumer behavior. How old a consumer is generally indicates what products he or she may be interested in purchasing. Consumer tastes in food, clothing, cars, furniture, and recreation are often age related.

Related to a person's age is his or her place in the family life cycle. As Chapter 8 explains in more detail, the *family life cycle* is an orderly series of stages through which consumers' attitudes and behavioral tendencies evolve through maturity, experience, and changing income and status. Marketers often define their target markets in terms of family life cycle, such as "young singles," "young married couples with children," and "middle-aged married couples without children." For instance, young singles spend more than average on alcoholic beverages, education, and entertainment. New parents typically increase their spending on health care, clothing, housing, and food and decrease their spending on alcohol, education, and transportation. Households with older children spend more on food, entertainment, personal care products, and education, as well as cars and gasoline. After their children leave home, spending by older couples on vehicles, women's clothing, health care, and long-distance calls typically increases.

For instance, the presence of children in the home is the most significant determinant of the type of vehicle that's driven off the new car lot. Parents are the ultimate need-driven car consumers, requiring larger cars and trucks to haul their children and all their belongings. It comes as no surprise then that for all households with children, SUVs rank either first or second among new-vehicle purchases, followed by minivans.

Marketers should also be aware of the many nontraditional life cycle paths that are common today and provide insights into the needs and wants of such consumers as divorced parents, lifelong singles, and childless couples. Three decades ago, married couples with children under the age of 18 accounted for about half of U.S. households. Today, such families make up only 23 percent of all households, while people living alone or with nonfamily members represent more than 30 percent. Furthermore, according to the U.S. Census Bureau, the number of single-mother households grew by 25 percent over the last decade. The shift toward more single-parent households is part of a broader societal change that has put more women on the career track. Although many marketers continue to be wary of targeting nontraditional families, Charles Schwab targeted single mothers in an advertising campaign featuring Sarah Ferguson, the Duchess of York and a divorced mom. The idea was to appeal to single mothers' heightened awareness of the need for financial self-sufficiency.

Life Events Another way to look at the life cycle is to look at major events in one's life over time. Life-changing events can occur at any time. A few examples are death of a spouse, moving, birth or adoption of a child, retirement, job loss, divorce, and marriage. Typically, such events are quite stressful, and consumers will often take steps to minimize that stress. Many times, life-changing events will mean new consumption patterns. For example, a recently divorced person may try to improve his or her appearance by joining a health club and dieting. Someone moving to a different city will need a new dentist, grocery store, auto service center, and doctor, among other things. Marketers realize that life events often mean a chance to gain a new customer. The Welcome Wagon offers free gifts and services for area newcomers. Lowe's sends out a discount coupon to those moving to a new community. And when you put your home on the market, very quickly you start getting flyers from moving companies promising a great price on moving your household goods.

Personality, Self-Concept, and Lifestyle

Each consumer has a unique personality. **Personality** is a broad concept that can be thought of as a way of organizing and grouping how an individual typically reacts to situations. Thus, personality combines psychological makeup and environmental forces. It includes people's underlying dispositions, especially their most dominant characteristics. Although personality is one of the least useful concepts in the study of consumer behavior, some marketers believe personality influences the types and brands of products purchased. For instance, the type of car, clothes, or jewelry a consumer buys may reflect one or more personality traits.

Self-concept, or self-perception, is how consumers perceive themselves. Self-concept includes attitudes, perceptions, beliefs, and self-evaluations. Although self-concept may change, the change is often gradual. Through self-concept, people define their identity, which in turn provides for consistent and coherent behavior.

Self-concept combines the **ideal self-image** (the way an individual would like to be perceived) and the **real self-image** (how an individual actually perceives himself or herself). Generally, we try to raise our real self-image toward our ideal (or at least narrow the gap). Consumers seldom buy products that jeopardize their self-image. For example, someone who sees herself as a trendsetter wouldn't buy clothing that doesn't project a contemporary image.

Human behavior depends largely on self-concept. Because consumers want to protect their identity as individuals, the products they buy, the stores they patronize, and the credit cards they carry support their self-image. No other product quite reflects a person's self-image as much as the car he or she drives. For example, many young consumers do not like family sedans like the Honda Accord or Toyota Camry and say they would buy one for their mom but not for themselves. Likewise, younger parents may avoid purchasing minivans because they do not want to sacrifice the youthful image they have of themselves just because they have new responsibilities. To combat decreasing sales, marketers of the Nissan Quest minivan decided to reposition it as something other than a "mom mobile" or "soccer mom car." They chose the ad copy "Passion built it. Passion will fill it up," followed by "What if we made a minivan that changed the way people think of minivans?"

By influencing the degree to which consumers perceive a good or service to be self-relevant, marketers

personality a way of organizing and grouping the consistencies of an individual's reactions to situations

self-concept how consumers perceive themselves in terms of attitudes, perceptions, beliefs, and self-evaluations

ideal self-image the way an individual would like to be perceived

real self-image the way an individual actually perceives himself or herself

LIFE STAGES VS. DEMOGRAPHICS

In a national survey of 1,440 people ages 13 to 54, researchers asked questions based on life stages rather than demographics to see if there were clear differences between groups. The groups used were teens, college students, recent graduates, single no kids, new nesters, established families, married couples with no children, and empty nesters. By organizing the categories this way, researchers were able to identify clear differences between the life stage groups, some of which fall into the same demographic category. For example, new nesters and married couples with no children are two life stage groups that both fall into the Generation Y demographic group. Looking at those groups in terms of life stages, however, reveals different preferences. New nesters value and are satisfied with social networking to keep in touch with friends and family, whereas childless couples are less satisfied with social networking with family and friends and use the tools primarily to expand professional networks. Many differences such as these appeared between these two life stages and were less apparent when researchers looked at them as one demographic group. (We'll examine life stages in more detail in Chapter 8.)[31]

SOURCE: Steve McClellan, "Are Demographics Dead?" *AdWeek*, February 23, 2010, www.adweek.com.

© WILLIAM CASEY/SHUTTERSTOCK.COM

perception the process by which people select, organize, and interpret stimuli into a meaningful and coherent picture

selective exposure the process whereby a consumer notices certain stimuli and ignores others

can affect consumers' motivation to learn about, shop for, and buy a certain brand. Marketers also consider self-concept important because it helps explain the relationship between individuals' perceptions of themselves and their consumer behavior.

Many companies now use psychographics to better understand their market segments. For many years, marketers selling products to mothers conveniently assumed that all moms were fairly homogeneous and concerned about the same things—the health and well-being of their children—and that they could all be reached with a similar message. But recent lifestyle research has shown that there are traditional, blended, and nontraditional moms, and companies like Procter & Gamble and Pillsbury are using strategies to reach these different types of mothers. Psychographics is also effective with other market segments. Psychographics and lifestyle segmentation are discussed in more detail in Chapter 8.

LO 8 Psychological Influences on Consumer Buying Decisions

An individual's buying decisions are further influenced by psychological factors: perception, motivation, learning, and beliefs and attitudes. These factors are what consumers use to interact with their world. They are the tools consumers use to recognize their feelings, gather and analyze information, formulate thoughts and opinions, and take action. Unlike the other three influences on consumer behavior, psychological influences can be affected by a person's environment because they are applied on specific occasions. For example, you will perceive different stimuli and process these stimuli in different ways depending on whether you are sitting in class concentrating on the instructor, sitting outside of class talking to friends, or sitting in your dorm room watching television.

Perception

The world is full of stimuli. A stimulus is any unit of input affecting one or more of the five senses: sight, smell, taste, touch, and hearing. The process by which

we select, organize, and interpret these stimuli into a meaningful and coherent picture is called **perception**. In essence, perception is how we see the world around us and how we recognize that we need some help in making a purchasing decision.

People cannot perceive every stimulus in their environment. Therefore, they use **selective exposure** to decide which stimuli to notice and which to ignore. A typical consumer is exposed to more than 2,500 advertising messages a day but notices only between 11 and 20.

The familiarity of an object, contrast, movement, intensity (such as increased volume), and smell are cues that influence perception. Consumers use these cues to identify and define products and brands. The shape of a product's packaging, such as Coca-Cola's signature contour bottle, can influence perception. Color is another cue, and it plays a key role in consumers' perceptions. Packaged foods manufacturers use color to trigger unconscious associations for grocery shoppers who typically make their shopping decisions in the blink of an eye. Ampacet, a world leader in color additives for plastics, reported in 2007 that nature-inspired colors and organic values were becoming more popular as the economy and global focus shifted from the tech-boom to the bio- or eco-boom. Ecological consequences and concerns have resulted in marketing initiatives such as "going green." Colors like natural greens, earthy browns, and strong yellows, as well as metallics such as steely silver, carbon black, gold, and copper, are popular for packaging. Color researchers speculate that technological overload has led to a resurgence in the appreciation of simple luxury. Color names for fabrics and makeup reflect that trend with names such as Grounded, Champagne Chic, and Serene Blue.[32]

What is perceived by consumers may also depend on the stimuli's vividness or shock value. Graphic warnings of the hazards associated with a product's use are perceived more readily and remembered more accurately than less vivid warnings or warnings that are written in text. "Sexier" ads excel at attracting the attention of younger consumers. Companies like American Apparel and Abercrombie & Fitch appeal to the 8-to-18 age group with ads that push the envelope by setting models in provocative poses and highlighting their intimates collections with push-up bras and panties saying "Eye Candy."[33] On the other hand, baby carrot farmers are using junk food packaging—or the perception of high-fat, much coveted food—to market baby carrots as a delicious snacking alternative. The campaign is aggressive and edgy, a stance marketers hope sticks to baby carrots, making them cool.[34]

Two other concepts closely related to selective exposure are selective distortion and selective retention. **Selective distortion** occurs when consumers change or distort information that conflicts with their feelings or beliefs. For example, suppose a college student buys a Microsoft Zune MP3 player. After the purchase, if the student gets new information about an alternative brand, such as an Apple iPod, he or she may distort the information to make it more consistent with the prior view that the Microsoft Zune is just as good as the iPod, if not better. Business travelers who fly often may distort or discount information about plane crashes because they must use air travel constantly in their jobs.

Selective retention is remembering only information that supports personal feelings or beliefs. The consumer forgets all information that may be inconsistent. After reading a pamphlet that contradicts one's political beliefs, for instance, a person may forget many of the points outlined in it. Similarly, consumers may see a news report on suspected illegal practices by their favorite retail store but soon forget the reason the store was featured on the news.

Which stimuli will be perceived often depends on the individual. People can be exposed to the same stimuli under identical conditions but perceive them very differently. For example, two people viewing a television commercial may have different interpretations of the advertising message. One person may be thoroughly engrossed by the message and become highly motivated to buy the product. Thirty seconds after the ad ends, the second person may not be able to recall the content of the message or even the product advertised.

Marketing Implications of Perception

Marketers must recognize the importance of cues, or signals, in consumers' perception of products. Marketing managers first identify the important attributes, such as price or quality, that the targeted consumers want in a product and then design signals to communicate these attributes. For example, consumers will pay more for candy in expensive-looking foil packages. But shiny labels on wine bottles sig-

© MATTHEW COLE/SHUTTERSTOCK.COM

nify less expensive wines; dull labels indicate more expensive wines. Marketers also often use price as a signal to consumers that the product is of higher quality than competing products. Of course, brand names send signals to consumers. The brand names of Close-Up toothpaste, DieHard batteries, and Caress moisturizing soap, for example, identify important product qualities. Names chosen for search engines and sites on the Internet, such as Yahoo!, Amazon.com, and Excite, are intended to convey excitement, intensity, and vastness.

Consumers also associate quality and reliability with certain brand names. Companies watch their brand identity closely, in large part because a strong link has been established between perceived brand value and customer loyalty. Brand names that consistently enjoy high perceived value from consumers include Kodak, Disney, National Geographic, Mercedes-Benz, and Fisher-Price. Naming a product after a place can also add perceived value by association. Brand names using the words Santa Fe, Dakota, or Texas convey a sense of openness, freedom, and youth, but products named after other locations might conjure up images of pollution and crime. Marketing managers are also interested in the *threshold level of perception*, the minimum difference in a stimulus that the consumer will notice. This concept is sometimes referred to as the "just-noticeable difference." For example, how much would Apple have to drop the price of its iPod Shuffle before consumers recognized it as a bargain—$25? $50? or more? One study found that the just-noticeable difference in a stimulus is about a 20 percent change. For example, consumers will likely notice a 20 percent price decrease more quickly than one of only 15 percent. This marketing principle can be applied to other marketing variables as well, such as package size or loudness of a broadcast advertisement.[35]

Besides changing such stimuli as price, package size, and volume, marketers can change the product or attempt to reposition its image. But marketers must be careful when adding features. How many new services will discounter Target need to add before consumers perceive

selective distortion a process whereby a consumer changes or distorts information that conflicts with his or her feelings or beliefs

selective retention a process whereby a consumer remembers only that information that supports his or her personal beliefs

motive a driving force that causes a person to take action to satisfy specific needs

Maslow's hierarchy of needs a method of classifying human needs and motivations into five categories in ascending order of importance: physiological, safety, social, esteem, and self-actualization

it as a full-service department store? How many sporty features will General Motors have to add to a basic two-door sedan before consumers start perceiving it as a sports car?

Marketing managers who intend to do business in global markets should be aware of how foreign consumers perceive their products. For instance, in Japan, product labels are often written in English or French, even though they may not translate into anything meaningful. Many Japanese associate foreign words on product labels with the exotic, the expensive, and high quality.

Marketers have often been suspected of sending advertising messages subconsciously to consumers in what is known as *subliminal perception*. The controversy began when a researcher claimed to have increased popcorn and Coca-Cola sales at a movie theater after flashing "Eat popcorn" and "Drink Coca-Cola" on the screen every five seconds for 1/300th of a second, although the audience did not consciously recognize the messages. Almost immediately consumer protection groups became concerned that advertisers were brainwashing consumers, and this practice was pronounced illegal in California and Canada. Although the researcher later admitted to making up the data and scientists have been unable to replicate the study since, consumers are still wary of hidden messages that advertisers may be sending.

Motivation

By studying motivation, marketers can analyze the major forces influencing consumers to buy or not buy products. When you buy a product, you usually do so to fulfill some kind of need. These needs become motives when aroused sufficiently. For instance, suppose this morning you were so hungry before class that you needed to eat something. In response to that need, you stopped at Subway for a breakfast sandwich. In other words, you were motivated by hunger to stop at Subway. A **motive** is the driving force that causes a person to take action to satisfy specific needs.

Why are people driven by particular needs at particular times? One popular theory is **Maslow's hierarchy of needs**, shown in Exhibit 6.6, which arranges needs in ascending order of importance: physiological, safety, social, esteem, and self-actualization. As a person fulfills one need, a higher-level need becomes more important.

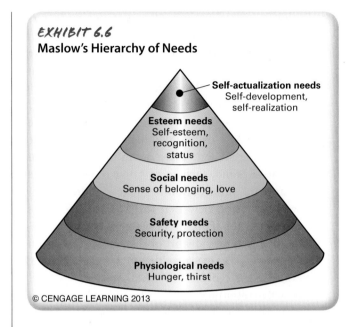

EXHIBIT 6.6
Maslow's Hierarchy of Needs

- **Self-actualization needs** Self-development, self-realization
- **Esteem needs** Self-esteem, recognition, status
- **Social needs** Sense of belonging, love
- **Safety needs** Security, protection
- **Physiological needs** Hunger, thirst

© CENGAGE LEARNING 2013

The most basic human needs—that is, the needs for food, water, and shelter—are *physiological*. Because they are essential to survival, these needs must be satisfied first. Ads showing a juicy hamburger or a runner gulping down Gatorade after a marathon are examples of appeals to satisfy the physiological needs of hunger and thirst.

Safety needs include security and freedom from pain and discomfort. Marketers sometimes appeal to consumers' fears and anxieties about safety to sell their products. For example, aware of the aging population's health fears, the retail medical imaging centers Heart Check America and HealthScreen America advertise that they offer consumers a full body scan for early detection of health problems such as coronary disease and cancer. On the other hand, some companies or industries advertise to allay consumer fears. For example, in the wake of the September 11 terrorist attacks, the airline industry found itself having to conduct an image campaign to reassure consumers about the safety of air travel.

After physiological and safety needs have been fulfilled, *social needs*—especially love and a sense of belonging—become the focus. Love includes acceptance by one's peers, as well as sex and romantic love. Marketing managers probably appeal more to this need than to any other. Ads for clothes, cosmetics, and vacation packages suggest that buying the product can bring love. The need to belong is also a favorite of marketers, especially those marketing products to teens. Teens consider Apple's iPod to be not only their favorite branded product but also something that defines their generation. Given the group's need for customization within a controlled environment, this love for Apple makes sense. Millennials' relationship with their parents is completely different from that of previous generations, and staying connected with family and friends is a priority. For marketers, this means understanding how to maximize crowdsourcing and peer-to-peer networks. For example, Relayrides offers the first peer-to-peer car-sharing where a person can borrow a neighbor's car for a quick trip to the store, and lenders can make up to $250 a month loaning out their cars.[36]

Love is acceptance without regard to one's contribution. Esteem is acceptance based on one's contribution to the group. *Self-esteem needs* include self-respect and a sense of accomplishment. Esteem needs also include prestige, fame, and recognition of one's accomplishments. Montblanc pens, Mercedes-Benz automobiles, and Neiman Marcus stores all appeal to esteem needs.

The highest human need is *self-actualization*. It refers to finding self-fulfillment and self-expression, reaching the point in life at which "people are what they feel they should be." Maslow felt that very few people ever attain this level. Even so, advertisements may focus on this type of need. For example, American Express ads convey the message that acquiring its card is one of the highest attainments in life. Microsoft appealed to consumers' needs for self-actualization when it chose "I'm a PC and Windows 7 was my idea" as the slogan for Windows 7; similarly, the U.S. Army changed its slogan from "Be all that you can be" to "Army of One."

Learning

Almost all consumer behavior results from **learning**, which is the process that creates changes in behavior through experience and practice. It is not possible to observe learning directly, but we can infer when it has occurred by a person's actions. For example, suppose you see an advertisement for a new and improved cold medicine. If you go to the store that day and buy that remedy, we infer that you have learned something about the cold medicine.

There are two types of learning: experiential and conceptual. *Experiential learning* occurs when an experience changes your behavior. For example, if the new cold medicine does not relieve your symptoms, you may not buy that brand again. *Conceptual learning*, which is not acquired through direct experience, is the second type of learning. Assume, for example,

that you are standing at a soft drink machine and notice a new diet flavor with an artificial sweetener. Because someone has told you that diet beverages leave an aftertaste, you choose a different drink. You have learned that you would not like this new diet drink without ever trying it.

Reinforcement and repetition boost learning. Reinforcement can be positive or negative. If you see a vendor selling frozen yogurt (stimulus), buy it (response), and find the yogurt to be quite refreshing (reward), your behavior has been positively reinforced. On the other hand, if you buy a new flavor of yogurt and it does not taste good (negative reinforcement), you will not buy that flavor of yogurt again (response). Without positive or negative reinforcement, a person will not be motivated to repeat the behavior pattern or to avoid it. Thus, if a new brand evokes neutral feelings, some marketing activity, such as a price change or an increase in promotion, may be required to induce further consumption. Learning theory is helpful in reminding marketers that concrete and timely actions are what reinforce desired consumer behavior.

Repetition is a key strategy in promotional campaigns because it can lead to increased learning. Most marketers use repetitious advertising so that consumers will learn what their unique advantage is over the competition. Generally, to heighten learning, advertising messages should be spread out over time rather than clustered together.

A related learning concept useful to marketing managers is **stimulus generalization**. In theory, stimulus generalization occurs when one response is extended to a second stimulus similar to the first. Marketers often use a successful, well-known brand name for a family of products because it gives consumers familiarity with and knowledge about each product in the family. Such brand name families spur the introduction of new products and facilitate the sale of existing items. Oxo relies on consumers' familiarity with its popular kitchen and household products to sell office and medical supplies; Sony's film division relies on name recognition from its home technology, such as the PlayStation. Clorox bathroom cleaner relies on familiarity with Clorox bleach, and Dove shampoo relies on familiarity with Dove soap. Branding is examined in more detail in Chapter 10.

Another form of stimulus generalization occurs when retailers or wholesalers design their packages to

learning a process that creates changes in behavior, immediate or expected, through experience and practice

stimulus generalization a form of learning that occurs when one response is extended to a second stimulus similar to the first

stimulus discrimination a learned ability to differentiate among similar products

belief an organized pattern of knowledge that an individual holds as true about his or her world

attitude a learned tendency to respond consistently toward a given object

resemble well-known manufacturers' brands. Such imitation often confuses consumers, who buy the imitation thinking it's the original.

The opposite of stimulus generalization is **stimulus discrimination**, which means learning to differentiate among similar products. Consumers may perceive one product as more rewarding or stimulating. For example, some consumers prefer Coca-Cola and others prefer Pepsi. Many insist they can taste a difference between the two brands.

With some types of products—such as aspirin, gasoline, bleach, and paper towels—marketers rely on promotion to point out brand differences that consumers would otherwise not recognize. This process, called *product differentiation*, is discussed in more detail in Chapter 8. Usually, product differentiation is based on superficial differences. For example, Bayer tells consumers that it's the aspirin "doctors recommend most."

Beliefs and Attitudes

Beliefs and attitudes are closely linked to values. A **belief** is an organized pattern of knowledge that an individual holds as true about his or her world. A consumer may believe that Sony's Cyber-shot camera takes the best HD video, is easiest to use, and is the most reasonably priced. These beliefs may be based on knowledge, faith, or hearsay. Consumers tend to develop a set of beliefs about a product's attributes and then, through these beliefs, form a *brand image*—a set of beliefs about a particular brand. In turn, the brand image shapes consumers' attitudes toward the product.

An **attitude** is a learned tendency to respond consistently toward a given object, such as a brand. Attitudes rest on an individual's value system, which represents personal standards of good and bad, right and wrong, and so forth; therefore, attitudes tend to be more enduring and complex than beliefs.

For an example of the nature of attitudes, consider the differing attitudes

CUSTOMERS WHO INSIST THEY TASTE A DIFFERENCE BETWEEN COKE AND PEPSI EXPERIENCE STIMULUS DISCRIMINATION.

of consumers around the world toward the practice of purchasing on credit. Americans have long been enthusiastic about charging goods and services and are willing to pay high interest rates for the privilege of postponing payment. To many European consumers, doing what amounts to taking out a loan—even a small one—to pay for anything seems absurd. Germans especially are reluctant to buy on credit. Italy has a sophisticated credit and banking system well suited to handling credit cards, but Italians prefer to carry cash, often huge wads of it. Although most Japanese consumers have credit cards, card purchases amount to less than 1 percent of all consumer transactions. The Japanese have long looked down on credit purchases but acquire cards to use while traveling abroad.

If a good or service is meeting its profit goals, positive attitudes toward the product merely need to be reinforced. If the brand is not succeeding, however, the marketing manager must strive to change target consumers' attitudes toward it. Changes in attitude tend to grow out of an individual's attempt to reconcile long-held values with a constant stream of new information. This change can be accomplished in three ways: changing beliefs about the brand's attributes, changing the relative importance of these beliefs, and adding new beliefs.

Changing Beliefs about Attributes

The first approach is to turn neutral, negative, or incorrect beliefs about product attributes into positive ones. Hotmail, which debuted in 1996 and quickly garnered wide usage, is now perceived as less modern than other e-mail services, such as Gmail. To combat growing negative perceptions, Microsoft revamped the Hotmail site to make it more modern and to integrate it as part of its Windows Live program. The Windows Live program offers free, modern programs that allow users to manage multimedia, chatting, blogs, and e-mail. The new Windows Live Hotmail features include the ability to watch videos from YouTube and Hulu from within your e-mail, and even automatically track U.S. Postal Service. packages when an e-mail contains a tracking number. These features

© ISTOCKPHOTO.COM/DONALD ERICKSON

make Hotmail an updated, modern choice for personal e-mail. To change people's lingering beliefs about Hotmail, Microsoft launched a massive marketing campaign to demonstrate Hotmail's updated, modern features.[37]

Changing beliefs about a service can be more difficult because service attributes are intangible. Convincing consumers to switch hairstylists or lawyers or to go to a mall dental clinic can be much more difficult than getting them to change brands of razor blades. Image, which is also largely intangible, significantly determines service patronage. Service marketing is explored in detail in Chapter 12.

Changing the Importance of Beliefs The second approach to modifying attitudes is to change the relative importance of beliefs about an attribute. J.Crew was suffering from plummeting sales in 2003, due in part to a frumpy, preppy persona, but has risen to new profits by offering luxurious basics, such as tailored basic dresses and cashmere sweaters. An endorsement from Michelle Obama further elevated the brand.[38] Marketers can also emphasize the importance of some beliefs over others. For example, McDonald's has been fingered as the culprit for Americans' obesity. But, now the chain offers a large line of salads and healthy meals and side options, hoping to demonstrate its ability to serve healthier options to customers who want them.[39]

Adding New Beliefs The third approach to transforming attitudes is to add new beliefs. Although changes in consumption patterns often come slowly, cereal marketers are betting that consumers will eventually warm up to the idea of cereal as a snack. A print ad for General Mills' Cookie Crisp cereal features a boy popping the sugary nuggets into his mouth while he does his homework. Koch Industries, the manufacturer of Dixie paper products, is also attempting to add new beliefs about the uses of its paper plates and cups with an advertising campaign aimed at positioning its product as a "home cleanup replacement." Commercials pitch Dixie paper plates as an alternative to washing dishes after everyday meals and not just for picnics.

U.S. companies attempting to market their goods overseas may need to help consumers add new beliefs about a product in general. Coca-Cola and PepsiCo have both found it challenging to sell their diet cola brands to consumers in India partly because diet foods of any kind are a new concept in that country where malnutrition was widespread until recently. Indians also have deep-rooted attitudes that anything labeled "diet" is meant for a sick person, such as a diabetic. As a general rule, most Indians are not diet conscious, preferring food prepared in the traditional manner that tastes good. Indians are also suspicious of the artificial sweeteners used in diet colas. India's Health Ministry has required warning labels on cans and bottles of Diet Coke and Diet Pepsi saying "Not Recommended for Children."[40]

STUDY TOOLS CHAPTER 6

Flip to the end of your textbook to:

❑ **Rip out Chapter Review Card**

Log in to the CourseMate for MKTG at cengagebrain.com to:

❑ **Review Key Terms Flash Cards (Print or Online)**

❑ **Review Audio and Visual Summaries**

❑ **Complete both Practice Quizzes to prepare for tests**

❑ **Play "Beat the Clock" and "Quizbowl" to master concepts**

❑ **Complete "Crossword Puzzle" to review key terms**

❑ **Watch the video on "Scholfield Honda" for a real company example on Consumer Decision Making**

CHAPTER 7 **Business** Marketing

> The key characteristic distinguishing business products from consumer products is intended use, not physical form.

LO 1 What Is Business Marketing?

AFTER YOU FINISH THIS CHAPTER, GO TO PAGE 127 FOR STUDY TOOLS

Business marketing (also called **industrial marketing**) is the marketing of goods and services to individuals and organizations for purposes other than personal consumption. The sale of a PC to your college or university is an example of business marketing. Business products include those that are used to manufacture other products, become part of another product, or aid the normal operations of an organization. The key characteristic distinguishing business products from consumer products is intended use, not physical characteristics.

How do you distinguish between a consumer product and a business product? A product that is purchased for personal or family consumption or as a gift is a consumer good. If that same product, such as a PC or a cell phone, is bought for use in a business, it is a business product. Some common items that are sold as both consumer goods and business products are office supplies (e.g., pens, paper, staple removers). Some items, such as forklifts, are more commonly sold as business products than as consumer goods. A survey by HubSpot revealed that the two primary marketing goals of U.S. business marketers' Web sites are making sales and attracting customers, clients, and other new business.[1]

The size of the business market in the United States and most other countries substantially exceeds that of the consumer market. In the business market, a single customer can account for a huge volume of purchases. For example, IBM's

> **business marketing (industrial marketing)** the marketing of goods and services to individuals and organizations for purposes other than personal consumption

What do you think?

Salespeople make shopping an uncomfortable experience.

1 2 3 4 5 6 7
STRONGLY DISAGREE   STRONGLY AGREE

Find out what others think at the CourseMate for MKTG. Log in at cengagebrain.com.

© SEAN GALLUP/GETTY IMAGES

business-to-business electronic commerce the use of the Internet to facilitate the exchange of goods, services, and information between organizations

purchasing department spends more than $40 billion annually on business products. Procter & Gamble, Apple, Merck, Dell, and Kimberly Clark each spend more than half of their annual revenue on business products.[2]

Some large firms that produce goods such as steel, computer memory chips, or production equipment market exclusively to business customers. Other firms market to both businesses and to consumers. Hewlett-Packard marketed exclusively to business customers in the past, but now markets laser printers and personal computers to consumers. Sony, traditionally a consumer marketer, now sells office automation products to businesses. Both companies have had to make organizational and marketing changes to expand into the new market categories.

LO 2 Business Marketing on the Internet

The use of the Internet to facilitate activities between organizations is called **business-to-business electronic commerce** (B-to-B or B2B e-commerce). This method of conducting business has evolved and grown rapidly throughout its short history. In 1995, the commercial Web sites that did exist were static. Only a few had data-retrieval capabilities. Frames, tables, and styles were not available. Security of any sort was rare, and streaming video did not exist. Today, B2B sites look more like consumer sites with social media and community building applications. Before the Internet, customers had to call Dow Chemical and request a specification sheet for the products they were considering. The information would arrive a few days later by mail. After choosing a product, the customer could then place an order by calling Dow (during business hours, of course). Now, such information is available through MyAccount@Dow, which provides information tailored to the customer's requirements, such as secure internal monitoring

TWITTER IS HELPFUL IN MAINTAINING CONTACTS WITH NETWORKS!

of a customer's chemical tank levels. When tanks reach a predetermined level, reordering can be automatically triggered.[3]

Companies selling to business buyers face the same challenges as all marketers, including determining who, exactly, the market is and how best to reach them. This is particularly difficult in business marketing because business has rapidly moved online. A recent report from Forrester Research, "B2B US Interactive Marketing Forecast 2009–2014," predicted that interactive spending by B-to-B marketers will reach $4.8 billion by 2014. In 2010, spending was approximately $2.3 billion. Some of the expected increase can be attributed to companies looking to bypass more expensive offline tactics and use more measurable online tactics.[4] Most B-to-B marketers primarily use e-mail marketing, SEO organic, online ads and banners, search key words, webinars, and viral videos to attract business customers.

The reviews on social media are mixed. Some B-to-B marketers feel that social media are not as useful to them as to business-to-consumer (B-to-C) marketers.[5] But other experts see growth in social media use as B-to-B marketers use opportunities to generate quality leads. Most of the spending is allocated to creating customer community (32 percent); podcasts (20 percent) and blogs (18 percent) to convey thought leadership; and Twitter (14 percent).[6] It is clear from some companies' Web sites that they are embracing new tools and applications. The primary tools used by B-to-B marketers are blogs, social networking sites, Twitter, video streaming sites, and mobile marketing. B-to-B marketers are experimenting with how to effectively use these media to build relationships with business customers. For example, YouTube has a "how to" guide for B-to-B marketers about effectively using online videos to promote their brands. LinkedIn, a social networking site, is seen as a repository for finding new talent for companies.[7]

Each year, BtoBonline.com identifies ten business marketing Web sites that are particularly good examples of how companies can use the Web to communicate with customers. Exhibit 7.1 identifies the ten great Web sites for 2010. Many of these companies have also been recognized in past years for effectively communicating with their target markets.[8]

Measuring Online Success

Most marketers use some sort of web analytics (like Google Analytics or an enterprise system like Omniture) to determine which

© PHILIPPE WIDLING/DESIGN PICS/JUPITERIMAGES / © ISTOCKPHOTO.COM/GEOFFREY HOLMAN

EXHIBIT 7.1
Ten Great Web Sites

URL	Company	Target Audience
www.accenture.com	Accenture	C-level executives at large companies, government organizations, and job seekers
www.airclic.com	Airclic	C-level supply chain and logistics decision makers across 13 industries, customers, current and prospective partners, media, investors, and influencers
www.dropbox.com	Dropbox	Businesses, consumers, and mobile productivity users
www.freightcenter.com	FreightCenter, Inc.	Small to midsize shippers, with some focus on enterprise shippers
www.ixda.org	Interaction Design Association	Recruiters and members
www.istockphoto.com	iStockphoto	Businesses, designers, and bloggers
www.macktrucks.com	Mack Trucks	Dealers and prospective Mack Truck buyers, including truckers, construction companies, refuse haulers, and other commerical companies
www.sas.com	SAS Institute, Inc.	Current and prospective customers, community members, employees, potential employees, and media
www.shawfloors.com	Shaw Floors	Architects, interior designers, resellers, retailers, and consumers
www.tyco.com	Tyco International	Prospective and current employees, investment community, customers, and community partners

SOURCE: Karen J. Bannan, "10 Great b2b Sites," *BtoB Magazine*, online, September 13, 2010, www.btobonline.com/article/20100913/FREE/309139988 /10-great-b-to-b-sites.

activities generate leads and then use that information to make the Web site more effective. Metrics include external search traffic, internal search engine analytics, and key word search results. Three of the most important measurements of online success are recency, frequency, and monetary value. *Recency* relates to the fact that customers who have made a purchase recently are more likely to purchase again in the near future than customers who haven't purchased for a while. *Frequency* data help marketers identify frequent purchasers who are definitely more likely to repeat their purchasing behavior in the future. The *monetary value* of sales is important because big spenders can be the most profitable customers for a business.

One common way of evaluating a Web application, Web site, or other piece of interactive technology is to evaluate its **stickiness** factor by combining frequency data with the length of time a visitor spent on the Web site (duration) and the number of site pages viewed during each visit (total site reach). For example, Apple's iCloud, which allows users to remotely store all content in the cloud and access it from any Apple device, increases user stickiness in the Apple software systems, meaning users will use all Apple software for long periods of time.[9]

$$STICKINESS = FREQUENCY \times DURATION \times SITE\ REACH$$

By measuring the stickiness factor of a Web site before and after a design or function change, the marketer can quickly determine whether visitors embraced the change. By adding purchase information to determine the level of stickiness needed to provide a desired purchase volume, the marketer gains an even more precise understanding of how a site change affected business. An almost endless number of factor combinations can be created to provide a quantitative method for determining buyer behavior online. First, though, the marketer must determine what measures are required and which factors can be combined to arrive at those measurements.[10]

stickiness a measure of a Web site's effectiveness; calculated by multiplying the frequency of visits by the duration of a visit by the number of pages viewed during each visit (site reach)

Trends in B-to-B Internet Marketing

Social media usage in B-to-B marketing and B-to-C marketing has been the largest marketing trend in the past five years. It requires vigilant adjustment to keep

disintermediation
the elimination of intermediaries such as wholesalers or distributers from a marketing channel

track of new applications and platforms, as well as constant evaluation to determine whether these new avenues are beneficial to (or used by) customers. While 43 percent of marketers are measuring social media on some level, it is still a work in progress for many B-to-B marketers.

Many marketers use social media to create awareness and build relationships and community rather than generate leads. As various platforms, such as mobile and video grow, marketers must develop new ways to measure campaign effectiveness across those platforms. According to a survey by BtoB and the Web Analytics Association, social media measurement was low for mobile (17 percent) and video (14 percent) and high for Web site traffic (88 percent) and e-mail campaigns (76 percent).[11] Because e-mail and Web sites have been in use by marketers longer, analytics to measure various metrics are more developed for those platforms. Some metrics that are particularly useful for social media are awareness, engagement, and conversion. Awareness is the attention that social media attracts, such as the number of followers or fans. Engagement refers to the interactions between the brand and the audience such as comments, retweets, and searches. Conversions occur when action is taken.[12] Each of these metrics affects the return on investment.

As the increasing use of social media indicates, over the past decade marketers have become more and more sophisticated in the use of the Internet. Exhibit 7.2 compares three prominent Internet business marketing strategy initiatives from the late 1990s compared to five that are currently being pursued. Companies have had to transition from "We have a Web site because our customer does" to having a site that attracts, interests, satisfies, informs, and retains customers. New applications that provide additional information about present and potential customers; increase efficiency; lower costs; increase supply chain efficiency; or enhance customer retention, loyalty, and trust are being developed each year. Chapter 21, Customer Relationship Management, describes several of these applications. Increasingly, business customers expect suppliers to know them personally, keep tabs on people's movement within their company, and offer personal interaction through social media, e-mail, and personal mailers.[13]

One term in Exhibit 7.2 that may be unfamiliar is **disintermediation**, which means eliminating intermediaries such as wholesalers or distributors from a marketing channel.[14] A prime example of disintermediation is Dell, which sells directly to business buyers

TOP SOCIAL MEDIA PLATFORMS FOR B-TO-B MARKETERS

© DMITRIY SHIRONOSOV/SHUTTERSTOCK.COM

BtoB magazine surveyed 577 B-to-B marketers on their favorite social media platforms at work, and while LinkedIn, Facebook, and Twitter were used by nearly all of the marketers, LinkedIn was their favorite social media tool (chosen by 26 percent of respondents). Runners up were Facebook (20 percent), blogs (19 percent), customer communities (14 percent), Twitter, (13 percent), and YouTube (7 percent).

Those who didn't use social media marketing cited difficulty in convincing top management of its usefulness. This could be due in part to lack of measurable success metrics or simply poor understanding of the medium.[15]

SOURCE: "Emerging Trends in B-to-B Social Media Marketing: Insights from the Field," *BtoB*, April 2011, 6–9.

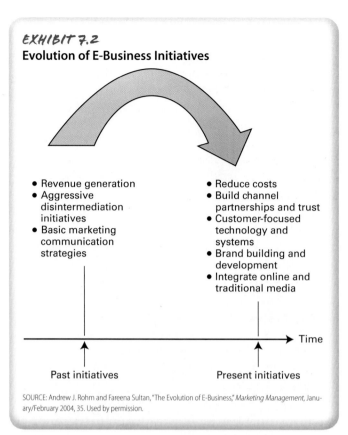

EXHIBIT 7.2
Evolution of E-Business Initiatives

- Revenue generation
- Aggressive disintermediation initiatives
- Basic marketing communication strategies

- Reduce costs
- Build channel partnerships and trust
- Customer-focused technology and systems
- Brand building and development
- Integrate online and traditional media

Time

Past initiatives — Present initiatives

SOURCE: Andrew J. Rohm and Fareena Sultan, "The Evolution of E-Business," *Marketing Management*, January/February 2004, 35. Used by permission.

line of products and services to focus entirely on helping corporate customers expand consumer offerings, including offering networking products and solutions.[16]

LO 3 Relationship Marketing and Strategic Alliances

As explained in Chapter 1, relationship marketing is a strategy that entails seeking and establishing ongoing partnerships with customers. Relationship marketing has become an important business marketing strategy as customers have become more demanding and competition has become more intense. Loyal customers are also more profitable than those who are price sensitive and perceive little or no difference among brands or suppliers.

Relationship marketing is increasingly important as business suppliers use platforms like Facebook, Twitter, and other social networking sites to advertise themselves to businesses. The social networking sites encourage businesses to shop around and research options for all their needs. This means that for many suppliers, retaining their current customers has become a primary focus, whereas acquiring new customers was the focus in the past. Maintaining a steady dialogue between the supplier and the customer is a proven way to gain repeat business.[17]

Building long-term relationships with customers offers companies a way to build competitive advantage that is hard for competitors to copy. For example, the FedEx PowerShip program includes a series of automated shipping, tracking, and invoicing systems that save customers time and money while solidifying their loyalty to FedEx. This produces a win-win situation.

Strategic Alliances

A **strategic alliance**, sometimes called a **strategic partnership**, is a cooperative agreement between business firms. Strategic alliances can take the form of licensing or distribution agreements, joint ventures, research and development consortia, and partnerships. They may be between manufacturers,

and consumers. Dell is now using Twitter to sell its overstock inventory. Large retailers such as Walmart use a disintermediation strategy to help reduce costs and prices.

A few years ago, many people thought the Internet would eliminate the need for distributors. Why would customers pay a distributor's markup when they could buy directly from the manufacturer with a few mouse clicks? Yet Internet disintermediation has occurred less frequently than many expected. The reason is that distributors often perform important functions such as providing credit, aggregation of supplies from multiple sources, delivery, and processing returns.

Many business customers, especially small firms, depend on knowledgeable distributors for information and advice that is not available to them online. You will notice in Exhibit 7.2 that building channel partnerships and trust has replaced aggressive disintermediation initiatives as a priority for most firms. Some firms have followed disintermediation with **reintermediation**, the reintroduction of an intermediary between producers and users. They realized that providing direct online purchasing only was similar to having only one store in a city selling a popular brand. For example, Cisco is dropping its direct-to-consumer

reintermediation the reintroduction of an intermediary between producers and users

strategic alliance (strategic partnership) a cooperative agreement between business firms

relationship commitment a firm's belief that an ongoing relationship with another firm is so important that the relationship warrants maximum efforts at maintaining it indefinitely

trust the condition that exists when one party has confidence in an exchange partner's reliability and integrity

manufacturers and customers, manufacturers and suppliers, and manufacturers and channel intermediaries.

Business marketers form strategic alliances to strengthen operations and better compete. Honest Tea, a leader in the sustainable, organic beverage market, accepted a partnership with Coca-Cola in order to gain access to the beverage giant's larger, established distributors and get Honest Tea's healthier drinks into schools and supermarkets. Coca-Cola, now the largest shareholder of Honest Tea, encourages the brand to continue its pursuit of sustainable, organic, fair-trade beverages by providing new, top-of-the-line equipment set to Honest Tea's specifications.[18]

Sometimes alliance partners are fierce competitors. For instance, in the face of rising fuel prices and increasing business competition from Delta Airlines, Singapore Airlines and Virgin Australia have teamed up to offer greater range for both airlines. Virgin's expansive Australian and Pacific routes will give Singapore Airlines access to the lucrative Australia–United States route, and Virgin will have access to 70 new routes. The companies will also collaborate on pricing and a frequent flyer program, hoping to increase their share in the business traveler market.[19]

Other alliances are formed between companies that operate in completely different industries. For example, MasterCard and Avis Budget Group formed an alliance to provide MasterCard users discounts on services provided by Budget and Avis car rental services. MasterCard users prefer discounts in the travel sector, and the alliance gives Budget and Avis an opportunity to increase market share in the $4 billion-a-year U.S. car rental market.[20] Exhibit 7.3 demonstrates the benefits Starbucks and Green Mountain Coffee receive from each other through their strategic alliance.

For an alliance to succeed in the long term, it must be built on commitment and trust. **Relationship commitment** means that a firm believes an ongoing relationship with some other firm is so important that it warrants maximum efforts at maintaining it indefinitely.[21] A perceived breakdown in commitment by one of the parties often leads to a breakdown in the relationship.

Trust exists when one party has confidence in an exchange partner's reliability and integrity.[22] Some alliances fail when participants lack trust in their trading partners. For instance, General Motors,

IF YOU ORDER IT WE WILL COME.
FOOD AND DRINKS ON DEMAND. THIS IS HOW TO FLY.

GRAB A SEAT AT VIRGINAMERICA.COM
SAN FRANCISCO : LAS VEGAS : LOS ANGELES : NEW YORK : SAN DIEGO : SEATTLE : WASHINGTON, D.C.

Virgin america

© AP IMAGES/PRNEWSFOTO/VIRGIN AMERICA

Ford, DaimlerChrysler, Nissan Motor Company, and Renault SA created an Internet automobile parts exchange, called Covisint, that they hoped would make $300 billion in sales per year. But the auto industry is characterized by mistrust between buyers and sellers, and the alliance never got a strong foothold. After three years, and hundreds of millions of dollars invested, the exchange was floundering. The investment money was nearly gone, and the workforce had been reduced by 35 percent. Automobile industry suppliers did not trust Covisint, resulting in its failure.

Relationships in Other Cultures

Although the terms *relationship marketing* and *strategic alliances* are fairly new, and popularized mostly by American business executives and educators, the concepts have long been familiar in other cultures. Businesses in China, Japan, Korea, Mexico, and much of Europe rely heavily on personal relationships. Chapter 21 explores customer relationship management in detail.

In Japan, for example, exchange between firms is based on personal relationships that are developed

EXHIBIT 7.3
Strategic Alliance: Starbucks and Green Mountain

	Gives		Gets
	Starbucks Branded Coffee Starbucks ground coffee has worldwide recognition and a strong market share.		*Market Share* Starbucks worldwide recognition allows Green Mountain to steal market share from other single-pod brands that don't carry Starbucks brand coffee.
	Starbucks Customers Starbucks customers are willing to brew at home and tend to be affluent.		*Stronger Brand Recognition* By offering the high-value Keurig brewing machine at Starbucks stores, Green Mountain is able to give its Keurig line stronger branding.
	Existing Green Mountain Customers Current Green Mountain customers own Keurig machines and brew single-pod coffee.		*Market Share* Focused access to Keurig machine users in homes and businesses increases Starbucks presence in those markets.
	Technology Keurig machines and single-pod brewing technology		*Expanded Product Offering* By selling Keurig machines and coffee pods in retail stores, Starbucks can offer more products and more ways to drink Starbucks coffee.

© AP IMAGES/TOBY TALBOT / © AP IMAGES/TED S. WARREN / © AP IMAGES/TOBY TALBOT / © AP IMAGES/TED S. WARREN

through what is called *amae*, or indulgent dependency. *Amae* is the feeling of nurturing concern for, and dependence upon, another. Reciprocity and personal relationships contribute to *amae*. Relationships between companies can develop into a *keiretsu*—a network of interlocking corporate affiliates. Within a *keiretsu*, executives may sit on the boards of their customers or their suppliers. Members of a *keiretsu* trade with each other whenever possible and often engage in joint product development, finance, and marketing activity. For example, the Toyota Group *keiretsu* includes 14 core companies and another 170 that receive preferential treatment. Toyota holds an equity position in many of these 170 member firms and is represented on many of their boards of directors.

Many firms have found that the best way to compete in Asian countries is to form relationships with Asian firms. For example, German automaker Volkswagen has an alliance with Suzuki Motor Corporation to work on developing new hybrid and electric vehicles under both brands.[23]

LO4 Major Categories of Business Customers

The business market consists of four major categories of customers: producers, resellers, governments, and institutions.

Producers

The producer segment of the business market includes profit-oriented individuals and organizations that use purchased goods and services to produce other products, to incorporate into other products, or to facilitate the daily operations of the organization. Examples of producers include construction, manufacturing, transportation, finance, real estate, and food service firms. In the United States, there are more than 13 million firms in the producer segment of the business market. Some

keiretsu a network of interlocking corporate affiliates

original equipment manufacturers (OEMs) individuals and organizations that buy business goods and incorporate them into the products they produce for eventual sale to other producers or to consumers

of these firms are small, and others are among the world's largest businesses.

Producers are often called **original equipment manufacturers** or **OEMs**. This term includes all individuals and organizations that buy business goods and incorporate them into the products they produce for eventual sale to other producers or to consumers. Companies such as General Motors that buy steel, paint, tires, and batteries are said to be OEMs.

© AP IMAGES/PRNEWSFOTO/ALTAIR ENGINEERING

Resellers

The reseller market includes retail and wholesale businesses that buy finished goods and resell them for a profit. A retailer sells mainly to final consumers; wholesalers sell mostly to retailers and other organizational customers. There are approximately 1.5 million retailers and 500,000 wholesalers operating in the United States. Consumer product firms like Procter & Gamble, Kraft Foods, and Coca-Cola sell directly to large retailers and retail chains and through wholesalers to smaller retail units. Retailing is explored in detail in Chapter 15.

Business product distributors are wholesalers that buy business products and resell them to business customers. They often carry thousands of items in stock and employ sales forces to call on business customers. Businesses that wish to buy a gross of pencils or a hundred pounds of fertilizer typically purchase these items from local distributors rather than directly from manufacturers such as Empire Pencil or Dow Chemical.

Governments

A third major segment of the business market is government. Government organizations include thousands of federal, state, and local buying units. They make up what may be the largest single market for goods and services in the world, estimated at $5.5 trillion in 2010.[24]

Marketing to government agencies can be an overwhelming undertaking, but companies that learn how the system works can position themselves to win lucrative contracts and build lasting, rewarding relationships.[25] Contracts for government purchases are often put out for bid. Interested vendors submit bids (usually sealed) to provide specified products during a particular time. Sometimes the lowest bidder is awarded the contract. When the lowest bidder is not awarded the contract, strong evidence must be presented to justify the decision. Grounds for rejecting the lowest bid include lack of experience, inadequate financing, or poor past performance. Bidding allows all potential suppliers a fair chance at winning government contracts and helps ensure that public funds are spent wisely.

Federal Government Name just about any good or service and chances are that someone in the federal government uses it. The U.S. federal government buys goods and services valued at more than $600 billion per year, making it the world's largest customer.

Although much of the federal government's buying is centralized, no single federal agency contracts for all the government's requirements, and no single buyer in any agency purchases all that the agency needs. We can view the federal government as a combination of several large companies with overlapping responsibilities and thousands of small independent units. One popular source of information about government procurement is *Commerce Business Daily*. Until recently, businesses hoping to sell to the federal government found the document unorganized, and it often arrived too late to be useful. The online version (www.cbd-net.com) is timelier and lets contractors find leads using key word searches. Other examples of publications designed to explain how to do business with the federal government include *Doing Business with the General Services Administration*, *Selling to the Military*, and *Selling to the U.S. Air Force*.

State, County, and City Government Selling to states, counties, and cities can be less frustrating for both small and large vendors than selling to the federal government. Paperwork is typically simpler and more manageable than it is at the federal level. On the other hand, vendors must decide which of the more than 82,000 government units are likely to buy their wares. State and local buying agencies include school districts, highway departments, government-operated hospitals, and housing agencies.

Institutions

The fourth major segment of the business market consists of institutions that seek to achieve goals other than the standard business goals of profit, market share, and return on investment. This segment includes schools, hospitals, colleges and universities, churches, labor unions, fraternal organizations, civic clubs, foundations, and other so-called nonbusiness organizations. Xerox offers educational and medical institutions the same prices as government agencies (the lowest that Xerox offers) and has a separate sales force that calls on these customers.

LO 5 The North American Industry Classification System

The **North American Industry Classification System (NAICS)** is an industry classification system introduced in 1997 to replace the standard industrial classification system (SIC). NAICS (pronounced *nakes*) is a system for classifying North American business establishments. The system, developed jointly by the United States, Canada, and Mexico, provides a common industry classification system for the North American Free

How NAICS Works

The more digits in the NAICS code, the more homogeneous the groups at that level.

NAICS Level	NAICS Code	Description
Sector	51	Information
Subsector	513	Broadcasting and telecommunications
Industry group	5133	Telecommunications
Industry	51332	Wireless telecommunications carriers, except satellite
Industry subdivision	513321	Paging

Trade Agreement (NAFTA) partners. Goods- or service-producing firms that use identical or similar production processes are grouped together.

NAICS is an extremely valuable tool for business marketers engaged in analyzing, segmenting, and targeting markets. Each classification group is relatively homogeneous in terms of raw materials required, components used, manufacturing processes employed, and problems faced. The more digits in a code, the more homogeneous the group. Therefore, if a supplier understands the needs and requirements of a few firms within a classification, requirements can be projected for all firms in that category. The number, size, and geographic dispersion of firms can also be identified. This information can be converted to market potential estimates, market share estimates, and sales forecasts. It can also be used for identifying potential new customers. NAICS codes can help identify firms that may be prospective users of a supplier's goods and services. For a complete listing of all NAICS codes, see www.naics.com/search.htm.

North American Industry Classification System (NAICS) a detailed numbering system developed by the United States, Canada, and Mexico to classify North American business establishments by their main production processes

derived demand the demand for business products

LO 6 Business versus Consumer Markets

The basic philosophy and practice of marketing are the same whether the customer is a business organization or a consumer. Business markets do, however, have characteristics different from consumer markets.

Demand

Consumer demand for products is quite different from demand in the business market. Unlike consumer demand, business demand is derived, inelastic, joint, and fluctuating.

Derived Demand The demand for business products is called **derived demand** because organizations buy products to be used in producing their customers' products. For instance, the number of drills or lathes that a manufacturing firm needs is "derived from," or based upon the demand for, products that are produced using these machines. Because demand is derived, business marketers must carefully monitor

joint demand the demand for two or more items used together in a final product

multiplier effect (accelerator principle) phenomenon in which a small increase or decrease in consumer demand can produce a much larger change in demand for the facilities and equipment needed to make the consumer product

demand patterns and changing preferences in final consumer markets, even though their customers are not in those markets. Moreover, business marketers must carefully monitor their customers' forecasts, because derived demand is based on expectations of future demand for those customers' products.

Some business marketers not only monitor final consumer demand and customer forecasts but also try to influence final consumer demand. Aluminum producers use television and magazine advertisements to point out the convenience and recycling opportunities that aluminum offers to consumers who can choose to purchase soft drinks in either aluminum or plastic containers.

Inelastic Demand The demand for many business products is inelastic with regard to price. *Inelastic demand* means that an increase or decrease in the price of the product will not significantly affect demand for the product. This will be discussed further in Chapter 19.

The price of a product used in the production of, or as part of, a final product is often a minor portion of the final product's total price. Therefore, demand for the final consumer product is not affected. If the price of automobile paint or spark plugs rises significantly, say, 200 percent in one year, do you think the number of new automobiles sold that year will be affected? Probably not.

Joint Demand **Joint demand** occurs when two or more items are used together in a final product. For example, a decline in the availability of memory chips will slow production of microcomputers, which will in turn reduce the demand for disk drives. Likewise, the demand for Apple operating systems exists as long as there is demand for Apple computers. Sales of the two products are directly linked.

Fluctuating Demand The demand for business products—particularly new plants and equipment—tends to be less stable than the demand for consumer products. A small increase or decrease in consumer demand can produce a much larger change in demand for the facilities and equipment needed to make the consumer product. Economists refer to this phenomenon as the **multiplier effect** (or **accelerator principle**).

Cummins Engine Company, a producer of heavy-duty diesel engines, uses sophisticated surface grinders to make parts. Suppose Cummins is using 20 surface grinders. Each machine lasts about ten years. Purchases have been timed so 2 machines will wear out and be replaced annually. If the demand for engine parts does not change, 2 grinders will be bought this year. If the demand for parts declines slightly, only 18 grinders may be needed and Cummins won't replace the worn ones. However, suppose that next year demand returns to previous levels plus a little more. To meet the new level of demand, Cummins will need to replace the two machines that wore out in the first year, the two that wore out in the second year, plus one or more additional machines. The multiplier effect works this way in many industries, producing highly fluctuating demand for business products.

Purchase Volume

Business customers buy in much larger quantities than consumers. Just think how large an order Kellogg's typically places for the wheat bran and raisins used to manufacture Raisin Bran. Or, consider that Enterprise Rent-A-Car purchases 500 electric cars from Nissan at one time.[26]

Number of Customers

Business marketers usually have far fewer customers than consumer marketers. The advantage is that it is a lot easier to identify prospective buyers, monitor current customers' needs and levels of satisfaction, and personally attend to existing customers. The main disadvantage is that each customer becomes crucial—especially for those manufacturers that have only one customer. In many cases, this customer is the U.S. government. The success or failure of one bid can make the difference between prosperity and bankruptcy. Boeing, trying to

The success or failure of one bid can make the difference between prosperity and bankruptcy.

© ISTOCKPHOTO.COM/DMITRY OSHCHEPKOV

regain its position as the dominant tanker plane developer, vied for more than three years to win the U.S. Air Force's $35 billion bid to supply refueling planes. Its main competition was European Aeronautic Defence and Space Company, the world's other leading supplier of tanker planes.[27]

Location of Buyers

Business customers tend to be much more geographically concentrated than consumers. For instance, more than half the nation's business buyers are located in California, Illinois, Michigan, New Jersey, New York, Ohio, and Pennsylvania. The aircraft and microelectronics industries are concentrated on the West Coast, and many of the firms that supply the automobile manufacturing industry are located in and around Detroit.

Distribution Structure

Many consumer products pass through a distribution system that includes the producer, one or more wholesalers, and a retailer. In business marketing, however, because of many of the characteristics already mentioned, channels of distribution for business marketing are typically shorter. Direct channels, where manufacturers market directly to users, are much more common. The use of direct channels has increased dramatically in the past decade with the introduction of various Internet buying and selling schemes. One such technique is called a **business-to-business online exchange**, which is an electronic trading floor that provides companies with integrated links to their customers and suppliers. The goal of B2B exchanges is to simplify business purchasing and to make them more efficient. For example, Exostar claims more than half of the aerospace industry's firms as its customers and has more than 70,000 registered companies to support those customers.[28] Exchanges such as Exostar facilitate direct channel relationships between producers and their customers.

Nature of Buying

Unlike consumers, business buyers usually approach purchasing rather formally. Businesses use professionally trained purchasing agents or buyers who spend their entire career purchasing a limited number of items. They get to know the items and the sellers well. Some professional purchasers earn the designation of Certified Purchasing Manager (CPM) after participating in a rigorous certification program.

Nature of Buying Influence

Typically, more people are involved in a single business purchase decision than in a consumer purchase. Experts from fields as varied as quality control, marketing, and finance, as well as professional buyers and users, may be grouped in a buying center (discussed later in this chapter).

Type of Negotiations

Consumers are used to negotiating price on automobiles and real estate. In most cases, however, American consumers expect sellers to set the price and other conditions of sale, such as time of delivery and credit terms. In contrast, negotiating is common in business marketing. Buyers and sellers negotiate product specifications, delivery dates, payment terms, and other pricing matters. Sometimes these negotiations occur during many meetings over several months. Final contracts are often very long and detailed.

Use of Reciprocity

Business purchasers often choose to buy from their own customers, a practice known as **reciprocity**. For example, General Motors buys engines for use in its automobiles and trucks from BorgWarner, which in turn buys many of the automobiles and trucks it needs from General Motors. This practice is neither unethical nor illegal unless one party coerces the other and the result is unfair competition. Reciprocity is generally considered a reasonable business practice. If all possible suppliers sell a similar product for about the same price, doesn't it make sense to buy from those firms that buy from you?

Use of Leasing

Consumers normally buy products rather than lease them. But businesses commonly lease expensive equipment such as computers, construction equipment and vehicles, and automobiles. Leasing allows firms to reduce capital outflow, acquire a seller's latest products, receive better services, and gain tax advantages.

The lessor, the firm providing the product, may be either the manufacturer or an independent firm. The benefits to the lessor include greater total revenue from leasing compared to selling and an opportunity to do business with customers who cannot afford to buy.

business-to-business online exchange an electronic trading floor that provides companies with integrated links to their customers and suppliers

reciprocity a practice whereby business purchasers choose to buy from their own customers

major equipment (installations) capital goods such as large or expensive machines, mainframe computers, blast furnaces, generators, airplanes, and buildings

accessory equipment goods, such as portable tools and office equipment, that are less expensive and shorter-lived than major equipment

raw materials unprocessed extractive or agricultural products, such as mineral ore, lumber, wheat, corn, fruits, vegetables, and fish

Primary Promotional Method

Business marketers tend to emphasize personal selling in their promotion efforts, especially for expensive items, custom-designed products, large-volume purchases, and situations requiring negotiations. The sale of many business products requires a great deal of personal contact. Personal selling is discussed in more detail in Chapter 18.

LO7 Types of Business Products

Business products generally fall into one of the following seven categories, depending on their use: major equipment, accessory equipment, raw materials, component parts, processed materials, supplies, and business services.

Major Equipment

Major equipment includes capital goods such as large or expensive machines, mainframe computers, blast furnaces, generators, airplanes, and buildings. (These items are also commonly called **installations**.) Major equipment is depreciated over time rather than charged as an expense in the year it is purchased. In addition, major equipment is often custom designed for each customer. Personal selling is an important part of the marketing strategy for major equipment because distribution channels are almost always direct from the producer to the business user.

Accessory Equipment

Accessory equipment is generally less expensive and shorter-lived than major equipment. Examples include portable drills, power tools, microcomputers, and fax machines. Accessory equipment is often charged as an expense in the year it is bought rather than depreciated over its useful life. In contrast to major equipment, accessories are more often standardized and are usually bought by more customers. These customers tend to be widely dispersed. For example, all types of businesses buy microcomputers.

Local industrial distributors (wholesalers) play an important role in the marketing of accessory equipment because business buyers often purchase accessories from them. Regardless of where accessories are bought, advertising is a more vital promotional tool for accessory equipment than for major equipment.

Raw Materials

Raw materials are unprocessed extractive or agricultural products—for example, mineral ore, lumber, wheat, corn, fruits, vegetables, and fish. Raw materials become part of finished products. Extensive users, such as steel or lumber mills and food canners, generally buy huge

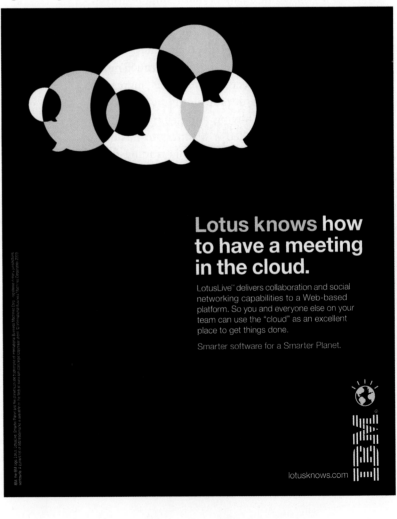

Many of IBM's products are major purchases and are customized according to a large business's computer and server needs.

Lotus knows how to have a meeting in the cloud.

LotusLive™ delivers collaboration and social networking capabilities to a Web-based platform. So you and everyone else on your team can use the "cloud" as an excellent place to get things done.

Smarter software for a Smarter Planet.

lotusknows.com

REPRINT COURTESY OF INTERNATIONAL BUSINESS MACHINES CORPORATION, © 2011 INTERNATIONAL BUSINESS MACHINES CORPORATION

quantities of raw materials. Because there is often a large number of relatively small sellers of raw materials, none can greatly influence price or supply. Thus, the market tends to set the price of raw materials, and individual producers have little pricing flexibility. Promotion is almost always via personal selling, and distribution channels are usually direct from producer to business user.

Component Parts

Component parts are either finished items ready for assembly or products that need very little processing before becoming part of some other product. Caterpillar diesel engines are component parts used in heavy-duty trucks. Other examples include spark plugs, tires, and electric motors for automobiles. A special feature of component parts is that they can retain their identity after becoming part of the final product. For example, automobile tires are clearly recognizable as part of a car. Moreover, because component parts often wear out, they may need to be replaced several times during the life of the final product. Thus, there are two important markets for many component parts: the original equipment manufacturer (OEM) market and the replacement market.

The availability of component parts is often a key factor in OEMs meeting their production deadlines. For example, Boeing has had to delay final assembly of Boeing 787 Dreamliners by more than three years because of slower than expected completion of components prior to their arrival at the final assembly line. In addition to delayed sales and customer disappointment and dissatisfaction, Boeing has already paid billions in penalties and has damaged credibility with customers. Despite the setbacks and the fact that there were only six Dreamliners flying in 2010, Boeing had 866 of the planes on back-order at that time.[29]

The difference between unit costs and selling prices in the OEM market is often small, but profits can be substantial because of volume buying.

The replacement market is composed of organizations and individuals buying component parts to replace worn-out parts. Because components often retain their identity in final products, users may choose to replace a component part with the same brand used by the manufacturer—for example, the same brand of automobile tires or battery. The replacement market operates differently from the OEM market, however. Whether replacement buyers are organizations or individuals, they tend to demonstrate the characteristics of consumer markets that were shown in Learning Outcome 6. Consider, for example, an automobile

replacement part. Purchase volume is usually small, and there are many customers, geographically dispersed, who typically buy from car dealers or parts stores. Negotiations do not occur, and neither reciprocity nor leasing is usually an issue.

Manufacturers of component parts often direct their advertising toward replacement buyers. Cooper Tire & Rubber, for example, makes and markets component parts—automobile and truck tires—for the replacement market only. General Motors and other carmakers compete with independent firms in the market for replacement automobile parts.

Processed Materials

Processed materials are products used directly in manufacturing other products. Unlike raw materials, they have had some processing. Examples include sheet metal, chemicals, specialty steel, treated lumber, corn syrup, and plastics. Unlike component parts, processed materials do not retain their identity in final products.

Most processed materials are marketed to OEMs or to distributors servicing the OEM market. Processed materials are generally bought according to customer specifications or to some industry standard, as is the case with steel and plywood. Price and service are important factors in choosing a vendor.

Supplies

Supplies are consumable items that do not become part of the final product—for example, lubricants, detergents, paper towels, pencils, and paper. Supplies are normally standardized items that purchasing agents routinely buy. Supplies typically have relatively short lives and are inexpensive compared to other business goods. Because supplies generally fall into one of three categories—maintenance, repair, or operating supplies—this category is often referred to as MRO items. Competition in the MRO market is intense. Bic and Paper Mate, for example, battle for business purchases of inexpensive ballpoint pens.

Business Services

Business services are expense items that do not become part of a final product. Businesses often retain outside providers to perform janitorial, advertising,

component parts either finished items ready for assembly or products that need very little processing before becoming part of some other product

processed materials products used directly in manufacturing other products

supplies consumable items that do not become part of the final product

business services expense items that do not become part of a final product

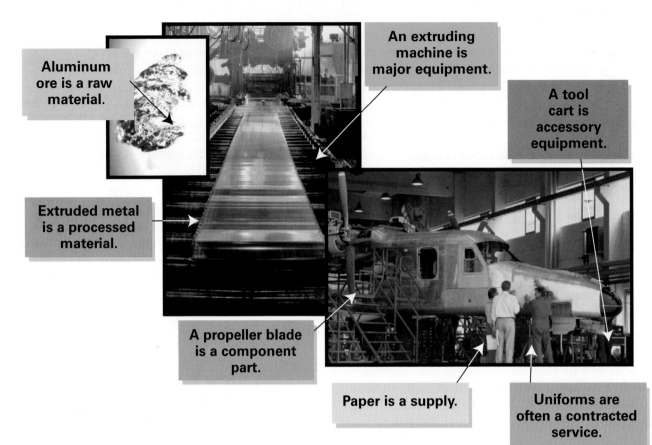

Aluminum ore is a raw material.

An extruding machine is major equipment.

A tool cart is accessory equipment.

Extruded metal is a processed material.

A propeller blade is a component part.

Paper is a supply.

Uniforms are often a contracted service.

PHOTOS COURTESY OF CHAPEL HOUSE PHOTOGRAPHY

buying center all those people in an organization who become involved in the purchase decision

legal, management consulting, marketing research, maintenance, and other services. Contracting an outside provider makes sense when it costs less than hiring or assigning an employee to perform the task and when an outside provider is needed for particular expertise.

LO 8 Business Buying Behavior

As you probably have already concluded, business buyers behave differently from consumers. Understanding how purchase decisions are made in organizations is a first step in developing a business selling strategy. Business buying behavior has five important aspects: buying centers, evaluative criteria, buying situations, business ethics, and customer service.

Buying Centers

In many cases, more than one person is involved in a purchase decision. Identifying who these people are and the roles they play greatly enhances the salesperson's chances for success.[30]

A **buying center** includes all those people in an organization who become involved in the purchase decision. Membership and influence vary from company to company. For instance, in engineering-dominated firms like Bell Helicopter, the buying center may consist almost entirely of engineers. In marketing-oriented firms like Toyota and IBM, marketing and engineering have almost equal authority. In consumer goods firms like Procter & Gamble, product managers and other marketing decision makers may dominate the buying center. In a small manufacturing company, almost everyone may be a member.

The number of people involved in a buying center varies with the complexity and importance of a purchase decision. The composition of the buying group will usually change from one purchase to another and sometimes even during various stages of the buying process. To make matters more complicated, buying centers do not appear on formal organization charts.

For example, even though a formal committee may have been set up to choose a new plant site, it is only part of the buying center. Other people, like the company president, often play informal yet powerful roles. In a lengthy decision-making process, such as finding a new plant location, some members may drop out of the buying center when they can no longer play a useful role. Others whose talents are needed then become part of the center. No formal announcement of "who is in" and "who is out" is ever made.

Roles in the Buying Center As in family purchasing decisions, several people may each play a role in the business purchase process.

» *Initiator:* the person who first suggests making a purchase.

» *Influencers/evaluators:* people who influence the buying decision. They often help define specifications and provide information for evaluating options. Technical personnel are especially important as influencers.

» *Gatekeepers:* group members who regulate the flow of information. Frequently, the purchasing agent views the gatekeeping role as a source of his or her power. A secretary may also act as a gatekeeper by determining which vendors get an appointment with a buyer.

» *Decider:* the person who has the formal or informal power to choose or approve the selection of the supplier or brand. In complex situations, it is often difficult to determine who makes the final decision.

» *Purchaser:* the person who actually negotiates the purchase. It could be anyone from the president of the company to the purchasing agent, depending on the importance of the decision.

» *Users:* members of the organization who will actually use the product. Users often initiate the buying process and help define product specifications.

Implications of Buying Centers for the Marketing Manager Successful vendors realize the importance of identifying who is in the decision-making unit, each member's relative influence in the buying decision, and each member's evaluative criteria. Successful selling strategies often focus on determining the most important buying influences and tailoring sales presentations to the evaluative criteria most important to these buying center members. For example, Loctite Corporation, the manufacturer of Super Glue and industrial adhesives and sealants, found that engineers were the most important influencers and deciders in adhesive and sealant purchase decisions. As a result, Loctite focused its marketing efforts on production and maintenance engineers.

Evaluative Criteria

Business buyers evaluate products and suppliers against three important criteria: quality, service, and price—in that order.

Quality In this case, quality refers to technical suitability. A superior tool can do a better job in the production process, and superior packaging can increase dealer and consumer acceptance of a brand. Evaluation of quality also applies to the salesperson and the salesperson's firm. Business buyers want to deal with reputable salespeople and companies that are financially responsible. Quality improvement should be part of every organization's marketing strategy.

Service Almost as much as they want satisfactory products, business buyers want satisfactory service. A purchase offers several opportunities for service. Suppose a vendor is selling heavy equipment. Prepurchase service could include a survey of the buyer's needs. After thorough analysis of the survey findings, the vendor could prepare a report and recommendations in the form of a purchasing proposal. If a purchase results, postpurchase service might consist of installing the equipment and training those who will be using it. Postsale services may also include maintenance and repairs. Another service that business buyers seek is dependability of supply. They must be able to count on delivery of what was ordered when it is scheduled to be delivered. Buyers also welcome services that help them sell their finished products. Services of this sort are especially appropriate when the seller's product is an identifiable part of the buyer's end product.

Price Business buyers want to buy at low prices—at the lowest prices, under most circumstances. However, a buyer who pressures a supplier to cut prices to a point at which the supplier loses money on the sale almost forces shortcuts on quality. The buyer also may, in effect, force the supplier to quit selling to him or her. Then a new source of supply will have to be found.

Buying Situations

Often, business firms, especially manufacturers, must decide whether to make something or buy it from an outside supplier. The decision is essentially one of economics. Can an item of similar quality be bought at a lower price elsewhere? If not, is manufacturing it in-house the best use of limited company resources? For example, Briggs & Stratton Corporation, a major manufacturer of four-cycle engines, might be able to save $150,000 annually on outside purchases by spending $500,000 on the equipment needed to produce gas throttles internally. Yet Briggs & Stratton could also use that $500,000 to upgrade its carburetor assembly line, which would save $225,000 annually. If a firm does

new buy a situation requiring the purchase of a product for the first time

modified rebuy a situation in which the purchaser wants some change in the original good or service

straight rebuy a situation in which the purchaser reorders the same goods or services without looking for new information or investigating other suppliers

decide to buy a product instead of making it, the purchase will be a new buy, a modified rebuy, or a straight rebuy.

New Buy A **new buy** is a situation requiring the purchase of a product for the first time. For example, suppose a manufacturing company needs a better way to page its managers while they are working on the shop floor. Currently, each of the several managers has a distinct ring—for example, two short and one long—that sounds over the plant intercom whenever he or she is being paged by anyone in the factory. The company decides to replace its buzzer system of paging with handheld wireless radio technology that will allow managers to communicate immediately with the department initiating the page. This situation represents the greatest opportunity for new vendors. No long-term relationship has been established for this product, specifications may be somewhat fluid, and buyers are generally more open to new vendors.

If the new item is a raw material or a critical component part, the buyer cannot afford to run out of supply. The seller must be able to convince the buyer that the seller's firm can consistently deliver a high-quality product on time.

Modified Rebuy A **modified rebuy** is normally less critical and less time-consuming than a new buy. In a modified rebuy situation, the purchaser wants some change in the original good or service. It may be a new color, greater tensile strength in a component part, more respondents in a marketing research study, or additional services in a janitorial contract.

Because the two parties are familiar with each other and credibility has been established, the buyer and seller can concentrate on the specifics of the modification. But in some cases, modified rebuys are open to outside bidders. The purchaser uses this strategy to ensure that the new terms are competitive. An example would be the manufacturing company buying radios with a vibrating feature for managers who have trouble hearing the ring over the factory noise. The firm may open the bidding to examine the price and quality offerings of several suppliers.

Straight Rebuy A **straight rebuy** is a situation vendors prefer. The purchaser is not looking for new information or other suppliers. An order is placed and the product is provided as in previous orders. Usually, a straight rebuy is routine because the terms of the purchase have been agreed to in earlier negotiations. An example would be the previously cited manufacturing company purchasing additional radios for new managers from the same supplier on a regular basis.

One common instrument used in straight rebuy situations is the purchasing contract. Purchasing contracts are used with products that are bought often and in high volume. In essence, the purchasing contract makes the buyer's decision-making routine and promises the salesperson a sure sale. The advantage to the buyer is a quick, confident decision and, to the salesperson, reduced or eliminated competition. Suppliers must remember not to take straight rebuy relationships for granted. Retaining existing customers is much easier than attracting new ones.

Business Ethics

As we noted in Chapter 3, ethics refers to the moral principles or values that generally govern the conduct of an individual or a group. Ethics can also be viewed as the standard of behavior by which conduct is judged.

Although we have heard a lot about corporate misbehavior in recent years, most people, and most companies, follow ethical practices. To help achieve this, over half of all major corporations offer ethics training to employees. Many companies also have codes of ethics that help guide buyers and sellers. For example, Home Depot has a clearly written code of ethics available on its corporate Web site that acts as an ethical guide for all its employees.

Customer Service

Business marketers are increasingly recognizing the benefits of developing a formal system to monitor customer opinions and perceptions of the quality of customer service. Companies such as McDonald's, L.L. Bean, and Lexus build their strategies not only around products but also around a few highly developed service skills. These companies understand that keeping current customers satisfied is just as important as attracting new ones, if not more so. Leading-edge firms are obsessed not only with delivering high-quality customer service but also with

© ISTOCKPHOTO.COM/JAMIE SHIELDS

measuring satisfaction, loyalty, relationship quality, and other indicators of nonfinancial performance.

Most firms find it necessary to develop measures unique to their own strategies, value propositions, and target markets. For example, Anderson Corporation assesses the loyalty of its trade customers by their willingness to continue carrying its windows and doors, recommend its products to colleagues and customers, increase their volume with the company, and put its products in their own homes. Basically, each firm's measures should not only ask "What are your expectations?" and "How are we doing?" but should also reflect what the firm wants its customers to do.

Some customers are more valuable than others. They may have greater value because they spend more, buy higher-margin products, have a well-known name, or have the potential of becoming a bigger customer in the future. Some companies selectively provide different levels of service to customers based on their value to the business. By giving the most valuable customers superior service, a firm is more likely to keep them happy, hopefully increasing retention of these high-value customers and maximizing the total business value they generate over time.

To achieve this goal, the firm must be able to divide customers into two or more groups based on their value. It must also create and apply policies that govern how service will be allocated among groups. Policies might establish which customers' phone calls get "fast tracked" and which customers are directed to use the Web and/or voice self-service, how specific e-mail questions are routed, and who is given access to online chat and who isn't.[31]

Providing different customers with different levels of service is a very sensitive matter. It must be handled very carefully and very discreetly to avoid offending lesser-value, but still important, customers.

STUDY TOOLS
CHAPTER 7

Flip to the back of your textbook to:
- ❑ **Rip out Chapter Review Card**

Log in to the CourseMate for MKTG at cengagebrain.com to:
- ❑ **Review Key Terms Flash Cards (Print or Online)**
- ❑ **Review Audio and Visual Summaries**
- ❑ **Complete both Practice Quizzes to prepare for tests**
- ❑ **Play "Beat the Clock" and "Quizbowl" to master concepts**
- ❑ **Complete "Crossword Puzzle" to review key terms**
- ❑ **Watch the video on "Flight 001" for a real company example on Business Marketing**

Segmenting and Targeting Markets

> Market segmentation plays a key role in the marketing strategy of almost all successful organizations.

LO1 Market Segmentation

AFTER YOU FINISH THIS CHAPTER, GO TO PAGE 145 FOR STUDY TOOLS

The term *market* means different things to different people. We are all familiar with the supermarket, stock market, labor market, fish market, and flea market. All these types of markets share several characteristics. First, they are composed of people (consumer markets) or organizations (business markets). Second, these people or organizations have wants and needs that can be satisfied by particular product categories. Third, they have the ability to buy the products they seek. Fourth, they are willing to exchange their resources, usually money or credit, for desired products. In sum, a **market** is (1) people or organizations with (2) needs or wants and with (3) the ability and (4) the willingness to buy. A group of people or an organization that lacks any one of these characteristics is not a market.

Within a market, a **market segment** is a subgroup of people or organizations sharing one or more characteristics that cause them to have similar product needs. At one extreme, we can define every person and every organization in the world as a market segment because each is unique. At the other extreme, we can define the entire consumer market as one large market segment and the business market as another large segment. All people have some similar characteristics and needs, as do all organizations.

market people or organizations with needs or wants and the ability and willingness to buy

market segment a subgroup of people or organizations sharing one or more characteristics that cause them to have similar product needs

What do you think?

It's pretty obvious when advertising is aimed at a certain group.

1 2 3 4 5 6 7
STRONGLY DISAGREE   STRONGLY AGREE

Find out what others think at the CourseMate for MKTG. Log in at cengagebrain.com.

© ISTOCKPHOTO.COM/RUBBERBALL

market segmentation the process of dividing a market into meaningful, relatively similar, and identifiable segments or groups

From a marketing perspective, market segments can be described as somewhere between the two extremes. The process of dividing a market into meaningful, relatively similar, and identifiable segments or groups is called **market segmentation**. The purpose of market segmentation is to enable the marketer to tailor marketing mixes to meet the needs of one or more specific segments.

LO 2 The Importance of Market Segmentation

Until the 1960s, few firms practiced market segmentation. When they did, it was more likely a haphazard effort than a formal marketing strategy. Before 1960, for example, the Coca-Cola Company produced only one beverage and aimed it at the entire soft drink market. Today, Coca-Cola offers more than a dozen different products to market segments based on diverse consumer preferences for flavors and calorie and caffeine content. Coca-Cola offers traditional soft drinks, energy drinks (including POWERade), flavored teas, fruit drinks (Fruitopia), and water (Dasani).

Market segmentation plays a key role in the marketing strategy of almost all successful organizations and is a powerful marketing tool for several reasons. Most important, nearly all markets include groups of people or organizations with different product needs and preferences. Market segmentation helps marketers define customer needs and wants more precisely. Because market segments differ in size and potential, segmentation helps decision makers to more accurately define marketing objectives and better allocate resources. In turn, performance can be better evaluated when objectives are more precise.

Chico's, a successful women's fashion retailer, thrives by marketing to women ages 35 to 55 who like to wear comfortable, yet stylish, clothing. It sells private label clothing that comes in just a few non-judgmental sizes: zero (standard sizes 4 to 6), one (8 to 10), two (10 to 12), and three (14 to 16). Nestlé has modified its portfolio to increase its market share in emerging economies, such as China, India, Malaysia, and Thailand. It sells food goods enriched with vitamins and has seen sales of enhanced milk products increase.[1]

LO 3 Criteria for Successful Segmentation

Marketers segment markets for three important reasons. First, segmentation enables marketers to identify groups of customers with similar needs and to analyze the characteristics and buying behavior of these groups. Second, segmentation provides marketers with information to help them design marketing mixes specifically matched with the characteristics and desires of one or more segments. Third, segmentation is consistent with the marketing concept of satisfying customer wants and needs while meeting the organization's objectives.

To be useful, a segmentation scheme must produce segments that meet four basic criteria:

1. *Substantiality:* A segment must be large enough to warrant developing and maintaining a special marketing mix. This criterion does not necessarily mean that a segment must have many potential customers. Marketers of custom-designed homes and business buildings, commercial airplanes, and large computer systems typically develop marketing programs tailored to each potential customer's needs. In most cases, however, a market segment needs many potential customers to make commercial sense. In the 1980s, home banking failed because not enough people owned personal computers. Today, a larger number of people own computers, and home banking is a thriving industry.

2. *Identifiability and measurability:* Segments must be identifiable and their size measurable. Data about the population within geographic boundaries, the number of people in various age categories, and other social and demographic characteristics are often easy to get, and they provide fairly concrete measures of segment size. Suppose that a social service agency wants to identify segments by their readiness to participate in a drug and alcohol program or in prenatal care. Unless the agency can measure how many people are willing, indifferent, or unwilling to participate, it will have trouble gauging whether there are enough people to justify setting up the service.

3. *Accessibility:* The firm must be able to reach members of targeted segments with customized marketing mixes. Some market segments are hard to reach—for example,

© IIRCONICUSSO/SHUTTERSTOCK.COM

senior citizens (especially those with reading or hearing disabilities), individuals who don't speak English, and the illiterate.

4. *Responsiveness:* Markets can be segmented using any criteria that seem logical. Unless one market segment responds to a marketing mix differently than other segments, however, that segment need not be treated separately. For instance, if all customers are equally price conscious about a product, there is no need to offer high-, medium-, and low-priced versions to different segments.

LO 4 Bases for Segmenting Consumer Markets

Marketers use **segmentation bases**, or **variables**, which are characteristics of individuals, groups, or organizations, to divide a total market into segments. The choice of segmentation bases is crucial because an inappropriate segmentation strategy may lead to lost sales and missed profit opportunities. The key is to identify bases that will produce substantial, measurable, and accessible segments that exhibit different response patterns to marketing mixes.

Markets can be segmented using a single variable, such as age group, or several variables, such as age group, gender, and education. Although it is less precise, single-variable segmentation has the advantage of being simpler and easier to use than multiple-variable segmentation. The disadvantages of multiple-variable segmentation are that it is often harder to use than single-variable segmentation; usable secondary data are less likely to be available; and as the number of segmentation bases increases, the size of individual segments decreases. Nevertheless, the current trend is toward using more rather than fewer variables to segment most markets. Multiple-variable segmentation is clearly more precise than single-variable segmentation.

Consumer goods marketers commonly use one or more of the following characteristics to segment markets: geography, demographics, psychographics, benefits sought, and usage rate.

Geographic Segmentation

Geographic segmentation refers to segmenting markets by region of a country or the world, market size, market density, or climate. Market density means the number of people within a unit of land, such as a census tract. Climate is commonly used for geographic segmentation because of its dramatic impact on residents' needs and purchasing behavior. Snowblowers, water and snow skis, clothing, and air-conditioning and heating systems are products with varying appeal, depending on climate.

Consumer goods companies take a regional approach to marketing for four reasons. First, many firms need to find new ways to generate sales because of sluggish and intensely competitive markets. Second, computerized checkout stations with scanners give retailers an accurate assessment of which brands sell best in their region. Third, many packaged-goods manufacturers are introducing new regional brands intended to appeal to local preferences. Fourth, a more regional approach allows consumer goods companies to react more quickly to competition. For many years, all Macy's stores carried the same merchandise, regardless of location. Now, the chain's "My Macy's" program tailors each store's merchandise mix to reflect local tastes. For example, the stores in Columbus, Ohio, carry more golf clothing than a typical store because of the area's many golf courses.[2] The strategy has paid off for Macy's; total sales increased by almost 5 percent between 2009 and 2010 in spite of the troubled economy during this time.[3]

Demographic Segmentation

Marketers often segment markets on the basis of demographic information because it is widely available and often related to consumers' buying and consuming behavior. Some common bases of **demographic segmentation** are age, gender, income, ethnic background, and family life cycle.

Age Segmentation Marketers use a variety of terms to refer to different age groups. Examples include newborns, infants, young children, tweens, Generation Y (teens, young adults), Generation X, baby boomers, and seniors. Age segmentation can be an important tool, as a brief exploration of the market potential of several age segments illustrates.

Through allowances, earnings, and gifts, children account for and influence a great deal of consumption. For example, young shoppers in the United States spend more than $200 billion of their own money

segmentation bases (variables) characteristics of individuals, groups, or organizations

geographic segmentation segmenting markets by region of a country or the world, market size, market density, or climate

demographic segmentation segmenting markets by age, gender, income, ethnic background, and family life cycle

One girl films a haul video of her recent shopping trip.

or offer gift cards for them to shop at their stores.[7]

Generation X is the group that was born after the baby boomers. Members of Generation X tend to be disloyal to brands and skeptical of big business. Many of them are parents, and they make purchasing decisions with thought for and input from their families. Xers desire an experience, not just a product. The desire to have an experience has led to an increase in multifunctional boutiques, particularly in Manhattan's Lower East Side, where the small shops vie for high-end shoppers. The Dressing Room, for example, is a bi-level store with a boutique upstairs, vintage clothing downstairs, and a full bar where customers can hang out.[8]

People born between 1946 and 1964 are often called "baby boomers." Boomers spend $2.1 trillion a year and represent half of all spending in the United States. For the next 18 years, one baby boomer will turn 60 every seven seconds. Boomers make up 49 percent of affluent households, and they want attention and service when they shop.[9] This group spends big money on goods and services such as travel, electronics, and automobiles. Baby boomers are not

and their parents' money each year on purchases for themselves and also have considerable influence over major family purchase decisions.[4] Teens in particular are technology savvy and very social consumers. Tweens desire to be kids but also want some of the fun of being a teenager. Many retailers serve this market with clothing that is similar in style to that worn by teenagers and young adults.

The members of the Generation Y market, or the millennial generation, were born between 1982 and 2003 and make up almost one-third of the U.S. population. This group not only has formidable purchasing power but is also more civic-minded than the baby boom generation. Seventy-four percent of millennials say they are more likely to pay attention to a company's overall message if the company has a deep commitment to a cause. The teens in this group are interested in apparel that enhances personalization and self-expression because they want their look to reflect their personalities and style.[5] College students (also part of the millennials) all have mobile phones and use them constantly to communicate and connect. Despite the potential marketing gold mine such a connected audience presents, a study showed many people in this group were highly negative toward ads on their phones.[6] This age group engages in its own peer-to-peer marketing through YouTube videos of unboxing or hauls. *Unboxing*, popular with new technology, is a video or article describing and reviewing new products. *Hauls* are videos in which the shopper (usually a female) shows off and reviews her purchases from the day. These videos reap millions of views and promote enough sales that some companies send free samples to the haulers for review

TAKING GIRL TALK TO A NEW LEVEL

Hallmark Cards has introduced a new collection called "Girlfriends." The new line of cards and gifts is designed to help women connect in a fun, humorous, and meaningful way. The cards and gifts address real-life situations that are both celebratory and challenging. The line conveys support, celebrates friendship, strengthens bonds, and reassures the recipient her friends are behind her no matter what.[10]

SOURCE: Hallmark Corporate Information, "New Hallmark Card Line Helps Women Celebrate Good Times and Convey Support in Tough Times," *Hallmark*, June 22, 2010.

© T14/ZUMA PRESS/NEWSCOM

© CREATISTA/SHUTTERSTOCK.COM

particularly brand loyal, and they are a very diverse group. Some are parents to infant children, and others are empty nesters.

Consumers born before 1946 represent people who are part of the war generation (ages 61 to 66), the Great Depression generation (ages 67 to 76), and the G.I. generation (age 77 and up). Many in this group view retirement not as a passive time, but as an active time they use to explore new knowledge, travel, volunteer, and spend time with family and friends. They are living longer and are healthier than older consumers 20 years ago. As consumers age, the do require some shopping modifications. Tesco, a British grocery store chain, is considering designing a store specifically to meet the needs of older shoppers. Music, nonslip floors, extra-wide aisles, brighter than usual lighting, and steps to assist older consumers in reaching high shelves are some the features being examined for inclusion.

Gender Segmentation In the United States, women make over 70 percent of purchases of consumer goods each year. They are an experienced purchasing group with the responsibility of purchasing the majority of household items. They also are increasingly part of what were once considered all-male markets, such as video games. In 2008, women made 48 percent of all video game purchases.[11] The video game industry has been forced to respond by developing more games with female protagonists and changing its advertising strategy. Design, fashion, and weight-loss games such as *Style Savvy* or *The Biggest Loser* are increasingly popular among women.[12] Marketers of products such as clothing, cosmetics, personal-care items, magazines, jewelry, and gifts still commonly segment markets by gender, and many of these marketers are going after the less-traditional male market. For example, L'Oreal and Procter & Gamble are focusing on the growing market of men's cosmetics with moisturizers, bronzers, hair dye, and shaving accessories. Men's grooming products sales reached $5.6 billion in 2009, up from $3.8 billion in 2004.[13] Even weight-loss programs, which currently have 90 percent female consumption, are starting to target men. Weight Watchers is trying to increase the number of men using its program to lose weight by offering a men-only version of its Web site and mobile applications, which research shows men prefer over the traditional Weight Watchers meetings. Men's programs have higher point totals (reflecting the male tendency to have leaner body mass) and more "cheat sheets" telling them how many points various foods cost.[14]

Income Segmentation Income is a popular demographic variable for segmenting markets because income level influences consumers' wants and determines their buying power. Many markets are segmented by income, including the markets for housing, clothing, automobiles, and food. Wholesale clubs Costco and Sam's Club appeal to many income segments. Harrison Group researchers found that the favorite stores of affluent households (those that earn more than $100,000 annually) are Costco and Target.[15] High-income customers looking for luxury want outstanding customer service. For example, fashion companies use computer technology to customize upscale products that are designed specifically for their wealthy customers' needs.[16] Other companies try to appeal to low-income customers. Walmart plans for more of its stores to offer financial services in "Money Centers" to its lower-income customers who do not have banks. These Money Centers will provide services such as cashing checks, paying bills and filling out tax forms.[17]

Ethnic Segmentation In the past, ethnic groups in the United States were expected to conform to a

Many companies are attempting to promote products to men in traditionally female markets.

IMAGE COURTESY OF THE ADVERTISING ARCHIVES

family life cycle (FLC) a series of stages determined by a combination of age, marital status, and the presence or absence of children

homogenized, Anglo-centric ideal. This was evident both in the marketing of mass-marketed products and in the selective way that films, television, advertisements, and popular music portrayed America's diverse population. Until the 1970s, ethnic foods were rarely sold except in specialty stores. The racial barrier in entertainment lasted nearly as long, except for supporting movie and television roles—often based on stereotypes dating back to the 19th century.[18] Increasing numbers of ethnic minorities and increased buying power have changed this. Hispanic Americans, African Americans, and Asian Americans are the three largest ethnic groups in the United States. In the American Southwest, Caucasian populations comprise less than half the population and have become the minority to

other ethnic groups combined. To meet the needs and wants of expanding ethnic populations, some companies, such as McDonald's and Kmart, make products geared toward a specific group. Kmart has teamed up with Sofia Vergara, a popular Colombian actress, to develop a clothing line to appeal to Hispanics.[19]

Family Life Cycle Segmentation The demographic factors of gender, age, and income often do not sufficiently explain why consumer buying behavior varies. Frequently, consumption patterns among people of the same age and gender differ because they are in different stages of the family life cycle. The **family life cycle (FLC)** is a series of stages determined by a combination of age, marital status, and the presence or absence of children.

The life cycle stage consisting of the married-couple household used to be considered the traditional family in the United States. Today, however, married couples make up less than half of households, down from nearly 80 percent in the 1950s. Single adults are increasingly in the majority. Already, unmarried Americans make up 42 percent of the workforce, 40 percent of home buyers, and one of the most potent consumer groups on record. Exhibit 8.1 on page 136 illustrates numerous FLC patterns and shows how families' needs, incomes, resources, and expenditures differ at each stage. The horizontal flow shows the traditional FLC. The lower part of the exhibit gives some of the characteristics and purchase patterns of families in each stage of the traditional life cycle. The exhibit also acknowledges that about half of all first marriages end in divorce. If young marrieds move into the young divorced stage, their consumption patterns often revert back to those of the young single stage of the cycle. About four out of five divorced persons remarry by middle age and reenter the traditional life cycle, as indicated by the "recycled flow" in the exhibit. Research has found that the overriding factor in describing baby boomer subsegments is the presence of children in the house. A Nielsen study discovered eight specific segments: four segments with children younger than 18 represented about 40 percent of the boomers, and four segments without children represented 60 percent.[20] Consumers are especially receptive to marketing efforts at certain points in the life cycle.

Psychographic Segmentation

Age, gender, income, ethnicity, FLC stage, and other demographic variables are usually helpful in developing segmentation strategies, but often they don't

"Yo quería dientes blancos como artista y el dentista, saludables. Su consejo, cambia a Colgate Total Plus Whitening"

Ahora están blancos y saludables.

IMAGE COURTESY OF THE ADVERTISING ARCHIVES

THE NEXT BIG SPENDERS

A new group is emerging as the spending elite—**singles.** In 2008, singles spent $2.2 trillion, which represented 35 percent of all consumer spending in that year. Most singles are younger than 45 and receptive to advertising, and they spend more time on the Internet than older demographic groups. While many marketers ignore this group, Norwegian Cruise Lines has gone out of its way to welcome singles. Most cruise ships don't have single-occupancy rooms, and if a solo patron goes on a cruise, he or she has traditionally been charged a supplemental fee for staying in a double-occupancy room. Norwegian Cruise Line's ship, the *Epic,* goes against that industry practice by offering 128 single-occupancy rooms with no extra fees.[21]

SOURCE: Andrew Adam Newman, "The Power of One," *Fortune,* April 19, 2010, 15–16.

© ARVIND BALARAMAN/SHUTTERSTOCK.COM

paint the entire picture. Demographics provide the skeleton, but psychographics add meat to the bones. **Psychographic segmentation** is market segmentation on the basis of the following psychographic segmentation variables:

▸▸ *Personality:* Personality reflects a person's traits, attitudes, and habits. Clothing is the ultimate personality descriptor. Fashionistas wear high-end, trendy clothes, and hipsters enjoy jeans and T-shirts with tennis shoes. People buy clothes that they feel represent their personalities and give others an idea of who they are.

▸▸ *Motives:* Marketers of baby products and life insurance appeal to consumers' emotional motives—namely, to care for their loved ones. Using appeals to economy, reliability, and dependability, carmakers like Subaru and Suzuki target customers with rational motives. Carmakers like Mercedes-Benz, Jaguar, and Cadillac appeal to customers with status-related motives.

▸▸ *Lifestyles:* Lifestyle segmentation divides people into groups according to the way they spend their time, the importance of the things around them, their beliefs, and socioeconomic characteristics such as income and education. For example, record stores specializing in vinyl are targeting young people who are listening to independent labels and often pride themselves on being independent of big business. LEED-certified appliances appeal to environmentally conscious "green" consumers. PepsiCo is promoting its no-calorie, sugar-free, flavored water, Aquafina Sparkling, to consumers who are health conscious.

▸▸ *Geodemographics:* **Geodemographic segmentation** clusters potential customers into neighborhood lifestyle categories. It combines geographic, demographic, and lifestyle segmentations. Geodemographic segmentation helps marketers develop marketing programs tailored to prospective buyers who live in small geographic regions, such as neighborhoods, or who have very specific lifestyle and demographic characteristics. For example, companies looking to win government manufacturing or technology contracts post cryptic billboards and posters on Washington, D.C. buses and Metro trains, as well as advertising their capabilities on local radio stations. The average commuter doesn't understand the cryptic acronyms, but government decision makers who see or hear the ads understand them and will award federal projects based on the ads—or so companies such as Northrop Grumman hope. Such a campaign could work only in an area where high levels of government decision makers commute regularly.[22]

Psychographic variables can be used individually to segment markets or be combined with other variables to provide more detailed descriptions of market segments. One approach is for marketers and advertisers to purchase information from a collector, such as eXelate Media, in order to reach the audience they want. eXelate, part of consumer research firm Nielsen, gathers information about Web-browsing habits through cookies placed on Web sites. Nielsen, using eXelate, organizes groups according to this information. One group, the "young digerati," includes 24- to 44-year-olds who

▸▸ are tech savvy,

▸▸ are affluent,

psychographic segmentation
segmenting markets on the basis of personality, motives, lifestyles, and geodemographics

geodemographic segmentation
segmenting potential customers into neighborhood lifestyle categories

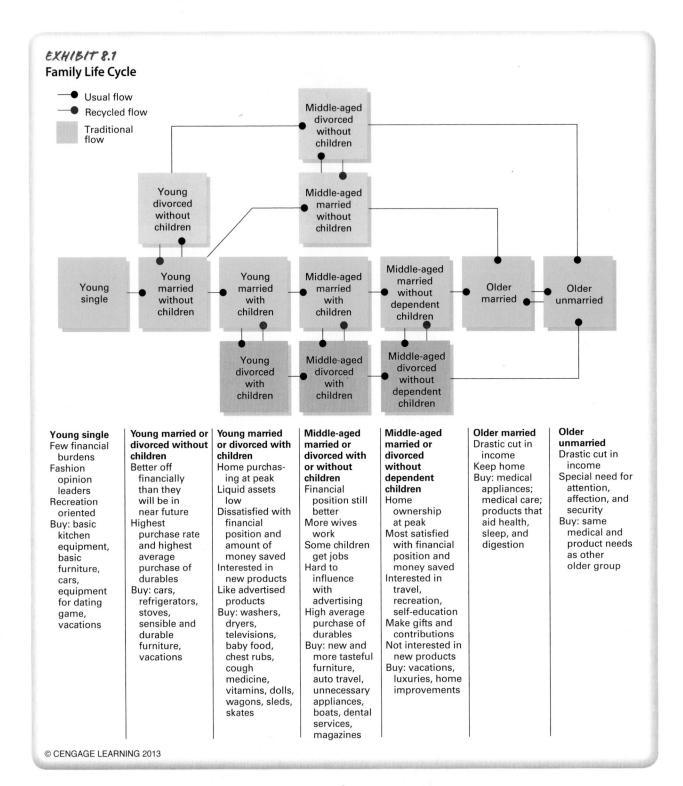

EXHIBIT 8.1
Family Life Cycle

- ●── Usual flow
- ●── Recycled flow
- ▢ Traditional flow

Middle-aged divorced without children

Young divorced without children

Middle-aged married without children

Young single

Young married without children

Young married with children

Middle-aged married with children

Middle-aged married without dependent children

Older married

Older unmarried

Young divorced with children

Middle-aged divorced with children

Middle-aged divorced without dependent children

Young single	Young married or divorced without children	Young married or divorced with children	Middle-aged married or divorced with or without children	Middle-aged married or divorced without dependent children	Older married	Older unmarried
Few financial burdens	Better off financially than they will be in near future	Home purchasing at peak	Financial position still better	Home ownership at peak	Drastic cut in income	Drastic cut in income
Fashion opinion leaders	Highest purchase rate and highest average purchase of durables	Liquid assets low	More wives work	Most satisfied with financial position and money saved	Keep home	Special need for attention, affection, and security
Recreation oriented	Buy: cars, refrigerators, stoves, sensible and durable furniture, vacations	Dissatisfied with financial position and amount of money saved	Some children get jobs	Interested in travel, recreation, self-education	Buy: medical appliances; medical care; products that aid health, sleep, and digestion	Buy: same medical and product needs as other older group
Buy: basic kitchen equipment, basic furniture, cars, equipment for dating game, vacations		Interested in new products	Hard to influence with advertising	Make gifts and contributions		
		Like advertised products	High average purchase of durables	Not interested in new products		
		Buy: washers, dryers, televisions, baby food, chest rubs, cough medicine, vitamins, dolls, wagons, sleds, skates	Buy: new and more tasteful furniture, auto travel, unnecessary appliances, boats, dental services, magazines	Buy: vacations, luxuries, home improvements		

© CENGAGE LEARNING 2013

---

benefit segmentation the process of grouping customers into market segments according to the benefits they seek from the product

- ▶ live in trendy condos,
- ▶ read the *Economist,* and
- ▶ have an annual income of $88,000.

An automaker can purchase that list and the list of people who visit car blogs and then target ads to the "young digerati" interested in cars.[23]

Benefit Segmentation

Benefit segmentation is the process of grouping customers into market segments according to the benefits they seek from the product. Most types of market segmentation are based on the assumption that this variable and customers' needs are related. Benefit segmentation is different because it groups potential customers on the basis of their needs or wants rather than some other characteristic, such as age or gender. The snack-food market, for example, can be divided into six benefit segments: nutritional snackers, weight watchers, guilty snackers, party snackers, indiscriminate snackers, and economical snackers.

Customer profiles can be developed by examining demographic information associated with people seeking certain benefits. This information can be used to match marketing strategies with selected target markets. The many different types of performance energy bars with various combinations of nutrients are aimed at consumers looking for different benefits. For example, PowerBar is designed for athletes looking for long-lasting fuel, while PowerBar Protein Plus is aimed at those who want extra protein for replenishing muscles after strength training. Carb Solutions High Protein Bars are for those on low-carb diets; Luna Bars are targeted to women who want a bar with fewer calories,

soy protein, and calcium; and Clif Bars are for people who want a natural bar with ingredients like rolled oats, soybeans, and organic soy flour.

Usage-Rate Segmentation

Usage-rate segmentation divides a market by the amount of product bought or consumed. Categories vary with the product, but they are likely to include some combination of the following: former users, potential users, first-time users, light or irregular users, medium users, and heavy users. Segmenting by usage rate enables marketers to focus their efforts on heavy users or to develop multiple marketing mixes aimed at different segments. Because heavy users often account for a sizable portion of all product sales, some marketers focus on the heavy-user segment.

The **80/20 principle** holds that 20 percent of all customers generate 80 percent of the demand. Although the percentages usually are not exact, the general idea often holds true. For example, in the fast-food industry, the heavy user accounts for only one of five fast-food patrons but makes about 60 percent of all visits to fast-food restaurants. The needs of heavy users differs from the needs of other usage-rate groups. They have intense needs for product and service selection and a variety of types of information, as well as an emotional attachment to the product category.[24]

Developing customers into heavy users is the goal behind many frequency/loyalty programs like the airlines' frequent flyer programs. Many supermarkets and other retailers have also designed loyalty programs that reward the heavy-user segment with deals available only to them, such as in-store coupon dispensing systems, loyalty card programs, and special price deals on selected merchandise.

usage-rate segmentation
dividing a market by the amount of product bought or consumed

80/20 principle
a principle holding that 20 percent of all customers generate 80 percent of the demand

Adidas's "Me, Myself" women's training campaign features WNBA MVP Candace Parker. The campaign encourages women with active lifestyles to share training successes and struggles with each other, while giving Adidas visibility within an active market.

© AP IMAGES/PRNEWSFOTO/ADIDAS

LO5 Bases for Segmenting Business Markets

The business market consists of four broad segments: producers, resellers, government, and institutions. (For a detailed discussion of the characteristics of these segments, see Chapter 7.) Whether marketers focus on only one or on all four of these segments, they

satisficers business customers who place an order with the first familiar supplier to satisfy product and delivery requirements

optimizers business customers who consider numerous suppliers (both familiar and unfamiliar) solicit bids, and study all proposals carefully before selecting one

are likely to find diversity among potential customers. Thus, further market segmentation offers just as many benefits to business marketers as it does to consumer product marketers.

Company Characteristics

Company characteristics, such as geographic location, type of company, company size, and product use, can be important segmentation variables. Some markets tend to be regional because buyers prefer to purchase from local suppliers, and distant suppliers may have difficulty competing in terms of price and service. Therefore, firms that sell to geographically concentrated industries benefit by locating close to their markets.

Segmenting by customer type allows business marketers to tailor their marketing mixes to the unique needs of particular types of organizations or industries. For example, Round-Table Companies teamed with SmarterComics to produce 50-page illustrated versions of the most popular business books such as *The Long Tail* by Chris Anderson and *How to Master the Art of Selling* by Tom Hopkins. Corey Michael Blake, founder of Round-Table, wanted to make the most-read business books available to time-pressed businesspeople. By condensing and illustrating popular business texts, Blake found a new market for comic books and extended the business book market.[25] Volume of purchase (heavy, moderate, light) is a commonly used basis for business segmentation. Another is the buying organization's size, which may affect its purchasing procedures, the types and quantities of products it needs, and its responses to different marketing mixes. Banks frequently offer different services, lines of credit, and overall attention to commercial customers based on their size. Many products, especially raw materials like steel, wood, and petroleum, have diverse applications. How customers use a product may influence the amount they buy, their buying criteria, and their selection of vendors. For example, a producer of springs may have customers who use the product in applications as diverse as making

machine tools, bicycles, surgical devices, office equipment, telephones, and missile systems.

Buying Processes

Many business marketers find it helpful to segment customers and prospective customers on the basis of how they buy. For example, companies can segment some business markets by ranking key purchasing criteria, such as price, quality, technical support, and service. Atlas Corporation has developed a commanding position in the industrial door market by providing customized products in just 4 weeks, which is much faster than the industry average of 12 to 15 weeks. Atlas's primary market is companies with an immediate need for customized doors.

The purchasing strategies of buyers may provide useful segments. Two purchasing profiles that have been identified are satisficers and optimizers. **Satisficers** contact familiar suppliers and place the order with the first one to satisfy product and delivery requirements. **Optimizers** consider numerous suppliers (both familiar and unfamiliar), solicit bids, and study all proposals carefully before selecting one.

The personal characteristics of the buyers themselves (their demographic characteristics, decision style, tolerance for risk, confidence level, job responsibilities, and so on) influence their buying behavior and thus offer a viable basis for segmenting some business markets. IBM computer buyers, for example, are sometimes characterized as being more risk averse than buyers of less expensive computers that perform essentially the same functions. In advertising, therefore, IBM stresses its reputation for high quality and reliability.

© PERTUSINAS/SHUTTERSTOCK.COM

LO 6 Steps in Segmenting a Market

The purpose of market segmentation, in both consumer and business markets, is to identify marketing opportunities.

1. *Select a market or product category for study:* Define the overall market or product category to be studied. It may be a market in which the firm already competes, a new but related market or product category, or a totally new market.

2. *Choose a basis or bases for segmenting the market:* This step requires managerial insight, creativity, and market knowledge. There are no scientific procedures for selecting segmentation variables. However, a successful segmentation scheme must produce segments that meet the four basic criteria discussed earlier in this chapter.

3. *Select segmentation descriptors:* After choosing one or more bases, the marketer must select the segmentation descriptors. Descriptors identify the specific segmentation variables to use. For example, if a company selects demographics as a basis of segmentation, it may use age, occupation, and income as descriptors. A company that selects usage segmentation needs to decide whether to go after heavy users, nonusers, or light users.

4. *Profile and analyze segments:* The profile should include the segments' size, expected growth, purchase frequency, current brand usage, brand loyalty, and long-term sales and profit potential. This information can then be used to rank potential market segments by profit opportunity, risk, consistency with organizational mission and objectives, and other factors important to the firm.

5. *Select target markets:* Selecting target markets is not a part of but a natural outcome of the segmentation process. It is a major decision that influences and often directly determines the firm's marketing mix. This topic is examined in greater detail later in this chapter.

6. *Design, implement, and maintain appropriate marketing mixes:* The marketing mix has been described as product, place (distribution), promotion, and pricing strategies intended to bring about mutually satisfying exchange relationships with target markets. These topics are explored in detail in Chapters 10 through 20.

Markets are dynamic, so it is important that companies proactively monitor their segmentation strategies over time. Often, once customers or prospects have been assigned to a segment, marketers think their task is done. Once customers are assigned to an age segment, for example, they stay there until they reach the next age bracket or category, which could be ten years in the future. Thus, the segmentation classifications are static, but the customers and prospects are changing. Dynamic segmentation approaches adjust to fit the changes that occur in customers' lives. BCBG uses BCBGeneration to target a younger crowd, and Aéropostale owns P.S., which sells clothing for children ages 7 to 12. However, some segments have too many players, and choosing to enter those kinds of segments can be particularly challenging. High-end denim has so many boutiques and brands that customers are tired of the volume.[26]

target market
a group of people or organizations for which an organization designs, implements, and maintains a marketing mix intended to meet the needs of that group, resulting in mutually satisfying exchanges

undifferentiated targeting strategy
a marketing approach that views the market as one big market with no individual segments and thus uses a single marketing mix

LO 7 Strategies for Selecting Target Markets

So far, this chapter has focused on the market segmentation process, which is only the first step in deciding whom to approach about buying a product. The next task is to choose one or more target markets. A **target market** is a group of people or organizations for which an organization designs, implements, and maintains a marketing mix intended to meet the needs of that group, resulting in mutually satisfying exchanges. Because most markets will include customers with different characteristics, lifestyles, backgrounds, and income levels, it is unlikely that a single marketing mix will attract all segments of the market. Thus, if a marketer wishes to appeal to more than one segment of the market, it must develop different marketing mixes. For example, Subaru's customer base consists of eco-conscious individuals who value freedom and buy experiences, not things. To attract younger, sportier consumers with similar values, Subaru is developing a small car, as well as a hybrid.[27] The three general strategies for selecting target markets—undifferentiated, concentrated, and multisegment targeting—are illustrated on the next page in Exhibit 8.2, which also illustrates the advantages and disadvantages of each targeting strategy.

Undifferentiated Targeting

A firm using an **undifferentiated targeting strategy** essentially adopts a mass-market philosophy, viewing the market as one big market with no individual

EXHIBIT 8.2
Advantages and Disadvantages of Target Marketing Strategies

Targeting Strategy	Advantages	Disadvantages
Undifferentiated Targeting	• Potential savings on production/marketing costs	• Unimaginative product offerings • Company more susceptible to competition
Concentrated Targeting	• Concentration of resources • Can better meet the needs of a narrowly defined segment • Allows some small firms to better compete with larger firms • Strong positioning	• Segments too small or changing • Large competitors may more effectively market to niche segment
Multisegment Targeting	• Greater financial success • Economies of scale in producing/marketing	• High costs • Cannibalization

© CENGAGE LEARNING 2013

ple of an undifferentiated targeting strategy: "They can have their car in any color they want, as long as it's black." At one time, Coca-Cola used this strategy with a single product and a single size of its familiar green bottle. Marketers of commodity products, such as flour and sugar, are also likely to use an undifferentiated targeting strategy.

One advantage of undifferentiated marketing is the potential for saving on production and marketing. Because only one item is produced, the firm should be able to achieve economies of mass production. Also, marketing costs may be lower when there is only one product to promote and a single channel of distribution. Too often, however, an undifferentiated strategy emerges by default rather than by design, reflecting a failure to consider the advantages of a segmented approach. The result is often sterile, unimaginative product offerings that have little appeal to anyone.

Another problem associated with undifferentiated targeting is that it makes the company more susceptible to competitive inroads. Hershey lost a big share of the candy market to Mars and other candy companies before it changed to a multisegment targeting strategy. Coca-Cola forfeited its position as the leading seller of cola drinks in supermarkets to PepsiCo in the late 1950s, when Pepsi began offering several sizes of containers.

You might think a firm producing a standard product such as toilet tissue would adopt an undifferentiated strategy. However, this market has industrial segments and consumer segments. Industrial buyers want an economical, single-ply product sold in boxes

segments. The firm uses one marketing mix for the entire market. A firm that adopts an undifferentiated targeting strategy assumes that individual customers have similar needs that can be met with a common marketing mix.

The first firm in an industry sometimes uses an undifferentiated targeting strategy. With no competition, the firm may not need to tailor marketing mixes to the preferences of market segments. Henry Ford's famous comment about the Model T is a classic exam-

of a hundred rolls. The consumer market demands a more versatile product in smaller quantities. Within the consumer market, the product is differentiated with designer print or no print, cushioned or non-cushioned, and economy priced or luxury priced. Fort Howard Corporation, the market share leader in industrial toilet paper, does not even sell to the consumer market.

Undifferentiated marketing can succeed in certain situations, though. A small grocery store in a small, isolated town may define all of the people who live in the town as its target market. It may offer one marketing mix and generally satisfy everyone in town. This strategy is not likely to be as effective if there are three or four grocery stores in town.

Concentrated Targeting

With a **concentrated targeting strategy**, a firm selects a market **niche** (one segment of a market) for targeting its marketing efforts. Because the firm is appealing to a single segment, it can concentrate on understanding the needs, motives, and satisfactions of that segment's members and on developing and maintaining a highly specialized marketing mix. Some firms find that concentrating resources and meeting the needs of a narrowly defined market segment is more profitable than spreading resources over several different segments.

Intelligentsia, a Chicago-based coffee roaster/retailer, targets serious coffee drinkers with hand-roasted, ground, and poured super-gourmet coffee or tea served by seriously educated baristas. The company also offers training classes for the at-home or out-of-town coffee aficionado. Starting price—$200 per class. America Online became one of the world's leading Internet providers by targeting Internet newcomers.

Small firms often adopt a concentrated targeting strategy to compete effectively with much larger firms. For example, Enterprise Rent-A-Car rose to number one in the car rental industry by catering to people with cars in the shop. It then expanded into the airport rental market. Some other firms use a concentrated strategy to establish a strong position in a desirable market segment. Porsche, for instance, targets an upscale automobile market through "class appeal, not mass appeal."

Concentrated targeting violates the old adage "Don't put all your eggs in one basket." If the chosen segment is too small or if it shrinks because of environmental changes, the firm may suffer negative consequences. For instance, OshKosh B'gosh was highly successful selling children's wear in the 1980s. It was so successful, however, that the children's line came to define OshKosh's image to the extent that the company could not sell clothes to anyone else. Attempts at marketing older children's clothing, women's casual clothes, and maternity wear were all abandoned. Recognizing it was in the children's wear business, the company expanded into products such as kids' shoes, children's eyewear, and plush toys.

A concentrated strategy can also be disastrous for a firm that is not successful in its narrowly defined target market. Before Procter & Gamble introduced Head & Shoulders shampoo, several small firms were already selling antidandruff shampoos. Head & Shoulders was introduced with a large promotional campaign, and the new brand captured over half the market immediately. Within a year, several of the firms that had been concentrating on this market segment went out of business.

Multisegment Targeting

A firm that chooses to serve two or more well-defined market segments and develops a distinct marketing mix for each has a **multisegment targeting strategy**. Walmart has historically followed a concentrated strategy that targeted lower-income segments. Recently, however, the company has segmented its customers into three core groups based on the type of value they seek at the stores. "Brand Aspirationals" are low-income customers who like to buy brand names such as KitchenAid, "Price-Sensitive Affluents" are wealthier shoppers who love deals, and "Value-Price Shoppers" like low prices and can't afford much more.[28]

Multisegment targeting offers many potential benefits to firms, including greater sales volume, higher profits, larger market share, and economies of scale in manufacturing and marketing. Yet it may also involve greater product design, production, promotion, inventory, marketing research, and management costs. Before deciding to use this strategy, firms should compare the benefits and costs of multisegment targeting to those of undifferentiated and concentrated targeting.

Another potential cost of multisegment targeting is **cannibalization**, which occurs when sales of a new

concentrated targeting strategy a strategy used to select one segment of a market for targeting marketing efforts

niche one segment of a market

multisegment targeting strategy a strategy that chooses two or more well-defined market segments and develops a distinct marketing mix for each

cannibalization a situation that occurs when sales of a new product cut into sales of a firm's existing products

one-to-one marketing an individualized marketing method that utilizes customer information to build long-term, personalized, and profitable relationships with each customer

product cut into sales of a firm's existing products. For example, Apple's iPhone and iPad may be causing sales of the iPod to drop, and there is some fear that the iPad will take away Mac sales, Apple's cash cow. The only evidence of those fears being realized is the 17 percent drop in sales of iPods since the release of the iPad.[29] In many cases, however, companies prefer to steal sales from their own brands rather than lose sales to a competitor. Also, in today's fast-paced world of Internet business, some companies are willing to cannibalize existing business to build new business.

LO 8 One-to-One Marketing

Most businesses today use a mass-marketing approach designed to increase *market share* by selling their products to the greatest number of people. For many businesses, however, it is more efficient and profitable to use one-to-one marketing to increase *share of customer*—in other words, to sell more products to each customer. **One-to-one marketing** is an individualized marketing method that utilizes customer information to build long-term, personalized, and profitable relationships with each customer. The goal is to reduce costs through customer retention and increase revenue through customer loyalty.

The difference between one-to-one marketing and the traditional mass-marketing approach can be compared to the difference between a rifle and a shotgun. If you have good aim, a rifle is the more efficient weapon to use. A shotgun, on the other hand, increases your odds of hitting the target when it is more difficult to focus. Instead of scattering messages far and wide across the spectrum of mass media (the shotgun approach), one-to-one marketers look for opportunities to communicate with each individual customer (the rifle approach).

A Dog's Life, a California company that makes organic pet treats, holds a monthly competition in

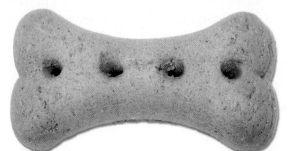

which users upload photos of their pets and vote on their favorites. The winning photo is featured for a month on bags of the dog treats. Customers can also pay $3 to $4 for customized treats, which include a photo of their choice on the package. Winners of the contest buy several bags, and the contests keep the brand in the social media news circuit.[30] Customers who customize have been found to be more loyal. Several factors suggest that personalized communications and product customization will continue to expand as more companies understand why and how their customers make and execute purchase decisions.

At least four trends will lead to the continuing growth of one-to-one marketing: *personalization*, *time savings*, *loyalty*, and *technology*.

▸▸ *Personalization:* One-size-fits-all marketing is no longer relevant. Consumers want to be treated as the individuals they are, with their own unique sets of needs and wants. By its personalized nature, one-to-one marketing can fulfill this desire.

▸▸ *Time savings:* Direct and personal marketing efforts will continue to grow to meet the needs of consumers who no longer have the time to spend shopping and making purchase decisions. With the personal and targeted nature of one-to-one marketing, consumers can spend less time making purchase decisions and more time doing the things that are important.

▸▸ *Loyalty:* Consumers will be loyal only to those companies and brands that have earned their loyalty and reinforced it at every purchase occasion. One-to-one marketing techniques focus on finding a firm's best customers, rewarding them for their loyalty, and thanking them for their business.

▸▸ *Technology:* Mass-media approaches will decline in importance as advances in market research and database technology allow marketers to collect detailed information on their customers. New technology offers one-to-one marketers a more cost-effective way to reach customers and enables businesses to personalize their messages. For example, MyYahoo.com greets each user by name and offers information in which the user has expressed interest. Similarly, RedEnvelope.com helps customers keep track of special occasions and offers personalized gift recommendations. With the help of database technology, one-to-one marketers can track their customers as individuals, even if they number in the millions.

One-to-one marketing is a huge commitment and often requires a 180-degree turnaround for marketers who spent the last half of the 20th century developing and implementing mass-marketing efforts. Although mass marketing will probably continue to be used,

© ISTOCKPHOTO.COM/LORI SPARKIA

especially to create brand awareness or to remind consumers of a product, the advantages of one-to-one marketing cannot be ignored.

LO9 Positioning

The development of any marketing mix depends on **positioning**, a process that influences potential customers' overall perception of a brand, product line, or organization in general. **Position** is the place a product, brand, or group of products occupies in consumers' minds relative to competing offerings. Consumer goods marketers are particularly concerned with positioning. Procter & Gamble, for example, markets 11 different laundry detergents, each with a unique position, such as allergen-free, softening, or ultra-concentrated.

Positioning assumes that consumers compare products on the basis of important features. Marketing efforts that emphasize irrelevant features are therefore likely to misfire. For example, Crystal Pepsi and a clear version of Coca-Cola's Tab failed because consumers perceived the "clear" positioning as more of a marketing gimmick than a benefit.

Effective positioning requires assessing the positions occupied by competing products, determining the important dimensions underlying these positions, and choosing a position in the market where the organization's marketing efforts will have the greatest impact. SuperJam positions itself as superior to other jams because it is 100 percent fruit, has no sugar added, and is made with super fruits such as blueberries and cranberries, which boast added health benefits. The recipe also comes from the creator's grandmother, adding a homespun element that separates it from other jams.[31] As the previous example illustrates, **product differentiation** is a positioning strategy that many firms use to distinguish their products from those of competitors. The distinctions can be either real or perceived. Tandem Computer designed machines with two central processing units and two memories for users who cannot afford for their computer systems to be down or databases to be lost (e.g., an airline reservation system). In this case, Tandem used product differentiation to create a product with very real advantages for the target market. However, many

everyday products, such as bleaches, aspirin, unleaded regular gasoline, and some soaps, are differentiated by such trivial means as brand names, packaging, color, smell, or "secret" additives. The marketer attempts to convince consumers that a particular brand is distinctive and that they should demand it over competing brands.

Some firms, instead of using product differentiation, position their products as being similar to competing products or brands. Two examples of this positioning are artificial sweeteners advertised as tasting like sugar and margarine tasting like butter.

Perceptual Mapping

Perceptual mapping is a means of displaying or graphing, in two or more dimensions, the location of products, brands, or groups of products in customers' minds. For example, Saks Incorporated, the department store chain, stumbled in sales when it tried to attract a younger core customer. To recover, Saks invested in research to determine its core customers in its 54 stores across the country. The perceptual map in Exhibit 8.3 on the next page shows how Saks uses customer demographics, such as age, spending habits, and shopping patterns, to build a matrix that charts the best mix of clothes and accessories to stock in each store.

© SUPERJAM

positioning developing a specific marketing mix to influence potential customers' overall perception of a brand, product line, or organization in general

position the place a product, brand, or group of products occupies in consumers' minds relative to competing offerings

product differentiation a positioning strategy that some firms use to distinguish their products from those of competitors

perceptual mapping a means of displaying or graphing, in two or more dimensions, the location of products, brands, or groups of products in customers' minds

repositioning

changing consumers' perceptions of a brand in relation to competing brands

Positioning Bases

Firms use a variety of bases for positioning, including the following:

▸▸ *Attribute:* A product is associated with an attribute, product feature, or customer benefit. In engineering its products, Seventh Generation focuses on removing common toxins and chemicals from household products to make them safe for everyone in the household.

▸▸ *Price and quality:* This positioning base may stress high price as a signal of quality or emphasize low price as an indication of value. Neiman Marcus uses the high-price strategy; Walmart has successfully followed the low-price and value strategy. The mass merchandiser Target has developed an interesting position based on price and quality. It is an "upscale discounter," sticking to low prices but offering higher quality and design than most discount chains.

▸▸ *Use or application:* Stressing uses or applications can be an effective means of positioning a product with buyers. Danone introduced its Kahlúa liqueur using advertising to point out 228 ways to consume the product. Snapple introduced a new drink called "Snapple a Day" that is intended for use as a meal replacement.

▸▸ *Product user:* This positioning base focuses on a personality or type of user. Gap Inc. has several different brands: Gap stores offer basic casual pieces, such as jeans and T-shirts to middle-of-the-road consumers at mid-level prices; Old Navy offers low-priced, trendy casual wear geared to youth and college-age groups; and Banana Republic is a luxury brand offering fashionable, luxurious business and casual wear to 25- to 35-year-olds.[32]

▸▸ *Product class:* The objective here is to position the product as being associated with a particular category of products—for example, positioning a margarine brand with butter. Alternatively, products can be disassociated with a category.

▸▸ *Competitor:* Positioning against competitors is part of any positioning strategy. Avis Rent A Car's positioning as number two compared to Hertz exemplifies positioning against specific competitors.

▸▸ *Emotion:* Positioning using emotion focuses on how the product makes customers feel. A number of companies use this approach. For example, Nike's "Just Do It" campaign didn't tell consumers what "it" is, but most got the emotional message of achievement and courage. The

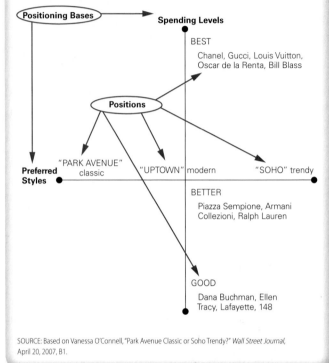

EXHIBIT 8.3

Perceptual Map and Positioning Strategy for Saks Department Stores

Positioning Bases → Spending Levels

BEST
Chanel, Gucci, Louis Vuitton, Oscar de la Renta, Bill Blass

Positions

Preferred Styles — "PARK AVENUE" classic — "UPTOWN" modern — "SOHO" trendy

BETTER
Piazza Sempione, Armani Collezioni, Ralph Lauren

GOOD
Dana Buchman, Ellen Tracy, Lafayette, 148

SOURCE: Based on Vanessa O'Connell, "Park Avenue Classic or Soho Trendy?" *Wall Street Journal*, April 20, 2007, B1.

creators of iPhone game *Bumpy Road* not only created a new way to play a game (by manipulating the world around a car, rather than manipulating the car), but they relied on a simple story about a precious little couple to differentiate *Bumpy Road* from other games.[33]

Repositioning

Sometimes products or companies are repositioned in order to sustain growth in slow markets or to correct positioning mistakes. **Repositioning** is changing consumers' perceptions of a brand in relation to competing brands. Post Foods, in an effort to revive its Grape Nuts cereal, repositioned it from a cereal for families and women to a cereal for men. Advertising in *Sports Illustrated* magazine featured men doing "tough things" such as walking a poodle with a pink collar and setting up a VCR followed by the new slogan "That Takes Grape Nuts."[34]

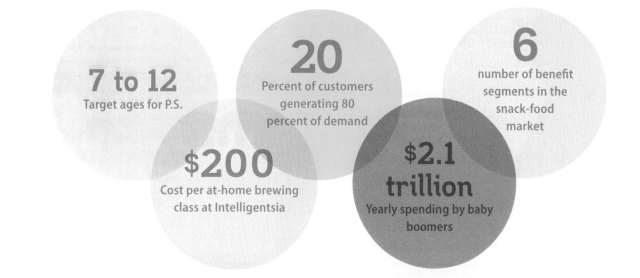

7 to 12
Target ages for P.S.

20
Percent of customers generating 80 percent of demand

6
number of benefit segments in the snack-food market

$200
Cost per at-home brewing class at Intelligentsia

$2.1 trillion
Yearly spending by baby boomers

STUDY TOOLS
CHAPTER 8

Flip to the back of your textbook to:

❏ **Rip out Chapter Review Card**

Log in to the CourseMate for MKTG at cengagebrain.com to:

❏ **Review Key Terms Flash Cards (Print or Online)**

❏ **Review Audio and Visual Summaries**

❏ **Complete both Practice Quizzes to prepare for tests**

❏ **Play "Beat the Clock" and "Quizbowl" to master concepts**

❏ **Complete "Crossword Puzzle" to review key terms**

❏ **Watch the video on "Numi Organic Tea" for a real company example on Segmenting and Targeting Markets**

Decision Support Systems

and Marketing Research

Whether a research project costs $200 or $2 million, the same general process should be followed.

AFTER YOU FINISH THIS CHAPTER, GO TO PAGE 163 FOR STUDY TOOLS

LO 1 Marketing Decision Support Systems

Accurate and timely information is the lifeblood of marketing decision making. Good information can help an organization maximize sales and efficiently use scarce company resources. To prepare and adjust marketing plans, managers need a system for gathering everyday information about developments in the marketing environment—that is, for gathering **marketing information**. The system most commonly used these days for gathering marketing information is called a *marketing decision support system*.

A marketing **decision support system (DSS)** is an interactive, flexible, computerized information system that enables managers to obtain and manipulate information as they are making decisions. A DSS bypasses the information-processing specialist and gives managers access to useful data from their own desks.

These are the characteristics of a true DSS:

▸▸ *Interactive:* Managers give simple instructions and see immediate results. The process is under their direct control. Managers don't have to wait for scheduled reports.

▸▸ *Flexible:* A DSS can sort, regroup, total, average, and manipulate the data in various ways. It will shift gears as the user changes topics, matching information to the problem at hand.

marketing information
everyday information about developments in the marketing environment that managers use to prepare and adjust marketing plans

decision support system (DSS)
an interactive, flexible, computerized information system that enables managers to obtain and manipulate information as they are making decisions

What do you think?

The Internet has made me more likely to take surveys for companies.

1 2 3 4 5 6 7
STRONGLY DISAGREE   STRONGLY AGREE

© ISTOCKPHOTO.COM/ZONECREATIVE

Find out what others think at the CourseMate for MKTG. Log in at cengagebrain.com.

database marketing the creation of a large computerized file of customers' and potential customers' profiles and purchase patterns

marketing research the process of planning, collecting, and analyzing data relevant to a marketing decision

▸▸ *Discovery oriented:* Managers can probe for trends, isolate problems, and ask "what if" questions.

▸▸ *Accessible:* Managers who aren't skilled with computers can easily learn how to use a DSS. Novice users should be able to choose a standard, or default, method of using the system. They can bypass optional features so they can work with the basic system right away while gradually learning to apply its advanced features.

Perhaps the fastest-growing use of a DSS is for **database marketing**, which is the creation of a large computerized file of customers' and potential customers' profiles and purchase patterns. It is usually the key tool for successful one-to-one marketing, which relies on very specific information about a market.

LO 2 The Role of Marketing Research

Marketing research is the process of planning, collecting, and analyzing data relevant to a marketing decision. The results of this analysis are then communicated to management. Thus, marketing research is the function that links the consumer, customer, and public to the marketer through information. Marketing research plays a key role in the marketing system. It provides decision makers with data on the effectiveness of the current marketing mix and insights for necessary changes. Furthermore, marketing research is a main data source for both management information systems and DSS. In other words, the findings of a marketing research project become data in a DSS.

Marketing research has three roles: descriptive, diagnostic, and predictive. Its *descriptive* role includes gathering and presenting factual statements. For example, what is the historic sales trend in the industry? What are consumers' attitudes toward a product and its advertising? Its *diagnostic* role includes explaining data, such as determining the impact on sales of a change in

EXHIBIT 9.1
The Marketing Research Process

1 Identify and formulate the problem/opportunity.

2 Plan the research design and gather secondary data.

3 Specify the sampling procedures.

4 Collect primary data.

5 Analyze the data.

6 Prepare and present the report.

7 Follow up.

© CENGAGE LEARNING 2013

the design of the package. Its *predictive* function is to address "what if" questions. For example, how can the researcher use the descriptive and diagnostic research to predict the results of a planned marketing decision?

LO 3 Steps in a Marketing Research Project

Virtually all firms that have adopted the marketing concept engage in some marketing research because it offers decision makers many benefits. Some companies spend millions on marketing research; others, particularly smaller firms, conduct informal, limited-scale research studies.

Whether a research project costs $200 or $2 million, the same general process should be followed. The marketing research process is a scientific approach to decision making that maximizes the chance of getting accurate and meaningful results. Exhibit 9.1 traces the seven steps in the research process, which begins with the recognition of a marketing problem or opportunity. As changes occur in the firm's external environment, marketing managers are faced with the questions, "Should we change the existing marketing mix?" and, if so, "How?" Marketing research may be used to evaluate product, promotion, distribution, or pricing alternatives.

After years of research, Procter & Gamble relaunched its ubiquitous hair care line Pantene in 2010. In 2009, Pantene's U.S. sales dropped 9 percent, more than the 3 percent decline for the shampoo market as a whole. P&G had already been working on ways to differentiate Pantene from other hair care lines but needed a specific place to focus its research.

Pantene researchers delved into women's reactions to "bad hair days," a challenging, subjective area that is lightly touched on by only a few other hair care companies. But P&G faced the problem head on, surveying women about their feelings when using certain hair products. The ultimate goal for Pantene was to help women have "good hair days." After one week using Pantene products, women using the new formula reported more joy than the control group. The company is still collecting sales figures, but with brighter packaging and slimmer product lines to ease consumer confusion, managers remain optimistic that their hallmark line will bounce back from the recession stronger than before.[1]

The Pantene story illustrates an important point about problem/opportunity definition. The **marketing research problem** is information oriented. It involves determining what information is needed and how that information can be obtained efficiently and effectively. The **marketing research objective**, then, is to provide insightful decision-making information. This requires specific pieces of information needed to solve the marketing research problem. Managers must combine this information with their own experience and other information to make proper decisions. Procter & Gamble's marketing research problem was to gather specific information about how a woman's hair affects her feelings and mood. The marketing research objectives were to reformulate Pantene to affect women's hair more positively and reposition the brand as an antidote to bad hair days.

In contrast, the **management decision problem** is action oriented. Management problems tend to be much broader in scope and far more general than marketing research problems, which must be narrowly defined and specific if the research effort is to be successful. Sometimes several research studies must be conducted to solve a broad management problem. For Pantene, the management decision problem was deciding how to win women back after the recession.

Marketing research enabled Procter & Gamble to reevaluate its Pantene brand, resulting in new packaging, a new formula, and a reduced number of products.

© TERRI MILLER/E-VISUAL COMMUNICATIONS, INC.

Secondary Data

A valuable tool throughout the research process but particularly in the problem/opportunity identification stage is **secondary data**—data previously collected for any purpose other than the one at hand. Secondary information originating within the company includes documents such as annual reports, reports to stockholders, product testing results perhaps made available to the news media, and house periodicals composed by the company's personnel for communication to employees, customers, or others. Often this information is incorporated into a company's internal database.

Innumerable outside sources of secondary information also exist, principally in the forms of government departments and agencies (federal, state, and local) that compile and publish summaries of business data. Trade and industry associations also publish secondary data. Still more data are available in business periodicals and other news media that regularly publish studies and articles on the economy, specific industries, and even individual companies. The unpublished summarized secondary information from these sources corresponds to internal reports, memos, or special-purpose analyses with limited circulation. Economic considerations or priorities in the organization may preclude publication of these summaries. Most of the sources listed above can be found on the Internet.

Secondary data save time and money if they help solve the researcher's problem. Even if the problem is not solved, secondary data have other advantages. They can aid in formulating the problem statement and suggest research methods and other types of data needed for solving the problem. In addition, secondary data can pinpoint the kinds of people to approach and their locations and serve as a basis of comparison for other data. The disadvantages of secondary data stem mainly from a mismatch between the researcher's unique problem and the purpose for which the secondary data were originally gathered, which are typically different. For example, a company wanted to determine the market potential for a fireplace log made of coal rather than compressed wood by-products. The researcher found plenty of secondary data

marketing research problem
determining what information is needed and how that information can be obtained efficiently and effectively

marketing research objective
the specific information needed to solve a marketing research problem; the objective should be to provide insightful decision-making information

management decision problem
a broad-based problem that uses marketing research in order for managers to take proper actions

secondary data
data previously collected for any purpose other than the one at hand

© KONSTANTIN YOLSHIN/SHUTTERSTOCK.COM

marketing research aggregator a company that acquires, catalogs, reformats, segments, and resells reports already published by marketing research firms

research design specifies which research questions must be answered, how and when the data will be gathered, and how the data will be analyzed

primary data information that is collected for the first time; used for solving the particular problem under investigation

about total wood consumed as fuel, quantities consumed in each state, and types of wood burned. Secondary data were also available about consumer attitudes and purchase patterns of wood by-product fireplace logs. The wealth of secondary data provided the researcher with many insights into the artificial log market. Yet nowhere was there any information that would tell the firm whether consumers would buy artificial logs made of coal.

The quality of secondary data may also pose a problem. Often secondary data sources do not give detailed information that would enable a researcher to assess their quality or relevance. Whenever possible, a researcher needs to address these important questions: Who gathered the data? Why were the data obtained? What methodology was used? How were classifications (such as heavy users versus light users) developed and defined? When was the information gathered?

The New Age of Secondary Information: The Internet

Although necessary in almost any research project, gathering secondary data has traditionally been a tedious and boring job. The researcher often had to write to government agencies, trade associations, or other secondary data providers and then wait days or weeks for a reply that might never come. Often, one or more trips to the library were required and the researcher might have found that needed reports were checked out or missing. Now, however, the rapid development of the Internet has eliminated much of the drudgery associated with the collection of secondary data.

Marketing Research Aggregators

The **marketing research aggregator** industry is a $120 million business that is growing about 6 percent a year. Companies in this field acquire, catalog, reformat, segment, and resell reports already pub-

lished by large and small marketing research firms. Even Amazon.com has added a marketing research aggregation area to its high-profile e-commerce site.

The role of aggregator firms is growing because their databases of research reports are getting bigger and more comprehensive—and more useful—as marketing research firms get more comfortable using resellers as a sales channel. Meanwhile, advances in Web technology are making the databases easier to search and deliveries speedier. By slicing and repackaging research reports into narrower, more specialized sections for resale to small- and medium-sized clients who often cannot afford to commission their own studies or buy full reports, the aggregators are essentially nurturing a new target market for the information. Some major aggregators are mindbranch.com, aarkstore.com, and usadata.com.

Planning the Research Design and Gathering Primary Data

Good secondary data can help researchers conduct a thorough situation analysis. With that information, researchers can list their unanswered questions and rank them. Researchers must then decide the exact information required to answer the questions. The **research design** specifies which research questions must be answered, how and when the data will be gathered, and how the data will be analyzed. Typically, the project budget is finalized after the research design has been approved.

Sometimes research questions can be answered by gathering more secondary data; otherwise, primary data may be needed. **Primary data**, or information collected for the first time, are used for solving the particular problem under investigation. The main advantage of primary data is that they will answer a specific research question that secondary data cannot answer. In Procter & Gamble's research for Pantene, managers used a psychological questionnaire to determine how hair products affected women's daily attitudes. For one week, one group of women used the old Pantene formula, and the other group used the new formula. This primary data revealed that women using the new Pantene felt more excited, proud, interested, and attentive than the other group—positive emotions that the Pantene research group could not have discovered through secondary research.[2] Moreover, primary data are current, and researchers know the source. Sometimes researchers gather the data themselves rather than assign projects to outside companies. Researchers also specify the methodology of the research. Secrecy can be maintained because the information is proprietary. In contrast, much secondary data is available to all interested parties for relatively small fees or free.

Gathering primary data is expensive; costs can range from a few thousand dollars for a limited survey to several million for a nationwide study. For instance, a nationwide, 15-minute telephone interview with 1,000 adult males can cost $50,000 for everything, including a data analysis and report. Because primary data gathering is so expensive, firms may cut back on the number of in-person interviews to save money and use an Internet study instead. Larger companies that conduct many research projects use another cost-saving technique. They *piggyback studies*, or gather data on two different projects using one questionnaire. Nevertheless, the disadvantages of primary data gathering are usually offset by the advantages. It is often the only way of solving a research problem. And with a variety of techniques available for research—including surveys, observations, and experiments—primary research can address almost any marketing question.

Survey Research The most popular technique for gathering primary data is **survey research**, in which a researcher interacts with people to obtain facts, opinions, and attitudes. Exhibit 9.2 summarizes the characteristics of traditional forms of survey research.

In-Home Personal Interviews Although in-home personal interviews often provide high-quality information, they tend to be very expensive because of the interviewers' travel time and mileage costs. Therefore, they are rapidly disappearing from the American and

survey research
the most popular technique for gathering primary data, in which a researcher interacts with people to obtain facts, opinions, and attitudes

EXHIBIT 9.2
Characteristics of Traditional Forms of Survey Research

Characteristic	In-Home Personal Interviews	Mall Intercept Interviews	Central-Location Telephone Interviews	Self-Administered and One-Time Mail Surveys	Mail Panel Surveys	Executive Interviews	Focus Groups
Cost	High	Moderate	Moderate	Low	Moderate	High	Low
Time span	Moderate	Moderate	Fast	Slow	Relatively slow	Moderate	Fast
Use of interviewer probes	Yes	Yes	Yes	No	Yes	Yes	Yes
Ability to show concepts to respondent	Yes (also taste tests)	Yes (also taste tests)	No	Yes	Yes	Yes	Yes
Management control over interviewer	Low	Moderate	High	N/A	N/A	Moderate	High
General data quality	High	Moderate	High to moderate	Moderate to low	Moderate	High	Moderate
Ability to collect large amounts of data	High	Moderate	Moderate to low	Low to moderate	Moderate	Moderate	Moderate
Ability to handle complex questionnaires	High	Moderate	High, if computer aided	Low	Low	High	N/A

© CENGAGE LEARNING 2013

mall intercept interview a survey research method that involves interviewing people in the common areas of shopping malls

computer-assisted personal interviewing an interviewing method in which the interviewer reads questions from a computer screen and enters the respondent's data directly into the computer

computer-assisted self-interviewing an interviewing method in which a mall interviewer intercepts and directs willing respondents to nearby computers where each respondent reads questions off a computer screen and directly keys his or her answers into a computer

central-location telephone (CLT) facility a specially designed phone room used to conduct telephone interviewing

executive interview a type of survey that involves interviewing businesspeople at their offices concerning industrial products or services

European researchers' survey toolbox. They are, however, still popular in many countries around the globe.

Mall Intercept Interviews The **mall intercept interview** is conducted in the common area of a shopping mall or in a market research office within the mall. To conduct this type of interview, the research firm rents office space in the mall or pays a significant daily fee. One drawback is that it is hard to get a representative sample of the population. One advantage is the ability of the interviewer to probe when necessary—a technique used to clarify a person's response and ask for more detailed information.

Mall intercept interviews must be brief. Only the shortest ones are conducted while respondents are standing. Usually, researchers invite respondents into the office for interviews, which are still generally less than 15 minutes long. The overall quality of mall intercept interviews is about the same as telephone interviews.

Marketing researchers are applying computer technology in mall interviewing. The first technique is **computer-assisted personal interviewing**. The researcher conducts in-person interviews, reads questions to the respondent off a computer screen, and directly keys the respondent's answers into the computer. A second approach is **computer-assisted self-interviewing**. A mall interviewer intercepts and directs willing respondents to nearby computers. Each respondent reads questions off a computer screen and directly keys his or her answers into a computer. The third use of technology is fully automated self-interviewing. Respondents are guided by interviewers or independently approach a centrally located computer station or kiosk, read questions off a screen, and directly key their answers into the station's computer.

Telephone Interviews Telephone interviews costs less than personal interviews, but cost is rapidly increasing due to respondent refusals to participate. Most telephone interviewing is conducted from a specially designed phone room called a **central-location telephone (CLT) facility**. A CLT facility has many phone lines, individual interviewing stations, headsets,

and sometimes monitoring equipment. The research firm typically will interview people nationwide from a single location. The federal "Do Not Call" law does not apply to survey research.

Most CLT facilities offer computer-assisted interviewing. The interviewer reads the questions from a computer screen and enters the respondent's data directly into the computer, saving time. Hallmark Cards found that an interviewer administered a printed questionnaire for its Shoebox greeting cards in 28 minutes. The same questionnaire administered with computer assistance took only 18 minutes. The researcher can stop the survey at any point and immediately print out the survey results, allowing the research design to be refined as necessary.

Mail Surveys Mail surveys have several benefits: relatively low cost, elimination of interviewers and field supervisors, centralized control, and actual or promised anonymity for respondents (which may draw more candid responses). A disadvantage is that mail questionnaires usually produce low response rates because certain elements of the population tend to respond more than others. The resulting sample may therefore not represent the surveyed population. Another serious problem with mail surveys is that no one probes respondents to clarify or elaborate on their answers.

Mail panels offer an alternative to the one-shot mail survey. A mail panel consists of a sample of households recruited to participate by mail for a given period. Panel members often receive gifts in return for their participation. Essentially, the panel is a sample used several times. In contrast to one-time mail surveys, the response rates from mail panels are high. Rates of 70 percent (of those who agree to participate) are not uncommon.

Executive Interviews An **executive interview** involves interviewing businesspeople at their offices concerning industrial products or services, a process that is very expensive. First, individuals involved in the purchase decision for the product in question must be identified and located, which can itself be expensive and time-consuming. Once a qualified person is located, the next step is to get that person to agree to be interviewed and to set a time for the interview.

Finally, an interviewer must go to the particular place at the appointed time. Long waits are frequently encountered; cancellations are not uncommon. This type of survey requires the very best interviewers because they are frequently interviewing on topics that they know very little about.

Focus Groups A **focus group** is a type of personal interviewing. Often recruited by random telephone screening, seven to ten people with certain desired characteristics form a focus group. These qualified consumers are usually offered an incentive (typically $30 to $50) to participate in a group discussion. The meeting place (sometimes resembling a living room, sometimes featuring a conference table) has audiotaping and perhaps videotaping equipment. It also likely has a viewing room with a one-way mirror so that clients (manufacturers or retailers) can watch the session. During the session, a moderator, hired by the research company, leads the group discussion. Focus groups can be used to gauge consumer response to a product or promotion and are occasionally used to brainstorm new product ideas or to screen concepts for new products. Focus groups also represent an efficient way of learning how products are actually used in the home. Panelists' descriptions of how they perform tasks highlight need gaps, which can improve an existing product or demonstrate how a new product might be received. It is estimated that over 600,000 focus groups are conducted around the world each year.[4]

Questionnaire Design All forms of survey research require a questionnaire. Questionnaires ensure that all respondents will be asked the same series of questions. Questionnaires include three basic types of questions: open-ended, closed-ended, and scaled-response. An **open-ended question** encourages an answer phrased in the respondent's own words. Researchers get a rich array of information based on the respondent's frame of reference (What do you think about the new flavor?). In contrast, a **closed-ended question** asks the respondent to make a selection from a limited list of responses. Closed-ended questions can either be what marketing researchers call *dichotomous* (Do you like the new flavor? Yes or No.) or *multiple choice*. A **scaled-response question** is a closed-ended question designed to measure the intensity of a respondent's answer. The "What do you think?" question that opened the chapter is a scaled-response question.

Closed-ended and scaled-response questions are easier to tabulate than open-ended questions because response choices are fixed. On the other hand, unless the researcher designs the closed-ended question very carefully, an important choice may be omitted.

A good question must be clear and concise and avoid ambiguous language. The answer to the question "Do you live within ten minutes of here?" depends on the mode of transportation (maybe the person walks), driving speed, perceived time, and other factors. Language should also be clear. As such, jargon should be avoided, and wording should be geared to the target audience. A question such as "What is the level of efficacy of your preponderant dishwasher powder?" would probably be greeted by a lot of blank stares. It would be much simpler to say "Are you (1) very satisfied, (2) somewhat satisfied, or (3) not satisfied with your current brand of dishwasher powder?"

Stating the survey's purpose at the beginning of the interview may improve clarity, but it may also

© TYLER OLSON/SHUTTERSTOCK.COM

A LIFE IN THE DAY OF THE CUSTOMER

Martin Lindstrom, a business consultant, has **revitalized ailing brands** and taught CEOs how to tweak products or target them in just the right way to make sales soar. His secret is simple: live with your customers. When Lindstrom is hired by a company, he goes and lives with its target audience—eats, sleeps, and plays with them. As a result, he can tell companies that 37 percent of teenagers eat a box of cereal on their first day of college in order to feel closer to home, and that 4 percent of people brush their teeth in the shower. Up close and personal market research gives marketers a true look into how their customers live and, properly applied, helps give them exactly what they need.[3]

SOURCE: Martin Lindstrom, "Want to Sell Product? Sleep With Your Customers," *Fast Company*, June 8, 2011.

focus group seven to ten people who participate in a group discussion led by a moderator

open-ended question an interview question that encourages an answer phrased in the respondent's own words

closed-ended question an interview question that asks the respondent to make a selection from a limited list of responses

scaled-response question a closed-ended question designed to measure the intensity of a respondent's answer

observation research a research method that relies on four types of observation: people watching people, people watching an activity, machines watching people, and machines watching an activity

mystery shoppers researchers posing as customers who gather observational data about a store

behavioral targeting (BT) a form of observation marketing research that combines a consumer's online activity with psychographic and demographic profiles compiled in databases

increase the chances of receiving biased responses. Many times, respondents will try to provide answers that they believe are "correct" or that the interviewer wants to hear. To avoid bias at the question level, researchers should avoid leading questions and adjectives that cause respondents to think of the topic in a certain way.

Finally, to ensure clarity, the interviewer should avoid asking two questions in one—for example, "How did you like the taste and texture of the Pepperidge Farm coffee cake?" This should be divided into two questions, one concerning taste and the other texture.

Observation Research In contrast to survey research, **observation research** depends on watching what people do. Specifically, it can be defined as the systematic process of recording the behavioral patterns of people, objects, and occurrences without questioning them. A market researcher using the observation technique witnesses and records information as events occur or compiles evidence from records of past events. Carried a step further, observation may involve watching people or phenomena and may be conducted by human observers or machines. Examples of these various observational situations are shown in Exhibit 9.3.

Two common forms of people-watching-people research are one-way mirror observations and mystery shoppers. A one-way mirror allows the researchers to see the participants, but the participants cannot see the researchers.

Mystery Shoppers **Mystery shoppers** are researchers posing as customers who gather observational data about a store (e.g., are the shelves neatly stocked?) and collect data about customer/employee interactions. The interaction is not an interview, and communication occurs only so that the mystery shopper can observe the actions and comments of the employee. Mystery shopping is, therefore, classified as an observational marketing research method even though communication is often involved.

Behavioral Targeting **Behavioral targeting (BT)** began as a simple process by placing cookies on users' browsers to track which Web sites they visited and

EXHIBIT 9.3
Observational Situations

Situation	Example
People watching people	Observers stationed in supermarkets watch consumers select frozen Mexican dinners; the purpose is to see how much comparison shopping people do at the point of purchase.
People watching an activity	An observer stationed at an intersection counts traffic moving in various directions.
Machines watching people	Movie or videotape cameras record behavior as in the people-watching-people example above.
Machines watching an activity	Traffic-counting machines monitor traffic flow.

© CENGAGE LEARNING 2013

ultimately match the user with ads they would most likely investigate. Today, BT combines a consumer's online activity with psychographic and demographic profiles compiled in databases (discussed in Chapters 4 and 8). Because of the potential effectiveness of BT advertising, its popularity is skyrocketing.

Social networking, which is discussed in depth in Chapter 22, is the fastest-growing area of BT. The information that a member of Google+ or Facebook shares, in combination with his or her demographic and psychographic information, becomes a very powerful tool for ad placement. Critics call this form of BT *conversational eavesdropping analysis*, but advocates call it *user-declared information targeting*.[5] It is an apt description because the information is posted by members in their profiles. Say Alex posts kayaking as an interest on his profile. Because he declared his interest, it is more concrete marketing knowledge. A note that someone from that computer's address visited a kayaking Web site is less concrete because anyone could have been using that computer. Both Facebook and MySpace allow marketers to target ads to members based upon profile information. Many large companies use BT. When PepsiCo wanted to promote Aquafina Alive on the Web, the company placed ads only on sites visited by people interested in healthy lifestyles.

Ethnographic Research Ethnographic research comes to marketing from the field of anthropology. The technique is becoming increasingly popular in commercial marketing research. **Ethnographic research**, or the study of human behavior in its natural context, involves observation of behavior and physical setting. Ethnographers directly observe the population they are studying. As "participant observers," ethnographers can use their intimacy with the people they are studying to gain richer, deeper insights into culture and behavior—in short, what makes people do what they do.

The at-home consumption market is one that eludes much research. Anthropologists and other observational researchers can't sit in people's homes and monitor which electronic devices they are using and how they use them. Questionnaires rely on one-time truthful responses and the respondent's memory. However, some of the nation's biggest media companies are hoping to get a look into people's homes by using iPhones to monitor media consumption. The Coalition for Innovative Media Measurement, a collaboration between media and ad industries to determine how consumers view media and which devices they use, is sponsoring the study. The company would give 1,000 participants iPhones with a special app that they would log into every 30 minutes and answer questions about their media activities. Respondents give frequent updates on what and how they are consuming music and television, whether it is through streaming or downloading, on computers or television, or from subscription services or free. This type of research may be the closest researchers have come to living with research participants and to understanding how Americans consume media. Knowing how Americans watch programs would allow the media and ad industries to tailor delivery to the consumer and use the Internet to their advantage, rather than be left behind with outdated business models.[6]

Virtual Shopping Advances in computer technology have enabled researchers to simulate an actual retail store environment on a computer screen. Depending on the type of simulation, a shopper can "pick up" a package by touching its image on the monitor and rotate it to examine all sides. Like buying on most online retailers, the shopper touches the shopping cart to add an item to the basket. During the shopping process, the computer unobtrusively records the amount of time the consumer spends shopping in each product category, the time the consumer spends examining each side of a product, the

quantity of the product the consumer purchases, and the order in which items are purchased.

Computer-simulated environments like this one offer a number of advantages over older research methods. First, the virtual store duplicates the distracting clutter of an actual market. Layouts can even be modified to reflect various types of retailers, such as drugstores or supermarkets, meaning that consumers can shop in an environment with a realistic level of complexity and variety. Second, researchers can set up and alter the tests very quickly. Data collection is also fast and error free because the information generated by the purchase is automatically tabulated and stored by the computer. Third, production costs are low because displays are created electronically. Once the hardware and software are in place, the cost of a test is largely a function of the number of respondents, who generally are given a small incentive to participate. Fourth, the simulation has a high degree of flexibility. It can be used to test entirely new marketing concepts or to fine-tune existing programs.[7]

Virtual shopping research is growing rapidly as companies such as Cadbury, Nestlé, PepsiCo, and Clorox realize the benefits from this type of observation research.[8] About 150,000 new consumer packaged goods were introduced in the United States in 2010.[9] All are vying for very limited retail shelf space. Any process, such as virtual shopping, that can speed product development time and lower costs is always welcomed by manufacturers.

Experiments An **experiment** is a method a researcher can use to gather primary data. The researcher alters one or more variables—price, package design, shelf space, advertising theme, advertising expenditures— while observing the effects of those alterations on another variable (usually sales). The best experiments are those in which all factors are held constant except the ones being manipulated. The researcher can then

> **ethnographic research** the study of human behavior in its natural context; involves observation of behavior and physical setting
>
> **experiment** a method of gathering primary data in which the researcher alters one or more variables while observing the effects of those alterations on another variable

© COLIN ANDERSON/BLEND IMAGES/JUPITERIMAGES

sample a subset from a larger population

universe the population from which a sample will be drawn

probability sample a sample in which every element in the population has a known statistical likelihood of being selected

random sample a sample arranged in such a way that every element of the population has an equal chance of being selected as part of the sample

nonprobability sample any sample in which little or no attempt is made to get a representative cross section of the population

convenience sample a form of nonprobability sample using respondents who are convenient or readily accessible to the researcher—for example, employees, friends, or relatives

measurement error an error that occurs when there is a difference between the information desired by the researcher and the information provided by the measurement process

observe what changes in sales, for example, result from changes in the amount of money spent on advertising.

Specifying the Sampling Procedures

Once the researchers decide how they will collect primary data, their next step is to select the sampling procedures they will use. A firm can seldom take a census of all possible users of a new product, nor can they all be interviewed. Therefore, a firm must select a sample of the group to be interviewed. A **sample** is a subset from a larger population.

Several questions must be answered before a sampling plan is chosen. First, the population, or **universe**, of interest must be defined. This is the group from which the sample will be drawn. It should include all the people whose opinions, behavior, preferences, attitudes, and so on, are of interest to the marketer. For example, in a study whose purpose is to determine the market for a new canned dog food, the universe might be defined to include all current buyers of canned dog food.

After the universe has been defined, the next question is whether the sample must be representative of the population. If the answer is yes, a probability sample is needed. Otherwise, a nonprobability sample might be considered.

Probability Samples A **probability sample** is a sample in which every element in the population has a known statistical likelihood of being selected. Its most desirable feature is that scientific rules

can be used to ensure that the sample represents the population.

One type of probability sample is a **random sample**—a sample arranged in such a way that every element of the population has an equal chance of being selected as part of the sample. For example, suppose a university is interested in getting a cross section of student opinions on a proposed sports complex to be built using student activity fees. If the university can acquire an up-to-date list of all the enrolled students, it can draw a random sample by using random numbers from a table (found in most statistics books) to select students from the list. Common forms of probability and nonprobability samples are shown in Exhibit 9.4.

Nonprobability Samples Any sample in which little or no attempt is made to get a representative cross section of the population can be considered a **nonprobability sample**. Therefore the probability of selection of each sampling unit is not known. A common form of a nonprobability sample is the **convenience sample**, which uses respondents who are convenient or readily accessible to the researcher—for instance, employees, friends, or relatives.

Nonprobability samples are acceptable as long as the researcher understands their nonrepresentative nature. Because of their lower cost, nonprobability samples are the basis of much marketing research.

Types of Errors Whenever a sample is used in marketing research, two major types of errors may occur: measurement error and sampling error. **Measurement error** occurs when there is a difference between the information desired by the researcher and the information provided by the measurement process. For example, people may tell an interviewer that they purchase Crest toothpaste when they do not.

SAMPLE

UNIVERSE

© PASHABO/SHUTTERSTOCK.COM / © GUY SHAPIRA/SHUTTERSTOCK.COM

EXHIBIT 9.4
Types of Samples

Probability Samples	
Simple Random Sample	Every member of the population has a known and equal chance of selection.
Stratified Sample	The population is divided into mutually exclusive groups (such as gender or age); then random samples are drawn from each group.
Cluster Sample	The population is divided into mutually exclusive groups (such as geographic areas); then a random sample of clusters is selected. The researcher then collects data from all the elements in the selected clusters or from a probability sample of elements within each selected cluster.
Systematic Sample	A list of the population is obtained—e.g., all persons with a checking account at XYZ Bank—and a skip interval is obtained by dividing the sample size by the population size. If the sample size is 100 and the bank has 1,000 customers, then the skip interval is 10. The beginning number is randomly chosen within the skip interval. If the beginning number is 8, then the skip pattern would be 8, 18, 28, ...
Nonprobability Samples	
Convenience Sample	The researcher selects the easiest population members from which to obtain information.
Judgment Sample	The researcher's selection criteria are based on personal judgment that the elements (persons) chosen will likely give accurate information.
Quota Sample	The researcher finds a prescribed number of people in several categories—e.g., owners of large dogs versus owners of small dogs. Respondents are not selected on probability sampling criteria.
Snowball Sample	Additional respondents are selected on the basis of referrals from the initial respondents. This method is used when a desired type of respondent is hard to find—e.g., persons who have taken round-the-world cruises in the last three years. This technique employs the old adage "Birds of a feather flock together."

© CENGAGE LEARNING 2013

Measurement error generally tends to be larger than sampling error.

Sampling error occurs when a sample somehow does not represent the target population. Sampling error can be one of several types. Nonresponse error occurs when the sample actually interviewed differs from the sample drawn. This error happens because the original people selected to be interviewed either refused to cooperate or were inaccessible.

Frame error, another type of sampling error, arises if the sample drawn from a population differs from the target population. For instance, suppose a telephone survey is conducted to find out Chicago beer drinkers' attitudes toward Coors. If a Chicago telephone directory is used as the *frame* (the device or list from which the respondents are selected), the survey will contain a frame error. Not all Chicago beer drinkers have phones, and many phone numbers are unlisted. An ideal sample (e.g., a sample with no frame error) matches all important characteristics of the target population to be surveyed. Could you find a perfect frame for Chicago beer drinkers?

Random error occurs when the selected sample is an imperfect representation of the overall population. Random error represents how accurately the chosen sample's true average (mean) value reflects the population's true average (mean) value. For example, we might take a random sample of beer drinkers in Chicago and find that 16 percent regularly drink Coors beer. The next day we might repeat the same sampling procedure and discover that 14 percent regularly drink Coors beer. The difference is due to random error. Error is common to all surveys, yet it is often not reported or is underreported. Typically, the only error mentioned in a written report is sampling error.

sampling error an error that occurs when a sample somehow does not represent the target population

frame error an error that occurs when a sample drawn from a population differs from the target population

random error an error that occurs when the selected sample is an imperfect representation of the overall population

field service firm
a firm that specializes in interviewing respondents on a subcontracted basis

cross-tabulation a method of analyzing data that lets the analyst look at the responses to one question in relation to the responses to one or more other questions

Collecting the Data

Marketing research field service firms collect most primary data. A **field service firm** specializes in interviewing respondents on a subcontracted basis. Many have offices, often in malls, throughout the country. A typical marketing research study involves data collection in several cities, which requires the marketer to work with a comparable number of field service firms. Besides conducting interviews, field service firms provide focus group facilities, mall intercept locations, test product storage, and kitchen facilities to prepare test food products.

Analyzing the Data

After collecting the data, the marketing researcher proceeds to the next step in the research process: data analysis. The purpose of this analysis is to interpret and draw conclusions from the mass of collected data. The marketing researcher tries to organize and analyze those data by using one or more techniques common to marketing research: one-way frequency counts, cross-tabulations, and more sophisticated statistical analysis. Of these three techniques, one-way frequency counts are the simplest. One-way frequency tables simply record the responses to a question. For example, the answers to the question "What brand of microwave popcorn do you buy most often?" would provide a one-way frequency distribution. One-way frequency tables are always done in data analysis, at least as a first step, because they provide the researcher with a general picture of the study's results. A **cross-tabulation** lets the analyst look at the responses to one question in relation to the responses to one or more other questions. For example, what is the association

between gender and the brand of microwave popcorn bought most frequently?

Researchers can use many other more powerful and sophisticated statistical techniques, such as hypothesis testing, measures of association, and regression analysis. A description of these techniques goes beyond the scope of this book but can be found in any good marketing research textbook. The use of sophisticated statistical techniques depends on the researchers' objectives and the nature of the data gathered.

Preparing and Presenting the Report

After data analysis has been completed, the researcher must prepare the report and communicate the conclusions and recommendations to management. This is a key step in the process. If the marketing researcher wants managers to carry out the recommendations, he or she must convince them that the results are credible and justified by the data collected.

Researchers are usually required to present both written and oral reports on the project. Today, the written report is no more than a copy of the Power-Point slides used in the oral presentation. Both reports should be tailored to the audience. They should begin with a clear, concise statement of the research objectives, followed by a complete, but brief and simple, explanation of the research design or methodology employed. A summary of major findings should come next. The conclusion of the report should also present recommendations to management.

Most people who enter marketing will become research users rather than research suppliers. Thus, they must know what to notice in a report. As with many other items we purchase, quality is not always readily apparent. Nor does a high price guarantee

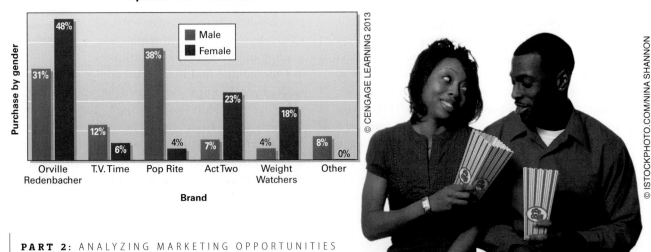

Popcorn Cross-Tabulation

© CENGAGE LEARNING 2013

© ISTOCKPHOTO.COM/NINA SHANNON

superior quality. The basis for measuring the quality of a marketing research report is the research proposal. Did the report meet the objectives established in the proposal? Was the methodology outlined in the proposal followed? Are the conclusions based on logical deductions from the data analysis? Do the recommendations seem prudent, given the conclusions?

Following Up

The final step in the marketing research process is to follow up. The researcher should determine why management did or did not carry out the recommendations in the report. Was sufficient decision-making information included? What could have been done to make the report more useful to management? A good rapport between the product manager, or whoever authorized the project, and the market researcher is essential. Often they must work together on many studies throughout the year.

Typically, the research process flows rather smoothly from one step to the next in the United States. However, conducting research in international markets can create a whole host of problems and challenges.

LO 4 The Profound Impact of the Internet on Marketing Research

Today, about one-fifth of the world's population is online. In the United States, 71 percent of the population is online, spanning every ethnic, socioeconomic, and educational divide.[10] Most managers accept that online research can, under appropriate conditions, accurately represent U.S. consumers as a whole. Non-adopters of the Internet tend to be older, low-income consumers (aged 65+ with household income less than $30,000), who do not tend to be the target market for many goods and services.[11]

More than 90 percent of America's marketing research companies conduct some form of online research. Online survey research has replaced computer-assisted telephone interviewing (CATI) as the most popular mode of data collection, though there is no evidence of this or other traditional survey methods being completely replaced by online sur-

veys.[12] Internet data collection is also rated as having the greatest potential for further growth.

Advantages of Internet Surveys

The huge growth in the popularity of Internet surveys is the result of the many advantages offered by the Internet. The specific advantages of Internet surveys are related to many factors:

▸▸ *Rapid development, real-time reporting:* Internet surveys can be broadcast to thousands of potential respondents simultaneously. Respondents complete surveys simultaneously; then results are tabulated and posted for corporate clients to view as the returns arrive. The result: survey results can be in a client's hands in significantly less time than would be required for traditional surveys.

▸▸ *Dramatically reduced costs:* The Internet can cut costs by 25 to 40 percent and provide results in half the time it takes to do traditional telephone surveys. Traditional survey methods are labor-intensive efforts incurring training, telecommunications, and management costs. Electronic methods eliminate these completely. While costs for traditional survey techniques rise proportionally with the number of interviews desired, electronic solicitations can grow in volume with little increase in project costs.

▸▸ *Personalized questions and data:* Internet surveys can be highly personalized for greater relevance to each respondent's own situation, thus speeding the response process.

▸▸ *Improved respondent participation:* Internet surveys take half as much time to complete as phone interviews, can be accomplished at the respondent's convenience (after work hours), and are much more stimulating and engaging. As a result, Internet surveys enjoy much higher response rates.

▸▸ *Contact with the hard-to-reach:* Certain groups—doctors, high-income professionals, top management in Global 2000 firms—are among the most surveyed on the planet and the most difficult to reach. Many of these groups are well represented online. Internet surveys provide convenient anytime/anywhere access that makes it easy for busy professionals to participate.

Uses of the Internet by Marketing Researchers

Marketing researchers are using the Internet to administer surveys, conduct focus groups, and perform a variety of other types of marketing research.

Methods of Conducting Online Surveys There are several basic methods for conducting online surveys: Web survey systems, survey design and Web hosting sites, and online panel providers.

Web Survey Systems Web survey systems are software systems specifically designed for Web questionnaire construction and delivery. They consist of an integrated questionnaire designer, Web server, database, and data delivery program, designed for use by non-programmers. The Web server distributes the questionnaire and files responses in a database. The user can query the server at any time via the Web for completion statistics, descriptive statistics on responses, and graphical displays of data. Some popular online survey research software packages are Sawtooth CiW, Infopoll, SurveyMonkey, and SurveyPro.

Survey Design and Web Hosting Sites Several Web sites allow the researcher to design a survey online without loading design software. The survey is then administered on the design site's server. Some offer tabulation and analysis packages as well. One popular site that offers Web hosting services is Vovici.

Online Panel Providers Often researchers use online panel providers for a ready-made sample population. Online panel providers such as Survey Sampling International and e-Rewards pre-recruit people who agree to participate in online market research surveys.

Some online panels are created for specific industries and may have a few thousand panel members, while the large commercial online panels have millions of people waiting to be surveyed. When people join online panels, they answer an extensive profiling questionnaire that enables the panel provider to target research efforts to panel members who meet specific criteria.

Online Focus Groups A relatively recent development in qualitative research is the online or cyber focus group. A number of organizations are currently offering this new means of conducting focus groups. The process is fairly simple. The research firm builds a database of respondents via a screening questionnaire on its Web site. When a client comes to a firm with a need for a particular focus group, the firm goes to its database and identifies individuals who appear to qualify. It sends an e-mail message to these individuals, asking them to log on to a particular site at a particular time scheduled for the group. The firm pays them an incentive for their participation.

The firm develops a discussion guide similar to the one used for a conventional focus group, and a moderator runs the group by typing in questions online for all to see. The group operates in an environment similar to that of a chat room so that all participants see all questions and all responses. The firm captures the complete text of the focus group and makes it available for review after the group has finished.

Online focus groups also allow respondents to view things such as a concept statement, a mockup of a print ad, or a short product demonstration video. The moderator simply provides a URL reference for the respondents to go to in another browser window. One of the risks of doing this, however, is that once respondents open another browser, they have "left the room" and the moderator may lose their attention; researchers must hope that respondents will return within the specified amount of time.

More advanced virtual focus group software reserves a frame (section) of the screen for stimuli to be shown. Here, the moderator has control over what is shown in the stimulus area. The advantage of this approach is that the respondent does not have to do any work to see the stimuli.

Advantages of Online Focus Groups Many advantages are claimed for cyber groups:

▸ *Better participation rates:* Typically, online focus groups can be conducted over the course of days; once participants are recruited, they are less likely to pull out due to time conflicts.

▸ *Cost-effectiveness:* Face-to-face focus groups incur costs for facility rental, airfare, hotel, and food. None of these costs is incurred with online focus groups.

▸ *Broad geographic scope:* Time is flexible online; respondents can be gathered from all over the world.

▸ *Accessibility:* Online focus groups give you access to individuals who otherwise might be difficult to recruit (e.g., business travelers, senior executives, mothers with infants).

▸ *Honesty:* From behind their screen names, respondents are anonymous to other respondents and tend to talk more freely about issues that might create inhibitions in a face-to-face group.

© ISTOCKPHOTO.COM/VALERIE LOISELEUX

Web Community Research, Text-Message-Based Research, and Blogging Assignments A Web community is a carefully selected group of consumers who agree to participate in an ongoing dialogue with a particular corporation.[13] All community interaction takes place on a custom-designed Web site. During the life of the community—which may last anywhere from six months to a year or more—community members respond to questions posed by the corporation on a regular basis. In addition to responding to the corporation's questions, community members talk to one another about topics that are of interest to them.

The popularity and power of Web communities initially came from several key benefits. They:

▸▸ engage customers in a space where they are comfortable, allowing clients to interact with them on a deeper level,

▸▸ achieve customer-derived innovations,

▸▸ establish brand advocates who are emotionally invested in a company's success, and

▸▸ offer real-time results, enabling clients to explore ideas that normal time constraints prohibit.

Additionally, Web communities help companies create a customer-focused organization by putting employees into direct contact with consumers from the comfort of their own desks, as well as providing cost-effective, flexible research.

Two other relatively recent developments in Internet marketing research are text-message-based research and blogging assignments. Text-message-based research allows marketers to text a basic question (What are you drinking with lunch today?) and a follow-up to respondents (On a scale of 1 to 9, how much do you like your drink?). Because mobile phones are so prevalent, this type of research can reach most demographics, and it is very quick, resulting in higher feedback rates. For blogging assignments, which are different from consumer-generated blogs (covered below), marketers assign respondents to write a brief blog entry each time they use the product being reviewed. These blogs can span any amount of time and offer marketers a closer look at how consumers interact with products. Additionally, because the technology is relatively inexpensive, assignments can be given to larger numbers of respondents. These blogs are not public and are viewable only by the respondent and the marketer.[14]

The Role of Consumer-Generated Media in Marketing Research

Consumer-generated media (CGM) are media that consumers generate themselves and share among themselves. CGM comes from various sources, such as blogs, message boards, review sites, and podcasts. Because it is consumer based, CGM is trusted more than traditional forms of advertising and promotion.[15]

CGM can be influenced but not controlled by marketers. Nielsen BuzzMetrics is the leading marketing research firm tracking CGM. BrandPulse is BuzzMetrics' most popular product. BrandPulse can tell a company how much "buzz" exists, where online discussion is taking place, the tone of the discussion, and which issues are most important. BrandPulse provides timely understanding of the opinions and trends affecting a company or brand. Depending on the information the customer needs, other BuzzMetrics products can go into further detail, such as detecting who would be a good candidate for relationship marketing programs.[16]

LO 5 Scanner-Based Research

Scanner-based research is a system for gathering information from a single group of respondents by continuously monitoring the advertising, promotion, and pricing they are exposed to and the things they buy. The variables measured are advertising campaigns, coupons, displays, and product prices. The result is a huge database of marketing efforts and consumer behavior.

The two major scanner-based suppliers are Information Resources, Inc. (IRI) and the A. C. Nielsen Company. Each has about half of the market. However, IRI is the founder of scanner-based research. IRI's first product is called **BehaviorScan**. A household panel (a group of 3,000 long-term participants in the research project) has been recruited and maintained in each BehaviorScan town. Each panel member shops with an ID card, which is presented at the checkout in scanner-equipped grocery stores and drugstores, allowing IRI to track electronically each household's purchases, item by item, over time. It uses microcomputers to measure television viewing in each panel household and can send special commercials to panel member television sets. With such a measure of household purchasing, it is possible to manipulate marketing variables, such as television advertising

consumer-generated media (CGM) media that consumers generate and share among themselves

scanner-based research a system for gathering information from a single group of respondents by continuously monitoring the advertising, promotion, and pricing they are exposed to and the things they buy

BehaviorScan a scanner-based research program that tracks the purchases of 3,000 households through store scanners in each research market

InfoScan a scanner-based sales-tracking service for the consumer packaged-goods industry

neuromarketing a field of marketing that studies the body's responses to marketing stimuli

or consumer promotions, or to introduce a new product and analyze real changes in consumer buying behavior.

IRI's most successful product is **InfoScan,** a scanner-based sales-tracking service for the consumer packaged-goods industry. Retail sales, detailed consumer purchasing information (including measurement of store loyalty and total grocery basket expenditures), and promotional activity by manufacturers and retailers are monitored and evaluated for all bar-coded products. Data are collected weekly from more than 70,000 supermarkets, drugstores, and mass merchandisers.[17]

Some companies have begun studying microscopic changes in skin moisture, heart rate, brain waves, and other biometrics to see how consumers react to things such as package designs and ads. This **neuromarketing** approach is a fresh attempt to better understand consumers' responses to promotion and purchase motivations.

LO 6 When Should Marketing Research Be Conducted?

When managers have several possible solutions to a problem, they should not instinctively call for marketing research. In fact, the first decision to make is whether to conduct marketing research at all.

Some companies have been conducting research in certain markets for many years. Such firms understand the characteristics of target customers and their likes and dislikes about existing products. Under these circumstances, further research would be repetitive and waste money. Procter & Gamble, for example, has extensive knowledge of the coffee market. After it conducted initial taste tests with Folgers Instant Coffee, P&G went into national distribution without further research. Sara Lee followed the same strategy with its frozen croissants, as did Quaker Oats with Chewy Granola Bars. This tactic, however, can backfire. Marketers may think they understand a particular market thoroughly and so bypass market research for a product, only to have the product fail and be withdrawn from the market.

If information were available and free, managers would rarely refuse more, but because marketing information can require a great deal of time and expense to accumulate, they might decide to forgo additional information. Ultimately, the willingness to acquire additional decision-making information depends on managers' perceptions of its quality, price, and timing. Research should be undertaken only when the expected value of the information is greater than the cost of obtaining it.

LO 7 Competitive Intelligence

Derived from military intelligence, competitive intelligence is an important tool for helping a firm overcome a competitor's advantage. Specifically, competitive

PICKING TEEN BRAINS FOR MUSIC HITS

Emory University scientists may have given the music industry the next new method of predicting which songs will be hits with teens. They measured **brain response** to a variety of songs and discovered that teenage brains found some songs more rewarding to hear, even if the listeners said that they didn't enjoy the song. Brain activity could accurately predict which songs would sell at least 20,000 copies, and 50 percent of the time, it accurately predicted which songs would sell more than 50,000 copies. This sort of instinct-based research is controversial and still in testing stages, but for the struggling music industry, the idea of having an accurate predictor of hits based on scientific scanning is worth investigating.[18]

SOURCE: Robert Lee Hotz, "Songs Stick in Teens' Heads," *Wall Street Journal,* June 13, 2011.

© ISTOCKPHOTO.COM/MATTJEACOCK

intelligence can help identify the advantage and play a major role in determining how it was achieved.

Competitive intelligence (CI) helps managers assess their competitors and their vendors in order to become more efficient and effective competitors. Intelligence is analyzed information. It becomes decision-making intelligence when it has implications for the organization. For example, a primary competitor may have plans to introduce a product with performance standards equal to those of the company gathering the information but with a 15 percent cost advantage. The new product will reach the market in eight months. This intelligence has important decision-making and policy consequences for management. CI and environmental scanning (see Chapter 2) combine to create marketing intelligence. Marketing intelligence is then used as input into a marketing decision support system.

The Internet is an important resource for gathering CI, but noncomputer sources can be equally valuable. Some examples include company salespeople, industry experts, CI consultants, government agencies, Uniform Commercial Code filings, suppliers, periodicals, the Yellow Pages, and industry trade shows.

competitive intelligence (CI)
an intelligence system that helps managers assess their competition and vendors in order to become more efficient and effective competitors

STUDY TOOLS — CHAPTER 9

Flip to the back of your textbook to:

❑ **Rip out Chapter Review Card**

Log in to the CourseMate for MKTG at cengagebrain.com to:

❑ **Review Key Terms Flash Cards (Print or Online)**

❑ **Review Audio and Visual Summaries**

❑ **Complete both Practice Quizzes to prepare for tests**

❑ **Play "Beat the Clock" and "Quizbowl" to master concepts**

❑ **Complete "Crossword Puzzle" to review key terms**

❑ **Watch the video on "Ogden Publications" for a real company example on Decision Support Systems and Marketing Research**

The product is the starting point in creating a marketing mix.

LO 1 What Is a Product?

AFTER YOU FINISH THIS CHAPTER, GO TO PAGE 177 FOR STUDY TOOLS

The product offering, the heart of an organization's marketing program, is usually the starting point in creating a marketing mix. A marketing manager cannot determine a price, design a promotion strategy, or create a distribution channel until the firm has a product to sell. Moreover, an excellent distribution channel, a persuasive promotion campaign, and a fair price have no value when the product offering is poor or inadequate.

A **product** may be defined as everything, both favorable and unfavorable, that a person receives in an exchange. A product may be a tangible good like a pair of shoes, a service like a haircut, an idea like "don't litter," or any combination of these three. Packaging, style, color, options, and size are some typical product features. Just as important are intangibles such as service, the seller's image, the manufacturer's reputation, and the way consumers believe others will view the product.

To most people, the term *product* means a tangible good. However, services and ideas are also products. (Chapter 12 focuses specifically on the unique aspects of marketing services.) The marketing process identified in Chapter 1 is the same whether the product marketed is a good, a service, an idea, or some combination of these.

product everything, both favorable and unfavorable, that a person receives in an exchange

© FELIPE DUPOUY/STONE/GETTY IMAGES

What do you think?

I pay attention to which brands I choose.

1 STRONGLY DISAGREE   2   3   4   5   6   7 STRONGLY AGREE

LO 2 Types of Consumer Products

Products can be classified as either business (industrial) or consumer products, depending on the buyer's intentions. The key distinction between the two types of products is their intended use. If the intended use is a business purpose, the product is classified as a business or industrial product. As explained in Chapter 7, a **business product**, or **industrial product**, is used to manufacture other goods or services, to facilitate an organization's operations, or to resell to other customers. A **consumer product** is bought to satisfy an individual's personal wants. Sometimes the same item can be classified as either a business or a consumer product, depending on its intended use. Examples include lightbulbs, pencils and paper, and computers.

We need to know about product classifications because business and consumer products are marketed differently. They are marketed to different target markets and tend to use different distribution, promotion, and pricing strategies.

Chapter 7 examined seven categories of business products: major equipment, accessory equipment, component parts, processed materials, raw materials, supplies, and services. This chapter examines an effective way of categorizing consumer products. Although there are several ways to classify them, the most popular approach includes these four types: convenience products, shopping products, specialty products, and unsought products. This approach classifies products according to how much effort is normally used to shop for them.

Convenience Products

A **convenience product** is a relatively inexpensive item that merits little shopping effort—that is, a consumer is unwilling to shop extensively for such an item. Candy, soft drinks, aspirin, small hardware items, dry cleaning, and car washes fall into the convenience product category.

business product (industrial product) a product used to manufacture other goods or services, to facilitate an organization's operations, or to resell to other customers

consumer product a product bought to satisfy an individual's personal wants

convenience product a relatively inexpensive item that merits little shopping effort

shopping product a product that requires comparison shopping because it is usually more expensive than a convenience product and is found in fewer stores

specialty product a particular item for which consumers search extensively and are very reluctant to accept substitutes

Business product or consumer product?

Consumers buy convenience products regularly, usually without much planning. Nevertheless, consumers do know the brand names of popular convenience products, such as Coca-Cola, Bayer aspirin, and Old Spice deodorant. Convenience products normally require wide distribution in order to sell sufficient quantities to meet profit goals. For example, the gum brand Extra is available everywhere, including Walmart, Walgreens, gas stations, newsstands, and vending machines.

Shopping Products

A **shopping product** is usually more expensive than a convenience product and is found in fewer stores. Consumers usually buy a shopping product only after comparing several brands or stores on style, practicality, price, and lifestyle compatibility. They are willing to invest some effort into this process to get the desired benefits.

There are two types of shopping products: homogeneous and heterogeneous. Consumers perceive *homogeneous* shopping products as basically similar—for example, washers, dryers, refrigerators, and televisions. With homogeneous shopping products, consumers typically look for the lowest-priced brand that has the desired features. For example, they might compare Kenmore, Whirlpool, and General Electric refrigerators.

In contrast, consumers perceive *heterogeneous* shopping products as essentially different—for example, furniture, clothing, housing, and universities. Consumers often have trouble comparing heterogeneous shopping products because the prices, quality, and features vary so much. The benefit of comparing heterogeneous shopping products is "finding the best product or brand for me"; this decision is often highly individual. For example, it would be difficult to compare a small, private college with a large, public university.

Specialty Products

When consumers search extensively for a particular item and are very reluctant to accept substitutes, that item is a **specialty product**. Omega watches, Rolls-Royce automobiles, Bose speakers, Ruth's Chris Steak House, and highly specialized forms of medical care are generally considered specialty products.

Marketers of specialty products often use selective, status-conscious advertising to maintain a prod-

© ISTOCKPHOTO.COM/MILOS LUZANIN

uct's exclusive image. Distribution is often limited to one or a very few outlets in a geographic area. Brand names and quality of service are often very important.

Unsought Products

A product unknown to the potential buyer or a known product that the buyer does not actively seek is referred to as an **unsought product**. New products fall into this category until advertising and distribution increase consumer awareness of them.

Some goods are always marketed as unsought items, especially needed products we do not like to think about or care to spend money on. Insurance, burial plots, and similar items require aggressive personal selling and highly persuasive advertising. Salespeople actively seek leads to potential buyers. Because consumers usually do not seek out this type of product, the company must go directly to them through a salesperson, direct mail, or direct response advertising.

LO 3 Product Items, Lines, and Mixes

Rarely does a company sell a single product. More often, it sells a variety of things. A **product item** is a specific version of a product that can be designated as a distinct offering among an organization's products.

Campbell's Cream of Chicken soup is an example of a product item (see Exhibit 10.1).

A group of closely related product items is called a **product line**. For example, the column in Exhibit 10.1 titled "Soups" represents one of Campbell's product lines. Different container sizes and shapes also distinguish items in a product line. Diet Coke, for example, is available in cans and various plastic containers. Each size and each container are separate product items.

An organization's **product mix** includes all the products it sells. All Campbell's products—soups, sauces, frozen entrées, beverages, and biscuits—constitute its product mix. Each product item in the product mix may require a separate marketing strategy. In some cases, however, product lines and even entire product mixes share some marketing strategy components. UPS promotes its various services by demonstrating its commitment to its line of work with the tagline "We [heart] Logistics." Organizations derive several benefits from organizing related items into product lines:

▸▸ *Advertising economies:* Product lines provide economies of scale in advertising. Several products can be advertised under the umbrella of the line. Campbell's can talk about its soup being "M'm, M'm, Good!" and promote the entire line.

unsought product a product unknown to the potential buyer or a known product that the buyer does not actively seek

product item a specific version of a product that can be designated as a distinct offering among an organization's products

product line a group of closely related product items

product mix all products that an organization sells

EXHIBIT 10.1
Campbell's Product Lines and Product Mix

	Soups	Sauces	Frozen Entrées	Beverages	Biscuits
	Cream of Chicken	Cheddar Cheese	Macaroni and Cheese	Tomato Juice	Arnott's:
	Cream of Mushroom	Alfredo	Golden Chicken	V-Fusion	Water Cracker
	Vegetable Beef	Italian Tomato	Fricassee	Juices	Butternut Snap
	Chicken Noodle	Hollandaise	Traditional Lasagna	V8 Splash	Chocolate Ripple
	Tomato				Spicy Fruit Roll
	Bean with Bacon				Chocolate
	Minestrone				Wheaten
	Clam Chowder				
	French Onion				
	and more . . .				

Width of the Product Mix (spanning all product lines)

Depth of the Product Lines — **DEPTH**

SOURCE: Campbell's Web site: http://www.campbellsoup.com.

product mix width
the number of product lines an organization offers

product line depth the number of product items in a product line

product modification
changing one or more of a product's characteristics

▸▸ *Package uniformity:* A product line can benefit from package uniformity. All packages in the line may have a common look and still keep their individual identities. Again, Campbell's soup is a good example.

▸▸ *Standardized components:* Product lines allow firms to standardize components, thus reducing manufacturing and inventory costs. For example, General Motors uses the same parts on many automobile makes and models.

▸▸ *Efficient sales and distribution:* A product line enables sales personnel for companies like Procter & Gamble to provide a full range of choices to customers. Distributors and retailers are often more inclined to stock the company's products if it offers a full line. Transportation and warehousing costs are likely to be lower for a product line than for a collection of individual items.

▸▸ *Equivalent quality:* Purchasers usually expect and believe that all products in a line are about equal in quality. Consumers expect that all Campbell's soups and all Gillette razors will be of similar quality.

Product mix width (or breadth) refers to the number of product lines an organization offers. In Exhibit 10.1, for example, the width of Campbell's product mix is five product lines. **Product line depth** is the number of product items in a product line. As shown in Exhibit 10.1, the sauces product line consists of four product items; the frozen entrée product line includes three product items.

Firms increase the *width* of their product mix to diversify risk. To generate sales and boost profits, firms spread risk across many product lines rather than depend on only one or two. Firms also widen their product mix to capitalize on established reputations. The Fiber One cereal brand extended its name to include yogurt, bread, baking mixes, granola bars, and cottage cheese.

Firms increase the *depth* of their product lines to attract buyers with different preferences, to increase sales and profits by further segmenting the market, to capitalize on economies of scale in production and marketing, and to even out seasonal sales patterns. LG's line of Optimus Smartphones has ten different options, including the Optimus Chic, which is aimed at fashionistas who appreciate sleek curves on their phones.[1]

Adjustments to Product Items, Lines, and Mixes

Over time, firms change product items, lines, and mixes to take advantage of new technical or product devel-

DeBeers uses simple, powerful language to show consumers that for important life decisions (such as marriage), DeBeers provides a quality product that will last a lifetime.

opments or to respond to changes in the environment. They may adjust by modifying products, repositioning products, or extending or contracting product lines.

Product Modification Marketing managers must decide if and when to modify existing products. **Product modification** changes one or more of a product's characteristics:

▸▸ *Quality modification:* change in a product's dependability or durability. Reducing a product's quality may let the manufacturer lower the price and appeal to target markets unable to afford the original product. Conversely, increasing quality can help the firm compete with rival firms. For example, Barnes & Noble offers a color version of its Nook that runs Android apps, allowing it to compete with Apple as well as netbook makers, such as Dell and Asus. Increasing quality can also result in increased brand loyalty, greater ability to raise prices, or new opportunities for market segmentation.

▸▸ *Functional modification:* change in a product's versatility, effectiveness, convenience, or safety. Dish Network and DIRECTV can now provide satellite service to multiple units in apartment buildings with one dish. Previously, each company had to hang a satellite for each unit, which could be unsightly and against apartment codes, but functional improvements in the technology now make satellite service a viable apartment option.[2]

▸▸ *Style modification:* aesthetic product change rather than a quality or functional change. Clothing and auto manufacturers commonly use style modifications to motivate customers to replace products before they are worn out.

Planned obsolescence is a term commonly used to describe the practice of modifying products so that those that have already been sold become obsolete before they actually need replacement. For example, products such as printers and cell phones become obsolete because technology changes so quickly.

Some argue that planned obsolescence is wasteful; some claim it is unethical. Marketers respond that consumers favor style modifications because they like changes in the appearance of goods such as clothing and cars. Marketers also contend that consumers, not manufacturers and marketers, decide when styles are obsolete.

Repositioning Repositioning, as Chapter 8 explained, involves changing consumers' perceptions of a brand. Laundry detergent Woolite is trying to reposition itself as an everyday laundry detergent that will benefit all fabrics, rather than being just for delicate blacks or handwashing. Its new campaign, directed by horror film director and metal musician Rob Zombie, mimics creepy horror films and shows a deformed man "torturing" clothes by stretching, shrinking, and exposing them to bright lights. The company says the goal is to interest women ages 25 to 40 by recalling the horror films of their youth. The ads stand out for being dark and bleak in an industry characterized by Snuggle the bear and cheerful women washing bright clothing.[3] Changing demographics, declining sales, or changes in the social environment often motivate firms to reposition established brands. Disney's 1951 animated *Alice in Wonderland* was a family-friendly cartoon, but in 2010, Disney repositioned Alice by teaming with Tim Burton. They brought Alice, now 19 years old, back to Wonderland in a dark, live-action adventure. To capitalize on Alice's new, dark look, Disney targeted 12- to 22-year-olds with merchandise in Hot Topic, a retail chain with a Goth following.[4]

Product Line Extensions A **product line extension** occurs when a company's management decides to add products to an existing product line in order to compete more broadly in the industry. Hasbro/Mattel has added a series of games using the Scrabble name, some without boards or tiles, such as Scrabble Slam and a version with proper noun usage called Scrabble Trickster.[5]

A company can add too many products, or demand can change for the type of products that were introduced over time. When this happens, a product line is overextended. Product lines can be overextended when:

▸▸ Some products in the line do not contribute to profits because of low sales or cannibalize sales of other items in the line.

▸▸ Manufacturing or marketing resources are disproportionately allocated to slow-moving products.

▸▸ Some items in the line are obsolete because of new product entries in the line or new products offered by competitors.

Product Line Contraction Sometimes, marketers can get carried away with product extensions. (Does the world really need 31 varieties of Head & Shoulders shampoo?) Contracting product lines is a strategic way to deal with overextension. For example, when Procter & Gamble's Pantene brand lost 9 percent of sales in 2009, P&G marketing research showed that shoppers were overwhelmed by the wall of white. Pantene had 165 different products grouped into 14 collections. In an effort to regain the lost sales, P&G cut product offerings to 120 items in four groups.[6]

Three major benefits are likely when a firm contracts overextended product lines. First, resources become concentrated on the most important products. Second, managers no longer waste resources trying to improve the sales and profits of poorly performing products. Third, new product items have a greater chance of being successful because more financial and human resources are available to manage them.

LO 4 Branding

The success of any business or consumer product depends in part on the target market's ability to distinguish one product from another. Branding is the main tool marketers use to distinguish their products from those of the competition.

planned obsolescence the practice of modifying products so those that have already been sold become obsolete before they actually need replacement

product line extension adding additional products to an existing product line in order to compete more broadly in the industry

brand a name, term, symbol, design, or combination thereof that identifies a seller's products and differentiates them from competitors' products

brand name that part of a brand that can be spoken, including letters, words, and numbers

brand mark the elements of a brand that cannot be spoken

brand equity the value of company and brand names

global brand a brand that obtains at least a third of its earnings from outside its home country, is recognizable outside its home base of customers, and has publicly available marketing and financial data

brand loyalty consistent preference for one brand over all others

manufacturer's brand the brand name of a manufacturer

private brand a brand name owned by a wholesaler or a retailer

A **brand** is a name, term, symbol, design, or combination thereof that identifies a seller's products and differentiates them from competitors' products. A **brand name** is that part of a brand that can be spoken, including letters (GM, YMCA), words (Chevrolet), and numbers (WD-40, 7-Eleven). The elements of a brand that cannot be spoken are called the **brand mark**—for example, the well-known Mercedes-Benz and Delta Air Lines symbols.

Benefits of Branding

Branding has three main purposes: product identification, repeat sales, and new-product sales. The most important purpose is *product identification*. Branding allows marketers to distinguish their products from all others. Many brand names are familiar to consumers and indicate quality.

The term **brand equity** refers to the value of company and brand names. A brand that has high awareness, perceived quality, and brand loyalty among customers has high brand equity. Starbucks, Subaru, and Apple are companies with high brand equity. A brand with strong brand equity is a valuable asset. For example, Oprah Winfrey leverages her personal brand (her name) to sell her magazines; create shows (Dr. Phil owes his celebrity to her); and develop schools, charities, and cable networks.[7]

The term **global brand** refers to a brand that obtains at least a third of its earnings from outside its home country, is recognizable outside its home base of customers, and has publicly available marketing and financial data. Yum! Brands, which owns Pizza Hut, KFC, and Taco Bell, is a good example of a company that has developed strong global brands. Yum! believes that it has to adapt its restaurants to local tastes and different cultural and political climates. In Japan, for instance, KFC sells tempura crispy strips. In northern England, KFC focuses on gravy and potatoes, and in Thailand it offers rice with soy or sweet chili sauce.

The best generator of *repeat sales* is satisfied customers. Branding helps consumers identify products they wish to buy again and avoid those they do not. **Brand loyalty**, a consistent preference for one brand over all others, is quite high in some product categories. More than half the consumers in product categories such as cigarettes, mayonnaise, toothpaste, coffee, headache remedies, bath soap, and ketchup are loyal to one brand. Many students go to college and purchase the same brands they used at home rather than choosing by price. Brand identity is essential to developing brand loyalty.

The third main purpose of branding is to *facilitate new-product sales*. Having a well-known and respected company and brand name is extremely useful when introducing new products.

Branding Strategies

Firms face complex branding decisions. Firms may choose to follow a policy of using manufacturers' brands, private (distributor) brands, or both. In either case, they must then decide among a policy of individual branding (different brands for different products), family branding (common names for different products), or a combination of individual branding and family branding.

Manufacturers' Brands versus Private Brands The brand name of a manufacturer—such as Kodak, La-Z-Boy, and Fruit of the Loom—is called a **manufacturer's brand**. Sometimes "national brand" is used as a synonym for "manufacturer's brand." This term is not always accurate, however, because many manufacturers serve only regional markets. Using "manufacturer's brand" precisely defines the brand's owner.

A **private brand**, also known as a private label or store brand, is a brand name owned by a wholesaler or a retailer. Walmart's Great Value brand is a popular private label. Walgreens sells Walgreens brand products, and this year it is advertising them on television and with several bloggers. The company emphasizes the comparison with brand name quality with a satisfaction guarantee.[8] Perceptions about quality are part of the reason for the success of private brands. Nielsen Company reported that unit sales of private label goods increased 8 percent from 2008 to 2010,

© SAD/SHUTTERSTOCK.COM

while sales of brand name products decreased about 4 percent. Another recent study found that 63 percent of consumers plan to buy private labels even after the economy rebounds.[9]

Retailers love consumers' greater acceptance of private brands. Because overhead is low and there are no marketing costs, private label products bring 10 percent higher profit margins, on average, than manufacturers' brands. More than that, a trusted store brand can differentiate a chain from its competitors. Exhibit 10.2 illustrates key issues that wholesalers and retailers should consider in deciding whether to sell manufacturers' brands or private brands. Many firms offer a combination of both. Instead of marketing private brands as cheaper and inferior to manufacturers' brands, many retailers are creating and promoting their own **captive brands**. These brands carry no evidence of the store's affiliation, are manufactured by a third party, and are sold exclusively at the chains. This strategy allows the retailer to ask a price similar to manufacturers' brands, and the captive brands are typically displayed alongside mainstream products. For example, Private Selection® is Kroger's line of products designed to meet consumer desire for upscale brands. Private Selection® boasts that it will meet or beat the manufacturers' brands in terms of quality.[10]

Individual Brands versus Family Brands Many companies use different brand names for different products, a practice referred to as **individual branding**. Companies use individual brands when their products vary greatly in use or performance. For instance, it would not make sense to use the same brand name for a pair of dress socks and a baseball bat. Procter & Gamble targets different segments of the laundry detergent market with Bold, Cheer, Dash, Dreft, Era, Gain, Ivory Snow, Oxydol, Solo, and Tide.

In contrast, a company that markets several different products under the same brand name is practicing **family branding**. Jack Daniel's family brand includes whiskey, coffee, mustard, playing cards, and clothing lines.

Co-branding **Co-branding** entails placing two or more brand names on a product or its package. Three common types of co-branding are ingredient branding, cooperative branding, and complementary branding. *Ingredient branding* identifies the brand of a part that makes up the product—for example, Procter & Gamble has developed Mr. Clean Disinfecting Wipes with Febreze (a scent) Freshness. Febreze is also

captive brand a brand manufactured by a third party for an exclusive retailer, without evidence of that retailer's affiliation

individual branding using different brand names for different products

family branding marketing several different products under the same brand name

co-branding placing two or more brand names on a product or its package

---

EXHIBIT 10.2

Comparison of Manufacturers' and Private Brands from the Reseller's Perspective

Key Advantages of Carrying Manufacturers' Brands	Key Advantages of Carrying Private Brands
• Heavy advertising to the consumer by manufacturers such as Procter & Gamble helps develop strong consumer loyalties.	• A wholesaler or retailer can usually earn higher profits on its own brand. In addition, because the private brand is exclusive, there is less pressure to mark down the price to meet competition.
• Well-known manufacturers' brands, such as Kodak and Fisher-Price, can attract new customers and enhance the dealer's (wholesaler's or retailer's) prestige.	• A manufacturer can decide to drop a brand or a reseller at any time or even become a direct competitor to its dealers.
• Many manufacturers offer rapid delivery, enabling the dealer to carry less inventory.	• A private brand ties the customer to the wholesaler or retailer. A person who wants a DieHard battery must go to Sears.
• If a dealer happens to sell a manufacturer's brand of poor quality, the customer may simply switch brands and remain loyal to the dealer.	• Wholesalers and retailers have no control over the intensity of distribution of manufacturers' brands. Walmart store managers don't have to worry about competing with other sellers of Sam's American Choice products or Ol' Roy dog food. They know that these brands are sold only in Walmart and Sam's Club stores.

© CENGAGE LEARNING 2013

trademark the exclusive right to use a brand or part of a brand

service mark a trademark for a service

generic product name identifies a product by class or type and cannot be trademarked

co-branded with Tide, Bounce, and Downy.[11] *Cooperative branding* occurs when two brands receiving equal treatment (in the context of an advertisement) borrow from each other's brand equity. A promotional contest jointly sponsored by Ramada Inn, American Express, and Continental Airlines used cooperative branding. Guests at Ramada who paid with an American Express card were automatically entered in a contest and were eligible to win more than a hundred getaways for two at any Ramada in the continental United States and round-trip airfare from Continental. Finally, with *complementary branding*, products are advertised or marketed together to suggest usage, such as a spirits brand (Seagram's) and a compatible mixer (7-Up).

Co-branding is a useful strategy when a combination of brand names enhances the prestige or perceived value of a product or when it benefits brand owners and users. For example, people perceive a higher value for a Glad trash bag that has Febreze between its two layers of plastic than for Ruffies trash bags that use baking soda to block odor.[12] Co-branding may be used to increase a company's presence in markets where it has little or no market share.

IMAGE COURTESY OF THE ADVERTISING ARCHIVES

GET BETTER, FASTER.
GET FREE.

NIKE FREE'S ENGINEERED FLEXIBILITY HELPS IGNITE THE MUSCLES IN YOUR BODY FROM THE GROUND UP FOR IMPROVED STRENGTH, BALANCE AND FLEXIBILITY – SO YOU CAN GET EVEN MORE FROM YOUR WORKOUT. AND WHEN COMBINED WITH ONE OF THE 60 CUSTOM BUILT WORKOUTS FROM THE NEW NIKE TRAINING CLUB APP, YOU CAN REACH YOUR GOALS WHATEVER THEY ARE. EVER WANTED A PERSONAL TRAINER IN YOUR POCKET? NOW YOU'VE GOT ONE.

NIKE FREE
NIKE.COM/FREE

This ad promotes Nike+iPod software that allows walkers and runners to keep track of the distance and pace of workouts.

Trademarks

A **trademark** is the exclusive right to use a brand or part of a brand. Others are prohibited from using the brand without permission. A **service mark** performs the same function for services, such as H&R Block and Weight Watchers. Parts of a brand or other product identification may qualify for trademark protection. Some examples are:

▸▸ Sounds, such as the MGM lion's roar.

▸▸ Shapes, such as the Jeep front grille and the Coca-Cola bottle.

▸▸ Ornamental colors or designs, such as the decoration on Nike tennis shoes, the black-and-copper color combination of a Duracell battery, Levi's small tag on the left side of the rear pocket of its jeans, or the cutoff black cone on the top of Cross pens.

▸▸ Catchy phrases, such as Prudential's "Own a piece of the rock," Mountain Dew's "Do the Dew," and Nike's "Just Do It!"

▸▸ Abbreviations, such as Bud, Coke, or The Met.

It is important to understand that trademark rights come from use rather than registration. An intent-to-use application is filed with the U.S. Patent and Trademark Office, and a company must have a genuine intention to use the mark when it files and must actually use it within three years of the granting of the application. Trademark protection typically lasts for ten years.[13] To renew the trademark, the company must prove it is using the mark. Rights to a trademark last as long as the mark is used. Normally, if the firm does not use it for two years, the trademark is considered abandoned, and a new user can claim exclusive ownership of the mark.

In November 1999, legislation went into effect that explicitly applies trademark law to the online world. This law includes financial penalties for those who violate trademarks or register an otherwise trademarked term as a domain name.[14]

Companies that fail to protect their trademarks face the possibility that their product names will become generic. A **generic product name** identifies a product by class or type and cannot be trademarked. Former brand names that were not sufficiently protected by their owners and were subsequently declared to be generic product names by U.S. courts include aspirin, cellophane, linoleum, thermos, kerosene, monopoly, cola, and shredded wheat.

Companies such as Rolls-Royce, Cross, Xerox, Levi Strauss, Frigidaire, and McDonald's aggressively enforce their trademarks. Rolls-Royce, Coca-Cola, and Xerox even run newspaper and magazine ads stating that their names are trademarks and should not be used as descriptive or generic terms. When Apple introduced its cloud-based storage services, iCloud, a company called iCloud Communications, which offers similar services and has been in business since 2005, filed a trademark infringement lawsuit against Apple. iCloud Communications claims that Apple's iCloud not only is confusing potential customers, but is actively detracting from iCloud Communications' business.[15]

To try to stem the number of trademark infringements, violations carry steep penalties. Despite the risk of incurring a penalty, infringement lawsuits are still common. Serious conflict can occur when brand names resemble one another too closely. Bacardi's Havana Club rum won a trademark victory over Pernod Ricard in 2010. Pernod also sells Havana Club rum outside the United States. Bacardi only sells Havana Club rum in the United States and Puerto Rico, where

it is distilled, so there is little brand overlap in their respective markets, but the trademark dispute has been going on since 1996. Pernod filed an appeal after the 2010 decision.[16]

Companies must also contend with fake or unauthorized brands. Knockoffs of trademarked clothing lines are easy to find in cheap shops all over the world, and loose imitations are found in some reputable department stores as well. Golf equipment counterfeited in China has recently become more common, accounting for a cumulative price tag of more than $590,000 in 2011. As online shopping has increased, counterfeiters are more frequently selling directly to the customer.[17]

In Europe, you can sue counterfeiters only if your brand, logo, or trademark is formally registered. Until recently, formal registration was required in each country in which a company sought protection. A company can now register its trademark in all European Union (EU) member countries with one application.

LO5 Packaging

Packages have always served a practical function— that is, they hold contents together and protect goods as they move through the distribution channel. Today, however, packaging is also a container for promoting the product and making it easier and safer to use.

Packaging Functions

The three most important functions of packaging are to contain and protect products; promote products; and facilitate the storage, use, and convenience of products. A fourth function of packaging that is becoming increasingly important is to facilitate recycling and reduce environmental damage.

Containing and Protecting Products The most obvious function of packaging is to contain products that are liquid, granular, or otherwise divisible. Packaging also enables manufacturers, wholesalers, and retailers to market products in specific quantities, such as ounces.

Physical protection is another obvious function of packaging. Most products are handled several times between the time they are manufactured, harvested, or otherwise produced and the time they are consumed or used. Many products are also shipped, stored, and inspected several times between production and

Julius Sämann Ltd., which owns the rights to the famous LITTLE TREES air fresheners, and CAR-FRESHNER Corporation, its U.S. licensee, use ads like this one to discourage unauthorized copying of their intellectual property.

This is privately owned property.

So is **this,**

and **this,**

and **this,**

and **this...**

...no matter how you use it.

The LITTLE TREES® design is a registered trademark. This means it can only be used by the trademark owner (that's us) and those who have permission. In other words, it is illegal for you to use our trademark without our consent. To ask permission, e-mail legal@little-trees.com.

www.little-trees.com

The Tree design, LITTLE TREES and CAR-FRESHNER are trademarks. © 2011 by Julius Sämann Ltd.

THE TREE DESIGN, LITTLE TREES AND CAR-FRESHNER ARE TRADEMARKS OF JULIUS SÄMANN LTD. AND ARE USED WITH PERMISSION. © 2011 JULIUS SÄMANN LTD.

consumption. Some, like milk, need to be refrigerated. Others, like beer, are sensitive to light. Still others, like medicines and bandages, need to be kept sterile. Packages protect products from breakage, evaporation, spillage, spoilage, light, heat, cold, infestation, and many other conditions.

Promoting Products Packaging does more than identify the brand, list the ingredients, specify features, and give directions. A package differentiates a product from competing products and may associate a new product with a family of other products from the same manufacturer. Miracle Whip recently redesigned its packaging with a more youthful style, using just its initials (MW) to encourage 18- to 35-year-olds to use the tangy mayo alternative and to differentiate the brand from other mayonnaise packages. The package redesign dovetailed with a marketing campaign spreading the word that mayo is "boring" through billboards in EA's *Skate 3* video game and product placement in Lady Gaga music videos.[18]

Packages use designs, colors, shapes, and materials to try to influence consumers' perceptions and buying behavior. For example, marketing research shows that health-conscious consumers are likely to think that any food is probably good for them as long as it comes in green packaging. Packaging can also influence consumer perceptions of quality and/or prestige—it even has a measurable effect on sales. For example, P&G designers strategically focus on package designs in order to attract consumers while they are shopping. Designers spent time researching consumer preferences and behaviors before P&G's new Febreze Home Collection was developed. Since introducing the line, P&G gained two share points in the air freshener category.[19]

Facilitating Storage, Use, and Convenience Wholesalers and retailers prefer packages that are easy to ship, store, and stock on shelves. They also like packages that protect products, prevent spoilage or breakage, and extend the product's shelf life.

Consumers' requirements for storage, use, and convenience cover many dimensions. Consumers are constantly seeking items that are easy to handle, open, and reclose, although some consumers want packages that are tamperproof or childproof. Research indicates that hard-to-open packages are among consumers' top complaints—especially when it comes to clamshell electronics packaging. As oil prices force the cost of plastics used in packaging skyward, companies such as Target and Walmart are pushing suppliers to do away with excess packaging. Clamshell packaged items have been the first to experience repackaging—lightbulbs, Swiss army knives, USB cables, and scissors are being packed with less plastic, making them easier to access and keeping costs down.[20] Such packaging innovations as zipper tear strips, hinged lids, tab slots, screw-on tops, and pour spouts were introduced to solve these and other problems. Easy openings are especially important for kids and aging baby boomers.

STEALING BACK NOSES

Kleenex brand, with its dominant share of the facial tissue market, has seen some losses to less expensive store brands over the past year. However, Kleenex has a packaging advantage over its imitators: Kleenex sells style along with its facial tissue. During the summer months, Kleenex sells wedge-shaped tissue boxes that look like fruit slices: watermelon, orange, and lime slices. Each box looks fetching on a picnic table, and the triangular size fits more easily among other picnic items than the traditional square box. Kleenex also offers wallpaper-inspired boxes and a number of other seasonal varieties of the tissue holders. The result: not only does Kleenex have a 43 percent market share, but only 12 percent of customers cover their Kleenex boxes, down from 16 percent in 1986.[21]

SOURCE: Andrew Newman, "A Sharp Focus on Design When the Package is Part of the Product," *New York Times*, July 8, 2010.

© TERRI MILLER/E-VISUAL COMMUNICATIONS, INC.

Some firms use packaging to segment markets. For example, a C&H sugar carton with an easy-to-pour, reclosable top is targeted to consumers who don't do a lot of baking and are willing to pay at least 20 cents more for the package. Different-sized packages appeal to heavy, moderate, and light users. Campbell's soup is packaged in single-serving cans aimed at the elderly and singles market segments. Packaging convenience can increase a product's utility and, therefore, its market share and profits.

Facilitating Recycling and Reducing Environmental Damage One of the most important packaging issues today is eco-consciousness, a trend that has recently been in and out of consumer and media attention. Studies conflict as to whether consumers will pay more for eco-friendly packaging, though consumers repeatedly iterate the desire to purchase such products. One New Jersey marketing firm released a study revealing that, while customers reported increased interest in buying products made from recycled materials, only 17 percent said that they checked a package to see if it was recyclable before buying it.[22] Some firms use their packaging to target environmentally concerned market segments. For example, in Canada Frito-Lay introduced 100 percent compostable bags for SunChips with a label from the Biodegradable Products Institute (BPI) to remind consumers to compost the chip bags. BPI has a labeling program that certifies that the products carrying the label will degrade completely in commercial compost facilities. Programs like these help educate manufacturers, legislators, and consumers about the benefits of composting and how to do it.[23]

Labeling

An integral part of any package is its label. Labeling generally takes one of two forms: persuasive or informational. **Persuasive labeling** focuses on a promotional theme or logo, and consumer information is secondary. Note that the standard promotional claims—such as "new," "improved," and "super"—are no longer very persuasive. Consumers have been saturated with "newness" and thus discount these claims.

Informational labeling, in contrast, is designed to help consumers make proper product selections and lower their cognitive dissonance after the purchase. Most major furniture manufacturers affix labels to their wares that explain the products' construction features, such as type of frame, number of coils, and fabric characteristics. The Nutritional Labeling and Education Act of 1990 mandated detailed nutritional information on most food packages and standards for health claims on food packaging. An important outcome of this legislation has been guidelines from the Food and Drug Administration for using terms such as *low fat*, *light*, *reduced cholesterol*, *low sodium*, *low calorie*, *low carb*, and *fresh*. Getting the right information is very important to consumers, and one company wants to help consumers shop smart. NuVal, LLC ranks supermarket products on a scale from 1 to 100 based on nutritional information presented in on-pack labels. A higher score indicates higher nutritional value. The NuVal score is placed on the shelf label next to the price in stores paying a licensing fee. The scores allow consumers to easily compare the nutritional elements of packaged foods.[24]

Greenwashing There are numerous products in every product category that use *greenwashing* to try and sell products. Greenwashing is when a product or company attempts to give the impression of environmental friendliness whether or not it is environmentally friendly.

As consumer demand for "green" products appeared to escalate, "green" certifications proliferated. Companies could create their own certifications and logos, resulting in more than 300 possible certification labels, ranging in price from free to thousands of dollars. Consumer distrust and confusion caused the Federal Trade Commission to issue new rules. Starting in late 2011, new regulations apply to labeling products with "green" certification logos. If the same company that produced the product performed the certification, that relationship must be clearly marked. This benefits organizations such as Green Seal, which uses unbiased, third-party scientists and experts to verify claims about emissions or biodegradability, and hopes to increase consumer confidence in "green" products.[25]

Universal Product Codes

The **universal product codes (UPCs)** that appear on most items in supermarkets and other high-volume outlets were first introduced in 1974. Because the numerical codes appear as a series of thick and thin vertical lines, they are often called *bar codes*. The lines are read by computerized optical scanners that match codes with brand names, package sizes, and prices.

persuasive labeling a type of package labeling that focuses on a promotional theme or logo, and consumer information is secondary

informational labeling a type of package labeling designed to help consumers make proper product selections and lower their cognitive dissonance after the purchase

universal product codes (UPCs) a series of thick and thin vertical lines (bar codes), readable by computerized optical scanners, that represent numbers used to track products

NOT MILK?

As health concerns and alternative eating styles increase, so do the varieties of milk and dairy alternatives. These products are made from **plant-based products** and include soy milk, rice milk, almond milk, cheese alternatives, and soy-based ice creams. The National Milk Producers Federation (NMPF) has petitioned the Food and Drug Administration (FDA) to stop producers of nondairy foods from using terms such as *milk, cheese,* and *ice cream* because they do not accurately describe the products and might cause consumer confusion. The NMPF contends that rather than using the traditional dairy names, these products should be labeled "artificial milk" or "imitation milk."[26]

SOURCES: Sherry F. Colb, "'Not Milk?': Dairy Petitions the FDA to Block Labels Like 'Soy Milk' on Non-Dairy Products," *Findlaw*, May 12, 2010; Betsy Friauf, "Not Milk?" *Star-Telegram*, July 24, 2010, D1.

© SMIT/SHUTTERSTOCK.COM

They also print information on cash register tapes and help retailers rapidly and accurately prepare records of customer purchases, control inventories, and track sales. The UPC system and scanners are also used in scanner-based research (see Chapter 9).

LO 6 Global Issues in Branding and Packaging

When planning to enter a foreign market with an existing product, a firm has three options for handling the brand name:

▸▸ *One brand name everywhere:* This strategy is useful when the company markets mainly one product and the brand name does not have negative connotations in any local market. The Coca-Cola Company uses a one-brand-name strategy in more than 195 countries around the world. The advantages of a one-brand-name strategy are greater identification of the product from market to market and ease of coordinating promotion from market to market.

▸▸ *Adaptations and modifications:* A one-brand-name strategy is not possible when the name cannot be pronounced in the local language, when the brand name is owned by someone else, or when the brand name has a negative or vulgar connotation in the local language. The Iranian detergent "Barf," for example, might encounter some problems in the U.S. market.

▸▸ *Different brand names in different markets:* Local brand names are often used when translation or pronunciation problems occur, when the marketer wants the brand to appear to be a local brand, or when regulations require localization. Gillette's Silkience hair conditioner is called Soyance in France and Sientel in Italy. Coca-Cola's Sprite brand had to be renamed Kin in Korea to satisfy a government prohibition on the unnecessary use of foreign words.

In addition to global branding decisions, companies must consider global packaging needs. Three aspects of packaging that are especially important in international marketing are labeling, aesthetics, and climate considerations. The major *labeling* concern is properly translating ingredient, promotional, and instructional information on labels. Care must also be employed in meeting all local labeling requirements. Several years ago, an Italian judge ordered that all bottles of Coca-Cola be removed from retail shelves because the ingredients were not properly labeled. Labeling is also harder in countries like Belgium and Finland, which require packaging to be bilingual.

Package *aesthetics* may also require some attention. Even though simple visual elements of the brand, such as a symbol or logo, can be a standardizing element across products and countries, marketers must stay attuned to cultural traits in host countries. For example, colors may have different connotations. Red is associated with witchcraft in some countries, green may be a sign of danger, and white may be symbolic of death. Such cultural differences could necessitate a packaging change if colors are chosen for another country's interpretation. In the United States, green typically symbolizes an eco-friendly product, but that packaging could keep customers away in a country where green indicates danger. Aesthetics also influence package size. Soft drinks are not sold in six-packs in countries that lack refrigeration. In some countries, products such as detergent may be bought only in small quantities because of a lack of storage space. Other products, such as cigarettes, may be bought in small quantities, and even single units, because of the low purchasing power of buyers.

Extreme climates and long-distance shipping necessitate sturdier and more durable packages for goods sold overseas. Spillage, spoilage, and breakage are all more important concerns when products are shipped long distances or frequently handled during shipping and storage. Packages may also have to ensure a longer product life if the time between production and consumption lengthens significantly.

LO7 Product Warranties

Just as a package is designed to protect the product, a **warranty** protects the buyer and gives essential information about the product. A warranty confirms the quality or performance of a good or service. An **express warranty** is a written guarantee. Express warranties range from simple statements—such as "100-percent cotton" (a guarantee of quality) and "complete satisfaction guaranteed" (a statement of performance)—to extensive documents written in technical language. In contrast, an **implied warranty** is an unwritten guarantee that the good or service is fit for the purpose for which it was sold. All sales have an implied warranty under the Uniform Commercial Code.

Congress passed the Magnuson-Moss Warranty–Federal Trade Commission Improvement Act in 1975 to help consumers understand warranties and get action from manufacturers and dealers. A manufacturer that promises a full warranty must meet certain minimum standards, including repair "within a reasonable time and without charge" of any defects and replacement of the merchandise or a full refund if the product does not work "after a reasonable number of attempts" at repair. Any warranty that does not live up to this tough prescription must be "conspicuously" promoted as a limited warranty.

> **warranty** a confirmation of the quality or performance of a good or service
>
> **express warranty** a written guarantee
>
> **implied warranty** an unwritten guarantee that the good or service is fit for the purpose for which it was sold

STUDY TOOLS CHAPTER 10

Flip to the back of your textbook to:

❏ **Rip out Chapter Review Card**

Log in to the CourseMate for MKTG at cengagebrain.com to:

❏ **Review Key Terms Flash Cards (Print or Online)**

❏ **Review Audio and Visual Summaries**

❏ **Complete both Practice Quizzes to prepare for tests**

❏ **Play "Beat the Clock" and "Quizbowl" to master concepts**

❏ **Complete "Crossword Puzzle" to review key terms**

❏ **Watch the video on "Recycline" for a real company example on Product Concepts**

The average fast-moving consumer goods company introduces 70 to 80 new products per year.

AFTER YOU FINISH THIS CHAPTER, GO TO PAGE 192 FOR STUDY TOOLS

© JASPER WHITE/STONE/GETTY IMAGES

LO 1 The Importance of New Products

New products are important to sustain growth, increase revenues and profits, and replace obsolete items. Research by *Business Week* and the Boston Consulting Group revealed that the world's 25 most innovative companies have higher average stock returns and higher average revenue growth than companies that were not included in this group.[1] The *Bloomberg Businessweek*–Boston Consulting Group's list includes firms such as Apple, Google, Microsoft, IBM, and Toyota.[2] These firms are known for innovative products. Other firms on the list are known for innovative business models, innovative customer experience, and/or innovative processes.[3]

new product a product new to the world, the market, the producer, the seller, or some combination of these

Categories of New Products

The term **new product** is somewhat confusing because its meaning varies widely. Actually, the term has several "correct" definitions. A product can be new to the world, to the market, to the producer or seller, or some combination of these. There are six categories of new products:

▸▸ *New-to-the-world products (also called discontinuous innovations):* These products create an entirely new market. For example, a new virtual cane uses sonarlike technology and vibrations to give blind and visually impaired users an idea of the spatial layout of a room. The strength of the vibrations indicates the proximity of obstacles. This product is

What do you think?

Getting the newest products is always extremely exciting.

1 | 2 | 3 | 4 | 5 | 6 | 7
STRONGLY DISAGREE   STRONGLY AGREE

Find out what others think at the CourseMate for MKTG. Log in at cengagebrain.com.

intended to be a techonological replacement for traditional canes.[4] New-to-the-world products represent the smallest category of new products.

▸▸ *New product lines:* These products, which the firm has not previously offered, allow it to enter an established market. For example, Moleskine's first products were simple black-covered journals. Since then, the company has expanded into pens, travel bags, and even digital creative tools available on the iPhone and iPad.[5]

▸▸ *Additions to existing product lines:* This category includes new products that supplement a firm's established line. Nintendo added to its Wii line of consoles by introducing the Wii U, which uses a new controller with a touch screen, expanding the way that gamers can interact within the game.

▸▸ *Improvements or revisions of existing products:* The "new and improved" product may be significantly or only slightly changed. Procter & Gamble's new "Dry Max" technology for Pampers Swaddlers and Cruisers diapers, Ariel and Dash laundry detergents with Actilift to help prevent stains from setting, and a reformulation of Pantene shampoo/conditioner are examples of new and improved products.[6]

Pepsi introduced a new skinny can at New York Fashion Week, which classifies as a new product with new packaging.

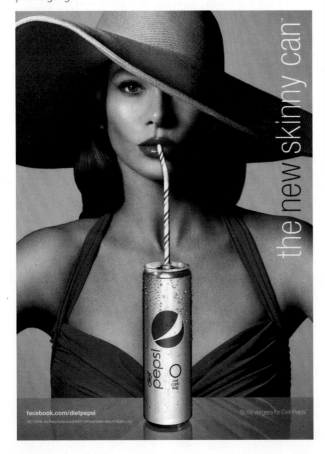

the new skinny can™

diet pepsi O cal carb sug

facebook.com/dietpepsi

Sofia Vergara for Diet Pepsi™

▸▸ *Repositioned products:* These are existing products targeted at new markets or market segments, or ones repositioned to change the current market's perception of the product or company, which may be done to boost declining sales. Spanish leather-goods brand Loewe, known for its studded, tasseled, and patterned handbags, is hoping to change how customers think of the brand and reposition the brand for simplicity with a leather version of a brown paper shopping bag without tassels, pockets, clasps, or finery.[7] Clothing retailer Talbots decided to reposition from an outlet targeted at middle- and upper-class suburban ladies to a more youthful position. Its research revealed that women 65 years of age and older thought the brand was for "someone older." Talbots is working on a complete merchandise and image overhaul.[8]

▸▸ *Lower-priced products:* This category refers to products that provide performance similar to competing brands at a lower price. HP LaserJet 3100 is a scanner, copier, printer, and fax machine combined. This new product is priced lower than many conventional color copiers and much lower than the combined price of the four items purchased separately.

LO 2 The New-Product Development Process

The management consulting firm Booz Allen Hamilton has studied the new-product development process for more than 30 years. Analyzing five major studies undertaken during this period, the firm has concluded that the companies most likely to succeed in developing and introducing new products are those that take the following actions:

▸▸ Make the long-term commitment needed to support innovation and new-product development.

▸▸ Use a company-specific approach, driven by corporate objectives and strategies, with a well-defined new-product strategy at its core.

▸▸ Capitalize on experience to achieve and maintain competitive advantage.

▸▸ Establish an environment—a management style, organizational structure, and degree of top management support—conducive to achieving company-specific new-product and corporate objectives.

Most companies follow a formal new-product development process, usually starting with a new-

IMAGE COURTESY OF THE ADVERTISING ARCHIVES

product strategy. Exhibit 11.1 traces the seven-step process, which is discussed in detail in this section. The exhibit is funnel shaped to highlight the fact that each stage acts as a screen. The purpose is to filter out unworkable ideas.

New-Product Strategy

A **new-product strategy** links the new-product development process with the objectives of the marketing department, the business unit, and the corporation. A new-product strategy must be compatible with these objectives, and in turn, all three of the objectives must be consistent with one another.

A new-product strategy is part of the organization's overall marketing strategy. It sharpens the focus and provides general guidelines for generating, screening, and evaluating new-product ideas. The new-product strategy specifies the roles that new products must play in the organization's overall plan and describes the characteristics of products the organization wants to offer and the markets it wants to serve.

In the traditional development process of new products, many versions of a core idea are discussed, tested, winnowed, and retested until a winning product emerges. Businesses should expect four out of five new products to fail under a strict traditional model.[9] Nevertheless, companies continue to work to innovate. Following a slow year in 2009, leading firms such as Procter & Gamble, Kimberly-Clark, Energizer Holdings, and Unilever committed to increasing new-product activity in 2010.[10]

new-product strategy a plan that links the new-product development process with the objectives of the marketing department, the business unit, and the corporation

Idea Generation

New-product ideas come from many sources, including customers, employees, distributors, competitors, vendors, research and development (R&D), and consultants.

▸ *Customers:* The marketing concept suggests that customers' wants and needs should be the springboard for developing new products. Companies can derive insight from listening to Internet chatter or reading blogs, which often indicate early trends or areas consumers are interested in seeing develop or change. Another approach for generating new-product ideas is using what some companies are calling "customer innovation centers." The idea is to provide a forum for meeting with customers and directly involving them in the innovation process. Dr. John Horn, vice president for research and development in a 3M division, says that the goal is to understand what customers are trying to accomplish instead of what they say they need.[11] Customers might be better at designing products than elite teams of product designers.

▸ *Employees:* Marketing personnel—advertising and marketing research employees, as well as salespeople—often create new-product ideas because they analyze and are involved in the marketplace. Encouraging employees from different divisions to exchange ideas is also a useful strategy. When the R&D team at West Paw Design had writer's block, the team held a contest for the company's 36 employees to design and produce a prototype for a new product. Now it's an annual contest, and the prototype with the most votes enters the development process. Many don't make it to stores, but some do, like the Eco Nap, a dog bed made out of recycled materials, created by a team in the shipping department. The result is an influx of ideas and encouragement across disciplines.[12]

Some firms reward employees for coming up with creative new ideas. In *Bloomberg Businessweek's* annual ranking of the most innovative companies, 15 of the top 50 are Asian, up from only 5 in 2006. The increase isn't surprising when you look at the

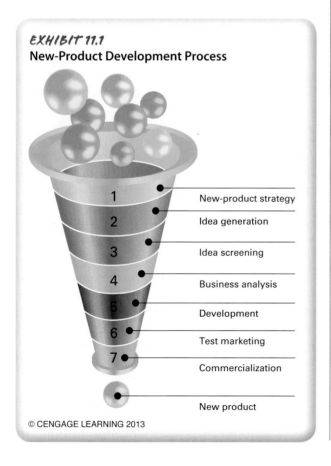

EXHIBIT 11.1
New-Product Development Process

1	New-product strategy
2	Idea generation
3	Idea screening
4	Business analysis
5	Development
6	Test marketing
7	Commercialization
	New product

© CENGAGE LEARNING 2013

© VITALY TITOV & MARIA SIDELNKOVA/SHUTTERSTOCK.COM

product development a marketing strategy that entails the creation of marketable new products; the process of converting applications for new technologies into marketable products

brainstorming the process of getting a group to think of unlimited ways to vary a product or solve a problem

screening the first filter in the product development process, which eliminates ideas that are inconsistent with the organization's new-product strategy or are obviously inappropriate for some other reason

concept test a test to evaluate a new-product idea, usually before any prototype has been created

importance upper-level executives place on innovation. In China, 95 percent said that innovation was key to economic growth. Only 72 percent of U.S. upper-level executives agreed. There is a similar trend in spending on innovation—88 percent of Chinese executives plan to increase their innovation budgets, but only 48 percent of U.S. executives said the same thing.[13]

▸ *Distributors:* A well-trained sales force routinely asks distributors about needs that are not being met. Because they are closer to end users, distributors are often more aware of customer needs than are manufacturers. The inspiration for Rubbermaid's Sidekick, a litter-free lunch box, came from a distributor who suggested that the company place some of its plastic containers inside a lunch box and sell the box as an alternative to plastic wrap and paper bags.

▸ *Vendors:* 7-Eleven, Inc. regularly forges partnerships with vendors to create proprietary products. Coca-Cola invented the flavor blue vanilla for a 7-Eleven Slurpee drink, and the matching Laffy Taffy Blue Vanilla Rope candy was developed by Nestlé's Wonka division exclusively for 7-Eleven.

▸ *Competitors:* No firms rely solely on internally generated ideas for new products. A big part of any organization's marketing intelligence system should be monitoring the performance of competitors' products. One purpose of competitive monitoring is to determine which, if any, of the competitors' products should be copied. There is plenty of information about competitors on the Internet. For example, AltaVista (www.altavista.com) is a powerful index tool that can be used to locate information about products and companies. Fuld & Company's competitive intelligence guide provides links to a variety of market intelligence sites.

▸ *Research and development:* R&D is carried out in four distinct ways. You learned about basic research and applied research in Chapter 4. The other two ways are product development and product modification. **Product development** goes beyond applied research by converting applications into marketable products. Product modification makes cosmetic or functional changes in existing products. Many new-product breakthroughs come from R&D activities

IBM has research and innovation labs all over the world, and in 2010 the company announced plans to open a new one in São Paulo, Brazil. The goal is to increase sales in rapidly emerging markets like Brazil, and to help Brazil find ways to manage and encourage growth. IBM will help Brazil extract natural resources with new technology developed for the area. IBM then hopes to export those new advances to China and India. By having innovation centers located all over the world, IBM is able to increase its network and generate new ideas based on how different countries operate.[14]

▸ *Consultants:* Outside consultants are always available to examine a business and recommend product ideas. Examples include the Weston Group, Booz Allen Hamilton, and Management Decisions. Traditionally, consultants determine whether a company has a balanced portfolio of products and, if not, what new-product ideas are needed to offset the imbalance. General Mills' Web site at https://openinnovation.generalmills.com includes interactive features that let independent inventors and food scientists know what topics the company is interested in pursuing. If General Mills likes an idea it receives, it may pursue a licensing or joint venture arrangement.[15]

Creativity is the wellspring of new-product ideas, regardless of who comes up with them. A variety of approaches and techniques have been developed to stimulate creative thinking. The two considered most useful for generating new-product ideas are brainstorming and focus-group exercises. The goal of **brainstorming** is to get a group to think of unlimited ways to vary a product or solve a problem. Group members avoid criticism of an idea, no matter how ridiculous it may seem. Objective evaluation is postponed. The sheer quantity of ideas is what matters. As noted in Chapter 9, an objective of focus-group interviews is to stimulate insightful comments through group interaction. In the industrial market, machine tools, keyboard designs, aircraft interiors, and backhoe accessories have evolved from focus groups.

Idea Screening

After new ideas have been generated, they pass through the first filter in the product development process. This stage, called **screening**, eliminates ideas that are inconsistent with the organization's new-product strategy or are obviously inappropriate for some other reason. The new-product committee, the new-product department, or some other formally appointed group performs the screening review. General Motors' Advanced Portfolio Exploration Group (APEx) knows that only one out of every twenty new car concepts developed by the group will ever become a reality. That's not a bad percentage. In the pharmaceutical business, the percentage is much lower. Most new-product ideas are rejected at the screening stage.

Concept tests are often used at the screening stage to rate concept (or product) alternatives. A **concept test** evaluates a new-product idea, usually before any prototype has been created. Typically, researchers get consumer reactions to descriptions and visual representations of a proposed product.

Concept tests are considered fairly good predictors of success for line extensions. They have also been relatively precise predictors of success for new products that are not copycat items, are not easily classified into existing product categories, and do not require major changes in consumer behavior—such as Betty Crocker Tuna Helper and Libby's Fruit Float. However, concept tests are usually inaccurate in predicting the success of new products that create new consumption patterns and require major changes in consumer behavior—such as microwave ovens, VCRs, computers, and word processors.

Business Analysis

New-product ideas that survive the initial screening process move to the **business analysis** stage, where preliminary figures for demand, cost, sales, and profitability are calculated. For the first time, costs and revenues are estimated and compared. Depending on the nature of the product and the company, this process may be simple or complex.

The newness of the product, the size of the market, and the nature of the competition all affect the accuracy of revenue projections. In an established market like soft drinks, industry estimates of total market size are available. Forecasting market share for a new entry is a bigger challenge.

Analyzing overall economic trends and their impact on estimated sales is especially important in product categories that are sensitive to fluctuations in the business cycle. If consumers view the economy as uncertain and risky, they will put off buying durable goods such as major home appliances, automobiles, and homes. Likewise, business buyers postpone major equipment purchases if they expect a recession. Understanding the market potential is important because costs increase dramatically once a product idea enters the development stage.

Development

In the early stage of **development**, the R&D or engineering department may develop a prototype of the product. During this stage, the firm should start sketching a marketing strategy. The marketing department should decide on the product's packaging, branding, labeling, and so forth. In addition, it should map out preliminary promotion, price, and distribution strategies. The feasibility of manufacturing the product at

© FENG YU/SHUTTERSTOCK.COM

COMMON QUESTIONS IN THE BUSINESS ANALYSIS STAGE

- ▸▸ What is the likely demand for the product?
- ▸▸ What impact would the new product probably have on total sales, profits, market share, and return on investment?
- ▸▸ How would the introduction of the product affect existing products? Would the new product cannibalize existing products?
- ▸▸ Would current customers benefit from the product?
- ▸▸ Would the product enhance the image of the company's overall product mix?
- ▸▸ Would the new product affect current employees in any way? Would it lead to increasing or reducing the size of the workforce?
- ▸▸ What new facilities, if any, would be needed?
- ▸▸ How might competitors respond?
- ▸▸ What is the risk of failure? Is the company willing to take the risk?

an acceptable cost should be thoroughly examined. The development stage can last a long time and thus be very expensive. It took 10 years to develop Crest toothpaste, 15 years to develop the Polaroid Colorpack camera and the Xerox copy machine, 18 years to develop Minute Rice, and 51 years to develop the television. Gillette

business analysis
the second stage of the screening process where preliminary figures for demand, cost, sales, and profitability are calculated

development
the stage in the product development process in which a prototype is developed and a marketing strategy is outlined

simultaneous product development a team-oriented approach to new-product development

test marketing the limited introduction of a product and a marketing program to determine the reactions of potential customers in a market situation

developed three shaving systems over a 27-year period (Trac II, Atra, and Sensor) before introducing the Mach3 in 1998 and Fusion in 2006.[16]

The development process works best when all the involved areas (R&D, marketing, engineering, production, and even suppliers) work together rather than sequentially, a process called **simultaneous product development**. This approach allows firms to shorten the development process and reduce costs. With simultaneous product development, all relevant functional areas and outside suppliers participate in all stages of the development process. Rather than proceeding through highly structured stages, the cross-functional team operates in unison. Involving key suppliers early in the process capitalizes on their knowledge and enables them to develop critical component parts.

The Internet is a useful tool for implementing simultaneous product development. On the Web, multiple partners from a variety of locations can meet regularly to assess new-product ideas, analyze markets and demographics, and review cost information. Ideas judged to be feasible can quickly be converted into new products. Without the Internet, it would be impossible to conduct simultaneous product development from different parts of the world. Global R&D is important for two reasons. First, large companies have become global and are no longer focused only on one market. Global R&D is necessary to connect with customers in different parts of the world. Second, companies want to tap into the world's best talent—which isn't always found in the United States.[17]

Some firms use online brain trusts to solve technical problems. InnoCentive, Inc. is a network of 80,000 self-selected science problem solvers in 173 countries. Its clients include NASA, *Popular Science,* and *The Economist.* When one of InnoCentive's partners selects an idea for development, it no longer tries to develop the idea from the ground up with its own resources and time. Instead, it issues a brief to its network of thinkers, researchers, technology entrepreneurs, and inventors around the world, hoping to generate dialogue, suggestions, and solutions.

Innovative firms are also gathering a variety of R&D input from customers online. Threadless, a T-shirt company, and Ryz, an athletic shoe manufacturer, ask consumers to vote online for their favorites. The companies use these results to determine the products they sell over the Internet.[18]

In 2009, to increase customer satisfaction, Procter & Gamble began developing a new formula for its Pantene hair care line using extensive scientific research.

© TERRI MILLER/ E-VISUAL COMMUNICATIONS, INC.

Laboratory tests are often conducted on prototype models during the development stage. User safety is an important aspect of laboratory testing, which actually subjects products to much more severe treatment than is expected by end users. The Consumer Product Safety Act of 1972 requires manufacturers to conduct a "reasonable testing program" to ensure that their products conform to established safety standards.

Many products that test well in the laboratory are also tried out in homes or businesses. Examples of product categories well suited for such use tests include human and pet food products, household cleaning products, and industrial chemicals and supplies. These products are all relatively inexpensive, and their performance characteristics are apparent to users. For example, Procter & Gamble tests a variety of personal and home-care products in the community around its Cincinnati, Ohio, headquarters.

Test Marketing

After products and marketing programs have been developed, they are usually tested in the marketplace. **Test marketing** is the limited introduction of a product and a marketing program to determine the reactions of potential customers in a market situation. Test marketing allows management to evaluate alternative strategies and to assess how well the various aspects of the marketing mix fit together. Even established products are test marketed to assess new marketing strategies.

The cities chosen as test sites should reflect market conditions in the new product's projected market area. Yet no "magic city" exists that can universally represent market conditions, and a product's success in one city doesn't guarantee that it will be a nationwide hit. When selecting test market cities, researchers should therefore find locations where the demographics and purchasing habits mirror the overall market. The company should also have good distribution in test cities. When Chick-fil-A wanted to test its new spicy chicken sandwich, it used Baltimore, Maryland, as its test market because that city is representative of the restaurant chain's other markets across the country. Baltimore also has good distribution and customers with a history of talking to the company. And the area generates more revenue per store than any other market.[19] Moreover, test locations should be isolated from the media. If the television stations in a particular market reach a very large area outside that market, the advertising used for the test product may pull in many consumers from outside the market. The product may then appear more successful than it really is.

The High Costs of Test Marketing Test marketing frequently takes one year or longer, and costs can exceed $1 million. Some products remain in test markets even longer. Google plans to test-market an ultra-high-speed broadband network in one or more communities at a competitive price. The search giant plans to test its fiber-to-the-home concept by providing up to 500,000 homes with 1-gigabyte-per-second broadband access. Communities in every state except Delaware have requested to be one of the test markets. Topeka, Kansas, even changed its name to Google, Kansas, for a month in an effort to be chosen.[20] Despite the cost, many firms believe it is better to fail in a test market than in a national introduction. Because test marketing is so expensive, some companies do not test line extensions of well-known brands.

The high cost of test marketing is not just financial. One unavoidable problem is that test marketing exposes the new product and its marketing mix to competitors before its introduction. Thus, the element of surprise is lost. Competitors can also sabotage or "jam" a testing program by introducing their own sales promotion, pricing, or advertising campaign. The purpose is to hide or distort the normal conditions that the testing firm might expect in the market.

Government regulation can also affect test marketing, particularly in the tobacco industry. With steadily declining U.S. cigarette sales, Reynolds American (maker of Camel cigarettes) hoped to diversify with smokeless, spitless tobacco in the form of dissolvable lozenges, sticks, and strips. Testing for Camel Orbs, a pressed tobacco lozenge that looks similar to a small breath mint, hit roadblocks from several protest groups, who said that the candy-like shape and the bright packaging would encourage children to try—and get hooked on—the product. The Food and Drug Administration asked Reynolds to provide research on the use of the product by people under age 25 and their perceptions of it. Stricter legislation on how tobacco products can be marketed also limits a test market's awareness of the product.[21]

Alternatives to Test Marketing Many firms are looking for cheaper, faster, safer alternatives to traditional test marketing. In the early 1980s, Information Resources, Inc. pioneered one alternative: scanner-based research (discussed in Chapter 9). A typical supermarket scanner test costs about $300,000. Another alternative to traditional test marketing is **simulated (laboratory) market testing**. Advertising and other promotional materials for several products, including the test product, are shown to members of the product's target market. These people are then taken to shop at a mock or real store, where their purchases are recorded. Shopper behavior, including repeat purchasing, is monitored to assess the product's likely performance under true market conditions. Research firms offer simulated market tests for $25,000 to $100,000, compared to $1 million or more for full-scale test marketing.

The Internet offers a fast, cost-effective way to conduct test marketing. Procter & Gamble uses the Internet to assess customer demand for potential new products. Many products that are not available in grocery stores or drugstores can be sampled from P&G's Web site devoted to samples and coupons, www.pgeverydaysolutions.com.[22]

Despite these alternatives, most firms still consider test marketing essential for most new products. The high price of failure simply prohibits the widespread introduction of most new products without testing.

simulated (laboratory) market testing the presentation of advertising and other promotional materials for several products, including a test product, to members of the product's target market

Commercialization

commercialization
the decision to market a product

The final stage in the new-product development process is **commercialization**, the decision to market a product. The decision to commercialize the product sets several tasks in motion: ordering production materials and equipment, starting production, building inventories, shipping the product to field distribution points, training the sales force, announcing the new product to the trade, and advertising to potential customers.

The time from the initial commercialization decision to the product's actual introduction varies. It can range from a few weeks for simple products that use existing equipment to several years for technical products that require custom manufacturing equipment. And the total cost of development and initial introduction can be staggering. Gillette spent $750 million developing Mach3, and the first-year marketing budget for the new three-blade razor was $300 million.

The most important factor in successful new-product introduction is a good match between the product and market needs—as the marketing concept would predict. Successful new products deliver a meaningful and perceivable benefit to a sizable number of people or organizations and are different in some meaningful way from their intended substitutes. Firms that routinely experience success in new-product introductions tend to share the following characteristics:

» A history of listening carefully to customers

» An obsession with producing the best product possible

» A vision of what the market will be like in the future

» Strong leadership

» A commitment to new-product development

» A project-based team approach to new-product development

» Getting every aspect of the product development process right

A $35 IPAD: NO WAY!

India has unveiled the prototype of a basic **touch-screen tablet.** It is aimed at students and costs only 1,500 rupees, or $35.

The Indian government hopes to find a manufacturer that can mass-produce the tablet and keep the costs down (or even lower them). The tablet's functions include word processing, Web browsing, and videoconferencing. It has a solar power option, too—important for India's energy-starved rural communities—although it costs extra.

Some view the tablet as India's response to MIT's $100 computer aimed at children in developing nations. When MIT's offering proved too expensive, India took on the challenge of building a truly affordable computer. The human resource development minister turned to students and professors at India's elite technical universities to develop the $35 tablet. India plans to subsidize the cost of the tablet for its students, bringing the purchase price down to around $20. Falling hardware costs and intelligent design make the price plausible, and further cost reductions may be possible in the future. The tablet doesn't have a hard disk but uses a memory card, much like a camera or mobile phone. The tablet design cuts hardware costs, as does the use of open-source software. The next step is to manufacture the tablet and bring it to the people.[23]

SOURCE: Erika Kinetz, "iPad? No—IndiaPad," *Fort Worth Star-Telegram*, July 24, 2010, 9B.

© OLEKSIY MARK/SHUTTERSTOCK.COM

LO 3 Global Issues in New-Product Development

Increasing globalization of markets and competition provides a reason for multinational firms to consider new-product development from a worldwide perspective. A firm that starts with a global strategy is better able to develop products that are marketable worldwide. In many multinational corporations, every product is developed for potential worldwide distribution, and unique market requirements are satisfied during development whenever possible.

Some global marketers design their products to meet regulations in their major markets and then, if necessary, meet smaller markets' requirements country by country. Nissan develops lead-country car models that, with minor changes, can be sold in most markets. With this approach, Nissan has been able to reduce the number of its basic models from 48 to 18. Some products, however, have little potential for global market penetration without modification. In other cases, companies cannot sell their products at affordable prices and still make a profit in many countries.

LO 4 The Spread of New Products

Managers have a better chance of successfully marketing products if they understand how consumers learn about and adopt products.

Diffusion of Innovation

An **innovation** is a product perceived as new by a potential adopter. It really doesn't matter whether the product is "new to the world" or some other category of new product. If it is new to a potential adopter, it is an innovation in this context. **Diffusion** is the process by which the adoption of an innovation spreads.

Five categories of adopters participate in the diffusion process:

▸ *Innovators:* the first 2.5 percent of all those who adopt the product. Innovators are eager to try new ideas and products, almost as an obsession. In addition to having higher incomes, they are more worldly and more active outside their community than noninnovators. They rely less on group norms and are more self-confident. Because they are well educated, they are more likely to get their information from scientific sources and experts. Innovators are characterized as being venturesome.

▸ *Early adopters:* the next 13.5 percent to adopt the product. Although early adopters are not the very first, they do adopt early in the product's life cycle. Compared to innovators, they rely much more on group norms and values. They are also more oriented to the local community, in contrast to the innovators' worldly outlook. Early adopters are more likely than innovators to be opinion leaders because of their closer affiliation with groups. Early adopters are a new product's best friends.[24] The respect of others is a dominant characteristic of early adopters.

▸ *Early majority:* the next 34 percent to adopt. The early majority weighs the pros and cons before adopting a new product. They are likely to collect more information and evaluate more brands than early adopters, thereby extending the adoption process. They rely on the group for information but are unlikely to be opinion leaders themselves. Instead, they tend to be opinion leaders' friends and neighbors. The early majority is an important link in the process of diffusing new ideas because they are positioned between earlier and later adopters. A dominant characteristic of the early majority is deliberateness.

▸ *Late majority:* the next 34 percent to adopt. The late majority adopts a new product because most of their

innovation a product perceived as new by a potential adopter

diffusion the process by which the adoption of an innovation spreads

I CAN'T WAIT TO GET MY SAMSUNG GALAXY SG2 ...

© ISTOCKPHOTO.COM/VASKO MIOKOVIC PHOTOGRAPHY / © ISTOCKPHOTO.COM/GEOFFREY HOLMAN

friends have already adopted it. Because they also rely on group norms, their adoption stems from pressure to conform. This group tends to be older and below average in income and education. They depend mainly on word-of-mouth communication rather than on the mass media. The dominant characteristic of the late majority is skepticism.

▸▸ *Laggards:* the final 16 percent to adopt. Like innovators, laggards do not rely on group norms. Their independence is rooted in their ties to tradition. Thus, the past heavily influences their decisions. By the time laggards adopt an innovation, it has probably been outmoded and replaced by something else. For example, they may have bought their first black-and-white television set after color television was already widely diffused. Laggards have the longest adoption time and the lowest socioeconomic status. They tend to be suspicious of new products and alienated from a rapidly advancing society. The dominant value of laggards is tradition. Marketers typically ignore laggards, who do not seem to be motivated by advertising or personal selling and are virtually impossible to reach online.

Note that some product categories may never be adopted by 100 percent of the population. The adopter categories refer to all of those who will eventually adopt a product, not the entire population.

Product Characteristics and the Rate of Adoption

Five product characteristics can be used to predict and explain the rate of acceptance and diffusion of a new product:

▸▸ *Complexity:* the degree of difficulty involved in understanding and using a new product. The more complex the product, the slower is its diffusion.

▸▸ *Compatibility:* the degree to which the new product is consistent with existing values and product knowledge, past experiences, and current needs. Incompatible products diffuse more slowly than compatible products.

▸▸ *Relative advantage:* the degree to which a product is perceived as superior to existing substitutes. Because it can store and play back thousands of songs, the iPod has a clear relative advantage over the portable CD player.

▸▸ *Observability:* the degree to which the benefits or other results of using the product can be observed by others and communicated to target customers. For instance, fashion items and automobiles are highly visible and more observable than personal-care items.

▸▸ *"Trialability":* the degree to which a product can be tried on a limited basis. It is much easier to try a new toothpaste or breakfast cereal than a new automobile or microcomputer.

Marketing Implications of the Adoption Process

Two types of communication aid the diffusion process: *word-of-mouth communication* among consumers and communication from marketers to consumers. Word-of-mouth communication within and across groups speeds diffusion. Opinion leaders discuss new products with their followers and with other opinion leaders. Marketers must therefore ensure that opinion leaders have the types of information desired in the media that they use. Suppliers of some products, such as professional and health care services, rely almost solely on word-of-mouth communication for new business.

COURTESY OF DYSON INC.

Dyson vacuums are held in high esteem and are very successful products, in part because of their effective advertising campaigns. This ad demonstrates the innovative structure of the Dyson Ball, which makes the chore of vacuuming more efficient and easier.

A vacuum with wheels makes you go back and forth.

Vacuums still have wheels that make it hard work to move around objects and unnecessarily difficult to vacuum in corners.

A ball just turns.

dyson ball

No more awkward turns.

www.dyson.com

The second type of communication aiding the diffusion process is *communication directly from the marketer to potential adopters*. Messages directed toward early adopters should normally use different appeals than messages directed toward the early majority, the late majority, or the laggards. Early adopters are more important than innovators because they make up a larger group, are more socially active, and are usually opinion leaders.

As the focus of a promotional campaign shifts from early adopters to the early majority and the late majority, marketers should study the dominant characteristics, buying behavior, and media characteristics of these target markets. Then they should revise messages and media strategy to fit. The diffusion model helps guide marketers in developing and implementing promotion strategy.

LO5 Product Life Cycles

The **product life cycle (PLC) is one of the most familiar concepts in marketing.** Few other general concepts have been so widely discussed. Although some researchers and consultants have challenged the theoretical basis and managerial value of the PLC, many believe it is a useful marketing management diagnostic tool and a general guide for marketing planning in various life cycle stages.[25]

The PLC is a biological metaphor that traces the stages of a product's acceptance, from its introduction (birth) to its decline (death). As Exhibit 11.2 shows, a product progresses through four major stages: introduction, growth, maturity, and decline.

The PLC concept can be used to analyze a brand, a product form, or a product category. The PLC for a product form is usually longer than the PLC for any one brand. The exception would be a brand that was the first and last competitor in a product form market. In that situation, the brand and product form life cycles would be equal in length. Product categories have the longest life cycles. A **product category** includes all brands that satisfy a particular type of need such as shaving products, passenger automobiles, or soft drinks.

The time a product spends in any one stage of the life cycle may vary dramatically. Some products,

product life cycle (PLC) a concept that provides a way to trace the stages of a product's acceptance, from its introduction (birth) to its decline (death)

product category all brands that satisfy a particular type of need

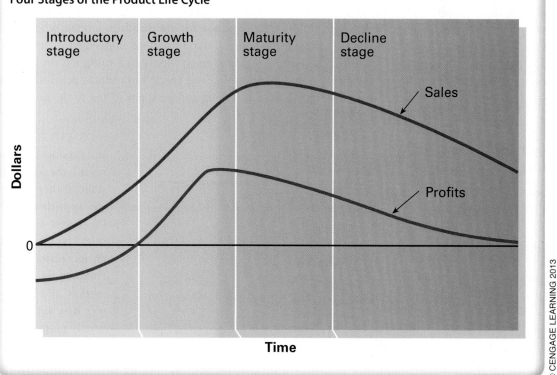

EXHIBIT 11.2
Four Stages of the Product Life Cycle

Introductory stage | Growth stage | Maturity stage | Decline stage

Dollars

Sales

Profits

0

Time

© CENGAGE LEARNING 2013

introductory
stage the full-scale launch
of a new product into the
marketplace

growth stage the
second stage of the product life
cycle when sales typically grow
at an increasing rate, many
competitors enter the market,
large companies may start to
acquire small pioneering firms,
and profits are healthy

such as fad items, move through the entire cycle in weeks. Fads are typically characterized by a sudden and unpredictable spike in sales followed by a rather abrupt decline.[26] Examples of fad items are Silly Bandz, Beanie Babies, and Crocs. Other products, such as electric clothes washers and dryers, stay in the maturity stage for decades. Exhibit 11.2 illustrates the typical life cycle for a consumer durable good, such as a washer or dryer. In contrast, Exhibit 11.3 below illustrates typical life cycles for styles (such as formal, business, or casual clothing), fashions (such as miniskirts or baggy jeans), and fads (such as leopard-print clothing). Changes in a product, its uses, its image, or its positioning can extend that product's life cycle.

The PLC concept does not tell managers the length of a product's life cycle or its duration in any stage. It does not dictate marketing strategy. It is simply a tool to help marketers forecast future events and suggest appropriate strategies.

Introductory Stage

The **introductory stage** of the PLC represents the full-scale launch of a new product into the marketplace. Computer databases for personal use, room-deodorizing air-conditioning filters, and wind-powered home electric generators are all product categories that have recently entered the PLC. A high failure rate, little competition, frequent product modification, and limited distribution typify the introductory stage of the PLC.

Marketing costs in the introductory stage are normally high for several reasons. High dealer margins are often needed to obtain adequate distribution, and incentives are needed to get consumers to try the new product. Advertising expenses are high because of the need to educate consumers about the new product's benefits. Production costs are also often high in this stage, as product and manufacturing flaws are identified and corrected and efforts are undertaken to develop mass production economies.

Sales normally increase slowly during the introductory stage. Moreover, profits are usually negative because of R&D costs, factory tooling, and high introduction costs. The length of the introductory phase is largely determined by product characteristics, such as the product's advantages over substitute products, the educational effort required to make the product known, and management's commitment of resources to the new item. A short introductory period is usually preferred to help reduce the impact of negative earnings and cash flows. As soon as the product gets off the ground, the financial burden should begin to diminish. Also, a short introduction helps dispel some of the uncertainty as to whether the new product will be successful.

Promotion strategy in the introductory stage focuses on developing product awareness and informing consumers about the product category's potential benefits. At this stage, the communication challenge is to stimulate primary demand—demand for the product in general rather than for a specific brand. Intensive personal selling is often required to gain acceptance for the product among wholesalers and retailers. Promotion of convenience products often requires heavy consumer sampling and couponing. Shopping and specialty products demand educational advertising and personal selling to the final consumer.

Growth Stage

If a product category survives the introductory stage, it then advances to the **growth stage** of the life cycle. In this stage, sales typically grow at an increasing rate, many competitors enter the market, and large companies may start to acquire small pioneering firms. Profits rise rapidly in the growth stage, reach their peak, and begin declining

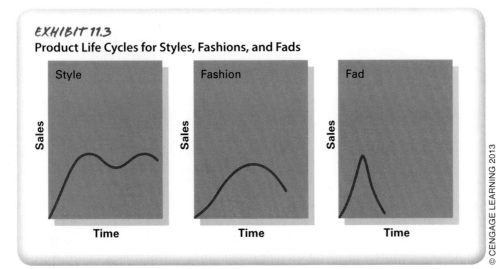

EXHIBIT 11.3
Product Life Cycles for Styles, Fashions, and Fads

Style — Sales / Time

Fashion — Sales / Time

Fad — Sales / Time

© CENGAGE LEARNING 2013

© DEKLOFENAK/SHUTTERSTOCK.COM

maturity stage a period during which sales increase at a decreasing rate
decline stage a long-run drop in sales

as competition intensifies. Emphasis switches from primary demand promotion (e.g., promoting personal digital assistants, or PDAs) to aggressive brand advertising and communication of the differences between brands (e.g., promoting BlackBerry versus Palm).

Distribution becomes a major key to success during the growth stage, as well as in later stages. Manufacturers scramble to sign up dealers and distributors and to build long-term relationships. Without adequate distribution, it is impossible to establish a strong market position.

XFit, a stretch denim material, has paired with denim labels to get its product to retailers. The stretch denim market has 35 percent of the market, and customers want a jean that holds its shape but fits comfortably. XFit relies on designers to label jeans with information about the benefits of XFit. If the label doesn't resonate with customers or differentiate the material from other stretch denims, XFit will lose its place in the stretch fiber market.[27]

Maturity Stage

A period during which sales increase at a decreasing rate signals the beginning of the **maturity stage** of the life cycle. New users cannot be added indefinitely, and sooner or later the market approaches saturation. Normally, this is the longest stage of the PLC. Many major household appliances are in the maturity stage of their life cycles.

For shopping products such as durable goods and electronics, and many specialty products, annual models begin to appear during the maturity stage. Product lines are lengthened to appeal to additional market segments. Service and repair assume more important roles as manufacturers strive to distinguish their products from others. Product design changes tend to become stylistic (How can the product be made different?) rather than functional (How can the product be made better?).

As prices and profits continue to fall, marginal competitors start dropping out of the market. Dealer margins also shrink, resulting in less shelf space for mature items, lower dealer inventories, and a general reluctance to promote the product. Thus, promotion to dealers often intensifies during this stage in order to retain loyalty.

Heavy consumer promotion by the manufacturer is also required to maintain market share. Cutthroat competition during this stage can lead to price wars. Another characteristic of the maturity stage is the emergence of "niche marketers" that target narrow, well-defined, underserved segments of a market.

Decline Stage

A long-run drop in sales signals the beginning of the **decline stage**. The rate of decline is governed by how rapidly consumer tastes change or substitute products are adopted. Many convenience products and fad items lose their market overnight, leaving large inventories of unsold items, such as designer jeans. Others die more slowly. Landline telephone service is an example of a product in the decline stage of the product life cycle. After peaking at about 141 million in 2000, the number of U.S. home phones fell to 78 million by the end of 2008, according to the Federal Communications Commission.[28] People abandoning landlines to go wireless and households replacing landlines with Internet phones have both contributed to this long-term decline.

Some firms have developed successful strategies for marketing products in the decline stage of the PLC. They eliminate all nonessential marketing expenses and let sales decline as more and more customers discontinue purchasing the products. Eventually, the product is withdrawn from the market.

Some firms practice what management sage Peter Drucker has called "organized abandonment," which is based upon a periodic audit of all goods and services that a firm markets. One key question is, if we weren't already marketing the product, would we be willing to introduce it now? If the answer is "no," the product should be carefully considered as a candidate for elimination from the product mix.[29]

Implications for Marketing Management

The PLC concept encourages marketing managers to plan so that they can take the initiative instead of reacting to past events. The PLC is especially useful as a predicting or forecasting tool. Because products pass through distinctive stages, it is often possible to estimate a product's location on the curve using historical data. Profits, like sales, tend to follow a predictable path over a product's life cycle.

Exhibit 11.4 shows the relationship between the adopter categories and stages of the PLC. Note that the various categories of adopters first buy products in different stages of the life cycle. Almost all sales in the maturity and decline stages represent repeat purchasing.

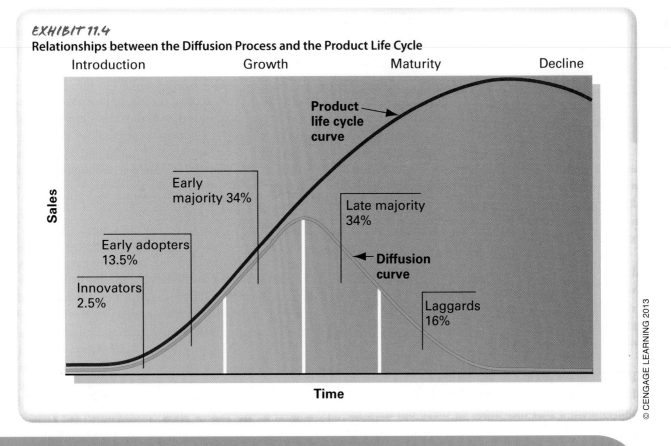

EXHIBIT 11.4

Relationships between the Diffusion Process and the Product Life Cycle

Introduction | Growth | Maturity | Decline

Sales

Product life cycle curve

Early majority 34%

Early adopters 13.5%

Innovators 2.5%

Late majority 34%

◄ Diffusion curve

Laggards 16%

Time

© CENGAGE LEARNING 2013

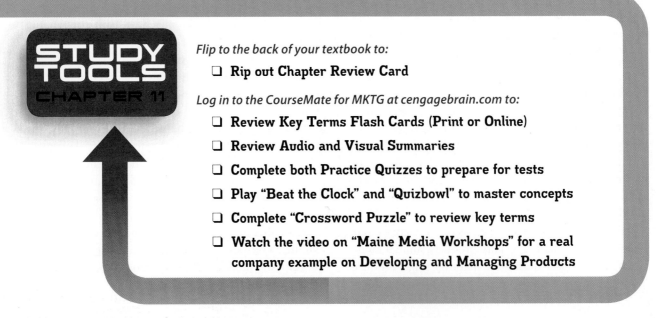

STUDY TOOLS CHAPTER 11

Flip to the back of your textbook to:

❏ **Rip out Chapter Review Card**

Log in to the CourseMate for MKTG at cengagebrain.com to:

❏ **Review Key Terms Flash Cards (Print or Online)**

❏ **Review Audio and Visual Summaries**

❏ **Complete both Practice Quizzes to prepare for tests**

❏ **Play "Beat the Clock" and "Quizbowl" to master concepts**

❏ **Complete "Crossword Puzzle" to review key terms**

❏ **Watch the video on "Maine Media Workshops" for a real company example on Developing and Managing Products**

VCR sales dropped rapidly in the face of growing DVD competition.

Maturity ③

Diffusion and Growth ②

Decline ④

Introduction of the VCR ①

DVDs now dominate the product category ⑤

Life Cycle of the VCR ·········►

1977 VHS first sold in the United States

1992 100 millionth VCR sold

1997 First DVD titles released in the United States

2000 VCR sales peak at 23 million units

2001 DVD dollar sales surpass VHS sales

2006 More households own DVD players than VCRs

| ☐ 525/60 | PCM 1, 2 | ☐ STEREO | ☐ MONO |
| ☐ 625/50 | PCM 3, 4 | ☐ STEREO | ☐ MONO |

DVDs are under pressure from streaming video services like Netflix, Roku, Apple TV, and Hulu.

© ISTOCKPHOTO.COM/RUSM / © ISTOCKPHOTO.COM/EUTOCH / © ISTOCKPHOTO.COM/JASON STITT / © ISTOCKPHOTO.COM/ ERICSPHOTOGRAPHY / © ISTOCKPHOTO.COM/CHRISTIAN J. STEWART / © ISTOCKPHOTO.COM/AHMED REFAAT / © ISTOCK-PHOTO.COM/ALEKSEJS JEVSEJENKO

CHAPTER 12

Services and Nonprofit Organization Marketing

Nearly 80 percent of employed people will be in the service industry between 2008 and 2018.

LO 1 The Importance of Services

AFTER YOU FINISH THIS CHAPTER, GO TO **PAGE 207** FOR **STUDY TOOLS**

A **service** is the result of applying human or mechanical efforts to people or objects. Services involve a deed, a performance, or an effort that cannot be physically possessed. Today, the service sector substantially influences the U.S. economy. According to the Bureau of Labor Statistics, the service industry will account for 95 percent of the total employment increase between 2008 and 2018, and nearly 80 percent of employed people will be in the service industry.[1] The demand for services is expected to continue. Much of this demand results from demographics. An aging population will need nurses, home health care workers, physical therapists, and social workers. Demand for information managers, such as computer engineers and systems analysts, will also increase. There is also a growing market for service companies worldwide.

service the result of applying human or mechanical efforts to people or objects

The marketing process described in Chapter 1 is the same for all types of products, whether they are goods or services. In addition, although a comparison of goods and services marketing can be beneficial, in reality it is hard to distinguish clearly between manufacturing and service firms. Indeed, many manufacturing firms can point to service as a major factor in their success. For example, maintenance and repair services offered by the manufacturer are important to buyers of copy machines. Nevertheless, services have some unique characteristics that distinguish them from goods, and marketing strategies need to be adjusted for these characteristics.

What do you think?

Most jobs have something to do with service.

| 1 | 2 | 3 | 4 | 5 | 6 | 7 |

STRONGLY DISAGREE   STRONGLY AGREE

© PETER DAZELEY/PHOTOGRAPHER'S CHOICE/GETTY IMAGES

Find out what others think at the CourseMate for MKTG. Log in at cengagebrain.com. | 195

LO 2 How Services Differ from Goods

Services have four unique characteristics that distinguish them from goods. Services are intangible, inseparable, heterogeneous, and perishable.

Intangibility

The basic difference between services and goods is that services are intangible performances. Because of their **intangibility**, they cannot be touched, seen, tasted, heard, or felt in the same manner that goods can be sensed.

Evaluating the quality of services before or even after making a purchase is harder than evaluating the quality of goods because, compared to goods, services tend to exhibit fewer search qualities. A **search quality** is a characteristic that can be easily assessed before purchase—for instance, the color of an appliance or automobile. At the same time, services tend to exhibit more experience and credence qualities. An **experience quality** is a characteristic that can be assessed only after use, such as the quality of a meal in a restaurant. A **credence quality** is a characteristic that consumers may have difficulty assessing even after purchase because they do not have the necessary knowledge or experience. Medical and consulting services are examples of services that exhibit credence qualities.

These characteristics also make it harder for marketers to communicate the benefits of an intangible service than to communicate the benefits of tangible goods. Thus, marketers often rely on tangible cues to communicate a service's nature and quality. For example, Travelers Insurance Company uses an umbrella symbol as a tangible reminder of the protection that insurance provides.

The facilities that customers visit, or from which services are delivered, are a critical tangible part of the total service offering. Messages about the organization are communicated to customers through such elements as the decor, the clutter or neatness of service areas, and the staff's manners and dress. In order to make a hotel stay a defined all-sensory experience, many hotels are using ambient scenting to create a unique experience. And because scent triggers specific emotions and brain function, some hotels, like the Mandarin Oriental Miami, use different scents in different areas to create an ideal environment. Its conference rooms are perfumed with a blend called Meeting Sense that claims to enhance productivity.[2]

Inseparability

Goods are produced, sold, and then consumed. In contrast, services are often sold, produced, and consumed at the same time. In other words, their production and consumption are inseparable activities. This **inseparability** means that, because consumers must be present during the production of services like haircuts or surgery, they are actually involved in the production of the services they buy. That type of consumer involvement is rare in goods manufacturing.

Simultaneous production and consumption also means that services normally cannot be produced in a centralized location and consumed in decentralized locations, as goods typically are. Services are also inseparable from the perspective of the service provider. Thus, the quality of service that firms are able to deliver depends on the quality of their employees.

Heterogeneity

One great strength of McDonald's is consistency. Whether customers order a Big Mac in Chicago or Seattle, they know exactly what they are going to get. This is not the case with many service providers. Because services have greater **heterogeneity** or variability of inputs and outputs, they tend to be less

intangibility the inability of services to be touched, seen, tasted, heard, or felt in the same manner that goods can be sensed

search quality a characteristic that can be easily assessed before purchase

experience quality a characteristic that can be assessed only after use

credence quality a characteristic that consumers may have difficulty assessing even after purchase because they do not have the necessary knowledge or experience

inseparability the inability of the production and consumption of a service to be separated; consumers must be present during the production

heterogeneity the variability of the inputs and outputs of services, which causes services to tend to be less standardized and uniform than goods

© ISTOCKPHOTO.COM/CHRIS GRAMLY

standardized and uniform than goods. For example, physicians in a group practice or barbers in a barber shop differ within each group in their technical and interpersonal skills. Because services tend to be labor intensive and production and consumption are inseparable, consistency and quality control can be hard to achieve.

Standardization and training help increase consistency and reliability. Marriott is known for standardizing its hotels down to the smallest detail—from how much bleach is used to clean the floor to which flushers are on bathroom toilets. These standards for high-quality service across the company's different hotel chains allow travelers to have confidence that their hotel will meet expectations.[3]

Perishability

Perishability is the fourth characteristic of services. **Perishability** refers to the inability of services to be stored, warehoused, or inventoried. An empty hotel room or airplane seat produces no revenue that day. The revenue is lost. Yet service organizations are often forced to turn away full-price customers during peak periods.

One of the most important challenges in many service industries is finding ways to synchronize supply and demand. The philosophy that some revenue is better than none has prompted many hotels to offer deep discounts on weekends and during the off-season.

LO 3 Service Quality

Because of the four unique characteristics of services, service quality is more difficult to define and measure than is the quality of tangible goods. Business executives rank the improvement of service quality as one of the most critical challenges facing them today.

Research has shown that customers evaluate service quality by the following five components:[4]

▸▸ *Reliability:* the ability to perform the service dependably, accurately, and consistently. Reliability is performing the service right the first time. This component has been found to be the one most important to consumers.

▸▸ *Responsiveness:* the ability to provide prompt service. Examples of responsiveness include calling the customer back quickly, serving lunch fast to someone who is in a hurry, or mailing a transaction slip immediately. The ultimate in responsiveness is offering service 24 hours a day, seven days a week.

▸▸ *Assurance:* the knowledge and courtesy of employees and their ability to convey trust. Skilled employees who treat customers with respect and make customers feel that they can trust the firm exemplify assurance.

▸▸ *Empathy:* caring, individualized attention to customers. Firms whose employees recognize customers and learn their specific requirements are providing empathy.

▸▸ *Tangibles:* the physical evidence of the service. The tangible parts of a service include the physical facilities, tools, and equipment used to provide the service, as well as the appearance of personnel.

Overall service quality is measured by combining customers' evaluations for all five components.

The Gap Model of Service Quality

A model of service quality called the **gap model** identifies five gaps that can cause problems in service delivery and influence customer evaluations of service quality.[5] These gaps are illustrated in Exhibit 12.1 on the next page:

▸▸ *Gap 1:* the gap between what customers want and what management thinks customers want. This gap results from a lack of understanding or a misinterpretation of the customers' needs, wants, or desires. A firm that does little or no customer satisfaction research is likely to experience this gap. To close gap 1, firms must stay

perishability the inability of services to be stored, warehoused, or inventoried

reliability the ability to perform a service dependably, accurately, and consistently

responsiveness the ability to provide prompt service

assurance the knowledge and courtesy of employees and their ability to convey trust

empathy caring, individualized attention to customers

tangibles the physical evidence of a service, including the physical facilities, tools, and equipment used to provide the service

gap model a model identifying five gaps that can cause problems in service delivery and influence customer evaluations of service quality

© ISTOCKPHOTO.COM/AUKE HOLWERDA

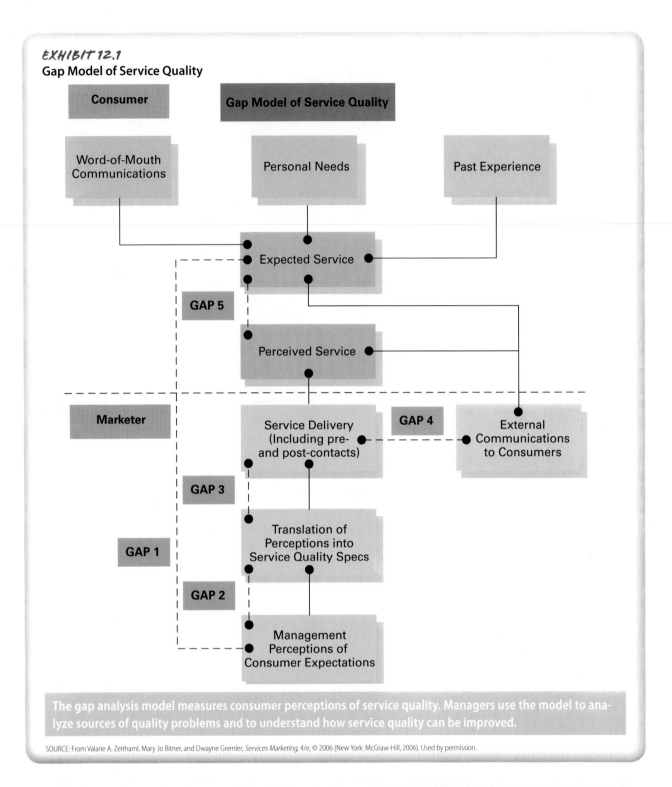

EXHIBIT 12.1
Gap Model of Service Quality

The gap analysis model measures consumer perceptions of service quality. Managers use the model to analyze sources of quality problems and to understand how service quality can be improved.

SOURCE: From Valarie A. Zeithaml, Mary Jo Bitner, and Dwayne Gremler, *Services Marketing*, 4/e, © 2006 (New York: McGraw-Hill, 2006). Used by permission.

attuned to customer wishes by researching customer needs and satisfaction.

▸▸ *Gap 2:* the gap between what management thinks customers want and the quality specifications that management develops to provide the service. Essentially, this gap is the result of management's inability to translate customers' needs into delivery systems within the firm. For example, KFC used to rate its managers according

to "chicken efficiency," or how much chicken they threw away at closing; customers who came in late would either have to wait for chicken to be cooked or settle for chicken several hours old.

▸▸ *Gap 3:* the gap between the service quality specifications and the service that is actually provided. If both gaps 1 and 2 have been closed, then gap 3 is due to the inability of management and employees to do what should be done. Management needs to ensure that employees have the skills and the proper tools to perform their jobs. Other techniques that help to close gap 3 are training employees so they know what management expects and encouraging teamwork. Nick's Pizza & Pub in Chicago has attracted visitors from everywhere who have heard about how the company hires and trains its employees. Among other things, the company interviews candidates twice and gives them a personality test. Role-playing is common. The training program is rigorous and ongoing. In an industry where annual employee turnover is typically 200 percent, Nick's turnover is just 20 percent. And customers love the service—on three occasions, waitresses have received tips of $1,000.[6]

▸▸ *Gap 4:* the gap between what the company provides and what the customer is told it provides. This is clearly a communication gap. It may include misleading or deceptive advertising campaigns promising more than the firm can deliver or doing "whatever it takes" to get the business. To close this gap, companies need to create realistic customer expectations through honest,

accurate communication about what the firms can provide.

▸▸ *Gap 5:* the gap between the service that customers receive and the service they want. This gap can be positive or negative. For example, if a patient expects to wait 20 minutes in the physician's office before seeing the physician but actually waits only 10 minutes, the patient's evaluation of service quality will be high. However, a 40-minute wait would result in a lower evaluation.

When one or more of these gaps is large, service quality is perceived as low. As the gaps shrink, service quality perception improves. USAA, a financial-services organization that serves military families, is great at closing gap 1. It knows what its highly mobile customers who face unique financial challenges need. For example, the company was the first bank to allow iPhone deposits, it texts balances to soldiers in the field, and it heavily discounts customers' car insurance while they are deployed overseas.[7]

LO4 Marketing Mixes for Services

Services' unique characteristics—intangibility, inseparability of production and consumption, heterogeneity, and perishability—make marketing more challenging. Elements of the marketing mix (product, place, promotion, and pricing) need to be adjusted to meet the special needs created by these characteristics.

Product (Service) Strategy

A product, as defined in Chapter 10, is everything a person receives in an exchange. In the case of a service organization, the product offering is intangible and consists in large part of a process or a series of processes. Product strategies for service offerings include decisions on the type of process involved, core and supplementary services, standardization or customization of the service product, and the service mix.

Service as a Process Two broad categories of things get processed in service organizations: people and objects. In some cases, the process is physical, or tangible, while in others the process is intangible. Based on these characteristics, service processes can be placed into one of four categories:[8]

▸▸ *People processing* takes place when the service is directed at a customer. Examples are transportation services and health care.

Retallack Lodge uses humor in its advertisements to encourage skiers to take advantage of its skiing, snowboarding, and lodge services.

COURTESY OF PHIL PINFOLD—RETALLACK LODGE

core service the most basic benefit the consumer is buying

supplementary services a group of services that support or enhance the core service

mass customization a strategy that uses technology to deliver customized services on a mass basis

▶▶ *Possession processing* occurs when the service is directed at customers' physical possessions. Examples are lawn care, dry cleaning, and veterinary services.

▶▶ *Mental stimulus processing* refers to services directed at people's minds. Examples are theater performances and education.

▶▶ *Information processing* describes services that use technology or brainpower directed at a customer's assets. Examples are insurance and consulting.

Because customers' experiences and involvement differ for each of these types of services, marketing strategies may also differ. For example, people-processing services require customers to enter the *service factory*, which is a physical location, such as an aircraft, a physician's office, or a hair salon. In contrast, possession-processing services typically do not require the presence of the customer in the service factory. Marketing strategies for the former would therefore focus more on an attractive, comfortable physical environment and employee training on employee–customer interaction issues than would strategies for the latter.

Core and Supplementary Service Products The service offering can be viewed as a bundle of activities that includes the **core service**, which is the most basic benefit the customer is buying, and a group of **supplementary services** that support or enhance the core service. Exhibit 12.2 illustrates these concepts for an overnight stay at a luxury hotel. The core service is overnight rental of a bedroom, which involves people processing. The supplementary services, some of which involve information processing, include reservations, check-ins and check-outs, room service, and meals.

In many service industries, the core service becomes a commodity as competition increases. Thus, firms usually emphasize supplementary services to create a competitive advantage. On the other hand, some firms are positioning themselves in the marketplace by greatly reducing supplementary services.

Customization/Standardization An important issue in developing the service offering is whether to customize or standardize it. Customized services are more flexible and respond to individual customers' needs. They also usually command a higher price. Standardized services are more efficient and cost less.

Instead of choosing to either standardize or customize a service, a firm may incorporate elements of

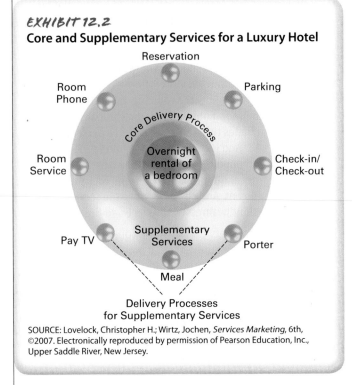

EXHIBIT 12.2
Core and Supplementary Services for a Luxury Hotel

SOURCE: Lovelock, Christopher H.; Wirtz, Jochen, *Services Marketing*, 6th, ©2007. Electronically reproduced by permission of Pearson Education, Inc., Upper Saddle River, New Jersey.

both by adopting an emerging strategy called **mass customization**. Mass customization uses technology to deliver customized services on a mass basis, which results in giving each customer whatever she or he asks for. For example, based on the popularity of the Old Spice Guy commercials, Reddit (a social news aggregator) and Isaiah Mustafa (the Old Spice Guy) developed a customizable voice mail generator that allows you to choose, based on gender, what the Old Spice Guy says as your voice mail greeting. Customers can build an entire outgoing message and can customize the final sign-off phrase with one of these four options: "I'm on a horse," "I'm on a phone," "SWAN DIVE," and "This voice mail is now diamonds."[9]

Personalization services can generate privacy questions and be controversial when implemented without customer approval. Facebook's Instant Personalization (IP) service is automatically checked on user profiles and imports profile data onto certain Web sites upon the user's next visit. For example, when a user visits Pandora, the online streaming radio service, it will immediately begin playing music by bands that she has "liked" on her Facebook profile. IP also links real names and other public Facebook information to partner Web sites and other Facebook users. Unless a user turns off Web site–specific settings, she will automatically be publicizing information on her profile (location, name, phone number, etc.) when she uses sites like Pandora, Microsoft docs, and Yelp.[10]

The Service Mix Most service organizations market more than one service. For example, TruGreen offers lawn care, shrub care, carpet cleaning, and industrial lawn services. Each organization's service mix represents a set of opportunities, risks, and challenges. Each part of the service mix should make a different contribution to achieving the firm's goals. To succeed, each service may also need a different level of financial support. Designing a service strategy therefore means deciding what new services to introduce to which target market, what existing services to maintain, and what services to eliminate.

Place (Distribution) Strategy

Distribution strategies for service organizations must focus on such issues as convenience, number of outlets, direct versus indirect distribution, location, and scheduling. A key factor influencing the selection of a service provider is *convenience*. For example, infirm or elderly patients would probably prefer to use a doctor who makes house calls.

An important distribution objective for many service firms is the number of outlets to use or the number of outlets to open during a certain time. Generally, the intensity of distribution should meet, but not exceed, the target market's needs and preferences. Having too few outlets may inconvenience customers; having too many outlets may boost costs unnecessarily. Intensity of distribution may also depend on the image desired. Having only a few outlets may make the service seem more exclusive or selective.

The next service distribution decision is whether to distribute services to end users *directly* or *indirectly* through other firms. Because of the intangible nature of services, many service firms have to use direct distribution or franchising. Examples include legal, medical, accounting, and personal-care services. The newest form of direct distribution is the Internet. Most major

airlines are now using online services to sell tickets directly to consumers, which results in lower distribution costs for the airlines. Other firms with standardized service packages have developed indirect channels using independent intermediaries. For example, Bank of America offers teller and loan services to customers in small satellite facilities at Albertsons grocery stores in Texas.

The *location* of a service most clearly reveals the relationship between its target market strategy and distribution strategy. For time-dependent service providers such as airlines, physicians, and dentists, *scheduling* is often a more important factor.

Promotion Strategy

Consumers and business users have more trouble evaluating services than goods because services are less tangible. In turn, marketers have more trouble promoting intangible services than tangible goods. Here are four promotion strategies they can try:

▸ *Stressing tangible cues:* A tangible cue is a concrete symbol of the service offering. To make their intangible services more tangible, hotels turn down the bedcovers and put mints on the pillows. DoubleTree hotels offer their guests a warm chocolate chip cookie as they check in.

▸ *Using personal information sources:* A personal information source is someone consumers are familiar with (such

Celebrity endorsement can decrease perceived risk in choosing a service. For example, John Travolta endorses Breitling watches for their quality and endurance.

IMAGE COURTESY OF THE ADVERTISING ARCHIVES

as a celebrity) or someone they admire or can relate to personally. Service firms may seek to simulate positive word-of-mouth communication among present and prospective customers by using real customers in their ads.

▸▸ *Creating a strong organizational image:* One way to create an image is to manage the evidence, including the physical environment of the service facility, the appearance of the service employees, and the tangible items associated with a service (such as stationery, bills, and business cards). For example, McDonald's Golden Arches are instantly recognizable. Another way to create an image is through branding.

▸▸ *Engaging in postpurchase communication:* Postpurchase communication refers to the follow-up activities that a service firm might engage in after a customer transaction. Postcard surveys, telephone calls, and other types of follow-up show customers that their feedback matters.

Price Strategy

Considerations in pricing a service are similar to the pricing considerations to be discussed in Chapters 19 and 20. However, the unique characteristics of services present two special pricing challenges.

First, in order to price a service, it is important to define the unit of service consumption. For example, should pricing be based on completing a specific service task (cutting a customer's hair), or should it be time based (how long it takes to cut a customer's hair)? Some services include the consumption of goods, such as food and beverages. Restaurants charge customers for food and drink rather than the use of a table and chairs.

Second, for services that are composed of multiple elements, the issue is whether pricing should be based on a "bundle" of elements or whether each element should be priced separately. A bundled price may be preferable when consumers dislike having to pay "extra" for every part of the service (e.g., paying extra for baggage or food on an airplane), and it is simpler for the firm to administer. Alternatively, customers may not want to pay for service elements they do not use. Many furniture stores now have "unbundled" delivery charges from the price of the furniture. Customers who wish to can pick up the furniture at the store, saving on the delivery fee.

Marketers should set performance objectives when pricing each service. Three categories of pricing objectives have been suggested:[11]

▸▸ *Revenue-oriented pricing* focuses on maximizing the surplus of income over costs. A limitation of this approach is that determining costs can be difficult for many services.

▸▸ *Operations-oriented pricing* seeks to match supply and demand by varying prices. For example, matching hotel demand to the number of available rooms can be achieved by raising prices at peak times and decreasing them during slow times.

▸▸ *Patronage-oriented pricing* tries to maximize the number of customers using the service. Thus, prices vary with different market segments' ability to pay, and methods of payment (such as credit) are offered that increase the likelihood of a purchase.

A firm may need to use more than one type of pricing objective. In fact, all three objectives probably need to be included to some degree in a pricing strategy, although the importance of each type may vary depending on the type of service provided, the prices that competitors are charging, the differing ability of various customer segments to pay, or the opportunity to negotiate price. For customized services (such as construction services), customers may also have the ability to negotiate a price.

LO 5 Relationship Marketing in Services

Many services involve ongoing interaction between the service organization and the customer. Thus, they can benefit from relationship marketing, the strategy described in Chapter 1, as a means of attracting, developing, and retaining customer relationships. The idea is to develop strong loyalty by creating satisfied customers who will buy additional services from the firm and are unlikely to switch to a competitor. Satisfied customers are also likely to engage in positive word-of-mouth communication, thereby helping to bring in new customers.

Many businesses have found that it is more cost-effective to hang on to the customers they have than to focus only on attracting new ones. A bank executive, for example, found that increasing customer retention by 2 percent can have the same effect on profits as reducing costs by 10 percent.

Services that purchasers receive on a continuing basis (e.g., cable television, banking, insurance) can be considered membership services. This type of service naturally lends itself to relationship marketing. When services involve discrete transactions (e.g., in a movie theater, at a restaurant, or on public transportation), it may be more difficult to build membership-type relationships with customers. Nevertheless, services involving discrete transactions may be transformed into membership relationships using marketing tools. For example, the service could be sold in bulk (e.g., a theater series subscription or a commuter pass on public transportation). Or a service firm could offer special benefits to customers who choose to register with the firm (e.g., loyalty programs for hotels and airlines). The service firm that has a more formalized relationship with its customers has an advantage because it knows who its customers are and how and when they use the services offered.[12]

Relationship marketing can be practiced at three levels:[13]

▸▸ *Level 1:* The firm uses pricing incentives to encourage customers to continue doing business with it. Frequent flyer programs are an example of level 1 relationship marketing. This level of relationship marketing is the least effective in the long term because its price-based advantage is easily imitated by other firms.

▸▸ *Level 2:* This level of relationship marketing also uses pricing incentives but seeks to build social bonds with customers. The firm stays in touch with customers, learns about their needs, and designs services to meet those needs. Level 2 relationship marketing is often more effective than level 1 relationship marketing.

▸▸ *Level 3:* At this level, the firm again uses financial and social bonds but adds structural bonds to the formula. Structural bonds are developed by offering value-added services that are not readily available from other firms. USA Network developed many fans with its interactive, program-based games, but to encourage people to share the games and shows they enjoy, USA started the Character Rewards program. Players accrue points as they watch videos, share links, and play games. Points are redeemable for in-universe, virtual goods or real goods from the network store. The program also gives USA insight as to what shows viewers enjoy the most, which ultimately leads to more enjoyable programming.[14]

LO 6 Internal Marketing in Service Firms

Services are performances, so the quality of a firm's employees is an important part of building long-term relationships with customers. Employees who like their jobs and are satisfied with the firm they work

PERSON-LESS HOTEL CHECK-IN

Hotel check-in lines can be long at convention hubs and tourist locations such as Las Vegas. To combat long lines and dissatisfied customers, many hotels are working to get their most loyal customers into their rooms more quickly—and without standing in line. One method is using permanent keys. The keys, usually a loyalty member's card, use RFID chips that can be remotely turned on and off and programmed with the new room number to unlock a hotel room. The room number is texted to the customer, who can go directly to the room upon arrival and use the loyalty card to unlock the door. Starwood hotels and Hyatt Gold Passport loyalty card holders have been the first to receive the new perma-key loyalty cards. Another innovation is tone-based locks, which open only when a specific tone is played through a cell phone. To open the door, the customer calls the number received in a text and holds the phone up to the lock on the door; when the lock recognizes the tone, it unlocks. Hotels aren't abandoning their loyal customers, however. When a customer opens the door for the first time, the front desk is notified and calls the room to check that everything is to standard. Excellent customer service without the line is the ultimate loyalty reward.[15]

SOURCE: Andrea Petersen, "Hotels Encourage Guests to Throw Away Their Keys," *Wall Street Journal,* June 9, 2011. © 2011.

© JAKUB PAVLINEC/SHUTTERSTOCK.COM

internal marketing treating employees as customers and developing systems and benefits that satisfy their needs

nonprofit organization an organization that exists to achieve some goal other than the usual business goals of profit, market share, or return on investment

for are more likely to deliver superior service to customers. In other words, a firm that makes its employees happy has a better chance of retaining customers. Thus, it is critical that service firms practice **internal marketing**, which means treating employees as customers and developing systems and benefits that satisfy their needs. To satisfy employees, companies have designed and instituted a wide variety of programs such as flextime, on-site day care, and concierge services. Biomark, a company specializing in electronic wildlife tags, offers employees opportunities to work in the field tagging fish and animals and located its headquarters so as to minimize commuting time for the largest number of employees.[16]

vice firms market intangible products, and both often require the customer to be present during the production process. Both for-profit and nonprofit services vary greatly from producer to producer and from day to day, even from the same producer.

LO7 Global Issues in Services Marketing

The international marketing of services is a major part of global business, and the United States has become the world's largest exporter of services. Competition in international services is increasing rapidly, however. To be successful in the global marketplace, service firms must first determine the nature of their core product. Then the marketing mix elements (additional services, place, promotion, pricing, distribution) should be designed to take into account each country's cultural, technological, and political environment.

Because of their competitive advantages, many U.S. service industries have been able to enter the global marketplace. U.S. banks, for example, have advantages in customer service and collections management.

LO8 Nonprofit Organization Marketing

A **nonprofit organization** is an organization that exists to achieve some goal other than the usual business goals of profit, market share, or return on investment. Both nonprofit organizations and private-sector ser-

Taxes have become the single biggest item in the American family budget.

© ISTOCKPHOTO.COM/VALENTIN MOSICHEV/ © EDYTA PAWLOWSKA/SHUTTERSTOCK.COM

Few people realize that nonprofit organizations account for more than 20 percent of the economic activity in the United States. The cost of government (i.e., taxes), the predominant form of nonprofit organization, has become the biggest single item in the American family budget—more than housing, food, or health care. Together, federal, state, and local governments collect tax revenues that amount to more than a third of the U.S. gross domestic product. In addition to government entities, nonprofit organizations include hundreds of thousands of private museums, theaters, schools, and churches.

What Is Nonprofit Organization Marketing?

Nonprofit organization marketing is the effort by nonprofit organizations to bring about mutually satisfying exchanges with target markets. Although these organizations vary substantially in size and purpose and operate in different environments, most perform the following marketing activities:

» Identify the customers they wish to serve or attract (although they usually use other terms, such as clients, patients, members, or sponsors)

» Explicitly or implicitly specify objectives

» Develop, manage, and eliminate programs and services

» Decide on prices to charge (although they use other terms, such as fees, donations, tuition, fares, fines, or rates)

» Schedule events or programs, and determine where they will be held or where services will be offered

» Communicate their availability through brochures, signs, public service announcements, or advertisements

Often, the nonprofit organizations that carry out these functions do not realize they are engaged in marketing.

Unique Aspects of Nonprofit Organization Marketing Strategies

Like their counterparts in business organizations, nonprofit managers develop marketing strategies to bring about mutually satisfying exchanges with target markets. However, marketing in nonprofit organizations is unique in many ways—including the setting of marketing objectives, the selection of target markets, and the development of appropriate marketing mixes.

Objectives In the private sector, the profit motive is both an objective for guiding decisions and a criterion for evaluating results. Nonprofit organizations do not seek to make a profit for redistribution to owners or shareholders. Rather, their focus is often on generating enough funds to cover expenses.

Most nonprofit organizations are expected to provide equitable, effective, and efficient services that respond to the wants and preferences of multiple constituencies. These include users, payers, donors, politicians, appointed officials, the media, and the general public. Nonprofit organizations cannot measure their success or failure in strictly financial terms.

The lack of a financial "bottom line" and the existence of multiple, diverse, intangible, and sometimes vague or conflicting objectives make prioritizing objectives, making decisions, and evaluating performance hard for nonprofit managers. They must often use approaches different from the ones commonly used in the private sector.

Target Markets Three issues relating to target markets are unique to nonprofit organizations:

» *Apathetic or strongly opposed targets:* Private-sector organizations usually give priority to developing those market segments that are most likely to respond to particular offerings. In contrast, nonprofit organizations must often target those who are apathetic about or strongly opposed to receiving their services, such as vaccinations and psychological counseling.

» *Pressure to adopt undifferentiated segmentation strategies:* Nonprofit organizations often adopt undifferentiated strategies (see Chapter 8) by default. Sometimes they fail to recognize the advantages of targeting, or an undifferentiated approach may appear to offer economies of scale and low per-capita costs. In other instances, nonprofit organizations are pressured or required to serve the maximum number of people by targeting the average user.

» *Complementary positioning:* The main role of many nonprofit organizations is to provide services, with available resources, to those who are not adequately served by private-sector organizations. As a result, the nonprofit organization must often complement, rather than compete with, the efforts of others. The positioning task is to identify underserved market segments and to develop marketing programs that match their needs rather than target the niches that may be most profitable. For example, a university library may see itself as complementing the services of the public library rather than as competing with it.

Product Decisions There are three product-related distinctions between business and nonprofit organizations:

nonprofit organization marketing the effort by nonprofit organizations to bring about mutually satisfying exchanges with target markets

State departments of tourism can develop advertisements based on a clear understanding of what the state has to offer and what current tourists enjoy doing there. For example, this ad for Nevada shows beautiful mountains for skiing and the correct pronunciation of the state's name.

▸▸ *Benefit complexity:* Nonprofit organizations often market complex behaviors or ideas. Examples include the need to exercise or eat right and the need to quit smoking. The benefits that a person receives are complex, long term, and intangible, and therefore are more difficult to communicate to consumers.

▸▸ *Benefit strength:* The benefit strength of many nonprofit offerings is quite weak or indirect. What are the direct, personal benefits to you of driving 55 miles per hour or donating blood? In contrast, most private-sector service organizations can offer customers direct, personal benefits in an exchange relationship.

▸▸ *Involvement:* Many nonprofit organizations market products that elicit very low involvement ("Prevent forest fires") or very high involvement ("Stop smoking"). The typical range for private-sector goods is much narrower. Traditional promotional tools may be inadequate to motivate adoption of either low- or high-involvement products.

public service advertisement (PSA) an announcement that promotes a program of a federal, state, or local government or of a nonprofit organization

Place (Distribution) Decisions A nonprofit organization's capacity for distributing its service offerings to potential customer groups when and where they want them is typically a key variable in determining the success of those service offerings. For example, many large universities have one or more satellite campus locations to provide easier access for students in other areas. Some educational institutions also offer classes to students at off-campus locations via interactive video technology or at home via the Internet.

The extent to which a service depends on fixed facilities has important implications for distribution decisions. Services like rail transit and lake fishing can be delivered only at specific points. Many nonprofit services, however, do not depend on special facilities.

Promotion Decisions Many nonprofit organizations are explicitly or implicitly prohibited from advertising, thus limiting their promotion options. Most federal agencies fall into this category. Other nonprofit organizations simply do not have the resources to retain advertising agencies, promotion consultants, or marketing staff. However, nonprofit organizations have a few special promotion resources to call on:

▸▸ *Professional volunteers:* Nonprofit organizations often seek out marketing, sales, and advertising professionals to help them develop and implement promotion strategies. In some instances, an advertising agency donates its services in exchange for potential long-term benefits. Donated services create goodwill; personal contacts; and general awareness of the donor's organization, reputation, and competency.

▸▸ *Sales promotion activities:* Sales promotion activities that make use of existing services or other resources are increasingly being used to draw attention to the offerings of nonprofit organizations. Sometimes nonprofit charities even team up with other companies for promotional activities.

▸▸ *Public service advertising:* A **public service advertisement (PSA)** is an announcement that promotes a program of a federal, state, or local government or of a nonprofit organization. Unlike a commercial advertiser, the sponsor of the PSA does not pay for the time or space. Instead, it is donated by the medium. The Advertising Council's PSAs are some of the most memorable advertisements of all time. For example, Smokey the Bear reminds everyone to be careful not to start wildfires.

Pricing Decisions Five key characteristics distinguish the pricing decisions of nonprofit organizations from those of the profit sector:

▸▸ *Pricing objectives:* The main pricing objective in the profit sector is revenue or, more specifically, profit

COURTESY OF THE AMERICAN ACADEMY OF ORTHOPAEDIC SURGEONS AND THE ORTHOPAEDIC TRAUMA ASSOCIATION (2010.)

maximization, sales maximization, or target return on sales or investment. Many nonprofit organizations must also be concerned about revenue. Often, however, nonprofit organizations seek to either partially or fully defray costs rather than to achieve a profit for distribution to stockholders. Nonprofit organizations also seek to redistribute income—for instance, through taxation and sliding-scale fees. Moreover, they strive to allocate resources fairly among individuals or households or across geographic or political boundaries.

▸▸ *Nonfinancial prices:* In many nonprofit situations, consumers are not charged a monetary price but instead must absorb nonmonetary costs. The importance of those costs is illustrated by the large number of eligible citizens who do not take advantage of so-called "free" services for the poor. In many public assistance programs, about half the people who are eligible don't participate. Nonmonetary costs include time, embarrassment, and effort.

▸▸ *Indirect payment:* Indirect payment through taxes is common to marketers of "free" services, such as libraries, fire protection, and police protection. Indirect payment is not a common practice in the profit sector.

GET THE MESSAGE.
TEXTING WHILE DRIVING IS A DEADLY DISTRACTION.

AUTO ALLIANCE
DRIVING INNOVATION®

OTA ORTHOPAEDIC TRAUMA ASSOCIATION

AAOS AMERICAN ACADEMY OF ORTHOPAEDIC SURGEONS

Join the conversation.
Visit DecideToDrive.org.

▸▸ *Separation between payers and users:* By design, the services of many charitable organizations are provided for those who are relatively poor and largely paid for by those who are better off financially. Although examples of separation between payers and users can be found in the profit sector (such as insurance claims), the practice is much less prevalent.

▸▸ *Below-cost pricing:* An example of below-cost pricing is university tuition. Virtually all private and public colleges and universities price their services below full cost.

Flip to the back of your textbook to:

❑ **Rip out Chapter Review Card**

Log in to the CourseMate for MKTG at cengagebrain.com to:

❑ **Review Key Terms Flash Cards (Print or Online)**

❑ **Review Audio and Visual Summaries**

❑ **Complete both Practice Quizzes to prepare for tests**

❑ **Play "Beat the Clock" and "Quizbowl" to master concepts**

❑ **Complete "Crossword Puzzle" to review key terms**

❑ **Watch the video on "Kodak" for a real company example on Services and Nonprofit Organization Marketing**

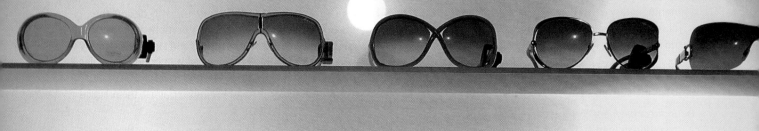

Marketing channels facilitate the physical movement of goods through the supply chain.

© CHRISTIAN BEIRLE GONZÁLEZ/FLICKR/GETTY IMAGES

AFTER YOU FINISH THIS CHAPTER, GO TO PAGE 223 FOR STUDY TOOLS

LO1 Marketing Channels

A marketing channel can be viewed as a large canal or pipeline through which products, their ownership, communication, financing and payment, and accompanying risk flow to the consumer. Formally, a **marketing channel** (also called a **channel of distribution**) is a business structure of interdependent organizations that reach from the point of product origin to the consumer with the purpose of moving products to their final consumption destination. Marketing channels facilitate the physical movement of goods through the supply chain, representing "place" or "distribution" in the marketing mix (product, price, promotion, and place) and encompassing the processes involved in getting the right product to the right place at the right time.

Many different types of organizations participate in marketing channels. **Channel members** (also called *intermediaries*, *resellers*, and *middlemen*) negotiate with one another, buy and sell products, and facilitate the change of ownership between buyer and seller in

marketing channel (channel of distribution)
a set of interdependent organizations that eases the transfer of ownership as products move from producer to business user or consumer

channel members
all parties in the marketing channel who negotiate with one another, buy and sell products, and facilitate the change of ownership between buyer and seller in the course of moving the product from the manufacturer into the hands of the final consumer

What do you think?

The way a product gets to me is only important if it isn't working correctly.

2   3   4   5   6   7

STRONGLY DISAGREE   STRONGLY AGREE

Find out what others think at the CourseMate for MKTG. Log in at cengagebrain.com.

209

discrepancy of quantity the difference between the amount of product produced and the amount an end user wants to buy

discrepancy of assortment the lack of all the items a customer needs to receive full satisfaction from a product or products

temporal discrepancy a situation that occurs when a product is produced but a customer is not ready to buy it

the course of moving the product from the manufacturer into the hands of the final consumer. As products move to the final consumer, channel members facilitate the distribution process by providing specialization and division of labor, overcoming discrepancies, and providing contact efficiency.

Providing Specialization and Division of Labor

According to the concept of *specialization and division of labor*, breaking down a complex task into smaller, simpler ones and allocating them to specialists will create greater efficiency and lower average production costs. Manufacturers achieve economies of scale through the use of efficient equipment capable of producing large quantities of a single product.

Marketing channels can also attain economies of scale through specialization and division of labor by aiding producers who lack the motivation, financing, or expertise to market directly to end users or consumers. In some cases, as with most consumer convenience goods, such as soft drinks, the cost of marketing directly to millions of consumers—taking and shipping individual orders—is prohibitive. For this reason, producers hire channel members, such as wholesalers and retailers, to do what the producers are not equipped to do or what channel members are better prepared to do. Channel members can do some things more efficiently than producers because they have built good relationships with their customers. Therefore, their specialized expertise enhances the overall performance of the channel.

Overcoming Discrepancies

Marketing channels also aid in overcoming discrepancies of quantity, assortment, time, and space created by economies of scale in production. For example, assume that J.M. Smucker Company can efficiently produce its Hungry Jack instant pancake mix only at a rate of 5,000 units in a typical day. Not even the most ardent pancake fan could consume that amount in a year, much less in a day. The quantity produced to achieve low unit costs has created a **discrepancy of quantity**, which is the difference between the amount of product produced and the amount an end user wants to

buy. By storing the product and distributing it in the appropriate amounts, marketing channels overcome quantity discrepancies by making products available in the quantities that consumers desire.

Mass production creates not only discrepancies of quantity but also discrepancies of assortment. A **discrepancy of assortment** occurs when a consumer does not have all of the items needed to receive full satisfaction from a product. For pancakes to provide maximum satisfaction, several other products are required to complete the assortment. At the very least, most people want a knife, fork, plate, butter, and syrup. Even though J.M. Smucker is a large consumer product company, it does not come close to providing the optimal assortment to go with its Hungry Jack pancakes. To overcome discrepancies of assortment, marketing channels assemble in one place many of the products necessary to complete a consumer's needed assortment.

A **temporal discrepancy** is created when a product is produced but a consumer is not ready to buy it. Marketing channels overcome temporal discrepancies by maintaining inventories in anticipation of demand. For example, manufacturers of seasonal merchandise, such as Christmas or Halloween decorations, are in operation all year even though consumer demand is concentrated during certain months of the year.

Furthermore, because mass production requires many potential buyers, markets are usually scat-

© CHRISTI TOLBERT/SHUTTERSTOCK.COM

tered over large geographic regions, creating a **spatial discrepancy**. Often global, or at least nationwide, markets are needed to absorb the outputs of mass producers. Marketing channels overcome spatial discrepancies by making products available in locations convenient to consumers. For example, if all the Hungry Jack pancake mix is produced in Boise, Idaho, then J.M. Smucker must use an intermediary to distribute the product to other regions of the United States.

Providing Contact Efficiency

The third need fulfilled by marketing channels is that they provide contact efficiency by reducing the number of stores customers must shop in to complete their purchases. Suppose you had to buy your milk at a dairy and your meat at a stockyard. You would spend a great deal of time, money, and energy just shopping for a few groceries. Marketing channels simplify distribution by cutting the number of transactions required to get products from manufacturers to consumers and making an assortment of goods available in one location.

Consider the example illustrated in Exhibit 13.1 on the next page. Four consumers each want to buy a television set. Without a retail intermediary like Best Buy, television manufacturers JVC, Zenith, Sony, Toshiba, and RCA would each have to make four contacts to reach the four consumers who are in the target market, for a total of 20 transactions. However, when Best Buy acts as an intermediary between the producer and consumers, each producer has to make only one contact, reducing the number to nine transactions. Each producer sells to one retailer rather than to four consumers. In turn, consumers buy from one retailer instead of from five producers. Information technology has enhanced contact efficiency by making information on products and services easily available over the Internet. Shoppers can find the best bargains without physically searching for them.

spatial discrepancy the difference between the location of a producer and the location of widely scattered markets

retailer a channel intermediary that sells mainly to consumers

merchant wholesaler an institution that buys goods from manufacturers and resells them to businesses, government agencies, and other wholesalers or retailers and that receives and takes title to goods, stores them in its own warehouses, and later ships them

DISTRIBUTING MEDICATION TO THE WORLD'S SUFFERING

Spatial discrepancies can be life threatening, particularly when distributing medication. The distribution of the child-friendly malaria drug in developing countries suffers from spatial discrepancy, especially in Africa, where 200 million people fall ill with malaria yearly. The size and location of the African market have led to this spatial discrepancy for the drug, which is mass-produced in Switzerland. To overcome this discrepancy, companies have partnered with nonprofits and governments to distribute the medication through national medical centers and hospitals in Africa. The combined efforts of these groups have made a much-needed drug available to people who otherwise might not have access to it.[1]

© VLADNIK/SHUTTERSTOCK.COM

SOURCE: Robert Guth, "New Child-Friendly Malaria Drug Presents Distribution Challenge," *Wall Street Journal*, January 27, 2009, © 2009.

LO 2 Channel Intermediaries and Their Functions

Intermediaries in a channel negotiate with one another, facilitate the change of ownership between buyers and sellers, and physically move products from the manufacturer to the final consumer. The most prominent difference separating intermediaries is whether they take title to the product. *Taking title* means they own the merchandise and control the terms of the sale—for example, price and delivery date. Retailers and merchant wholesalers are examples of intermediaries that take title to products in the marketing channel and resell them. **Retailers** are firms that sell mainly to consumers. Retailers will be discussed in more detail in Chapter 15.

Merchant wholesalers are organizations that facilitate the movement of products and services from the manufacturer to producers, resellers, governments, institutions, and retailers. All merchant wholesalers take title to the goods they sell, and most of them

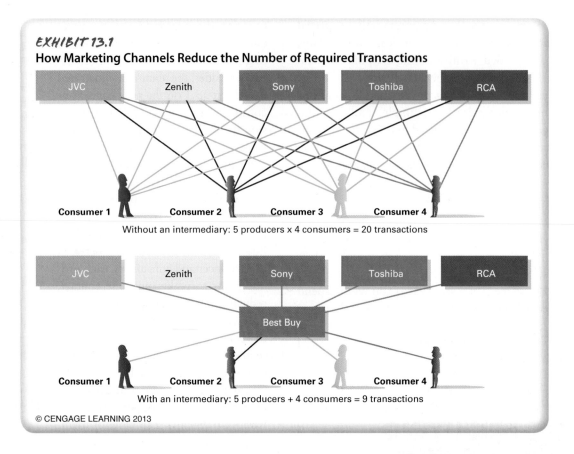

EXHIBIT 13.1
How Marketing Channels Reduce the Number of Required Transactions

JVC | Zenith | Sony | Toshiba | RCA

Consumer 1   Consumer 2   Consumer 3   Consumer 4

Without an intermediary: 5 producers x 4 consumers = 20 transactions

JVC | Zenith | Sony | Toshiba | RCA

Best Buy

Consumer 1   Consumer 2   Consumer 3   Consumer 4

With an intermediary: 5 producers + 4 consumers = 9 transactions

© CENGAGE LEARNING 2013

operate one or more warehouses where they receive goods, store them, and later reship them. Customers are mostly small- or medium-sized retailers, but merchant wholesalers also market to manufacturers and institutional clients.

Other intermediaries do not take title to goods and services they market but do facilitate the exchange of ownership between sellers and buyers. **Agents and brokers** simply facilitate the sale of a product from producer to end user by representing retailers, wholesalers, or manufacturers. Title reflects ownership, and ownership usually implies control. Unlike wholesalers, agents or brokers only facilitate sales and generally have little input into the terms of the sale. They do, however, get a fee or commission based on sales volume. For example, when selling a home, the owner usually hires a real estate agent who then brings potential buyers to see the house. The agent facilitates the sale by bringing the buyer and owner together but never actually takes ownership of the home.

Variations in channel structures are due in large part to variations in the numbers and types of wholesaling intermediaries. Generally, product characteristics, buyer considerations,

agents and brokers wholesaling intermediaries who do not take title to a product but facilitate its sale from producer to end user by representing retailers, wholesalers, or manufacturers

and market conditions determine the type of intermediary the manufacturer should use.

▶▶ *Product characteristics* that may require a certain type of wholesaling intermediary include whether the product is standardized or customized, the complexity of the product, and the gross margin of the product. For example, a customized product such as insurance is sold through an insurance agent or broker who may represent one or multiple companies. In contrast, a standardized product such as gum is sold through a merchant wholesaler that takes possession of the gum and reships it to the appropriate retailers.

▶▶ *Buyer considerations* affecting the wholesaler choice include how often the product is purchased and how long the buyer is willing to wait to receive the product. For example, at the beginning of the school term, a student may be willing to wait a few days for a textbook to get a lower price by ordering online. Thus, this type of product can be distributed directly. But if the student waits to buy the book until right before an exam and needs the book immediately, it will have to be purchased at the school bookstore.

▶▶ *Market characteristics* determining the wholesaler type include how many buyers are in the market and whether they are concentrated in a general location or are widely dispersed. Gum and textbooks, for example, are produced in one location and consumed in many other locations. Therefore, a merchant wholesaler is needed to distribute the products. In contrast, in a home sale, the buyer and seller are localized in one area, which facilitates the use of an agent/broker relationship.

Channel Functions Performed by Intermediaries

Retailing and wholesaling intermediaries in marketing channels perform several essential functions that make the flow of goods between producer and buyer possible. The three basic functions that intermediaries perform are summarized in Exhibit 13.2.

Transactional functions involve contacting and communicating with prospective buyers to make them aware of existing products and explain their features, advantages, and benefits. Intermediaries in the channel also provide *logistical* functions. **Logistics** is the efficient and cost-effective forward and reverse flow and storage of goods, services, and related information into, through, and out of channel member companies. Logistics functions typically include transportation and storage of assets, as well as their sorting, accumulation, consolidation, and/or allocation for the purpose of conforming to customer requirements. For example, grading agricultural products typifies the sorting-out

process, while consolidation of many lots of grade A eggs from different sources into one lot illustrates the accumulation process. Supermarkets or other retailers perform the assorting function by assembling thousands of different items that match their customers' desires. Similarly, while large companies typically have direct channels, many small companies depend on wholesalers to promote and distribute their products.

The third basic channel function, *facilitating*, includes research and financing. Research provides information about channel members and consumers by getting answers to key questions: Who are the buyers? Where are they located? Why do they buy? Financing ensures that channel members have the money to keep products moving through the channel to the ultimate consumer.

Although individual members can be added to or deleted from a channel, someone must still perform these essential functions.

logistics the efficient and cost-effective forward and reverse flow and storage of goods, services, and related information into, through, and out of channel member companies

© MIRRORMERE/SHUTTERSTOCK.COM

EXHIBIT 13.2
Marketing Channel Functions Performed by Intermediaries

Type of Function	Description
Transactional Functions	**Contacting and promoting:** Contacting potential customers, promoting products, and soliciting orders
	Negotiating: Determining how many goods or services to buy and sell, type of transportation to use, when to deliver, and method and timing of payment
	Risk taking: Assuming the risk of owning inventory
Logistical Functions	**Physically distributing:** Transporting and sorting goods to overcome temporal and spatial discrepancies
	Storing: Maintaining inventories and protecting goods
	Sorting: Overcoming discrepancies of quantity and assortment by
	Sorting out: Breaking down a heterogeneous supply into separate homogeneous stocks
	Accumulating: Combining similar stocks into a larger homogeneous supply
	Allocating: Breaking a homogeneous supply into smaller and smaller lots ("breaking bulk")
	Assorting: Combining products into collections or assortments that buyers want available at one place
Facilitating Functions	**Researching:** Gathering information about other channel members and consumers
	Financing: Extending credit and other financial services to facilitate the flow of goods through the channel to the final consumer

© CENGAGE LEARNING 2013

direct channel a distribution channel in which producers sell directly to consumers

They can be performed by producers, end users, or consumers; channel intermediaries such as wholesalers and retailers; and sometimes nonmember channel participants. For example, if a manufacturer decides to eliminate its private fleet of trucks, it must still have a way to move the goods to the wholesaler. This task may be accomplished by the wholesaler, which may have its own fleet of trucks, or by a nonmember channel participant, such as an independent trucking firm. Nonmembers also provide many other essential functions that may at one time have been provided by a channel member. For example, research firms may perform the research function, advertising agencies may provide the promotion function, transportation and storage firms may provide the physical distribution function, and banks may perform the financing function.

LO 3 Channel Structures

A product can take many routes to reach its final consumer. Marketers search for the most efficient channel from the many alternatives available. Marketing a consumer convenience good such as gum or candy differs from marketing a specialty good like a Prada handbag. The next sections discuss the structures of typical and alternative marketing channels for consumer and business-to-business products.

Channels for Consumer Products

Exhibit 13.3 illustrates the four ways manufacturers can route products to consumers. Producers use the **direct channel** to sell directly to consumers. Direct marketing activities—including telemarketing, mail-order and catalog shopping, and forms of electronic retailing such as online shopping and shop-at-home television networks—are a good example of this type of channel structure. There are no intermediaries. Producer-owned stores and fac-

tory outlet stores—like Sherwin-Williams, Polo Ralph Lauren, Oneida, and WestPoint Home—are examples of direct channels. Direct channels can be appealing for a number of businesses. In an effort to compete with Apple Stores, Microsoft is creating its own stores to sell directly to consumers. While the direct channel will allow Microsoft to interact directly with consumers, it also exposes Microsoft to some risks. Microsoft stores will now be responsible for managing the inventory in a direct channel, which could result in damages, theft, and obsolescence—problems Microsoft has less experience than Apple in handling and that were previously handled by an intermediary.[2]

By contrast, an *agent/broker channel* is fairly complicated and typically used in markets with many small manufacturers and many retailers that lack the resources to find each other. Agents or brokers bring manufacturers and wholesalers together for negotiations, but they do not take title to merchandise. Ownership passes directly to one or more wholesalers and then to retailers. Finally, retailers sell to the ultimate consumer of the product. For example, a food broker represents buyers and sellers of grocery products. The broker acts on behalf of many different producers and negotiates the sale of their products to wholesalers that specialize in foodstuffs. These wholesalers in turn sell to grocers and convenience stores.

Most consumer products are sold through distribution channels similar to the other two alternatives: the retailer channel and the wholesaler channel. A *retailer*

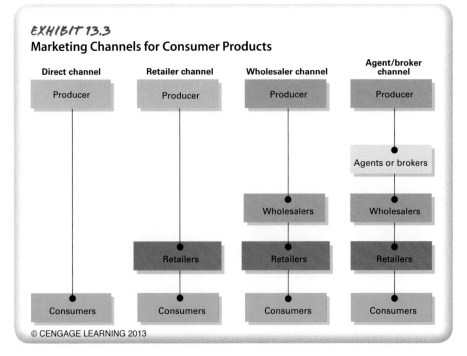

EXHIBIT 13.3
Marketing Channels for Consumer Products

Direct channel	Retailer channel	Wholesaler channel	Agent/broker channel
Producer	Producer	Producer	Producer
			Agents or brokers
		Wholesalers	Wholesalers
	Retailers	Retailers	Retailers
Consumers	Consumers	Consumers	Consumers

© CENGAGE LEARNING 2013

channel is most common when the retailer is large and can buy in large quantities directly from the manufacturer. Walmart, Sears, and car dealers are examples of retailers that often bypass a wholesaler. A *wholesaler channel* is commonly used for low-cost items that are frequently purchased, such as candy, cigarettes, and magazines.

Channels for Business and Industrial Products

As Exhibit 13.4 illustrates, five channel structures are common in business and industrial markets. First, *direct channels* are typical in business and industrial markets. For example, manufacturers buy large quantities of raw materials, major equipment, processed materials, and supplies directly from other manufacturers. Manufacturers that require suppliers to meet detailed technical specifications often prefer direct channels. Apple used a direct channel to purchase chips for its iPad. To ensure that Toshiba would deliver flash memory chips for iPad construction, Apple paid the chip maker $500 million in July 2009—well in advance of the April 2010 release. Such guarantees happen most efficiently through the direct communication made possible by using a direct channel.[3] The channel from producer to government buyers is also a direct channel. Since much government buying is done through bidding, a direct channel is attractive.

Companies selling standardized items of moderate or low value often rely on *industrial distributors*. In many ways, an industrial distributor is like a supermarket for organizations. Industrial distributors are wholesalers and channel members that buy and take title to products. Moreover, they usually keep inventories of their products and sell and service them. Often small manufacturers cannot afford to employ their own sales force. Instead, they rely on manufacturers' representatives or selling agents to sell to either industrial distributors or users.

The Internet has enabled virtual distributors to emerge and has forced traditional industrial distributors to expand their business model. Many manufacturers and consumers are bypassing distributors and going direct, often via the Internet. Companies looking to drop the intermediary from the supply chain have created exchanges. Retailers use the Worldwide Retail Exchange to make purchases that in the past would have required telephone, fax, or face-to-face sales calls, and in so doing, they save approximately 15 percent in their purchasing costs. Finally, a third type of Internet marketplace is a private exchange. With a *private exchange*, a company creates a network that connects its business with those of its suppliers. Some large companies prefer private exchanges because they provide tighter security over transactions, especially when negotiating complex contracts.

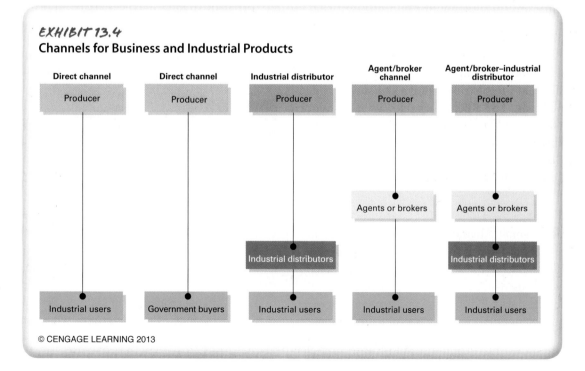

EXHIBIT 13.4
Channels for Business and Industrial Products

© CENGAGE LEARNING 2013

Alternative Channel Arrangements

dual distribution (multiple distribution) the use of two or more channels to distribute the same product to target markets

strategic channel alliance a cooperative agreement between business firms to use the other's already established distribution channel

Rarely does a producer use just one type of channel to move its product. It usually employs several different or alternative channels, which include multiple channels, nontraditional channels, and strategic channel alliances.

Multiple Channels When a producer selects two or more channels to distribute the same product to target markets, this arrangement is called **dual distribution** (or **multiple distribution**). As more people embrace online shopping, an increasing number of retailers are using multiple distribution channels. For example, companies such as The Limited, which includes Express, Victoria's Secret, and Bath and Body Works, sell in-store, online, and through catalogs. An emerging trend is ordering online for in-store pickup. Large chains such as Walmart, Lowes, and Best Buy offer this multichannel distribution for customer convenience.

Nontraditional Channels Often nontraditional channel arrangements help differentiate a firm's product from the competition. Nontraditional channels include the Internet, mail-order channels, or infomercials. Although nontraditional channels may limit a brand's coverage, they can give a producer serving a niche market a way to gain market access and customer attention without having to establish channel intermediaries. Nontraditional channels can also provide another avenue of sales for larger firms. For example, Redbox uses kiosks in Walgreens, Kroger, and McDonald's to distribute movies to shoppers at those locations. The Redbox enables users to rent movies for a 24-hour period for $1.00 each and return them to any Redbox kiosk. Customers can also go online to reserve movies at Redbox kiosks to ensure their preferred selection is available when wanted.[4]

Strategic Channel Alliances Companies often form **strategic channel alliances**, which enable them to use another manufacturer's already-established channel. Alliances are used most often when the creation of marketing channel relationships may be too expensive and time consuming. Verizon Wireless and the National Football League signed a contract allowing Verizon to broadcast live Sunday afternoon football games to mobile subscribers. Subscribers will receive access to a mobile version of the NFL's dedicated football channel called the RedZone. This is the first time the NFL has broadcast live Sunday games to mobile devices.[5]

Alliances can also prove more efficient when a company wants to run promotions. PepsiCo purchased its two major bottlers and has since been able to work directly with retailers to create store-specific bundles for grocery stores (12-packs of Pepsi and large bags of chips) and for convenience stores (single bottles of Pepsi and small bags of chips). The purchase of its bottlers has also made it easier for Pepsi to work directly with stores to provide store-specific merchandise, like bringing Mexican brands to stores in San Antonio, Texas, that cater to Hispanics.[6]

Strategic channel alliances are proving to be more successful for growing businesses than mergers and acquisitions. This is especially true in global markets where cultural differences, distance, and other barriers can prove challenging.

LO 4 Making Channel Strategy Decisions

Devising a marketing channel strategy requires several critical decisions. Managers must decide what role distribution will play in the overall marketing strategy. In addition, they must be sure that the channel strategy chosen is consistent with product, promotion, and pricing strategies. In making these decisions, marketing managers must determine what factors will influence the choice of channel and what level of distribution intensity will be appropriate.

© KRISTA KENNELL/SIPA PRESS VIA AP IMAGES

Factors Affecting Channel Choice

Managers must answer many questions before choosing a marketing channel. The final choice depends on the analysis of several factors, which often interact. These factors can be grouped as market factors, product factors, and producer factors.

Market Factors Among the most important market factors affecting the choice of distribution channel are target customer considerations. Specifically, managers should answer the following questions: Who are the potential customers? What do they buy? Where do they buy? When do they buy? How do they buy? Additionally, the choice of channel depends on whether the producer is selling to consumers or to industrial customers. Industrial customers' buying habits are very different from those of consumers. Industrial customers tend to buy in larger quantities and require more customer service.

The geographic location and size of the market are also important to channel selection. As a rule, if the target market is concentrated in one or more specific areas, then direct selling through a sales force is appropriate. When markets are more widely dispersed, intermediaries would be less expensive. The size of the market also influences channel choice. Generally, larger markets require more intermediaries.

Product Factors Products that are more complex, customized, and expensive tend to benefit from shorter and more direct marketing channels. These types of products sell better through a direct sales force. Examples include pharmaceuticals, scientific instruments, airplanes, and mainframe computer systems. On the other hand, the more standardized a product is, the longer its distribution channel can be and the greater the number of intermediaries that can be involved. For example, with the exception of flavor and shape, the formula for chewing gum is about the same from producer to producer. Chewing gum is also very inexpensive. As a result, the distribution channel for gum tends to involve many wholesalers and retailers.

The product's life cycle is also an important factor in choosing a marketing channel. In fact, the choice of channel may change over the life of the product. As products become more common and less intimidating to potential users, producers tend to look for alternative channels.

Another factor is the delicacy of the product. Perishable products such as vegetables and milk have a relatively short life span. Fragile products like china and crystal require a minimum amount of handling. Therefore, both require fairly short marketing channels. Online retailers such as eBay facilitate the sale of unusual or difficult-to-find products that benefit from a direct channel.

Producer Factors Several factors pertaining to the producer itself are important to the selection of a marketing channel. In general, producers with large financial, managerial, and marketing resources are better able to use more direct channels. These producers have the ability to hire and train their own sales forces, warehouse their own goods, and extend credit to their customers. Smaller or weaker firms, on the

LESS DELICATE PRODUCTS HAVE MORE CHANNEL FLEXIBILITY.

FRAGILE PRODUCTS REQUIRE SHORT CHANNELS.

© IVONNE WIERINK/SHUTTERSTOCK.COM; © KARAM MIRI/SHUTTERSTOCK.COM

intensive distribution a form of distribution aimed at having a product available in every outlet where target customers might want to buy it

selective distribution a form of distribution achieved by screening dealers to eliminate all but a few in any single area

exclusive distribution a form of distribution that establishes one or a few dealers within a given area

other hand, must rely on intermediaries to provide these services for them. Compared to producers with only one or two product lines, producers that sell several products in a related area are able to choose channels that are more direct. Sales expenses then can be spread over more products.

A producer's desire to control pricing, positioning, brand image, and customer support also tends to influence channel selection. For instance, firms that sell products with exclusive brand images, such as designer perfumes and clothing, usually avoid channels in which discount retailers are present. Manufacturers of upscale products, such as Gucci (handbags) and Godiva (chocolates), may sell their wares only in expensive stores in order to maintain an image of exclusivity. Many producers have opted to risk their image, however, and test sales in discount channels. Levi Strauss expanded its distribution to include JCPenney, Sears, and Walmart.

Levels of Distribution Intensity

Organizations have three options for intensity of distribution: intensive distribution, selective distribution, or exclusive distribution.

Intensive Distribution Intensive distribution is a form of distribution aimed at maximum market coverage. The manufacturer tries to have the product available in every outlet where potential customers might want to buy it. If buyers are unwilling to search for a product (as is true of convenience goods and operating supplies), the product must be very accessible to buyers. A low-value product that is purchased frequently may require a lengthy channel. For example, candy, chips, and other snack foods, which are found in almost every type of retail store, are typically sold to retailers in small quantities by food or candy wholesalers.

Most manufacturers pursuing an intensive distribution strategy sell to a large percentage of the wholesalers willing to stock their products. Retailers' willingness (or unwillingness) to handle items tends to control the manufacturer's ability to achieve intensive distribution. For example, a retailer already carrying ten brands of gum may show little enthusiasm for one more brand.

Selective Distribution The next level of distribution is **selective distribution**, which is achieved by screening

dealers and retailers to eliminate all but a few in any single area. Because only a few are chosen, the consumer must seek out the product. For example, HBO selectively distributes its popular TV shows through a series of its own subscription-based channels (HBO, HBO on Demand, and HBO Go for mobile devices) and sells subscriptions or single episodes through Apple, Amazon, and Sony's online stores. HBO does not stream through Netflix or Blockbuster, two of the more popular rental options, electing to have interested viewers buy rather than rent.[7] Selective distribution strategies often hinge on a manufacturer's desire to maintain a superior product image so as to be able to charge a premium price. DKNY clothing, for instance, is sold only in select retail outlets, mainly full-price department stores. Manufacturers sometimes expand selective distribution strategies, believing that doing so will enhance revenues without diminishing their product's image. The celebrity fragrance industry generally introduces a fragrance, such as the new fragrance from Lady Gaga, exclusively at department store makeup counters. After roughly a year, or when sales have begun declining, the fragrance is released to larger discount retailers, such as Walmart and Target. Such a strategy combines the initial exclusivity and elevated product image with the extended spike in sales from wider distribution.[8]

Exclusive Distribution The most restrictive form of market coverage is **exclusive distribution**, which entails only one or a few dealers within a given area. Because buyers may have to search or travel extensively to buy the product, exclusive distribution is usually confined to consumer specialty goods, a few shopping goods, and major industrial equipment. Products such as Rolls-Royce automobiles, Chris-Craft power boats, and Pettibone tower cranes are distributed under exclusive arrangements.

Retailers and wholesalers may be unwilling to commit the time and money necessary to promote and service a product unless the manufacturer guarantees them an exclusive territory. This arrangement shields the dealer from direct competition and enables it to be the main beneficiary of the manufacturer's promotion efforts in that geographic area. With exclusive distribution, channels of communication are usually well established because the manufacturer works with a limited number of dealers rather than many accounts.

Exclusive distribution also takes place within a retailer's store rather than a geographic area—for example, when a retailer agrees not to sell a manufacturer's competing brands.

© AP IMAGES/PRNEWSFOTO/ICONIX BRAND GROUP, INC.

LO5 Types of Channel Relationships

A marketing channel is more than a set of institutions linked by economic ties. Social relationships play an important role in building unity among channel members. Marketing managers should carefully consider the types of relationships they choose to foster between their company and other companies and in doing so pay close attention to the benefits and hazards associated with each relationship type. Relationships among channel members range from "loose" to "tight," taking the form of a continuum stretching from single transactions to complex interdependent relationships such as partnerships or alliances. The choice of relationship type is important for channel management because each relationship type carries with it different levels of time, financial, and resource investment. There are three basic types of relationships, organized here by degree of closeness:

▸ *Arm's-length relationships* are considered by channel members to be temporary or one-time-only and often

Actress and recording artist Vanessa Hudgens appears in Candie's Spring 2011 multimedia marketing campaign. Candie's brand is sold exclusively at Kohl's and typically uses big stars to drive customers to Kohl's stores.

arise from a sudden or unique need. These relationships are characterized by the companies' unwillingness or lack of ability to develop a closer type of relationship. Both parties typically retain their independence and pursue only their own interests while attempting to benefit from the goods or services provided by the other. A major weakness of arm's-length relationships is the potential for opportunism. Opportunistic behavior may occur when the members do not have a common goal; when members have not formed a formal relationship; when one company is more dependent on the other than vice versa; or when there is uncertainty within the relationship and the market.

▸ *Cooperative relationships*, generally administered using some kind of formal contract, are used when a company wants less ambiguity but doesn't want the long-term and/or capital investment necessary in an integrated relationship. Cooperative relationships tend to be more flexible than integrated relationships but are more structured than arm's-length relationships, and they include nonequity agreements such as franchising and licensing as well as joint ventures and strategic alliances.

▸ *Integrated relationships* are closely bonded relationships characterized by formal arrangements that explicitly define the relationships of the channel members. These relationships may take two forms. With vertical integration, all the related channel members are owned by a single legal entity, whereas in a supply chain, several companies act as one. Coca-Cola and PepsiCo have both announced and negotiated deals to take over their respective bottling company suppliers. Both companies want to have more flexibility and control of their products and bottling plants so that they can better serve their customers.[9] Supply chains are discussed in detail in Chapter 14.

Based on these descriptions, it might seem that integrated relationships would be the preferred relationship type in almost all company-to-company channel settings. However, highly integrated relationships also come with some significant costs and hazards. For example, the single-owner model is somewhat risky because a large amount of capital assets must be purchased or leased (requiring a

arm's-length relationship a relationship between companies that is loose, characterized by low relational investment and trust, and usually taking the form of a series of discrete transactions with no or low expectation of future interaction or service

cooperative relationship a relationship between companies that takes the form of informal partnership with moderate levels of trust and information sharing as needed to further each company's goals

integrated relationship a relationship between companies that is tightly connected, with linked processes across and between firm boundaries and high levels of trust and interfirm commitment

potentially huge initial cash outlay), and the failure of any portion of the business may not only result in the economic loss of that portion but may also reduce the value of the other business units (or render them totally worthless). Because these trade-offs are sometimes hard to justify, companies often look for the sort of "happy medium" of cooperative relationships.

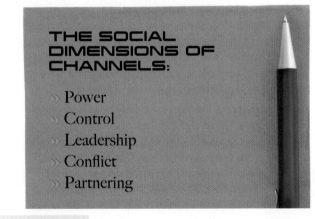

LO 6 Managing Channel Relationships

In addition to considering the multiple different types of channel relationships and their costs and benefits, managers must also be aware of the social dimensions that are constantly affecting their relationships. The basic social dimensions of channels are power, control, leadership, conflict, and partnering.

THE SOCIAL DIMENSIONS OF CHANNELS:

» Power
» Control
» Leadership
» Conflict
» Partnering

channel power
the capacity of a particular marketing channel member to control or influence the behavior of other channel members

channel control a situation that occurs when one marketing channel member intentionally affects another member's behavior

channel leader (channel captain) a member of a marketing channel that exercises authority and power over the activities of other channel members

channel conflict a clash of goals and methods between distribution channel members

Channel Power, Control, and Leadership

Channel power is a channel member's ability to control or influence the behavior of other channel members. **Channel control** occurs when one channel member's power affects another member's behavior. To achieve control, a channel member assumes channel leadership and exercises authority and power. This member is termed the **channel leader**, or **channel captain**. In one marketing channel, a manufacturer may be the leader because it controls new-product designs and product availability. In another, a retailer may be the channel leader because it wields power and control over the retail price, inventory levels, and postsale service. Apple is the current channel leader for tablets and is using its power to dictate subscription terms for magazine and app developers. Sales must be made from within an app available through Apple's App Store (giving Apple 30 percent of the sale), and apps cannot link to an outside Web page where the product is sold unless that product is offered for the same or a lower price in iTunes.[10]

Channel Conflict

Inequitable channel relationships often lead to **channel conflict**, which is a clash of goals and methods among the members of a distribution channel. In a broad context, conflict may not be bad. Often it arises because staid, traditional channel members refuse to keep pace with the times. Removing an outdated intermediary may result in reduced costs for the entire channel. The Internet has forced many intermediaries to offer services such as merchandise tracking and inventory availability online.

Conflicts among channel members can be due to many different situations and factors. Oftentimes, conflict arises because channel members have conflicting goals. For instance, athletic footwear retailers want to sell as many shoes as possible in order to maximize profits, regardless of whether the shoe is manufactured by Nike, Adidas, or Saucony, but the Nike manufacturer wants a certain sales volume and market share in each market. Magazine publishers often offer discounts and deals to subscribers via e-mail or mail. However, Apple's subscription service through iTunes does not release any subscriber information to the publisher unless the user opts in to receive offers. Apple's goal of consumer protection is at odds with the publishers' desire to sell magazine subscriptions.[11]

Conflict can also arise when channel members fail to fulfill expectations of other channel members—for example, when a franchisee does not follow the rules set down by the franchisor, or when communications channels break down between channel members. Further, ideological differences and different perceptions of reality can also cause conflict among channel members. For instance, when it comes to return policies, a retailer's "the customer is always right" perspective will likely conflict with a wholesaler or manufacturer's perspective that people try to get something for nothing.

© ISTOCKPHOTO.COM/TRAVELLINGLIGHT

Conflict within a channel can be either horizontal or vertical. **Horizontal conflict** occurs among channel members on the same level, such as two or more different wholesalers or two or more different retailers that handle the same manufacturer's brands. This type of channel conflict is found most often when manufacturers practice dual or multiple distribution strategies. When Apple changed its distribution strategy and began opening its own stores, it angered its traditional retail partners, some of whom ultimately filed lawsuits against the company. Horizontal conflict can also occur when some channel members feel that other members on the same level are being treated differently by the manufacturer.

Many marketers and customers regard horizontal conflict as healthy competition. Much more serious is **vertical conflict**, which occurs between different levels in a marketing channel, most typically between the manufacturer and wholesaler or the manufacturer and retailer. Producer-versus-wholesaler conflict occurs when the producer chooses to bypass the wholesaler and deal directly with the consumer or retailer.

Dual distribution strategies can also cause vertical conflict in the channel. As CVS begins to open its new Beauty 360 stores, which will be adjacent to existing CVS stores, the drugstore chain has to be careful not to cannabalize its existing beauty business or offend current prestige beauty suppliers that sell in CVS. Beauty 360 is targeted to niche and affluent customers who have never shopped in CVS stores. CVS hopes to avoid any vertical conflict by differentiating its brands for each of its store formats.[12]

Channel Partnering

Regardless of the locus of power, channel members rely heavily on one another. **Channel partnering**, or **channel cooperation**, is the joint effort of all channel members to create a channel that serves customers and creates a competitive advantage. Channel partnering is vital if each member is to gain something from other members. By cooperating, retailers, wholesalers, manufacturers, and suppliers can speed up inventory replenishment, improve customer service, and reduce the total cost of the marketing channel.

Channel alliances and partnerships help managers create the parallel flow of materials and information required to leverage the channel's intellectual, material, and marketing resources. The rapid growth in channel partnering is due to new enabling technology and the need to lower costs.

> **horizontal conflict** a channel conflict that occurs among channel members on the same level
>
> **vertical conflict** a channel conflict that occurs between different levels in a marketing channel, most typically between the manufacturer and wholesaler or between the manufacturer and retailer
>
> **channel partnering (channel cooperation)** the joint effort of all channel members to create a channel that serves customers and creates a competitive advantage

RESISTING THE LOUIS VUITTON MODEL

© ADISA/SHUTTERSTOCK.COM

SOURCE: Carol Matlack, "Handbags at the Barricades," *Bloomberg Businessweek*, © 2011, March 28–April 3, 2011, 80–83.

Louis Vuitton, owned by LVMH, was once known for handcrafted luxury accessories, but now is famous for its signature print, which is mass-produced in highly automated factories. This move toward automation in luxury goods is a result of the increasingly consolidated luxury market, which consists of three big groups: LVMH, PPR (maker of Gucci products), and Richemont (Cartier). Hermés, maker of luxurious scarves and handbags, remains one of the few brand name designers that isn't a subsidiary of one of those groups. This independence allows Hermés to handcraft its products—each bag is crafted by one person, who spends roughly 13 hours on one bag. However, the largely family-owned business is struggling to remain independent from the channel leaders. Bernard Arnault of LVMH recently revealed that he owns 20 percent of the Hermés shares, giving him more control over how Hermés is run. Now the 72 adult descendants of Hermés are banding together to resist the move to automation and consolidation under LMVH.[13]

LO7 Channels and Distribution Decisions for Global Markets

With the spread of free trade agreements and treaties in recent decades, such as the European Union and the North American Free Trade Agreement (NAFTA), global marketing channels and management of the channels have become increasingly important to U.S. companies that export their products or manufacture abroad.

Developing Global Marketing Channels

Executives should recognize the unique cultural, economic, institutional, and legal aspects of each market before trying to design marketing channels in foreign countries. Manufacturers introducing products in global markets have to decide whether the product will be marketed directly, mostly by company salespeople, or through independent foreign intermediaries, such as agents and distributors. Using company salespeople generally provides more control and is less risky than using foreign intermediaries. However, setting up a sales force in a foreign country also entails a greater commitment, both financially and organizationally.

Marketers should be aware that channel structures and types abroad may differ from those in the United States. For instance, the more highly developed a nation is economically, the more specialized are its channel types. Therefore, a marketer wishing to sell in Germany or Japan will have several channel types to choose from. Conversely, developing countries such as Ethiopia, India, and Venezuela have limited channel types available, and they tend to shun the large-scale formats popular in the United States and Western Europe.

Some countries also enact economic policies that directly or indirectly regulate channel choices. For example, due to the size of India's market, many companies are interested in operating there. India does not explicitly prohibit foreign retailers from entering its market, but it protects its businesses by levying heavy taxes on foreign retailers. To address this issue, many companies, including Mercedes-Benz, Toyota, and General Motors, have entered joint ventures with local Indian companies. Through these joint ventures, foreign companies are able to compete effectively in India's available distribution channels.[14]

© AP IMAGES/LIONEL CIRONNEAU

The fasion industry works diligently to protect its designers by running ads such as this one to deter people from buying knock-offs in the street.

Marketers must also be aware that many countries have "gray" marketing channels in which products are distributed through unauthorized channel intermediaries. It is estimated that sales of counterfeit luxury items like Prada handbags and Big Bertha golf clubs have reached almost $2 billion a year. The Internet has also proved to be a way for pirates to circumvent authorized distribution channels, especially in the case of popular prescription drugs.

LO8 Channels and Distribution Decisions for Services

The fastest-growing part of our economy is the service sector. Although distribution in the service sector is difficult to visualize, the same skills, techniques, and strategies used to manage inventory can also be used to manage service inventory—for instance, hospital beds, bank accounts, or airline seats. The quality of the planning and execution of distribution can have a major impact on costs and customer satisfaction.

One thing that sets service distribution apart from traditional manufacturing distribution is that in a service environment, production and consumption are simultaneous. In manufacturing, a production setback can often be remedied by using safety stock or a faster mode of transportation. Such substitution is not possible with a service. The benefits of a service are also relatively intangible—that is, a consumer normally can't see the benefits of a service, such as a doctor's physical exam, but normally can see the benefits provided by a product, such as cold medicine relieving a stuffy nose.

Because service industries are so customer oriented, customer service is a priority. To manage customer relationships, many service providers, such as insurance carriers, physicians, hair salons, and financial services, use technology to schedule appointments, manage accounts, and disburse information. Service distribution focuses on four main areas:

▸▸ *Minimizing wait times:* Minimizing the amount of time customers wait in line is a key factor in maintaining the quality of service. Researchers report that people tend to overestimate the amount of time they spend waiting in line and that unexplained waits seem longer than explained waits.

▸▸ *Managing service capacity:* If service firms don't have the capacity to meet demand, they must either turn down some prospective customers, let service levels slip, or expand capacity. For instance, at tax time a tax preparation firm may have so many customers desiring its services that it has to either turn business away or add temporary offices or preparers.

▸▸ *Improving service delivery:* Service firms are now experimenting with different distribution channels for their services. Choosing the right distribution channel can increase the times that services are available or add to customer convenience. The Internet is fast becoming an alternative channel for delivering services. Consumers can now purchase plane tickets, plan a vacation cruise, reserve a hotel room, pay bills, purchase mutual funds, and receive electronic newspapers in cyberspace.

▸▸ *Establishing channel-wide network coherence:* Because services are to some degree intangible, service firms also find it necessary to standardize their service quality across different geographic regions in order to maintain their brand image. Having network coherence means that suppliers, service processes, and customer service have quality standards that are maintained regardless of where the service is purchased or consumed.

STUDY TOOLS — **CHAPTER 13**

Flip to the back of your textbook to:
❑ **Rip out Chapter Review Card**

Log in to the CourseMate for MKTG at cengagebrain.com to:
❑ **Review Key Terms Flash Cards (Print or Online)**
❑ **Review Audio and Visual Summaries**
❑ **Complete both Practice Quizzes to prepare for tests**
❑ **Play "Beat the Clock" and "Quizbowl" to master concepts**
❑ **Complete "Crossword Puzzle" to review key terms**
❑ **Watch the video on "Taza Chocolate" for a real company example on Marketing Channels**

Supply Chain
Management

In today's marketplace, products are being driven by customers.

LO1 Supply Chains and Supply Chain Management

AFTER YOU FINISH THIS CHAPTER, GO TO PAGE 237 FOR STUDY TOOLS

Many modern companies are turning to supply chain management for competitive advantage. A company's **supply chain** includes all of the companies involved in all of the upstream and downstream flows of products, services, finances, and information, from initial suppliers (the point of origin) to the ultimate customer (the point of consumption). The goal of **supply chain management** is to coordinate and integrate all of the activities performed by supply chain members into a seamless process, from the source to the point of consumption, ultimately giving supply chain managers "total visibility" of the supply chain both inside and outside the firm. The philosophy behind supply chain management is that by visualizing the entire supply chain, supply chain managers can maximize strengths and efficiencies at each level of the process to create a highly competitive, customer-driven supply system that is able to respond immediately to changes in supply and demand.

Supply chain management is completely customer driven. In the mass production era, manufacturers produced standardized products that were "pushed"

supply chain the connected chain of all of the business entities, both internal and external to the company, that perform or support the logistics function

supply chain management a management system that coordinates and integrates all of the activities performed by supply chain members into a seamless process, from the source to the point of consumption, resulting in enhanced customer and economic value

What do you think?

I purchase more merchandise online than in stores.

1 2 3 4 5 6 7
STRONGLY DISAGREE   STRONGLY AGREE

Find out what others think at the CourseMate for MKTG. Log in at cengagebrain.com.

© ADAM DUCKWORTH/ALAMY

supply chain integration when multiple firms in a supply chain coordinate their activities and processes so that they are seamlessly linked to one another in an effort to satisfy the customer

down through the supply channel to the consumer. In today's marketplace, however, products are being driven by customers, who expect to receive product configurations and services matched to their unique needs. The focus is on pulling products into the marketplace and partnering with members of the supply chain to enhance customer value. Supply chain relationships between the automobile manufacturers and the after-market auto-parts industry make it possible to customize an automobile.[1]

This reversal of the flow of demand from a "push" to a "pull" has resulted in a radical reformulation of market expectations and traditional marketing, production, and distribution functions. Integrated channel partnerships allow companies to respond with the unique product configuration and mix of services demanded by the customer. Today, supply chain management is both a *communicator* of customer demand that extends from the point of sale all the way back to the supplier, and a *physical flow* process that engineers the timely and cost-effective movement of goods through the entire supply pipeline.

Benefits of Supply Chain Management

Supply chain management is a key means of differentiation for a firm and a critical component in marketing and corporate strategy. Companies that focus on supply chain management commonly report lower inventory, transportation, warehousing, and packaging costs; greater supply chain flexibility; improved customer service; and higher revenues. Research has shown a clear relationship between supply chain performance and profitability.

For example, to combat the recession, Goodyear implemented supply chain management improvements that resulted in reductions in inventory of $1 billion in 2009.[2]

LO 2 Supply Chain Integration

A key principle of supply chain management is that multiple firms work together to perform tasks as a single, unified system rather than as several individual companies acting in isolation. Companies in

a world-class supply chain combine their resources, capabilities, and innovations such that they are used for the best interest of the entire chain as a whole, with the goal being that overall performance of the supply chain will be greater than the sum of its parts. As firms become increasingly supply chain oriented, they develop management practices that are consistent with this systems approach.

Management practices that are reflective of a highly coordinated effort between supply chain partners are said to be "integrated." In other words, **supply chain integration** occurs when multiple firms in a supply chain coordinate their activities and processes so that they are seamlessly linked to one another in an effort to satisfy the customer. In a world-class supply chain, the customer may not know where the business activities of one firm or business unit end and where those of another begin—all the participating firms and business units appear to be reading from the same script.

In the practice of world-class supply chain management, six types of integration are sought by firms interested in providing top-level service to customers:[3]

▸▸ *Relationship integration* is the ability of two or more companies to develop social connections that serve to guide their interactions when working together. More specifically, relationship integration is the capability to develop and maintain a shared mental framework

Relationally integrated supply chains have a set of rules, policies, and/or procedures that dictate how firms will work together, and specify how conflicts among supply chain partners will be resolved.

© MAX BLAIN/SHUTTERSTOCK.COM

across companies that describes how they will depend on one another when working together. This includes the ways in which they will collaborate on activities or projects so that the customer gains the maximum amount of total value possible from the supply chain.

▸▸ *Measurement integration* reflects the idea that performance assessments should be transparent and measurable across the borders of different business units and firms, and should also assess the performance of the supply chain as a whole while holding each individual firm or business unit accountable for meeting its own goals.

▸▸ *Technology and planning integration* refers to the creation and maintenance of information technology systems that connect managers across and through the firms in the supply chain; it requires information hardware and software systems that can exchange information when needed between customers, suppliers, and internal operational areas of each of the supply chain partners.

▸▸ *Material and service supplier integration* requires firms to link seamlessly to those outsiders that provide goods and services to them so that they can streamline work processes and thereby provide smooth, high-quality customer experiences. Both sides need to have a common vision of the total value creation process and be willing to share the responsibility for satisfying customer requirements to make supplier integration successful.

▸▸ *Internal operations integration* is the result of capabilities development toward the goal of linking internally performed work into a seamless process that stretches across departmental and/or functional boundaries with the goal of satisfying customer requirements.

▸▸ *Customer integration* is a competency that enables firms to offer long-lasting, distinctive, value-added offerings to those customers who represent the greatest value to the firm or supply chain. Highly customer-integrated firms assess their own capabilities and then match them to customers whose desires they can meet and who offer large enough sales potential for the linkage to be profitable over the long term.

Firms' success in achieving each of these types of integration is very important. Highly integrated supply chains (those that are successful in achieving many or all of these types of integration) have been shown to be better at satisfying customers, managing costs, delivering high-quality products, enhancing productivity, and utilizing company or business unit assets, all of which translate into greater profitability for the firms and their partners working together in the supply chain.

LO 3 The Key Processes of Supply Chain Management

When firms practice good supply chain management, their functional departments or areas, such as marketing, research and development, and/or production, are integrated both within and across the linked firms. Integration, then, is "how" excellent supply chain management works. The business processes on which the linked firms work together represent the "what" of supply chain management—they are the objects of focus on which firms, departments, areas, and people work together when seeking to reduce supply chain costs or generate additional revenues. **Business processes** are composed of bundles of interconnected activities that stretch across firms in the supply chain; they represent key areas that some or all of the involved firms are constantly working on in order to reduce costs and/or generate revenues for everyone throughout supply chain management. There are eight critical business processes on which supply chain managers must focus:

1. Customer relationship management
2. Customer service management
3. Demand management
4. Order fulfillment
5. Manufacturing flow management
6. Supplier relationship management
7. Product development and commercialization
8. Returns management[4]

Customer Relationship Management

The **customer relationship management (CRM) process** (discussed further in Chapter 21) allows companies to prioritize their marketing focus on different customer groups according to each group's long-term value to the company or supply chain. Once higher-value customers are identified, firms should focus on providing customized products and better service to this group than to others. The CRM

business processes bundles of interconnected activities that stretch across firms in the supply chain

customer relationship management (CRM) process allows companies to prioritize their marketing focus on different customer groups according to each group's long-term value to the company or supply chain

customer service management process presents a multi-company, unified response system to the customer whenever complaints, concerns, questions, or comments are voiced

demand management process seeks to align supply and demand throughout the supply chain by anticipating customer requirements at each level and creating demand-related plans of action prior to actual customer purchasing behavior

order fulfillment process a highly integrated process, often requiring persons from multiple companies and multiple functions to come together and coordinate to create customer satisfaction at a given place and time

process includes both segmentation of customers by value and the generation of customer loyalty for the most attractive segments—key activities that are enabled through customer integration. This process provides a set of comprehensive principles for the initiation and maintenance of customer relationships and is often carried out with the assistance of specialized CRM computer software.

Customer Service Management

Whereas the CRM process is designed to identify and build relationships with good customers, the customer service management process is designed to ensure that those customer relationships remain strong. The **customer service management process** presents a multi-company, unified response system to the customer whenever complaints, concerns, questions, or comments are voiced. When the process is well executed, it can have a strong positive impact on revenues, often as a result of quick positive response to negative customer feedback, and sometimes even in the form of additional sales gained through the additional customer contact. Customers expect service from the moment a product is purchased until it is disposed of, and the customer service management process allows for touch points between the buyer and seller throughout this life cycle. The use of customer

care software enables companies to enhance their customer service management process.

Demand Management

The **demand management process** seeks to align supply and demand throughout the supply chain by anticipating customer requirements at each level and creating demand-related plans of action prior to actual customer purchasing behavior. At the same time, demand management seeks to minimize the costs of serving multiple types of customers who have variable wants and needs. In other words, the demand management process allows companies in the supply chain to satisfy customers in the most efficient and effective ways possible. The activities such as collecting customer data, forecasting future demand, and developing activities that serve to "smooth out" demand help bring available inventory into alignment with customer desires. Though it is very difficult to predict exactly what items and quantities customers will buy prior to purchase, demand management can ease the pressure on the production process and allow companies to satisfy most of their customers through greater flexibility in manufacturing, marketing, and sales programs. However, much of the uncertainty in demand planning can be mitigated by conducting collaborative planning, forecasting, and replenishment (CPFR) activities with the company's customers and suppliers. Because of inefficiencies in the manufacturing and ordering processes, General Mills had an abundance of inventory of its Fruit Roll-Ups and Gushers fruit snacks. By combining the overstock into "mystery" fruit snacks pouches, General Mills created the sixth-fastest-selling fruit snack on the market![5]

Order Fulfillment

One of the most fundamental processes in supply chain management is the order fulfillment process, which involves generating, filling, delivering, and providing on-the-spot service for customer orders. The **order fulfillment process** is a highly integrated process, often requiring persons from multiple companies and multiple functions to come together and coordinate to create customer satisfaction at a given place and time. The best order fulfillment processes reduce the time between order and customer receipt as much as possible while ensuring that the customer receives exactly what he or she wants. The shorter lead times are beneficial in that they allow firms to carry reduced inventory levels and free up cash

© JAMES STEIDL/SHUTTERSTOCK.COM

© ISTOCKPHOTO.COM/DONALD ERICKSON

that can be used on other projects. Overall, the order fulfillment process involves understanding both internal capabilities and external customer needs, and matching these together so that the supply chain maximizes profits while minimizing costs and waste.

When the order fulfillment process is managed diligently, the amount of time between order placement and receipt of the customer's payment following order shipment (known as the order-to-cash cycle) is minimized as much as possible. Since many firms do not view order fulfillment as a core competency (versus, for example, product development or marketing), they often outsource this function to a third-party logistics firm (3PL) that specializes in the order fulfillment process. The 3PL becomes a semi-permanent part of the firm's supply chain and is assigned to manage one or more specialized functions. When employed for order fulfillment, the 3PL is contracted to manage the firm's order fulfillment process from beginning to end, thereby freeing up the firm's time and resources so that they can be expended on core business activities. Many times 3PLs constitute a firm's only interaction with the customer, so they need to represent the needs and interests of the entire firm and supply chain. Developing and training these employees to be empowered and respond to the customer's needs in the best interest of the supply chain is becoming increasingly important.[6]

Manufacturing Flow Management

The **manufacturing flow management process** is concerned with ensuring that firms in the supply chain have the needed resources to manufacture with flexibility and to move products through a multi-stage production process. Firms with flexible manufacturing have the ability to create a wide variety of goods and/or services with minimized costs associated with changing production techniques. The manufacturing flow process includes much more than simple production of goods and services—it means creating flexible agreements with suppliers and shippers so that unexpected demand bursts can be accommodated.

The goals of the manufacturing flow management process are centered on leveraging the capabilities held by multiple members of the supply chain to improve overall manufacturing output in terms of quality, delivery speed, and flexibility, all of which tie to profitability.

Supplier Relationship Management

The **supplier relationship management process** is closely related to the manufacturing flow management process and contains several characteristics that parallel the customer relationship management process. The manufacturing flow management process is highly dependent on supplier relationships for flexibility. Furthermore, in a way similar to that found in the customer relationship management process, supplier relationship management provides structural support for developing and maintaining relationships with suppliers. Thus, by integrating these two ideas, supplier relationship management supports manufacturing flow by identifying and maintaining relationships with highly valued suppliers. Just as firms benefit from developing close-knit, integrated relationships with customers, close-knit, integrated relationships with suppliers provide a means through which performance advantages can be gained.

The management of supplier relationships is a key step toward ensuring that firms' manufacturing resources are available. Thus, the supplier relationship management process has a direct impact on each supply chain member's bottom-line financial performance.

PepsiCo decided it needed more control over major parts of its supply chain and purchased two of its major

manufacturing flow management process concerned with ensuring that firms in the supply chain have the needed resources to manufacture with flexibility and to move products through a multi-stage production process

supplier relationship management process supports manufacturing flow by identifying and maintaining relationships with highly valued suppliers

product development and commercialization process includes the group of activities that facilitates the joint development and marketing of new offerings among a group of supply chain partner firms

returns management process enables firms to manage volumes of returned product efficiently while minimizing returns-related costs and maximizing the value of the returned assets to the firms in the supply chain

logistics the process of strategically managing the efficient flow and storage of raw materials, in-process inventory, and finished goods from point of origin to point of consumption

bottlers. As a result, Pepsi is able to work more closely with its retailers.[7]

Product Development and Commercialization

The **product development and commercialization process** (discussed in detail in Chapter 11) includes the group of activities that facilitates the joint development and marketing of new offerings among a group of supply chain partner firms. In many cases, new products and services are not the sole responsibility of a single firm that serves as inventor, engineer, builder, marketer, and sales agent; rather, they are often the product of a multicompany collaboration with multiple firms and business units playing unique roles in new-product development, testing, and launch activities, among others. The capability for developing and introducing new offerings quickly is key for competitive success versus rival firms, so it is often advantageous to involve many supply chain partners in the effort. The process requires the close cooperation of suppliers and customers who provide input throughout the process and serve as advisers and co-producers for the new offering(s).

Returns Management

The final supply chain management process deals with situations in which customers choose to return a product to the retailer or supplier, thereby creating a reversed flow of goods within the supply chain. The **returns management process** enables firms to manage volumes of returned product efficiently while minimizing returns-related costs and maximizing the value of the returned assets to the firms in the supply chain. Returns have the potential to affect a firm's financial position in a major and negative way if mishandled. In certain industries, such as apparel e-retailing, returns can amount to as much as 40 percent of sales volume.

In addition to the value of managing returns from a pure asset-recovery perspective, many firms are discovering that returns management also creates additional marketing and customer service touch points that can be leveraged for added customer value above and beyond normal sales and promotion-driven encounters. Handling returns gives the company an additional opportunity to please the customer, and customers who have positive experiences with the returns management process can become very confident buyers who are willing to reorder, since they know any problems they encounter with purchases will be quickly and fairly rectified. In addition, the returns management process allows the firm to recognize weaknesses in product design and/or areas for potential improvement through the direct customer feedback that initiates the process.

LO 4 Managing the Logistical Components of the Supply Chain

Critical to any supply chain is orchestrating the physical means by which products move through it. Logistics is the process of strategically managing the efficient flow and storage of raw materials, in-process inventory, and finished goods from point of origin to point of consumption. As mentioned earlier, supply chain management coordinates and integrates all of the activities performed by supply chain members

In certain industries, such as apparel e-retailing, returns can amount to as much as 40 percent of sales volume.

© ISTOCKPHOTO.COM/MARIA TOUTOUDAKI

© ISTOCKPHOTO.COM/SUBJUG

into a seamless process. The supply chain consists of several interrelated and integrated logistical components: (1) sourcing and procurement of raw materials and supplies, (2) production scheduling, (3) order processing, (4) inventory control, (5) warehousing and materials handling, and (6) transportation.

The **logistics information system** is the link connecting all of the logistics components of the supply chain. The components of the system include, for example, software for materials acquisition and handling, warehouse-management and enterprise-wide solutions, data storage and integration in data warehouses, mobile communications, electronic data interchange, radio frequency identification (RFID) chips, and the Internet. Working together, the components of the logistics information system are the fundamental enablers of successful supply chain management.

The **supply chain team**, in concert with the logistics information system, orchestrates the movement of goods, services, and information from the source to the consumer. Supply chain teams typically cut across organizational boundaries, embracing all parties who participate in moving the product to market. The best supply chain teams also move beyond the organization to include the external participants in the chain, such as suppliers, transportation carriers, and third-party logistics suppliers. Members of the supply chain communicate, coordinate, and cooperate extensively.

Sourcing and Procurement

One of the most important links in the supply chain is that between the manufacturer and the supplier. Purchasing professionals are on the front lines of supply chain management. Purchasing departments plan purchasing strategies, develop specifications, select suppliers, and negotiate price and service levels.

The goal of most sourcing and procurement activities is to reduce the costs of raw materials and supplies. Purchasing professionals have traditionally relied on tough negotiations to get the lowest price possible from suppliers of raw materials, supplies, and components. Perhaps the biggest contribution purchasing can make to supply chain management, however, is in the area of vendor relations. Companies can use the purchasing function to strategically manage suppliers in order to reduce the total cost of materials and services. Through enhanced vendor relations, buyers and sellers can develop cooperative relationships that reduce

> REMEMBER: The supply chain consists of several components:
> 1. sourcing and procurement of raw materials and supplies,
> 2. production scheduling,
> 3. order processing,
> 4. inventory control,
> 5. warehousing and materials handling, and
> 6. transportation.

logistics information system the link that connects all the logistics functions of the supply chain

supply chain team an entire group of individuals who orchestrate the movement of goods, services, and information from the source to the consumer

mass customization (build-to-order) a production method whereby products are not made until an order is placed by the customer; products are made according to customer specifications

costs and improve efficiency with the aim of lowering prices and enhancing profits. By integrating suppliers into their companies' businesses, purchasing managers have become better able to streamline purchasing processes, manage inventory levels, and reduce overall costs of the sourcing and procurement operations.

Production Scheduling

In traditional mass-market manufacturing, production begins when forecasts call for additional products to be made or when inventory control systems signal low inventory levels. The firm then makes a product and transports the finished goods to its own warehouses or those of intermediaries, where the goods wait to be ordered by retailers or customers. For example, many types of convenience goods, such as toothpaste, deodorant, and detergent, are manufactured based on past sales and demand and then sent to retailers to resell. Production scheduling based on pushing a product down to the consumer obviously has its disadvantages, the most notable being that companies risk making products that may become obsolete or that consumers don't want in the first place.

In a customer "pull" manufacturing environment, which is growing in popularity, production of goods or services is not scheduled until an order is placed by the customer specifying the desired configuration. This process, known as **mass customization**, or **build-to-order**, uniquely tailors mass-market goods and services to the needs of the individuals who buy them. Companies as diverse as BMW, Dell, Levi Strauss, Mattel, and a host of Web-based businesses are adopting mass customization to maintain or obtain a competitive edge.

As more companies move toward mass customization of goods—and away from mass marketing

just-in-time production (JIT)

a process that redefines and simplifies manufacturing by reducing inventory levels and delivering raw materials at the precise time they are needed on the production line

of them—the need to stay on top of consumer demand is forcing manufacturers to make their supply chains more flexible. Flexibility is critical to a manufacturer's success when dramatic swings in demand occur. To meet consumers' demand for customized products, companies are forced to adapt their manufacturing approach or even create a completely new process. Despite the fact that most car companies have a section on their Web site where customers can "build and price" their own car, build-to-order vehicles in the United States comprise less than 5 percent of total car sales. BMW is hoping that customization will help it surpass Lexus as the leading luxury car brand in the United States. Encouraging buyers to customize their BMWs is more challenging in the United States than in Germany. Whereas build-to-order cars are common in Europe, U.S. consumers are accustomed to driving away in their new cars, so BMW is working with its dealerships to promote the build-to-order models.[8]

Just-in-Time Manufacturing An important manufacturing process common today among manufacturers is just-in-time manufacturing. Borrowed from the Japanese, **just-in-time production (JIT)**, sometimes called *lean production*, requires manufacturers to work closely with suppliers and transportation providers to get necessary items to the assembly line or factory floor at the precise time they are needed for production. For the manufacturer, JIT means that raw materials arrive at the assembly line in guaranteed working order "just in time" to be installed, and finished products are generally shipped to the customer immediately after completion. For the supplier, JIT means supplying customers with products in just a few days, or even a few hours, rather than weeks. For the ultimate consumer, JIT means lower costs, shorter lead times, and products that more closely meet the consumer's needs.

Many clothing retailers are working to shorten lead times because they were left with large amounts of unsold stock after the recession, and many are now trying to shorten their supply chain even further using a method called *chasing*. Chasing happens when a buyer orders a small amount of product to test in stores, and if the product sells well, the buyer quickly places a larger order with the supplier and requires the new order to be delivered even faster. Aéropostale uses

EXPOSING THE RISKS OF JIT MANUFACTURING

In the aftermath of the devastating **earthquake** that rocked **Japan** in March 2011 and knocked many of its factories out of production for a significant amount of time, automotive and electronics companies based around the world are feeling the pinch. Why? Japan is responsible for 25 percent of the world's silicon production. Many parts (from small chips to airplane wings) are on extreme back order or are too intricate and complex to be manufactured by anyone else. Boeing relies on Japanese manufacturing for 35 percent of its 787 jet. General Motors closed a plant in Shreveport, Louisiana, because of parts shortages. Honda stopped taking new car orders from U.S. dealers. Deere halted delivery of mining and excavating equipment. In total, according to *Bloomberg*

Businessweek, more than 130 plants closed to wait for parts after the earthquake. Nevertheless, even though using JIT manufacturing means that any interruption will cause production to stop within days (sometimes hours), the cost savings allow U.S. manufacturers to operate competitively with other manufacturers around the world. Despite the risks, the cost of not using JIT manufacturing is just too high for many companies to change to a different manufacturing model.[9]

SOURCE: Thomas Black, Susanna Ray, Aaron Ricadela, et al., "Downside of Just-In-Time Inventory," *Bloomberg Businessweek*, March 28–April 3, 2011, 17–18.

© PETER ENDIG/DPA/PICTURE-ALLIANCE/NEWSCOM

this method to ensure that product moves through its stores quickly and with minimum discounting. However, rising cotton prices, shipping restrictions, and factories wary of small orders are causing prices to rise and making chasing difficult. Aéropostale combats these challenges by working directly with cotton mills and ensuring that factories have a steady stream of orders, even if they are small.[10]

Order Processing

The order is often the catalyst that sets the supply chain in motion, especially in build-to-order environments. The **order processing system** processes the requirements of the customer and sends the information into the supply chain via the logistics information system. The order goes to the manufacturer's warehouse. If the product is in stock, the order is filled, and arrangements are made to ship it. If the product is not in stock, the order triggers a replenishment request that finds its way to the factory floor.

Proper order processing is critical to good service. As an order enters the system, management must monitor two flows: the flow of goods and the flow of information. Good communication among sales representatives, office personnel, and warehouse and shipping personnel is essential to correct order processing. Shipping incorrect merchandise or partially filled orders can create just as much dissatisfaction as stockouts or slow deliveries. The flow of goods and information must be continually monitored so that mistakes can be corrected before an invoice is prepared and the merchandise shipped.

Order processing is becoming more automated through the use of computer technology known as **electronic data interchange (EDI)**. The basic idea of EDI is to replace the paper documents that usually accompany business transactions, such as purchase orders and invoices, with electronic transmission of the needed information. A typical EDI message includes all the information that would traditionally be included on a paper invoice, such as product code, quantity, and transportation details. The information is usually sent via private networks, which are more secure and reliable than the networks used for standard e-mail messages. Most important, the information can be read and processed by computers, significantly reducing costs and increasing efficiency. Companies that use EDI can reduce inventory levels, improve cash flow, streamline operations, and increase the speed and accuracy of information transmission. EDI also creates a closer relationship between buyers and sellers.

Inventory Control

The **inventory control system** develops and maintains an adequate assortment of materials or products to meet a manufacturer's or a customer's demands. Inventory decisions, for both raw materials and finished goods, have a big impact on supply chain costs and the level of service provided. If too many products are kept in inventory, costs increase—as do risks of obsolescence, theft, and damage. If too few products are kept on hand, then the company risks product shortages and angry customers, and ultimately lost sales. The goal of inventory management, therefore, is to keep inventory levels as low as possible while maintaining an adequate supply of goods to meet customer demand. Nordstrom has implemented a new inventory management system that fills online orders from distribution hubs or stores near the customer. By sending product to the customer from the nearest possible point, Nordstrom increases its shipping efficiency and better manages its inventory.[11]

Managing inventory from the supplier to the manufacturer is called **materials requirement planning (MRP)**, or **materials management**. This system also encompasses the sourcing and procurement operations, signaling when raw materials, supplies, or components will need to be replenished for the production of more goods. The system that manages the finished goods inventory from manufacturer to end user is commonly referred to as **distribution resource planning (DRP)**.

Both inventory systems use various inputs, such as sales forecasts, available inventory, outstanding orders, lead times, and mode of transportation to be used, to determine what needs to be done to replenish goods at all points in the supply chain. Marketers identify demand at each level in the supply chain, from the retailer back up the chain to the manufacturer, and use EDI to transmit important information throughout the channel.

Some inventory replenishment systems use little or no forecasting. These **automatic replenishment programs** trigger shipments only when a good is sold

order processing system a system whereby orders are entered into the supply chain and filled

electronic data interchange (EDI) information technology that replaces the paper documents that usually accompany business transactions, such as purchase orders and invoices, with electronic transmission of the needed information to reduce inventory levels, improve cash flow, streamline operations, and increase the speed and accuracy of information transmission

inventory control system a method of developing and maintaining an adequate assortment of materials or products to meet a manufacturer's or a customer's demand

materials requirement planning (MRP; materials management) an inventory control system that manages the replenishment of raw materials, supplies, and components from the supplier to the manufacturer

distribution resource planning (DRP) an inventory control system that manages the replenishment of goods from the manufacturer to the final consumer

automatic replenishment program a real-time inventory system that triggers shipments only when a good is sold to the end user

materials-handling system a method of moving inventory into, within, and out of the warehouse

to the end user and use an EDI link connected with bar-code scanners so that the supplier can view inventory in real time. When stock at the customer's location drops below predetermined levels, the supplier takes responsibility for restocking the shelves or the warehouse. This process often results in lower inventory levels.

Warehousing and Materials Handling

Although JIT manufacturing processes may eliminate the need to warehouse many raw materials, manufacturers may often keep some safety stock on hand in the event of an emergency, such as a strike at a supplier's plant or a catastrophic event that temporarily stops the flow of raw materials to the production line. Likewise, the final user may not need or want the goods at the same time the manufacturer produces and wants to sell them. Products such as grain and corn are produced seasonally, but consumers demand them year-round. Other products such as Christmas ornaments and turkeys are produced year-round, but consumers do not want them until autumn or winter. Therefore, management must have a storage system to hold these products until they are shipped.

Storage helps manufacturers manage supply and demand, or production and consumption. It provides time utility to buyers and sellers, which means that the seller stores the product until the buyer wants or needs it. But storing additional product does have disadvantages, including the costs of insurance on the stored product, taxes, obsolescence or spoilage, theft, and warehouse operating costs. Another drawback is opportunity costs—that is, the opportunities lost because money is tied up in stored product instead of being used for something else.

Because businesses are focusing on cutting supply chain costs, the warehousing industry is investing in services using sophisticated tracking technology such as materials-handling systems. An effective **materials-handling system** moves inventory into, within, and out of the warehouse quickly with minimal handling. With a manual, nonautomated materials-handling system, a product may be handled more than a dozen times. Each time it is handled, the cost and risk of damage increase; each lifting of a product stresses its packaging. Consequently, most manufacturers today have moved to automated systems. Scanners quickly identify goods entering and leaving a warehouse

Some items like Christmas ornaments are produced year-round, but only purchased seasonally.

through bar codes affixed to the packaging. Automatic storage and retrieval systems store and pick goods in the warehouse or distribution center. Automated materials-handling systems decrease product handling, ensure accurate placement of product, and improve the accuracy of order picking and the rates of on-time shipment. For example, Dell uses a computer system called OptiPlex to run its factories. The computer software receives orders, sends requests for parts to suppliers, orders components, organizes assembly of the product, and even arranges for the product to be shipped. Instead of hundreds of workers, often fewer than six are working at a Dell factory at one time. An order for a few hundred computers can be filled in less than eight hours using the automated system. With the OptiPlex system, productivity has increased dramatically.

Transportation

Transportation typically accounts for 5 to 10 percent of the price of goods. Supply chain logisticians must decide which mode of transportation to use to move products from supplier to producer and from producer to buyer. These decisions are, of course, related to all other logistics decisions. The five major modes of transportation are railroads, motor carriers, pipelines, water transportation, and airways. Maersk, a global container shipping line, has drastically reduced the cost of shipping overseas by manufacturing container ships that can carry 18,000 containers (each one 20 feet long) at once. These ships are the largest ever built. Larger ships have a greater economy of scale (meaning that they can transport so many more items that the price per item decreases drastically), enabling companies to ship a greater variety of items, from wheat and trucks to iPods and powdered milk.[12] Supply chain managers generally choose a mode of transportation on the basis of several criteria:

© JOANNA ZOPOTH-LIPIEJKO/SHUTTERSTOCK.COM

▸▸ *Cost:* The total amount a specific carrier charges to move the product from the point of origin to the destination.

▸▸ *Transit time:* The total time a carrier has possession of goods, including the time required for pickup and delivery, handling, and movement between the point of origin and the destination.

▸▸ *Reliability:* The consistency with which the carrier delivers goods on time and in acceptable condition.

▸▸ *Capability:* The ability of the carrier to provide the appropriate equipment and conditions for moving specific kinds of goods, such as those that must be transported in a controlled environment (e.g., under refrigeration).

▸▸ *Accessibility:* A carrier's ability to move goods over a specific route or network.

▸▸ *Traceability:* The relative ease with which a shipment can be located and transferred.

The mode of transportation used depends on the needs of the shipper as they relate to these six criteria. Exhibit 14.1 compares the basic modes of transportation based on these criteria.

In many cases, especially in a JIT manufacturing environment, the transportation network replaces the warehouse or eliminates the expense of storing inventories as goods are timed to arrive the moment they're needed on the assembly line or for shipment to customers.

LO 5 Trends in Supply Chain Management

Several technological advances and business trends are affecting the job of the supply chain manager today. Three of the most important trends are advanced computer technology, outsourcing of logistics functions, and electronic distribution.

Advanced Computer Technology

Advanced computer technology has boosted the efficiency of logistics dramatically with tools such as automatic identification systems (auto ID) using bar coding and radio frequency technology, communications technology, and supply chain software sys-

tems that help synchronize the flow of goods and information with customer demand. At Amazon.com's state-of-the-art fulfillment centers, technology is used to maximize efficiency. Incoming product is immediately sent to the first available empty shelf space. That means a shipment of golf balls could end up next to *Best American Short Stories 2011*. As online orders come in, pickers, the employees who gather items from the warehouse, are given a list of items, a cart, and a route to follow, calculated by a computer gun to exactly fill the cart and to take the picker on the most efficient route through the warehouse. Once the cart is filled, the pickers drop items into bins that route to packaging. Packaging is also computer regulated—as a product comes up for packing, a computer indicates which of the company's 15 different standard package sizes is the best fit for the order.[13]

Smart tags are another type of advanced computer technology that is helping companies manage their supply chains. Walmart is beginning to require its clothing suppliers to put smart tags on the hang tags found on most items of clothing so that it can see if any pieces are missing in stores or in shipments. Previously, Walmart tracked pallets or boxes, allowing it to track shipments on a large level, but not to track individual items. The individual tags also allow Walmart to track individual pieces back to the manufacturer. Walmart hopes to use this itemized technology to reduce shoplifting and employee theft and to increase sales. American Apparel tested similar technology and saw individual store sales rise as much as 14.3 percent over stores without the smart tags. When theft is reduced, merchandise that shoplifters tend to target remains available for sale, increasing a store's likelihood of having better sales figures.[14]

EXHIBIT 14.1
Criteria for Ranking Modes of Transportation

	Highest				Lowest
Relative Cost	Air	Truck	Rail	Pipe	Water
Transit Time	Water	Rail	Pipe	Truck	Air
Reliability	Pipe	Truck	Rail	Air	Water
Capability	Water	Rail	Truck	Air	Pipe
Accessibility	Truck	Rail	Air	Water	Pipe
Traceability	Air	Truck	Rail	Water	Pipe

© CENGAGE LEARNING 2013

outsourcing (contract logistics)

a manufacturer's or supplier's use of an independent third party to manage an entire function of the logistics system, such as transportation, warehousing, or order processing

electronic distribution a

distribution technique that includes any kind of product or service that can be distributed electronically, whether over traditional forms such as fiber-optic cable or through satellite transmission of electronic signals

Outsourcing Logistics Functions

External partners are becoming increasingly important in the efficient deployment of supply chain management. **Outsourcing**, or **contract logistics**, is a rapidly growing segment of the distribution industry in which a manufacturer or supplier turns over the entire function of buying and managing transportation or another function of the supply chain, such as warehousing, to an independent third party. To focus on their core competencies, companies are turning their logistics functions over to firms with expertise in that area. Partners create and manage entire solutions for getting products where they need to be, when they need to be there. Because a logistics provider is focused, clients receive service in a timely, efficient manner, thereby increasing their level of satisfaction and boosting their perception of added value to a company's offerings.

Third-party contract logistics allow companies to cut inventories, locate stock at fewer plants and distribution centers, and still provide the same level of service or even better. The companies then can refocus investment on their core business. In the hospitality industry, Avendra negotiates with suppliers to obtain virtually everything that a hotel might need, from food and beverages to golf course maintenance. By relying on Avendra to manage many aspects of the supply chain, hotels like Fairmont Hotels & Resorts and InterContinental Hotels Group can concentrate on their core function—providing hospitality. In an effort to reduce inventory costs, speed up delivery, or better meet customer requirements, many firms are taking outsourcing one step further by allowing business partners to take over the final assembly of their product or its packaging.

Electronic Distribution

Electronic distribution is the most recent development in the logistics arena. Broadly defined, **electronic distribution** includes any kind of product or service that can be distributed electronically, whether over traditional forms such as fiber-optic cable or through satellite transmission of electronic signals. Companies like eTrade, iTunes, and Movies.com have built their business models around electronic distribution.

Green Supply Chain Management

In response to the need for firms to both gain cost savings and act as leaders in protecting the natural environment, many are adopting green supply chain management principles as a key part of their supply chain strategy. Green supply chain management involves the integration of environmentally conscious thinking into all phases of key supply chain management processes. Such activities include green materials sourcing; the design of products with consideration given to their environmental impact based on packaging, shipment, and use; and end-of-life management for products including easy recycling and/or clean disposal. By enacting green supply chain management principles, firms hope to simultaneously generate cost savings and protect our natural resources from excess pollution, damage, and/or wastefulness.

A wire manufacturer in Georgia called Southwire converted one-

Computer gun specifies pickup route

Cart, filled exactly

© JOSHUA LOTT/BLOOMBERG VIA GETTY IMAGES / COURTESY OF CHAPEL HOUSE PHOTOGRAPHY

© 2006 AVERY DENNISON. ALL RIGHTS RESERVED.

If your supply chain were this simple, any RFID tag would do.

We understand your world. That's why we provide real-world RFID solutions. With more than 70 years' experience in related industries, Avery Dennison is uniquely qualified to turn the promise of RFID into reality. Our expertise in pressure-sensitive adhesives, roll-to-roll manufacturing, electronic tags and multi-layered label construction has helped us to create an expanding portfolio of highly reliable, competitively priced Gen 2 products. In fact, our RFID Division Atlanta Technical Development Center simulates a wide variety of challenging real-world conditions to ensure that our RFID products will deliver consistently across your supply chain.

For solutions to your real-world RFID needs, call 866-803-RFID or visit www.rfid.averydennison.com.

©2006 Avery Dennison Corporation. All rights reserved. Intelligent™ Label Technology is a trademark of Avery Dennison Corporation.

AVERY DENNISON

Businesses need strong logistical allies who already have shipping expertise so that they can trust their partners to get the job done. Using the correct tools, such as Avery products, makes the logistics easier.

third of its delivery fleet to hybrid vehicles, eliminated nearly all lead additives from its products, and reduced its landfill waste by 27 percent. Southwire supplies Pacific Gas & Electric, which is taking part in an industry alliance to further green its supply chain.[15]

Global Logistics and Supply Chain Management

Global markets present their own sets of logistical challenges. It is critical for importers of any size to understand and cope with the legalities of trade in other countries. Shippers and distributors must be aware of the permits, licenses, and registrations they may need to acquire and, depending on the type of product they are importing, the tariffs, quotas, and other regulations that apply in each country. This multitude of different rules is why multinational companies are so committed to working through the World Trade Organization to develop a global set of rules and to encourage countries to participate.

Transportation can also be a major issue for companies dealing with global supply chains. Uncertainty regarding shipping usually tops the list of reasons companies, especially smaller ones, resist international markets. In some instances, poor infrastructure makes transportation dangerous and unreliable. And the process of moving goods across the borders of even the most industrialized nations can still be complicated by government regulations.

STUDY TOOLS
CHAPTER 14

Flip to the back of your textbook to:

❏ **Rip out Chapter Review Card**

Log in to the CourseMate for MKTG at cengagebrain.com to:

❏ **Review Key Terms Flash Cards (Print or Online)**

❏ **Review Audio and Visual Summaries**

❏ **Complete both Practice Quizzes to prepare for tests**

❏ **Play "Beat the Clock" and "Quizbowl" to master concepts**

❏ **Complete "Crossword Puzzle" to review key terms**

❏ **Watch the video on "Recycline" for a real company example on Supply Chain Management**

CHAPTER **15** **Retailing**

When we shop for groceries, hair styling, clothes, books, and other products and services, we are involved in retailing.

AFTER YOU FINISH THIS CHAPTER, GO TO PAGE 255 FOR STUDY TOOLS

© KARIN SMEDS/GORILLA CREATIVE IMAGES/GETTY IMAGES

LO 1 The Role of Retailing

Retailing—all the activities directly related to the sale of goods and services to the ultimate consumer for personal, nonbusiness use—has enhanced the quality of our daily lives. When we shop for groceries, hair styling, clothes, books, and many other products and services, we are involved in retailing. The millions of goods and services provided by retailers mirror the needs and styles of U.S. society.

Retailing affects all of us directly or indirectly. The retailing industry is one of the largest employers in the United States. There are over 1.5 million U.S. retailers employing more than 15 million people—about one in five American workers—and the industry is expected to grow to over 16.5 million by 2018.[1] In addition, retail trade accounts for 10.8 percent of all U.S. employment, and almost 12 percent of all businesses in 2009 were classified as retail according to NAICS.[2] At the store level, retailing is still largely a mom-and-pop business. Almost nine out of ten retail companies employ fewer than 20 employees, and according to the National Retail Federation, over 90 percent of all retailers operate just one store.[3]

The U.S. economy depends heavily on retailing. Approximately two-thirds of the U.S. gross domestic product was estimated to come from retail activity in early 2010.[4] Although most retailers are quite small, a few giant organizations dominate the industry, most notably Walmart, whose annual U.S. sales are greater than the sales of the four next largest U.S. retailers combined.

> **retailing** all the activities directly related to the sale of goods and services to the ultimate consumer for personal, nonbusiness use

What do you think?

I enjoy seeing mall exhibits while shopping.

1   2   3   4   5   6   7
STRONGLY DISAGREE   STRONGLY AGREE

Find out what others think at the CourseMate for MKTG. Log in at cengagebrain.com.

Classification of Retail Operations

independent retailer a retailer owned by a single person or partnership and not operated as part of a larger retail institution

chain store a store that is part of a group of the same stores owned and operated by a single organization

franchise the right to operate a business or to sell a product

A retail establishment can be classified according to its ownership, level of service, product assortment, and price. Specifically, retailers use the latter three variables to position themselves in the competitive marketplace. (As noted in Chapter 8, positioning is the strategy used to influence how consumers perceive one product in relation to all competing products.) These three variables can be combined in several ways to create distinctly different retail operations. Exhibit 15.1 lists the major types of retail stores discussed in this chapter and classifies them by level of service, product assortment, price, and gross margin.

Ownership

Retailers can be broadly classified by form of ownership: independent, part of a chain, or franchise outlet. An **independent retailer** is a retailer owned by a single person or partnership and not operated as part of a larger retail institution. Around the world, most retailers are independent, operating one or a few stores in their community. Local florists and ethnic food markets typically fit this classification.

A **chain store** is part of a group of the same stores owned and operated by a single organization. Under this form of ownership, many administrative tasks are handled by the home office for the entire chain. The home office also buys most of the merchandise sold in the stores. Gap and Starbucks are examples of chains.

Franchises are owned and operated by individuals but are licensed by a larger supporting organization, such as Subway and Quiznos. The franchising approach combines the advantages of independent ownership with those of the chain store organization.

Level of Service

The level of service that retailers provide can be classified along a continuum, from full-service to self-service. Some retailers, such as exclusive clothing stores, offer high levels of service. They provide alterations, credit, delivery, consulting, liberal return policies, layaway, gift wrapping, and personal shopping. Retailers like factory outlets and warehouse clubs offer virtually no services.

Product Assortment

The third basis for positioning or classifying stores is by the breadth and depth of their product line. Specialty stores—for example, Best Buy, Toys"R"Us, or GameStop—have the most concentrated product assortments, usually carrying single or narrow product lines, but with considerable depth. On the other end of the spectrum, full-line discounters typically carry broad assortments of merchandise with limited depth. For example, Target carries automotive supplies, household cleaning products, and pet food. Typically, though, it carries only four or five brands of dog food. In contrast, a specialty pet store, like PetSmart, may carry as many as 20 brands in a large variety of flavors, shapes, and sizes.

EXHIBIT 15.1
Types of Stores and Their Characteristics

Type of Retailer	Level of Service	Product Assortment	Price	Gross Margin
Department store	Moderately high to high	Broad	Moderate to high	Moderately high
Specialty store	High	Narrow	Moderate to high	High
Supermarket	Low	Broad	Moderate	Low
Drugstore	Low to moderate	Medium	Moderate	Low
Convenience store	Low	Medium to narrow	Moderately high	Moderately high
Full-line discount store	Moderate to low	Medium to broad	Moderately low	Moderately low
Specialty discount store	Moderate to low	Medium to broad	Moderately low to low	Moderately low
Warehouse club	Low	Broad	Low to very low	Low
Off-price retailer	Low	Medium to narrow	Low	Low
Restaurant	Low to high	Narrow	Low to high	Low to high

© CENGAGE LEARNING 2013

Stores often modify their product assortment in order to accommodate environmental factors. During the recent recession, Saks broadened its product assortment to include entry-level-priced items, which are less expensive than the company's traditional luxury offerings. Over the last year, however, Saks has seen sales increase dramatically, so it is expanding its offerings of higher-priced luxury items once more as spending continues to increase.[5]

Other retailers, such as factory outlet stores, may carry only part of a single line. Nike stores sell only certain items of its own brand. Discount specialty stores like Home Depot or Rack Room Shoes carry a broad assortment in concentrated product lines, such as building and home supplies or shoes.

Price

Price is a fourth way to position retail stores. Traditional department stores and specialty stores typically charge the full "suggested retail price." In contrast, discounters, factory outlets, and off-price retailers use low prices to lure shoppers.

When you see prices like $425, $340, or $225 for a handbag, you might expect to be shopping at a designer boutique. But mid-level mall stores like Talbots, Abercrombie & Fitch, and Ann Taylor are looking to attract the accessory shopper by offering handbags at near-designer prices. Clothing and other accessories vary in price at these retailers, but when the average price of an item sold is $95 at Talbots, $65 at Abercrombie & Fitch, and $40 at Ann Taylor, retailing a handbag for $425, $340, or $225, respectively, may push the price positions of these mid-level retailers to a higher level and cause them to lose their core customers.[6]

The last column in Exhibit 15.1 shows the typical **gross margin**—how much the retailer makes as a percentage of sales after the cost of the goods sold is subtracted. The level of the gross margin and the price level generally match. For example, a traditional jewelry store has high prices and high gross margins. A factory outlet has low prices and low gross margins. Markdowns on merchandise during sale periods and price wars among competitors, when stores lower prices on certain items in an effort to win customers, cause gross margins to decline.

LO3 Major Types of Retail Operations

Traditionally, there have been several distinct types of retail stores, with each offering a different product assortment, type of service, and price level according to its customers' shopping preferences. In a recent trend, however, retailers are experimenting with alternative formats that make it harder to classify them. For instance, supermarkets are expanding their nonfood items and services, discounters are adding groceries, drugstores are becoming more like convenience stores, and department stores are experimenting with smaller stores. Nevertheless, many stores still fall into the basic types.

Department Stores

A **department store** carries a wide variety of shopping and specialty goods, including apparel, cosmetics, housewares, electronics, and sometimes furniture. Purchases are generally made within each department rather than at one central checkout area. Each department is treated as a separate buying center to achieve economies in promotion, buying, service, and control. Each department is usually headed by a **buyer**, a department head who not only selects the merchandise for his or her department but may also be responsible for promotion and for personnel. For a consistent, uniform store image, central management sets broad policies about the types of merchandise carried and price ranges. Central management is also responsible for the overall advertising program, credit policies, store expansion, customer service, and so on. Large independent department stores are rare today. Most are owned by national chains. Macy's (formerly known as Federated Department Stores, Inc.), JCPenney, Sears, Dillard's, and Nordstrom are some of the largest U.S. department store chains.

Specialty Stores

Specialty store formats allow retailers to refine their segmentation strategies and tailor their merchandise to specific target markets. A **specialty store** is not only a type of store but also a method of retail operations—namely, specializing in a given type of merchandise. Examples include children's clothing, baked goods, and pet supplies. A typical specialty store carries a deeper but narrower assortment of specialty merchandise than a department store. Generally, specialty stores' knowledgeable salesclerks offer more attentive customer service. The format has become very powerful in the apparel market and other areas.

gross margin the amount of money the retailer makes as a percentage of sales after the cost of goods sold is subtracted

department store a store housing several departments under one roof

buyer a department head who selects the merchandise for his or her department and may also be responsible for promotion and personnel

specialty store a retail store specializing in a given type of merchandise

supermarket a large, departmentalized, self-service retailer that specializes in food and some nonfood items

scrambled merchandising the tendency to offer a wide variety of nontraditional goods and services under one roof

drugstore a retail store that stocks pharmacy-related products and services as its main draw

In fact, consumers buy more clothing from specialty stores than from any other type of retailer. The Children's Place, Williams-Sonoma, and Foot Locker are examples of successful chain specialty retailers.

Consumers usually consider price to be secondary in specialty outlets. Instead, the distinctive merchandise, the store's physical appearance, and the caliber of the staff determine its popularity. Burberry customers pay higher prices than those found in competitors' shops for the iconic golden plaid fabric designs that accentuate its key items. The higher prices are justified by the luxurious retail atmosphere and high quality service. Burberry's sales rose over 20 percent even during the 2009 recession year.[7]

Because of their attention to the customer and limited product line, manufacturers often favor introducing new products in small specialty stores before moving on to larger retail and department stores.

Supermarkets

U.S. consumers spend about 10 percent of their disposable income in *supermarkets*. **Supermarkets** are large, departmentalized, self-service retailers that specialize in food and some nonfood items. Demographic and lifestyle changes have affected the supermarket industry, as families eat out more or are just too busy to prepare meals at home. Since 2007, though, economic conditions have forced many families to resume eating

at home, and many supermarkets have experienced a 2 to 3 percent upswing in sales, following several years of declining sales.[8]

Conventional supermarkets are being replaced by bigger *superstores*, which are usually twice the size of supermarkets. Superstores meet the needs of today's customers for convenience, variety, and service by offering one-stop shopping for many food and nonfood needs, as well as many services—including pharmacies, flower shops, salad bars, in-store bakeries, take-out food sections, sit-down restaurants, health food sections, video rentals, dry cleaning services, shoe repair, photo processing, and banking. Some even offer family dentistry or optical shops, and many now have gas stations. This tendency to offer a wide variety of nontraditional goods and services under one roof is called **scrambled merchandising**.

To stand out in an increasingly competitive marketplace, many supermarket chains are tailoring marketing strategies to appeal to specific consumer segments. Most notable is the shift toward *loyalty marketing programs* that reward loyal customers carrying frequent shopper cards with discounts or gifts. Once scanned at the checkout, frequent shopper cards help supermarket retailers electronically track shoppers' buying habits.

Drugstores

Drugstores stock pharmacy-related products and services as their main draw, but they also carry an extensive selection of over-the-counter (OTC) medications, cosmetics, health and beauty aids, seasonal merchandise, specialty items such as greeting cards and a limited selection of toys, and some nonrefrigerated convenience foods. As competition has increased from mass merchandisers and supermarkets with their own pharmacies, as well as from direct mail prescription services, drugstores have added services such as 24-hour, drive-through pharmacies and low-cost health clinics staffed by nurse practitioners.

Demographic trends in the United States look favorable for the drugstore industry. The average 60-year-old purchases 15 prescriptions per year, nearly twice as many as the average 30-year-old. Because baby boomers are attentive to their health and keenly sensitive about their looks, the increased traffic at the pharmacy counter in the future should also spur sales in other traditionally strong drugstore merchandise categories, most notably OTC drugs, vitamins, and health and beauty aids.

© ALEX SEGRE/ALAMY

Convenience Stores

A **convenience store** can be defined as a miniature supermarket, carrying only a limited line of high-turnover convenience goods. These self-service stores are typically located near residential areas and are open 24 hours a day, seven days a week. Convenience stores offer exactly what their name implies: convenient location, long hours, fast service. The customer pays a surcharge for convenience, so prices are almost always higher at a convenience store than at a supermarket.

In response to recent heavy competition from gas stations and supermarkets, convenience store operators have changed their strategy. They have expanded their offerings of nonfood items with video rentals and health and beauty aids and added upscale sandwich and salad lines and more fresh produce. Some convenience stores are even selling Pizza Hut, Subway, and Taco Bell products prepared in the store.

Discount Stores

A **discount store** is a retailer that competes on the basis of low prices, high turnover, and high volume. Discounters can be classified into four major categories: full-line discount stores, specialty discount stores, warehouse membership clubs, and off-price retailers.

Full-Line Discount Stores Compared to traditional department stores, **full-line discount stores** offer consumers very limited service and carry a much broader assortment of well-known, nationally branded "hard goods," including housewares, toys, automotive parts, hardware, sporting goods, garden items, and clothing. As with department stores, national chains dominate the discounters. Full-line discounters are often called mass merchandisers. **Mass merchandising** is the retailing strategy whereby retailers use moderate to low prices on large quantities of merchandise and lower levels of service to stimulate high turnover of products.

Walmart is the largest full-line discount store in terms of sales. Today, it has more than 8,300 stores on four continents, and its "Save money. Live better" slogan, designed to target a more affluent customer, is leading the way for other discount stores to draw in the middle-class shopper. Walmart has also become a formidable retailing giant in online shopping, concentrating on toys and electronics. With tie-ins to its stores across the country, Walmart offers online shopping with in-store kiosks linking to the site and the ability to handle returns and exchanges from Internet sales at its physical stores. A key differentiator in Walmart's brand has been its environmentally

friendly approach while still offering everyday low prices; the retailer believes it will be supplied by 100 percent renewable energy and create zero net landfill waste in the near future, thus disproving the myth that a large retailer cannot be both environmentally friendly and profitable simultaneously.[9]

Supercenters combine a full line of groceries and general merchandise with a wide range of services, including pharmacy, dry cleaning, portrait studios, photo finishing, hair salons, optical shops, and restaurants—all in one location. For supercenter operators such as Target, food is a customer magnet that sharply increases the store's overall volume, while taking customers away from traditional supermarkets.

Specialty Discount Stores Another discount niche includes the single-line **specialty discount stores**—for example, stores selling sporting goods, electronics, auto parts, office supplies, housewares, or toys. These stores offer a nearly complete selection of single-line merchandise and use self-service, discount prices,

convenience store
a miniature supermarket, carrying only a limited line of high-turnover convenience goods

discount store a retailer that competes on the basis of low prices, high turnover, and high volume

full-line discount store a retailer that offers consumers very limited service and carries a broad assortment of well-known, nationally branded "hard goods"

mass merchandising a retailing strategy using moderate to low prices on large quantities of merchandise and lower levels of service to stimulate high turnover of products

supercenter a retail store that combines groceries and general merchandise goods with a wide range of services

specialty discount store a retail store that offers a nearly complete selection of single-line merchandise and uses self-service, discount prices, high volume, and high turnover

Target is one example of a popular full-line discount retailer.

© AP IMAGES/PAUL SAKUMA

T.J.Maxx offers few services, in keeping with its classification as a discount retailer.

© LEE WALTERS/ALAMY

category killer a specialty discount store that heavily dominates its narrow merchandise segment

warehouse membership club a limited-service merchant wholesaler that sells a limited selection of brand name appliances, household items, and groceries on a cash-and-carry basis to members, usually small businesses and groups

off-price retailer a retailer that sells at prices 25 percent or more below traditional department store prices because it pays cash for its stock and usually doesn't ask for return privileges

factory outlet an off-price retailer that is owned and operated by a manufacturer

high volume, and high turnover to their advantage. A **category killer** is a specialty discount store that heavily dominates its narrow merchandise segment. Examples include Best Buy in electronics, Staples and Office Depot in office supplies, and IKEA in home furnishings.

Category killers have emerged in other specialty segments as well, creating retailing empires in highly fragmented mom-and-pop markets. For instance, the home improvement industry, which for years was served by professional builders and small hardware stores, is now dominated by Home Depot and Lowe's. Category-dominant retailers like these serve their customers by offering a large selection of merchandise, stores that make shopping easy, and low prices every day, which eliminate the need for time-consuming comparison shopping.

Warehouse Membership Clubs A **warehouse membership club** is a limited-service merchant wholesaler that sells a limited selection of brand name appliances, household items, and groceries. These are usually sold in bulk from warehouse outlets on a cash-and-carry basis to members only. Individual members of warehouse clubs are charged low or no membership fees. Warehouse club members tend to be better educated and more affluent and have larger households than regular supermarket shoppers. These core customers use warehouse clubs to stock up on staples; then they go to specialty outlets or food stores for perishables. Currently, the leading stores in this category are Walmart's Sam's Club, Costco, and BJ's Wholesale Club.

Off-Price Retailers An **off-price retailer** sells at prices 25 percent or more below traditional department store prices because it pays cash for its stock and usually doesn't ask for return privileges. Off-price retailers buy manufacturers' overruns at cost or even less. They also absorb goods from bankrupt stores, irregular merchandise, and unsold end-of-season output. Nevertheless, much off-price retailer merchandise consists of first-quality, current goods. Because buyers for off-price retailers purchase only what is available or what they can get a good deal on, merchandise

styles and brands often change monthly. Today, there are hundreds of off-price retailers, the best known being T.J.Maxx, Ross Stores, Marshalls, HomeGoods, and Tuesday Morning.

Factory outlets are an interesting variation on the off-price concept. A **factory outlet** is an off-price retailer that is owned and operated by a manufacturer. Thus, it carries one line of merchandise—its own. Each season, from 5 to 10 percent of a manufacturer's output does not sell through regular distribution channels because it consists of closeouts (merchandise being discontinued), factory seconds, and canceled orders. With factory outlets, manufacturers can regulate where their surplus is sold, and they can realize higher profit margins than they would by disposing of the goods through independent wholesalers and retailers. Factory outlet malls typically locate in out-of-the-way rural areas or near vacation destinations. Most are situated 10 to 15 miles from urban or suburban shopping areas so that manufacturers don't alienate their department store accounts by selling the same goods virtually next door at a discount. Saks Fifth Avenue Off 5th and Nordstrom Rack are considered luxury outlets and target a different, more aspirational audience.

Restaurants

Restaurants straddle the line between retailing establishments and service establishments. Restaurants do sell tangible products—food and drink—but they also provide a valuable service for consumers in the form of food preparation and food service. Most restaurants could even fall into the definition of a specialty retailer given that most concentrate their menu offerings on a distinctive type of cuisine—for example, Olive Garden Italian restaurants and Starbucks coffeehouses.

Eating out is an important part of Americans' daily activities and is growing in strength. According to the National Restaurant Association, more than 70 billion meals are eaten in restaurants or cafeterias annually in nearly one million locations. Food eaten away from home accounts for about 49 percent ($2,698 per household) of the annual household food budget. The trend toward eating out has been fueled by the increase in working mothers and dual-income families who have more money to eat out and less time to shop and prepare meals at home.[10]

The restaurant industry is one of the most entrepreneurial and competitive in U.S. commerce. Because barriers to entering the restaurant industry are low, the opportunity appeals to many people. The risks, however, are great. Over 50 percent of all new restaurants fail within the first year of operation. Restaurants face competition not only from other restaurants but also from the consumer who can easily choose to cook at home. Competition has fostered innovation and ever-changing menus in most segments of the restaurant industry. Many restaurants are now competing directly with supermarkets by offering takeout and delivery in an effort to capture more of the home meal replacement market.

LO 4 Nonstore Retailing

The retailing formats discussed so far have been in-store methods, in which customers must physically shop at stores. In contrast, **nonstore retailing** is shopping without visiting a store. Because consumers demand convenience, nonstore retailing is currently growing faster than in-store retailing. The major forms of nonstore retailing are automatic vending, direct retailing, direct marketing, and electronic retailing.

Automatic Vending

A low-profile yet important form of retailing is **automatic vending**, the use of machines to offer goods for sale—for example, the soft drink, candy, or snack vending machines found in college cafeterias and office buildings. Vending is the most pervasive retail business in the United States. Recent estimates suggest that credit card technology is already available in over 11.5 million vending machines of different types, and in fact the cards themselves may soon be unnecessary—customers will be able to make purchases

An emerging trend in vending payment is the ability to use cell phones to purchase products.

with Smartphones or using biometric devices linking retina scan patterns or thumbprints directly to credit accounts at major banks.[11] Consumers are willing to pay higher prices for products from a convenient vending machine than for the same products in a traditional retail setting.

Retailers are constantly seeking new opportunities to sell via vending. Many vending machines today sell nontraditional kinds of merchandise such as DVDs, digital cameras, perfumes, and even ice cream.

Direct Retailing

In **direct retailing**, representatives sell products door-to-door, office-to-office, or at home sales parties. Companies like Avon and The Pampered Chef have used this approach for years. But recently direct retailers' sales have suffered as women have entered the workforce. Although most direct sellers like Avon and Tupperware still advocate the party plan method, the realities of the marketplace have forced them to be more creative in reaching their target customer. Direct sales representatives now hold parties in offices, parks, and even parking lots. Others hold informal gatherings where shoppers can drop in at their convenience or offer self-improvement classes. Many direct retailers are also turning to direct mail, telephone, or more traditional retailing venues to find new avenues to their customers and increase sales. Despite some

nonstore retailing shopping without visiting a store

automatic vending the use of machines to offer goods for sale

direct retailing the selling of products by representatives who work door-to-door, office-to-office, or at home sales parties

© YOSHIKAZU TSUNO/AFP/GETTY IMAGES

direct marketing (direct response marketing) techniques used to get consumers to make a purchase from their home, office, or other nonretail setting

telemarketing the use of the telephone to sell directly to consumers

difficulties in reaching busy customers, large companies that are not traditionally direct retailers have been won over by the promise of word-of-mouth sales. House Party, a company specializing in organizing home sales parties, awards hostesses parties based on the market to which the client wants to appeal. Corporate clients such as Procter & Gamble, Kraft Foods, McDonald's, and Schwan Food pay House Party $250,000 for 2,000 parties where the hostess and guests receive free coupons and merchandise, all in the hopes they will become brand advocates and spread the word.[12]

Direct retailers are also using the Internet as a channel to reach more customers and increase sales. Amway launched Quixtar.com, an online channel for its products that generated over $1 billion in revenues in its first year. Customers access the site using a unique referral number for each Amway rep, a system that ensures that the reps earn their commissions.

Direct Marketing

According to the Direct Marketing Association, every year U.S companies spend more than $167 billion on direct marketing, representing over 17 percent of their marketing expenditures, and generate about $1.93 trillion in sales.[13] **Direct marketing**, sometimes called **direct response marketing**, refers to the techniques used to get consumers to make a purchase from their home, office, or other nonretail setting. Those techniques include telemarketing, direct mail, catalogs and mail order, and electronic retailing. Shoppers using

these methods are less bound by traditional shopping situations. Time-strapped consumers and those who live in rural or suburban areas are most likely to be direct response shoppers because they value the convenience and flexibility that direct marketing provides.

Telemarketing Telemarketing is the use of the telephone to sell directly to consumers. It consists of outbound sales calls, usually unsolicited, and inbound calls—that is, orders through toll-free 800 numbers or fee-based 900 numbers. The use of telemarketing is not at all insignificant in modern marketing; recent estimates indicate that U.S. companies will spend over $15 billion on inbound and outbound calls by 2015.[14]

Rising postage rates and decreasing long-distance phone rates have made *outbound* telemarketing an attractive direct marketing technique. Skyrocketing field sales costs have also led marketing managers to use outbound telemarketing. Searching for ways to keep costs under control, marketing managers have learned how to pinpoint prospects quickly, zero in on serious buyers, and keep in close touch with regular customers. Meanwhile, they are reserving expensive, time-consuming, in-person calls for closing sales. So many consumers complained about outbound telemarketing, however, that Congress passed legislation establishing a national "do not call" list of consumers who do not want to receive unsolicited telephone calls. The telemarketing law, however, exempts nonprofits, so some companies have set up nonprofit subsidiaries to continue their calling activities. Some industry experts say the lists help them by eliminating nonbuyers, but others believe this legislation could have a long-term negative effect on telemarketing sales.[15]

Inbound telemarketing programs, which use 800 and 900 numbers, are mainly used to take orders, generate leads, and provide customer service. Inbound 800 telemarketing has successfully supplemented direct response television, radio, and print advertising for more than 25 years. The more recently introduced 900 numbers, which customers pay to call, are gaining popularity as a cost-effective way for companies to target customers. One of the major benefits of 900 numbers is that they allow marketers to generate qualified responses. Although the charge may reduce the total volume of calls, the calls that do come are from customers who have a true interest in the product.

Direct Mail Direct mail can be the most efficient or the least efficient retailing method, depending on the quality of the mailing list and the effectiveness of the

© JEAN-PHILIPPE KSIAZEK/AFP/GETTY IMAGES

mailing piece. With direct mail, marketers can precisely target their customers according to demographics, geographics, and even psychographics. Good mailing lists come from an internal database or are available from list brokers for about $35 to $150 per thousand names.

Direct mailers are becoming more sophisticated in targeting the "right" customers. Using statistical methods to analyze census data, lifestyle and financial information, and past purchase and credit history, direct mailers can pick out those most likely to buy their products. So, despite increases in postal rates and raw material and logistics costs, U.S. direct mail services were up over 14 percent in 2010 and are expected to surpass $25 billion annually by 2015.[16]

Catalogs and Mail Order Merchants send more than 20 billion catalogs a year to U.S. consumers.[17] Although women make up the bulk of catalog shoppers, the percentage of male catalog shoppers has recently soared. As changing demographics have shifted more of the shopping responsibility to men, they are viewing shopping via catalog, mail order, and the Internet as more sensible than a trip to the mall. Often, interested consumers will flip through a traditional paper catalog to get ideas before placing their orders online.

Successful catalogs usually are created and designed for highly segmented markets. Certain types of retailers are using mail order successfully. For example, computer manufacturers have discovered that mail order is a lucrative way to sell personal computers to home and small-business users, evidenced by the huge successes of Dell, which has used its direct business model to become a $59 billion company and the number one PC seller worldwide. With a global market share of about 13 percent, it sells about $50 million in computers and equipment through its online catalog every day.[18]

Electronic Retailing

Electronic retailing includes online retailing and the 24-hour, shop-at-home television networks.

Online Retailing For years, shopping at home meant looking through catalogs and then placing an order over the telephone. For many people today, however, it now means turning on a computer, surfing retail Web sites, and selecting and ordering products online with the click of a mouse. **Online retailing**, or *e-tailing*, is a type of shopping available to consumers with personal computers and access to the Internet. Online sales increased by more than 12 percent last year and are expected to continue to increase by at least 10 percent annually through 2015.[19]

Online retailing has exploded in the last several years as consumers have found this type of shopping convenient and, in many instances, less costly. Consumers can shop without leaving home, choose from a wide selection of merchants, use shopping comparison services to search the Web for the best price, and then have the items delivered to their doorsteps. As a result of improved technology and convenience, online shopping continues to grow at a rapid pace, with online sales accounting for roughly 8 percent of total retail sales. Online retailing is also increasing in popularity outside the United States.

Most traditional retailers have now jumped on the Internet bandwagon, allowing shoppers to purchase the same merchandise found in their stores from their Web site and even allowing customers to purchase some items online and pick them up in stores. Online retailing also fits well with traditional catalog companies, such as Lands' End and Eddie Bauer, that already have established distribution networks. Many shoppers like retail Web sites because they can recommend products and offer customized packages.

As the popularity of online retailing grows, it is becoming critical that retailers be online and that their stores, Web sites, and catalogs be closely integrated. Customers expect to find the same brands, products, and prices whether they purchase online, on the phone, or in a store. Therefore, retailers are increasingly using in-store kiosks to help tie the channels together for greater customer service.

Popular e-tailers don't necessarily have to have a physical presence in the market. Bluefly.com,

© IWONA GRODZKA /SHUTTERSTOCK.COM

online retailing a type of shopping available to consumers with personal computers and access to the Internet

franchisor the originator of a trade name, product, methods of operation, and the like that grants operating rights to another party to sell its product

franchisee an individual or business that is granted the right to sell another party's product

Zappos.com, and eBay have created tremendously successful formulas without selling in a single retail store.

Shop-at-Home Networks The shop-at-home television networks are specialized forms of direct response marketing. These shows display merchandise, with the retail price, to home viewers. Viewers can phone in their orders directly on a toll-free line and shop with a credit card. The shop-at-home industry has quickly grown into a multi-billion-dollar business with a loyal customer following. Shop-at-home networks can reach nearly every home with a television set. The best-known shop-at-home networks are HSN (formerly the Home Shopping Network) and the QVC (Quality, Value, Convenience) Network. Home shopping networks attract a broad audience through diverse programming and product offerings and are now adding new products to appeal to more affluent audiences. HSN features a range of personalities selling their own brands and products. For instance, Padma Lakshmi, host of the popular television show *Top Chef*, has a collection of teas, spices, and kitchenware called Easy Exotic.[20]

LO 5 Franchising

A *franchise* is a continuing relationship in which a franchiser grants to a franchisee the business rights to operate or sell a product. The **franchisor** originates the trade name, product, methods of operation, and so on. The **franchisee**, in return, pays the franchisor for the right to use its name, product, or business methods. A franchise agreement between the two parties usually lasts for 10 to 20 years, at which time the agreement can be renewed if both parties are agreeable.

To be granted the rights to a franchise, a franchisee usually pays an initial, one-time franchise fee. The amount of this fee depends solely on the individual franchisor, but it generally ranges from $50,000 to $250,000 or higher. In addition to this initial franchise fee, the franchisee is expected to pay royalty fees, usually in the range of 3 to 7 percent of gross revenues, but occasionally as high as 12 percent or more. The franchisee may also be expected to pay advertising fees, which usually cover the cost of promotional materials and, if the franchise organization is large enough, regional or national advertising. A McDonald's franchise, for example, costs an initial $45,000 per store plus a monthly fee based upon the restaurant's sales performance and base rent. In addition, a new McDonald's franchisee can expect start-up costs for equipment and pre-opening expenses to range from $506,000 to over $1.6 million, for a total investment of up to roughly $1.8 million for a new store.[21] The size of the restaurant facility, area of the country, inventory, selection of kitchen equipment, signage, and style of decor and landscaping affect new restaurant costs. Fees such as these are typical for all major franchisers, including Burger King and Subway.

Two basic forms of franchises are used today: product and trade name franchising and business format franchising. In *product and trade name franchising*, a dealer agrees to sell certain products provided by a manufacturer or a wholesaler. This approach has been used most widely in the auto and truck, soft drink bottling, tire, and gasoline service industries. For example, a local tire retailer may hold a franchise to sell Michelin tires.

© JOAO VIRISSIMO/SHUTTERSTOCK.COM

Top Ten Franchisors

1. Subway
2. McDonald's
3. 7-Eleven, Inc.
4. Hampton Inn/Hampton Inn & Suites
5. Supercuts
6. H&R Block
7. Dunkin' Donuts
8. Jani-King
9. Servpro
10. ampm

SOURCE: "Franchise 500: Top 10 Franchises," *Entrepreneur*, January 2010, www.entrepreneur.com/franchise500/index.html.

Business format franchising is an ongoing business relationship between a franchisor and a franchisee. Typically, a franchiser "sells" a franchisee the rights to use the franchisor's format or approach to doing business. This form of franchising has rapidly expanded since the 1950s through retailing, restaurant, food-service, hotel and motel, printing, and real estate franchises.

LO 6 Retail Marketing Strategy

Retailers must develop marketing strategies based on overall goals and strategic plans. Retailing goals might include more traffic, higher sales of a specific item, a more upscale image, or heightened public awareness of the retail operation. The strategies that retailers use to obtain their goals might include a sale, updated decor, or a new advertisement. The key tasks in strategic retailing are defining and selecting a target market and developing the retailing mix to successfully meet the needs of the chosen target market.

Defining a Target Market

The first and foremost task in developing a retail strategy is to define the target market. This process begins with market segmentation, the topic of Chapter 8. Successful retailing has always been based on knowing the customer. Sometimes retailing chains flounder when management loses sight of the customers the stores should be serving.

Target markets in retailing are often defined by demographics, geographics, and psychographics. For instance, Sportsgirl, a casual fashion e-tailer in Australia, targets young women from their teens to their thirties, who have a higher-than-average income, read fashion magazines, and favor high-end designers. By understanding who its customers are, the company has been able to design a Web site and a mobile application that instantaneously sends an image of clothing that a customer is considering to her friends' mobile devices for input, opinions, or approval

before the customer makes the final purchase.[22] Determining a target market is a prerequisite to creating the retailing mix. For example, Target's merchandising approach for sporting goods is to match its product assortment to the demographics of the local store and region.

retailing mix a combination of the six Ps—product, place, promotion, price, presentation, and personnel—to sell goods and services to the ultimate consumer

Choosing the Retailing Mix

Retailers combine the elements of the retailing mix to come up with a single retailing method to attract the target market. The **retailing mix** consists of six Ps: the four Ps of the marketing mix (product, place, promotion, and price) plus presentation and personnel (see Exhibit 15.2).

The combination of the six Ps projects a store's image, which influences consumers' perceptions. Using these impressions of stores, shoppers position one store against another. A retail marketing manager must make sure that the store's positioning is compatible with the target customers' expectations. As discussed at the beginning of the chapter, retail stores can be positioned on three broad dimensions: service provided by store personnel, product assortment, and price. Management should use everything else—place, presentation, and promotion—to fine-tune the basic positioning of the store.

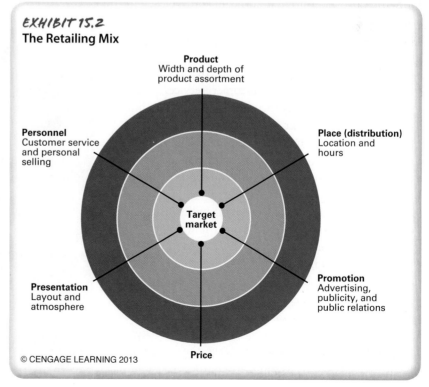

EXHIBIT 15.2
The Retailing Mix

Product
Width and depth of product assortment

Place (distribution)
Location and hours

Promotion
Advertising, publicity, and public relations

Price

Presentation
Layout and atmosphere

Personnel
Customer service and personal selling

Target market

© CENGAGE LEARNING 2013

© NY1/NY1/ZUMA PRESS/NEWSCOM

product offering
the mix of products offered to the consumer by the retailer; also called the *product assortment* or *merchandise mix*

The Product Offering The first element in the retailing mix is the **product offering**, also called the *product assortment* or *merchandise mix*. Retailers decide what to sell on the basis of what their target market wants to buy. They can base their decision on market research, past sales, fashion trends, customer requests, and other sources. A recent approach, called *data mining*, uses complex mathematical models to help retailers make better product mix decisions. Dillard's, Target, and Walmart use data mining to determine which products to stock at what price, how to manage markdowns, and how to advertise to draw target customers.

Developing a product offering is essentially a question of the width and depth of the product assortment. *Width* refers to the assortment of products offered; *depth* refers to the number of different brands offered within each assortment. Price, store design, displays, and service are important to consumers in determining where to shop, but the most critical factor is merchandise selection. This reasoning also holds true for online retailers. Amazon.com, for instance, is building the world's biggest online department store so that shoppers can get whatever they want with one click on their Web browsers. Like a traditional department store or mass merchandiser, Amazon offers considerable width in its product assortment with millions of different items, including books, music, toys, videos, tools and hardware, health and beauty aids, electronics, and software. Conversely, online specialty retailers, such as 1-800-Flowers.com and Polo.com, focus on a single category of merchandise, hoping to attract loyal customers with a larger depth of products at lower prices and excellent customer service. Many online retailers purposely focus on single product line niches that could never garner enough foot traffic to support a traditional brick-and-mortar store. For instance, Web sites such as bugbitingplants.com and petflytrap.com sell and ship live carnivorous plants in the United States.

After determining what products will satisfy target customers' desires, retailers must find sources of supply and evaluate the products. When the right products are found, the retail buyer negotiates a purchase contract. The buying function can either be performed in-house or be delegated to an outside firm. The goods must then be moved from the seller to the retailer, which means shipping, storing, and stocking the inventory. The trick is to manage the inventory by cutting prices to move slow goods and by keeping adequate supplies of hot-selling items in stock. As in all good systems, the final step is to evaluate the entire process to seek more efficient methods and eliminate problems and bottlenecks.

Promotion Strategy Retail promotion strategy includes advertising, public relations and publicity, and sales promotion. The goal is to help position the store in consumers' minds. Retailers design intriguing ads, stage special events, and develop promotions aimed at their target markets. Today's grand openings are a carefully orchestrated blend of advertising, merchandising, goodwill, and glitter. All the elements of an opening—press coverage, special events, media advertising, and store displays—are carefully planned.

Retailers' advertising is carried out mostly at the local level. Local advertising by retailers usually provides specific information about their stores, such as location, merchandise, hours, prices, and special sales. In contrast, national retail advertising generally focuses on image. For example, Target uses advertisements similar to designer fashion advertisements to depict high-quality goods. Paired with the ubiquitous red target and tag line "Expect more. Pay less," Target is demonstrating that it sells products that consumers normally aspire to own at prices they can afford.

Heidi Klum and other Victoria's Secret models celebrate at an opening ceremony for a New York store. The popular and lovely women are part of the Victoria's Secret promotion strategy.

Target's advertising campaign also takes advantage of cooperative advertising, another popular retail advertising practice. Traditionally, marketers would pay retailers to feature their products in store mailers, or a marketer would develop a television campaign for the product and simply tack on several retailers' names at the end. But Target's advertising makes use of a more collaborative trend by integrating products such as Tide laundry detergent or Coca-Cola into the actual campaign. Another common form of cooperative advertising involves promotion of exclusive products. For example, Target hires famous young designers for temporary partnerships, during which they develop reasonably priced product lines available exclusively at Target stores.

The Proper Location The retailing axiom "location, location, location" has long emphasized the importance of place to the retail mix. The location decision is important first because the retailer is making a large, semi-permanent commitment of resources that can reduce its future flexibility. Second, the location will affect the store's future growth and profitability.

Site location begins by choosing a community. Important factors to consider are the area's economic growth potential, the amount of competition, and geography. For instance, retailers like T.J.Maxx and Walmart often build stores in new communities that are still under development. Fast-food restaurants tend to place a priority on locations with other fast-food restaurants because being located in clusters helps to draw customers for each restaurant. However, even after careful research, the perfect position can be elusive in the face of changing markets. For example, Wendy's found, when attempting to enter the competitive breakfast business, that its locations weren't positioned on the right side of the road to attract the bulk of commuters looking for breakfast.[23] Finally, for many retailers geography remains the most important factor in choosing a community. For example, Starbucks looks for densely populated urban communities for its stores.

After settling on a geographic region or community, retailers must choose a specific site. In addition to growth potential, the important factors to consider are neighborhood socioeconomic characteristics, traffic flows, land costs, zoning regulations, and public transportation. A particular site's visibility, parking, entrance and exit locations, accessibility, and safety and security issues are also important considerations. Additionally, a retailer should consider how its store will fit into the surrounding environment. Retail decision makers probably would not locate a Dollar General store next door to a Neiman Marcus department store.

Retailers face one final decision about location: whether to have a freestanding unit or to become a tenant in a shopping center or mall.

destination store a store that consumers purposely plan to visit

Freestanding Stores An isolated, freestanding location can be used by large retailers like Walmart or Target and sellers of shopping goods like furniture and cars because they are "destination" stores. A **destination store** is a store consumers seek out and purposely plan to visit. An isolated store location may have the advantages of low site cost or rent and no nearby competitors. On the other hand, it may be hard to attract customers to a freestanding location, and no other retailers are around to share costs.

Freestanding units are increasing in popularity as retailers strive to make their stores more convenient to access, more enticing to shop, and more profitable. Freestanding sites now account for more than half of all retail construction starts in the United States as more and more retailers are deciding not to locate in pedestrian malls. Perhaps the greatest reason for developing a freestanding site is greater visibility. Retailers often feel they get lost in huge centers and malls, but freestanding units can help stores develop an identity with shoppers. Also, an aggressive expansion plan may not allow time to wait for shopping centers to be built. Drugstore chains like Walgreens have been purposefully relocating their existing shopping center stores to freestanding sites, especially street corner sites for drive-through accessibility.

Shopping Centers Shopping centers first appeared in the 1950s when the U.S. population started migrating to the suburbs. The first shopping centers were *strip centers*, typically located along busy streets. They usually included a supermarket, a variety store, and perhaps a few specialty stores. Then *community shopping centers* emerged, with one or two small department stores, more specialty stores, a couple of restaurants, and several apparel stores. These community shopping centers provided off-street parking and a broader variety of merchandise.

Regional malls offering a much wider variety of merchandise started appearing in the mid-1970s. Regional malls are either entirely enclosed or roofed to allow shopping in any weather. Most are landscaped

atmosphere the overall impression conveyed by a store's physical layout, decor, and surroundings

with trees, fountains, sculptures, and the like to enhance the shopping environment. They have acres of free parking. The *anchor stores* or *generator stores* (often major department stores) are usually located at opposite ends of the mall to create heavy foot traffic.

According to shopping center developers, *lifestyle centers* are emerging as the newest generation of shopping centers. Lifestyle centers typically combine outdoor shopping areas composed of upscale retailers and restaurants, with plazas, fountains, and pedestrian streets. They appeal to retail developers looking for an alternative to the traditional shopping mall, a concept rapidly losing favor among shoppers.

GET YOUR MALL-ON

Online shopping has decreased foot traffic in regional malls. To counteract the trend, **shopping malls** around the United States have rolled out Smartphone apps that allow shoppers to load mall directories and help find their cars. And these useful features are just the beginning. One app, called ShopKick, offers reward points to users who go to certain malls and visit participating stores. With 875 points, users receive a $25 gift card to one of the participating retailers. Some mall owners are hoping to offer a deal-a-day feature on the app, further encouraging people participating in the offer to go to the mall.[24]

SOURCE: Kris Hudson, "Malls Test Apps to Aid Shoppers," *Wall Street Journal*, April 26, 2011, B6.

Store within a Store Many smaller specialty lines are opening shops inside larger stores to expand their retail opportunities without risking investment in a separate store. Mango, a European retailer looking to expand into the United States, is launching MNG by Mango in JCPenney stores.[25]

Pop-Up Shops Pop-up shops—tiny, temporary stores that stay in one location only for a few months—are a growing trend. They help retailers reach a wide market while avoiding high rent at retail locations. Pop-up shops have become the marketing tool du jour for large companies. Procter & Gamble opened a 4,000-foot pop-up shop in Manhattan where everything was free—even full Covergirl makeovers and Head & Shoulders shampoos and stylings. The goal was to demonstrate the experience of P&G products and build brand loyalty.[26]

Retail Prices Another important element in the retailing mix is price. Retailing's ultimate goal is to sell products to consumers, and the right price is critical in ensuring sales. Because retail prices are usually based on the cost of the merchandise, an essential part of pricing is efficient and timely buying.

Price is also a key element in a retail store's positioning strategy. Higher prices often indicate a level of quality and help reinforce the prestigious image of retailers, as they do for Lord & Taylor and Neiman Marcus. On the other hand, discounters and off-price retailers, such as Target and T.J.Maxx, offer a good value for the money. There are even stores, such as Dollar Tree, where everything costs $1. Dollar Tree's single-price-point strategy is aimed at getting customers to make impulse purchases through what analysts call the "wow factor"—the excitement of discovering that an item costs only a dollar.

Presentation of the Retail Store The presentation of a retail store helps determine the store's image and positions the retail store in consumers' minds. For instance, a retailer that wants to position itself as an upscale store would use a lavish or sophisticated presentation.

The main element of a store's presentation is its **atmosphere**, the overall impression conveyed by a store's physical layout, decor, and surroundings. The atmosphere might create a relaxed or busy feeling, a sense of luxury or efficiency, a friendly or cold attitude, a sense of organization or clutter, or a fun or serious mood. Urban Outfitters stores, targeted to Generation Y consumers, use raw concrete, original brick, rusted steel, and unfinished wood to convey an urban feel.

The layout of retail stores is a key factor in their success. The goal is to use all of the store's space effectively, including aisles, fixtures, merchandise displays,

© V. J. MATTHEW/SHUTTERSTOCK.COM

and nonselling areas. In addition to making shopping easy and convenient for the customer, an effective layout has a powerful influence on traffic patterns and purchasing behavior.

Layout also includes where products are placed in the store. Many technologically advanced retailers are using a technique called *market-basket analysis* to sift through the data collected by their point-of-purchase scanning equipment. The analysis looks for products that are commonly purchased together to help retailers find ideal locations for each product. Walmart uses market-basket analysis to determine where in the store to stock products for customer convenience. Kleenex tissues, for example, are in the paper-goods aisle and beside the cold medicines.

These are the most influential factors in creating a store's atmosphere:

▸▸ *Employee type and density:* Employee type refers to an employee's general characteristics—for instance, neat, friendly, knowledgeable, or service oriented. Density is the number of employees per thousand square feet of selling space. Whereas low employee density creates a "do-it-yourself," casual atmosphere, high employee density denotes readiness to serve the customer's every whim.

▸▸ *Merchandise type and density:* A prestigious retailer like Nordstrom or Neiman Marcus carries the best brand names and displays them in a neat, uncluttered arrangement. Discounters and off-price retailers often carry seconds or out-of-season goods crowded into small spaces and hung on long racks by category—tops, pants, skirts, etc.—creating the impression that "We've got so much stuff, we're practically giving it away."

▸▸ *Fixture type and density:* Fixtures can be elegant (rich woods) or trendy (chrome and smoked glass); they can even consist of old, beat-up tables, as in an antiques store. The fixtures should be consistent with the general atmosphere the store is trying to create.

▸▸ *Sound:* Sound can be pleasant or unpleasant for a customer. Music can entice customers to stay in the store longer and buy more or eat quickly and leave a table for others. It can also control the pace of the store traffic, create an image, and attract or direct the shopper's attention.

© IDEA FOR LIFE/SHUTTERSTOCK.COM
© INTI ST. CLAIR/DIGITAL VISION/JUPITERIMAGES

Anatomy of a Fitting room

A screen or closet offers a place to store unwanted items so they won't clutter the fitting room.

Assisted shoppers are twice as likely to make a purchase.

The changing room is private, well lit, spacious, and clean. Some store use whiteboards to write shoppers' names on the door of the fitting room, offering a personalized touch.

Mirrors with movable panels encourage shoppers to step into the shared space, where assistants can make add-on sales and further interact with the customer.

Rugs break up a room and make it more colorful and inviting, which encourages customers to stay longer in the store.

Comfortable couches or chairs offer shoppers a place to rest.

SOURCE: Elizabeth Holmes and Ray Smith, "Why Are Fitting Rooms So Awful?" *Wall Street Journal*, April 6, 2011, D1.

- *Odors:* Smell can either stimulate or detract from sales. Research suggests that people evaluate merchandise more positively, spend more time shopping, and are generally in a better mood when an agreeable odor is present. Retailers use fragrances as an extension of their retail strategy.

- *Visual factors:* Colors can create a mood or focus attention and therefore are an important factor in atmosphere. Red, yellow, and orange are considered warm colors and are used when a feeling of warmth and closeness is desired. Cool colors like blue, green, and violet are used to open up closed-in places and create an air of elegance and cleanliness. Many retailers have found that natural lighting, either from windows or skylights, can lead to increased sales. Outdoor lighting can also affect consumer patronage.

Personnel and Customer Service People are a unique aspect of retailing. Most retail sales involve a customer–salesperson relationship, if only briefly. When customers shop at a grocery store, the cashiers check and bag their groceries. When customers shop at a prestigious clothier, the salesclerks may assist in the fitting process, offer alteration services, wrap purchases, and even serve champagne. Sales personnel provide their customers with the amount of service prescribed by the retail strategy of the store.

Retail salespeople serve another important selling function: They persuade shoppers to buy. They must therefore be able to persuade customers that what they are selling is what the customer needs. Salespeople are trained in two common selling techniques: trading up and suggestion selling. *Trading up* means persuading customers to buy a higher-priced item than they originally intended to purchase. To avoid selling customers something they do not need or want, however, salespeople should take care when practicing trading-up techniques. *Suggestion selling,* a common practice among most retailers, seeks to broaden customers' original purchases with related items. For example, if you buy a new printer at Office Depot, the sales representative will ask if you would like to purchase paper, a USB cable, and/or extra ink cartridges. Suggestion selling by sales or service associates should always help shoppers recognize true needs rather than sell them unwanted merchandise.

Providing great customer service is one of the most challenging elements in the retail mix because customer expectations for service vary greatly. What customers expect in a department store is very different from what they expect in a discount store. Customer expectations also change. Ten years ago, shoppers wanted personal one-on-one attention. Today, most customers are happy to help themselves as long as they can easily find what they need.

Customer service is also critical for online retailers. Online shoppers expect a retailer's Web site to be user-friendly, with readily available products and an easy return process. Therefore, customer-friendly retailers like Bluefly.com design their sites to give their customers the information they need regarding new products and sales. Other companies like Amazon.com and LandsEnd.com offer product recommendations and personal shoppers. Some retailers with online, catalog, and traditional brick-and-mortar stores, such as Lands' End and Williams-Sonoma, now allow customers to return goods bought through the catalog or online to their traditional store to make returns easier.

LO7 New Developments in Retailing

In an effort to better serve their customers and attract new ones, retailers are constantly adopting new strategies. Two recent developments are interactivity and m-commerce.

Interactivity

Adding interactivity to the retail environment is one of the most popular strategies in retailing in the past few years. Small retailers as well as national chains are using interactivity in stores to differentiate themselves from the competition. The new interactive trend gets customers involved rather than just catching their eye. For example, Build-a-Bear enables customers to make their own stuffed animals by choosing which animals to stuff and then dressing and naming them.

M-Commerce

M-commerce (mobile e-commerce) enables consumers using wireless mobile devices to connect to the Internet and shop. M-commerce enjoyed early success overseas and has been gaining acceptance and popularity in the United States. Essentially, m-commerce goes beyond text message advertisements to allow consumers to purchase goods and services using wireless mobile devices, such as mobile telephones, pagers, personal digital assistants (PDAs), and handheld computers. M-commerce users adopt the new technology because it saves time and offers more convenience in a greater number of locations. Vending machines are an important venue for m-commerce. Coca-Cola's Intelligent Vending, a "cashless" payment system, accepts credit cards, RFID devices, and hotel room keys and can be accessed via cell phone.[27]

THE GENIUS BEHIND APPLE'S GENIUS BAR (AND ITS STORES)

© KATHERINE WELLES/SHUTTERSTOCK.COM

In an environment where physical stores are seeing flat or declining sales, Apple's sales per square foot have soared well above those of other luxury retailers. Apple's people and its stores project a casual and carefree atmosphere. The lighting is pleasant, the setting is open and airy, the employees are enthusiastic about Apple's products, the Genius Bar is knowledgeable, and everyone is positive. Why? It is part of each Apple Store employee's training. Sales associates are trained to help customers solve problems. Training manuals even detail what sales associates should say to emotional customers. Positivity is reinforced as sales associates learn proper word choice: Apple's Genius Bar geniuses never say "unfortunately," but instead say "as it turns out." Sales associates don't correct customers who mispronounce product names. Employees even applaud customers as they leave with just-released products. It all adds up to a retail experience that Apple customers love, which they show by purchasing products in Apple Stores.[28]

SOURCE: Yukari Iwatani Kane and Ian Sherr, "Secrets from Apple's Genius Bar," *Wall Street Journal,* June 15, 2011.

M-Commerce Growth Potential **M-commerce** is part of a bigger trend in which mobile technology allows people to complete tasks on the go that they used to do at a desktop computer. Many major companies, ranging from Polo Ralph Lauren to Sears, already offer shopping on mobile phones, and the growth potential is huge. Currently, 3.5 percent of North American mobile phone users have made online purchases via their phones.[29] There are nearly 260 million data-capable mobile devices, 62 million of which are fully Web-enabled Smartphones or 3G-enabled laptops.[30] The gap between the number of Smartphones owned and Smartphones used for purchases is expected to close.

STUDY TOOLS CHAPTER 15

Flip to the back of your textbook to:
- ❏ **Rip out Chapter Review Card**

Log in to the CourseMate for MKTG at cengagebrain.com to:
- ❏ **Review Key Terms Flash Cards (Print or Online)**
- ❏ **Review Audio and Visual Summaries**
- ❏ **Complete both Practice Quizzes to prepare for tests**
- ❏ **Play "Beat the Clock" and "Quizbowl" to master concepts**
- ❏ **Complete "Crossword Puzzle" to review key terms**
- ❏ **Watch the video on "Sephora" for a real company example on Retailing**

Promotional Planning for Competitive Advantage

Few goods or services can survive in the marketplace without effective promotion.

AFTER YOU FINISH THIS CHAPTER, GO TO PAGE 273 FOR STUDY TOOLS

LO1 The Role of Promotion in the Marketing Mix

Few goods or services, no matter how well developed, priced, or distributed, can survive in the marketplace without effective **promotion**—communication by marketers that informs, persuades, and reminds potential buyers of a product in order to influence an opinion or elicit a response.

Promotional strategy is a plan for the optimal use of the elements of promotion: advertising, public relations, personal selling, sales promotion, and social media. As Exhibit 16.1 on the next page shows, the marketing manager determines the goals of the company's promotional strategy in light of the firm's overall goals for the marketing mix—product, place (distribution), promotion, and price. Using these overall goals, marketers combine the elements of the promotional strategy (the promotional mix) into a coordinated plan. The promotion plan then becomes an integral part of the marketing strategy for reaching the target market.

The main function of a marketer's promotional strategy is to convince target customers that the goods and services offered provide a competitive advantage over the competition. A **competitive advantage** is the set of unique features of a company and its products that are perceived by the target market as significant and superior to those of the competition. Such features can include

promotion communication by marketers that informs, persuades, and reminds potential buyers of a product in order to influence an opinion or elicit a response

promotional strategy a plan for the optimal use of the elements of promotion: advertising, public relations, personal selling, sales promotion, and social media

competitive advantage one or more unique aspects of an organization that cause target consumers to patronize that firm rather than competitors

What do you think?

Time taken to communicate is time well spent.

1	2	3	4	5	6	7
STRONGLY DISAGREE						STRONGLY AGREE

Find out what others think at CourseMate for MKTG. Log in at cengagebrain.com.

© ASGER CARLSEN/STONE+/GETTY IMAGES

communication the process by which we exchange or share meaning through a common set of symbols

high product quality, rapid delivery, low prices, excellent service, or a feature not offered by the competition. For example, Toyota's Lexus line resonates with customers because it offers Mercedes-quality cars at a lower price. The luxury line implies that the driver is successful enough to buy what she wants and sensible enough to get a great price on it. The savvy, affluent customer position has given Lexus a competitive advantage in the luxury car market.[1] Thus, promotion is a vital part of the marketing mix, informing consumers of a product's benefits and thereby positioning the product in the marketplace.

LO2 Marketing Communication

Promotional strategy is closely related to the process of communication. As humans, we assign meaning to feelings, ideas, facts, attitudes, and emotions. **Communication** is the process by which meanings are exchanged or shared through a common set of symbols. When a company develops a new product, changes an old one, or simply tries to increase sales of an existing good or service, it must communicate

EXHIBIT 16.1
Role of Promotion in the Marketing Mix

- Overall marketing objectives
- Marketing mix
  - Product
  - Place (distribution)
  - Promotion
  - Price
- Promotional mix
  - Advertising
  - Public relations
  - Sales promotion
  - Personal selling
  - Social media
- Promotion plan
- Target market

© CENGAGE LEARNING 2013

its selling message to potential customers. Marketers communicate information about the firm and its products to the target market and various publics through its promotion programs.

Domino's Pizza recently had a serious communications problem. After customer complaints about the quality of its product (and a disturbing video featuring one of its employees doing things to the pizza that was posted on YouTube and went viral), the company decided to do something that no other company had done—it promoted the complaints in advertising and social media. Working with ad agency Crispin, Porter & Bogusky, Domino's embraced authenticity by announcing that its pizza photos would not have "fancy touch ups" and encouraged consumers to take photos of their pizza and post them to a new Web site. Dubbed the "Pizza Turnaround," the campaign featured the CEO reacting (and apologizing) to consumer complaints about the "crust tasting like cardboard" and the "sauce tasting like ketchup." Domino's changed its recipe and positioned the brand as "real" and "authentic," an old positioning base to be sure, but one that was particularly relevant given consumer mistrust of advertising and corporations in general. And it worked. Sales increased 14 per-

© AP IMAGES/PRNEWSFOTO/DOMINO'S PIZZA

DOMINO'S // PIZZA TRACKER POLL RESULTS

cent from one quarter to the next, and research showed the ads were some of the most effective in years.[2]

Communication can be divided into two major categories: interpersonal communication and mass communication. **Interpersonal communication** is direct, face-to-face communication between two or more people. When communicating face-to-face, people see the other person's reaction and can respond almost immediately. A salesperson speaking directly with a client is an example of an interpersonal marketing communication.

Mass communication involves communicating a concept or message to large audiences. A great deal of marketing communication is directed to consumers as a whole, usually through a mass medium such as television or newspapers. When a company advertises, it generally does not personally know the people with whom it is trying to communicate. Furthermore, the company often cannot respond immediately to consumers' reactions to its messages (unless they are using social media or other Internet-based marketing tools). Instead, the marketing manager must wait to see whether people are reacting positively or negatively to the mass-communicated promotion. Any clutter from competitors' messages or other distractions in the environment can reduce the effectiveness of the mass-communication effort.

process. In an interpersonal conversation, the sender may be a parent, a friend, or a salesperson. For an advertisement, press release, or social media campaign, the sender is the company or organization itself. For example, to take advantage of the World Cup and gain market share in Africa against Pepsi, Coca-Cola launched a huge marketing campaign called "What's Your Celebration?" inspired by Roger Milla, a former Cameroon soccer player, and the famous, impromptu celebration dance that he did after scoring a goal in the 1990 World Cup. Coca-Cola used Milla's dance to encourage everyone to loosen up with Coke and embrace the joys of the World Cup. In addition to asking people "what's your celebration?" Coca-Cola worked with Somalian-born singer K'Naan to create a catchy, inspiring song to play at the soccer games that incorporated Coke's iconic five-note melody. The song, "Wavin' Flag," became the top download on iTunes and the unofficial anthem of the 2010 World Cup, as well as a key part of Coca-Cola's message of celebration.[3]

Encoding is the conversion of the sender's ideas and thoughts into a message, usually in the form of words or

interpersonal communication direct, face-to-face communication between two or more people

mass communication the communication of a concept or message to large audiences

sender the originator of the message in the communication process

encoding the conversion of a sender's ideas and thoughts into a message, usually in the form of words or signs

The Communication Process

Marketers are both senders and receivers of messages. As *senders*, marketers attempt to inform, persuade, and remind the target market to adopt courses of action compatible with the need to promote the purchase of goods and services. As *receivers*, marketers attune themselves to the target market in order to develop the appropriate messages, adapt existing messages, and spot new communication opportunities. In this way, most marketing communication is a two-way, rather than one-way, process. The two-way nature of the communication process is shown in Exhibit 16.2.

The Sender and Encoding The **sender** is the originator of the message in the communication

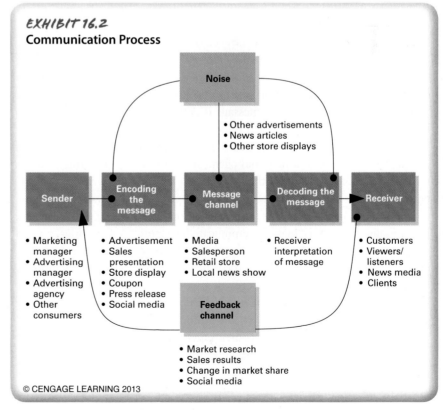

EXHIBIT 16.2
Communication Process

Noise
• Other advertisements
• News articles
• Other store displays

Sender → Encoding the message → Message channel → Decoding the message → Receiver

Sender
• Marketing manager
• Advertising manager
• Advertising agency
• Other consumers

Encoding the message
• Advertisement
• Sales presentation
• Store display
• Coupon
• Press release
• Social media

Message channel
• Media
• Salesperson
• Retail store
• Local news show

Decoding the message
• Receiver interpretation of message

Receiver
• Customers
• Viewers/listeners
• News media
• Clients

Feedback channel
• Market research
• Sales results
• Change in market share
• Social media

© CENGAGE LEARNING 2013

channel a medium of communication—such as a voice, radio, or newspaper—for transmitting a message
noise anything that interferes with, distorts, or slows down the transmission of information
receiver the person who decodes a message
decoding interpretation of the language and symbols sent by the source through a channel

signs. Coca-Cola encoded the "What's Your Celebration?" message into the song "Wavin' Flag" and into ads showing various teams and their goal celebrations, from backflips to coordinated slides, and fans dancing and waving flags. Fans were then encouraged to upload their own celebration videos on Coca-Cola's World Cup Web site, http://celebrations.coca-cola.com. On the Web site, in the commercials, and during games, the drum beats and catchy rhythms of "Wavin' Flag" encouraged celebration with Coke.[4]

A basic principle of encoding is that what matters is not what the source says but what the receiver hears. One way of conveying a message that the receiver will hear properly is to use concrete words and pictures.

Message Transmission Transmission of a message requires a **channel**—a voice, radio, newspaper, computer, Smartphone, or other communication medium. A facial expression or gesture can also serve as a channel. Coca-Cola used South African restaurants as one of its channels to get the "What's Your Celebration?" campaign to the African people. The company donated televisions encased in red plastic and Coke-themed tables to more than 1,000 South African restaurants so they could show the games and bring people together. Coca-Cola also sponsored the World Cup Trophy Tour, which allowed soccer fans in 84 countries (50 in Africa) to take pictures with the cup, attend concerts, play games, and watch 3D soccer highlights celebrating the history of the game.

Reception occurs when the message is detected by the receiver and enters his or her frame of reference. In a two-way conversation such as a sales pitch given by a sales representative to a potential client, reception is normally high. Similarly, when the message is a recommendation from a friend, the reception is high as well. In contrast, the desired receivers may or may not detect the message when it is mass communicated because most media are cluttered by **noise**—anything that interferes with, distorts, or slows down the transmission of information. In some media overcrowded with advertisers, such as newspapers and television, the noise level is high and the reception level is low. For example, competing network advertisements, other entertainment option advertisements, or other programming on the network itself might hamper reception of Coca-Cola's advertising campaign message. Transmission can also

be hindered by situational factors such as physical surroundings like light, sound, location, and weather; the presence of other people; consumer multi-tasking, or the temporary moods consumers might bring to the situation. Mass communication may not even reach all the right consumers. Because Coca-Cola was targeting an event with a dedicated audience of soccer fans, it was more likely that the target audience experienced the "What's Your Celebration?" campaign, particularly the "Wavin' Flag" song with Coke's jingle in it. However, other Coke ads may run when the target audience of soccer viewers is not watching.

The Receiver and Decoding Marketers communicate their message through a channel to customers, or **receivers**, who will decode the message. It is important to note that there can be multiple receivers as consumers share their experiences and their recommendations online through social networks and other types of social media. These conversations online are becoming an increasingly influential way to promote products and services. **Decoding** is the interpretation of the language and symbols sent by the source through a channel. Common understanding between two communicators, or a common frame of reference, is required for effective communication. Therefore, marketing managers must ensure a proper match between the message to be conveyed and the target market's attitudes and ideas.

Even though a message has been received, it will not necessarily be properly decoded—or even seen, viewed, or heard—because of selective exposure, distortion, and retention. Even when people receive a message, they tend to manipulate, alter, and modify it to reflect their own biases, needs, knowledge, and culture. Differences in age, social class, education, culture, and ethnicity can lead to miscommunication. Further, because people don't always listen or read carefully, they can easily misinterpret what is said or written. In fact, researchers have found that consumers misunderstand a large proportion of both printed and televised communications. Bright colors and bold graphics have been shown to increase consumers' comprehension of marketing communication. Even these techniques are not foolproof, however.

Marketers targeting consumers in foreign countries must also worry about the translation and possible miscommunication of their promotional messages by other cultures. Global marketers must decide whether to standardize or customize the message for each global market in which they sell. Coke's "What's Your Celebration?" campaign was very similar all over the world, though the company released the Roger Milla ads at different times of the year before the World Cup began. Coca-Cola also promoted its POWERade brand through the World Cup, targeting individual countries by featuring individual members of each country's team in POWERade print ads. For Coca-Cola, being highly visible before and during one of the world's most watched events paid off with 5 percent worldwide growth for the period including the World Cup.[5]

Feedback In interpersonal communication, the receiver's response to a message is direct **feedback** to the source. Feedback may be verbal, as in saying "I agree," or nonverbal, as in nodding, smiling, frowning, or gesturing.

Because mass communicators like Coca-Cola are often cut off from direct feedback, they must rely on market research or analysis of viewer responses for indirect feedback. Coca-Cola might use such measurements as the percentage of television viewers who recognized, recalled, or stated that they were exposed to the company's messages. Indirect feedback enables mass communicators to decide whether to continue, modify, or drop a message. Web sites also facilitate feedback. Coca-Cola used its World Cup Web site as a place where people could upload their celebrations. Each video suggested a person who responded positively to the "What's Your Celebration?" campaign.

With the increase in online advertising, marketers are able to get more feedback than before the Internet became such a driving social force. Using analytics, marketers can see how long a consumer stays on a

Web site or which pages they view. Moreover, social media enable instant feedback by allowing companies, such as JCPenney and Comcast, to respond to consumers' posts on Facebook and to complaints posted on Twitter.

feedback the receiver's response to a message

As the preceding paragraph implies, the Internet and social media have had an impact on the communication model. That model shows the feedback channel as primarily impersonal and numbers driven. In the traditional communication process, marketers can see the results of consumer behavior (e.g., a drop or rise in sales), but are able to explain those changes only by using their judgment. When marketers launch a social media campaign, they create an unfiltered feedback channel. Social media campaigns enable marketers to personalize the feedback channel by opening the door for direct conversation with consumers. However, because social media are in real time and are public, any negative posts or complaints are highly visible. Thus, many companies have a crisis communication strategy to deal with negative information.

LO 3 The Goals of Promotion

People communicate with one another for many reasons. They seek amusement, ask for help, give assistance or instructions, provide information, and express ideas and thoughts. Promotion, on the other

© N44/ZUMA PRESS/NEWSCOM

hand, seeks to modify behavior and thoughts in some way. For example, promoters may try to persuade consumers to eat at Burger King rather than at McDonald's. Promotion also strives to reinforce existing behavior—for instance, getting consumers to continue dining at Burger King once they have switched. The source (the seller) hopes to project a favorable image or to motivate purchase of the company's goods and services.

Promotion can perform one or more of three tasks: *inform* the target audience, *persuade* the target audience, or *remind* the target audience. Often a marketer will try to accomplish two or more of these tasks at the same time.

Informing

Informative promotion seeks to convert an existing need into a want or to stimulate interest in a new product. It is generally more prevalent during the early stages of the product life cycle. People typically will not buy a product or service or support a non-profit organization until they know its purpose and its benefits to them. Informative messages are important for promoting complex and technical products such as automobiles, computers, and investment services. For example, when Apple released the iPhone, its touch screen functions were new to the Smartphone category. To inform consumers of the phone's features and how it worked, Apple ran a series of commercials showing a hand manipulating the phone. The voiceover provided information about the benefits of the phone by telling a story around how the iPhone makes life easier. Similar commercials have run for the iPad to inform consumers about the benefits of a larger touch screen. Informative promotion is also important for a "new" brand being introduced into an "old" product class. The new product cannot establish itself against more mature products unless potential buyers are aware of it, value its benefits, and understand its positioning in the marketplace.

Persuading

Persuasive promotion is designed to stimulate a purchase or an action. Persuasion normally becomes the main promotion goal when the product enters the growth stage of its life cycle. By this time, the target market should have general product awareness and some knowledge of how the product can fulfill its wants. Therefore, the promotional task switches from informing consumers about the product category to persuading them to buy the company's brand rather

© AP IMAGES/PRNEWSFOTO/APPLE

than that of the competitor. At this time, the promotional message emphasizes the product's real and perceived competitive advantages, often appealing to emotional needs such as love, belonging, self-esteem, and ego satisfaction. For example, advertisers of phones using the Android operating system are trying to persuade users to purchase their phone instead of an iPhone (or even instead of another brand of Android phone). Advertising messages, therefore, are highlighting the unique technological benefits of Android phones, such as a faster processor or larger screen.

Persuasion can also be an important goal for very competitive mature product categories such as many household items and soft drinks. In a marketplace characterized by many competitors, the promotional message often encourages brand switching and aims to convert some buyers into loyal users. Critics believe that some promotional messages and techniques can be too persuasive, causing consumers to buy products and services they don't really need.

Reminding

Reminder promotion is used to keep the product and brand name in the public's mind. This type of promotion prevails during the maturity stage of the life cycle. It assumes that the target market has already been persuaded of the merits of the good or service. Its purpose is simply to trigger a memory. Crest toothpaste and other consumer products often use reminder promotion.

LO 4 The Promotional Mix

Most promotional strategies use several ingredients—which may include advertising, public relations, sales promotion, personal selling, and social media—to reach a target market. That combination is called the **promotional mix**. The proper promotional mix is the one that management believes will meet the needs of the target market and fulfill the organization's overall goals. The more funds allocated to each promotional ingredient and the more managerial emphasis placed on each technique, the more important that element is thought to be in the overall mix.

Advertising

Almost all companies selling a good or a service use advertising, whether in the form of a multi-million-dollar campaign or a simple classified ad in a newspaper. **Advertising** is any form of impersonal paid communication in which the sponsor or company is identified. Traditional media—such as television, radio, newspapers, magazines, books, direct mail, billboards, and transit cards (advertisements on buses and taxis and at bus stops)—are most commonly used to transmit advertisements to consumers. With the increasing fragmentation of traditional media choices, marketers are using new methods, such as Web sites, e-mail, blogs, and interactive video kiosks located in department stores and supermarkets, to send their advertisements to consumers. However, as the Internet becomes a more vital component of many companies' promotion and marketing mixes, consumers and lawmakers are increasingly concerned about possible violations of consumers' privacy. Social networking sites like Facebook are having to re-examine their privacy policies.

One of the primary benefits of advertising is its ability to communicate to a large number of people at one time. Cost per contact, therefore, is typically very low. Advertising has the advantage of being able to reach the masses (e.g., through national television networks), but it can also be microtargeted to small groups of potential customers, such as television ads on a targeted cable network. Although the *cost per contact* in advertising is very low, the *total cost* to advertise is typically very high. This hurdle tends to restrict advertising on a national basis. Chapter 17 examines advertising in greater detail.

Public Relations

Concerned about how they are perceived by their target markets, organizations often spend large sums to build a positive public image. **Public relations** is the marketing function that evaluates public attitudes, identifies areas within the organization the public may be interested in, and executes a program of action to earn public understanding and acceptance. Public relations helps an organization communicate with its customers, suppliers, stockholders, government officials, employees, and the community in which it operates. Marketers use public relations not only to maintain a positive image but also to educate the public about the company's goals and objectives, introduce new products, and help support the sales effort.

A public relations program can generate favorable **publicity**—public information about a company, product, service, or issue appearing in the mass media as a news item. Organizations generally do not pay for the publicity and are not identified as the source of the information, but they can benefit tremendously from it. Social media sites like Twitter can provide large amounts of publicity quickly. For example, in 2011 John Greene, a young-adult fiction author, tweeted the name of his next book, *The Fault in Our Stars* (due out in spring 2012), on Twitter, Tumblr, and YouPants.org; promised to sign all pre-orders; and read an excerpt on a live YouTube show. Soon after, fans began discussing pre-ordering on Twitter and designing dust jackets for the book. The same day *The Fault in Our Stars* became the number one seller on Amazon.com and Barnes & Noble.com.[6]

Although organizations do not directly pay for publicity, it should not be viewed as free. Preparing news releases, staging special events, and persuading media personnel to broadcast or print publicity messages costs money. Public relations and publicity are examined further in Chapter 17.

Sales Promotion

Sales promotion consists of all marketing activities—other than personal selling, advertising, and public relations—that stimulate consumer purchasing and

promotional mix the combination of promotional tools—including advertising, public relations, personal selling, sales promotion, and social media—used to reach the target market and fulfill the organization's overall goals

advertising impersonal, one-way mass communication about a product or organization that is paid for by a marketer

public relations the marketing function that evaluates public attitudes, identifies areas within the organization the public may be interested in, and executes a program of action to earn public understanding and acceptance

publicity public information about a company, product, service, or issue appearing in the mass media as a news item

sales promotion marketing activities—other than personal selling, advertising, and public relations—that stimulate consumer buying and dealer effectiveness

personal selling
a purchase situation involving a personal, paid-for communication between two people in an attempt to influence each other

dealer effectiveness. Sales promotion is generally a short-run tool used to stimulate immediate increases in demand. Sales promotion can be aimed at end consumers, trade customers, or a company's employees. Sales promotions include free samples, contests, premiums, trade shows, vacation giveaways, and coupons. A popular promotion for restaurants is free food. A Denny's restaurant promotion awarded the winner Grand Slam breakfasts for a year—52 servings of the breakfast. Denny's recoups the loss rather quickly because the winner usually brings paying customers along. Many companies, including KFC, have found that customers continue to eat at the restaurants even after the winning term of their prize expires.[7]

Marketers often use sales promotion to improve the effectiveness of other ingredients in the promotional mix, especially advertising and personal selling. Research shows that sales promotion complements advertising by yielding faster sales responses.[8]

Personal Selling

Personal selling is a purchase situation involving a personal, paid-for communication between two people in an attempt to influence each other. In this dyad, both the buyer and the seller have specific objectives they wish to accomplish. The buyer may need to minimize cost or assure a quality product, for instance, while the salesperson may need to maximize revenue and profits.

Traditional methods of personal selling include a planned presentation to one or more prospective buyers for the purpose of making a sale. Whether it takes place face-to-face or over the phone, personal selling attempts to persuade the buyer to accept a point of view. For example, a car salesperson may try to persuade a car buyer that a particular model is superior to a competing model in certain features, such as gas mileage. Once the buyer is somewhat convinced, the salesperson may attempt to elicit some action from the buyer, such as a test-drive or a purchase. Frequently, in this traditional view of personal selling, the objectives of the salesperson are at the expense of the buyer, creating a win–lose outcome.

More current notions on personal selling emphasize the relationship that develops between a salesperson and a buyer. Initially, this concept was more typical in business-to-business selling situations, involving the sale of products like heavy machinery or computer systems. More recently, both business-to-business and business-to-consumer selling focus on building long-term relationships rather than on making a one-time sale.

Relationship selling emphasizes a win–win outcome and the accomplishment of mutual objectives that benefit both buyer and salesperson in the long term. Rather than focusing on a quick sale, relation-

CULTURAL SAVIOR AND ACCESSORY MAKER: TOD'S

Italian luxury accessory maker Tod's recently donated $36.5 million for the restoration of the Colosseum in Rome. Tod's mission of promoting Italian production and quality is in line with the donation to restore one of Italy's most visible and best-known landmarks. The company will be the only sponsor, but there will be no advertising on any scaffolding during the work. Tod's CEO, Diego Della Valle, is committed to encouraging other businesses to donate funds for the restoration of other Italian cultural icons. The donation has increased Tod's visibility around the world due to the Colosseum's iconic status. Della Valle has mentioned that Tod's may also contribute to the restoration of other historic landmarks in the cities of Pompeii, Florence, and Venice.[9]

SOURCE: Luisa Zargani, "Della Valle Hopes Colosseum Just First Italian Restoration," *Women's Wear Daily*, June 24, 2011, 3.

© VICHIE81/SHUTTERSTOCK.COM

© ISTOCKPHOTO.COM/ATTATOR

ship selling attempts to create a long-term, committed relationship based on trust, increased customer loyalty, and a continuation of the relationship between the salesperson and the customer. Personal selling, like other promotional mix elements, is increasingly dependent on the Internet. Most companies use their Web sites to attract potential buyers seeking information on products and services and to drive customers to their physical locations where personal selling can close the sale. Personal selling is discussed further in Chapter 18.

Social Media

Social media are promotion tools used to facilitate conversations among people online. When used by marketers, these tools facilitate consumer empowerment. For the first time, consumers are able to speak directly to other consumers, the company, and Web communities. Social media include blogs (online journals), microblogs (Twitter), podcasting (online audio shows), vodcasts (online videos and newscasts, especially on YouTube), and social networks such as Facebook and LinkedIn. Initially, these tools were used primarily by individuals for self-expression. For example, a lawyer might develop a blog to talk about politics because that is her hobby. Or a college freshman might develop a profile on Facebook to stay in touch with his high school friends. But soon, businesses saw that these tools could be used to engage with consumers as well. The rise of blogging, for example, has created a completely new way for marketers to manage their image, connect with consumers, and generate interest in and desire for their companies' products. Now marketers are using social media as integral aspects of their campaigns and as a way to extend the benefits of their traditional media. Social media are discussed in more detail in Chapter 22.

The Communication Process and the Promotional Mix

The five elements of the promotional mix differ in their ability to affect the target audience. For instance, promotional mix elements may communicate with the consumer directly or indirectly. The message may flow one way or two ways. Feedback may be fast or slow, a little or a lot. Likewise, the communicator may have varying degrees of control over message delivery, content, and flexibility. Exhibit 16.3 on the next page outlines characteristics among the promotional mix elements with respect to mode of communication, marketer's control over the communication process,

amount and speed of feedback, direction of message flow, marketer's control over the message, identification of the sender, speed in reaching large audiences, and message flexibility.

From Exhibit 16.3, you can see that most elements of the promotional mix are indirect and impersonal when used to communicate with a target market, providing only one direction of message flow. For example, advertising, public relations, and sales promotion are generally impersonal, one-way means of mass communication. Because they provide no opportunity for direct feedback, it is more difficult to adapt these promotional elements to changing consumer preferences, individual differences, and personal goals.

Personal selling, on the other hand, is personal, two-way communication. The salesperson receives immediate feedback from the consumer and can adjust the message in response. Personal selling, however, is very slow in dispersing the marketer's message to large audiences. Because a salesperson can communicate to only one person or a small group of persons at one time, it is a poor choice if the marketer wants to send a message to many potential buyers. Social media are also considered two-way communication, though not quite as immediate as personal selling. Social media can disperse messages to a wide audience and allow for engagement and feedback from customers through Twitter, Facebook, and blog posts.

LO 5 Promotional Goals and the AIDA Concept

The ultimate goal of any promotion is to get someone to buy a good or service or, in the case of nonprofit organizations, to take some action (e.g., donate

EXHIBIT 16.3
Characteristics of the Elements in the Promotional Mix

	Advertising	Public Relations	Sales Promotion	Personal Selling	Social Media
Mode of Communication	Indirect and impersonal	Usually indirect and impersonal	Usually indirect and impersonal	Direct and face-to-face	Indirect but instant
Communicator Control over Situation	Low	Moderate to low	Moderate to low	High	Moderate
Amount of Feedback	Little	Little	Little to moderate	Much	Much
Speed of Feedback	Delayed	Delayed	Varies	Immediate	Intermediate
Direction of Message	One-way	One-way	Mostly one-way	Two-way	Two-way, multiple ways
Control over Message Content	Yes	No	Yes	Yes	Varies, generally no
Identification of Sponsor	Yes	No	Yes	Yes	Yes
Speed in Reaching Large Audience	Fast	Usually fast	Fast	Slow	Fast
Message Flexibility	Same message to all audiences	Usually no direct control over message audiences	Same message to varied targets	Tailored to prospective buyer	Some of the most targeted opportunities

© CENGAGE LEARNING 2013

AIDA concept a model that outlines the process for achieving promotional goals in terms of stages of consumer involvement with the message; the acronym stands for attention, interest, desire, and action

blood). A classic model for reaching promotional goals is called the **AIDA concept**.[10] The acronym stands for *attention, interest, desire,* and *action*—the stages of consumer involvement with a promotional message.

This model proposes that consumers respond to marketing messages in a cognitive (thinking), affective (feeling), and conative (doing) sequence. First, a promotion manager may focus on attracting a consumer's *attention* by training a salesperson to use a friendly greeting and approach, or by using loud volume, bold headlines, movement, bright colors, and the like in an advertisement. Next, a good sales presentation, demonstration, or advertisement creates *interest* in the product and then, by illustrating how the product's features will satisfy the consumer's needs, arouses *desire*. Finally, a special offer or a strong closing sales pitch may be used to obtain purchase *action*.

The AIDA concept assumes that promotion propels consumers along the following four steps in the purchase-decision process:

1. *Attention:* The advertiser must first gain the attention of the target market. A firm cannot sell something if the

market does not know that the good or service exists. When Apple introduced the iPad, it quickly became one of the largest electronics product launches in history. To create awareness and gain attention for its revolutionary tablet computer, Apple not only used traditional media advertising but also contacted influential bloggers and journalists so that they would write about the product in blogs, newspapers, and magazines. Because the iPad was a brand extension of the Apple computer, it

© ISTOCKPHOTO.COM/KYOSHINO

required less effort than an entirely new brand would have. At the same time, because the iPad was an innovative new product line, the promotion had to get customers' attention and create awareness of a new idea from an established company.

2   *Interest:* Simple awareness of a brand seldom leads to a sale. The next step is to create interest in the product. A print ad cannot tell potential customers all the features of the iPad. Therefore, Apple had to arrange iPad demonstrations and target messages to innovators and early adopters to create interest in the new tablet computer. To do this, Apple used both online videos on YouTube and personal demonstrations in Apple Stores. The iPad also received extensive media coverage from both online and traditional media outlets.

3   *Desire:* Potential customers for the Apple iPad may like the concept of a portable tablet computer, but they may not necessarily think that it is better than a laptop or Smartphone. Therefore, Apple had to create brand preference with the iTunes Music Store, apps, multiple functionality, power, light weight, and other features of the iPad. Specifically, Apple had to convince potential customers that the iPad was the best solution to their desire for a combination tablet computer and Smartphone.

4   *Action:* Some potential target market customers may have been persuaded to buy an iPad but had yet to make the actual purchase. To motivate them to take action, Apple continued advertising to communicate the features and benefits more effectively. And the strategy worked. In less than three months, the iPad sold more than 3 million units; more than half a million of these sales came during launch week despite the average $429 price tag.[11]

Most buyers involved in high-involvement purchase situations pass through the four stages of the AIDA model on the way to making a purchase. The promoter's task is to determine where on the purchase ladder most of the target consumers are located and design a promotion plan to meet their needs. For example, if Apple learned from its market research that many potential customers were in the desire stage but had not yet bought an iPad for some reason, then Apple could place advertising on Google and perhaps in video games to target younger individuals, who are the primary target market, with messages to motivate them to buy an iPad.

The AIDA concept does not explain how all promotions influence purchase decisions. The model suggests that promotional effectiveness can be measured in terms of consumers progressing from one stage to the next. However, the order of stages in the model, as well as whether consumers go through all steps, has been much debated. A purchase can occur without interest or desire, perhaps when a low-involvement product is bought on impulse. Regardless of the order of the stages or consumers' progression through these stages, the AIDA concept helps marketers by suggesting which promotional strategy will be most effective.[12]

AIDA and the Promotional Mix

Exhibit 16.4 depicts the relationship between the promotional mix and the AIDA model. It shows that although advertising does have an impact in the later stages, it is most useful in gaining attention for goods or services. In contrast, personal selling reaches fewer people at first. Salespeople are more effective at creating customer interest for merchandise or a service and at creating desire. For example, advertising may help a potential computer purchaser gain knowledge about competing brands, but the salesperson may be the one who actually encourages the buyer to decide a particular brand is the best choice. The salesperson also has the advantage of having the computer physically there to demonstrate its capabilities to the buyer.

Public relations has its greatest impact in gaining attention for a company, good, or service. Many companies can attract attention and build goodwill by sponsoring community events that benefit a worthy cause such as antidrug and antigang programs. Such sponsorships project a positive image of the firm and its products into the minds of consumers and potential consumers. Book publishers push to get their titles on the best-seller lists of major publications, such as *Publishers Weekly* or the *New York Times*. Book authors also make appearances on talk shows and at bookstores to personally sign books and speak to fans.

Sales promotion's greatest strength is in creating strong desire and purchase intent. Coupons and other price-off promotions are techniques used to persuade

EXHIBIT 16.4 **The Promotional Mix and AIDA**

	Attention	Interest	Desire	Action
Advertising	●	●	○	●
Public Relations	●	●	○	●
Sales Promotion	○	○	●	○
Personal Selling	○	●	●	●
Social Media	●	●	○	○

● Very effective ○ Somewhat effective ● Not effective

© ISTOCKPHOTO.COM/CRAFTVISION

integrated marketing communications (IMC) the careful coordination of all promotional messages for a product or a service to ensure the consistency of messages at every contact point at which a company meets the consumer

customers to buy new products. Frequent buyer sales promotion programs, popular among retailers, allow consumers to accumulate points or dollars that can later be redeemed for goods. Frequent buyer programs tend to increase purchase intent and loyalty and encourage repeat purchases.

Social media are a strong way to gain attention and interest in a brand, particularly if content goes viral. It can then reach a massive audience. Social media are also effective at engaging with customers and enabling companies to maintain interest in the brand if properly managed.

LO 6 Integrated Marketing Communications

Ideally, marketing communications from each promotional mix element (personal selling, advertising, sales promotion, social media, and public relations) should be integrated—that is, the message reaching the consumer should be the same regardless of whether it is from an advertisement, a salesperson in the field, a magazine article, a Facebook fan page, or a coupon in a newspaper insert.

From the consumer's standpoint, a company's communications are already integrated. Consumers do not think in terms of the five elements of promotion: personal selling, advertising, sales promotion, public relations, and social media. Instead, everything is an "ad." The only people who recognize the distinctions among these communications elements are the marketers themselves. Unfortunately, many marketers neglect this fact when planning promotional messages and fail to integrate their communication efforts from one element to the next. The most common rift typically occurs between personal selling and the other elements of the promotional mix.

This unintegrated, disjointed approach to promotion has propelled many companies to adopt the concept of **integrated marketing communications (IMC)**. IMC is the careful coordination of all promotional messages—traditional advertising, direct marketing, social media, interactive, public relations, sales promotion, personal selling, event marketing, and other communications—for a product or service to assure the consistency of messages at every contact point where a company meets the consumer. Following the concept of IMC, marketing managers carefully work out the roles that various promotional elements will play in the marketing mix. Timing of promotional activities is coordinated, and the results of each campaign are carefully monitored to improve future use of the promotional mix tools. Typically, a marketing communications director is appointed who has overall responsibility for integrating the company's marketing communications.

Procter & Gamble's Old Spice was competing in a very mature and competitive market of men's products (like deodorant and body wash). Sales had been declin-

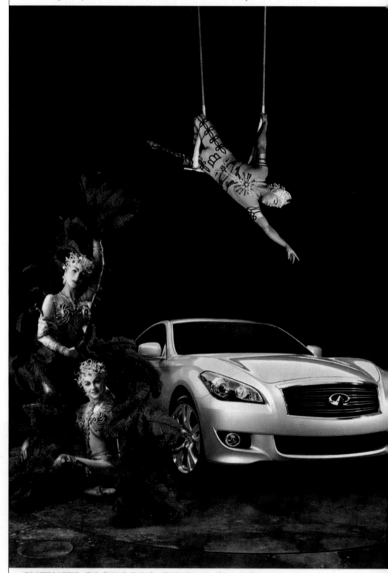

© AP IMAGES/PRNEWSFOTO/INFINITI

Infiniti has announced that it has partnered with Cirque du Soleil to become an official sponsor of the entertainment group and its exclusive automotive partner.

INFINITI SPONSORS CIRQUE DU SOLEIL (232/10)
Photos: Camirand Costumes: Dominique Lemieux © 2003, 2006 Cirque du Soleil
For further information please contact Infiniti Communications on +41 21 822 4950/30
© Copyright for editorial use only

ing until ad agency Weiden & Kennedy (of Nike fame) developed a TV spot called "The man your man could smell like" with former football player Isaiah Mustafa. The TV spot aired online during the Super Bowl and was viewed by millions of people. Soon it became not only a pop culture phenomenon but also a viral blockbuster. The overall campaign included coupons; public relations; coverage on blogs, Facebook, and Twitter; as well as print advertising and television advertising. However, what sent this campaign over the top was pure genius. Old Spice solicited questions for the "Old Spice Guy" via Twitter and Facebook and then had Mustafa "answer" the questions using short videoclips online—186 clips to be exact. The videos have been viewed hundreds of millions of times on YouTube, making the Old Spice YouTube channel one of the most popular channels. The results? Sales increased 107 percent, and Old Spice now has more than a million fans on Facebook, thousands of Twitter followers, higher Web site traffic, and press coverage valued at close to one billion impressions. This campaign leveraged a television spot by extending its life online and by engaging consumers online.[13]

The IMC concept has been growing in popularity for several reasons. First, the proliferation of thousands of media choices beyond traditional television has made promotion a more complicated task. Instead of promoting a product just through mass-media options, like television and magazines, promotional messages today can appear in many varied sources. Further, the mass market has also fragmented—more selectively segmented markets and an increase in niche marketing have replaced the traditional broad market groups that marketers promoted to in years past. Finally, marketers have slashed their advertising spending in favor of promotional techniques that generate immediate sales responses and those that are more easily measured, such as direct marketing. Online advertising has earned a bigger share of the budget as well due to its measurability. Thus, the interest in IMC is largely a reaction to the scrutiny that marketing communications has come under and, particularly, to suggestions that uncoordinated promotional activity leads to a strategy that is wasteful and inefficient.

LO7 Factors Affecting the Promotional Mix

Promotional mixes vary a great deal from one product and one industry to the next. Normally, advertising and personal selling are used to promote goods and services, supported and supplemented by sales promotion. Public relations helps develop a positive image for the organization and the product line. Social media have been used more for consumer goods, but business-to-business marketers are increasingly using these media. A firm may choose not to use all five promotional elements in its promotional mix, or it may choose to use them in varying degrees. The particular promotional mix chosen by a firm for a product or service depends on several factors: the nature of the product, the stage in the product life cycle, target market characteristics, the type of buying decision, funds available for promotion, and whether a push or a pull strategy will be used.

Nature of the Product

Characteristics of the product itself can influence the promotional mix. For instance, a product can be classified as either a business product or a consumer product. (Refer to Chapters 7 and 10.) As business products are often custom-tailored to the buyer's exact specifications, they are often not well suited to mass promotion. Therefore, producers of most business goods, such as computer systems or industrial machinery, rely more heavily on personal selling than on advertising. Advertising, however, still serves a purpose in promoting business goods. Advertising in trade media can help locate potential customers for the sales force. For example, print media advertising often includes coupons soliciting the potential customer to "fill this out for more detailed information."

In contrast, because consumer products generally are not custom-made, they do not require the selling efforts of a company representative who can tailor them to the user's needs. Thus, consumer goods are promoted mainly through advertising or social media to create brand familiarity. Television and radio advertising, consumer-oriented magazines, and increasingly the Internet and other highly targeted media are used to promote consumer goods, especially nondurables. Sales promotion, the brand name, and the product's packaging are about twice as important for consumer goods as for business products. Persuasive personal selling is important at the retail level for goods such as automobiles and appliances.

The costs and risks associated with a product also influence the promotional mix. As a general rule, when the costs or risks of buying and using a product increase, personal selling becomes more important. In fact, inexpensive items cannot support the cost of a salesperson's time and effort unless the potential volume is high. On the other hand, expensive and complex machinery, cars, and new homes represent a considerable investment. A salesperson must assure buyers that they are spending their money wisely and not taking an undue financial risk.

Social risk is an issue as well. Many consumer goods are not products of great social importance because they do not reflect social position. People do not experience much social risk in buying a loaf of bread. However, buying many specialty products such as jewelry and clothing involves a social risk. Many consumers depend on sales personnel for guidance in making the "proper" choice.

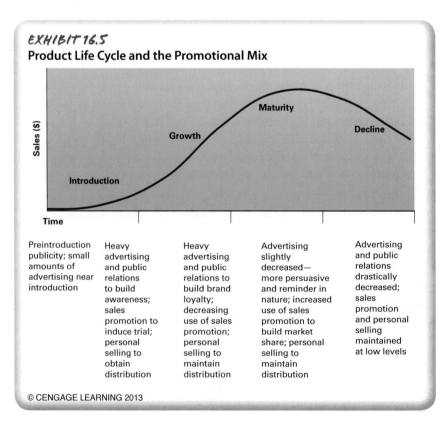

Many consumers depend on salespeople for help making the choice that is right for them.

Stages in the Product Life Cycle

The product's stage in its life cycle is a big factor in designing a promotional mix (see Exhibit 16.5). During the *introduction stage*, the basic goal of promotion is to inform the target audience that the product is available. Initially, the emphasis is on the general product class—for example, Smartphones. This emphasis gradually changes to gaining attention for a particular brand, such as Apple, Nokia, Samsung, Sony Ericsson, or Motorola. Typically, both extensive advertising and public relations inform the target audience of the product class or brand and heighten awareness levels. Sales promotion encourages early trial of the product, and personal selling gets retailers to carry the product.

When the product reaches the *growth stage* of the life cycle, the promotion blend may shift. Often a change is necessary because different types of potential buy-

ers are targeted. Although advertising and public relations continue to be major elements of the promotional mix, sales promotion can be reduced because consumers need fewer incentives to purchase. The promotional strategy is to emphasize the product's differential advantage over the competition. Persuasive promotion is used to build and maintain brand loyalty during the growth stage. By this stage, personal selling has usually succeeded in getting adequate distribution for the product.

As the product reaches the *maturity stage* of its life cycle, competition becomes fiercer, and thus persuasive and reminder advertising are more strongly emphasized. Sales promotion comes back into focus as product sellers try to increase their market share.

All promotion, especially advertising, is reduced as the product enters the *decline stage*. Nevertheless,

EXHIBIT 16.5
Product Life Cycle and the Promotional Mix

| Preintroduction publicity; small amounts of advertising near introduction | Heavy advertising and public relations to build awareness; sales promotion to induce trial; personal selling to obtain distribution | Heavy advertising and public relations to build brand loyalty; decreasing use of sales promotion; personal selling to maintain distribution | Advertising slightly decreased— more persuasive and reminder in nature; increased use of sales promotion to build market share; personal selling to maintain distribution | Advertising and public relations drastically decreased; sales promotion and personal selling maintained at low levels |

© CENGAGE LEARNING 2013

© ISTOCKPHOTO.COM/ŠTĚPÁN KAPL

personal selling and sales promotion efforts may be maintained, particularly at the retail level.

Target Market Characteristics

A target market characterized by widely scattered potential customers, highly informed buyers, and brand-loyal repeat purchasers generally requires a promotional mix with more advertising and sales promotion and less personal selling. Sometimes, however, personal selling is required even when buyers are well informed and geographically dispersed. Although industrial installations may be sold to well-educated people with extensive work experience, salespeople must be present to explain the product and work out the details of the purchase agreement.

Often firms sell goods and services in markets where potential customers are hard to locate. Print advertising can be used to find them. The reader is invited to go online, call, or mail in a reply card for more information. As the online queries, calls, or cards are received, salespeople are sent to visit the potential customers.

Type of Buying Decision

The promotional mix also depends on the type of buying decision—for example, a routine decision or a complex decision. For routine consumer decisions like buying toothpaste, the most effective promotion calls attention to the brand or reminds the consumer about the brand. Advertising and, especially, sales promotion are the most productive promotion tools to use for routine decisions.

If the decision is neither routine nor complex, advertising and public relations help establish awareness for the good or service. Suppose a man is looking for a bottle of wine to serve to his dinner guests. As a beer drinker, he is not familiar with wines, yet he has read an article in a popular magazine about the Robert Mondavi winery and has seen an advertisement for the wine. He may be more likely to buy this brand because he is already aware of it. Online reviews are often important in this type of buying decision as well because the consumer has any number of other consumers' reviews easily accessible.

In contrast, consumers making complex buying decisions are more extensively involved. They rely on large amounts of information to help them reach a purchase decision. Personal selling is most effective in helping these consumers decide. For example, consumers thinking about buying a car typically research the car online using corporate and third-party Web sites. However, few people buy a car without visiting the

© PEPSICO INC./FRITO-LAY NORTH AMERICA

Lay's calls attention to its commitment to natural ingredients as a distinguishing attribute to help customers make a routine buying decision—purchasing Lay's snack food.

When does nature surprise you with unexpected flavor?

When you use all natural ingredients from start to finish.

MADE WITH ALL NATURAL INGREDIENTS · NO MSG · NO PRESERVATIVES · NO ARTIFICIAL FLAVORS

Sun Chips GARDEN SALSA

Tostitos HINT OF LIME

Lay's Garden Tomato & Basil

push strategy a marketing strategy that uses aggressive personal selling and trade advertising to convince a wholesaler or a retailer to carry and sell particular merchandise

dealership. They depend on a salesperson to provide the information they need to reach a decision. In addition to online resources, print advertising may also be used for high-involvement purchase decisions because it can often provide a large amount of information to the consumer.

Available Funds

Money, or the lack of it, may easily be the most important factor in determining the promotional mix. A small, undercapitalized manufacturer may rely heavily on free publicity if its product is unique. If the situation warrants a sales force, a financially strained firm may turn to manufacturers' agents, who work on a commission basis with no advances or expense accounts. Even well-capitalized organizations may not be able to afford the advertising rates of publications like *Time Magazine*, *Reader's Digest*, and the *Wall Street Journal*, or the cost of running television commercials during *The Big Bang Theory*, *American Idol*, or the Super Bowl. The price of a high-profile advertisement in these media could support several salespeople for an entire year.

When funds are available to permit a mix of promotional elements, a firm will generally try to optimize its return on promotion dollars while minimizing the *cost per contact*, or the cost of reaching one member of the target market. In general, the cost per contact is very high for personal selling, public relations, and sales promotions like sampling and demonstrations. On the other hand, given the number of people national advertising and social media reach, they have a very low cost per contact. Usually, there is a trade-off among the funds available, the number of people in the target market, the quality of communication needed, and the relative costs of the promotional elements. There are plenty of low-cost options available to companies without a huge budget. Many of these include online strategies and public relations efforts, in which the company relies on free publicity.

Push and Pull Strategies

The last factor that affects the promotional mix is whether a push or a pull promotional strategy will be used. Manufacturers may use aggressive personal selling and trade advertising to convince a wholesaler or a retailer to carry and sell their merchandise. This approach is known as a **push strategy** (see Exhibit 16.6). The wholesaler, in turn, must often push the merchandise forward by persuading the retailer to handle the goods. The retailer then uses advertising, displays, and other forms of promotion to convince the consumer to buy the "pushed" products. Walmart uses aggressive discounts to consumers to push product out of its stores, such as selling 40-ounce bottles of Heinz ketchup for $1, or offering specials on holidays, like discounting sodas or meat for Labor Day barbeques.[14] This concept also applies to services.

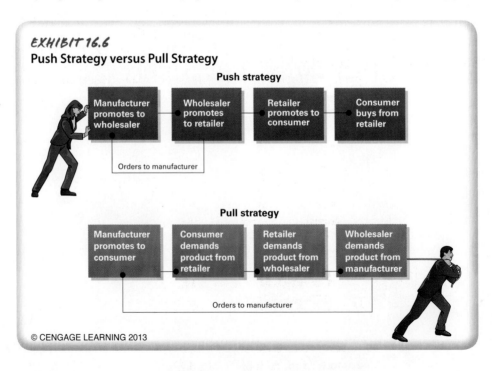

EXHIBIT 16.6
Push Strategy versus Pull Strategy

Push strategy

Manufacturer promotes to wholesaler → Wholesaler promotes to retailer → Retailer promotes to consumer → Consumer buys from retailer

Orders to manufacturer

Pull strategy

Manufacturer promotes to consumer → Consumer demands product from retailer → Retailer demands product from wholesaler → Wholesaler demands product from manufacturer

Orders to manufacturer

© CENGAGE LEARNING 2013

At the other extreme is a **pull strategy**, which stimulates consumer demand to obtain product distribution. Rather than trying to sell to the wholesaler, the manufacturer using a pull strategy focuses its promotional efforts on end consumers or opinion leaders. A classic example of a pull strategy is the heavy advertising and promotion of sugary breakfast cereals on children's television programs. The demand created from such major advertising campaigns is likely to "pull" demand from children (and then their parents) and encourage retailers to stock those cereals in their stores. As consumers begin demanding the product, the retailer orders the merchandise from the wholesaler. The wholesaler, confronted with rising demand, then places an order for the "pulled" merchandise from the manufacturer. Consumer demand pulls the product through the channel of distribution (see Exhibit 16.6). Heavy sampling, introductory consumer advertising, cents-off campaigns, and couponing are part of a pull strategy.

Rarely does a company use a pull or a push strategy exclusively. Instead, the mix will emphasize one of these strategies. For example, pharmaceutical companies generally use a push strategy, through personal selling and trade advertising, to promote their drugs and therapies to physicians. Sales presentations and advertisements in medical journals give physicians the detailed information they need to prescribe medication to their patients. Most pharmaceutical companies supplement their push promotional strategy with a pull strategy targeted directly to potential patients through advertisements in consumer magazines and on television.

pull strategy a marketing strategy that stimulates consumer demand to obtain product distribution

STUDY TOOLS
CHAPTER 16

Flip to the end of your textbook to:

❑ **Rip out Chapter Review Card**

Log in to the CourseMate for MKTG at cengagebrain.com to:

❑ **Review Key Terms Flash Cards (Print or Online)**

❑ **Review Audio and Visual Summaries**

❑ **Complete both Practice Quizzes to prepare for tests**

❑ **Play "Beat the Clock" and "Quizbowl" to master concepts**

❑ **Complete "Crossword Puzzle" to review key terms**

❑ **Watch the video on "Ogden Publications" for a real company example on Promotional Planning for Competitive Advantage**

CHAPTER **17** Advertising and Public Relations

The top 100 global marketers spend more than $125.3 billion on measured media.

AFTER YOU FINISH THIS CHAPTER, GO TO PAGE 292 FOR STUDY TOOLS

LO 1   The Effects of Advertising

Advertising was defined in Chapter 16 as impersonal, one-way mass communication about a product or organization that is paid for by a marketer. It is a popular form of promotion, especially for consumer packaged goods and services. Advertising expenditures typically increase annually but have fallen in recent years. In 2009, 30 companies each spent more than $1 billion, with the top 100 global marketers spending more than $125.3 billion overall on measured media. The top five spenders were Procter & Gamble ($4.2 billion), Verizon ($3 billion), AT&T ($2.7 billion), General Motors ($2.2 billion), and Pfizer ($2 billion).[1]

Advertising and marketing services, agencies, and other firms that provide marketing and communications services to marketers employ an estimated 1.4 million people including those working in media advertising, such as newspapers, broadcast and cable TV, radio, magazines, and Internet media companies.[2] Employment in both areas has decreased in recent years due primarily to economic conditions and much lower newspaper employment.

The amount of money budgeted for advertising by some firms is staggering. As noted above, Procter & Gamble, Verizon, AT&T, General Motors, and Pfizer each spend from $2 billion to more than $4 billion annually in the United States on national advertising alone. If local advertising, sales promotion, and public relations were included, these figures would be much higher. More than 100 companies each spend in excess of $300 million every year on advertising.[3] Spending on advertising varies by industry.

What do you think?

Television advertising helps me to know which brands have the features I am looking for.

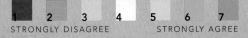

1   2   3   4   5   6   7

STRONGLY DISAGREE   STRONGLY AGREE

Find out what others think at the CourseMate for MKTG. Log in at cengagebrain.com.

© RICHARD LEVINE/ALAMY

advertising response function
a phenomenon in which spending for advertising and sales promotion increases sales or market share up to a certain level but then produces diminishing returns

institutional advertising a form of advertising designed to enhance a company's image rather than promote a particular product

product advertising a form of advertising that touts the benefits of a specific good or service

Advertising and Market Share

The most successful consumer brands, like Ivory soap and Coca-Cola, were built over many years by heavy advertising and marketing investments long ago. Today's advertising dollars for successful consumer brands are spent on maintaining brand awareness and market share.

New brands with a small market share tend to spend proportionately more for advertising and sales promotion than those with a large market share, typically for two reasons. First, beyond a certain level of spending for advertising and sales promotion, diminishing returns set in. That is, sales and market share improvements slow down and eventually decrease no matter how much is spent on advertising and sales promotion. This phenomenon is called the **advertising response function**. Understanding the advertising response function helps marketers use budgets wisely. A market leader like Johnson & Johnson's Neutrogena typically spends proportionately less on advertising than a newer line such as Jergens' Natural Glow moisturizer brand. Neutrogena has already captured the attention of the majority of its target market. It only needs to remind customers of its product.

The second reason new brands tend to require higher spending for advertising and sales promotion is that a certain minimum level of exposure is needed to measurably affect purchase habits. If Jergens advertised its Natural Glow moisturizers in only one or two publications and bought only one or two television spots, it would not achieve the exposure needed to penetrate consumers' perceptual defenses and affect purchase intentions.

The Effects of Advertising on Consumers

Advertising affects consumers' daily lives, informing them about products and services and influencing their attitudes, beliefs, and ultimately their purchases. Advertising affects the television programs people watch, the content of the newspapers they read, the politicians they elect, the medicines they take, and the toys their children play with. Consequently, the influence of advertising on the U.S. socioeconomic system has been the subject of extensive debate in nearly all corners of society.

Though advertising cannot change consumers' deeply rooted values and attitudes, advertising may succeed in transforming a person's negative attitude toward a product into a positive one. For instance, serious or dramatic advertisements are more effective at changing consumers' negative attitudes. Humorous ads, on the other hand, have been shown to be more effective at shaping attitudes when consumers already have a positive image of an advertised brand.[4]

Advertising also reinforces positive attitudes toward brands. When consumers have a neutral or favorable frame of reference toward a product or brand, advertising often positively influences them. When consumers are already highly loyal to a brand, they may buy more of it when advertising and promotion for that brand increase.[5] This is why market leaders spend billions of dollars annually to reinforce and remind their loyal customers about the benefits of their products. For example, Kellogg's spent between $30 and $40 million advertising its Kashi brand in 2009.[6]

Advertising can also affect the way consumers rank a brand's attributes. For example, in years past, car ads emphasized such brand attributes as roominess, speed, and low maintenance. Today, however, car marketers have added safety, versatility, customization, and fuel efficiency to the list.

LO 2 Major Types of Advertising

A firm's promotional objectives determine the type of advertising it uses. If the goal of the promotion plan is to improve the image of the company or the industry, **institutional advertising** may be used. In contrast, if the advertiser wants to enhance the sales of a specific good or service, **product advertising** is used.

Institutional Advertising

Historically, advertising in the United States has been product oriented. Today, however, companies market multiple products and need a different type of advertising. Institutional advertising, or corporate advertising, promotes the corporation as a whole and is designed to establish, change, or maintain the corporation's identity. It usually does not ask the audience to do anything but maintain a favorable attitude toward the advertiser and its goods and services.

A form of institutional advertising called **advocacy advertising** is typically used to safeguard against negative consumer attitudes and to enhance the company's credibility among consumers who already favor its position. Corporations often use advocacy advertising to express their views on controversial issues. At other times, firms' advocacy campaigns react to criticism or blame, some in direct response to criticism by the media. For example, oil and gas companies typically get blamed for high gas prices and high profits. One of the largest oil companies, Chevron Corporation, recently launched a campaign called "The Power of Human Energy" (www.chevron.com) to highlight the different areas of energy the company is investing in aside from oil exploration.

Other advocacy campaigns may try to ward off increased regulation, damaging legislation, or an unfavorable outcome in a lawsuit. For example, as BP worked to stop the oil leak in the Gulf of Mexico, the company was also spending $50 million on television advertising. One advertisement featured then-CEO Tony Hayward apologizing for the spill and promising that BP would pay for the cleanup. BP hoped to quell some of the anger against the company by positioning itself as a company that had made a terrible mistake but was working very hard to correct it.[7]

advocacy advertising a form of advertising in which an organization expresses its views on controversial issues or responds to media attacks

Product Advertising

Unlike institutional advertising, product advertising promotes the benefits of a specific good or service. The product's stage in its life cycle often determines which type of product advertising is used: pioneering

ADVERTISING OUTSIDE THE BOX

© ISTOCKPHOTO.COM/LINEARCURVES

MMM, fresh new gym smell!

A new gym in Boston, Massachusetts, called GymIt, was struggling to develop its brand and grow its clientele, even though its prices were significantly lower than those of most big box, designer gyms ($19.99/month and no contract versus $40/month and a one-year contract in some gyms). To get the word out about its no-frills gym where customers can work out without being distracted by big box gym promotions, tanning beds, and social club activities, GymIt teamed up with Small Army, a Boston advertising agency specializing in out-of-the-box campaigns. Small Army and GymIt developed a story for the gym: Gyms are for working out; therefore, we provide a space for working out. The tagline, "GymIt. Get In, Work Out," features the same simplicity and efficiency that customers find at the well-equipped, air-conditioned gym. The mascot is a white figure, no hands, no feet, no eyes—just a GymIt headband. He runs around Boston drumming up interest in the gym by handing out headbands saying "Hot New Fitness Trend: Not Getting Ripped Off." Small Army made sure that all the copy and the mascot screamed minimalism and were easy to understand—just as GymIt is an easy place to work out. The campaign worked—despite using only nontraditional channels such as social media and the mascot, GymIt's numbers have skyrocketed, and publicity about the mascot has reached news channels around Boston.[8]

SOURCE: "Small Army Marketing Campaign Helps Boston Gym Have a Strong Opening," *PRWeb*, May 31, 2011.

pioneering advertising a form of advertising designed to stimulate primary demand for a new product or product category

competitive advertising a form of advertising designed to influence demand for a specific brand

comparative advertising a form of advertising that compares two or more specifically named or shown competing brands on one or more specific attributes

advertising, competitive advertising, or comparative advertising.

Pioneering Advertising **Pioneering advertising** is intended to stimulate primary demand for a new product or product category. Heavily used during the introductory stage of the product life cycle, pioneering advertising offers consumers in-depth information about the benefits of the product class. Pioneering advertising also seeks to create interest. Manufacturers and sellers of e-readers have been increasing their advertising volume to create a market for the new technology. For instance, Barnes & Noble launched Internet, print, radio, and television ad campaigns to promote and inform readers about its Nook e-reader. The campaign marked the first time Barnes & Noble had advertised on television since its 1996 campaign announcing its new Web site. Similarly, Amazon.com spent $18 million to promote its Kindle e-reader in print and online.[9]

Competitive Advertising Firms use competitive or brand advertising when a product enters the growth phase of the product life cycle and other companies begin to enter the marketplace. Instead of building demand for the product category, the goal of **competitive advertising** is to influence demand for a specific brand. Often, promotion becomes less informative and appeals more to emotions during this phase. Generally, this is where an emphasis on branding begins. Advertisements focus on showing subtle differences between brands, building recall of a brand name, and creating a favorable attitude toward the brand. GEICO uses competitive advertising that discusses the attributes of the brand, how little time it takes to get a quote, how much customers can save, and the ease of submitting a claim. All of its campaigns use humor to promote the brand above others in the industry but without actively comparing GEICO with other insurance companies.

Comparative Advertising **Comparative advertising** directly or indirectly compares two or more competing brands on one or more specific attributes. Some advertisers even use comparative advertising against their own brands. Products experiencing slow growth or those entering the marketplace against strong competitors are more likely to employ comparative claims in their advertising. In contrast to GEICO's

IT STARTS WITH SHARPIE.

PLAIN JANE TO STAINED. WITH NEW STAINED BY SHARPIE.™
FLEXIBLE BRUSH TIPS. FLUID DESIGNS.
D.I.Y. QUEEN ERICA DOMESEK OF P.S.—I MADE THIS...,
USES STAINED BY SHARPIE™ TO CREATE ENDLESS D.I.Y. FASHION
POSSIBILITIES. IN 8 FABRIC INKS. WHAT ARE YOU GONNA START?

Sharpie
uncap what's inside.
sharpie.com

WG4501 ©2011 Newell Rubbermaid Office Products

© AP IMAGES/PRNEWSFOTO/SHARPIE

This ad for Sharpie Stained positions the pens against traditional fabric paint as an effective way to channel creativity onto fabric, but without a strict comparison with fabric paint. This is an example of competitive advertising.

"15 minutes can save you 15 percent or more on car insurance" tagline that doesn't explicitly mention any other insurance company, 21st Century Insurance takes on its major competitors directly in its "door dings" television ad campaign. The ad features two cars, one labeled GEICO, the other 21st Century. A man wielding a huge mallet puts dings in the doors of both cars, and "since both cars are covered, both get the same repairs."[10] Then the commercial goes on to explain that 21st Century Insurance customers who switch from GEICO save an average of $480 a year, and those switching from Progressive and Allstate save an average of $528 a year.[11] 21st Century is explicitly comparing its insurance rates with those of its main competitors and capitalizing on customers' desire for great coverage at the lowest prices.

Before the 1970s, comparative advertising was allowed only if the competing brand was veiled and unidentified. In 1971, however, the Federal Trade Commission (FTC) fostered the growth of comparative advertising by saying that the advertising provided information to the customer and that advertisers were more skillful than the government in communicating this information. Federal rulings prohibit advertisers from falsely describing competitors' products and allow competitors to sue if ads show their products or mention their brand names in an incorrect or false manner. FTC rules also apply to advertisers making false claims about their own products.

LO3 Creative Decisions in Advertising

Advertising strategies are typically organized around an advertising campaign. An **advertising campaign** is a series of related advertisements focusing on a common theme, slogan, and set of advertising appeals. It is a specific advertising effort for a particular product that extends for a defined period of time.

Before any creative work can begin on an advertising campaign, it is important to determine what goals or objectives the advertising should achieve. An **advertising objective** identifies the specific communication task that a campaign should accomplish for a specified target audience during a specified period. The objectives of a specific advertising campaign often depend on the overall corporate objectives and the product being advertised.

The DAGMAR approach (Defining Advertising Goals for Measured Advertising Results) is one method of setting objectives. According to this method, all advertising objectives should precisely define the target audience, the desired percentage change in some specified measure of effectiveness, and the time frame in which that change is to occur.

Once objectives are defined, creative work can begin on the advertising campaign. Advertising campaigns often follow the AIDA model, which was discussed in Chapter 16. Depending on where consumers are in the AIDA process, the creative development of an advertising campaign might focus on creating attention, arousing interest, stimulating desire, or ultimately leading to the action of buying the product. Specifically, creative decisions include identifying product benefits, developing and evaluating advertising appeals, executing the message, and evaluating the effectiveness of the campaign.

Identifying Product Benefits

A well-known rule of thumb in the advertising industry is "Sell the sizzle, not the steak"—that is, in advertising, the goal is to sell the benefits of the product, not its attributes. Consumers don't buy attributes, they buy benefits. An attribute is simply a feature of the product such as its easy-open package, special formulation, or new lower price. A benefit is what consumers will receive or achieve by using the product such as convenience or ease of use. A benefit should answer the consumer's question "What's in it for me?" Benefits might be such things as pleasure, improved health, savings, or relief. A quick test to determine whether you are offering attributes or benefits in your advertising is to ask "So?" Consider this example:

▶ *Attribute:* "With just 10 calories per serving, Propel hydrates and contains Vitamins C & E, B Vitamins, and antioxidants. Propel is conveniently available in both ready-to-drink and powder form." "So . . . ?"

COURTESY OF EGGLAND'S BEST, INC.

Eggland's Best lists the attributes of its eggs. The implied benefit is more nutritious eggs, which are better for customers.

advertising campaign a series of related advertisements focusing on a common theme, slogan, and set of advertising appeals

advertising objective a specific communication task that a campaign should accomplish for a specified target audience during a specified period

advertising appeal a reason for a person to buy a product

unique selling proposition a desirable, exclusive, and believable advertising appeal selected as the theme for a campaign

▶▶ *Benefit:* "So . . . Propel fuels real women who are energized and empowered by physical activity and understand their need to replenish, energize, and protect in all aspects of their lives."[12]

Developing and Evaluating Advertising Appeals

An **advertising appeal** identifies a reason for a person to buy a product. Developing advertising appeals, a challenging task, is typically the responsibility of the creative team (e.g., art directors and copywriters) in the advertising agency. Advertising appeals typically play off consumers' emotions or address some need or want the consumer has.

Advertising campaigns can focus on one or more advertising appeals. Often the appeals are quite general, thus allowing the firm to develop a number of subthemes or mini campaigns using both advertising and sales promotion. Several possible advertising appeals are listed in Exhibit 17.1.

Choosing the best appeal from those developed usually requires market research. Criteria for evaluation include desirability, exclusiveness, and believability. The appeal first must make a positive impression on and be desirable to the target market. It must also be exclusive or unique. Consumers must be able to distinguish the advertiser's message from competitors' messages. Most important, the appeal should be believable. An appeal that makes extravagant claims not only wastes promotional dollars but also creates ill will for the advertiser.

The advertising appeal selected for the campaign becomes what advertisers call its **unique selling proposition**. The unique selling position often becomes all or part of the campaign's slogan. For example, K-Swiss's new Tube line of workout shoes has teamed with HBO's *Eastbound and Down* to create an ad campaign starring the main character of the show, Kenny Powers, a washed-up pitcher with a foul mouth and an overblown confidence in his awesomeness. The campaign features Powers as the CEO of K-Swiss and his marketing decisions on how to make the brand relevant (or in his words, "making marketing that touches my audience deep inside").[13] K-Swiss is using humor to appeal to its target audience of young males, and the unique selling position for Tubes is that they will help you perform like Powers's all-star athlete employees. The campaign sparked a 250 percent sales increase for K-Swiss and helped bring *Eastbound and Down* into a more mainstream consciousness.[14]

EXHIBIT 17.1
Common Advertising Appeals

Appeal	Goal
Profit	Lets consumers know whether the product will save them money, make them money, or keep them from losing money.
Health	Appeals to those who are body conscious or who want to be healthy; love or romance is used often in selling cosmetics and perfumes.
Fear	Can center around social embarrassment, growing old, or losing one's health; because of its power, requires advertiser to exercise care in execution.
Admiration	Frequently highlights celebrity spokespeople.
Convenience	Is often used for fast-food restaurants and microwave foods.
Fun and Pleasure	Are the keys to advertising vacations, beer, amusement parks, and more.
Vanity and Egotism	Are used most often for expensive or conspicuous items such as cars and clothing.
Environmental Consciousness	Centers around protecting the environment and being considerate of others in the community.

© CENGAGE LEARNING 2013

Executing the Message

Message execution is the way an advertisement portrays its information. In general, the AIDA plan (see Chapter 16) is a good blueprint for executing an advertising message. Any ad should immediately draw the reader's, viewer's, or listener's attention. The advertiser must then use the message to hold interest, create desire for the good or service, and ultimately motivate a purchase.

The style in which the message is executed is one of the most creative elements of an advertisement. Exhibit 17.2 lists some examples of executional styles used by advertisers. Executional styles often dictate what type of media is to be employed to convey the message. For example, scientific executional styles lend themselves well to print advertising where more information can be conveyed. Testimonials by athletes are one of the more popular executional styles.

Injecting humor into an advertisement is a popular and effective executional style. Humorous executional styles are more often used in radio and television advertising than in print or magazine advertising where humor is less easily communicated. Humorous ads are typically used for lower-risk, low-involvement, routine purchases such as candy, cigarettes, and casual jeans than for higher-risk purchases or those that are expensive, durable, or flamboyant.[15]

Sometimes a company will modify its executional styles to make its advertising more effective. For decades, Procter & Gamble has advertised shampoo in China using a demonstrational executional style. Television ads demonstrated how the science of shampoo worked and then showed a woman with nice, shiny hair. Because today's urban Chinese no longer make solely utilitarian purchases, P&G now uses emotional appeals in its advertisements. One shows a woman emerging from an animated cocoon as a sophisticated butterfly while a voice purrs, "Head & Shoulders metamorphosis—new life for hair."[16]

Post-Campaign Evaluation

Evaluating an advertising campaign can be the most demanding task facing advertisers. How can an advertiser assess if the campaign led to an increase in sales or market share or elevated awareness of the product? Many advertising campaigns aim to create an image for the good or service instead of asking for action, so their real effect is

---

EXHIBIT 17.2
Eleven Common Executional Styles for Advertising

Executional Style	Description
Slice-of-Life	Depicts people in normal settings, such as at the dinner table or in their car. McDonald's often uses slice-of-life styles showing youngsters munching on french fries from Happy Meals on family outings.
Lifestyle	Shows how well the product will fit in with the consumer's lifestyle. As his Volkswagen Jetta moves through the streets of the French Quarter, a Gen X driver inserts a techno music CD and marvels at how the rhythms of the world mimic the ambient vibe inside his vehicle.
Spokesperson/ Testimonial	Can feature a celebrity, company official, or typical consumer making a testimonial or endorsing a product. Sheryl Crow represented Revlon's Colorist hair coloring, while Beyoncé Knowles was named the new face of American Express. Dell, Inc. founder Michael Dell touts his vision of the customer experience via Dell in television ads.
Fantasy	Creates a fantasy for the viewer built around use of the product. Carmakers often use this style to let viewers fantasize about how they would feel speeding around tight corners or down long country roads in their cars.
Humorous	Advertisers often use humor in their ads, such as Snickers' "Not Going Anywhere for a While" campaign featuring hundreds of souls waiting, sometimes impatiently, to get into heaven.
Real/Animated Product Symbols	Creates a character that represents the product in advertisements, such as the Energizer Bunny or Starkist's Charlie the Tuna. GEICO's suave gecko and disgruntled cavemen became cult classics for the insurance company.
Mood or Image	Builds a mood or image around the product, such as peace, love, or beauty. De Beers ads depicting shadowy silhouettes wearing diamond engagement rings and diamond necklaces portrayed passion and intimacy while extolling that "a diamond is forever."
Demonstration	Shows consumers the expected benefit. Many consumer products use this technique. Laundry detergent spots are famous for demonstrating how their product will clean clothes whiter and brighter. Fort James Corporation demonstrated in television commercials how its Dixie Rinse & ReUse disposable stoneware product line can stand up to the heat of a blowtorch and survive a cycle in a clothes washer.
Musical	Conveys the message of the advertisement through song. For example, Nike's ads depicted a marathoner's tortured feet and a surfer's thigh scarred by a shark attack while strains of Joe Cocker's "You Are So Beautiful" could be heard in the background.
Scientific	Uses research or scientific evidence to give a brand superiority over competitors. Pain relievers like Advil, Bayer, and Excedrin use scientific evidence in their ads.

© CENGAGE LEARNING 2013

medium the channel used to convey a message to a target market

media planning the series of decisions advertisers make regarding the selection and use of media, allowing the marketer to optimally and cost-effectively communicate the message to the target audience

unknown. So many variables shape the effectiveness of an ad that advertisers often must guess whether their money has been well spent. Nonetheless, marketers spend considerable time studying advertising effectiveness and its probable impact on sales, market share, or awareness.

Testing ad effectiveness can be done before and/or after the campaign. Before a campaign is released, marketing managers use pretests to determine the best advertising appeal, layout, and media vehicle. After advertisers implement a campaign, they use several monitoring techniques to determine whether the campaign has met its original goals. Even if a campaign has been highly successful, advertisers still typically do a postcampaign analysis to identify how the campaign might have been more efficient and what factors contributed to its success.

LO 4 Media Decisions in Advertising

A major decision for advertisers is the choice of **medium**—the channel used to convey a message to a

This scooter ad uses quirky humor to sell a scooter (a low-involvement purchase).

"Oh Bugger..."

target market. **Media planning**, therefore, is the series of decisions advertisers make regarding the selection and use of media, enabling the marketer to optimally and cost-effectively communicate the message to the target audience. Specifically, advertisers must determine which types of media will best communicate the benefits of their product or service to the target audience and when and for how long the advertisement will run.

Promotional objectives and the appeal and executional style of the advertising strongly affect the selection of media. Both creative and media decisions are made at the same time: Creative work cannot be completed without knowing which medium will be used to convey the message to the target market. In many cases, the advertising objectives dictate the medium and the creative approach to be used. For example, if the objective is to demonstrate how fast a product operates, a television commercial that shows this action may be the best choice.

U.S. advertisers spend roughly $300 billion annually on media monitored by national reporting services—newspapers, magazines, radio, television, the Internet, and outdoor. The remainder is spent on unmonitored media, such as direct mail, trade exhibits, cooperative advertising, brochures, coupons, catalogs, and special events. In 2008, about 48 percent of every media dollar went toward TV ads (cable, syndicated, spot, and network), 19 percent to magazines, 2.7 percent to outdoor advertizing, and about 16.5 percent for newspaper ads.[17] But these traditional mass-market media are declining in usage as more targeted media are growing. Between 2008 and 2010, spending on magazine advertising declined and Internet advertising rose to 12.6 percent of global ad spending.[18]

Media Types

Advertising media are channels that advertisers use in mass communication. The six major advertising media are newspapers, magazines, radio, television, the Internet, and outdoor media. Exhibit 17.3 summarizes the advantages and disadvantages of some of these major channels. In recent years, however, alternative media channels have emerged that give advertisers innovative ways to reach their target audience and avoid advertising clutter.

Newspapers Newspapers are one of the oldest forms of media. The advantages of newspaper advertising include geographic flexibility and timeliness. Because copywriters can usually prepare newspaper ads quickly and at a reasonable cost, local merchants can reach their

EXHIBIT 17.3
Advantages and Disadvantages of Major Advertising Media

Medium	Advantages	Disadvantages
Newspapers	Geographic selectivity and flexibility; short-term advertiser commitments; news value and immediacy; year-round readership; high individual market coverage; co-op and local tie-in availability; short lead time	Little demographic selectivity; limited color capabilities; low pass-along rate; may be expensive
Magazines	Good reproduction, especially for color; demographic selectivity; regional selectivity; local market selectivity; relatively long advertising life; high pass-along rate	Long-term advertiser commitments; slow audience buildup; limited demonstration capabilities; lack of urgency; long lead time
Radio	Low cost; immediacy of message; can be scheduled on short notice; relatively no seasonal change in audience; highly portable; short-term advertiser commitments; entertainment carryover	No visual treatment; short advertising life of message; high frequency required to generate comprehension and retention; distractions from background sound; commercial clutter
Television	Ability to reach a wide, diverse audience; low cost per thousand; creative opportunities for demonstration; immediacy of messages; entertainment carryover; demographic selectivity with cable stations	Short life of message; some consumer skepticism about claims; high campaign cost; little demographic selectivity with network stations; long-term advertiser commitments; long lead times required for production; commercial clutter
Internet	Fastest-growing medium; ability to reach a narrow target audience; relatively short lead time required for creating Web-based advertising; moderate cost; ability to measure ad effectiveness; ability to engage consumers through search engine marketing, social media, display advertising, and mobile marketing	Most ad exposure relies on "click-through" from display ads; measurement for social media needs much improvement; not all consumers have access to the Internet, and many consumers are not using social media
Outdoor Media	Repetition; moderate cost; flexibility; geographic selectivity	Short message; lack of demographic selectivity; high "noise" level distracting audience

© CENGAGE LEARNING 2013

target market almost daily. Although there has been a decline in circulation as well as in the number of newspapers nationally, there are still several major newspapers including *The Wall Street Journal, USA Today, New York Times, Los Angeles Times* and *The Washington Post*. But most newspapers are local. Because newspapers are generally a mass-market medium, however, they may not be the best vehicle for marketers trying to reach a very narrow market. Newspaper advertising also encounters a lot of distractions from competing ads and news stories. Therefore, one company's ad may not be particularly visible.

The main sources of newspaper ad revenue are local retailers, classified ads, and cooperative advertising. In **cooperative advertising**, the manufacturer and the retailer split the costs of advertising the manufacturer's brand. For example, Estee Lauder may split the cost of an advertisement with Macy's department store provided that the ad focuses on Estee Lauder's products. One reason manufacturers use cooperative advertising is the impracticality of listing all their dealers in national advertising. Also, cooperative advertising encourages retailers to devote more effort to the manufacturer's lines.

Magazines Magazines are another traditional medium that has been successful. Some of the top magazines according to circulation include *AARP, Better Homes and Gardens, Reader's Digest, National Geographic,* and *Good Housekeeping*. However, compared to the cost of other media, the cost per contact in magazine advertising is usually high. The cost per

cooperative advertising an arrangement in which the manufacturer and the retailer split the costs of advertising the manufacturer's brand

infomercial a
30-minute or longer
advertisement that looks more
like a television talk show than
a sales pitch

potential customer may be much lower, however, because magazines are often targeted to specialized audiences and thus reach more potential customers.

One of the main advantages of magazine advertising is its market selectivity. Magazines are published for virtually every market segment. For instance, *Lucky* is a leading fashion magazine; *ESPN the Magazine* is a successful sports magazine; *Essence* is targeted toward African American women; *Marketing News* is a trade magazine for the marketing professional; and *The Source* is a niche publication geared to young urbanites with a passion for hip-hop music.

Radio Radio has several strengths as an advertising medium: selectivity and audience segmentation, a large out-of-home audience, low unit and production costs, timeliness, and geographic flexibility. Local advertisers are the most frequent users of radio advertising, contributing over 75 percent of all radio ad revenue. Like newspapers, radio also lends itself well to cooperative advertising.

As Americans become more mobile and pressed for time, network television and newspapers have lost viewers and readers, particularly in the youth market, but radio is experiencing a resurgence in popularity because its immediate, portable nature meshes so well with a fast-paced lifestyle. The ability to target specific demographic groups is a major selling point for radio stations, attracting advertisers pursuing narrowly defined audiences that are more likely to respond to certain kinds of ads and products. Radio listeners tend to listen habitually and at predictable times, with the most popular being "drive time," when commuters form a vast captive audience. Finally, satellite radio (e.g., Sirius XM) has attracted new audiences that are exposed to ads, which previously were not allowed on that format.

Television Television broadcasters include network television, independent stations, cable television, and direct broadcast satellite television. Network television reaches a wide and diverse market, and cable television and direct broadcast satellite systems, such as DIRECTV and Dish Network, broadcast a multitude of channels devoted to highly segmented markets. Because of its targeted channels, cable television is often characterized as "narrowcasting" by media buyers.

Advertising time on television can be very expensive, especially for network and popular cable channels. Special events and first-run prime-time shows for top-ranked television programs command the highest rates for a typical 30-second spot, with the least expensive ads costing about $300,000 and the more expensive ones $500,000. A 30-second spot during the Super Bowl runs between $2.8 and $3 million, which companies are willing to pay. Fox sold all of its advertising spots for the 2011 Super Bowl three months before the big game.[19]

One of the more successful recent television formats to emerge is the **infomercial**, a 30-minute or longer advertisement, which is relatively inexpensive to produce and air. Advertisers say the infomercial is an ideal way to present complicated information to potential customers, which other advertising vehicles typically don't allow time to do. Some companies are now producing infomercials with a more polished look, which is being embraced by mainstream marketers.

Probably the most significant trend to affect television advertising is the rise in popularity of digital video recorders (DVRs) like TiVo. For every hour of television programming, an average of 15 minutes is

© ARTPOSE ADAM BORKOWSKI/SHUTTERSTOCK.COM

dedicated to nonprogram material (ads, public service announcements, and network promotions), so the popularity of DVRs among ad-weary viewers is hardly surprising. Like marketers and advertisers, networks are also highly concerned about ad skipping. If consumers are not watching advertisements, then marketers will spend a greater proportion of their advertising budgets on alternative media, and a critical revenue stream for networks will disappear. The Coalition for Innovative Media Measurement is attempting to work with set-top box providers like TiVo to access their data and see how consumers are behaving in relation to recording and watching television through the set-top box. Nielsen, a research company, is also working to monitor home-media usage through in-home measurement tools. By understanding where consumer attention lies, companies will be able to target audiences in an increasingly fragmented media market.[20] To keep audiences from fast forwarding through commercials or changing the channel, some channels run short segments with characters or participants from shows with extra, non-essential content. For example, Bravo and Lifetime run short segments during commercial breaks with participants from the reality shows *Top Chef* and *Project Runway* that show participant reactions to challenges or lifestyle segments about the participants interacting with each other.[21]

The Internet With ad revenues exceeding $22 billion annually, the Internet has become a solid advertising medium. In 2009, marketers spent more to advertise online than in magazines—12.6 percent of global ad spending was online, and 10.3 percent was in magazines.[22] Internet advertising is becoming more versatile and able to target specific groups. Google offers the ability to *audience buy;* advertisers can purchase ad space targeted to a highly specific group, such as women ages 18 to 34 who like basketball.[23]

Popular Internet sites and search engines generally sell advertising space to marketers to promote their goods and services. Internet surfers click on these ads to be linked to more information about the advertised product or service. Both leading advertisers and companies whose ad budgets are not as large have become big Internet advertisers.

One of the most popular approaches for Internet advertising is search engine ads. Marketers' primary objective in using search engine ads is to enhance brand awareness. They do this through paid placement of ads tied to key words used in search engines—when

someone clicks on the ad, the advertiser pays the search engine a fee. Search engine advertising accounts for half of all money spent on Internet advertising. Search engines also generate nearly half of all Internet ad revenue. Display and banner ads are the next largest source of Internet revenue.[24]

advergaming placing advertising messages in Web-based or video games to advertise or promote a product, service, organization, or issue

Advergaming Another popular Internet advertising format is **advergaming**, in which companies put ad messages in Web-based or video games (on PlayStation or Wii) to advertise or promote a product, service, organization, or issue. Sometimes the entire game amounts to a virtual commercial; other times advertisers sponsor games or buy ad space for a product placement in them. Many of these are social games, played on Facebook or similar sites, where players can interact with one another. Social gaming has an audience of more than 300 million, and they will spend $4.9 billion inside games this year.[25] Showtime is cashing in on social gaming by licensing its popular show *Weeds* for a game called "Weeds Social Club," which lets users grow and distribute virtual marijuana. Players can spend actual money on "favors" that allow them to purchase upscale virtual goods such as TVs and wine. Ecko Code developed the game and is also developing games for other Showtime hits such as *Dexter*. Ecko Code expects players to spend at least one million (real) dollars a month inside each show's game.[26]

Outdoor Media Outdoor or out-of-home advertising is a flexible, low-cost medium that may take a variety of forms. Examples include billboards, skywriting, giant inflatables, mini billboards in malls and on bus stop shelters, signs in sports arenas, and lighted moving signs in bus terminals and airports, as well as ads painted on cars, trucks, buses, water towers, manhole covers, drinking glass coasters, and even people, called "living advertising." The plywood scaffolding surrounding downtown construction sites often holds ads, which in places like Manhattan's Times Square, can reach over a million viewers a day.

Outdoor advertising reaches a broad and diverse market and is therefore ideal for promoting convenience products and services as well as directing consumers to local businesses. One of outdoor advertising's main advantages over other media is that its exposure frequency is very high, yet the amount of clutter from competing ads is very low. Outdoor

media mix the combination of media to be used for a promotional campaign

advertising also can be customized to local marketing needs, which is why local businesses are the leading outdoor advertisers in any given region.

Alternative Media To cut through the clutter of traditional advertising media, advertisers are developing new media vehicles, like shopping carts in grocery stores, computer screen savers, DVDs, CDs, interactive kiosks in department stores, advertisements run before movies at the cinema, posters on bathroom stalls, and "advertainments"—mini movies that promote a product and are shown via the Internet.

Marketers are looking for more innovative ways to reach captive and often bored commuters. For instance, subway systems are now showing ads via lighted boxes installed along tunnel walls. Other advertisers seek consumers at home. Some marketers have begun replacing hold music on customer service lines with advertisements and movie trailers. This strategy generates revenue for the company being called and catches undistracted consumers for advertisers. The trick is to amuse and interest this captive audience without annoying them during their 10- to 15-minute wait.[27]

Video games are emerging as an excellent medium for reaching males ages 18 to 34. Massive, Inc. started a video game advertising network and established a partnership with Nielsen Entertainment, Inc. to provide ad ratings. Massive can insert ads with full motion and sound into games played on Internet-connected computers. Massive has also developed a way to measure the effectiveness of its video game advertisements called AdEffx Action Lift for Gaming. In a recent partnership, after gamers saw Microsoft Bing ads in games, 71 percent recalled that they saw the ad, and 60 percent had a more favorable opinion of Bing.[28]

Cell phones are particularly useful for reaching the youth market. Mobile advertising has substantial upside potential, given that there are more than 4 billion cell phone users in the world, and an increasing number of those users have Smartphones or tablets that have Internet access. As devices such as the iPad continue to grow in popularity, the amount of mobile advertising spending in the United States will continue to grow. Spending on mobile ads increased nearly $100 million in 2009 to $416 million.[29]

Despite the growth potential, one problem with mobile advertising is that many consumers perceive current text-message advertisements as spam—and spam that costs them money for using data. When individual companies send text-message ads, the receiver is charged normal message rates, whether or not the text message is wanted. If wireless carriers such as Verizon or AT&T opted to make mobile advertisements free to receive and respond to, much of the potential in mobile advertising could be realized. Alcatel-Lucent developed a system to do just that. Users could sign up for ads through their carriers and would receive advertisements as texts, display ads, or multimedia without being charged for data usage. With this system, not only would carriers benefit from receiving revenue by charging companies for advertising (much like television and radio), but consumers could receive discounts or coupons to local services by responding to an initial (free) text.[30]

Media Selection Considerations

An important element in any advertising campaign is the **media mix**, the combination of media to be used. Media mix decisions are typically based on several

© ISTOCKPHOTO.COM/ROBERT LEHMANN

factors: cost per contact, cost per click, reach, frequency, target audience considerations, flexibility of the medium, noise level, and the life span of the medium.

Cost per contact, also referred to as **cost per thousand (CPM)**, is the cost of reaching one member of the target market. Naturally, as the size of the audience increases, so does the total cost. Cost per contact enables an advertiser to compare the relative costs of specific media vehicles, such as television versus radio or magazine versus newspaper, or more specifically, *Newsweek* versus *Time*. Thus, an advertiser debating whether to spend local advertising dollars for television spots or radio spots could consider the cost per contact of each. The advertiser might then pick the vehicle with the lowest cost per contact to maximize advertising punch for the money spent. **Cost per click** is the cost associated with a consumer clicking on a display or banner ad. Although there are several variations, this option enables the marketer to pay only for "engaged" consumers—those who opted to click on an ad.

Reach is the number of target consumers who are exposed to a commercial at least once during a specific period, usually four weeks. Media plans for product introductions and attempts at increasing brand awareness usually emphasize reach. For example, an advertiser might try to reach 70 percent of the target audience during the first three months of the campaign. Reach is related to a medium's ratings, generally referred to in the industry as *gross ratings points*, or GRP. A television program with a higher GRP means that more people are tuning in to the show and the reach is higher. Accordingly, as GRP increases for a particular medium, so does cost per contact.

Because the typical ad is short-lived and because often only a small portion of an ad may be perceived at one time, advertisers repeat their ads so that consumers will remember the message. **Frequency** is the number of times an individual is exposed to a given message during a specific period. Advertisers use average frequency to measure the intensity of a specific medium's coverage. For example, Coca-Cola might want an average exposure frequency of five for its POWERade television ads. That means that each of the television viewers who saw the ad saw it an average of five times.

Media selection is also a matter of matching the advertising medium with the product's target market. If marketers are trying to reach teenage females, they might select *Seventeen* magazine. A medium's ability to reach a precisely defined market is its **audience selectivity**. Some media vehicles, like general newspapers and network television, appeal to a wide cross section of the population. Others—such as *Brides*, *Popular Mechanics*, *Architectural Digest*, *Lucky*, MTV, ESPN, and Christian radio stations—appeal to very specific groups.

The *flexibility* of a medium can be extremely important to an advertiser. For example, because of layouts and design, the lead time for magazine advertising is considerably longer than for other media types and so is less flexible. By contrast, radio and Internet advertising provide maximum flexibility. If necessary, an advertiser can change a radio ad on the day it is aired.

Noise level is the level of distraction experienced by the target audience in a medium. Noise can be created by competing ads, as when a street is lined with billboards or when a television program is cluttered with competing ads. Whereas newspapers and magazines have a high noise level, direct mail is a private medium with a low noise level. Typically, no other advertising media or news stories compete for direct mail readers' attention.

Media have either a short or a long *life span*, which means that messages can either quickly fade or persist as tangible copy to be carefully studied. A radio

cost per contact (cost per thousand or CPM) the cost of reaching one member of the target market

cost per click the cost associated with a consumer clicking on a display or banner ad

reach the number of target consumers exposed to a commercial at least once during a specific period, usually four weeks

frequency the number of times an individual is exposed to a given message during a specific period

audience selectivity the ability of an advertising medium to reach a precisely defined market

A TELEVISION PROGRAM WITH A HIGHER **GRP** MEANS THAT MORE PEOPLE ARE **TUNING** IN TO THE **SHOW** AND THE **REACH** IS **HIGHER.**

media schedule
designation of the media, the specific publications or programs, and the insertion dates of advertising

continuous media schedule a media scheduling strategy in which advertising is run steadily throughout the advertising period; used for products in the later stages of the product life cycle

flighted media schedule a media scheduling strategy in which ads are run heavily every other month or every two weeks, to achieve a greater impact with an increased frequency and reach at those times

pulsing media schedule a media scheduling strategy that uses continuous scheduling throughout the year coupled with a flighted schedule during the best sales periods

commercial may last less than a minute, but advertisers can overcome this short life span by repeating radio ads often. In contrast, a magazine has a relatively long life span, which is further increased by a high pass-along rate.

Media planners have traditionally relied on the above factors in selecting an effective media mix, with reach, frequency, and cost often the overriding criteria. Well-established brands with familiar messages, however, probably need fewer exposures to be effective, while newer or unfamiliar brands likely need more exposures to become familiar. In addition, today's media planners have more media options than ever before. (Today, there are over 1,600 television stations across the country, whereas 40 years ago there were only three.)

The proliferation of media channels is causing *media fragmentation* and forcing media planners to pay as much attention to where they place their advertising as to how often the advertisement is repeated. That is, marketers should evaluate reach *and* frequency in assessing the effectiveness of advertising. In certain situations, it may be important to reach potential consumers through as many media vehicles as possible. When this approach is considered, however, the budget must be large enough to achieve sufficient levels of frequency to have an impact. In evaluating reach versus frequency, therefore, the media planner ultimately must select an approach that is most likely to result in the ad being understood and remembered when a purchase decision is being made.

Advertisers also evaluate the qualitative factors involved in media selection. These include such things as attention to the commercial and the program, involvement, program liking, lack of distractions, and other audience behaviors that affect the likelihood that a commercial message is being seen and, hopefully, absorbed. While advertisers can advertise their product in as many media as possible and repeat the ad as many times as they like, the ad still may not be effective if the audience is not paying attention. Research on audience attentiveness for television, for example, shows that the longer viewers stay tuned to a particular program, the more memorable they find the commercials. Contrary to long-held assumptions, "holding power" can be more important than ratings (the number of people tuning in to any part of the program) when selecting media vehicles. Top-ranked shows like *Mad Men*, *30 Rock*, and *Modern Family* draw many viewers, but those viewers may be unlikely to remember the commercials they watch, perhaps because they are so intensely focused on the shows themselves. Advertising spots during less popular shows, which reach fewer viewers and cost less, may be more likely to make a memorable impression with a limited audience.

Online advertising on sites that stream television shows, such as Hulu.com, is not giving advertisers the same revenue that they receive through traditional television advertising. Although companies continue to stream shows through their individual Web sites, Hulu.com has pulled shows such as *The Daily Show* and the *Colbert Report* because the ads were not generating enough money.[31]

Additional research highlights the benefits of cross-media advertising campaigns. Viewers who encounter ads both on traditional television and online are most likely to remember and respond to them. Listerine ran a recent campaign on ABC and ABC.com and found that its mouthwash sales increased 33 percent more among viewers who saw the ad in both places.[32]

Media Scheduling

After choosing the media for the advertising campaign, advertisers must schedule the ads. A **media schedule** designates the medium or media to be used (such as magazines, television, or radio), the specific vehicles (such as *People* magazine, the show *Mad Men* on television, or Rush Limbaugh's national radio program), and the insertion dates of the advertising.

There are four basic types of media schedules:

▸▸ Products in the later stages of the product life cycle, which are advertised on a reminder basis, use a **continuous media schedule**. A continuous schedule allows the advertising to run steadily throughout the advertising period. Examples include Ivory soap and Charmin toilet tissue, which may have an ad in the newspaper every Sunday and a television commercial on NBC every Wednesday at 7:30 p.m. over a three-month time period.

▸▸ With a **flighted media schedule**, the advertiser may schedule the ads heavily every other month or every two weeks to achieve a greater impact with an increased frequency and reach at those times. Movie studios might schedule television advertising on Wednesday and Thursday nights, when moviegoers are deciding which films to see that weekend.

▸▸ A **pulsing media schedule** combines continuous scheduling with flighting. Continuous advertising is simply heavier during the best sale periods. A retail department store may advertise on a year-round basis but place more advertising during certain sale periods such as Thanksgiving, Christmas, and back-to-school. For example, beer may be advertised more heavily during summer months and football season given the higher consumption levels.

▸▸ Certain times of the year call for a **seasonal media schedule**. Products like Sudafed cold tablets and Coppertone sunscreen, which are used more during certain times of the year, tend to follow a seasonal strategy.

New research comparing continuous media schedules versus flighted ones finds that continuous schedules for television advertisements are more effective than flighting in driving sales. The research suggests that it may be more important to get exposure as close as possible to the time when someone is going to make a purchase. Therefore, the advertiser should maintain a continuous schedule over as long a period of time as possible. Often called *recency planning*, this theory of scheduling is now commonly used for scheduling television advertising for frequently purchased products, such as Coca-Cola or Tide detergent. Recency planning's main premise is that advertising works by influencing the brand choice of people who are ready to buy. Mobile advertising may be one of the most promising tactics for contacting consumers when they are thinking about a specific product. For example, a GPS-enabled mobile phone can get text messages for area restaurants around lunchtime to advertise specials to professionals working in a big city.

seasonal media schedule a media scheduling strategy that runs advertising only during times of the year when the product is most likely to be used

THE RISE OF SOCIAL MEDIA CELEBRITY ENDORSEMENTS

© REX FEATURES VIA AP IMAGE

Celebrity endorsements sell products—that is why companies continue to shell out the big money for athletes and movie stars to use their products on camera. Today, a new class of celebrity has emerged with the popularity of social media such as YouTube. These celebrities, known by usernames such as iJustine, Rhett & Link, Smosh, Michelle Phan, and What the Buck, are raking in six figures of ad revenue from Google and commanding up to $20,000 for branded videos targeted to their thousands—even millions—of viewers and fans on YouTube.

These YouTube celebrities take the specific act that made them popular and use it to endorse the products they are hired to discuss: Michelle Phan works for Lancome and posts makeup tutorials using its products. Her re-creation of Lady Gaga's "Poker Face" makeup was viewed more that 14 million times in 10 months. Why do companies hire such homegrown, untrained people to market products? Marketers have discovered that "Web-video celebrities offer trusted voices and an engaged viewership." These YouTube stars have built up their reputations by engaging with their audiences in a personal way that brands struggle to achieve. They genuinely interact with fans on Facebook and Twitter as well as YouTube, and fans respond by following every video, tweet, and post. The biggest risk is that YouTube fame can be fleeting—many of these stars are replaced by others in a matter of months.[33]

SOURCES: Brian Morrisey, "YouTube Stars Brands Love," *Advertising Age*, November 7, 2010; Irene Slutsky, "Meet YouTube's Most In-Demand Brand Stars," *Advertising Age*, September 13, 2010.

product placement a public relations strategy that involves getting a product, service, or company name to appear in a movie, television show, radio program, magazine, newspaper, video game, video or audio clip, book, or commercial for another product; on the Internet; or at special events

LO 5 Public Relations

Public relations is the element in the promotional mix that evaluates public attitudes, identifies issues that may elicit public concern, and executes programs to gain public understanding and acceptance. Public relations is a vital link in a progressive company's marketing communication mix. Marketing managers plan solid public relations campaigns that fit into overall marketing plans and focus on targeted audiences. These campaigns strive to maintain a positive image of the corporation in the eyes of the public. As such, they should capitalize on the factors that enhance the firm's image and minimize the factors that could generate a negative image.

Publicity is the effort to capture media attention—for example, through articles or editorials in publications or through human-interest stories on radio or television programs. Corporations usually initiate publicity through press releases that further their public relations plans. A company about to introduce a new product or open a new store may send press releases to the media in the hope that the story will be published or broadcast. Savvy publicity can often create overnight sensations or build up a reserve of goodwill with consumers. Corporate donations and sponsorships can also create favorable publicity.

Public relations departments may perform any or all of the following functions:

▸▸ *Press relations:* Placing positive, newsworthy information in the news media or influential bloggers to attract attention to a product, a service, or a person associated with the firm or institution

▸▸ *Product publicity:* Publicizing specific products or services through a variety of traditional and online channels

▸▸ *Corporate communication:* Creating internal and external messages to promote a positive image of the firm or institution

▸▸ *Public affairs:* Building and maintaining local, national, or global community relations

▸▸ *Lobbying:* Influencing legislators and government officials to promote or defeat legislation and regulation

▸▸ *Employee and investor relations:* Maintaining positive relationships with employees, shareholders, and others in the financial community

▸▸ *Crisis management:* Responding to unfavorable publicity or a negative event

Major Public Relations Tools

Public relations professionals commonly use several tools, many of which require an active role on the part of the public relations professional, such as writing press releases and engaging in proactive media relations. Sometimes, however, these techniques create their own publicity.

New-Product Publicity Publicity is instrumental in introducing new products and services. Publicity can help advertisers explain what's different about their new product by prompting free news stories or positive word of mouth about it. During the introductory period, an especially innovative new product often needs more exposure than conventional, paid advertising affords. Public relations professionals write press releases or develop videos in an effort to generate news about their new product. They also jockey for exposure of their product or service at major events, on popular television and news shows, or in the hands of influential people. Consider the publicity Apple generated for the release of the iPad, which included press coverage in traditional media as well as online blogs and forums. That was a small aspect of the entire marketing campaign.

Product Placement Marketers are increasingly using product placement to reinforce brand awareness and create favorable attitudes. **Product placement** is a strategy that involves getting one's product, service, or name to appear in a movie, television show, radio program, magazine, newspaper, video game, video or audio clip, book, or commercial for another product; on the Internet; or at special events. Indeed, a product mention on the Oprah Winfrey show was linked to increased sales for many products, especially books. Including an actual product, such as a can of Pepsi, adds a sense of realism to a movie, television show, video game, book, or similar vehicle that cannot be created by a can simply marked "soda." Product placements are arranged through barter (trade of product for placement), through paid placements, or at no charge when the product is viewed as enhancing the vehicle it is placed in.

Product placement expenditures total about $5 billion annually, though that number decreased to $3.61 billion in 2009 due to smaller marketing budgets during the recession.[34] More than two-thirds of product placements are in movies and television shows, but placements in other alternative media are growing, particularly on the Internet and in video games. Digital technology now enables companies to "virtually" place their products in any audio or video production. Virtual placement not only reduces the cost of product placement for new productions but also enables companies to place their products in previously produced programs, such as reruns of television shows. Overall, companies obtain valuable product exposure, brand reinforcement, and increased sales through product placement, often at a much lower cost than in mass media like television ads.

Consumer Education Some major firms believe that educated consumers are better, more loyal customers. Financial planning firms often sponsor free educational seminars on money management, retirement planning, and investing in the hope that the seminar participants will choose the sponsoring organization for their future financial needs.

Sponsorship Sponsorships are increasing both in number and as a proportion of companies' marketing budgets, with spending reaching $16.51 billion during 2009 in the United States.[35] Probably the biggest reason for the increasing use of sponsorships is the difficulty of reaching audiences and differentiating a product from competing brands through the mass media.

With **sponsorship**, a company spends money to support an issue, cause, or event that is consistent with corporate objectives, such as improving brand awareness or enhancing corporate image. The biggest category is sports, which accounts for almost 68 percent of spending in sponsorships (valued at $11.6 billion annually).[36] Nonsports categories include entertainment tours and attractions, causes, arts, festivals, fairs and annual events, and association and membership organizations.

Although the most popular sponsorship events are still those involving sports, music, or the arts, companies have recently been turning to more specialized events such as tie-ins with schools, charities, and other community service organizations. Marketers sometimes even create their own events tied around their products. Eating competitions often do this—in this formerly trophy-only sport, prize money for the winners can now approach $500,000. P&G paid Joey Chestnut, a star hot dog eater, $100,000 to do a six-stop publicity tour and endorse Pepto-Bismol.[37]

Corporations sponsor issues as well as events. Sponsorship issues are quite diverse, but the three most popular are education, health care, and social programs. Firms often donate a percentage of sales or profits to a worthy cause favored by their target market.

Company Web Sites Companies increasingly are using the Internet in their public relations strategies. Company Web sites are used to introduce new products, provide information to the media including social

> **sponsorship** a public relations strategy in which a company spends money to support an issue, cause, or event that is consistent with corporate objectives, such as improving brand awareness or enhancing corporate image

© TACAR/SHUTTERSTOCK.COM

crisis management a coordinated effort to handle all the effects of unfavorable publicity or another unexpected unfavorable event

media news releases, promote existing products, obtain consumer feedback, communicate legislative and regulatory information, showcase upcoming events, provide links to related sites (including blogs, Facebook, and Twitter), release financial information, interact with customers and potential customers, and perform many more marketing activities. In addition, social media is playing a larger role in how companies interact with customers online, particularly through other sites like Facebook, Yelp or Twitter. Indeed, online reviews (good and bad) from opinion leaders and other consumers help marketers sway purchasing decisions in their favor. On Playstation.com, Sony has online support, events and promotions, game trailers, and new and updated product releases. The site also includes message boards where the gaming community exchanges tips on games, votes on lifestyle issues like music and videos, and learns about promotional events.[38]

More and more often, companies are also using blogs—both corporate and noncorporate—as a tool to manage their public images. Noncorporate blogs cannot be controlled, but marketers must monitor them to be aware of and respond to negative information and encourage positive content. In addition to "getting the message out," companies are using blogs to create communities of consumers who feel positively about the brand. The hope is that positive attitude toward the brand will build into strong word-of-mouth marketing.

Managing Unfavorable Publicity

Although marketers try to avoid unpleasant situations, crises do happen. In our free-press environment, publicity is not easily controlled, especially in a crisis. **Crisis management** is the coordinated effort to handle the effects of unfavorable publicity, ensuring fast and accurate communication in times of emergency.

When users found that holding the iPhone 4 a certain way caused poor reception and dropped calls, the media ran a slew of negative stories questioning the iPhone 4's design and usability. In his intial response to the negative publicity, Steve Jobs tried to deflect attacks on the design of the iPhone's antenna by attacking phones by Apple's competitors. Ultimately, however, Jobs and the Apple team offered full refunds on the iPhone 4 for unsatisfied customers or a free cover that helped alleviate the problems caused by the poorly designed antenna. The offers deflated the negative press, and by showing good faith to customers who purchased the phone, Apple may have increased loyalty for its products and its brand.[39]

STUDY TOOLS CHAPTER 17

Flip to the back of your textbook to:
- ❑ **Rip out Chapter Review Card**

Log in to the CourseMate for MKTG at cengagebrain.com to:
- ❑ **Review Key Terms Flash Cards (Print or Online)**
- ❑ **Review Audio and Visual Summaries**
- ❑ **Complete both Practice Quizzes to prepare for tests**
- ❑ **Play "Beat the Clock" and "Quizbowl" to master concepts**
- ❑ **Complete "Crossword Puzzle" to review key terms**
- ❑ **Watch the video on "Ogden Publications" for a real company example on Advertising and Public Relations**

WHY CHOOSE?

Every 4LTR Press solution comes complete with a visually engaging textbook in addition to an interactive eBook. Go to CourseMate for MKTG to begin using the eBook. Access at **www.cengagebrain.com**

Complete the Speak Up survey in CourseMate at
www.cengagebrain.com

Follow us at
www.facebook.com/4ltrpress

© iStockphoto.com/A-Digit | © Cengage Learning 2013

CHAPTER **18** Sales Promotion and Personal Selling

> Advertising offers the consumer a reason to buy; sales promotion offers an incentive to buy.

AFTER YOU FINISH THIS CHAPTER, GO TO PAGE 309 FOR STUDY TOOLS

LO 1 Sales Promotion

In addition to using advertising, public relations, and personal selling, marketing managers can use sales promotion to increase the effectiveness of their promotional efforts. *Sales promotion* consists of marketing communication activities, other than advertising, personal selling, and public relations, in which a short-term incentive motivates consumers or members of the distribution channel to purchase a good or service immediately, either by lowering the price or by adding value.

Advertising offers the consumer a reason to buy; sales promotion offers an incentive to buy. Sales promotion is usually cheaper than advertising and easier to measure. A major national television advertising campaign often costs $5 million or more to create, produce, and place. In contrast, promotional campaigns using the Internet or direct marketing methods can cost less than half that amount. It is also very difficult to determine how many people buy a product or service as a result of radio or television ads. With sales promotion, marketers know the precise number of coupons redeemed or the number of contest entries.

Sales promotion is usually targeted toward either of two distinctly different markets. **Consumer sales promotion** is targeted to the ultimate consumer market. **Trade sales promotion** is directed to members of the marketing channel, such as wholesalers and retailers. Sales promotion expenditures have been steadily increasing over the past several years as a result of increased competition, the ever-expanding array of available media choices, consumers and retailers demanding more deals from

consumer sales promotion sales promotion activities targeting the ultimate consumer

trade sales promotion sales promotion activities targeting a marketing channel member, such as a wholesaler or retailer

What do you think?

The money I can save by using coupons doesn't amount to much.

1   2   3   4   5   6   7

STRONGLY DISAGREE   STRONGLY AGREE

© ISTOCKPHOTO.COM/EJLA

Find out what others think at the CourseMate for MKTG. Log in at cengagebrain.com.

manufacturers, and the continued reliance on accountable and measurable marketing strategies. In addition, product and service marketers who have traditionally ignored sales promotion activities, such as power companies, have discovered the marketing power of sales promotion. In fact, annual expenditures on promotion marketing in the United States now exceed $400 billion. Direct mail is the most widely used promotional medium, accounting for 50 percent of annual promotional expenditures.[1]

The Objectives of Sales Promotion

Sales promotion usually has more effect on behavior than on attitudes. Immediate purchase is the goal of sales promotion, regardless of the form it takes. The objectives of a promotion depend on the general behavior of target consumers (see Exhibit 18.1). For example, marketers who are targeting loyal users of their product actually need to reinforce existing behavior or increase product usage. An effective tool for strengthening brand loyalty is the *frequent buyer program*, which rewards consumers for repeat purchases. Other types of promotions are more effective with customers prone to brand switching or with those who are loyal to a competitor's product. A cents-off coupon, free sample, or eye-catching display in a store will often entice shoppers to try a different brand.

Once marketers understand the dynamics occurring within their product category and have determined the particular consumers and consumer behaviors they want to influence, they can then go about selecting promotional tools to achieve these goals.

LO 2 Tools for Consumer Sales Promotion

Marketing managers must decide which consumer sales promotion devices to use in a specific campaign. The methods chosen must suit the objectives to ensure success of the overall promotion plan. The popular tools for consumer sales promotion discussed in the following pages have also been easily transferred to online versions to entice Internet users to visit sites, purchase products, or use services on the Web. With the increasing popularity of social

---

EXHIBIT 18.1
Types of Consumers and Sales Promotion Goals

Type of Buyer	Desired Results	Sales Promotion Examples
Loyal customers People who buy your product most or all of the time	Reinforce behavior, increase consumption, change purchase timing	• Loyalty marketing programs, such as frequent buyer cards or frequent shopper clubs • Bonus packs that give loyal consumers an incentive to stock up or premiums offered in return for proofs of purchase
Competitor's customers People who buy a competitor's product most or all of the time	Break loyalty, persuade to switch to your brand	• Sampling to introduce your product's superior qualities compared to their brand • Sweepstakes, contests, or premiums that create interest in the product
Brand switchers People who buy a variety of products in the category	Persuade to buy your brand more often	• Any promotion that lowers the price of the product, such as coupons, price-off packages, and bonus packs • Trade deals that help make the product more readily available than competing products
Price buyers People who consistently buy the least expensive brand	Appeal with low prices or supply added value that makes price less important	• Coupons, price-off packages, refunds, or trade deals that reduce the price of the brand to match that of the brand that would have been purchased

SOURCE: From *Sales Promotion Essentials*, 2nd ed., by Don E. Schultz, William A. Robinson, and Lisa A. Petrison. Reprinted by permission of NTC Publishing Group, 4255 Touhy Ave., Lincolnwood, IL 60048.

media, new formats for promotion are emerging. For example, Groupon.com is a Web site that presents deals to consumers, and once a predetermined number of people purchase a deal, it becomes active. To date, Groupon.com has amassed more than 25 million subscribers and features both national deals and local deals. The concept is so popular that several companies including Walmart have adopted the strategy (Walmart calls its version Crowdsaver) and are now offering deals to Facebook friends who then "like" the deals. When a certain number "like" a deal, it is activated. For example, Healthy Choice launched a coupon that increased in value as more people "liked" it on Facebook.[2]

Coupons and Rebates

A **coupon** is a certificate that entitles consumers to an immediate price reduction when the product is purchased. Coupons are a particularly good way to encourage product trial and repurchase. They are also likely to increase the amount of a product bought.

Intense competition in the consumer packaged goods category and the annual introduction of over 1,200 new products have contributed to this trend of coupon promotions. Though coupons are often criticized for reaching consumers who have no interest in the product or for encouraging repeat purchase by regular users, recent studies indicate that coupons promote new-product use and are likely to stimulate purchases.

Freestanding inserts (FSIs), the promotional coupons inserts found in newspapers, are the traditional way of circulating printed coupons. FSIs are used to distribute 85 percent of coupons. Such traditional types of coupon distribution, which also include direct mail and magazines, had been declining for several years, as consumers used fewer coupons. Recently, however, with the recession tightening consumer spending, coupons experienced the largest increase in usage in 17 years. In 2010, coupon redemptions surged 23 percent to 3.2

billion coupons. The highest redemption rate increase of 15.9 percent was experienced by Internet coupons, even though they account for only a relatively small share of coupon redemptions overall. Electronically dispensed coupons also experienced a redemption rate increase to 7.9 percent.[3]

In-store coupons have become popular because they are more likely to influence customers' buying decisions. Instant coupons on product packages, coupons distributed from on-shelf coupon-dispensing machines, and electronic coupons issued at the checkout counter now achieve much higher redemption rates than other coupons because consumers are making more in-store purchase decisions.

The Internet is changing the face of coupons. In addition to Internet coupon sites such as Valpak and Coolsavings.com and social coupon sites such as Groupon and LivingSocial, there are also deal sites like DealSurf.com that aggregate offers from disparate sites for convenience. Some small businesses, however, can be overwhelmed if huge numbers of people take advantage of the online offers. The New York smoothie shop Xoom, for example, had 900 of 1,300 coupons redeemed. Although Xoom did not lose money, the shop did not see much repeat business, which was the major goal of the promotion, according to the owner. Groupon and LivingSocial are now trying to target coupons to subscribers based on purchase history, in an effort to increase the 22 percent rate of return customers for companies that work with the sites.[4] As marketing tactics grow more sophisticated, however, coupons are no longer viewed as a stand-alone tactic but as an integral component of a larger promotional campaign. After experiencing very low return-customer rates from the Groupon coupon, Xoom teamed up with other local restaurants to work with a deal site specific to New York City to target local customers. Working with the local site, Xoom received a

coupon a certificate that entitles consumers to an immediate price reduction when they buy the product

© HAVESEEN/SHUTTERSTOCK.COM

rebate a cash refund given for the purchase of a product during a specific period

premium an extra item offered to the consumer, usually in exchange for some proof of purchase of the promoted product

loyalty marketing program a promotional program designed to build long-term, mutually beneficial relationships between a company and its key customers

frequent buyer program a loyalty program in which loyal consumers are rewarded for making multiple purchases of a particular good or service

more manageable number of coupon redemptions and built a stronger return-customer base.[5]

A **rebate** is similar to a coupon in that a rebate offers the purchaser a price reduction; however, because the purchaser must mail in a rebate form and usually some proof of purchase, the reward is not as immediate. Manufacturers prefer rebates for several reasons. Rebates allow manufacturers to offer price cuts to consumers directly. Manufacturers have more control over rebate promotions because they can be rolled out and shut off quickly. Further, because buyers must fill out forms with their names, addresses, and other data, manufacturers use rebate programs to build customer databases. Perhaps the best reason of all to offer rebates is that although rebates are particularly good at enticing purchase, most consumers never bother to redeem them. The Federal Trade Commission estimates that only half of consumers eligible for rebates collect them.[6]

Premiums

A **premium** is an extra item offered to the consumer, usually in exchange for some proof that the promoted product has been purchased. Premiums reinforce the consumer's purchase decision, increase consumption, and persuade nonusers to switch brands. The best example of the use of premiums is McDonald's Happy Meal, which rewards children with a small toy.

Premiums can also include more product for the regular price, such as two-for-the-price-of-one bonus packs or packages that include more of the product. Kellogg's, for instance, added two more pastries to its Pop Tarts without increasing the price in an effort to boost market share lost to private label brands and new competitors. The promotion was so successful the company decided to keep the additional product in its regular packaging. Another possibility is to attach a premium to the product's package, such as a small sample of a complementary hair product attached to a shampoo bottle.

Loyalty Marketing Programs

A **loyalty marketing program**, or **frequent buyer program**, rewards loyal consumers for making multiple purchases. The objective of loyalty marketing programs is to build long-term, mutually beneficial relationships between a company and its key customers.

There are more than 1.8 billion loyalty program memberships in the United States; the average household has signed up for 14 programs but actively participates in only 6 or 7 of them.[7] Popularized by the airline industry through frequent flyer programs, loyalty marketing enables companies to strategically invest sales promotion dollars in activities designed to capture greater profits from customers already loyal to the product or company. Despite continuing to struggle with overall company losses, the drugstore chain Rite Aid posted some same store sales increases over the previous year due to its Wellness+ loyalty card program. CEO John Standley reported that card members accounted for 67 percent of nonprescription sales in the first quarter of fiscal 2012 and that 50 percent of the Gold and Silver level members visit Rite Aid once a week.[8]

Co-branded credit cards are an increasingly popular loyalty marketing tool. In a recent year, almost one billion direct marketing appeals for a co-branded credit card were sent to potential customers in the United States. Target, Gap, Sony, and American Airlines are only a few of the companies sponsoring co-branded Visa, MasterCard, or American Express cards.

Through loyalty programs, shoppers receive discounts, alerts on new products, and other types of enticing offers. In exchange, retailers are able to build customer databases that help them better understand customer preferences.

Companies are increasingly using the Internet to build customer loyalty through e-mail and social media. Some customers feel that their rewards programs, especially hotel rewards programs, send too much spam e-mail. Hotel rewards programs can greatly benefit the business because an average loyalty member is twice as profitable as a nonmember, and an elite member can be up to 12 times as profitable as a nonmember. However, too much e-mail, overly complicated or restrictive programs, or rewards that aren't perceived as valuable can turn a loyal customer away from the program.[9] Some companies use social media sites to help customers earn rewards points. For example, Foursquare, a popular check-in site, has partnered with American Express to enable customers to check in and receive coupons or discounts in participating stores if they use their AmEx card. A customer checking in to Sports Authority through Foursquare receives a coupon for $20 off a purchase of $50 or more on his or her AmEx card. The credit is applied to the customer's AmEx account in two to three business days.[10]

Contests and Sweepstakes

Contests and sweepstakes are generally designed to create interest in a good or service, often to encourage brand switching. *Contests* are promotions in which participants use some skill or ability to compete for prizes. A consumer contest usually requires entrants to answer questions, complete sentences, or write a paragraph about the product and submit proof of purchase. Winning a *sweepstakes*, on the other hand, depends on chance and participation is free. Sweepstakes usually draw about ten times more entries than contests do.

While contests and sweepstakes may draw considerable interest and publicity, generally they are not effective tools for generating long-term sales. To increase their effectiveness, sales promotion managers must make certain the award will appeal to the target market. Offering several smaller prizes to many winners instead of one huge prize to just one person often will increase the effectiveness of the promotion, but there's no denying the attractiveness of a jackpot-type prize.

Reader's Digest is visiting towns around America to offer promotional and financial support. Individuals can suggest their town and also enter to win an RV, a trip, or cash.

COURTESY OF READER'S DIGEST

Sampling

Sampling allows the customer to try a product risk-free. In a recent study of sampling in Costco, researchers found that sampling increased sales by an average of 88 percent. Expensive items benefited most from sampling, and items under $10, particularly beverages, benefited least from sampling.[11]

Samples can be directly mailed to the customer, delivered door-to-door, packaged with another product, or demonstrated or distributed at a retail store or service outlet. Sampling at special events is a popular, effective, and high-profile distribution method that permits marketers to piggyback onto fun-based consumer activities—including sporting events, college fests, fairs and festivals, beach events, and chili cook-offs.

Distributing samples to specific location types, such as health clubs, churches, or doctors' offices, is one of the most efficient methods of sampling. What better way to get consumers to try a product than to offer a sample exactly when it is needed most? If someone visits a health club regularly, chances are he or she is a good prospect for a health food product or vitamin supplement. Health club instructors are handing out not only these products but also body wash, deodorant, and face cloths to sweating participants at the end of class. Online sampling is gaining momentum as Web communities bring people together with common interests in trying new products, often using blogs to spread the word. V8 allowed users who "liked" the newly launched Facebook product page for V8 V-Fusion to enter their information to receive a sample of the V8 V-Fusion + Tea.[12]

Point-of-Purchase Promotion

A **point-of-purchase (P-O-P) display** includes any promotional display set up at the retailer's location to build traffic, advertise the product, or induce impulse buying. P-O-P displays include shelf "talkers" (signs attached to store shelves), shelf extenders (attachments that extend shelves so products stand out), ads on grocery carts and bags, end-aisle and floor-stand displays, television monitors at supermarket checkout counters, in-store audio messages, and audiovisual displays. One big advantage of the P-O-P display is that it offers manufacturers a captive audience in retail stores. Another advantage is that between 70 and 80 percent of all retail purchase

sampling a promotional program that allows the consumer the opportunity to try a product or service for free

point-of-purchase (P-O-P) display a promotional display set up at the retailer's location to build traffic, advertise the product, or induce impulse buying

This 50 percent off sign is meant to entice customers to make impulse purchases.

decisions are made in-store, so P-O-P displays can be very effective, increasing sales by as much as 65 percent. Combine that sales increase with the effectiveness of spoken advertisements (such as television ads), and it could be an impressive selling force. Food Lion Supermarkets and other stores are experimenting with video P-O-P displays that run television commercials for the products closest to the screen. Some displays are motion activated; when customers walk near the screen, the commercial begins, catching their attention.[13] Other strategies to increase sales include adding cards to the tops of displays, changing messages on signs on the sides or bottoms of displays, adding inflatable or mobile displays, and using signs that advertise the brand's sports, movie, or charity tie-in.[14]

Online Sales Promotion

Online sales promotions have expanded dramatically in recent years. Marketers are now spending billions of dollars annually on such promotions. Sales promotions online have proved effective and cost-efficient, generating response rates three to five times higher than off-line promotions. The most effective types of online sales promotions are free merchandise, sweepstakes, free shipping with purchases, and coupons.

Eager to boost traffic, Internet retailers are busy giving away free services or equipment, such as PCs and travel, to lure consumers not only to their own

trade allowance
a price reduction offered by manufacturers to intermediaries, such as wholesalers and retailers

push money
money offered to channel intermediaries to encourage them to "push" products—that is, to encourage other members of the channel to sell the products

Web sites but to the Internet in general. Another goal is to add potential customers to their databases.

Marketers have discovered that online coupon distribution provides another vehicle for promoting their products. In addition, e-coupons can help marketers lure new customers. Online coupons often have a redemption rate of more than 20 percent, as much as ten times higher than for traditional coupons.[15] In fact, nearly 50 percent of consumers who make purchases online use coupons or discount promotional codes. With the speed of compiling data online, marketers can conduct tests in real time and measure the results in time to offer last-minute promotions and react to changing market conditions.[16]

Online versions of loyalty programs are also popping up, and although many types of companies have these programs, the most successful are those run by hotel and airline companies.

LO 3 Tools for Trade Sales Promotion

Whereas consumer promotions pull a product through the channel by creating demand, trade promotions *push* a product through the distribution channel (see Chapter 13). When selling to members of the distribution channel, manufacturers use many of the same sales promotion tools used in consumer promotions—such as sales contests, premiums, and P-O-P displays. Several tools, however, are unique to manufacturers and intermediaries:

▸▸ *Trade allowances:* A **trade allowance** is a price reduction offered by manufacturers to intermediaries such as wholesalers and retailers. The price reduction or rebate is given in exchange for doing something specific, such as allocating space for a new product or buying something during special periods. For example, a local Best Buy outlet could receive a special discount for running its own promotion on Sony surround sound systems.

▸▸ *Push money:* Intermediaries receive **push money** as a bonus for pushing the manufacturer's brand through the distribution channel. Often the push money is directed toward a retailer's salespeople. LinoColor, the leading high-end scanner company, produces a Picture Perfect Rewards catalog filled with merchandise retailers can purchase with points accrued for every LinoColor scanner they sell.

▸▸ *Training:* Sometimes a manufacturer will train an intermediary's personnel if the product is rather complex—as

© ISTOCKPHOTO.COM/JEAN GILL

frequently occurs in the computer and telecommunications industries. For example, representatives of a speaker manufacturer like Bang & Olufsen may train salespeople in how to demonstrate the new features of the latest models of sound systems to consumers.

▶▶ *Free merchandise:* Often a manufacturer offers retailers free merchandise in lieu of quantity discounts. Occasionally, free merchandise is used as payment for trade allowances normally provided through other sales promotions. Instead of giving a retailer a price reduction for buying a certain quantity of merchandise, the manufacturer may throw in extra merchandise "free" (i.e., at a cost that would equal the price reduction).

▶▶ *Store demonstrations:* Manufacturers can also arrange with retailers to perform an in-store demonstration. Food manufacturers often send representatives to grocery stores and supermarkets to let customers sample a product while shopping.

▶▶ *Business meetings, conventions, and trade shows:* Trade association meetings, conferences, and conventions are an important aspect of sales promotion and a growing, multi-billion-dollar market. At these shows, manufacturers, distributors, and other vendors have the chance to display their goods or describe their services to potential customers. Companies participate in trade shows to attract and identify new prospects, serve current customers, introduce new products, enhance corporate image, test the market response to new products, enhance corporate morale, and gather competitive product information.

Trade promotions are popular among manufacturers for many reasons. Trade sales promotion tools help manufacturers gain new distributors for their products, obtain wholesaler and retailer support for consumer sales promotions, build or reduce dealer inventories, and improve trade relations. Car manufacturers annually sponsor dozens of auto shows for consumers. The shows attract millions of consumers, providing dealers with increased store traffic as well as good leads.

LO4 Personal Selling

As mentioned in Chapter 16, *personal selling* is a purchase situation involving a personal, paid-for communication between two people in an attempt to influence each other. In a sense, all businesspeople are salespeople. An individual may become a plant manager, a chemist, an engineer, or a member of any profession and yet still have to sell. During a job search, applicants must "sell" themselves to prospective employers in an interview.

Personal selling offers several advantages over other forms of promotion:

▶▶ Personal selling provides a detailed explanation or demonstration of the product. This capability is especially needed for complex or new goods and services.

▶▶ The sales message can be varied according to the motivations and interests of each prospective customer. Moreover, when the prospect has questions or raises objections, the salesperson is there to provide explanations. In contrast, advertising and sales promotion can only respond to the objections the copywriter thinks are important to customers.

▶▶ Personal selling can be directed only to qualified prospects. Other forms of promotion include some unavoidable waste because many people in the audience are not prospective customers.

▶▶ Personal selling costs can be controlled by adjusting the size of the sales force (and resulting expenses) in one-person increments. On the other hand, advertising and sales promotion must often be purchased in fairly large amounts.

▶▶ Perhaps the most important advantage is that personal selling is considerably more effective than other forms of promotion in obtaining a sale and gaining a satisfied customer.

Personal selling may also work better than other forms of promotion given certain customer and product characteristics. Generally speaking, personal selling becomes more important as the number of potential

Beauty consultants often offer to demonstrate their products by giving makeovers or facials to potential customers.

© ISTOCKPHOTO.COM/ICONOGENIC

relationship selling (consultative selling) a sales practice that involves building, maintaining, and enhancing interactions with customers in order to develop long-term satisfaction through mutually beneficial partnerships

customers decreases, as the complexity of the product increases, and as the value of the product grows (see Exhibit 18.2). For highly complex goods, such as business jets or private communication systems, a salesperson is needed to determine the prospective customer's needs, explain the product's basic advantages, and propose the exact features and accessories that will meet the client's needs. Macy's, Nordstrom, Saks Fifth Avenue, and Barneys New York offer free personal shopping, whereby consultants pull clothing they feel will fit the customer's style and specified need. This free service encourages customers to continue using personal shoppers and develop a relationship with the store.[17] Technology now plays an important role in personal selling through the use of social media like LinkedIn and Facebook, as well as the use of blogs and Twitter to establish expertise within a field.

LO5 Relationship Selling

Until recently, marketing theory and practice concerning personal selling focused almost entirely on a planned presentation to prospective customers for the sole purpose of making the sale. Marketers were most concerned with making a one-time sale and then moving on to the next prospect. Traditional personal selling methods attempted to persuade the buyer to accept a point of view or convince the buyer to take some action. Frequently, the objectives of the salesperson were at the expense of the buyer, creating a win–lose outcome. Although this type of sales approach has not disappeared entirely, it is being used less and less often by professional salespeople.

In contrast, modern views of personal selling emphasize the relationship that develops between a salesperson and a buyer. **Relationship selling**, or **consultative selling**, is a multistage process that emphasizes personalization and empathy as key ingredients in identifying prospects and developing them as long-term, satisfied customers. With relationship selling, the objective is to build long-term branded relationships with consumers and buyers, so the focus is on building mutual trust between the buyer and seller through the delivery of anticipated, long-term, value-added benefits to the buyer.

Relationship or consultative salespeople, therefore, become consultants, partners, and problem solvers for their customers. They strive to build long-term relationships with key accounts by developing trust over time. The emphasis shifts from a one-time sale to a long-term relationship in which the salesperson works with the customer to develop solutions for enhancing the customer's bottom line. Research has shown that positive customer–salesperson relationships contribute to trust, increased customer loyalty, and the intent to continue the relationship with the salesperson.[18] Thus, relationship selling promotes a win–win situation for both buyer and seller.

The end result of relationship selling tends to be loyal customers who purchase from the company time after time. A relationship selling strategy focused on retaining customers costs a company less than constantly prospecting and selling to new customers.

Relationship selling is more typically used in selling situations for industrial-type goods, such as heavy machinery or computer systems, and services, such as airlines and insurance, than for consumer goods. Exhibit 18.3 lists the key differences between traditional personal selling and relationship or consultative selling. These differences will become more apparent as we explore the personal selling process later in the chapter.

EXHIBIT 18.2
Comparison of Personal Selling and Advertising/Sales Promotion

Personal selling is more important if . . .	Advertising and sales promotion are more important if . . .
The product has a high value.	The product has a low value.
It is a custom-made product.	It is a standardized product.
There are few customers.	There are many customers.
The product is technically complex.	The product is easy to understand.
Customers are concentrated.	Customers are geographically dispersed.
Examples: Insurance policies, custom windows, airplane engines	**Examples:** Soap, magazine subscriptions, cotton T-shirts

© CENGAGE LEARNING 2013

EXHIBIT 18.3
Key Differences between Traditional Selling and Relationship Selling

Traditional Personal Selling	Relationship or Consultative Selling
Sell products (goods and services)	Sell advice, assistance, and counsel
Focus on closing sales	Focus on improving the customer's bottom line
Limited sales planning	Consider sales planning as top priority
Spend most contact time telling customers about product	Spend most contact time attempting to build a problem-solving environment with the customer
Conduct "product-specific" needs assessment	Conduct discovery in the full scope of the customer's operations
"Lone wolf" approach to the account	Team approach to the account
Proposals and presentations based on pricing and product features	Proposals and presentations based on profit impact and strategic benefits to the customer
Sales follow-up is short term, focused on product delivery	Sales follow-up is long term, focused on long-term relationship enhancement

SOURCE: Robert M. Peterson, Patrick L. Schul, and George H. Lucas Jr., "Consultative Selling: Walking the Walk in the New Selling Environment," *National Conference on Sales Management Proceedings*, March 1996.

LO 6 Steps in the Selling Process

Completing a sale requires several steps. The **sales process**, or **sales cycle**, is simply the set of steps a salesperson goes through to sell a particular product or service. The sales process or cycle can be unique for each product or service, depending on the features of the product or service, characteristics of customer segments, and internal processes in place within the firm such as how leads are gathered.

Some sales take only a few minutes, but others may take much longer to complete. Sales of technical products like a Boeing or Airbus airplane and customized goods and services typically take many months, perhaps even years, to complete. On the other end of the spectrum, sales of less technical products like stationery are generally more routine and may take only a few days. Whether a salesperson spends a few minutes or a few years on a sale, there are seven basic steps in the personal selling process, outlined further in the following sections.

Like other forms of promotion, these steps of selling follow the AIDA concept discussed in Chapter 16. Once a salesperson has located a prospect with the authority to buy, he or she tries to get the prospect's attention. A thorough needs assessment turned into an effective sales proposal and presentation should generate interest. After developing the customer's initial desire (preferably during the presentation of the sales proposal), the salesperson seeks action in the close by trying to get an agreement to buy. Follow-up after the sale, the final step in the selling process, not only lowers cognitive dissonance (refer to Chapter 6) but also may open up opportunities to discuss future sales. Effective follow-up will also lead to repeat business in which the process may start all over again at the needs assessment step.

Traditional selling and relationship selling follow the same basic steps. They differ in the relative importance placed on key steps in the process. Traditional selling efforts are transaction oriented, focusing on generating as many leads as possible, making as many presentations as possible, and closing as many sales as possible. Minimal effort is placed on asking questions to identify customer needs and wants or matching these needs and wants to the benefits of the product or service. In contrast, salespeople practicing relationship selling emphasize an up-front investment in the time and effort needed to uncover each customer's specific needs and wants and meet them with the product or service offering. By doing their homework up front, salespeople create the conditions necessary for a relatively straightforward close. Look at each step of the selling process individually.

sales process (sales cycle) the set of steps a salesperson goes through in a particular organization to sell a particular product or service

lead generation (prospecting) identification of those firms and people most likely to buy the seller's offerings

referral a recommendation to a salesperson from a customer or business associate

networking a process of finding out about potential clients from friends, business contacts, coworkers, acquaintances, and fellow members in professional and civic organizations

cold calling a form of lead generation in which the salesperson approaches potential buyers without any prior knowledge of the prospects' needs or financial status

lead qualification determination of a sales prospect's (1) recognized need, (2) buying power, and (3) receptivity and accessibility

Step 1: Generating Leads

Initial groundwork must precede communication between the potential buyer and the salesperson. **Lead generation**, or **prospecting**, is the identification of those firms and people most likely to buy the seller's offerings. These firms or people become "sales leads" or "prospects."

Sales leads can be obtained in several different ways, most notably through advertising, trade shows and conventions, social media, webinars, or direct mail and telemarketing programs. Favorable publicity also helps to create leads. Company records of past client purchases are another excellent source of leads. Many sales professionals are also securing valuable leads from their firm's Web site.

Another way to gather a lead is through a **referral**—a recommendation from a customer or business associate. The advantages of referrals over other forms of prospecting include highly qualified leads, higher closing rates, larger initial transactions, and shorter sales cycles. Referrals typically are as much as ten times more productive in generating sales than are cold calls. Unfortunately, although most clients are willing to give referrals, many salespeople do not ask for them. Effective sales training can help to overcome this reluctance to ask for referrals. To increase the number of referrals, some companies even pay or send small gifts to customers or suppliers that provide referrals. Generating referrals is one area that social media and technology can usually make much more efficient.

Seven Steps in the Personal Selling Process

1. Generating leads
2. Qualifying leads
3. Approaching the customer and probing needs
4. Developing and proposing solutions
5. Handling objections
6. Closing the sale
7. Following up

Networking is using friends, business contacts, coworkers, acquaintances, and fellow members in professional and civic organizations to identify potential clients. Indeed, a number of national networking clubs have been started for the sole purpose of generating leads and providing valuable business advice. Increasingly, sales professionals are also using online networking sites such as LinkedIn to connect with targeted leads and clients around the world, 24 hours a day. Some of LinkedIn's estimated 30 million users have reported response rates between 50 and 60 percent, versus 3 percent from direct marketing efforts.[19]

Before the advent of more sophisticated methods of lead generation, such as direct mail and telemarketing, most prospecting was done through **cold calling**—a form of lead generation in which the salesperson approaches potential buyers without any prior knowledge of the prospects' needs or financial status. Although cold calling is still used in generating leads, many sales managers have realized the inefficiencies of having their top salespeople use their valuable selling time searching for the proverbial "needle in a haystack." Passing the job of cold calling to a lower-cost employee, typically an internal sales support person, allows salespeople to spend more time and use their relationship-building skills on prospects who have already been identified.

Step 2: Qualifying Leads

When a prospect shows interest in learning more about a product, the salesperson has the opportunity to follow up, or qualify, the lead. Personally visiting unqualified prospects wastes valuable salesperson time and company resources. Many leads often go unanswered because salespeople are given no indication as to how qualified the leads are in terms of interest and ability to purchase. Unqualified prospects give vague or incomplete answers to a salesperson's specific questions, try to evade questions on budgets, and request changes in standard procedures like prices or terms of sale. In contrast, qualified leads are real prospects who answer questions, value your time, and are realistic about money and when they are prepared to buy. Salespeople who are given accurate information on qualified leads are more than twice as likely to follow up.[20]

Lead qualification involves determining whether the prospect has three things:

▸▸ *A recognized need:* The most basic criterion for determining whether someone is a prospect for a product

© ISTOCKPHOTO.COM/ART12321 / © ISTOCKPHOTO.COM/EKELY

is a need that is not being satisfied. The salesperson should first consider prospects who are aware of a need but should not disregard prospects who have not yet recognized that they have one. With a little more information about the product, they may decide they do have a need for it. Preliminary interviews and questioning can often provide the salesperson with enough information to determine whether there is a need.

» *Buying power:* Buying power involves both authority to make the purchase decision and access to funds to pay for it. To avoid wasting time and money, the salesperson needs to identify the purchasing authority and his or her ability to pay before making a presentation. Organizational charts and information about a firm's credit standing can provide valuable clues.

» *Receptivity and accessibility:* The prospect must be willing to see the salesperson and be accessible to the salesperson. Some prospects simply refuse to see salespeople. Others, because of their stature in their organization, will see only a salesperson or sales manager with similar stature.

Often the task of lead qualification is handled by a telemarketing group or a sales support person who *prequalifies* the lead for the salesperson. Prequalification systems free sales representatives from the time-consuming task of following up on leads to determine need, buying power, and receptiveness. Prequalification systems may even set up initial appointments with the prospect for the salesperson. The result is more time for the sales force to spend in front of interested customers. Software is increasingly being utilized in lead qualification.

Companies are increasingly using their Web sites to qualify leads. When qualifying leads online, companies want visitors to register, indicate the products and services they are interested in, and provide information on their time frame and resources. Leads from the Internet can then be prioritized (those indicating a short time frame, for instance, are given a higher priority) and then transferred to salespeople. Enticing visitors to register also enables companies to customize future electronic interactions.

Step 3: Approaching the Customer and Probing Needs

Before approaching customers, the salesperson should learn as much as possible about the prospect's organization and its buyers. This process, called the **preapproach**, describes the "homework" that must be done by the salesperson before contacting the

prospect. This may include visiting company Web sites, consulting standard reference sources such as Moody's, Standard & Poor's, or Dun & Bradstreet, or contacting acquaintances or others who may have information about the prospect. Reading the prospect's social media sites (following the company's Twitter feed and reading its Facebook page or blogs) is a great way to get to know the company culture and learn more about daily activities.[21] Another preapproach task is to determine whether the actual approach should be a personal visit, a phone call, a letter, or some other form of communication.

During the sales approach, the salesperson either talks to the prospect or secures an appointment for a future time in which to probe the prospect further as to his or her needs. Relationship selling theorists suggest that salespeople should begin developing mutual trust with their prospect during the approach. Salespeople must sell themselves before they can sell the product. Small talk that projects sincerity and some suggestion of friendship is encouraged to build rapport with the prospect, but remarks that could be construed as insincere should be avoided.

The salesperson's ultimate goal during the approach is to conduct a **needs assessment** to find out as much as possible about the prospect's situation. The salesperson should be determining how to maximize the fit between what he or she can offer and what the prospective customer wants. As part of the needs assessment, the consultative salesperson must know everything there is to know about the following:

» *The product or service:* Product knowledge is the cornerstone for conducting a successful needs analysis. The consultative salesperson must be an expert on his or her product or service, including technical specifications, the product's features and benefits, pricing and billing procedures, warranty and service support, performance comparisons with the competition, other customers' experiences with the product, and current advertising and promotional campaign messages. For example, a salesperson who is attempting to sell a Xerox copier to a doctor's office should be very knowledgeable about Xerox's selection of copiers, their attributes, capabilities, technological specifications, and postpurchase servicing.

» *Customers and their needs:* The salesperson should know more about customers than he or she knows about him- or herself. That's the secret to relationship and consultative selling, where the salesperson acts not only as a

preapproach a process that describes the "homework" that must be done by a salesperson before he or she contacts a prospect

needs assessment a determination of the customer's specific needs and wants and the range of options the customer has for satisfying them

sales proposal a formal written document or professional presentation that outlines how the salesperson's product or service will meet or exceed the prospect's needs

sales presentation a formal meeting in which the salesperson presents a sales proposal to a prospective buyer

supplier of products and services but also as a trusted consultant and adviser. The professional salesperson brings each client business-building ideas and solutions to problems. For example, if the Xerox salesperson is asking the "right" questions, then he or she should be able to identify copy-related areas where the doctor's office is losing or wasting money. Rather than just selling a copier, the Xerox salesperson can act as a consultant on how the doctor's office can save money and time.

▸▸ *The competition:* The salesperson must know as much about the competitor's company and products as he or she knows about his or her own company. Competitive intelligence includes many factors: who the competitors are and what is known about them, how their products and services compare, advantages and disadvantages, and strengths and weaknesses. For example, if the Canon copy machine is less expensive than the Xerox copier, the doctor's office may be leaning toward purchasing the Canon. But if the Xerox salesperson can point out that the cost of long-term maintenance and toner cartridges is lower for the Xerox copier, offsetting its higher initial cost, the salesperson may be able to persuade the doctor's office to purchase the Xerox copier.

▸▸ *The industry:* Knowing the industry requires active research by the salesperson. This means attending industry and trade association meetings, reading articles published in industry and trade journals, keeping track of legislation and regulation that affect the industry, being aware of product alternatives and innovations from domestic and foreign competition, and having a feel for economic and financial conditions that may affect the industry. It is also important to be aware of economic downturns, as businesses may be looking for less expensive financing options.

Creating a *customer profile* during the approach helps salespeople optimize their time and resources. This profile is then used to help develop an intelligent analysis of the prospect's needs in preparation for the next step, developing and proposing solutions. Customer profile information is typically stored and manipulated using sales force automation software packages designed for use on laptop computers. Sales force automation software provides sales reps with a computerized and efficient method of collecting customer information for use during the entire sales process. Further, customer and sales data stored in a computer database can be easily shared among sales team members. The information can also be appended with industry statistics, sales or meeting notes, billing data, and other information that may be pertinent to the prospect or the prospect's company.

The more salespeople know about their prospects, the better they can meet their needs.

A salesperson should wrap up the sales approach and need-probing mission by summarizing the prospect's need, problem, and interest. The salesperson should also get a commitment from the customer to some kind of action, whether it's reading promotional material or agreeing to a demonstration. This commitment helps qualify the prospect further and justify additional time invested by the salesperson. The salesperson should reiterate the action he or she promises to take, such as sending information or calling back to provide answers to questions. The date and time of the next call should be set at the conclusion of the sales approach as well as an agenda for the next call in terms of what the salesperson hopes to accomplish, such as providing a demonstration or presenting a solution.

Step 4: Developing and Proposing Solutions

Once the salesperson has gathered the appropriate information about the client's needs and wants, the next step is to determine whether his or her company's products or services match the needs of the prospective customer. The salesperson then develops a solution, or possibly several solutions, in which the salesperson's product or service solves the client's problems or meets a specific need.

These solutions are typically presented to the client in the form of a sales proposal presented at a sales presentation. A **sales proposal** is a written document or professional presentation that outlines how the company's product or service will meet or exceed the client's needs. The **sales presentation** is the formal meeting in which the

This link looks like it has more information about our second lead.

© ISTOCKPHOTO.COM/GEHRING/ © ISTOCKPHOTO.COM/GEOFFREY HOLMAN

salesperson has the opportunity to present the sales proposal. The presentation should be explicitly tied to the prospect's expressed needs. Further, the prospect should be involved in the presentation by being encouraged to participate in demonstrations or by exposure to computer exercises, slides, video or audio, flip charts, photographs, and the like. Technology has become an important part of presenting solutions for many salespeople.

Because the salesperson often has only one opportunity to present solutions, the quality of both the sales proposal and the presentation can make or break the sale. Salespeople must be able to present the proposal and handle any customer objections confidently and professionally. For a powerful presentation, salespeople must be well prepared, use direct eye contact, ask open-ended questions, be poised, use hand gestures and voice inflection, focus on the customer's needs, incorporate visual elements that impart valuable information, know how to operate the audio/visual or computer equipment being used for the presentation, and make sure the equipment works.[22] Nothing dies faster than a boring presentation. Often customers are more likely to remember how salespeople present themselves than what they say.

Step 5: Handling Objections

Rarely does a prospect say "I'll buy it" right after a presentation. Instead, the prospect often raises objections or asks questions about the proposal and the product. The potential buyer may insist that the price is too high or that the good or service will not satisfy the present need.

One of the first lessons every salesperson learns is that objections to the product should not be taken personally as confrontations or insults. A good salesperson considers objections a legitimate part of the purchase decision. To handle objections effectively, the salesperson should anticipate specific objections such as concerns about price, fully investigate the objection with the customer, be aware of what the competition is offering, and, above all, stay calm.

Often salespeople can use objections to close the sale. If the customer tries to pit suppliers against each other to drive down the price, the salesperson should be prepared to point out weaknesses in the competitor's offer and stand by the quality in his or her own proposal.

Step 6: Closing the Sale

At the end of the presentation, the salesperson should ask the customer how he or she would like to proceed.

If the customer exhibits signs that he or she is ready to purchase and all questions have been answered and objections have been met, then the salesperson can try to close the sale. Customers often give signals during or after the presentation that they are ready to buy or are not interested. Examples include changes in facial expressions, gestures, and questions asked. The salesperson should look for these signals and respond appropriately.

Closing requires courage and skill. A salesperson should keep an open mind when asking for the sale and be prepared for both a yes and a no. The typical salesperson makes several hundred sales calls a year, many of which are repeat calls to the same client in an attempt to make a sale. Building a good relationship with the customer is very important. Often, if the salesperson has developed a strong relationship with the customer, only minimal efforts are needed to close a sale.

Negotiation often plays a key role in the closing of the sale. **Negotiation** is the process during which both the salesperson and the prospect offer special concessions in an attempt to arrive at a sales agreement. For example, the salesperson may offer a price cut, free installation, or a trial order. Effective negotiators, however, avoid using price as a negotiation tool. Because companies spend millions on advertising and product development to create value, when salespeople give in to price negotiations too quickly, it decreases the value of the product. Instead, effective salespeople should emphasize value to the customer, rendering price a nonissue. Salespeople should also be prepared to ask for trade-offs and try to avoid giving unilateral concessions. Moreover, if the customer asks for a 5 percent discount, the salesperson should ask for something in return, such as higher volume or more flexibility in delivery schedules.

More and more U.S. companies are expanding their marketing and selling efforts into global markets. Salespeople selling in foreign markets should tailor their presentation and closing styles to each market.

negotiation the process during which both the salesperson and the prospect offer special concessions in an attempt to arrive at a sales agreement

© ISTOCKPHOTO.COM/JACOB WACKERHAUSEN

follow-up the final step of the selling process, in which the salesperson ensures delivery schedules are met, goods or services perform as promised, and the buyers' employees are properly trained to use the products

Different personalities and skills will be successful in some countries and absolute failures in others. For instance, if a salesperson is an excellent closer and always focuses on the next sale, doing business in Latin America might be difficult because people there want to take a long time building a personal relationship with their suppliers.

Step 7: Following Up

Salespeople's responsibilities do not end with making the sales and placing the orders. One of the most important aspects of their jobs is **follow-up**—the final step in the selling process, in which they must ensure delivery schedules are met, goods or services perform as promised, and buyers' employees are properly trained to use the products.

In the traditional sales approach, follow-up with the customer is generally limited to successful product delivery and performance. A basic goal of relationship selling is to motivate customers to come back, again and again, by developing and nurturing long-term relationships. Exhibit 18.4 depicts the time involved in the sales process and how those elements relate to the traditional and relationship selling approaches.

Most businesses depend on repeat sales, and repeat sales depend on thorough and continued follow-up by the salesperson. When customers feel abandoned, cognitive dissonance arises and repeat sales decline. Today, this issue is more pertinent than ever because customers are far less loyal to brands and vendors. Buyers are more inclined to look for the best deal, especially when they experience poor postsale follow-up. Automated e-mail follow-up marketing—a combination of sales automation and Internet technology—is enhancing customer satisfaction as well as bringing in more business for some marketers. After the initial contact with a prospect, a software program automatically sends a series of personalized e-mail messages over a period of time.

The Impact of Technology on Personal Selling

Will the increasingly sophisticated technology now available at marketers' fingertips eliminate the need for salespeople? Experts agree that a relationship between the salesperson and customer will always be necessary. Technology, however, can certainly help to improve that relationship. Cell phones, laptops, pagers, e-mail, and electronic organizers allow salespeople to be more accessible to both clients and the company. Moreover, the Internet provides salespeople with vast resources of information on clients, competitors, and the industry.

E-business—buying, selling, marketing, collaborating with partners, and servicing customers electronically using the Internet—has had a significant impact on personal selling. Virtually all large companies and most medium and small companies are involved in e-commerce and consider it to be necessary to compete in today's marketplace. For customers, the Web has become a powerful tool, providing accurate and up-to-date information on products, pricing, and order status. The Internet also cost-effectively processes orders and service requests. Although on the surface the Internet might appear to be a threat to the job security of salespeople, the Web is actually freeing sales reps from tedious administrative tasks like shipping catalogs, placing routine orders, or tracking orders. This leaves them more time to focus on the needs of their clients.

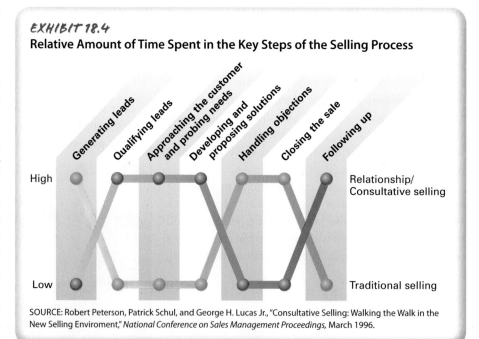

EXHIBIT 18.4
Relative Amount of Time Spent in the Key Steps of the Selling Process

SOURCE: Robert Peterson, Patrick Schul, and George H. Lucas Jr., "Consultative Selling: Walking the Walk in the New Selling Enviroment," *National Conference on Sales Management Proceedings*, March 1996.

HARNESSING WORD OF MOUTH AS A SALES TOOL

© ISTOCKPHOTO.COM/RUDYANTO WIJAYA

Roku, the maker of the original media streaming device, faces competition from Apple and Google, among others, for the growing market. Roku needed to get the word out about its easy-to-use, inexpensive, and fabulously reviewed product but lacked the financial prowess of Apple and Microsoft. So it turned to its fans: 25 percent of Roku's approximately one million users had encouraged a friend to buy a player. Now, Roku's refer-a-friend campaign rewards customers for recommending the players. Each person who buys a Roku player receives an e-mail with a personal link to share with friends. If a new customer purchases a Roku player through such a link, the original customer receives a free month's subscription to Netflix. The investment is paying off: in the first three months, 15,000 customers recommended Roku, and 1,500 purchased Roku through a friend's link.[23]

SOURCE: Jennifer Alsever, "Turning Customers into Salespeople," *Inc.*, July/August 2011.

STUDY TOOLS
CHAPTER 18

Flip to the back of your textbook to:

❏ **Rip out Chapter Review Card**

Log in to the CourseMate for MKTG at cengagebrain.com to:

❏ **Review Key Terms Flash Cards (Print or Online)**

❏ **Review Audio and Visual Summaries**

❏ **Complete both Practice Quizzes to prepare for tests**

❏ **Play "Beat the Clock" and "Quizbowl" to master concepts**

❏ **Complete "Crossword Puzzle" to review key terms**

❏ **Watch the video on "Scholfield Honda" for a real company example on Sales Promotion and Personal Selling**

Trying to set the right price is one of the most stressful and pressure-filled tasks of the marketing manager.

AFTER YOU FINISH THIS CHAPTER, GO TO **PAGE 327** FOR **STUDY TOOLS**

LO1 The Importance of Price

Price means one thing to the consumer and something else to the seller. To the consumer, it is the cost of something. To the seller, price is revenue—the primary source of profits. In the broadest sense, price allocates resources in a free-market economy. Marketing managers are frequently challenged by the task of price setting. Yet over the past two decades, managers have learned that meeting the challenge of setting the right price can have a significant impact on the firm's bottom line. Large organizations that successfully manage prices do so by creating a pricing infrastructure within the company. This means defining pricing goals, searching for ways to create greater customer value, assigning authority and responsibility for pricing decisions, and creating tools and systems to continually improve pricing decisions. Obtaining pricing excellence is a very worthwhile activity: a 1 percent improvement in the average price of goods and services leads to an 8.7 percent increase in net profits for the typical Global 1200 company.[1] The Global 1200 are the world's 1,200 largest public companies.

> **price** that which is given up in an exchange to acquire a good or service

What Is Price?

Price is that which is given up in an exchange to acquire a good or service. Price plays two roles in the evaluation of product alternatives: as a measure of sacrifice and as an information cue. To some degree, these are two opposing effects.[2]

What do you think?

I enjoy the prestige of buying a high-priced brand.

1 2 3 4 5 6 7
STRONGLY DISAGREE   STRONGLY AGREE

© AP IMAGES/THE CANADIAN PRESS, PAWEL DWULIT

Find out what others think at the CourseMate for MKTG. Log in at cengagebrain.com. |

The Sacrifice Effect of Price Price is, again, "that which is given up," which means what is sacrificed to get a good or service. In the United States, the sacrifice is usually money, but it can be other things as well. It may also be time lost while waiting to acquire the good or service. Price might also include "lost dignity" for individuals who lose their jobs and must rely on charity.

The Information Effect of Price Consumers do not always choose the lowest-priced product in a category, such as shoes, cars, or wine, even when the products are otherwise similar. One explanation of this behavior, based upon research, is that we infer quality information from price.[3] That is, higher quality equals higher price. The information effect of price may also extend to favorable price perceptions by others because higher prices can convey the prominence and status of the purchaser to other people. Thus, both a Swatch and a Rolex can tell time accurately, but they convey different meanings. The price–quality relationship will be discussed later in the chapter.

Value Is Based upon Perceived Satisfaction Consumers are interested in obtaining a "reasonable price." "Reasonable price" really means "perceived reasonable value" at the time of the transaction. The price paid is based on the satisfaction consumers *expect* to receive from a product and not necessarily the satisfaction they *actually* receive. Price can relate to anything with perceived value, not just money. When goods and services are exchanged, the trade is called *barter*.

The Importance of Price to Marketing Managers

As noted in the chapter introduction, prices are the key to revenues, which in turn are the key to profits for an organization. **Revenue** is the price charged to customers multiplied by the number of units sold. Revenue is what pays for every activity of the company: production, finance, sales, distribution, and so on. What's left over (if anything) is **profit**. Managers usually strive to charge a price that will earn a fair profit.

Price x Units = Revenue

revenue the price charged to customers multiplied by the number of units sold

profit revenue minus expenses

To earn a profit, managers must choose a price that is not too high or too low—a price that equals the perceived value to target consumers. If, in consumers' minds, a price is set too high, the perceived value will be less than the cost, and sale opportunities will be lost. Conversely, if a price is too low, the consumer may perceive it as a great value, but the firm loses revenue it could have earned.

Trying to set the right price is one of the most stressful and pressure-filled tasks of the marketing manager, as trends in the consumer market attest:

▸ Confronting a flood of new products, potential buyers carefully evaluate the price of each one against the value of existing products.

▸ The increased availability of bargain-priced private and generic brands has put downward pressure on overall prices.

▸ Many firms are trying to maintain or regain their market share by cutting prices.

▸ The Internet has made comparison shopping easier.

▸ The United States was in a recession from late 2007 until 2009 and was still recovering very slowly in 2011.

In the business market, buyers are also becoming more price sensitive and better informed. Computerized information systems enable organizational buyers to compare price and performance with great ease and accuracy. Improved communication and the increased use of direct marketing and computer-aided selling have also opened up many markets to new competitors. Finally, competition in general is increasing, so some installations, accessories, and component parts are being marketed like indistinguishable commodities.

LO 2 Pricing Objectives

To survive in today's highly competitive marketplace, companies need pricing objectives that are specific, attainable, and measurable. Realistic pricing goals then require periodic monitoring to determine the effectiveness of the company's strategy. For convenience, pricing objectives can be divided into three categories: profit oriented, sales oriented, and status quo.

Profit-Oriented Pricing Objectives

Profit-oriented objectives include profit maximization, satisfactory profits, and target return on investment.

Profit Maximization *Profit maximization* means setting prices so that total revenue is as large as possible relative to total costs. Profit maximization does not always signify unreasonably high prices, however. Both price and profits depend on the type of competitive environment a firm faces, such as whether it is in a monopoly position (being the only seller) or in a much more competitive situation. Also, remember that a firm cannot charge a price higher than the product's perceived value. Many firms do not have the accounting data they need for maximizing profits.

Sometimes managers say that their company is trying to maximize profits—in other words, trying to make as much money as possible. Although this goal may sound impressive to stockholders, it is not good enough for planning.

In attempting to maximize profits, managers can try to expand revenue by increasing customer satisfaction, or they can attempt to reduce costs by operating more efficiently. A third possibility is to attempt to do both. Some companies may focus too much on cost reduction at the expense of the customer, or rely so heavily on customer satisfaction to increase revenue that costs creep up unnecessarily. However, a company can maintain or slightly cut costs while increasing customer loyalty through customer service initiatives, loyalty programs, and customer relationship management programs and allocating fewer resources to programs that are designed to improve efficiency and reduce costs. Both types of programs, of course, are critical to the success of the firm.

Satisfactory Profits Satisfactory profits are a reasonable level of profits. Rather than maximizing profits, many organizations strive for profits that are satisfactory to the stockholders and management—in other words, a level of profits consistent with the level of risk an organization faces. In a risky industry, a satisfactory profit may be 35 percent. In a low-risk industry, it might be 7 percent.

Target Return on Investment The most common profit objective is a target **return on investment (ROI)**, sometimes called the firm's return on total assets. ROI measures management's overall effectiveness in generating profits with the available assets. The higher the firm's ROI, the better off the firm is. Many companies use a target ROI as their main pricing goal. In summary, ROI is a percentage that puts a firm's profits into perspective by showing profits relative to investment.

Return on investment is calculated as follows:

$$\text{Return on investment} = \frac{\text{Net profits after taxes}}{\text{Total assets}}$$

Assume that in 2012 Johnson Controls had assets of $4.5 million, net profits of $550,000, and a target ROI of 10 percent. This was the actual ROI:

$$\text{ROI} = \frac{\$550,000}{\$4,500,000} = 12.2 \text{ percent}$$

As you can see, the ROI for Johnson Controls exceeded its target, which indicates that the company prospered in 2012.

Comparing the 12.2 percent ROI with the industry average provides a more meaningful picture, however. Any ROI needs to be evaluated in terms of the competitive environment, risks in the industry, and economic conditions. Generally speaking, firms seek ROIs in the 10 to 30 percent range. In some industries, such as the grocery industry, however, a return of under 5 percent is common and acceptable.

A company with a target ROI can predetermine its desired level of profitability. The marketing manager can use the standard, such as 10 percent ROI, to determine whether a particular price and marketing mix are feasible. In addition, however, the manager must weigh the risk of a given strategy even if the return is in the acceptable range.

return on investment (ROI)
net profit after taxes divided by total assets

© OTNAYDUR/SHUTTERSTOCK.COM

EXHIBIT 19.1
Two Ways to Measure Market Share (Units and Revenue)

Company	Units Sold	Unit Price	Total Revenue	Unit Market Share	Revenue Market Share
A	1,000	$1.00	$1,000	50	25
B	200	4.00	800	10	20
C	500	2.00	1,000	25	25
D	300	4.00	1,200	15	30
Total	2,000		$4,000		

© CENGAGE LEARNING 2013

Sales-Oriented Pricing Objectives

market share a company's product sales as a percentage of total sales for that industry

Sales-oriented pricing objectives are based either on market share or on dollar or unit sales.

Market Share **Market share** is a company's product sales as a percentage of total sales for that industry. Sales can be reported in dollars or in units of product. It is very important to know whether market share is expressed in revenue or units because the results may be different. Consider four companies competing in an industry with 2,000 total unit sales and total industry revenue of $4 thousand (see Exhibit 19.1). Company A has the largest unit market share at 50 percent, but it has only 25 percent of the revenue market share. In contrast, company D has only a 15 percent unit share but the largest revenue share: 30 percent. Usually, market share is expressed in terms of revenue and not units.

Many companies believe that maintaining or increasing market share is an indicator of the effectiveness of their marketing mix. Larger market shares have indeed often meant higher profits, thanks to greater economies of scale, market power, and ability to compensate top-quality management. Conventional wisdom also says that market share and ROI are strongly related. For the most part they are; however, many companies with low market share survive and even prosper. To succeed with a low market share, companies need to compete in industries with slow growth and few product changes—for instance, industrial supplies. Otherwise, they must vie in an industry that makes frequently bought items, such as consumer convenience goods.

The conventional wisdom about market share and profitability isn't always reliable, however. Because of extreme competition in some industries, many market share leaders either do not reach their target ROI or actually lose money. Procter & Gamble switched from market share to ROI objectives after realizing that profits don't automatically follow from a large market share.

Still, the struggle for market share can be all-consuming for some companies. Kroger, the large food chain, is focusing on sales gains and not on increasing profits. In 2009, the grocer increased its national market share by 0.5 percent, which translated into $1 billion in new revenue. Kroger CEO David Dillon noted, "We are not opposed to having higher gross profits but fattening profits could cost Kroger shoppers and reduce brand equity."[4] Kroger expects to benefit from shopper loyalty as the economy improves. Research organizations like the Nielsen Company and Information Resources, Inc. provide excellent market share reports for many different industries. These reports enable companies to track their performance in various product categories over time.

Sales Maximization Rather than strive for market share, sometimes companies try to maximize sales. A firm with the objective of maximizing sales ignores profits, competition, and the marketing environment as long as sales are rising.

© AP IMAGES/KIICHIRO SATO

If a company is strapped for funds or faces an uncertain future, it may try to generate a maximum amount of cash in the short run. Management's task when using this objective is to calculate which price–quantity relationship generates the greatest cash revenue. Sales maximization can also be effectively used on a temporary basis to sell off excess inventory.

Maximization of cash should never be a long-run objective because cash maximization may mean little or no profitability.

Status Quo Pricing Objectives

Status quo pricing seeks to maintain existing prices or to meet the competition's prices. This third category of pricing objectives has the major advantage of requiring little planning. It is essentially a passive policy.

Often firms competing in an industry with an established price leader simply meet the competition's prices. These industries typically have fewer price wars than those with direct price competition. In other cases, managers regularly shop competitors' stores to ensure that their prices are comparable.

Status quo pricing often leads to suboptimal pricing. This occurs because the strategy ignores customers' perceived value of both the firm's goods or services and those offered by its competitors. Status quo pricing also ignores demand and costs. Although the policy is simple to implement, it can lead to a pricing disaster.

LO 3 The Demand Determinant of Price

After marketing managers establish pricing goals, they must set specific prices to reach those goals. The price they set for each product depends mostly on two factors: the demand for the good or service and the cost to the seller for that good or service. When pricing goals are mainly sales oriented, demand considerations usually dominate. Other factors, such as distribution and promotion strategies, perceived quality, needs of large customers, the Internet, and the stage of the product life cycle, can also influence price.

The Nature of Demand

Demand is the quantity of a product that will be sold in the market at various prices for a specified period. The quantity of a product that people will buy depends on its price. The higher the price, the fewer goods or services consumers will demand. Conversely, the lower the price, the more goods or services they will demand.

This trend is illustrated in the graph below, which shows the demand per week for gourmet cookies at a local retailer at various prices. This graph is called a *demand curve* (Exhibit 19.2a). The vertical axis of the graph shows different prices of gourmet cookies, measured in dollars per package. The horizontal axis measures the quantity of gourmet cookies that will be demanded per week at each price. For example, at a price of $2.50, 50 packages will be sold per week; at $1.00, consumers will demand 120 packages—as the *demand schedule* (Exhibit 19.2b) shows.

Notice how the demand curve slopes downward and to the right, which indicates that more gourmet cookies are demanded as the price is lowered. In other words, if cookie manufacturers put a greater quantity on the market, then their hope of selling all of it will be realized only by selling it at a lower price.

One reason more is sold at lower prices than at higher prices is that lower prices bring in new buyers. With each reduction in price, existing customers may also buy more.

> **status quo pricing** a pricing objective that maintains existing prices or meets the competition's prices
>
> **demand** the quantity of a product that will be sold in the market at various prices for a specified period

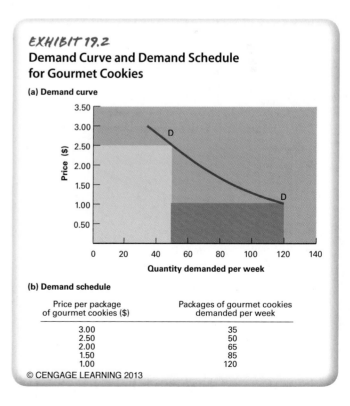

EXHIBIT 19.2

Demand Curve and Demand Schedule for Gourmet Cookies

(a) Demand curve

(b) Demand schedule

Price per package of gourmet cookies ($)	Packages of gourmet cookies demanded per week
3.00	35
2.50	50
2.00	65
1.50	85
1.00	120

© CENGAGE LEARNING 2013

supply the quantity of a product that will be offered to the market by a supplier at various prices for a specified period

price equilibrium the price at which demand and supply are equal

Supply is the quantity of a product that will be offered to the market by a supplier or suppliers at various prices for a specified period. The graph below illustrates the resulting *supply curve* (Exhibit 19.3a) for gourmet cookies. Unlike the falling demand curve, the supply curve for gourmet cookies slopes upward and to the right. At higher prices, gourmet cookie manufacturers will obtain more resources (flour, eggs, chocolate) and produce more gourmet cookies. If the price consumers are willing to pay for gourmet cookies increases, producers can afford to buy more ingredients.

Output tends to increase at higher prices because manufacturers can sell more cookies and earn greater profits. The *supply schedule* in Exhibit 19.3b shows that at $2, suppliers are willing to place 110 packages of gourmet cookies on the market, but they will offer 140 packages at a price of $3.

How Demand and Supply Establish Prices

At this point, combine the concepts of demand and supply to see how competitive market prices are determined. So far, the premise is that if the price is X, then consumers will purchase Y amount of gourmet cookies. The demand curve cannot predict consumption, nor can the supply curve alone forecast production. Instead, we need to look at what happens when supply and demand interact—as shown in Exhibit 19.4.

At a price of $3, the public would demand only 35 packages of gourmet cookies. However, suppliers stand ready to place 140 packages on the market at this price (data from the demand and supply schedules). If they do, they would create a surplus of 105 packages of gourmet cookies. How does a merchant eliminate a surplus? She lowers the price.

At a price of $1.00, 120 packages would be demanded, but only 25 would be placed on the market. A shortage of 95 units would be created. If a product is in short supply and consumers want it, how do they entice the dealer to part with one unit? They offer more money—that is, pay a higher price.

Now let's examine a price of $1.50. At this price, 85 packages are demanded and 85 are supplied. When demand and supply are equal, a state called **price equilibrium** is achieved. A temporary price below equilibrium—say, $1.00—results in a shortage because at that price the demand for gourmet cookies is greater than the available supply. Shortages put upward pressure on price. As long as demand and supply remain the same, however, temporary price increases or decreases tend to return to equilibrium. At equilibrium, there is no inclination for prices to rise or fall.

Prices may fluctuate during a trial-and-error period as the market for a good or service moves toward equilibrium. Sooner or later, however, demand and supply will settle into proper balance.

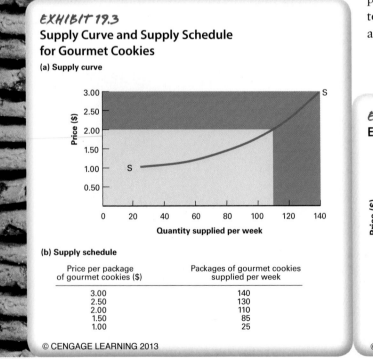

EXHIBIT 19.3
Supply Curve and Supply Schedule for Gourmet Cookies

(a) Supply curve

(b) Supply schedule

Price per package of gourmet cookies ($)	Packages of gourmet cookies supplied per week
3.00	140
2.50	130
2.00	110
1.50	85
1.00	25

© CENGAGE LEARNING 2013

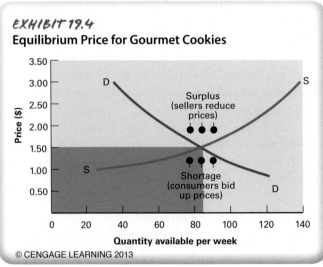

EXHIBIT 19.4
Equilibrium Price for Gourmet Cookies

© CENGAGE LEARNING 2013

Elasticity of Demand

To appreciate demand analysis, you should understand the concept of elasticity. **Elasticity of demand** refers to consumers' responsiveness or sensitivity to changes in price. **Elastic demand** is a situation in which consumer demand is sensitive to price changes. Conversely, **inelastic demand** means that an increase or a decrease in price will not significantly affect demand for the product.

Elasticity over the range of a demand curve can be measured by using this formula:

$$\text{Elasticity } (E) = \frac{\text{Percentage change in quantity demanded of good A}}{\text{Percentage change in price of good A}}$$

If E is greater than 1, demand is elastic.
If E is less than 1, demand is inelastic.
If E is equal to 1, demand is unitary.

Unitary elasticity means that an increase in sales exactly offsets a decrease in prices, so total revenue remains the same.

Elasticity can be measured by observing these changes in total revenue:

▸▸ If price goes down and revenue goes up, demand is elastic.

▸▸ If price goes down and revenue goes down, demand is inelastic.

▸▸ If price goes up and revenue goes up, demand is inelastic.

▸▸ If price goes up and revenue goes down, demand is elastic.

▸▸ If price goes up or down and revenue stays the same, elasticity is unitary.

The demand curve for Sony DVD players is very elastic. Decreasing the price of one of these players from $300 to $200 increases sales from 18,000 units

elasticity of demand consumers' responsiveness or sensitivity to changes in price

elastic demand a situation in which consumer demand is sensitive to changes in price

inelastic demand a situation in which an increase or a decrease in price will not significantly affect demand for the product

unitary elasticity a situation in which total revenue remains the same when prices change

ELASTICITY OF ELECTRICITY: NEW YORK CITY CASE STUDY

Many policy makers feel that demand for electricity is highly inelastic, but others argue that raising the cost of electricity will encourage energy conservation. New York City's electric rates provide an opportunity to test these two theories. About 1.75 million New York apartments have metered electricity, and their residents pay an average of 21 cents per kilowatt hour—one of the highest rates in the nation. In addition, New York has roughly 250,000 older apartments that have unlimited, unmetered electric power included in the rent. To determine the relationship between price and conservation, we can compare energy use in the unmetered apartments with energy use in the metered apartments. Demand for electricity is greater in the unmetered apartments. Without having to pay for metered use, some people, for example, leave their air conditioners running even when they are not at home. Yet even this increased demand is not unlimited. On average, electicity use is 30 percent higher in unmetered apartments than in metered ones. These numbers suggest that charging for electricity would provide an effective incentive for conservation. It also appears that demand for electricity is elastic, increasing as the price is lowered (or not charged) and decreasing as the price increases.[5]

SOURCE: Ed Dolan, "A Natural Experiment in Demand Elasticity: Metered vs Unmetered Electricity," *Ed Dolan's Econ Blog*, August 17, 2010.

© DEANHARTY/SHUTTERSTOCK.COM

to 59,000 units. Revenue increases from $5.4 million ($300 × 18,000) to $11.8 million ($200 × 59,000). The price decrease results in a large increase in sales and revenue.

Inelastic Demand When price and total revenue fall, demand is inelastic. When demand is inelastic, sellers can raise prices and increase total revenue. Often, items that are relatively inexpensive but convenient tend to have inelastic demand. Crops such as wheat, soybeans, and corn have inelastic demand. When there is a particularly productive year (as 2010 was in the United States), excess or bumper crops cause the prices of these crops to fall. But unless there is a drastic change in consumption rates, consumers won't readily buy greater amounts of grain, so revenue decreases with the price of the crops. If there is a crop shortage, prices escalate, but consumers still maintain the same level of demand because food is a necessity, and they will continue to purchase the more expensive crop.[6]

Elastic Demand In the previous example of Sony DVD players, when the price is dropped from $300 to $200, total revenue increases by $6.4 million ($11.8 million minus $5.4 million). An increase in total revenue when price falls indicates that demand is elastic. Let's measure Sony's elasticity of demand when the price drops from $300 to $200 by applying the formula presented earlier:

$$E = \frac{\text{Change in quantity/(Sum of quantities/2)}}{\text{Change in price/(Sum of prices/2)}}$$

$$E = \frac{(59,000 - 18,000)/[(59,000 + 18,000)/2]}{(\$300 - \$200)/[(\$300 + \$200)/2]}$$

$$E = \frac{41,000/38,500}{\$100/\$250}$$

$$E = \frac{1.065}{.4}$$

$$E = 2.66$$

Because E is greater than 1, demand is elastic.

Factors That Affect Elasticity Several factors affect elasticity of demand, including the following:

▶▶ *Availability of substitutes:* When many substitute products are available, the consumer can easily switch from one product to another, making demand elastic. The same is true in reverse: A person with complete renal failure will pay whatever is charged for a kidney transplant because there is no substitute.

▶▶ *Price relative to purchasing power:* If a price is so low that it is an inconsequential part of an individual's budget, demand will be inelastic.

▶▶ *Product durability:* Consumers often have the option of repairing durable products rather than replacing them, thus prolonging their useful life. In other words, people are sensitive to the price increase, and demand is elastic.

▶▶ *A product's other uses:* The greater the number of different uses for a product, the more elastic demand tends to be. If a product has only one use, as may be true of a new medicine, the quantity purchased probably will not vary as price varies. A person will consume only the prescribed quantity, regardless of price. On the other hand, a product like steel has many possible applications. As its price falls, steel becomes more economically feasible in a wider variety of applications, thereby making demand relatively elastic.

▶▶ *Rate of inflation:* Recent research has found that when a country's inflation rate (the rate at which the price level is rising) is high, demand becomes more elastic. In other words, rising price levels make consumers more price sensitive. During inflationary periods, consumers base their timing (when to buy) and quantity decisions on price promotions. This suggests that a brand gains additional sales or market share if the product is effectively promoted or if the marketing manager keeps the brand's price increases low relative to the inflation rate.[7]

Examples of both elastic and inelastic demand abound in everyday life. Recently, fans balked at high prices for concerts. Promoters lost money and some shows, including some by artists Christina Aguilera and Marc Anthony, were canceled. This is price elasticity in action. On the other hand, demand for

© A3615 PATRICK LUX DEUTSCH PRESSE AGENTUR/NEWSCOM

some tickets was highly inelastic. The Rolling Stones are still selling out concerts with tickets priced at up to $400.[8]

LO4 The Power of Yield Management Systems

When competitive pressures are high, a company must know when it can raise prices to maximize its revenues. More and more companies are turning to yield management systems, also known as revenue management systems, to help adjust prices. First developed in the airline industry, **yield management systems (YMS)** use complex mathematical software to profitably fill unused capacity. The software employs techniques such as discounting early purchases, limiting early sales at these discounted prices, and overbooking capacity. One of the key inputs in airlines' yield management systems is what has been the historical pattern of demand for a specific flight. Other service industries are now using YMS as well. Royal Caribbean Cruises, for example, uses its yield management system to adjust hundreds of prices through the course of a day.

Now YMS are spreading beyond service industries as their popularity increases. The lessons of airlines and hotels aren't entirely applicable to other industries, however, because plane seats and hotel beds are perishable—if they go empty, the revenue opportunity is lost forever. So it makes sense to slash prices to move toward capacity if it's possible to do so without reducing the prices that other customers pay. Cars and steel aren't so perishable, but the capacity to make them is. An underused factory is a lost revenue opportunity. So it makes sense to cut prices to use up capacity if it's possible to do so while getting other customers to pay full price.

Pharmacy chain Duane Reade uses DemandTec's algorithms to determine prices for two-thirds of the items it sells. For example, the software analyzed historical data and suggested a new system for pricing diapers. Now the price is related to the wearer's age. Diapers for infants are more expensive than those for toddlers. Since the system was instituted, diaper sales have increased so much that baby care revenues are up by 27 percent.[9]

LO5 The Cost Determinant of Price

Sometimes companies minimize or ignore the importance of demand and decide to price their products largely or solely on the basis of costs. Prices determined strictly on the basis of costs may be too high for the target market, thereby reducing or eliminating sales. On the other hand, cost-based prices may be too low, causing the firm to earn a lower return than it should. Nevertheless, costs should generally be part of any price determination, if only as a floor below which a good or service must not be priced in the long run.

The idea of cost may seem simple, but it is actually a multifaceted concept, especially for producers of goods and services. A **variable cost** is a cost that varies with changes in the level of output; an example of a variable cost is the cost of materials. In contrast, a **fixed cost** does not change as output is increased or decreased. Examples include rent and executives' salaries.

To compare the cost of production to the selling price of a product, it is helpful to calculate costs per unit, or average costs. **Average variable cost (AVC)** equals total variable costs divided by quantity of output. **Average total cost (ATC)** equals total costs divided by output. As the graph in Exhibit 19.5a on the next page shows, AVC and ATC are basically U-shaped curves. In contrast, average fixed cost (AFC) declines continually as output increases because total fixed costs are constant.

Marginal cost (MC) is the change in total costs associated with a one-unit change in output. Exhibit 19.5b shows that when output rises from seven to eight units, the change in total cost is from $640 to $750; therefore, MC is $110.

All the curves illustrated in Exhibit 19.5a have definite relationships:

▶▶ AVC plus AFC equals ATC.

▶▶ MC falls for a while and then turns upward, in this case with the fourth unit. At that point, diminishing returns set in, meaning that less output is produced for every additional dollar spent on variable input.

yield management systems (YMS) a technique for adjusting prices that uses complex mathematical software to profitably fill unused capacity by discounting early purchases, limiting early sales at these discounted prices, and overbooking capacity

variable cost a cost that varies with changes in the level of output

fixed cost a cost that does not change as output is increased or decreased

average variable cost (AVC) total variable costs divided by quantity of output

average total cost (ATC) total costs divided by quantity of output

marginal cost (MC) the change in total costs associated with a one-unit change in output

markup pricing the cost of buying the product from the producer, plus amounts for profit and for expenses not otherwise accounted for

▸▸ MC intersects both AVC and ATC at their lowest possible points.

▸▸ When MC is less than AVC or ATC, the incremental cost will continue to pull the averages down. Conversely, when MC is greater than AVC or ATC, it pulls the averages up, and ATC and AVC begin to rise.

▸▸ The minimum point on the ATC curve is the least cost point for a fixed-capacity firm, although it is not necessarily the most profitable point.

Costs can be used to set prices in a variety of ways. Markup pricing is relatively simple. Profit maximization pricing and break-even pricing make use of the more complicated concepts of cost.

Markup Pricing

Markup pricing, the most popular method used by wholesalers and retailers to establish a selling price, does not directly analyze the costs of production. Instead, **markup pricing** uses the cost of buying the

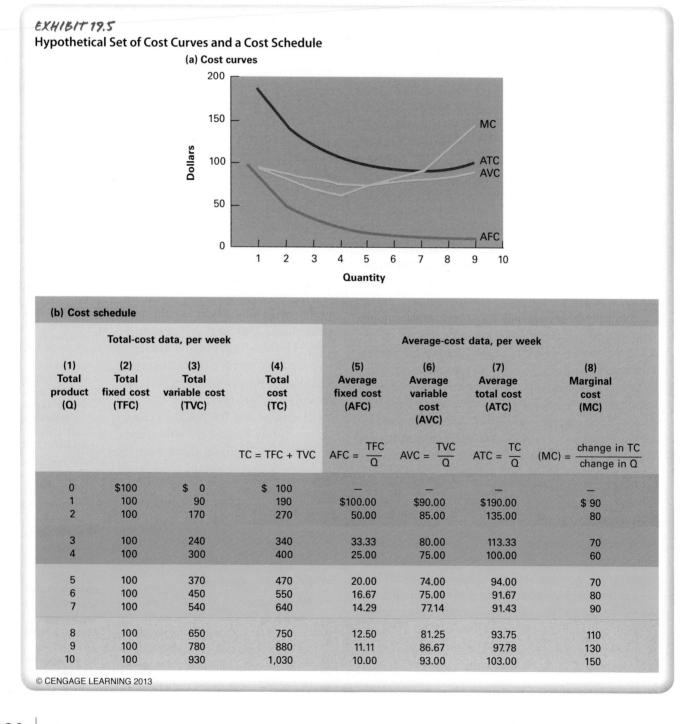

EXHIBIT 19.5
Hypothetical Set of Cost Curves and a Cost Schedule

(a) Cost curves

(b) Cost schedule

Total-cost data, per week				Average-cost data, per week			
(1) Total product (Q)	**(2)** Total fixed cost (TFC)	**(3)** Total variable cost (TVC)	**(4)** Total cost (TC)	**(5)** Average fixed cost (AFC)	**(6)** Average variable cost (AVC)	**(7)** Average total cost (ATC)	**(8)** Marginal cost (MC)
			$TC = TFC + TVC$	$AFC = \dfrac{TFC}{Q}$	$AVC = \dfrac{TVC}{Q}$	$ATC = \dfrac{TC}{Q}$	$(MC) = \dfrac{\text{change in TC}}{\text{change in Q}}$
0	$100	$ 0	$ 100	—	—	—	—
1	100	90	190	$100.00	$90.00	$190.00	$ 90
2	100	170	270	50.00	85.00	135.00	80
3	100	240	340	33.33	80.00	113.33	70
4	100	300	400	25.00	75.00	100.00	60
5	100	370	470	20.00	74.00	94.00	70
6	100	450	550	16.67	75.00	91.67	80
7	100	540	640	14.29	77.14	91.43	90
8	100	650	750	12.50	81.25	93.75	110
9	100	780	880	11.11	86.67	97.78	130
10	100	930	1,030	10.00	93.00	103.00	150

© CENGAGE LEARNING 2013

product from the producer, plus amounts for profit and for expenses not otherwise accounted for. The total determines the selling price.

A retailer, for example, adds a certain percentage to the cost of the merchandise received to arrive at the retail price. An item that costs the retailer $1.80 and is sold for $2.20 carries a markup of 40 cents, which is a markup of 22 percent of the cost ($0.40 ÷ $1.80). Retailers tend to discuss markup in terms of its percentage of the retail price—in this example, 18 percent ($0.40 ÷ $2.20). The difference between the retailer's cost and the selling price (40 cents) is the gross margin.

The formula for calculating the retail price given a certain desired markup is as follows:

$$\text{Retail price} = \frac{\text{Cost}}{1 - \text{Desired return on sales}}$$

$$= \frac{\$1.80}{1.00 - 0.18}$$

$$= \$2.20$$

If the retailer wants a 30 percent return, then:

$$\text{Retail price} = \frac{\$1.80}{1.00 - 0.30}$$

$$= \$2.57$$

The reason that retailers and others speak of markups on selling price is that many important figures in financial reports, such as gross sales and revenues, are sales figures, not cost figures.

To use markup based on cost or selling price effectively, the marketing manager must calculate an adequate gross margin—the amount added to cost to determine price. The margin must ultimately provide adequate funds to cover selling expenses and profit. Once an appropriate margin has been determined, the markup technique has the major advantage of being easy to employ.

Markups are often based on experience. For example, many small retailers mark up merchandise 100 percent over cost. (In other words, they double the cost.) This tactic is called **keystoning**. Some other factors that influence markups are the merchandise's appeal to customers, past response to the markup (an implicit demand consideration), the item's promotional value, the seasonality of the goods, their fashion appeal, the product's traditional selling price, and competition. Most retailers avoid any set markup because of such considerations as promotional value and seasonality.

Profit Maximization Pricing

Producers tend to use more complicated methods of setting prices than distributors use. One is **profit maximization**, which occurs when marginal revenue equals MC. You learned earlier that MC is the change in total costs associated with a one-unit change in output. Similarly, **marginal revenue (MR)** is the extra revenue associated with selling an extra unit of output. As long as the revenue of the last unit produced and sold is greater than the cost of the last unit produced and sold, the firm should continue manufacturing and selling the product.

Exhibit 19.6 shows the MRs and MCs for a hypothetical firm, using the cost data from Exhibit 19.5b. The profit-maximizing quantity, where MR = MC, is six units. You might say, "If profit is zero, why produce the sixth unit? Why not stop at five?" In fact, you would be right. The firm, however, would not know that the fifth unit would produce zero profits until it determined that profits were no longer increasing. Economists suggest producing up to the point where MR = MC. If MR is just one penny greater than MC, it will increase total profits.

Break-Even Pricing

Now let's take a closer look at the relationship between sales and cost. **Break-even analysis** determines what sales volume must be reached before the company breaks even (its total costs equal total revenue) and no profits are earned.

keystoning the practice of marking up prices by 100 percent, or doubling the cost

profit maximization a method of setting prices that occurs when marginal revenue equals marginal cost

marginal revenue (MR) the extra revenue associated with selling an extra unit of output or the change in total revenue with a one-unit change in output

break-even analysis a method of determining what sales volume must be reached before total revenue equals total costs

EXHIBIT 19.6
Point of Profit Maximization

Quantity	Marginal Revenue	Marginal Cost	Cumulative Total Profit
0	—	—	—
1	$140	$ 90	$ 50
2	130	80	100
3	105	70	135
4	95	60	170
5	85	70	185
*6	80	80	185
7	75	90	170
8	60	110	120
9	50	130	40
10	40	150	(70)

*Profit maximization.

© CENGAGE LEARNING 2013

The typical break-even model assumes a given fixed cost and a constant AVC. Suppose that Universal Sportswear, a hypothetical firm, has fixed costs of $2,000 and that the cost of labor and materials for each unit produced is 50 cents. Assume that it can sell up to 6,000 units of its product at $1 without having to lower its price.

Exhibit 19.7a illustrates Universal Sportswear's break-even point. As Exhibit 19.7b indicates, Universal Sportswear's total variable costs increase by 50 cents every time a new unit is produced, and total fixed costs remain constant at $2,000 regardless of the level of output. Therefore, for 4,000 units of output,

Universal Sportswear has $2,000 in fixed costs and $2,000 in total variable costs (4,000 units × $0.50), or $4,000 in total costs.

Revenue is also $4,000 (4,000 units × $1), giving a net profit of zero dollars at the break-even point of 4,000 units. Notice that once the firm gets past the break-even point, the gap between total revenue and total costs gets wider and wider because both functions are assumed to be linear.

The formula for calculating break-even quantities is simple:

$$\text{Break-even quantity} = \frac{\text{Total fixed costs}}{\text{Fixed cost contribution}}$$

EXHIBIT 19.7
Costs, Revenues, and Break-Even Point for Universal Sportswear

(a) Break-even point

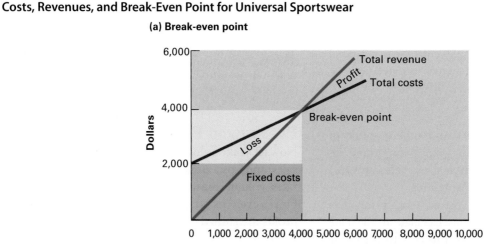

(b) Costs and revenues

Output	Total fixed costs	Average variable costs	Total variable costs	Average total costs	Average revenue (price)	Total revenue	Total costs	Profit or loss
500	$2,000	$0.50	$ 250	$4.50	$1.00	$ 500	$2,250	($1,750)
1,000	2,000	0.50	500	2.50	1.00	1,000	2,500	(1,500)
1,500	2,000	0.50	750	1.83	1.00	1,500	2,750	(1,250)
2,000	2,000	0.50	1,000	1.50	1.00	2,000	3,000	(1,000)
2,500	2,000	0.50	1,250	1.30	1.00	2,500	3,250	(750)
3,000	2,000	0.50	1,500	1.17	1.00	3,000	3,500	(500)
3,500	2,000	0.50	1,750	1.07	1.00	3,500	3,750	(250)
*4,000	2,000	0.50	2,000	1.00	1.00	4,000	4,000	0
4,500	2,000	0.50	2,250	0.94	1.00	4,500	4,250	250
5,000	2,000	0.50	2,500	0.90	1.00	5,000	4,500	500
5,500	2,000	0.50	2,750	0.86	1.00	5,500	4,750	750
6,000	2,000	0.50	3,000	0.83	1.00	6,000	5,000	1,000

*Break-even point

© CENGAGE LEARNING 2013

Fixed cost contribution is the price minus the AVC. Therefore, for Universal Sportswear,

$$\text{Break-even quantity} = \frac{\$2,000}{(\$1.00 - \$0.50)} = \frac{\$2,000}{\$0.50}$$
$$= 4,000 \text{ units}$$

The advantage of break-even analysis is that it provides a quick estimate of how much the firm must sell to break even and how much profit can be earned if a higher sales volume is obtained. If a firm is operating close to the break-even point, it may want to see what can be done to reduce costs or increase sales. Moreover, in a simple break-even analysis, it is not necessary to compute MCs and MRs because price and average cost per unit are assumed to be constant. Also, because accounting data for marginal cost and revenue are frequently unavailable, it is convenient not to have to depend on that information.

Break-even analysis is not without several important limitations. Sometimes it is hard to know whether a cost is fixed or variable. If labor wins a tough guaranteed-employment contract, are the resulting expenses a fixed cost? More important than cost determination is the fact that simple break-even analysis ignores demand. How does Universal Sportswear know it can sell 4,000 units at $1? Could it sell the same 4,000 units at $2 or even $5? Obviously, this information would profoundly affect the firm's pricing decisions.

LO 6 Other Determinants of Price

Other factors besides demand and costs can influence price. For example, the stages in the product life cycle, the competition, the product distribution strategy, the promotion strategy, and the perceived quality can all affect pricing.

Stages in the Product Life Cycle

As a product moves through its life cycle (see Chapter 11), the demand for the product and the competitive conditions tend to change:

▸▸ *Introductory stage:* Management usually sets prices high during the introductory stage. One reason is that it hopes to recover its development costs quickly. In addition, demand originates in the core of the market (the customers whose needs ideally match the product's attributes) and

thus is relatively inelastic. On the other hand, if the target market is highly price sensitive, management often finds it better to price the product at the market level or lower.

▸▸ *Growth stage:* As the product enters the growth stage, prices generally begin to stabilize for several reasons. First, competitors have entered the market, increasing the available supply. Second, the product has begun to appeal to a broader market, often lower-income groups. Finally, economies of scale are lowering costs, and the savings can be passed on to the consumer in the form of lower prices.

▸▸ *Maturity stage:* Maturity usually brings further price decreases as competition increases and inefficient, high-cost firms are eliminated. Distribution channels become a significant cost factor, however, because of the need to offer wide product lines for highly segmented markets, extensive service requirements, and the sheer number of dealers necessary to absorb high-volume production. The manufacturers that remain in the market toward the end of the maturity stage typically offer similar prices. At this stage, price increases are usually cost initiated, not demand initiated. Nor do price reductions in the late phase of maturity stimulate much demand. Because demand is limited and producers have similar cost structures, the remaining competitors will probably match price reductions.

▸▸ *Decline stage:* The final stage of the life cycle may see further price decreases as the few remaining competitors try to salvage the last vestiges of demand. When only one firm is left in the market, prices begin to stabilize. In fact, prices may eventually rise dramatically if the product survives and moves into the specialty goods category, as horse-drawn carriages and vinyl records have.

The Competition

Competition varies during the product life cycle, of course, and so at times it may strongly affect pricing decisions. Although a firm may not have any competition at first, the high prices it charges may eventually induce another firm to enter the market.

Often, in hotly competitive markets, price wars break out. Amazon.com has been increasing its online presence by offering more than just books, looking to become the go-to online e-tailer. Walmart answered Amazon's expansion by selling its most anticipated hardcovers online for just $10 each (an average hardcover sells for about $25). Later that day, Amazon matched the price. The battle continued until the prices stabilized with books selling for $9 at Amazon, $8.99 at Target, and $8.98 at Walmart. These prices have caused concern about the perceived value of

selling against the brand stocking well-known branded items at high prices in order to sell store brands at discounted prices

extranet a private electronic network that links a company with its suppliers and customers

books and the ability of independent bookstores to compete with the large chains selling the same books for up to 74 percent less than the list price.[10]

Distribution Strategy

An effective distribution network can often overcome other minor flaws in the marketing mix.[11] For example, although consumers may perceive a price as being slightly higher than normal, they may buy the product anyway if it is being sold at a convenient retail outlet.

Adequate distribution for a new product can often be attained by offering a larger-than-usual profit margin to distributors. A variation on this strategy is to give dealers a large trade allowance to help offset the costs of promotion and further stimulate demand at the retail level.

Manufacturers have gradually been losing control within the distribution channel to wholesalers and retailers, which often adopt pricing strategies that serve their own purposes. For instance, some distributors are **selling against the brand**: They place well-known brands on the shelves at high prices while offering other brands—typically, their private label brands, such as Kroger canned pears—at lower prices. Of course, sales of the higher-priced brands decline.

Wholesalers and retailers may also go outside traditional distribution channels to buy gray-market goods, as discussed in Chapter 13. Distributors obtain the goods through unauthorized channels for less than they would normally pay, so they can sell the goods with a bigger-than-normal markup or at a reduced price. Imports seem to be particularly susceptible to gray marketing. Although consumers might pay less for gray-market goods, they often find that the manufacturer won't honor the warranty.

Manufacturers can regain some control over price by using an exclusive distribution system, by franchising, or by avoiding doing business with price-cutting discounters. Manufacturers can also package merchandise with the selling price marked on it or place goods on consignment. The best way for manufacturers to control prices, however, is to develop brand loyalty in consumers by delivering quality and value.

The Impact of the Internet and Extranets

The Internet, **extranets** (private electronic networks), and wireless setups are linking people, machines, and companies around the globe—and connecting sellers and buyers as never before. These links are enabling

Target is using low-price and one-stop shopping advertising in its stores to convince shoppers that purchasing at Target is less expensive than purchasing at other discount retailers, such as Walmart.

© AP IMAGES/PAUL SAKUMA

buyers to quickly and easily compare products and prices, putting them in a better bargaining position. At the same time, the technology allows sellers to collect detailed data about customers' buying habits, preferences, and even spending limits so that sellers can tailor their products and prices.

Using Shopping Bots A shopping bot is a program that searches the Web for the best price for a particular item that you wish to purchase. *Bot* is short for *robot*. Shopping bots theoretically give pricing power to the consumer. The more information that the shopper has, the more efficient his or her purchase decision will be.

There are two general types of shopping bots. The first is the broad-based type that searches a wide range of product categories such as MySimon.com, DealTime.com, Bizrate.com, Pricegrabber.com, and PriceScan.com. These sites operate using a Yellow Pages type of model, in that they list every retailer they can find. The second is the niche-oriented type that searches for prices for only one type of product such as consumer electronics (CNET.com), books (Bookfinder.com), or travel-related services (Kayak.com).[12]

Most shopping bots give preferential listings to those e-retailers that pay for the privilege. These so-called merchant partners receive about 60 percent of the click-throughs.[13] Typically, the bot lists its merchant partners first, not the retailer offering the lowest price.

Internet Auctions The Internet auction business is huge. Among the most popular consumer auction sites are the following:

» *www.ubid.com:* Offers a large range of product categories. "My page" consolidates all of the user's activity in one place.

» *www.ebay.com:* The most popular auction site.

» *www.bidz.com:* Buys closeout deals in very large lots and offers them online in its no-reserve auctions.

Even though consumers are spending billions on Internet auctions, business-to-business auctions are likely to be the dominant form in the future. Recently, Whirlpool began holding online auctions. Participants bid on the price of the items that they would supply to Whirlpool but with a twist: They had to include the date when Whirlpool would have to pay for the items. The company wanted to see which suppliers would offer the longest grace period before requiring payment. Five auctions held over five months helped Whirlpool uncover savings of close to $2 million and more than doubled the grace period.

Whirlpool's success is a sign that the business-to-business auction world is shifting from haggling over prices to niggling over parameters of the deal. Warranties, delivery dates, transportation methods, customer support, financing options, and quality have all become bargaining chips.

Promotion Strategy

Price is often used as a promotional tool to increase consumer interest. Marketers at the Pittsburgh Zoo, for instance, have used a series of silly gimmicks to increase attendance. Some of the gimmicks for discounts include "friending" the zoo on Facebook or wearing a tie-dyed shirt. One day, the best mullet won a tour and runners-up earned a free haircut. And if you play along with these gimmicks, you get in to the zoo for $5.[14] The weekly flyers sent out by grocery stores in the Sunday newspaper advertise many products with special low prices. Crested Butte Ski Resort in Colorado made the unusual offer of free skiing between Thanksgiving and Christmas. Its only revenues were voluntary contributions from lodging and restaurant owners who benefited from the droves of skiers taking advantage of the promotion. Lodging during the slack period is now booked solid, and Crested Butte Resort no longer loses money during this time of the year.

Pricing can be a tool for trade promotions as well. For example, Levi's Dockers (casual men's pants) are very popular. Sensing an opportunity, rival pants maker Bugle Boy began offering similar pants at cheaper wholesale prices, which gave retailers a bigger gross margin than they were getting with Dockers. Levi Strauss had to either lower prices or risk its $400 million annual Dockers sales. Although Levi Strauss intended its cheapest Dockers to retail for $35, it started selling Dockers to retailers for $18 a pair. Retailers could then advertise Dockers at a very attractive retail price of $25.

Demands of Large Customers

Manufacturers find that their large customers such as department stores often make specific pricing demands that the suppliers must agree to. Department stores are making greater-than-ever demands on their

If you want to buy an airline ticket, where do you go? Straight to your preferred airline's Web site? Or do you do some comparison shopping on a site like Orbitz?

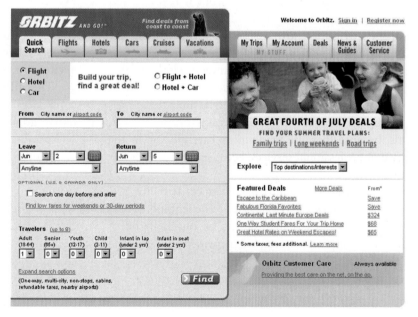

© AP IMAGES/PRNEWSFOTO/ORBITZ, INC.

prestige pricing
charging a high price to help
promote a high-quality image

suppliers to cover the heavy discounts and markdowns on their own selling floors. They want suppliers to guarantee their stores' profit margins, and they insist on cash rebates if the guarantee isn't met. They are also exacting fines for violations of ticketing, packing, and shipping rules. Cumulatively, the demands are nearly wiping out profits for all but the very biggest suppliers, according to fashion designers and garment makers.

When gas, grain, and dairy prices were exploding in 2008, you'd think the biggest seller of corn flakes and Cocoa Puffs would have been hit by rising food costs. But Walmart temporarily rolled back prices on hundreds of food items by as much as 30 percent. How? It pressured vendors to take costs out of the supply chain. "When our grocery suppliers bring price increases, we don't just accept them," said Walmart's general merchandise manager for perishables.[15]

The Relationship of Price to Quality

As mentioned at the beginning of the chapter, when a purchase decision involves great uncertainty, consumers tend to rely on a high price as a predictor of good quality. Reliance on price as an indicator of quality seems to occur for all products, but it reveals itself more strongly for some items than for others, particularly items geared toward the wealthy.[16] Among the products that benefit from this phenomenon are coffee, aspirin, salt, floor wax, shampoo, clothing, furniture, whiskey, and many services. In the absence of other information, people typically assume that prices are higher because the products contain better materials, because they are made more carefully, or, in the case of professional services, because the provider has more expertise.

Research has found that products that are perceived to be of high quality tend to benefit more from price promotions than products perceived to be of lower quality.[17] However, when perceived high- and lower-quality products are offered in settings where consumers have difficulty making comparisons, then price promotions have an equal effect on sales.

Comparisons are more difficult in end-of-aisle displays, feature advertising, and the like.

Knowledgeable merchants take these consumer attitudes into account when devising their pricing strategies. **Prestige pricing** is charging a high price to help promote a high-quality image. A successful prestige pricing strategy requires a retail price that is reasonably consistent with consumers' expectations. No one goes shopping at a Gucci's shop in New York and expects to pay $9.95 for a pair of loafers. In fact, demand would fall drastically at such a low price. In addition to prestige pricing, research has found two other basic effects associated with the price quality relationship: *hedonistic* and *allocative effects*.[18] High purchase prices may create feelings of pleasure and excitement associated with consuming higher-priced products. This is the hedonistic effect. Hedonistic consumption refers to pursuing emotional responses associated with using a product, such as pleasure, excitement, arousal, good feelings, and fun.

The allocative effect refers to the notion that consumers must allocate their budgets across alternative goods and services. The more you spend on one product, the less you have to spend on all others. Consumers sensitive to the allocative effects likely prefer low prices. However, managers must be aware that setting low prices or lowering prices with a discount may lower perceptions of product quality, prestige value, and hedonistic value. This is because of the negative cues associated with lower selling prices.[19]

Some companies, concerned about how counterfeits may affect their brands' images, are turning

© FANCY/SHUTTERSTOCK.COM

to high-end technology to combat increasingly professional counterfeit products. Companies such as Chanel and True Religion apparel (a high-end denim brand) are protecting their brands' prestige pricing and high-end names by using item-specific identification numbers (Chanel) and inserting security devices into seams in the product (True Religion). Both can be verified at official retailers, and Chanel recommends purchasing only through its Web site or official retailers to ensure authenticity. One company, Applied DNA Sciences, embeds botanical DNA in fibers in its client's products. Each brand receives unique DNA that can be identified under a special light.[20]

Some of the latest research on price–quality relationships has focused on consumer durable goods. The researchers first conducted a study to ascertain the dimensions of quality. These are (1) ease of use, (2) versatility (the ability of a product to perform more functions, or be more flexible), (3) durability, (4) serviceability (ease of obtaining quality repairs), (5) performance, and (6) prestige. The researchers found that when consumers focused on prestige and/or durability to assess quality, price was a strong indicator of perceived overall quality. Price was less important as an indicator of quality if the consumer was focusing on one of the other four dimensions of quality.[21]

STUDY TOOLS
CHAPTER 19

Flip to the back of your textbook to:

❑ **Rip out Chapter Review Card**

Log in to the CourseMate for MKTG at cengagebrain.com to:

❑ **Review Key Terms Flash Cards (Print or Online)**
❑ **Review Audio and Visual Summaries**
❑ **Complete both Practice Quizzes to prepare for tests**
❑ **Play "Beat the Clock" and "Quizbowl" to master concepts**
❑ **Complete "Crossword Puzzle" to review key terms**
❑ **Watch the video on "Evo" for a real company example on Pricing Concepts**

CHAPTER 20

Setting the Right Price

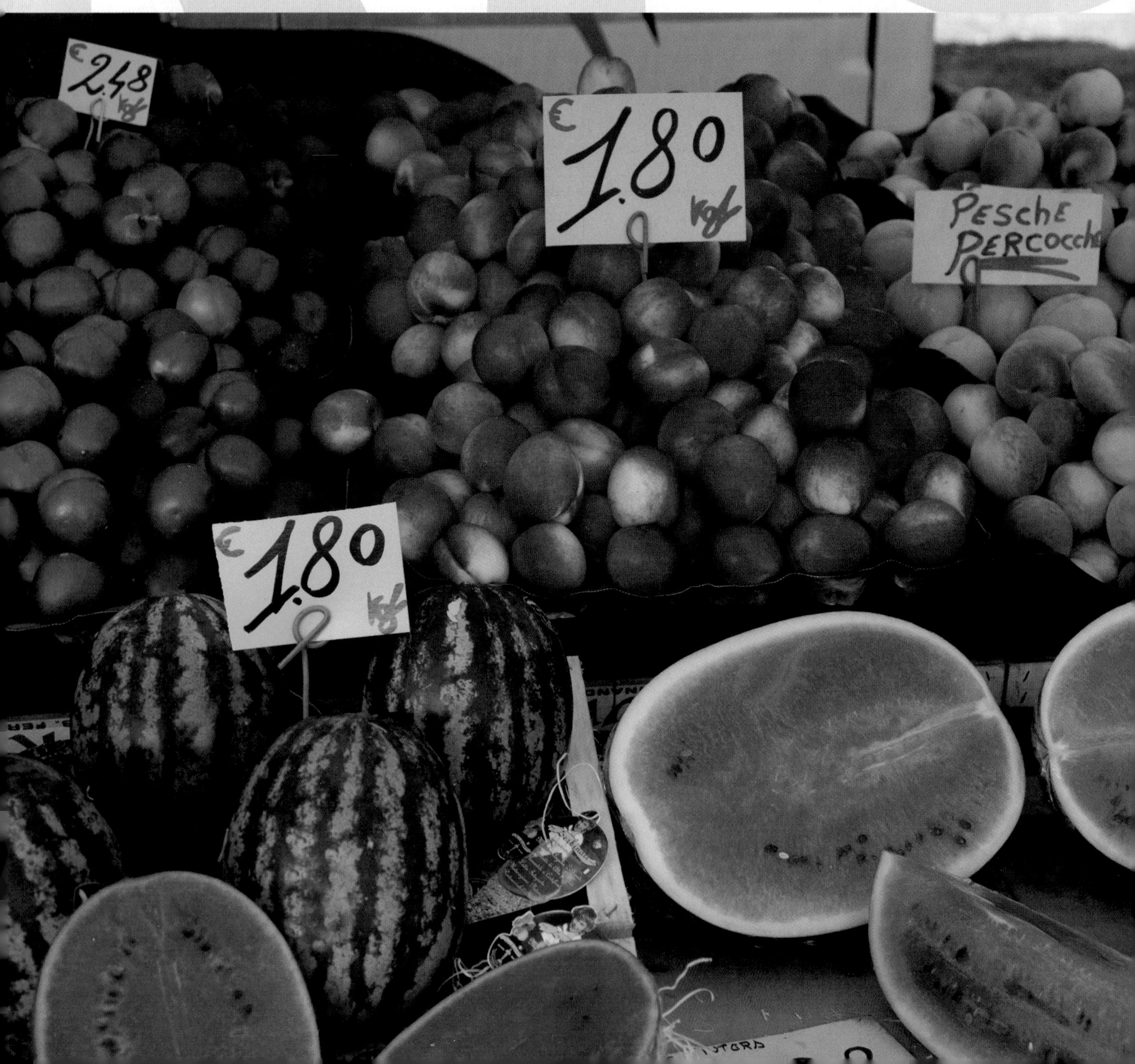

All pricing objectives have trade-offs that managers must weigh.

AFTER YOU FINISH THIS CHAPTER, GO TO PAGE 344 FOR STUDY TOOLS

LO 1 How to Set a Price on a Product

Setting the right price on a product is a four-step process, illustrated in Exhibit 20.1 on the next page and discussed throughout this chapter:

1. Establish pricing goals.
2. Estimate demand, costs, and profits.
3. Choose a price strategy to help determine a base price.
4. Fine-tune the base price with pricing tactics.

Establish Pricing Goals

The first step in setting the right price is to establish pricing goals. Recall from Chapter 19 that pricing objectives fall into three categories: profit oriented, sales oriented, and status quo. These goals are derived from the firm's overall objectives. A good understanding of the marketplace and of the consumer can sometimes tell a manager very quickly whether a goal is realistic.

All pricing objectives have trade-offs that managers must weigh. A profit maximization objective may require a bigger initial investment than the firm can commit to or wants to commit to. Reaching the desired market share often means sacrificing short-term profit because without careful management, long-term profit goals may not be met. Meeting the competition is the easiest pricing goal to implement. But can managers really afford to ignore demand and costs, the life cycle stage,

What do you think?

A person can save a lot of money by shopping around for bargains.

1 2 3 4 5 6 7
STRONGLY DISAGREE   STRONGLY AGREE

Find out what others think at the CourseMate for MKTG. Log in at cengagebrain.com.

© BUENA VISTA IMAGES/THE IMAGE BANK/GETTY IMAGES

price strategy a basic, long-term pricing framework that establishes the initial price for a product and the intended direction for price movements over the product life cycle

price skimming a pricing policy whereby a firm charges a high introductory price, often coupled with heavy promotion

and other considerations? When creating pricing objectives, managers must consider these trade-offs in light of the target customer, the environment, and the company's overall objectives.

Estimate Demand, Costs, and Profits

Chapter 19 explained that total revenue is a function of price and quantity demanded and that quantity demanded depends on elasticity. Elasticity is a function of the perceived value to the buyer relative to the price. The types of questions managers consider when conducting marketing research on demand and elasticity are key. Some questions for market research on demand and elasticity are:

» What price is so low that consumers would question the product's quality?

» What is the highest price at which the product would still be a bargain?

» What is the price at which the product is starting to get expensive?

» What is the price at which the product becomes too expensive to consider buying?[1]

After establishing pricing goals, managers should estimate total revenue at a variety of prices. Next, they should determine corresponding costs for each price. They are then ready to estimate how much profit, if any, and how much market share can be earned at each possible price. Managers can study the options in light of revenues, costs, and profits. In turn, this information can help determine which price can best meet the firm's pricing goals.

Choose a Price Strategy

The basic, long-term pricing framework for a good or service should be a logical extension of the pricing objectives. The marketing manager's chosen **price strategy** defines the initial price and gives direction for price movements over the product life cycle.

The price strategy sets a competitive price in a specific market segment, based on a well-defined positioning strategy. Changing a price level from premium to super premium may require a change in the product itself, the target customers served, the promotional strategy, or the distribution channels.

A company's freedom in pricing a new product and devising a price strategy depends on the market conditions and the other elements of the marketing mix. If a firm launches a new item resembling several others already on the market, its pricing freedom will be restricted. To succeed, the company will probably have to charge a price close to the average market price. In contrast, a firm that introduces a totally new product with no close substitutes will have considerable pricing freedom.

Despite its strategic value, pricing research is an underused tool. McKinsey & Company's Pricing Benchmark Survey estimated that only about 15 percent of companies do serious pricing research.[2]

Strategic pricing decisions tend to be made without an understanding of the likely buyer or the competitive response. Managers often make tactical pricing decisions without reviewing how they may fit into the firm's overall pricing or marketing strategy. Many companies make pricing decisions and changes without an existing process for managing the pricing activity. As a result, many of them do not have a serious pricing strategy and do not conduct pricing research to develop their strategy.[3]

Companies that do serious planning for creating a price strategy can select from three basic approaches: price skimming, penetration pricing, and status quo pricing.

EXHIBIT 20.1

Steps in Setting the Right Price on a Product

Establish pricing goals.

↓

Estimate demand, costs, and profits.

↓

Choose a price strategy to help determine a base price.

↓

Fine-tune the base price with pricing tactics.

↓

Results lead to the right price.

© CENGAGE LEARNING 2013

Price Skimming **Price skimming** is sometimes called a "market-plus" approach to pricing because it denotes a high price relative to the prices of competing products. The term *price skimming* is derived from the phrase "skimming the cream off the top." Companies often use this strategy for new products when the product is perceived by the target market as having unique advantages. Often companies will use skimming and then lower prices over time. This is called "sliding down the demand curve." Hardcover book publishers, such as HarperCollins, lower the price when the books are re-released in paperback. Other manufacturers

© CHARLES PLATIAU/REUTERS/LANDOV

A successful skimming strategy enables management to recover its product development costs quickly. Even if the market perceives an introductory price as too high, managers can lower the price. Firms often feel it is better to test the market at a high price and then lower the price if sales are too slow. Successful skimming strategies are not limited to products. Well-known athletes, lawyers, and hairstylists are experts at price skimming. Naturally, a skimming strategy will encourage competitors to enter the market.

A variation of skimming called anchoring can come into play in pricing a product line. The strategy typically is used by luxury retailers. An anchor is a high-priced product that may never sell but makes everything else look cheap by comparison. Thus, Ralph Lauren priced a "Ricky" alligator bag at $16,995, which made the "Tiffin" bag seem inexpensive at $2,595.[5]

Penetration Pricing Penetration pricing is at the opposite end of the spectrum from skimming. **Penetration pricing** means charging a relatively low price for a product as a way to reach the mass market. The low price is designed to capture a large share of a substantial market, resulting in lower production costs. If a marketing manager has made obtaining a large market share the firm's pricing objective, penetration pricing is a logical choice.

Penetration pricing does mean lower profit per unit, however. Therefore, to reach the break-even point, it requires a higher volume of sales than would a skimming policy. The recovery of product development costs may be slow. As you might expect, penetration pricing tends to discourage competition.

A penetration strategy tends to be effective in a price-sensitive market. Price should decline more rapidly when demand is elastic because the market can be expanded through a lower price. Also, price sensitivity and greater competitive pressure should lead to a lower initial price and a relatively slow decline in the price later to a stable low price.

Although Walmart is typically associated with penetration pricing, other chains have done an excellent job of following this strategy as well. Fast-food restaurants use dollar menus and low-priced foods to entice customers to visit one chain over another. McDonald's has been successful over competitor Burger King because McDonald's offers a wide range of food at various prices—low-priced snack wraps draw in customers, who may then decide to also get

> **penetration pricing** a pricing policy whereby a firm charges a relatively low price for a product initially as a way to reach the mass market

maintain skimming prices throughout a product's life cycle. A manager of the factory that produces Chanel purses (retailing for over $2,000 each) told one of your authors that it takes back unsold inventory and destroys it rather than selling it at a discount.

Price skimming works best when the market is willing to buy the product even though it carries an above-average price. For example, in 2011 there was significant buzz around the Chevy Volt, which led dealers to price the car above the $41,000 manufacturer's suggested retail price (MSRP)—some as high as $61,000. Today, however, the Volt faces more competition from other electric vehicles, such as the Nissan Leaf (MSRP $35,200). As a result, dealers are pricing the Volt closer to the new 2012 MSRP of $39,145.[4] Firms can also effectively use price skimming when a product is well protected legally, when it represents a technological breakthrough, or when it has in some other way blocked the entry of competitors. Managers may follow a skimming strategy when production cannot be expanded rapidly because of technological difficulties, shortages, or constraints imposed by the skill and time required to produce a product. As long as demand is greater than supply, skimming is an attainable strategy.

status quo pricing
charging a price identical to or very close to the competition's price

a more expensive item like a smoothie or a salad.[6]

If a firm has a low fixed cost structure and each sale provides a large contribution to those fixed costs, penetration pricing can boost sales and provide large increases in profits—but only if the market size grows or if competitors choose not to respond. Low prices can attract additional buyers to the market. The increased sales can justify production expansion or the adoption of new technologies, both of which can reduce costs. And, if firms have excess capacity, even low-priced business can provide incremental dollars toward fixed costs.

Penetration pricing can also be effective if an experience curve will cause costs per unit to drop significantly. The experience curve proposes that per-unit costs will go down as a firm's production experience increases. Manufacturers that fail to take advantage of these effects will find themselves at a competitive cost disadvantage relative to others that are further along the curve.

The big advantage of penetration pricing is that it typically discourages or blocks competition from entering a market. The disadvantage is that penetration means gearing up for mass production to sell a large volume at a low price. If the volume fails to materialize, the company will face huge losses from building or converting a factory to produce the failed product.

Penetration pricing can damage an entire industry's profit cycle if customers expect deep discounts if products do not sell or there is overstock. For example, the fashion industry suffered from inventory overflow during the recession and began deeply discounting inventory purchased before the economy took a nosedive. Because stores carried much of the same stock, their only option was to compete on price. Now, with the economy slowly recovering, the fashion industry is hoping to stabilize demand by offering fewer items, all at full price. JCPenney posted unexpected sales gains after introducing exclusive lines by Liz Claiborne and European designer Mango, which sold at full price.[7]

Sometimes, multinational firms will follow a skimming strategy in developed countries and a penetration strategy in developing countries. Procter & Gamble, for example, views low-income consumers in developing countries as crucial to its long-run growth strategy. The company known for its premium razors in developed countries has created the Gillette Guard, which costs 15 rupees (34 cents) and uses blades that cost 5 rupees (11 cents), for the India market. In contrast, P&G's Fusion Pro Glide razor system uses cartridges that sell for $16.99. In developing markets, P&G prices its products by determining what the consumer can afford and adjusting features and manufacturing processes to meet the target price. The Gillette Guard features a lightweight handle, which is preferred by Indian men, and eliminates the lubrication strip and colorful handle designs. P&G hopes that, as the Indian economy grows, customers will trade up to more expensive products.[8]

Status Quo Pricing The third basic price strategy a firm may choose is **status quo pricing**, also called meeting the competition or going rate pricing (see also

YOU CAN HAVE THIS FOR ONLY $0.00

Every day, we use services that cost us nothing. Google, Wikipedia, and open source software are available free of charge. Many popular Smartphone applications such as games are free but feature ad content that customers paying for the game won't see. One company in Brazil is taking free to another level. The Free Sample Club, in São Paulo, requires an annual registration fee of 50 reals, or about $28. Members can then go to the store and choose from 200 different products from over 130 companies. Customers are required to fill out online surveys, and the combination of free samples and survey feedback gives manufacturers a way to evaluate tastes and preferences through marketing research. Other firms participate in The Free Sample Club hoping to create ties and brand preference with a new group of consumers.[9]

SOURCE: Vivian Pereira, "Brazilians Embracing New Free-Sample Outlets," *International Herald Tribune*, July 10–11, 2010, 14.

© ANSON0618/SHUTTERSTOCK.COM

Chapter 19). It means charging a price identical to or very close to the competition's price.

Although status quo pricing has the advantage of simplicity, its disadvantage is that the strategy may ignore demand or cost or both. If the firm is comparatively small, however, meeting the competition may be the safest route to long-term survival.

LO 2 The Legality of Price Strategy

As we mentioned in Chapter 4, some pricing decisions are subject to government regulation. Among the issues that fall into this category are unfair trade practices, price fixing, price discrimination, and predatory pricing.

Unfair Trade Practices

In over half the states, **unfair trade practice acts** put a floor under wholesale and retail prices. Selling below cost in these states is illegal. Wholesalers and retailers must usually take a certain minimum percentage markup on their combined merchandise cost and transportation cost. The most common markup figures are 6 percent at the retail level and 2 percent at the wholesale level. If a specific wholesaler or retailer can provide "conclusive proof" that operating costs are lower than the minimum required figure, lower prices may be allowed.

The intent of unfair trade practice acts is to protect small local firms from giants like Walmart, which operates very efficiently on razor-thin profit margins. State enforcement of unfair trade practice laws has generally been lax, however, partly because low prices benefit local consumers.

Price Fixing

Price fixing is an agreement between two or more firms on the price they will charge for a product. Suppose two or more executives from competing firms meet to decide how much to charge for a product or to decide which of them will submit the lowest bid on a certain contract. Such practices are illegal under the Sherman Act and the Federal Trade Commission Act. Offenders have received fines and sometimes prison terms. Price fixing is one area where the law is quite clear, and the Justice Department's enforcement is vigorous.

International price fixing by private entities can be prosecuted under the antitrust laws of many countries. In April 2011, P&G and Unilever were fined roughly $450 million by the European Union for price fixing and pricing powdered laundry detergents at anticompetitive prices. The companies had been part of a coalition for reducing the amount of packaging in laundry detergent, but instead took the opportunity to protect market share and profit margins by agreeing to maintain prices despite smaller packaging.[10] In another example, in 2010, after nine years of investigations, New Zealand filed allegations against six transportation companies for allegedly fixing prices in international freight forwarding services to New Zealand. Under New Zealand's law, the penalty for a company found guilty of price fixing could be as much as $10 million to three times the company's net profit.[11] In 2011, three of the companies were fined a total of 5.2 million New Zealand dollars (U.S. $4.2 million).[12]

Most price-fixing cases focus on high prices charged to customers. A reverse form of price fixing occurs when powerful buyers force their suppliers' prices down. Recently, Maine blueberry growers alleged that four big processors conspired to push down the price they would pay for fresh wild berries. A state court jury agreed and awarded millions in damages.[13] Some price-fixing accusations are less clear-cut. For instance, Leegin Creative Leather Products sought to control its brand image by insisting that retailers charge a certain minimum price for its products. Leegin sued a boutique, Kay's Kloset, for offering its products at a lower price. The suit was decided in favor of

© STEPHEN COBURN/SHUTTERSTOCK.COM

unfair trade practice acts laws that prohibit wholesalers and retailers from selling below cost

price fixing an agreement between two or more firms on the price they will charge for a product

predatory pricing

the practice of charging a very low price for a product with the intent of driving competitors out of business or out of a market

Kay's, but appeals are ongoing and may influence the pricing and retail strategies of luxury goods companies trying to control their brand image.[14]

Price Discrimination

The Robinson-Patman Act of 1936 prohibits any firm from selling to two or more different buyers, within a reasonably short time, commodities (not services) of like grade and quality at different prices where the result would be to substantially lessen competition. The act also makes it illegal for a seller to offer two buyers different supplementary services and for buyers to use their purchasing power to force sellers into granting discriminatory prices or services. For a firm to violate the Robinson-Patman Act, it must meet the following six criteria:

1. There must be price discrimination—that is, the seller must charge different prices to different customers for the same product.

2. The transaction must occur in interstate commerce.

3. The seller must discriminate by price among two or more purchasers—that is, the seller must make two or more actual sales within a reasonably short time.

4. The products sold must be commodities or other tangible goods.

5. The products sold must be of like grade and quality, not necessarily identical. If the goods are truly interchangeable and substitutable, then they are of like grade and quality.

6. There must be significant competitive injury.

The Robinson-Patman Act provides three defenses for a seller charged with price discrimination (in each case the burden is on the seller to prove the defense):

▸▸ *Cost:* A firm can charge different prices to different customers if the prices represent manufacturing or quantity discount savings.

▸▸ *Market conditions:* Price variations are justified if designed to meet fluid product or market conditions. Examples include the deterioration of perishable goods, the obsolescence of seasonal products, a distress sale under court order, and a legitimate going-out-of-business sale.

▸▸ *Competition:* A reduction in price may be necessary to stay even with the competition. Specifically, if a competitor undercuts the price quoted by a seller to a buyer, the law authorizes the seller to lower the price charged to the buyer for the product in question.

Predatory Pricing

Predatory pricing is the practice of charging a very low price for a product with the intent of driving competitors out of business or out of a market. Once competitors have been driven out, the firm raises its prices. This practice is illegal under the Sherman Act and the Federal Trade Commission Act. To prove predatory pricing, the Justice Department must show that the predator—the destructive company—explicitly tried to ruin a competitor and that the predatory price was below the predator's average variable cost.

Prosecutions for predatory pricing suffered a major setback when a federal judge threw out a predatory pricing suit filed by the Justice Department against American Airlines. The Justice Department argued that the definition should be updated and that the test should be whether there was any business justification, other than driving away competitors, for American's aggressive pricing. Under that definition, the Justice Department attorneys thought they had a great case. Whenever a fledgling airline tried to get a toehold in the Dallas market, American would meet its fares and add flights. As soon as the rival retreated, American would jack its fares back up.

Under the average variable cost definition, however, the case would have been almost impossible to win. The reason is that like a high-tech industry, the airline industry has high fixed costs and low marginal costs. Once a flight is scheduled, the marginal cost of providing a seat for an additional passenger is almost zero. Thus, it is very difficult to prove that an airline is pricing below its average variable cost. The judge was

© ISTOCKPHOTO.COM/STEPHEN STRATHDEE

not impressed by the Justice Department's argument, however, and kept the average variable cost definition of predatory pricing.

LO3 Tactics for Fine-Tuning the Base Price

After managers understand both the legal and the marketing consequences of price strategies, they should set a **base price**—the general price level at which the company expects to sell the good or service. The general price level is correlated with the pricing policy: above the market (price skimming), at the market (status quo pricing), or below the market (penetration pricing). The final step, then, is to fine-tune the base price.

Fine-tuning techniques are short-run approaches that do not change the general price level. They do, however, result in changes within a general price level. These pricing tactics allow the firm to adjust for competition in certain markets, meet ever-changing government regulations, take advantage of unique demand situations, and meet promotional and positioning goals. Fine-tuning pricing tactics include various sorts of discounts, geographic pricing, and other pricing tactics.

Discounts, Allowances, Rebates, and Value-Based Pricing

A base price can be lowered through the use of discounts and the related tactics of allowances, rebates, low or zero percent financing, and value-based pricing. Managers use the various forms of discounts to encourage customers to do what they would not ordinarily do, such as paying cash rather than using credit, taking delivery out of season, or performing certain functions within a distribution channel.[15] The following are the most common tactics:

▸▸ *Quantity discounts:* When buyers get a lower price for buying in multiple units or above a specified dollar amount, they are receiving a **quantity discount**. A **cumulative quantity discount** is a deduction from list price that applies to the buyer's total purchases made during a specific period; it is intended to encourage customer loyalty. In contrast, a **noncumulative quantity discount** is a deduction from list price that applies to a single order rather than to the total volume of orders placed during a certain period. It is intended to encourage orders in large quantities.

▸▸ *Cash discounts:* A **cash discount** is a price reduction offered to a consumer, an industrial user, or a marketing intermediary in return for prompt payment of a bill. Prompt payment saves the seller carrying charges and billing expenses and allows the seller to avoid bad debt.

▸▸ *Functional discounts:* When distribution channel intermediaries, such as wholesalers or retailers, perform a service or function for the manufacturer, they must be compensated. This compensation, typically a percentage discount from the base price, is called a **functional discount** (or **trade discount**). Functional discounts vary greatly from channel to channel, depending on the tasks performed by the intermediary.

▸▸ *Seasonal discounts:* A **seasonal discount** is a price reduction for buying merchandise out of season. It shifts the storage function to the purchaser. Seasonal discounts also enable manufacturers to maintain a steady production schedule year-round.

▸▸ *Promotional allowances:* A **promotional allowance** (also known as a **trade allowance**) is a payment to a dealer for promoting the manufacturer's products. It is both a pricing tool and a promotional device. As a pricing tool, a promotional allowance is like a functional discount. If, for example, a retailer runs an ad for a manufacturer's product, the manufacturer may pay half the cost.

▸▸ *Rebates:* A **rebate** is a cash refund given for the purchase of a product during a specific period. The advantage of a rebate over a simple price reduction for stimulating demand is that a rebate is a temporary inducement that can be taken away without altering the basic price structure. A manufacturer that uses a simple price reduction for a short time may meet resistance when trying to restore the price to its original, higher level.

▸▸ *Zero percent financing:* During the mid and late 2000s, new-car sales receded. To get people back into the automobile showrooms, manufacturers offered zero percent financing, which enabled purchasers to borrow money to pay for new cars with no interest charge. The tactic created a huge increase in sales but not without cost to the manufacturers. A five-year interest-free car

base price the general price level at which the company expects to sell the good or service

quantity discount a price reduction offered to buyers buying in multiple units or above a specified dollar amount

cumulative quantity discount a deduction from list price that applies to the buyer's total purchases made during a specific period

noncumulative quantity discount a deduction from list price that applies to a single order rather than to the total volume of orders placed during a certain period

cash discount a price reduction offered to a consumer, an industrial user, or a marketing intermediary in return for prompt payment of a bill

functional discount (trade discount) a discount to wholesalers and retailers for performing channel functions

seasonal discount a price reduction for buying merchandise out of season

promotional allowance (trade allowance) a payment to a dealer for promoting the manufacturer's products

rebate a cash refund given for the purchase of a product during a specific period

value-based pricing setting the price at a level that seems to the customer to be a good price compared to the prices of other options

loan represented a cost of over $3,000 on a typical vehicle sold during a zero percent promotion.

Value-Based Pricing

Value-based pricing, also called *value pricing*, is a pricing strategy that has grown out of the quality movement. It became very popular during the recent recession. Instead of figuring prices based on costs or competitors' prices, it starts with the customer, considers the competition, and then determines the appropriate price. The basic assumption is that the firm is customer driven, seeking to understand the attributes customers want in the goods and services they buy and the value of that bundle of attributes to customers. Because very few firms operate in a pure monopoly, however, a marketer using value-based pricing must also determine the value of competitive offerings to customers. Customers determine the value of a product (not just its price) relative to the value of alternatives. In value-based pricing, therefore, the price of the product is set at a level that seems to the customer to be a good price compared with the prices of other options.

Shoppers in competitive markets are seeing prices fall as Walmart pushes rivals to match its value prices. The firm continued to up the ante in 2010 by further reducing prices on more than 10,000 items.[16] Such reduced prices have conditioned consumers to expect inexpensive goods every day. Customer expectations have pressured regional grocery chains to switch to value pricing. Traditionally, these chains offered weekly specials to attract shoppers and made up the lost profit through higher regular prices. For example, Safeway long banked on customers paying higher prices in return for top-quality fresh produce and upscale ambience. Now, even though it has cut its regular prices, Safeway is still more than 10 percent more expensive than Kroger. The result has been declines in both sales and profitability.[17]

Many companies responded to the recession of 2007–2009 by introducing value-pricing strategies. C.F. Martin, manufacturer of guitars favored by Elvis Presley, Gene Autry, and Eric Clapton, sells its average price guitar for around $2,000 to $3,000, with limited editions going for over $100,000. To avoid laying off skilled woodworkers during the recession, Martin released a solid wood version of a 1930s guitar model without frills such as inlays. Called the 1.Series model because of its simplicity, the guitar is priced at under $1,000. The company easily sold out its first year's output of 8,000 guitars.[18]

Pricing Products Too Low Sometimes managers price their products too low, thereby reducing company profits. This seems to happen for two reasons. First, managers attempt to buy market share through aggressive pricing. Usually, however, these price cuts are quickly met by competitors. Thus, any gain in market share is short-lived, and overall industry profits end up falling. Second, managers have a natural tendency to want to make decisions that can be justified objectively.

The problem is that companies often lack hard data on the complex determinants of profitability, such as the relationship between

In this advertisement, IKEA is using value-based pricing to bring customers into the store and to encourage shoppers to buy as much seating as they need.

NEW LOWER PRICE

KARLSTAD two chaises + sofa

$997

10 YEAR

Have a seat. Or two. Or three.

With the KARLSTAD series, you have the flexibility to create the perfect seating combination. Combine the different KARLSTAD pieces to create a solution that sits right with your home. Sink into an extra soft loveseat. Or pair it with an armchair or a free-standing chaise — whatever works best for you. You can even choose from a variety of legs and washable covers. So go ahead, find your comfort combination.

IKEA

IKEA-USA.com/KARLSTAD

KARLSTAD seating has a 10-year limited warranty. See **IKEA store** or **IKEA-USA.com**

COURTESY, SUSAN VAN ETTEN

PRICING PRODUCTS TOO LOW CAN REDUCE PROFITS.

© ISTOCKPHOTO.COM/NICOLAS LORAN

high-volume commodities with a competitive market and which were customized products with limited or no competition. Then they determined which products offered some unique value, such as faster delivery or better design. Parker's strategic pricing process led to some price cuts for its basic products and to price increases of more than 25 percent for its custom products. Parker's net income soared, from $130 million in 2002 to $830 million in 2007. Its return on investment capital rose from 7 percent to 21 percent over that same period.[20]

price changes and sales volumes, the link between demand levels and costs, and the likely responses of competitors to price changes. In contrast, companies usually have rich, unambiguous information on costs, sales, market share, and competitors' prices. As a result, managers tend to make pricing decisions based on current costs, projected short-term share gains, or current competitor prices rather than on long-term profitability.

The problem of "underpricing" can be solved by linking information about price, cost, and demand within the same decision support system. The demand data can be developed via marketing research. This will enable managers to get the hard data they need to calculate the effects of pricing decisions on profitability. Parker Hannifin Corporation makes industrial components used in everything from the space shuttle to a mechanism for tilting the model steamship used in the movie *Titanic*. The company was successful, but it was stuck in a profit-margin rut. It couldn't seem to improve its return on invested capital. Like most U.S. manufacturers, Parker used a "cost-plus" pricing method—calculating how much it cost to make a product and adding a flat percentage on top, usually 35 percent. Then its new CEO, Donald Washkewicz, decided to start thinking less like a "widget maker" and more like a retailer.[19] That meant that Parker Hannifin started determining its prices by what a consumer was willing to pay instead of by what a product cost to make. Washkewicz had his new "pricing gurus" determine which products were

Geographic Pricing

Because many sellers ship their wares to a nationwide or even a worldwide market, the cost of freight can greatly affect the total cost of a product. Sellers may use several different geographic pricing tactics to moderate the impact of freight costs on distant customers. The following methods of geographic pricing are the most common:

▸▸ *FOB origin pricing:* **FOB origin pricing**, also called *FOB factory* or *FOB shipping point,* is a price tactic that requires the buyer to absorb the freight costs from the shipping point ("free on board"). The farther buyers are from sellers, the more they pay, because transportation costs generally increase with the distance merchandise is shipped.

▸▸ *Uniform delivered pricing:* If the marketing manager wants total costs, including freight, to be equal for all purchasers of identical products, the firm will adopt uniform delivered pricing, or "postage stamp" pricing. With **uniform delivered pricing**, the seller pays the actual freight charges and bills every purchaser an identical, flat freight charge.

▸▸ *Zone pricing:* A marketing manager who wants to equalize total costs among buyers within large geographic areas—but not necessarily all of the seller's market area—may modify the base price with a zone-pricing tactic. **Zone pricing** is a modification of uniform delivered pricing. Rather than using a uniform freight rate for the entire United States (or its total market), the firm divides it into segments or zones and charges a flat freight rate to all customers in a given zone. The U.S. Postal Service's parcel post rate structure is probably the best-known zone-pricing system in the country.

FOB origin pricing a price tactic that requires the buyer to absorb the freight costs from the shipping point ("free on board")

uniform delivered pricing a price tactic in which the seller pays the actual freight charges and bills every purchaser an identical, flat freight charge

zone pricing a modification of uniform delivered pricing that divides the United States (or the total market) into segments or zones and charges a flat freight rate to all customers in a given zone

freight absorption pricing a price tactic in which the seller pays all or part of the actual freight charges and does not pass them on to the buyer

basing-point pricing a price tactic that charges freight from a given (basing) point, regardless of the city from which the goods are shipped

single-price tactic a price tactic that offers all goods and services at the same price (or perhaps two or three prices)

flexible pricing (variable pricing) a price tactic in which different customers pay different prices for essentially the same merchandise bought in equal quantities

▸ *Freight absorption pricing:* In **freight absorption pricing**, the seller pays all or part of the actual freight charges and does not pass them on to the buyer. The manager may use this tactic in intensely competitive areas or as a way to break into new market areas.

▸ *Basing-point pricing:* With **basing-point pricing**, the seller designates a location as a basing point and charges all buyers the freight cost from that point, regardless of the city from which the goods are shipped. Thanks to several adverse court rulings, basing-point pricing has waned in popularity. Freight fees charged when none were actually incurred, called *phantom freight,* have been declared illegal.

Other Pricing Tactics

Unlike geographic pricing, other pricing tactics are unique and defy neat categorization. Managers use these tactics for various reasons—for example, to stimulate demand for specific products, to increase store patronage, and to offer a wider variety of merchandise at a specific price point. "Other" pricing tactics include a single-price tactic, flexible pricing, professional services pricing, price lining, leader pricing, bait pricing, odd–even pricing, price bundling, and two-part pricing.

Single-Price Tactic A merchant using a **single-price tactic** offers all goods and services at the same price (or perhaps two or three prices). Apple hopes to mimic the early success of iTunes' single-price tactic in television show and movie rentals. iTunes now rents high-definition television shows for 99 cents and new movie releases for $4.99.[21]

Single-price selling removes price comparisons from the buyer's decision-making process. The retailer enjoys the benefits of a simplified pricing system and minimal clerical errors. However, continually rising costs are a headache for retailers following this strategy. In times of inflation, they must frequently raise the selling price.

Sometimes using a single price tactic can open the door for competition. For years, UPS prided itself on charging one price to all its customers. But when FedEx entered the market, one reason for its swift success was its variable pricing, which recognized inherent value differences between customers, orders

(parcels versus messages), and times of delivery (8 a.m. versus afternoon).[22]

Flexible Pricing **Flexible pricing** (or **variable pricing**) means that different customers pay different prices for essentially the same merchandise bought in equal quantities. This tactic is often found in the sale of shopping goods, specialty merchandise, and most industrial goods except supply items. Car dealers and many appliance retailers commonly follow the practice. It allows the seller to adjust for competition by meeting another seller's price. Thus, a marketing manager with a status quo pricing objective might readily adopt the tactic. Flexible pricing also enables the seller to close a sale with price-conscious consumers.

The obvious disadvantages of flexible pricing are the lack of consistent profit margins, the potential ill will of high-paying purchasers, the tendency for salespeople to automatically lower the price to make a sale, and the possibility of a price war among sellers.

Trade-Ins Flexible pricing and trade-ins often go hand in hand. About 57 percent of all new car sales involve a trade-in.[23] Trade-ins occur for other products as well, such as musical instruments, sporting goods, jewelry, and some appliances. If a trade-in is involved, the consumer must negotiate two prices, one for the new product and one for the existing product. The existence of a trade-in raises several questions for the purchaser. For example, will the new product's price differ depending on whether there is a trade-in? Are consumers better off trading in their used product toward the purchase of the new one from the same retailer, or should they keep the two transactions separate by dealing with different retailers? Several car buying guides, such as Edmunds.com and Autotrader.com, advise consumers to keep the two transactions separate.[24]

Recent research found that trade-in customers tend to care more about the trade-in value they receive than the price they pay for the new product. Thus, these buyers tend to pay more than purchasers without a trade-in. Analysis of data from the automobile market found that, on average, trade-in customers end up paying $452 more than customers who simply buy a new car from a dealer.[25]

Professional Services Pricing Professional services pricing is used by people with lengthy experience, training, and often certification by a licensing board—for example, lawyers, physicians, and family counselors.

Professionals sometimes charge customers at an hourly rate, but sometimes fees are based on the solution of a problem or performance of an act (such as an eye examination) rather than on the actual time involved.

Those who use professional pricing have an ethical responsibility not to overcharge a customer. Because demand is sometimes highly inelastic, such as when a person requires heart surgery to survive, there may be a temptation to charge "all the traffic will bear."[26]

Price Lining When a seller establishes a series of prices for a type of merchandise, it creates a price line. **Price lining** is the practice of offering a product line with several items at specific price points. Wireless providers use price lining for cellphones that are purchased with a two-year contract. The top tier is priced at $299 (the highest the market will pay), and subsequent tiers are $249, $199, $149, $99, and $49. Apple's iTunes has moved single-track purchases from a flat fee to a price line structure. The most popular tracks are $1.29 each, with less popular tracks priced at 99 cents or 69 cents.

Price lining reduces confusion for both the salesperson and the consumer. The buyer may be offered a wider variety of merchandise at each established price. Price lines may also enable a seller to reach several market segments. For buyers, the question of price may be quite simple: All they have to do is find a suitable product at the predetermined price. Moreover, price lining is a valuable tactic for the marketing manager, because the firm may be able to carry a smaller total inventory than it could without price lines. The results may include fewer markdowns, simplified purchasing, and lower inventory carrying charges.

Professionals, such as legal advisers, have an ethical responsibility to price services fairly.

© GINA SANDERS/SHUTTERSTOCK.COM

Price lines also present drawbacks, especially if costs are continually rising. Sellers can offset rising costs in three ways. First, they can begin stocking lower-quality merchandise at each price point. Second, sellers can change the prices, although frequent price line changes confuse buyers. Third, sellers can accept lower profit margins and hold quality and prices constant. This third alternative has short-run benefits, but its long-run handicaps may drive sellers out of business.

AT&T has set up a two-tiered price line for its Smartphone broadband users. Instead of charging $30 a month for unlimited use, AT&T now offers 200 megabytes for $15 a month or two gigabytes for $25, with added charges if the customer exceeds the ceiling. AT&T says that 98 percent of its customers consume less than two gigabytes a month.[27] Verizon also uses a tiered access plan. To date, Sprint Nextel and T-Mobile are staying with a flat rate price in an attempt to win market share.[28]

Leader Pricing **Leader pricing** (or **loss-leader pricing**) is an attempt by the marketing manager to attract customers by selling a product near or even below cost in the hope that shoppers will buy other items once they are in the store. This type of pricing appears weekly in the newspaper advertising of supermarkets. Leader pricing is normally used on well-known items that consumers can easily recognize as bargains. The trend of geo-social loss leader campaigns is growing in popularity as companies see how successful leader pricing is at enticing people to buy. Gap recently offered a coupon through social coupon site Groupon that used leader pricing. The coupon offered $50 worth of merchandise at Gap for $25. Gap grossed $11 million in coupon sales, selling as many as 534 of the coupons a minute.[29] Gap did not release sales data for the coupon's impact, but many bloggers believed that the back-to-school shopping season would result in shoppers spending more than $50 when they visited Gap.[30]

Leader pricing is not limited to products. Health clubs offer a one-month free trial as a loss leader.

Bait Pricing In contrast to leader pricing, which is a genuine attempt to give the consumer a reduced price, bait pricing is deceptive. **Bait pricing** tries to

price lining the practice of offering a product line with several items at specific price points

leader pricing (loss-leader pricing) a price tactic in which a product is sold near or even below cost in the hope that shoppers will buy other items once they are in the store

bait pricing a price tactic that tries to get consumers into a store through false or misleading price advertising and then uses high-pressure selling to persuade consumers to buy more expensive merchandise

odd–even pricing (psychological pricing) a price tactic that uses odd-numbered prices to connote bargains and even-numbered prices to imply quality

price bundling marketing two or more products in a single package for a special price

unbundling reducing the bundle of services that comes with the basic product

get consumers into a store through false or misleading price advertising and then uses high-pressure selling to persuade them to buy more expensive merchandise. You may have seen this ad or a similar one:

> REPOSSESSED . . . Singer slant-needle sewing machine . . . take over 8 payments of $5.10 per month . . . ABC Sewing Center.

This is bait. When a customer goes in to see the machine, a salesperson says that it has just been sold or else shows the prospective buyer a piece of junk. Then the salesperson says, "But I've got a really good deal on this fine new model." This is the switch that may cause a susceptible consumer to walk out with a $400 machine. The Federal Trade Commission considers bait pricing a deceptive act and has banned its use in interstate commerce. Most states also ban bait pricing, but sometimes enforcement is lax.

Odd–Even Pricing **Odd–even pricing** (or **psychological pricing**) means pricing at odd-numbered prices to connote a bargain and pricing at even-numbered prices to imply quality. For years, many retailers have priced their products in odd numbers—for example, $99.95—to make consumers feel they are paying a lower price for the product. Even-numbered pricing is often used for "prestige" items, such as a fine perfume at $100 a bottle or a good watch at $500. The demand curve for such items would also be sawtoothed, except that the outside edges would represent even-numbered prices and, therefore, elastic demand.

Price Bundling **Price bundling** is marketing two or more products in a single package for a special price. For example, Microsoft offers "suites" of software that bundle spreadsheets, word processing, graphics, e-mail, Internet access, and groupware for networks of microcomputers. Price bundling can stimulate demand for the bundled items if the target market perceives the price as a good value.

Services like hotels and airlines sell a perishable commodity (hotel rooms and airline seats) with relatively constant fixed costs. Bundling can be an important income stream for these businesses because the variable cost tends to be low—for instance, the cost of

cleaning a hotel room. Therefore, most of the revenue can help cover fixed costs and generate profits.

Bundling has also been used in the telecommunications industry. Companies offer local service, long distance, DSL Internet service, wireless, and even cable television in various menus of bundling. Telecom companies use bundling as a way to protect their market share and fight off competition by locking customers into a group of services. For consumers, comparison shopping may be difficult since they may not be able to determine how much they are really paying for each component of the bundle. A related price tactic is **unbundling**, or reducing the bundle of services that comes with the basic product. To help hold the line on costs, some stores require customers to pay for gift wrapping. Airlines charge for selecting a good seat, food, and checked baggage, all services that used to be bundled into the price of the ticket.

Clearly, price bundling can influence consumers' purchase behavior. But what about the decision to consume a particular bundled product or service? Some research has focused on how people consume certain bundled products or services. According to this research, the key to consumption behavior is how closely consumers can link the costs and benefits of the exchange.[31] In complex transactions like a holiday package, it may be unclear which costs are paying for which benefits. In such cases, consumers tend to mentally downplay their up-front costs for the bundled product, so they may be more likely to forgo a benefit that's part of the bundle, like a free dinner.

Similarly, when people buy season tickets to a concert series, sporting event, or other activity, the sunk costs (price of the bundle) and the pending benefit (going to see an event) become decoupled. This reduces the likelihood of consumption of the event over time.

Theatergoers who purchase tickets to a single play are almost certain to use those tickets. This is consistent with the idea that in a one-to-one transaction (i.e., one payment, one benefit), the costs and benefits of that transaction are tightly coupled, resulting in strong sunk cost pressure to consume the pending benefit.

A theater manager might expect a no-show rate of 20 percent when the percentage of season ticket holders is high, but a no-show rate of only 5 percent when the percentage of season ticket holders is low. With a high number of season ticket holders, a manager could oversell performances and maximize the revenue for the theater.

© PHOTODISC/GETTY IMAGES

The physical format of the transaction also figures in. A ski lift pass in the form of a booklet of tickets strengthens the cost–benefit link for consumers, whereas a single pass for multiple ski lifts weakens that link.

Though price bundling of services can result in a lower rate of total consumption of that service, the same is not necessarily true for products. Consider the purchase of an expensive bottle of wine. When the wine is purchased as a single unit, its cost and eventual benefit are tightly coupled. As a result, the cost of the wine will be important, and a person will likely reserve that wine for a special occasion. When purchased as part of a bundle (e.g., as part of a case of wine), however, the cost and benefit of that individual bottle of wine will likely become decoupled, reducing the impact of the cost on eventual consumption. Thus, in contrast to the price bundling of services, the price bundling of physical goods could lead to an increase in product consumption.

Two-Part Pricing **Two-part pricing** means establishing two separate charges to consume a single good or service. Airlines have moved to a two-part pricing system, charging the base ticket price, then offering passengers additional perks such as meals, extra leg room, in-flight movies, and trip insurance for additional costs. Last year these fees resulted in approximately $22 billion in revenue for the airline industry.[32]

Consumers sometimes prefer two-part pricing because they are uncertain about the number and the types of activities they might use at places like an amusement park. Also, the people who use a service most often pay a higher total price. Two-part pricing can increase a seller's revenue by attracting consumers who would not pay a high fee even for unlimited use. For example, a health club might be able to sell only 100 memberships at $700 annually with unlimited use of facilities, for a total revenue of $70,000. However, it could sell 900 memberships at $200 with a guarantee of using the racquetball courts ten times a month. Every use over ten would require the member to pay a $5 fee. Thus, membership revenue would provide a base of $180,000, with some additional usage fees throughout the year.

Research has shown that when consumers are thinking of buying a good or service with two-part pricing, they may mentally process the base price, such as a membership fee, more thoroughly than the extra fee or surcharge (playing a game of tennis). Thus, they can underestimate the total price compared with when prices are not partitioned.[33] The researchers also found that low-perceived benefit components should be priced relatively low and vice versa. Consumers find a higher total price more acceptable when the high-benefit component is priced high than when the low-benefit component is priced high. For example, assume John joins a health club and swims at the club four times a month. John really enjoys working out and views being a member of the club as part of a healthy lifestyle (high value). He also swims after a workout once a week to unwind and relax. For John, swimming is not that important but is enjoyable (low value). If the club charges $60 a month dues and $5 per swim, John perceives this as acceptable. According to the research, John would find it less attractive if the monthly dues were $40 and each swim was $10. Yet the total cost is the same!

Pay What You Want To many people, paying what you want or what you think something is worth is a very risky tactic. Obviously, it wouldn't work for expensive durables like automobiles.

> **two-part pricing** a price tactic that charges two separate amounts to consume a single good or service

Bundles, like season theater tickets, decouple the up-front cost from the pending benefits.

© FERENC SZELEPCSENYI/SHUTTERSTOCK.COM

consumer penalty
an extra fee paid by the consumer for violating the terms of the purchase agreement

product line pricing setting prices for an entire line of products

joint costs costs that are shared in the manufacturing and marketing of several products in a product line

Imagine someone paying $1 for a new BMW! Yet this model has worked in varying degrees in restaurants and other service businesses. One of your authors has patronized a restaurant close to campus that uses "pay what you think it is worth." After several years, the restaurant is still in business. The owner says that the average lunch donation is around $8. Social pressures can come into play in a "pay what you want" environment because an individual doesn't want to appear poor or cheap to his or her peers. Radiohead's 2007 album *In Rainbows* allowed online purchasers to pay as much or as little as they wanted to download the digital album.

Consumer Penalties

More and more businesses are adopting **consumer penalties**—extra fees paid by consumers for violating the terms of a purchase agreement. Businesses impose consumer penalties for two reasons: They will allegedly (1) suffer an irrevocable revenue loss and/or (2) incur significant additional transaction costs should customers be unable or unwilling to complete their purchase obligations. For the company, these customer payments are part of doing business in a highly competitive marketplace. With profit margins in many companies increasingly coming under pressure, organizations are looking to stem losses resulting from customers not meeting their obligations. However, the perceived unfairness of a penalty may affect some consumers' willingness to patronize a business in the future.

LO 4 Product Line Pricing

Product line pricing is setting prices for an entire line of products. Compared to setting the right price on a single product, product line pricing encompasses broader concerns. In product line pricing, the marketing manager tries to achieve maximum profits or other goals for the entire line rather than for a single component of the line.

Relationships among Products

The manager must first determine the type of relationship that exists among the various products in a line:

▸ If items are *complementary,* an increase in the sale of one good causes an increase in demand for the complementary product, and vice versa. For example, the sale of ski poles depends on the demand for skis, making these two items complementary.

▸ Two products in a line can also be *substitutes* for each other. If buyers buy one item in the line, they are less likely to buy a second item in the line.

▸ A *neutral* relationship can also exist between two products. In other words, demand for one of the products is unrelated to demand for the other.

Joint Costs

Joint costs are costs that are shared in the manufacturing and marketing of several products in a product line. These costs pose a unique problem in product pricing (e.g., the production of televisions that combine TVs and Blu-ray players).

Any assignment of joint costs must be somewhat subjective because costs are actually shared. Suppose a company produces two products, X and Y, in a common production process, with joint costs allocated on a weight basis. Product X weighs 1,000 pounds, and product Y weighs 500 pounds. Thus, costs are allocated on the basis of $2 for X for every $1 for Y. Gross margins (sales less the cost of goods sold) might then be as follows:

	Product X	Product Y	Total
Sales	$20,000	$6,000	$26,000
Less cost of goods sold	15,000	7,500	22,500
Gross margin	$ 5,000	($1,500)	$ 3,500

This statement reveals a loss of $1,500 on product Y. However, the firm must realize that overall it earned a $3,500 profit on the two items in the line. Also, weight may not be the right way to allocate the joint costs. Instead, the firm might use other bases, including market value or quantity sold.

LO 5 Pricing during Difficult Economic Times

Pricing is always an important aspect of marketing, but it is especially crucial in times of inflation and recession. The firm that does not adjust to economic trends may lose ground that it can never make up.

Inflation

When the economy is characterized by high inflation, special pricing tactics are often necessary. They can be subdivided into cost-oriented and demand-oriented tactics.

Cost-Oriented Tactics One popular cost-oriented tactic is *culling products with a low profit margin* from the product line. However, this tactic may backfire for three reasons:

▸▸ A high volume of sales on an item with a low profit margin may still make the item highly profitable.

▸▸ Eliminating a product from a product line may reduce economies of scale, thereby lowering the margins on other items.

▸▸ Eliminating the product may affect the price-quality image of the entire line.

Another popular cost-oriented tactic is **delayed-quotation pricing**, which is used for industrial installations and many accessory items. Price is not set on the product until the item is either finished or delivered. Long production lead times force many firms to adopt this policy during periods of inflation. Builders of nuclear power plants, ships, airports, and office towers sometimes use delayed-quotation tactics.

Escalator pricing is similar to delayed-quotation pricing in that the final selling price reflects cost increases incurred between the time an order is placed and the time delivery is made. An escalator clause allows for price increases (usually across the board) based on the cost-of-living index or some other formula. As with any price increase, management's ability to implement such a policy is based on inelastic demand for the product. Often it is used only for extremely complex products that take a long time to produce or with new customers. Another tactic growing in popularity is to hold prices constant but add new fees.

Any cost-oriented pricing policy that tries to maintain a fixed gross margin under all conditions can lead to a vicious circle. For example, a price increase will result in decreased demand, which in turn increases production costs (because of lost economies of scale). Increased production costs require a further price increase, leading to further diminished demand, and so on.

Demand-Oriented Tactics Demand-oriented pricing tactics use price to reflect changing patterns of demand caused by inflation or high interest rates. Cost changes are considered, of course, but mostly in the context of how increased prices will affect demand.

Price shading is the use of discounts by salespeople to increase demand for one or more products in a line. Often, shading becomes habitual and is done routinely without much forethought. To make the demand for a good or service more inelastic and to create buyer dependency, a company can use several strategies:

▸▸ *Cultivate selected demand:* Marketing managers can target prosperous customers who will pay extra for convenience or service. In cultivating close relationships with affluent organizational customers, marketing managers should avoid putting themselves at the mercy of a dominant firm. They can more easily raise prices when an account is readily replaceable. Finally, in companies where engineers exert more influence than purchasing departments do, performance is favored over price. Often a preferred vendor's pricing range expands if other suppliers prove technically unsatisfactory.

▸▸ *Create unique offerings:* Marketing managers should study buyers' needs. If the seller can design distinctive goods or services uniquely fitting buyers' activities, equipment, and procedures, a mutually beneficial relationship will evolve. By satisfying targeted buyers in a superior way, marketing managers can make them dependent. Cereal manufacturers have been able to pass along costs by marketing unique value-added or multi-ingredient cereals.

▸▸ *Change the package design:* Another way companies pass on higher costs is to shrink product sizes but keep prices the same. Skippy added an inwardly curved bottom to its peanut butter packaging, reducing volume slightly, but maintained the same price.[34]

▸▸ *Heighten buyer dependence:* Owens Corning Fiberglass supplies an integrated insulation service that includes commercial and scientific training for distributors and seminars for end users. This practice freezes out competition and supports higher prices.

---

delayed-quotation pricing
a price tactic used for industrial installations and many accessory items in which a firm price is not set until the item is either finished or delivered

escalator pricing
a price tactic in which the final selling price reflects cost increases incurred between the time the order is placed and the time delivery is made

price shading the use of discounts by salespeople to increase demand for one or more products in a line

© MIKE KEMP/RUBBERBALL/PHOTOLIBRARY

Recession

As discussed in Chapter 4, a recession is a period of reduced economic activity, such as occurred in the United States in 2007–2009. Reduced demand for goods and services, along with higher rates of unemployment, is a common trait of a recession. Yet astute marketers can often find opportunity during recessions. A recession is an excellent time to build market share because competitors are struggling to make ends meet.

According to pricing strategy consultants Paul Hunt and Greg Thomas, using pricing research to adjust prices during a recession or difficult economic conditions can result in a profit improvement of 20 percent, sometimes more.[35]

Two effective pricing tactics to hold or build market share during a recession are value-based pricing and bundling. *Value-based pricing*, discussed earlier in the chapter, stresses to customers that they are getting a good value for their money.

Bundling or *unbundling* can also stimulate demand during a recession. If features are added to a bundle, consumers may perceive the offering as having greater value. Conversely, companies can unbundle offerings and lower base prices to stimulate demand.

Recessions are a good time for marketing managers to study the demand for individual items in a product line and the revenue they produce. Pruning unprofitable items can save resources to be better used elsewhere.

Prices often fall during a recession as competitors try desperately to maintain demand for their wares. Even if demand remains constant, falling prices mean lower profits or no profits. Falling prices, therefore, are a natural incentive to lower costs. During the past recession, companies implemented new technology to improve efficiency and then slashed payrolls. They also discovered that suppliers were an excellent source of cost savings; the cost of purchased materials accounts for slightly more than half of most U.S. manufacturers' expenses. Specific strategies that companies use with suppliers include the following:

- ▸▸ *Renegotiating contracts:* Sending suppliers letters demanding price cuts of 5 percent or more; putting out for rebid the contracts of those that refuse to cut costs.

- ▸▸ *Offering help:* Dispatching teams of experts to suppliers' plants to help reorganize and suggest other productivity-boosting changes; working with suppliers to make parts simpler and cheaper to produce.

- ▸▸ *Keeping the pressure on:* To make sure that improvements continue, setting annual, across-the-board cost reduction targets, often of 5 percent or more a year.

- ▸▸ *Paring down suppliers:* To improve economies of scale, slashing the overall number of suppliers, sometimes by up to 80 percent, and boosting purchases from those that remain.

STUDY TOOLS CHAPTER 20

Flip to the back of your textbook to:
- ❑ **Rip out Chapter Review Card**

Log in to the CourseMate for MKTG at cengagebrain.com to:
- ❑ **Review Key Terms Flash Cards (Print or Online)**
- ❑ **Review Audio and Visual Summaries**
- ❑ **Complete both Practice Quizzes to prepare for tests**
- ❑ **Play "Beat the Clock" and "Quizbowl" to master concepts**
- ❑ **Complete "Crossword Puzzle" to review key terms**
- ❑ **Watch the video on "Whirlpool" for a real company example on Setting the Right Price**

ANATOMY OF Product Line Pricing: McDonald's Menu

There would probably be little demand for a menu item that was out of the price/value range established by other items in McDonald's product line. For example, a $10 burger would be well out of the price range that McDonald's customers expect for that product class.

1 ... offers several related products.

2 ... sells related products individually and in combinations.

©2007–2008 MCDONALD'S

What would you pay for a fast-food burger?
$1 $2 $3 $~~10~~

3 ... offers a line of products of various sizes, qualities, and prices.

4 ... presents a limited number of prices for all its product offerings.

CHAPTER **21** Customer Relationship Management (CRM)

> CRM is often described as a closed-loop system that builds relationships with customers.

LO1 What Is Customer Relationship Management?

AFTER YOU FINISH THIS CHAPTER, GO TO **PAGE 359** FOR **STUDY TOOLS**

Customer relationship management is the ultimate goal of a new trend in marketing that focuses on understanding customers as individuals instead of as part of a group. To do so, marketers are making their communications more customer specific. This movement initially was popularized as one-to-one marketing. But CRM is a much broader approach to understanding and serving customer needs than is one-to-one marketing.

Customer relationship management (CRM) is a company-wide business strategy designed to optimize profitability, revenue, and customer satisfaction by focusing on highly defined and precise customer groups. This is accomplished by organizing the company around customer segments, establishing and tracking customer interactions with the company, fostering customer-satisfying behaviors, and linking all processes of the company from its customers through its suppliers. The difference between CRM and traditional mass marketing can be compared to shooting a rifle versus a shotgun. Instead of scattering messages far and wide across the spectrum of mass media (the shotgun approach), CRM marketers now are homing in on ways to effectively communicate with each customer (the rifle approach).

customer relationship management (CRM) a company-wide business strategy designed to optimize profitability, revenue, and customer satisfaction by focusing on highly defined and precise customer groups

What do you think?

I often complain when I'm dissatisfied with a business or a product because I feel it is my duty to do so.

1 2 3 4 5 6 7
STRONGLY DISAGREE   STRONGLY AGREE

Find out what others think at the CourseMate for MKTG. Log in at cengagebrain.com.

© DIEGO CERVO/SHUTTERSTOCK.COM

The Customer Relationship Management Cycle

On the surface, CRM may resemble a simplistic customer service strategy. But, though customer service is part of the CRM process, it is only a small part of a totally integrated approach to building customer relationships. CRM is often described as a closed-loop system that builds relationships with customers. Exhibit 21.1 illustrates this closed-loop system, one that is continuous and circular with no predefined starting or end point.[1]

To initiate the CRM cycle, a company must *identify customer relationships with the organization*. This may simply entail learning who the customers are or where they are located, or it may require more detailed information about the products and services they are using. VCC, an international retail construction company, invested in Smartphones and iPads equipped with CRM tools from IBM for VCC's business managers. These tools, such as Mobile Edge, allow business managers to upload data, identify prospects, and even highlight leads for work that is similar to existing projects, which encourages efficient lead follow-up.[2] In addition to basic demographic information, the types of information gathered include how frequently consumers purchase goods, how much they purchase, and how far they drive.

Next, the company must *understand the interactions with current customers*. Companies accomplish this by collecting data on all types of communications a customer has with the company. IBM's mobile technologies enable field managers to quickly locate and understand all previous interactions with a client without memorizing printouts or guessing in the field. Mobile technology gives VCC managers access to key information that allows them to answer customer queries and take specific courses of action based on previous decisions. In this phase, companies build on the initial information collected and develop a more useful database.

Using this knowledge of its customers and their interactions, the company then *captures relevant customer data on interactions*. After meeting with a potential or current client, VCC business managers can immediately upload information about the meeting, including decisions reached, proposals made, and data for the project, directly to the construction company's central database.

How can marketers realistically analyze and communicate with individual customers? The answer lies in how information technology is used to implement the CRM system. Fundamentally, a CRM approach is no more than the relationship cultivated by a salesperson with the customer. A successful salesperson builds a relationship over time, constantly thinks about what the customer needs and wants, and is mindful of the trends and patterns in the customer's purchase history. The salesperson may also inform, educate, and instruct the customer about new products, technology, or applications in anticipation of the customer's future needs or requirements.

This kind of thoughtful attention is the basis of successful CRM systems. Information technology is used not only to enhance the collection of customer data, but also to *store and integrate customer data* throughout the company and, ultimately, to "get to know" customers on a more personal level. Customer data are the firsthand responses that are obtained from customers through investigation or by asking direct questions. These initial data, which might include individual answers to questionnaires, responses on warranty cards, or lists of purchases recorded by electronic cash registers, have not yet been analyzed or interpreted.

The value of customer data depends on its consistency and on the system used to store it. Obtaining high-quality, actionable data from various sources is a key element in any CRM system. VCC works with IBM to maintain a well-organized CRM app so the business managers in the field have the

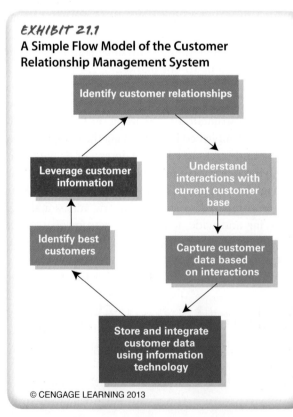

EXHIBIT 21.1

A Simple Flow Model of the Customer Relationship Management System

- Identify customer relationships
- Understand interactions with current customer base
- Capture customer data based on interactions
- Store and integrate customer data using information technology
- Identify best customers
- Leverage customer information

© CENGAGE LEARNING 2013

most relevant information to maintain customer relationships. Different kinds of database management software are available, from extremely high-tech, expensive, custom-designed databases to standardized programs.

Every customer wants to be a company's main priority. Yet not all customers are equally important in the eyes of a business. Consequently, the company must *identify its profitable and unprofitable customers*. Data mining is an analytical process that compiles actionable data about the purchase habits of a firm's current and potential customers. Essentially, data mining transforms customer data into customer information a company can use to make managerial decisions. For example, after VCC secures a new job, the iExtensions app flags similar opportunities as high priorities. Those flags are relayed to other business managers to pursue as well-qualfied leads.

© ISTOCKPHOTO.COM/SERGEY GALUSHKO

Once customer data are analyzed and transformed into usable information, the information must be *leveraged*. The CRM system sends the customer information to all areas of a business because the customer interacts with all aspects of the business. Essentially, the company is trying to enhance customer relationships by getting the right information to the right person in the right place at the right time.

VCC has found that getting timely customer information to its business managers has been profitable in several ways: New client business is up 40 percent; employees are working 400 fewer hours each month; and VCC has added clients in government, schools, and hospitals.[3]

Implementing a Customer Relationship Management System

Our discussion of a CRM system has assumed two key points. First, customers take center stage in any organization. Second, the business must manage the customer relationship across all points of customer contact throughout the entire organization. In the next sections, we examine how a CRM system is implemented and follow the progression depicted in Exhibit 21.1 as we explain each step in greater detail.

Identify Customer Relationships

Companies that have a CRM system follow a customer-centric focus or model. **Customer-centric** is an internal management philosophy similar to the marketing concept discussed in Chapter 1. Under this philosophy, the company customizes its product and service offering based on data generated through interactions between the customer and the company. This philosophy transcends all functional areas of the business, producing an internal system where all of the company's decisions and actions are a direct result of customer information.

A customer-centric company builds long-lasting relationships by focusing on what satisfies and retains valuable customers. For example, in Charlottesville, Virginia, Bill Crutchfield owns and operates a small electronics retailer called Crutchfield. The company has five stars on Yelp and is the only business to be awarded BizRate's Circle of Excellence award 11 years in a row for excellent online service. Crutchfield does this by imagining how a customer feels when he or she gets home with a new electronics product and has no idea how to install it. To ensure that all 500 employees can help a customer install or troubleshoot any of its products over the phone, Crutchfield engineers dissect each product and develop booklets with the product's specifications. Customer service representatives, salespeople, and tech support all receive the detailed information and use it to calm anxious customers or to direct new customers to the products that best fit their needs. Crutchfield even provides step-by-step, car-model-specific installation instructions for car stereos with pictures of Crutchfield mechanics installing the stereo in the vehicle. Customers love the service—besides ranking the company highly, they have kept it in business for 37 years without a single layoff.[4]

Customer-centric companies continually learn ways to enhance their product and service offerings. **Learning** in a CRM environment involves collecting customer information through comments and feedback on product and service performance.

Each unit of a business typically has its own way of recording what it learns and perhaps even its own

customer-centric
a philosophy under which the company customizes its product and service offering based on data generated through interactions between the customer and the company

learning an informal process of collecting customer data through customer comments and feedback on product or service performance

knowledge management the process by which learned information from customers is centralized and shared in order to enhance the relationship between customers and the organization

empowerment delegation of authority to solve customers' problems quickly—usually by the first person the customer notifies regarding the problem

interaction the point at which a customer and a company representative exchange information and develop learning relationships

customer information system. The departments' different interests make it difficult to pull all of the customer information together in one place using a common format. To overcome this problem, companies using CRM rely on knowledge management. **Knowledge management** is a process by which customer information is centralized and shared in order to enhance the relationship between customers and the organization. Information collected includes experiential observations, comments, customer actions, and qualitative facts about the customer.

As Chapter 1 explained, empowerment involves delegating authority to solve customers' problems. In other words, **empowerment** is the latitude organizations give their representatives to negotiate mutually satisfying commitments with customers. Usually, organizational representatives are able to make changes during interactions with customers through phone, fax, e-mail, Web communication, or face-to-face.

An **interaction** occurs when a customer and a company representative exchange information and develop learning relationships. With CRM, the customer—not the organization—defines the terms of the interaction, often by stating his or her preferences. The organization responds by designing products and services around customers' desired experiences. Starbucks implemented a Web site specifically for customers to suggest ideas for new products, ways to modify the Starbucks experience, and new opportunities for community involvement. Many customers posted that the noise level made by the blenders in Starbucks stores was negatively affecting the otherwise welcoming atmosphere. In response, Starbucks rolled out new, quiet blenders to all its stores. Starbucks has also responded to the call for healthy breakfast items and fresh fruit with oatmeal cups, egg white sandwiches, and a selection of fruit.[5]

The success of CRM—building lasting and profitable relationships—can be directly measured by the effectiveness of the interaction between the customer and the organization. In fact, what further differentiates CRM from other strategic initiatives is the organization's ability to establish and manage interactions with its current customer base. The more latitude (empowerment) a company gives its representatives, the more likely the interaction will conclude in a way that satisfies the customer.

For example, if a flight experiences a delay or is re-routed, or if there are other anomalies, Southwest Airlines e-mails all the customers on the flight within 24 hours. Each e-mail has a brief sincere apology, a short explanation, and a gift (usually a voucher). After a flight to Chicago was diverted to Milwaukee, Southwest sent an e-mail explaining that a sensor in the landing flaps went off, so the pilots needed to use a longer runway. Educating customers about why something happened has resulted in Southwest Airlines having the lowest customer complaint rate of all the major carriers. Delta Airlines, with the worst rating, receives more than nine times as many complaints as Southwest.[6]

LO3 Understand Interactions of the Current Customer Base

The *interaction* between the customer and the organization is the foundation on which a CRM system is built. Only through effective interactions can organizations learn about the expectations of their customers, generate and manage knowledge about them, negotiate mutually satisfying commitments, and build long-term relationships.

Exhibit 21.2 illustrates the customer-centric approach for managing customer interactions. Following a customer-centric approach, an interaction can occur through a formal or direct communication channel, such as a phone, the Internet, or a salesperson. Any activity or touch point a customer has with an organization, either directly or indirectly, constitutes an interaction.

© RUBBERBALL/JUPITERIMAGES

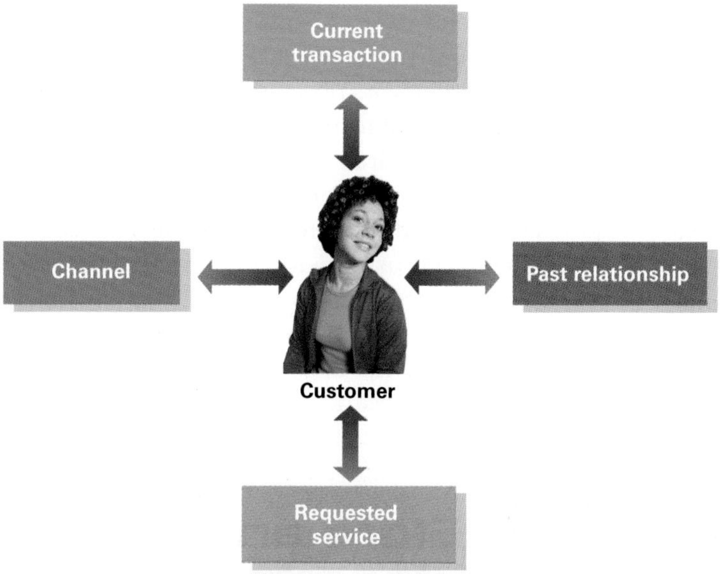

© IMAGE SOURCE/JUPITERIMAGES.

EXHIBIT 21.2
Customer-Centric Approach for Managing Customer Interactions

Companies that effectively manage customer interactions recognize that data provided by customers affect a wide variety of **touch points**. In a CRM system, touch points are all areas of a business where customers have contact with the company and data might be gathered. Touch points might include a customer registering for a particular service; a customer communicating with customer service for product information; a customer completing and returning the warranty information card for a product; or a customer talking with salespeople, delivery personnel, and product installers. Data gathered at these touch points, once interpreted, provide information that affects touch points inside the company. Interpreted information may be redirected to marketing research to develop profiles of extended warranty purchasers, to production to analyze recurring problems and repair components, and to accounting to establish cost-control models for repair service calls.

Web-based interactions are an increasingly popular touch point for customers to communicate with companies on their own terms. Web users can evaluate and purchase products, make reservations, input preferential data, and provide customer feedback on services and products. Data from these Web-based interactions are then captured, compiled, and used to segment customers, refine marketing efforts, develop new products, and deliver a degree of individual customization to improve customer relationships.

As social media have become more popular, many companies have begun to use these media for "social" CRM.[7] Essentially, social CRM takes the most successful aspects of traditional CRM, such as behavioral targeting, and expands them to include ways to engage customers through social media. This new paradigm includes a new customer recommendation value called the net promoter score. The net promoter score measures how much a customer influences the behavior of other customers through recommendations on social media. Social CRM also enables marketers to focus more on the relationship aspect of CRM. For example, REI empowers customers to "carve your own adventure" through its YouTube channel. Jet Blue uses Facebook and Twitter to provide advice and updates to travelers. To use social CRM effectively, companies must understand what sites customers use, whether they post opinions, and the major influencers in the category.

Another touch point is through **point-of-sale interactions** in stores or at information kiosks. Many point-of-sale software programs enable customers to easily provide information about themselves without feeling violated. The information is then used for marketing and merchandising activities, and to accurately identify the store's best customers and the types of products they buy. Data collected at point-of-sale interactions are also used to increase customer satisfaction through the development of in-store services and customer recognition promotions.

touch points all possible areas of a business where customers communicate with that business

point-of-sale interactions communications between customers and organizations that occur at the point of sale, normally in a store

LO 4 Capture Customer Data

Vast amounts of data can be obtained from the interactions between an organization and its customers. Therefore, in a CRM system, the issue is not how much data can be obtained, but rather what types of data should be acquired and how the data can effectively be used for relationship enhancement.

The traditional approach for acquiring data from customers is through channel interactions. Channel

data warehouse
a central repository for data from various functional areas of the organization that are stored and inventoried on a centralized computer system so that the information can be shared across all functional departments of the business

database a collection of data, especially one that can be accessed and manipulated by computer software

interactions include store visits, conversations with salespeople, interactions via the Web, traditional phone conversations, and wireless communications. In a CRM system, channel interactions are viewed as prime information sources based on the channel selected to initiate the interaction rather than on the data acquired. For example, when Frank Eliason was director of digital care at the Internet service provider Comcast, he monitored the microblogs on Twitter for customer complaints. Twitter offered different ways for him to interact with unhappy customers within the platform. Frank could reply directly in a message that the public could see, or he could send a private message to obtain their phone numbers so that Comcast software could check for Internet connection problems. Either way, Frank's helpful responses through the same medium where he received the complaints earned him followers on Twitter and enabled problems to be resolved quickly, making customers happy.[8] In some cases, companies use online chat to answer questions customers have about products they are looking for. For example, 24 Hour Fitness has an online chat window that opens when a potential customer begins to review the Web site. If the visitor remains on the site, the online chat window asks if he or she needs help finding something specific.

Interactions between the company and the customer facilitate the collection of large amounts of data. Companies can obtain not only simple contact information (name, address, phone number) but also data pertaining to the customer's current relationship with the organization—past purchase history, quantity and frequency of purchases, average amount spent on purchases, sensitivity to promotional activities, and so forth.

In this manner, a lot of information can be captured from one individual customer across several touch points. Multiply this by the thousands of customers across all of the touch points with an organization, and the volume of data can rapidly become unmanageable for company personnel. The large volume of data resulting from a CRM initiative can be managed effectively only through technology. Once customer data are collected, the question of who owns those data becomes extremely salient. In its privacy statement, Toysmart.com declared that it would never sell information registered at its Web site, including children's names and birth dates, to a third party. When the company filed for bankruptcy protection, it said the information collected constituted a company asset that needed to be sold off to pay creditors. Despite the outrage at this announcement, many dot-com companies closing their doors found they had little in the way of assets and followed Toysmart's lead.

LO5 Store and Integrate Customer Data

Customer data are only as valuable as the system in which the data are stored and the consistency and accuracy of the data captured. Gathering data is further complicated by the fact that data needed by one unit of the organization, such as sales and marketing, are often generated by another area of the business or even a third-party supplier, such as an independent marketing research firm. Thus, companies must use information technology to capture, store, and integrate strategically important customer information. This process of centralizing data in a CRM system is referred to as data warehousing.

A **data warehouse** is a central repository (*database*) of customer data collected by an organization. Essentially, it is a large computerized file of all information collected in the previous phase of the CRM process—for example, information collected in channel, transaction, and product/service touch points. The core of the data warehouse is the **database**, a collection of data, especially one that can be accessed and manipulated by computer software. The CRM database focuses on collecting vital statistics on consumers, their purchasing habits, transactions methods, and product usage in a centralized repository that is accessible by all functional areas of a company. By utilizing a data warehouse, marketing managers can quickly access vast amounts of information required to make decisions.

© ANDRESR/SHUTTERSTOCK.COM

When a company builds its database, usually the first step is to develop a list. A **response list** is based on customers who have indicated interest in a product or service, whereas a compiled list is created by an outside company that has collected names and contact information for potential consumers. Response lists tend to be especially valuable because past behavior is a strong predictor of future behavior and because consumers who have indicated interest in the product or service are more prone to purchase. Companies may find it valuable to enhance their customer records with information about the customers' or prospective customers' demographics and lifestyle characteristics. They can often accomplish this by augmenting the records with compiled lists. **Compiled lists** are created by an outside company that has collected names and contact information for potential consumers. This information is usually obtained from telephone directories and membership rosters of various groups. Lists range from those owned by large list companies, such as Dun & Bradstreet for business-to-business data and RR Donnelley and R.L. Polk for consumer lists, to small groups or associations that are willing to sell their membership lists. Indeed, many lists are compiled from people who have opted in to the list after they have purchased a related product. Data compiled by large data-gathering companies usually are very accurate.

In this phase, companies are usually collecting channel, transaction, and product/service information such as store, salesperson, communication channel, contact information, relationship, and brands.

A customer database becomes even more useful to marketing managers when it is enhanced to include more than simply a customer's or prospect's name, address, telephone number, and transaction history. Database enhancement involves purchasing information on customers or prospects to better describe their needs or determine how responsive they might be to marketing programs. Types of enhancement data typically include demographic, lifestyle, or behavioral information.

Database enhancement can increase the effectiveness of marketing programs. By learning more about their best and most profitable customers, marketers can maximize the effectiveness of marketing communications and cross-selling. Database enhancement also helps a company find new prospects.

Multinational companies building worldwide databases often face difficult problems when pulling together internal data about their customers. Differences in language, computer systems, and data-collection methods can be huge obstacles to overcome. Despite the challenges, many global companies are committed to building databases.

LO6 Identify the Best Customers

CRM manages interactions between a company and its customers. To be successful, companies must identify customers who yield high profits or potential profits. To do so, significant amounts of data must be gathered from customers, stored and integrated in the data warehouse, and then analyzed and interpreted for common patterns that can identify homogeneous customers who are different from other customer segments. Because not all customers are the same, organizations need to develop interactions that target *individual* customer needs and wants. Recall from Chapter 8 the 80/20 principle—80 percent of a company's revenue is generated by 20 percent of its customers. Therefore, the question becomes, how do we identify the 20 percent of our customer base that contributes 80 percent of our revenue? In a CRM system, the answer is data mining.

Data Mining

Data mining is used to find hidden patterns and relationships in the customer data stored in the data warehouse. It is a data analysis approach that identifies patterns of characteristics that relate to particular customers or customer groups. Although businesses have been conducting such analyses for many years, the procedures typically were performed on small data sets containing as few as 300 to 400 customers. Today, with the development of sophisticated data warehouses, millions of customers' shopping patterns can be analyzed.

Using data mining, marketers can search the data warehouse, capture relevant data, categorize significant characteristics, and develop customer profiles. When using data mining, it is important to remember that the real value is in the company's ability to transform its data from operational bits and bytes into information marketers need for successful marketing strategies. Companies must analyze the data to identify and

response list a customer list that includes the names and addresses of individuals who have responded to an offer of some kind, such as by mail, telephone, direct response television, product rebates, contests or sweepstakes, or billing inserts

compiled list a customer list developed by gathering names and addresses from telephone directories and membership rosters, usually enhanced with information from public records, such as census data, auto registrations, birth announcements, business start-ups, or bankruptcies

ADVERTISING THAT KNOWS WHERE (AND WHEN) YOU WORK

Despite an initial outcry from consumer privacy advocates, a controversial profiling technology known as **"deep packet scanning"** is making a comeback, but with tweaks that companies Phorm and Kindsight hope will quiet the advocates. Deep packet scanning is scanning technology that can read, analyze, and store information contained in all packets of information sent through Internet service providers (ISPs). More traditional "cookies" can only track Web browsing, but deep packet scanning can track any data traveling across the Internet. Both Phorm and Kindsight promise not to analyze sensitive Internet dealings or e-mails, and they do not sell names or sensitive personal information. Nevertheless, the technology tracks so much detail that it will be able to generate profiles for different users of the same computer and can even tell if the user is on for work or for play. Kindsight and Phorm require users to opt in to this level of tracking and offer incentives to do so: Kindsight offers a free security service, and Phorm offers free customized Web content tailored to the user's interest. Users will also receive highly targeted ads designed to appeal to their specific interests. ISPs hope that the new opt-in policies go over well in market tests—they hope to cash in on the ad revenue that can be generated from highly targeted ads. Kindsight and Phorm are both working with ISPs to gain access to their data packets. In return, the ISPs receive a portion of the ad revenue generated from the specific profiling (for which advertisers will pay more).[9]

SOURCE: Steve Stecklow and Paul Sonne, "Shunned Profiling Method on the Verge of Comeback," *Wall Street Journal*, November 14, 2010, A1, A14.

© SHAWN HEMPEL/SHUTTERSTOCK.COM

profile the best customers, calculate their lifetime value, and ultimately predict purchasing behavior through statistical modeling. Sense Networks recently introduced a New York mobile phone app called CabSense. CabSense uses data from more than 90 million cab rides in 3,000 taxis to tell the user the most likely spot to find an unoccupied taxi based on the user's current location. GPS and Google maps determine the user's location, and CabSense ranks nearby intersections by the likelihood of finding an open taxi.[10]

Before the information is leveraged, several types of analysis are often run on the data. These analyses include customer segmentation, recency-frequency-monetary analysis, lifetime value analysis, and predictive modeling.

Customer Segmentation Recall that *customer segmentation* is the process of breaking large groups of customers into smaller, more homogeneous groups. This type of analysis generates a "profile" or picture of the customers' similar demographic, geographic, and psychographic traits as well as their previous purchase behavior; it focuses particularly on the best customers. Profiles of the best customers can be compared and contrasted with other customer segments. For example, a bank could segment consumers on frequency of usage, credit, age, and turnover.

Once a profile of the best customer is developed using these criteria, it can be used to screen other potential consumers. Similarly, customer profiles can be used to introduce customers selectively to specific marketing actions. For example, open-minded young customers can be introduced to home banking. See Chapter 8 for a detailed discussion of segmentation.

Recency-Frequency-Monetary Analysis (RFM) Customers who have purchased recently and often and have spent considerable money are more likely to purchase again. Recency-frequency-monetary analysis (RFM) identifies those customers most likely to purchase again because they have bought recently, bought frequently, or spent a specified amount of money with the firm. Firms develop equations to identify the "best customers" (often the top 20 percent of the customer base) by assigning a score to customer records in the database on how often, how recently, and how much they have spent. Customers are then ranked to determine which ones move to the top of the list and which ones fall to the bottom. The ranking provides the basis for maximizing profits because it enables the firm to use the information in its customer database to select those persons who have proved to be good sources of revenue.

Lifetime Value Analysis (LTV) Recency, frequency, and monetary data can also be used to create a lifetime value model on customers in the database. Whereas RFM looks at how valuable a customer currently is to a company, **lifetime value analysis (LTV)** projects the future value of the customer over a period of years. One of the basic assumptions in any lifetime value calculation is that marketing to repeat customers is more profitable than marketing to first-time buyers. That is, it costs more to find a new customer in terms of promotion and gaining trust than to sell more to a customer who is already loyal.

Customer lifetime value has a number of benefits. It shows marketers how much they can spend to *acquire* new customers, it tells them the level of spending to *retain* customers, and it facilitates targeting new customers who look as though they will be profitable customers. Some marketers have taken CRM's lifetime value analysis one step further by implementing customer value management (CVM) strategies. The goal is to determine which individual customers are most valuable so that their total lifetime purchasing can be maximized. CVM requires a series of "value exchanges" that reward customers for providing personal information and use the information to encourage customers to make additional purchases or renew ongoing services. Chris Zane, owner of Zane's Cycles, an independent bicycle shop

© NUTTAKIT/SHUTTERSTOCK.COM / © ISTOCKPHOTO.COM/UTEHIL

in Connecticut, banks on great customer service to encourage customers to spend their lifetime bicycle money in his store. He offers the price of a child's first bike toward an upgrade every year until he or she reaches a 20-inch wheel. Zane's makes money only after the family purchases a second full-price bike but has earned a lifetime customer.[11]

Predictive Modeling The ability to reasonably predict future customer behavior gives marketers a significant competitive advantage. Through **predictive modeling**, marketers try to determine, based on some past set of occurrences, what the odds are that some other occurrence, such as an Internet inquiry or purchase, will take place in the future. SPSS Predictive Marketing is one tool marketers can use to answer questions about their consumers. The software requires minimal knowledge of statistical analysis. Users operate from a prebuilt model, which generates profiles in three to four days. SPSS also has an online product that predicts Web site users' behavior.

lifetime value analysis (LTV) a data manipulation technique that projects the future value of the customer over a period of years using the assumption that marketing to repeat customers is more profitable than marketing to first-time buyers

predictive modeling a data manipulation technique in which marketers try to determine, based on some past set of occurrences, what the odds are that some other occurrence, such as a response or purchase, will take place in the future

THIS WAY FOR A LIFETIME OF BIKES.

LO7 Leverage Customer Information

Data mining identifies the most profitable customers and prospects. Managers can then design tailored marketing strategies to best appeal to the identified segments. In CRM, this is commonly referred to as leveraging customer information to facilitate enhanced relationships with customers. Exhibit 21.3 shows some common CRM marketing database applications.

Campaign Management

Through campaign management, all areas of the company participate in the development of programs targeted to customers. **Campaign management** involves monitoring and leveraging customer interactions to sell a company's products and to increase customer service. Campaigns are based directly on data obtained from customers through various interactions. Campaign management includes monitoring the success of the communications based on customer reactions through sales, orders, callbacks to the company, and the like. If a campaign appears unsuccessful, it is evaluated and changed to better achieve the company's desired objective.

Campaign management involves developing customized product and service offerings for the appropriate customer segment, pricing these offerings attractively, and communicating these offers in a manner that enhances customer relationships. Customizing product and service offerings requires managing multiple interactions with customers, as well as giving priority to those products and services that are viewed as most desirable for a specifically designated customer. Even within a highly defined market segment, individual customer differences will emerge. Therefore, interactions among customers must focus on individual experiences, expectations, and desires.

campaign management
developing product or service offerings customized for the appropriate customer segment and then pricing and communicating these offerings for the purpose of enhancing customer relationships

Retaining Loyal Customers

If a company has identified its best customers, then it should make every effort to maintain and increase their loyalty. When a company retains an additional 5 percent of its customers each year, profits will increase by as much as 25 percent. What's more,

EXHIBIT 21.3

Common CRM Marketing Database Applications

CRM Marketing Database

- Campaign management
- Retaining loyal customers
- Cross-selling other products or services
- Designing targeted marketing communications
- Reinforcing customer purchase decisions
- Inducing product trial by new customers
- Increasing effectiveness of distribution channel marketing
- Improving customer service

© CENGAGE LEARNING 2013

improving customer retention by a mere 2 percent can decrease costs by as much as 10 percent.[12]

Loyalty programs reward loyal customers for making multiple purchases. The objective is to build long-term mutually beneficial relationships between a company and its key customers. Marriott, Hilton, and Starwood Hotels, for instance, reward their best customers with special perks not available to customers who stay less frequently. Travelers who spend a specified number of nights per year receive reservation guarantees, welcome gifts like fruit baskets and wine in their rooms, and access to concierge lounges. In addition to rewarding good customers, loyalty programs provide businesses with a wealth of information about their customers and shopping trends that can be used to make future business decisions.

RedBox, whose movie rental kiosks are found in supermarkets and McDonald's, sends its customers a birthday e-mail with a special promotion code for a free movie rental. Personal touches like this may give RedBox an edge over Netflix for movie rental services.[13]

Cross-Selling Other Products and Services

CRM provides many opportunities to cross-sell related products. Marketers can use the database to match product profiles and consumer profiles so that they can cross-sell customers products that match their demographic, lifestyle, or behavioral characteristics. DesignWorks NY, a graphic design and marketing communications firm, sends a letter to each of its customers. That letter has a checklist of all the services offered by DesignWorks with the services already used by the customer checked off. The letter helps develop relationships, reminds customers of their experience with DesignWorks, and cross-sells other services to an established customer. Clients respond positively and often sign on for additional services.[14]

Internet companies use product and customer profiling to reveal cross-selling opportunities while a customer is surfing their site. Past purchases on a particular Web site and the site a surfer comes from give online marketers clues about the surfer's interests and what items to cross-sell.

Designing Targeted Marketing Communications

Using transaction and purchase data, a database allows marketers to track customers' relationships to the company's products and services and modify the marketing message accordingly. Sense Network has an app called CitySense in San Francisco that determines your demographic based on your activities and creates a live map showing the locations of people with the similar demographic. Sense Network hopes to use this algorithm to help businesses target groups of people with tailored ads. For example, a user who spends time at inexpensive restaurants, late-night clubs, and college campuses is tracked as a student. Ads for textbooks could be sent to users with these traits and not to users with traits more typical of, say, business people, thereby creating less spam.[15]

Customers can also be segmented into infrequent users, moderate users, and heavy users.

A segmented communications strategy can then be developed based on which group the customer falls into. Communications to infrequent users might encourage repeat purchases through a direct incentive such as a limited-time price discount for ordering again. Communications to moderate users may use fewer incentives and more reinforcement of past purchase decisions. Communications to heavy users would be designed around loyalty and reinforcement of the purchase rather than price promotions.

Reinforcing Customer Purchase Decisions

As you learned in Chapter 6, cognitive dissonance is the feeling consumers get when they recognize an inconsistency between their values and opinions and their purchase behavior. In other words, they doubt the soundness of their purchase decision and often feel anxious. CRM offers marketers an excellent opportunity to reach out to customers to reinforce the purchase decision. By thanking customers for their purchases and telling them they are important, marketers can help cement a long-term, profitable relationship.

Updating customers periodically about the status of their order reinforces purchase decisions. Postsale e-mails also afford the chance to provide more customer service or cross-sell other products.

Subaru has a new way to encourage customer loyalty, which is one of the carmaker's strengths. Subaru owners can submit their cars' vehicle identification numbers (VINs) to purchase loyalty badges that affix to their Subarus. The main badge is a number showing how many Subarus that person has owned, and supplementary badges show that person's interests/

infrequent user   heavy user   moderate user

© ISTOCKPHOTO.COM/SAD444

achievements, such as skiing, hiking, music, mileage, or gardening. The program allows Subaru drivers to show pride in their purchase and be part of a group, both of which are strong ways to offset cognitive dissonance.[16]

Inducing Product Trial by New Customers

Although significant time and money are expended on encouraging repeat purchases by the best customers, a marketing database is also used to identify new customers. Because a firm using a marketing database already has a profile of its best customers, it can easily use the results of modeling to profile potential customers. EATEL, a regional telecommunications firm, uses modeling to identify prospective residential and commercial telephone customers and successfully attract their business.

Marketing managers generally use demographic and behavioral data overlaid on existing customer data to develop a detailed customer profile that is a powerful tool for evaluating lists of prospects. For instance, if a firm's best customers are 35 to 50 years of age, live in suburban areas, and enjoy mountain climbing, then the company can find prospects already in its database or customers who currently are identified as using a competitor's product that match this profile.

Increasing Effectiveness of Distribution Channel Marketing

In Chapter 13, you learned that a marketing channel is a business structure of interdependent organizations, such as wholesalers and retailers, that moves a product from the producer to the ultimate consumer. Most marketers rely on indirect channels to move their products to the end user. Thus, marketers often lose touch with the customer as an individual since the relationship is really between the retailer and the consumer. Marketers in this predicament often view their customers as aggregate statistics because specific customer information is difficult to gather.

With CRM databases, manufacturers now have a tool to gain insight into who is buying their products. Instead of simply unloading products into the distribution channel and leaving marketing and relationship building to dealers, auto manufacturers today are using Web sites to keep in touch with customers and prospects, learn about their lifestyles and hobbies, understand their vehicle needs, and develop relationships in the hope that these consumers will reward them with brand loyalty in the future. BMW and other vehicle manufacturers have databases with names of millions of consumers who have expressed an interest in their products.

With many brick-and-mortar stores setting up shop online, companies are now challenged to monitor purchases of customers who shop both in the store and online. This concept is referred to as multichannel marketing. After Lands' End determined that multichannel customers are the most valuable, the company targeted marketing campaigns toward retaining these customers and increased sales significantly.

Companies are also using radio frequency identification (RFID) technology to improve distribution. The technology uses a microchip with an antenna that tracks anything from a soda can to a car. A computer can locate the product anywhere. The main implication of this technology is that companies will enjoy a reduction in theft and loss of merchandise shipments and will always know where merchandise is in the distribution channel. Moreover, as this technology is further developed, marketers will be able to gather essential information related to product usage and consumption.[17]

Improving Customer Service

CRM marketing techniques increasingly are being used to improve customer service. Amazon.com uses several Web site tools that get customers to return. For example, customers can build wish lists of items, much like a gift registry, so friends and family can make purchases for birthday and other occasions. Amazon also offers recommendations for products based on past purchase and search behavior. These recommendations are listed when a registered customer logs on to the site. Finally, Amazon stores all customer payment and shipping information so customers can make a purchase with one click and then track the shipment. Amazon makes the process of searching for and purchasing books and other products easy and efficient.

Privacy Concerns and CRM

Before rushing out to invest in a CRM system and build a database, marketers should consider consumers' reactions to the growing use of databases. Many Americans and customers abroad are concerned about databases because of the potential for invasion of privacy. The sheer volume of information aggregated in databases makes it vulnerable to unauthorized access and use. A fundamental aspect of marketing using CRM databases is providing valuable services

to customers based on knowledge of what customers really value. It is critical, however, that marketers remember that these relationships should be built on trust. Although database technology enables marketers to compile ever-richer information about their customers that can be used to build and manage relationships, if these customers feel their privacy is being violated, then the relationship becomes a liability.

The popularity of the Internet for e-commerce and customer data collection and as a repository for sensitive customer data has alarmed privacy-minded customers. Online users complain loudly about being "spammed," and Web surfers, including children, are routinely asked to divulge personal information to access certain screens or purchase goods or services. Many users are unaware of how personal information is collected, used, and distributed. The government actively sells huge amounts of personal information to list companies. Hospitals sell the names of women who just gave birth on their premises. Consumer credit databases are often used by credit card marketers to prescreen targets for solicitations. Online and off-line privacy concerns are growing and ultimately will have to be dealt with by businesses and regulators.

Privacy policies for companies in the United States are largely voluntary, and regulations on how personal data are collected and used are being developed. But collecting data on consumers outside the United States is a different matter. For database marketers venturing beyond U.S. borders, success requires careful navigation of foreign privacy laws. For example, under the European Union's (EU) European Data Protection Directive, any business that trades with a European organization must comply with the EU's rules for handling information about individuals or risk prosecution. More than 50 nations have or are developing privacy legislation. Europe has the strictest legislation regarding the collection and use of customer data, and other countries are looking to that legislation when formulating their policies.

STUDY TOOLS
CHAPTER 21

Flip to the back of your textbook to:

❏ **Rip out Chapter Review Card**

Log in to the CourseMate for MKTG at cengagebrain.com to:

❏ **Review Key Terms Flash Cards (Print or Online)**

❏ **Review Audio and Visual Summaries**

❏ **Complete both Practice Quizzes to prepare for tests**

❏ **Play "Beat the Clock" and "Quizbowl" to master concepts**

❏ **Complete "Crossword Puzzle" to review key terms**

❏ **Watch the video on "Method" for a real company example on Customer Relationship Management**

For most people, social media are meant to be a social experience, not a marketing experience.

AFTER YOU FINISH THIS CHAPTER, GO TO PAGE 377 FOR STUDY TOOLS

LO1 What Are Social Media?

The most exciting thing to happen to marketing and promotion is the increasing use of online technology to promote brands, particularly using social media. Social media have changed the way that marketers can communicate with their brands—from mass messages to intimate conversations. As marketing moves into social media, marketers must remember that for most people, social media are meant to be a social experience, not a marketing experience. In fact, the term *social media* means different things to different people, though most people think it refers to digital technology. Brian Solis, of FutureWorks, defines **social media** as "any tool or service that uses the Internet to facilitate conversations."[1] However, social media can also be defined relative to traditional advertising like television and magazines: Whereas traditional marketing media offer a mass-media method of interacting with consumers, social media offer more one-to-one ways to meet consumers.

Social media have several implications for marketers and how they can interact with their customers. First, marketers must realize that they often do not control the content on social media sites. Consumers are sharing their thoughts, wishes, and experiences about brands with the world through social media. Because of this level of visibility and discussion, marketers must realize that having a great ad campaign is not enough—the product or service must be great, too.

social media any tool or service that uses the Internet to facilitate conversations

What do you think?

Marketers are adept at using social media as a marketing tool.

| 1 | 2 | 3 | 4 | 5 | 6 | 7 |

STRONGLY DISAGREE   STRONGLY AGREE

Find out what others think at the CourseMate for MKTG. Log in at cengagebrain.com.

© OLENA CHERNENKO/VETTA/GETTY IMAGES

Second, the ability to share experiences quickly and with such large numbers of people amplifies the impact of word of mouth in a way that can eventually affect a company's bottom line. This has huge ramifications for customer service. For example, Dave Carroll complained that his guitar was damaged by baggage handlers on a 2008 United Airlines flight—damage for which United refused to compensate him. Fed up, Carroll wrote a song, performed it, and posted the resulting music video decrying United's customer service. More than 3 million people watched the video, and it elicited 14,000 comments. United's stock price decreased 10 percent.[2] Thus, through the power of one unhappy customer, less-than-excellent customer service negatively affected consumer confidence and market value for United Airlines.

Third, social media allow marketers to listen. Domino's Pizza listened to much of what was being posted about its product (and it was not nice) and then decided to take that information and change its product. Social media, along with traditional marketing research, allowed Domino's to gain the insight needed to completely reinvent its pizza. And Domino's then used the simple act of transparency to launch an award-winning promotional campaign.

Fourth, social media also provide more sophisticated methods of measuring how marketers meet and interact with consumers than traditional advertising does. Currently, social media include tools and platforms like social networks, blogs, microblogs, and media sharing sites, which can be accessed through a growing number of devices such as computers, laptops, Smartphones, e-readers, tablets, and netbooks. This technology changes daily, offering consumers new ways to experience social media platforms, which must constantly innovate to keep up with consumer demands.

Finally, social media allow marketers to have much more direct and meaningful conversations with customers. Social media offer a form of relationship building that will ultimately bring the customer and brand closer.

At the basic level, consumers of social media want to exchange information, collaborate with others, and have conversations. Social media have changed how and where conversations take place, making human interaction global through popular technology. Research shows that more than 73 percent of active online users have read a blog and more than half belong to at least one social network. Marketing consultant John Haydon says, "The real value of social media is that it exponentially leverages word-of-mouth."[3] Clearly, conversations are happening online; it is up to the marketer to decide if engaging in those conversations will be profitable and to find the most effective method of entering the conversation.

Marketers are interested in online communication because it is wildly popular; brands, companies, individuals, and celebrities promote their messages online. Today, Lady Gaga reigns as the queen of social media: She holds the record for the living person with the most Facebook fans; on Twitter she directly interacts with her 14 million followers (a number that will likely be even greater by the time you read this); the music video for the song "Bad Romance" holds the title of most viewed video ever on YouTube. Lady Gaga's celebrity is due in large part to being a highly effective brand—her messages resonate with audiences worldwide, and she makes her brand easily accessible through popular social media platforms. Her carefully crafted social media strategy has translated into real money: Lady Gaga debuted on the Forbes Celebrity 100 Power List for 2010 at number 4, earning more than $62 million (including her corporate sponsorships and endorsements) in the preceding 12 months.[4] As far as brands go, very few marketers

© AP PHOTO/CHRIS PIZZELLO

have leveraged social media to drive sales of core products better than Lady Gaga.[5]

How Consumers Use Social Media

Before beginning to understand how to leverage social media for brand building, it is important to understand what consumers are using and how they are using it. Hoping to replicate some of Lady Gaga's social media success, many marketers are looking to get their message on the fastest-growing social media platform—Facebook. Facebook originated as a community for college students that opened to the general public as its popularity grew. It now has hundreds of millions of users: If Facebook were a country, it would be the third largest in the world. Growth in new profiles is highest among baby boomers, who use Facebook as a way to connect with old friends and keep up with family. Other social networks, like Hi5 and Bebo, offer an alternative for other demographics. Hi5 offers a wide variety of social games (covered later

in this chapter), adding two or three each week. Bebo is popular with tweens and teens, though that age group is increasingly moving to Facebook.

Videos are one of the most popular tools by which marketers reach consumers, and YouTube is by far the largest online video repository—it has more content than any major television network. Due to its connection with Google, YouTube offers a powerful search tool as well.[6] Flickr is a popular photo sharing site, where millions of people upload new photos daily. Twitter boasts hundreds of millions of registered users who together post a daily average of billions of tweets. Technorati tracks hundreds of millions of blogs and indexes an estimated 2 million new blog posts per day.[7] More than half of Technorati's active users have uploaded photos, and almost a quarter have uploaded videos. The bottom line, according to Universal McCann's Comparative Study on Social Media Trends, is that "if you are online, you are using social media."[8]

THE FICKLE NATURE OF SOCIAL MEDIA CONSUMPTION

Myspace was the virtual hub for the social media generation until Facebook usurped its title and wooed away its youthful contingent with a cleaner interface. Myspace reached its peak in December 2008, when it was attracting nearly 76 million unique visitors each month. Since late 2009, however, Myspace has lost more than 1 million U.S. users a month. What happened? In part, Myspace grew too quickly without understanding what consumers wanted. Parents came to mistrust it and perceived it as "seedy." Mostly, though, users wanted what Facebook offered: a safe, uncluttered, ad-free (at the time) place where they could interact with the people they wanted to interact with. What initially attracted users to Myspace (the freedom to code your own page, play with widgets and music, freely explore other people's pages) became too much and drove users away—and when they left, the advertisers left, too. In 2009, Myspace generated $470 million in advertising; the projection for 2011 was only $184 million. In 2011, Myspace was sold to Specific Media for $35 million, a far cry from the 2005 sale to News Corporation for $580 million. Specific Media hopes to continue the site as a music- and band-

focused hub, but as other come-and-gone social media sites can attest, bringing back users is a difficult task. A social media site grows quickly, as influencers pull in all their peers, but they also pull them away at the first sign of trouble or something new on the horizon—a trend that current social media darlings such as Twitter and LinkedIn should notice. It took only one year for Facebook to eclipse Myspace, and it has taken less than two years for Myspace to lose hundreds of millions of dollars and users.[9]

SOURCES: Felix Gillette, "The Rise and Inglorious Fall of Myspace," *Bloomberg Businessweek*, June 27–July 3, 2011, 54–59; Brian Stelter, "News Corporation Sells Myspace for $35 Million," *New York Times*, June 29, 2011, http://mediadecoder.blogs.nytimes.com/2011/06/29/news-corp-sells-myspace-to-specific-media-for-35-million.

© CHRIS JACKSON/GETTY IMAGES

social commerce
a subset of e-commerce that involves the interaction and user contribution aspects of social online media to assist online buying and selling of products and services

Increased usage of alternative platforms like Smartphones and tablet computers has further contributed to the proliferation of social media usage. In the United States, 90 percent of 18- to 29-year-olds own mobile phones. Among this group, 95 percent have sent a text message, 65 percent have accessed the Internet, and at least 23 percent have accessed a social networking site using their phones.[10] In April 2010, Apple released the much anticipated iPad tablet computer and has since been unable to keep up with demand, selling more than 9 million iPads in 2011.[11] More than 8,500 native iPad apps (many of which connect to social networks) are available for download, and within the first two months of the tablet's release, 35 million downloads had already been recorded.[12] The overall impact of tablet computing on social media (and thus the discipline of marketing) is yet to be seen, but given the incredible impact that the Smartphone has had in its short life span, tablets could prove to be game changing.

Social Commerce A new area of growth in social media is **social commerce**, which combines social media with the basics of e-commerce. Social commerce is a subset of e-commerce that involves the interaction and user contribution aspects of social online media to assist online buying and selling of products and services.[13] Basically, social commerce relies on user-generated content on Web sites to assist consumers with purchases. On Polyvore.com, members create collages of photographs of clothing items to create a fashionable look. Photographs come from various retailers and include accessories, clothes, shoes, and makeup. Once a look is complete, other members view the look and can click on the individual items to see prices and retailers. Social commerce sites often include ratings and recommendations (like Amazon) and social shopping tools (like Groupon). In fact, Groupon is one of the fastest-growing social media tools and continues to revolutionize the way that consumers access deals. In general, social commerce sites are designed to help consumers make more informed decisions on purchases or services.

Social Media and Integrated Marketing Communications

While marketers typically employ a social media strategy alongside traditional channels like print and broadcast, many budget pendulums are swinging toward social media. In the U.S. Interactive Marketing Forecast, 2009–2014, Forrester Research predicted that mobile marketing, social media, e-mail marketing, display advertising, and search marketing would grow from 13 percent of advertising spending in 2010 to more than 21 percent of spending by 2014. The bulk of this budget will still go to search marketing (almost doubling by 2014), but substantial investments will also be made in mobile marketing and social media.[14]

A unique consequence of social media is the widespread shift from one-to-many communication to many-to-many communication. Instead of simply putting a brand advertisement on television with no means for feedback, marketers can use social media to have conversations with consumers, forge deeper relationships, and build brand loyalty. Social media also allow consumers to connect with each other, share opinions, and collaborate on new ideas according to their interests. With the growth of mommy blogs that discuss child rearing and often review products, the popularity of mom-focused social networking site CafeMom.com is not surprising. The site offers conversation, advice, friendship, and entertainment (CAFE) and features groups on such varied topics as raising boys, recipe swaps, interior decorating, and marriage. CafeMom also hosts a blog with celebrity gossip, recipes, and child-rearing news. Thus, the site provides a centralized location for advertisers who want to reach mothers. CafeMom hopes to have a

© ISTOCKPHOTO.COM/LISE GAGNE

spinoff site geared toward Hispanic moms, one of the fastest-growing demographics in the United States.[15]

With social media, the audience is often in control of the message, the medium, the response, or all three. This distribution of control is often difficult for companies to adjust to, but the focus of social marketing is unavoidably on the audience, and the brand must adapt to succeed. The interaction between producer and consumer becomes less about entertaining and more about listening, influencing, and engaging. One example is Dorito's "Crash the Super Bowl" campaign. The company allows consumers to make television ads, post them on the Web site www.crashthesuperbowl .com, and vote for their favorite ads. The winning ads air during the Super Bowl.

In 2009, Hewlett-Packard used social media to avert a public relations (PR) crisis after a video claiming that HP was racist garnered 2 million views on YouTube. Because it was aware of its customers' social dialogues, HP learned about the groundswell early on and was able to quell the story before it gained too much momentum.[16] Mountain Dew's marketing team tested the limits of consumer control and the power of social media by moving the brand's advertising almost entirely online. The team tapped into the brand's core consumer demographic—18- to 39-year-old males with strong Facebook, Myspace, and YouTube presences—to build line extensions and help choose a marketing partner.

Using consumers to develop and market product is called **crowdsourcing**. Crowdsourcing describes how the input of many people can be leveraged to make decisions that used to be based on the input of only a few people.[17] Companies get feedback on marketing campaigns, new-product ideas, and other marketing decisions by asking customers to weigh in. One company called Talenthouse is offering up the crowd to help musicians fulfill all sorts of needs—from someone to photograph a tour to designing a dress for lead singers. Talenthouse has users submit work to be voted on by Facebook peers. The winner gets the job (though the musician has the final say in who wins). Some musicians see Talenthouse as a way to gain publicity or to help young artists: Paul McCartney set up a contest for Talenthouse competitors to design a piece of art inspired by his music. The winner received $1,000 and various merchandise, and the work was displayed in the London art gallery Idea Generation.[18] Crowdsourcing offers a way for companies to engage heavy users of a brand and receive input, which in turn increases those users' brand advocacy and lessens

the likelihood that a change will be disliked enough to drive away loyal customers.

LO2 Creating and Leveraging a Social Media Campaign

Social media is an exciting new field, and its potential for expanding a brand's impact is enormous. Because the costs are often minimal and the learning curve is relatively low, some organizations are tempted to dive headfirst into social media. However, as with any marketing campaign, it is always important to start with a strategy. For most organizations, this means starting with a marketing or communications plan, as covered in Chapter 2. Important evaluative areas such as situation analysis, objectives, and evaluation are still key. It is important to link communication objectives (for example, improving customer service) to the most effective social media tools (for example, Twitter) and to be able to measure the results to determine if the objectives were met. It is also important to understand the various types of media involved.

The new communication paradigm created by a shift to social media marketing raises questions about categorization. In light of the convergence of traditional and digital media, researchers have explored different ways that interactive marketers can categorize media types. One such researcher, Sean Corcoran of Forrester Research, devised a distinction among owned, earned, and paid media. **Owned media** are online content that an organization creates and controls. Owned media include blogs, Web sites, Facebook pages, and other social media presences. The purpose of owned media is to develop deeper relationships with customers. **Earned media** is a PR term connoting free media such as mainstream media coverage. In an interactive space, media are earned through word of mouth or online buzz about something the brand is doing. Earned media include viral videos, retweets, comments on blogs, and other forms of customer feedback resulting from a social media presence. **Paid media** are content paid for by the company to be placed online. Paid media are

crowdsourcing using consumers to develop and market products

owned media online content that an organization creates and controls

earned media a public relations term connoting free media such as mainstream media coverage

paid media content paid for by a company to be placed online similar to marketing efforts that utilize traditional media, like newspaper, magazine, and television advertisements. In an interactive space, paid media include display advertising, paid search words, and other types of direct online advertising.[19]

To leverage all three types of media, marketers must follow a few key guidelines. First, they must maximize owned media by reaching out beyond their existing Web sites to create portfolios of digital touch points. This is especially true for brands with tight budgets, as the organization may not be able to afford much paid media. Second, marketers must recognize that aptitude at public and media relations no longer translates into earned media. Instead, marketers must learn how to listen and respond to stakeholders. This will stimulate word of mouth. Finally, marketers must understand that paid media are not dead but should serve as a catalyst to drive customer engagement.[20] If balanced correctly, all three types of media can be powerful tools for interactive marketers.

A wine lover tastes a glass of red wine during an online wine tasting. People from all parts of Germany regularly meet online to taste wine and exchange opinions via Twitter, generating earned media buzz for the winery whose wine they are drinking.

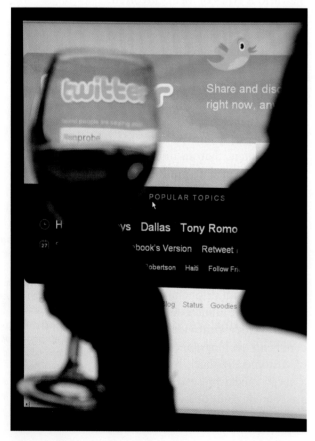

The Listening System

The first action a marketing team should take when initiating a social media campaign is simple—it should just listen. Customers are on social media and assume that the brand is there as well. They expect a new level of engagement with brands. Developing an effective listening system is necessary to both understanding and engaging an online audience. Marketers must not only hear what is being said about the brand, the industry, the competition, and the customer, but they must also pay attention to who is saying what and act upon that information. The specific ways that customers and noncustomers rate, rank, critique, praise, deride, recommend, snub, and generally discuss brands are all important. Thus, social media have created a new method of market research: These are customers telling marketers what they want and need (and don't want and need).

Negative comments and complaints are of particular importance, both because they can illuminate unknown brand flaws and because they are the comments that tend to go viral. Listening is important because consumers believe that if negative comments about a brand go unanswered, that brand is insincere, and consumers will take their business elsewhere. Online tools such as Google Alerts, Google Blog Search, Twitter Search, SiteVolume, Social Mention, and Socialcast are extremely helpful in the development of efficient, effective listening.

In Exhibit 22.1, social media strategist Jeremiah Owyang and Jim Sterne outline eight stages of effective listening. Listening to customers communicate about one's own brand can be very revealing, but social media are also a great way to monitor competitors' online presences, fans, and followers. Paying attention to the ways that competing brands attract and engage with their customers can be particularly enlightening for both small businesses and global brands.

Social Media Objectives

After establishing a listening platform, the organization should develop a list of objectives for its social media team to accomplish. These objectives must be developed with a clear understanding of how social media change the communication dynamic with and for customers. Remember—attempting to reach a mass audience with a static message will never be as successful as influencing people through conversation. Marketing managers must set objectives that reflect this reality. Here are some practical ideas that marketing managers should consider when setting social media objectives:

▸▸ *Listen and learn:* Monitor what is being said about the brand and competitors, and glean insights about audi-

© Z1031/JAN WOITAS/DPA/CORBIS

EXHIBIT 22.1
Eight Stages of Effective Listening

Stage	Description	Resources Required	Purpose
Stage 1: Without objective	The organization has established a listening system but has no goals.	Social media notification tools (Google Alerts)	Keep up with brand and competitor information.
Stage 2: Tracking brand mentions	The organization tracks mentions in social space but has no guidance on next steps.	A listening platform with key word report capabilities (Radian6)	Track discussions, understand sentiment, and identify influencers to improve overall marketing strategy.
Stage 3: Identifying market risks and opportunities	The organization seeks discussions online that may result in identification of problems and opportunities.	A listening platform with a large staff dedicated to the client (Converseon)	Staff seeks out discussions and reports to other teams, like product development and sales. These teams then engage the customers directly or conduct further research.
Stage 4: Improving campaign efficiency	The organization uses tools to get real-time data on marketing efficiency.	Web analytics software (Google Analytics)	See a wealth of information about consumers' behavior on their Web sites (and social media).
Stage 5: Measuring customer satisfaction	The organization collects information about satisfaction, including measures of sentiment.	Insight platforms that offer online focus group solutions	Measure impact of satisfaction or frustration during interaction.
Stage 6: Responding to customer inquiry	The organization identifies customers where they are (e.g., Twitter).	A customer service team is allowed to make real-time responses.	Generate high sense of satisfaction for customer but generates public complaints.
Stage 7: Better understanding of customers	The organization adds social information to demographics and psychographics to gain a better profile.	Social customer relationship management (CRM) systems to sync data	Social CRM marries database and social media to create a powerful analytical tool. (See Chapter 21 for more on CRM.)
Stage 8: Being proactive and anticipating customer demands	The organization examines previous patterns of data and social behavior to anticipate needs.	Advanced customer database with predictive application (yet to be created)	Modify social media strategy to preempt consumer behavior modifications based on trends.

SOURCES: Jeremiah Owyang, "Web Strategy Matrix: The Eight Stages of Listening," *Web Strategy,* November 10, 2009, www.web-strategist.com/blog/2009/11/10/evolution-the-eight-stages-of-listening/; Jim Sterne, *Social Media Metrics* (Hoboken, NJ: John Wiley & Sons, 2010).

ences. Use online tools and do research to implement the best social media practices. If you have established a listening strategy, this objective should already be accomplished.

▶▶ *Build relationships and awareness:* Open dialogues with stakeholders by giving them compelling content across a variety of media. Engage in conversations, and answer customers' questions candidly. This will both increase Web traffic and boost your search engine ranking. This is where crowdsourcing can be useful for product development and communication campaign feedback.

▶▶ *Promote products and services:* The clearest path to increasing the bottom line using social media is to get customers talking about products and services, which ultimately translates into sales.

▶▶ *Manage your reputation:* Develop and improve the brand's reputation by responding to comments and criticism that appear on blogs and forums. Additionally, organizations can position themselves as helpful and benevolent by participating in other forums and discussions. Social media make it much easier to establish and communicate expertise.

▶▶ *Improve customer service:* Customer comments about products and services will not always be positive. Use social media to search out displeased customers and engage them directly in order to solve their service issues.

LO 3 Evaluation and Measurement of Social Media

Social media have the potential to revolutionize the way organizations communicate with stakeholders. Given the relative ease and efficiency with which organizations can use social media, a positive return on investment (ROI) is likely for many—if not most—organizations. A Forrester Research report found that 95 percent of marketers planned to increase or maintain their investments in social media. However, though they understand that it is a worthwhile investment, most marketers have not been able to figure out how to measure the benefits of social media. As social media evolve, so do the measurements and metrics that track them.[21] Yet, as with traditional advertising, marketers lack hard evidence as to the relative effectiveness of these tools. Some marketers accept this unknown variable and focus on the fact that social media are less about ROI than about deepening relationships with customers; others work tirelessly to better understand the measurement of social media's effectiveness.

While literally hundreds of metrics have been developed to measure social media's value, these metrics are meaningless unless they are tied to key performance indicators.[22] For example, a local coffee shop manager may measure the success of her social media presence by the raw number of friends on Facebook and followers on Twitter she has accumulated. But these numbers depend entirely on context. The rate of accumulation, investment per fan and follower, and comparison to similarly sized coffee shops are all important variables to consider. Without context, measurements are meaningless.

LO 4 Social Behavior of Consumers

Social media have changed the way that people interact in their everyday lives. Some say that social media have made people smarter by giving people (especially children) access to so much information and interactivity. Social media allow people to stay in touch in ways never before experienced. Social media have also reinvented politics and civic engagement (social media played an important role in the 2008 presidential election and in the rise of the Tea Party movement in the 2010 elections). Social media have drastically changed the advertising business from an industry based on mass-media models (e.g., TV) to an industry based on relationships and conversations. This all has implications for how consumers use social media and the purposes for which they use those media.[23]

Once objectives have been determined and measurement tools have been implemented, it is important to identify the consumer who the marketer is trying to reach. Who is using social media? What types of social media do they use? How do they use social media? Are they just reading content, or do they actually create it? Does Facebook attract younger users? Do Twitter users retweet viral videos? These types of questions must be considered because they determine not only which tools will be most effective but also, more importantly, whether launching a social media campaign even makes sense for a particular organization.

Understanding an audience necessitates understanding how that audience uses social media. In *Groundswell*, Charlene Li and Josh Bernoff of Forrester Research identify six categories of social media users:

1 **Creators:** Those who produce and share online content like blogs, Web sites, articles, and videos

2 **Critics:** Those who post comments, ratings, and reviews of products and services on blogs and forums

To effectively market to a social media user, it is important to know whether she generates content or collects it.

© JOHN LUND/BLEND IMAGES/GETTY IMAGES

3 *Collectors:* Those who use RSS feeds to collect information and vote for Web sites online

4 *Joiners:* Those who maintain a social networking profile and visit other sites

5 *Spectators:* Those who read blogs, listen to podcasts, watch videos, and generally consume media

6 *Inactives:* Those who do none of these things[24]

A 2009 study determined that 24 percent of social media users functioned as creators, 37 percent functioned as critics, 21 percent functioned as collectors, 51 percent functioned as joiners, and 73 percent functioned as spectators. While participation in each of these categories had trended upward, inactives had decreased from 44 percent in 2007 to only 18 percent in 2009.[25] However, recent Forrester research shows that the number of people who contribute content is slowing down. Participation in most categories has fallen slightly, prompting analysts to recommend that marketers re-examine how they are engaging with their customers online.

Despite the apparent slowdown, research also shows that more social networking "rookies" are classified as joiners. Another bright spot is a new category, "conversationalists," or people who post status updates on social networking sites and microblogging services such as Twitter. Conversationalists represent 31 percent of users.[26] This type of classification gives marketers a general idea of who is using social media and how to engage them. It is similar to any type of market segmentation—especially the 80/20 rule. Those who are creating content and active on social media could be those consumers most likely to actively engage with a brand as well as actively post negative comments on social media. The critics and collectors make up most of this group. However, it is important not to miss the joiners and spectators because they are eager to follow and act on the comments of their fellow customers.

LO5 Social Media Tools: Consumer- and Corporate-Generated Content

Given that it is important for marketers to engage with customers on social media for the reasons mentioned earlier, there are a number of tools and platforms that can be employed as part of an organization's social media strategy. Blogs, microblogs, social networks, media creation and sharing sites, social news sites, location-based social networking sites, review sites, and virtual worlds and online gaming all have their place in a company's social marketing plan. These are all tools in a marketing manager's toolbox, available when applicable to the marketing plan but not necessarily to be used all at once. Because of the breakneck pace at which technology changes, this list of resources will surely look markedly different five years from now. More tools emerge every day, and branding strategies must keep up with the ever-changing world of technology. For now, the resources highlighted in this section remain a marketer's strongest set of platforms for conversing and strengthening relationships with customers.

Blogs

Blogs have become staples in many social media strategies and are often a brand's social media centerpiece. A **blog** is a publicly accessible Web page that functions as an interactive journal, whereby readers can post comments on the author's entries. Some experts believe that every company should have a blog that speaks to current and potential customers, not as consumers, but as people.[27] Blogs allows marketers to create content in the form of posts, which ideally build trust and a sense of authenticity in customers. Once posts are made, audience members can provide feedback through comments. Because it opens a dialogue and gives customers a voice, the comments section of a blog post is one of the most important avenues of conversation between brands and consumers.

Blogs can be divided into two broad categories: corporate and professional blogs, and noncorporate blogs such as personal blogs. **Corporate blogs** are sponsored by a company or one of its brands and are maintained by one or more of the company's employees. They disseminate marketing-controlled information and are effective platforms for developing thought leadership, fostering better relationships with stakeholders, maximizing search engine optimization, attracting new customers, endearing the organization with anecdotes and stories about brands, and providing an active forum for testing new ideas. Because blogs are designed to be updated daily, corporate blogs are dynamic and highly flexible, giving marketers the opportunity to adapt their messages

blog a publicly accessible Web page that functions as an interactive journal, whereby readers can post comments on the author's entries

corporate blogs blogs that are sponsored by a company or one of its brands and maintained by one or more of the company's employees

noncorporate blogs independent blogs that are not associated with the marketing efforts of any particular company or brand
microblogs blogs with strict post length limits

more frequently than any other communication channel.

Several brands use blogs effectively. GM's FastLane Blog (http://fastlane.gmblogs.com) is considered a corporate best. It is packed with audio, video, and photos and is organized into categories that offer something for everyone. One of FastLane Blog's biggest draws is its high-quality writing. Each reader comment is answered in a fun and pithy tone, encouraging participation and continued readership. Southwest Airlines (Nuts about Southwest, www.blogsouthwest.com) and Dell (which has created a hub for several blogs) also produce successful corporate blogs.

In contrast, **noncorporate blogs** are independent and not associated with the marketing efforts of any particular company or brand. Because these blogs contain information not controlled by marketers, they are perceived to be more authentic than corporate blogs. Mommy bloggers, women who review children's products and discuss family-related topics on their personal blogs, use noncorporate blogs. The goal of mommy blogs is to share parenting tips and experiences and become part of a community.

Because of the popularity of these and other types of blogs, many bloggers receive products and/or money from companies in exchange for a review. Many bloggers disclose where they received the product or if they were paid, but an affiliation is not always clear. Because of this, bloggers must disclose any financial relationship with a company per Federal Trade Commission rules. It is important for marketing managers to understand the rules behind complimentary products to bloggers as well as the high potential for social buzz; four out of five noncorporate bloggers post brand or product reviews. Even if a company does not have a formal social media strategy, chances are the brand is still out in the blogosphere, whether or not a marketing manager approached a blogger.

Microblogs

Microblogs are blogs that exchange smaller posts than traditional blogs. Twitter, the most popular microblogging platform, requires that posts be no more than 140 characters in length. However, there are several other platforms, including Jaiku, Tumblr, Plurk, and, of course, Facebook's status updates. These platforms allow users to post longer content, videos, images, and links. The content posted on microblogs ranges from five-paragraph news stories to scans of sandwiches

with the ingredients as captions (scanwiches.com). While Tumblr is growing rapidly, Twitter, originally designed as a short messaging system used for internal communication, is wildly popular and is used as a communication and research tool by individuals and brands around the world. Twitter is effective for disseminating breaking news, promoting longer blog posts and campaigns, sharing links, announcing events, and promoting sales. By following, retweeting, responding to potential customers' tweets, and tweeting content that inspires customers to engage the brand, corporate Twitter users can lay a foundation for meaningful two-way conversation quickly and effectively. Celebrities also flock to Twitter to interact with fans, discuss tour dates, and efficiently promote themselves directly to fans. Research has found that when operated correctly, corporate Twitter accounts are well respected and well received. Twitter can be used to build communities; aid in customer service; gain prospects; increase awareness; and, in the case of nonprofits, raise funds.

Sean Combs, aka P. Diddy, shows off his Twitter page. Combs uses Twitter as a blog to keep fans updated on his activities.

© JARED MILGRIM/CORBIS

A large part of Twitter's success stems from the fact that the platform is extremely versatile: Posts and private messages can be sent and received on most electronic, Internet-ready devices. To bring in revenue, Twitter is developing promoted tweets, which will be ads that appear in search results and user feeds both on Twitter.com and on third-party clients that access the service, such as TweetDeck, twhirl, TwitterBerry and Tweetie. Twitter is currently looking for a way to include promoted tweets that does not alienate consumers by interfering with their personal Twitter feed.[28]

The ways a business can use Twitter to successfully engage with customers are almost limitless. *Newsweek* uses its Tumblr account to drive traffic to its main Web site. Using funny, relevant content and a genuine voice, *Newsweek*'s blog was ranked as one of the best on Tumblr by the *Huffington Post*.[29]

Social Networks

Social networking sites allow individuals to connect—or network—with friends, peers, and business associates. Connections may be made around shared interests, shared environments, or personal relationships. Depending on the site, connected individuals may be able to send each other messages, track each other's activity, see each other's personal information, share multimedia, or comment on each other's blog and microblog posts. Depending on a marketing team's goals, there are several social networks that might be engaged as part of a social media strategy: Facebook is the largest and fastest-growing network; Hi5 caters to younger audiences; LinkedIn is geared toward professionals and businesses who use it to recruit professionals; and niche networks like Bebo, Last.fm, WeAreTeachers, BlackPlanet, and Match.com cater to specialized markets. There is a niche social network for just about every demographic and interest. Beyond those already established, an organization may decide to develop a brand-specific social network or community. Although each social networking site is different, some marketing goals can be accomplished on any such site. Given the right strategy, increasing awareness, targeting audiences, promoting products, forging relationships, highlighting expertise and leadership, attracting event participants, performing research, and generating new business are attainable marketing goals on any social network.

Facebook is by far the largest social networking site, and is popular with both individuals and groups. How an individual uses Facebook differs from the way a group or company uses Facebook, as you can see in Exhibit 22.2. While individual Facebook users create profiles, brands, organizations, and nonprofit causes operate as pages. As opposed to individual profiles, all pages are public and are thus subject to search engine indexing. By maintaining a popular Facebook page, a brand not only increases its social media presence, but it also helps to optimize search engine results. Pages often include photo and video albums, brand information, and links to external sites. The most useful page feature, however, is the Wall. The Wall allows a brand to communicate directly with fans via status updates, which enables marketers to build databases of interested stakeholders. When an individual becomes a fan of your organization or posts on your Wall, that information is shared with the individual's friends, creating a mini viral marketing campaign. Other Facebook marketing tools include groups, applications, and ads. Facebook is an extremely important platform for social marketers.

Facebook has proved to be fertile ground for new marketing ideas and campaigns. By creating a

social networking sites Web sites that allow individuals to connect—or network—with friends, peers, and business associates

EXHIBIT 22.2
Facebook Lingo

Non-Individual (Usually Corporate)	Individual
Page	Profile
Fan of a page, tells fan's friends that the user is a fan, creates mini viral campaign	Friend a person, send private messages, write on the Wall, see friend-only content
Public, searchable	Privacy options, not searchable unless user enabled

© CENGAGE LEARNING 2013

© ISTOCKPHOTO.COM/ED SWEETMAN

media sharing sites Web sites that allow users to upload and distribute multimedia content like videos and photos

social news sites Web sites that allow users to decide which content is promoted on a given Web site by voting that content up or down

Facebook application called Real or Fake, Adobe used the social network's built-in software platform to advertise student editions of the Photoshop photo editing software to college students. When users installed the Real or Fake application, they gained access to weekly images, which they were challenged to distinguish as authentic or digitally manipulated. After they took the challenge, users were directed to tutorials that demonstrated how the altered photos were manipulated using Photoshop. By the end of the campaign, Adobe had earned additional Facebook fans and had witnessed an increase in page views from 5,057 to 53,000 per week. More than 6 percent of Real or Fake users actually purchased the Photoshop software. Through this campaign, Adobe did not just establish a social media presence but also created a novel way to engage its fans.[30] Coca-Cola's Facebook page, boasting 5 million fans, was developed by two individuals in California. Rather than assuming its management, Coca-Cola decided to work with fans to maintain the page. Again, to succeed in social media, organizations must learn to share control with the customer.

LinkedIn features many of the same services as Facebook (profiles, status updates, private messages, company pages, and groups) but is oriented around business and professional connections. Unlike Facebook, LinkedIn features a question-and-answer forum, where users can ask for advice and share expertise in specific fields, and a file hosting service, where users can upload intellectual property like slides, presentations, and other shared documents.[31] LinkedIn is used primarily by professionals who wish to build their personal brands online and businesses that are recruiting employees and freelancers.

Media Sharing Sites

Media sharing sites allow users to upload and distribute multimedia content like videos and photos. Sites such as YouTube and Flickr are particularly useful to brands' social marketing strategies because they add a vibrant interactive channel on which to disseminate content. The distribution of user-generated content has changed markedly over the past few years. Today, organizations can tell compelling brand stories through videos, photos, and audio.

Photo sharing sites allow users to archive and share photos. Flickr, Picasa, TwitPic, Photobucket, Facebook, and Imgur all offer free photo hosting

services that can be utilized by individuals and businesses alike. For example, to strengthen its image of transparency and its relationship with potential donors, the American Red Cross maintained hundreds of Hurricane Katrina disaster photos and tracked sentiments about Red Cross services on Flickr throughout the crisis.[32]

Video creation and distribution have also gained popularity among marketers because of video's rich ability to tell stories. YouTube, the highest-trafficked video-based Web site and the sixth highest-trafficked site overall, allows users to upload and stream their videos to an enthusiastic and active community.[33] YouTube is not only large (in terms of visitors), but it also attracts a diverse base of users: Age and gender demographics are remarkably balanced.

Many entertainment companies and movie marketers have used YouTube as a showcase for new products, specials, and movie trailers. For example, Lions Gate Entertainment purchased ad space on the YouTube home page in 15 countries to promote the *Avatar* movie trailer. Some teen clothing brands like Forever 21 and JCPenney build followings on YouTube by posting hauls—videos made by teens that focus on fashion. Clearly, user-generated content can be a powerful tool for brands that can use it effectively.

A podcast, another type of user-generated media, is a digital audio or video file that is distributed serially for other people to listen to or watch. Podcasts can be streamed online, played on a computer, uploaded to a portable media player (like an iPod), or downloaded onto a Smartphone. Podcasts are like radio shows that are distributed through various means and not linked to a scheduled time slot. While they have not experienced the exponential growth rates of other digital platforms, podcasts have amassed a steadily growing number of loyal devotees. For example, Etsy, an online marketplace for handmade and vintage wares, offers a podcast series introducing favorite craftspeople to the world—driving business for those individuals.

Social News Sites

Social news sites allow users to decide which content is promoted on a given Web site by voting that content up or down. Users post news stories and multimedia on crowdsourced sites such as Reddit and Digg for the community to vote on. The more interest from readers, the higher the story or video is ranked. Marketers have found that these sites are useful for promoting campaigns, creating conversations around related issues, and building Web site traffic.[34] If content posted to a crowdsourced site is voted up, discussed, and shared enough to be listed among the most popular topics of the day, it can go viral across other sites and, eventually, the entire Web. Social bookmarking sites such as Delicious and StumbleUpon are similar to social news sites but the objective of their users is to collect, save, and share interesting and valuable links. On these sites, users categorize links with short, descriptive tags. Users can search the site's database of links by specific tags or can add their own tags to others' links. In this way, tags serve as the foundation for information gathering and sharing on social bookmarking sites.[35]

Location-Based Social Networking Sites

Considered by many to be the next big thing in social marketing, location sites like Gowalla and Loopt should be on every marketer's radar. Essentially, **location-based social networking sites** combine the fun of social networking with the utility of location-based GPS technology. Foursquare, one of the most popular location sites, treats location-based micronetworking as a game: Users earn badges and special statuses based on their number of visits to particular locations. Users can write and read short reviews and tips about businesses, organize meet-ups, and see which Foursquare-using friends are nearby. Foursquare updates can also be posted to linked Twitter and Facebook accounts for followers and friends to see. Location sites such

as Foursquare are particularly useful social marketing tools for local businesses, especially when combined with sales promotions like coupons, special offers, contests, and events. Location sites can be harnessed to forge lasting relationships with and deeply engrained loyalty in customers.[36] For example, a local restaurant can allow consumers to check in on Foursquare using their Smartphones and receive coupons for that day's purchases. Since the location site technology is relatively new, many brands are still figuring out how best to utilize Foursquare. Facebook added Places to capitalize on this location-based technology, which allows people to "check in" and share their location with their online friends. It will be interesting to see how use of this technology grows over time.

Review Sites

Individuals tend to trust other people's opinions when it comes to purchasing. According to Nielsen Media Research, more than 70 percent of consumers said that they trusted online consumer opinions. This percentage is much higher than that of consumers who trust traditional advertising. Based on the early work of Amazon and eBay to integrate user opinions into product and seller pages, countless Web sites allowing users to voice their opinions have sprung up across every segment of the Internet market. **Review sites** allow consumers to post, read, rate, and comment on opinions regarding all kinds of products and services. For example, Yelp, the most active local review directory on the Web, combines customer critiques of local businesses with business information and elements of social networking to create an engaging, informative experience. On Yelp, users scrutinize local restaurants, fitness centers, tattoo parlors, and other businesses, each of which has a detailed profile page. Business owners and representatives can edit their organizations' pages and respond to Yelp reviews both privately and publicly. Yelp even rewards its most popular (and prolific) reviewers by awarding them Elite status. Business will throw Elite-only parties to allow these esteemed Yelpers to try out their restaurant, hoping to receive a favorable review.[37] By giving marketers the opportunity to respond to their customers directly and put their businesses in a positive light, review sites certainly serve as useful tools for local and national businesses.

location-based social networking sites Web sites that combine the fun of social networking with the utility of location-based GPS technology

review sites Web sites that allow consumers to post, read, rate, and comment on opinions regarding all kinds of products and services

© HANDOUT/MCT/NEWSCOM

Virtual Worlds and Online Gaming

Virtual worlds and online gaming present additional opportunities for marketers to engage with consumers. These include massive multiplayer online games (MMOGs) such as *World of Warcraft* and *The Sims Online* as well as online communities (or virtual worlds) such as Second Life, Poptropica, and Habbo Hotel. Consultancy firm KZero Worldwide reported that almost 800 million people participate in some sort of virtual world experience, and the sector's annual revenue approaches $1 billion. Much of this revenue has come from in-game advertising—virtual world environments are often fertile grounds for branded content. Several businesses, such as IBM and consultancy firm Crayon, have developed profitable trade presences in Second Life. IBM has used its Second Life space to hold virtual conferences with more than 200 participants, while Crayon has held a number of virtual networking events and meet and greets in the virtual world.[38] Other organizations, such as the Centers for Disease Control and Prevention and the American Cancer Society, have held their own virtual events in Second Life. Although virtual worlds are unfamiliar to and even intimidating for many traditional marketers, the field is an important, viable, and growing consideration for social media marketing.

One area of growth is social gaming. Nearly 25 percent of people play games within social networking sites like Facebook or on mobile devices like the iPhone. Interestingly, the typical player is a 43-year-old woman with a full-time job and college education. Women are most likely to play with real-world friends or relatives as opposed to strangers. Most play multiple times per week, and more than 30 percent play daily. Facebook is by far the largest social network for gaming, though Hi5 is hoping to win over more users with its large variety of games. The top five games on Facebook are Farmville, Bejeweled Blitz, Texas Hold'em Poker, Café World, and Mafia Wars. Many play on mobile devices (and the demographic usually skews younger). Angry Birds sucks in users for 200 million minutes per day, and Zynga's City Ville entices more than 100 million people a month. These games are attractive because they can be played in just five minutes, perhaps while waiting for the train.[39] Because of the popularity of gaming with friends and relatives through these sites, marketers have to integrate their message based on the social network platforms and the demographic participating in social gaming.[40]

Another popular type of online gaming targets a different group—MMOGs target 18- to 34-year-old males. In these environments, thousands of people play

© GUSTAVO ARIAS R./LA NACION DE COSTA RICA/NEWSCOM

simultaneously, and the games have revenues of more than $400 billion annually. Regardless of the type of experience, brands must be creative in how they integrate into games. Social and real-world–like titles are the most appropriate for marketing and advertising (as opposed to fantasy games), and promotions typically include special events, competitions, and sweepstakes. In some games (like *Sims*), having ads increases the authenticity. For example, Nike offers shoes in *Sims Online* that allow the player to run faster.

LO 6 Social Media and Mobile Technology

While much of the excitement in social media has been based on Web sites and new technology uses, much of the growth lies in new platforms. These platforms include the multitude of Smartphones like iPhones and BlackBerrys as well as netbooks and iPads. The major implication of this development is that consumers now can access popular Web sites like Facebook, Mashable, Twitter, and Foursquare from all their various platforms.

Mobile and Smartphone Technology

More than 25 percent of the world's population—and more than 75 percent of the U.S. population—owns a mobile phone.[41] It is no surprise then that the mobile platform is such an effective marketing tool—especially when targeting a younger audience. In the 2008 presidential campaign, Barack Obama's staff utilized text messaging to raise funds and organize support from college students, while grassroots organizations such as DoSomething.org used messaging to alert young people to volunteering opportunities. Smartphones up the ante by allowing individuals to do nearly everything they can do with a computer—from anywhere. With a Smartphone in hand, reading a blog, writing an e-mail, scheduling a meeting, posting to Facebook, playing a multiplayer game, watching a video, taking a picture, using GPS, and surfing the Internet might all occur during one ten-minute car ride. Smartphone technology, often considered the crowning achievement in digital convergence and social media integration, has opened the door to modern mobile advertising as a viable marketing strategy.

According to an eMarketer survey, U.S. mobile marketing spending reached nearly $593 million in 2010 and is expected to grow. There are several reasons for the recent popularity of mobile marketing. First, an effort to standardize mobile platforms has resulted in a low barrier to entry. Second, especially given mobile marketing's younger audiences, there are more consumers than ever acclimating to once-worrisome privacy and pricing policies. Third, because most consumers carry their Smartphones with them at all times, mobile marketing is uniquely effective at garnering consumer attention in real time. Fourth, mobile marketing is measurable: Metrics and usage statistics make it an effective tool for gaining insight into consumer behavior. Finally, mobile marketing's response rate is higher than that of traditional media types like print and broadcast advertisement. Some common mobile marketing tools include:

▶▶ *SMS (short message service):* 160-character text messages sent to and from cell phones. SMS is typically integrated with other tools.

▶▶ *MMS (multimedia messaging service):* Similar to SMS but allows the attachment of images, videos, ringtones, and other multimedia to text messages.

▶▶ *Mobile Web sites (MOBI and WAP Web sites):* Web sites designed specifically for viewing and navigation on mobile devices.

▶▶ *Mobile ads:* Visual advertisements integrated into text messages, applications, and mobile Web sites. Mobile ads are often sold on a cost-per-click basis.

▶▶ *Bluetooth marketing:* A signal is sent to Bluetooth-enabled devices, which allows marketers to send targeted messages to users based on their geographic locations.

▶▶ *Smartphone applications (apps):* Software designed specifically for mobile and tablet devices. These apps include software to turn phones into scanners for various types of barcodes.

A popular recent application of Smartphone convenience and technology is a "quick response" (QR) code. When scanned by a Smartphone's QR reader, a QR code takes the user to a specific site with content about or a discount for products or services. Uses range from donating to a charity by scanning the code to simply checking out the company's Web site for more information. For example, Canadian coffee shop Ethical Bean Coffee company put QR codes on trains. The codes take customers to a mobile site with the coffee menu; customers can order a drink, and it will be ready at the nearest Ethical Bean location. By catering to the on-the-go commuter crowd, Ethical Bean saw a significant traffic boost.[42] Another Smartphone trend

© FRANCES M. ROBERTS/FRANCES M. ROBERTS/NEWSCOM

is called "near field communication" (NFC), which uses small chips hidden behind items like promotional posters that will transfer information about the show to NFC compatible devices that tap the poster. VH-1's *Basketball Wives* is one of the first large-scale campaigns to test NFC technology.[43]

Applications and Widgets

Given the widespread adoption of Apple's iPhone, RIM's BlackBerry line, Android-based phones, and other Smartphones, it's no surprise that millions of applications have been developed for the mobile market. Dozens of new and unique apps that harness mobile technology are added to mobile marketplaces every day. While many apps perform platform-specific tasks, others convert existing content into a mobile-ready format. Whether offering new or existing content, when an app is well branded and integrated into a company's overall marketing strategy, it can create buzz and generate customer engagement.

One organization that used its Smartphone apps effectively was Benjamin Moore Paint. The company focused on the fact that utility can be as effective a selling point as connectivity when it developed Color Capture, an app that allows iPhone users to match colors in photos to shades in the Benjamin Moore color collection. Users can also save their favorite colors and chip names for future use.[44]

Web widgets, also known as gadgets and badges, are software applications that run entirely within existing online platforms. Essentially, a Web widget allows a developer to embed a simple application such as a weather forecast, horoscope, or stock market ticker into a Web site, even if the developer did not write (or does not understand) the application's source code. From a marketing perspective, widgets allow customers to display company information (such as current promotions, coupons, or news) on their own Web sites. Widgets are often cheaper than apps to develop, can extend an organization's reach beyond existing platforms, will broaden the listening system, and can make an organization easier to find.[45]

Allowing customers to promote up-to-date marketing material on their own blogs and Web sites is very appealing, but before investing in a marketing-oriented widget, a number of questions should be considered:

▸▸ Does my organization regularly publish compelling content, such as news, daily specials, or coupons, on its Web site or blog?

▸▸ Does my content engage individuals or appeal to their needs as customers?

▸▸ Is my content likely to inspire conversations with the company or with other customers? Will customers want to share my content with others?

If you can answer yes to these questions, a widget may be an effective tool for your organization.

The Changing World of Social Media

As you read through the chapter, some of the trends that are noted may already seem ancient to you. The rate of change in social media is astounding—usage statistics change daily for sites like Facebook and Twitter. Some things that are in the rumor mill as we write this may have exploded in popularity; others may have fizzled out without even appearing on your radar. In Exhibit 22.3, we've listed some of the items that seem to be on the brink of exploding on to the social media scene. Take a moment to fill in the current state of each in the third column. Have you heard of it? Has it come and gone? Maybe it is still rumored, or maybe it has petered out. This exercise highlights not only the speed with which social media change but also the importance of keeping tabs on rumors. Doing so may result in a competitive advantage by being able to understand and invest in the next big social media site.

EXHIBIT 22.3
Social Media Trends

Trend	Change	Where Is It Now?
Facebook	Threaded commenting, up/down voting comments.	
Twitter	Promoted tweets.	
Facebook/Bing	Facebook-linked searching in Bing. Search pulls information from your profile to find more accurate information.	
Foursquare/Facebook Places/location-based applications	Facebook Places, Foursquare gaining popularity away from major cities.	
Google+	Just released, claimed by some to be a Facebook killer.	
Key Ring, CardStar, Google Wallet	Eliminate plastic loyalty cards and use Smartphones as a single digital repository for loyalty cards, credit cards, and other scannable or swipe-able cards typically found in a wallet.	
Stickybits, Bakodo	Ability to use barcode scanner on a Smartphone and QR code check-ins.	
Groupon, LivingSocial, Woot, and programs by Yelp, Zagat, and Open Table	Mainstream of the deal-a-day, social coupon trend.	

© CENGAGE LEARNING 2013

STUDY TOOLS CHAPTER 22

Flip to the back of your textbook to:

❑ **Rip out Chapter Review Card**

Log in to the CourseMate for MKTG at cengagebrain.com to:

❑ **Review Key Terms Flash Cards (Print or Online)**

❑ **Review Audio and Visual Summaries**

❑ **Complete both Practice Quizzes to prepare for tests**

❑ **Play "Beat the Clock" and "Quizbowl" to master concepts**

❑ **Complete "Crossword Puzzle" to review key terms**

❑ **Watch the video on "Mobile Marketing to Kids" for a real world example of Social Media and Marketing.**

ONE APPROACH.
70 UNIQUE SOLUTIONS.

www.cengage.com/4ltrpress

Endnotes

1

1. Announcement to the AMA Academic Council from Patricia K. Goodrich, Senior Director, Professional Development, American Marketing Association, October 25, 2007.

2. George Anderson, "Satisfied Workers Generate Greater Returns," *Retailwire*, January 16, 2008, www.retailwire.com.

3. David A. Kaplan, "The Best Company to Work For," *Fortune*, February 8, 2010, 57–64.

4. Philip Kotler and Kevin Lane Keller, *A Framework for Marketing Management*, 5th ed. (Upper Saddle River, NJ: Prentice-Hall, 2011), 4–5.

5. "Aggressive Deals Are Expected to Boost Toyota Sales 30 Percent in March," *Palm Beach Post*, March 12, 2010, www.palmbeachpost.com /money/aggressive-deals-are-expected-to-boost -toyota-sales-346358.html.

6. Inc. Staff, "10 Ways to Support Your Best Customers," *Inc.*, August 3, 2010, www.inc.com /guides/2010/07/10-ways-to-support-your-best -customers.html.

7. Kathy Grannic, "Zappos.com Tops in Customer Service, According to NRF Foundation/ American Express Survey," National Retail Federation, January 11, 2011, www.nrf.com /modules.php?name=News&op=viewlive&sp _id=1067.

8. Jena McGregor, "Customer Service Champs 2010," *Bloomberg Businessweek*, February 18, 2010, http://images.businessweek.com/ss/10/02 /0218_customer_service_champs/index.htm.

9. Tom Ryan, "Eco-Conscious Meets Cost-Conscious at P&G," *Retailwire*, March 22, 2010, www.retailwire.com/discussions/sngl_discussion .cfm/14373.

10. Ellen Byron and Suzanne Vranica, "'Green' Products to Get a Push," *Wall Street Journal*, January 11, 2010, B5.

11. "Recycle Guidelines," Best Buy, www.bestbuy .com/site/null/null/pcmcat174700050010.c?id =pcmcat174700050010 (Accessed March 30, 2011).

12. "Burt's Bees, Whole Foods Perceived Greenest US Brands," *environmentalleader.com*, June 9, 2010, www.environmentalleader.com/2010/06/09 /climate-change-identified-as-biggest-issue-for -global-consumers.

13. Yana Polikarpov, "Consumers Still Have Green Expectations," *Brandweek*, February 24, 2009, www.brandweek.com/bw/content_display /news-and-features/green-marketing/e3ia9e9c2b 958c051e5105490e4ff0dc43b.

14. "2010 Post-Recession Consumer Study," Ogilvy & Mather, March 15, 2010, www.ogilvy .com/News/Press-Releases/March-2010-Eyes -Wide-Open.aspx.

15. Anjali Athavaley, "What Makes a Mattress Cost $33,000?" *Wall Street Journal*, June 16, 2010, D1–D2.

16. Tim Donnelly, "How to Open a Business in Brooklyn," *Inc.*, June 28, 2010, www.inc.com /guides/2010/06/opening-a-business-in-brooklyn .html.

17. Inc. Staff, "10 Ways to Support Your Best Customers," August 3, 2010, www.inc.com/ guides/2010/07/10-ways-to-support-your-best-customers.html.

18. Phred Dvorak, "Next in Line for Reinvention: The Art of Selling," *Wall Street Journal*, January 28, 2008, B3.

19. Karen Aho, "The Customer Service Hall of Shame," *MSN*, May 18, 2010, http://articles .moneycentral.msn.com/Investing/Extra/the -customer-service-hall-of-shame-2010.aspx.

20. Ibid.

21. Emily Steel, "The Billboard That Knows," *Wall Street Journal*, February 28, 2011, http:// online.wsj.com/article/SB1000142405274870469 2904576167272357856608.html.

22. Jena McGregor, "USAA's Battle Plan," *Bloomberg Businessweek*, February 18, 2010, www.businessweek.com/magazine/content/10_09 /b4168040782858.htm.

23. Christopher Tkaczyk, "American Express," *Fortune*, August 16, 2010, 14.

24. Jeff Green and David Welch, "Cadillac Starts Putting on the Ritz," *Bloomberg Businessweek*, June 21–June 27, 2010, 24.

25. Samuel Fromartz, "Good Enough to Eat," *Fast Company*, September 2008, 29.

26. Katherine Barrett and Richard Greene, "Dashboard Confessionals, Eliminating Duplicative Services, and Henry Ford on Innovation," *Governing*, February 17, 2011, www.governing.com/topics/mgmt/Dashboard -Confessionals-Eliminating-Duplicative-Services -and-Henry-Ford-on-Innovation.html.

27. Courtney Rubin, "The Truth about Who's Using Twitter," *Inc.*, May 10, 2010, www.inc.com /news/articles/2010/05/twitter-just-as-well-known -as-facebook.html; Jessie Kunhardt, "The Best Publishers on Twitter and Facebook," *Huffington Post*, June 24, 2010, www.huffingtonpost .com/2010/06/24/the-best-publishers-on-tw_n _623364.html.

28. U.S. Census Bureau, "U.S. & World Population Clocks," www.census.gov/main/www /popclock.html (Accessed January 14, 2011).

2

1. Julie Naughton, "Macy's Reacts to Changing Consumer Shopping Habits," *Women's Wear Daily*, June 11, 2010, 6.

2. David Jolly, "Saab Sputter On, Saved by Two Chinese Automakers," *New York Times*, October 28, 2011, 23.

3. Nanette Byrnes, "Pepsi Brings in the Health Police," *Bloomberg Businessweek*, January 25, 2010, www.businessweek.com/magazine /content/10_04/b4164050511214.htm.

4. Elaine Wong, "Kraft Goes Beyond the Bagel," *Brandweek*, April 3, 2009, www .brandweek.com/bw/content_display /news-and-features/packaged-goods /e3id4d9d8e33174af5aa6460621107d2c8a.

5. Molly Prior, "CVS Comes Calling," *Women's Wear Daily*, June 11, 2010, 6.

6. David Kesmodel, "Pabst's Horse of a Different Color: Colt 45 Enters Controversial Ring," *Wall Street Journal*, March 18, 2011, http://online.wsj.com/article/SB10001424052748 704360404576206621165029478.html.

7. Arik Hesseldahl, "Why the Mac Is Still a Rock Star at Apple," *Bloomberg Businessweek*, June 28–July 4, 2010, 30.

8. Ina Fried, "Microsoft Pulls the Plug on Kin," *Cnet*, June 30, 2010, http://news.cnet.com/8301 -13860_3-20009336-56.html.

9. Hesseldahl, "Why the Mac Is Still a Rock Star at Apple."

10. Ben & Jerry's, "Ben & Jerry's Mission," www.benjerry.com/activism/mission-statement (Accessed March 30, 2011).

11. Connie Gugielmo and Aaron Ricadela, "Mulling Options, Dell Considers Going Private," *Bloomberg Businessweek*, June 21–June 27, 2010, 37–38.

12. Duane Stanford, "How PepsiCo Refreshed Its SoBe Water Brand," *Bloomberg Businessweek*, June 28–July 4, 2010, 15–16.

13. Alex Schleifer and Jonathan Anderson, "Lessons from Ikea," *UX Magazine*, January 12, 2010, www.uxmag.com/strategy/lessons-from-ikea.

14. Green B.E.A.N. Delivery, "Green B.E.A.N. Bins," October 11, 2010, www.greenbeandelivery .com/cincinnati/index.php/what-we-offer /farm-fresh-green-bins.

15. The Chef's Garden, "Our Story," July 2, 2010, www.chefs-garden.com/our-story; The Chef's Garden, "Research and Development," July 2, 2010, www.chefs-garden.com/research-and -development.

16. Austin Carr, "Netflix Reacts to Blockbuster's Boasts, iPhone App, and Hulu," *Fast Company*, June 11, 2010, www.fastcompany.com/1659085 /netflix-reacts-to-blockbuster-and-ceo-jim-keyes -speaks-on-iphone-app-and-competition-from-hu.

17. Kesmodel, "Pabst's Horse of a Different Color."

3

1. Marianne M. Jennings, *Business Ethics*, 5th ed. (Mason, OH: Thomson Higher Education, 2006), 5–6.

2. Based on Edward Stevens, *Business Ethics* (New York: Paulist Press, 1979). Used with permission of Paulist Press.

3. Anusorn Singhapakdi, Skott Vitell, and Kenneth Kraft, "Moral Intensity and Ethical Decision Making of Marketing Professionals," *Journal of Business Research*, 36, March 1996, 245–255; Ishmael Akaah and Edward Riordan, "Judgments of Marketing Professionals about Ethical Issues in Marketing Research: A Replication and Extension," *Journal of Marketing Research*, February 1989, 112–120; see also Shelby Hunt, Lawrence Chonko, and James Wilcox, "Ethical Problems of Marketing Researchers," *Journal of Marketing Research*, August 1984, 309–324; Kenneth Andrews, "Ethics in Practice," *Harvard Business Review*, September/October 1989, 99–104; Thomas Dunfee, Craig Smith, and William T. Ross, Jr., "Social Contracts and Marketing Ethics," *Journal of Marketing*, July 1999, 14–32; Jay Handleman and Stephen Arnold, "The Role of Marketing Actions with a Social Dimension: Appeals to the Institutional Environment," *Journal of Marketing*, July 1999, 33–48; and David Turnipseed, "Are Good Soldiers Good? Exploring the Link between Organizational Citizenship Behavior and Personal Ethics," *Journal of Business Research*, January 2002, 1–16.

4. "A Strong Ethical Culture Is Key to Cutting Misconduct on the Job," Ethics Resource Center, June 23, 2010, http://ethics.org/news/strong-ethical-culture-key-cutting-misconduct-job.

5. Ibid.

6. Susan Carey, "Snap, Crackle, Slap: FTC Forbids Rice Krispies Claim," *Wall Street Journal,* June 4, 2010, B1–B2.

7. Ibid.

8. Terry Mann, "Ethics Training for the Workplace," *eHow.com*, February 6, 2010, www.ehow.com.facts_5957733_ethics-training-workplace.html.

9. *2009 National Business Ethics Survey* (Arlington, Virginia: Ethics Resource Center) 2009, 9–12.

10. "Survey Says: Ethics Training Works," *All Business*, November 1, 2005, www.allbusiness.com/services/educational-services/4284114-1.html.

11. Dexter Roberts and Justin Blum, "Bribery Is Losing Its Charm in China,"*Bloomberg Businessweek*, July 12–July 18, 2010, 11.

12. Jeanne Moos, "Dodge vs. PETA," *CNN*, August 16, 2010, www.cnn.com/video/#/video/offbeat/2010/08/16/moos.invisible.monkey.vs.peta.cnn.

13. Marc Gunther, "Will Social Responsibility Harm Business?" *Wall Street Journal*, May 18, 2005, A2.

14. This section is adapted from Archie B. Carroll, "The Pyramid of Corporate Social Responsibility: Toward the Moral Management of Organizational Stakeholders," *Business Horizons*, July/August 1991, 39–48; see also Kirk Davidson, "Marketers Must Accept Greater Responsibilities," *Marketing News*, February 2, 1998, 6.

15. "SAM, Dow Jones Indexes and STOXX, Ltd. Announce Results of Dow Jones Sustainability Review," SAM Media Release, September 3, 2009; see also "What Is Sustainability?" June 7, 2010, www.About.com.

16. "Globally, Companies Are Giving Back," *HR Magazine*, June 1, 2007, 30.

17. "IBM Global Survey Shows Information Gap in 'Green'," *Sustainability Strategies,* June 1, 2009, www-03.ibm.com/press/us/en/pressrelease/27622.wss.

18. "United Nations Global Compact Annual Review—Anniversary Edition June 2010," United Nations Global Compact, June 2010, www.unglobalcompact.org/docs/news_events/8.1/UNGC_Annual_Review_2010.pdf.

19. "Secretary-General Opens Global Compact Leaders Summit as Business, Government, Civil Society Leaders Rally for Corporate Citizenship," UNESCAP Press Release, July 5, 2007, Press Release No. L/38/2007.

20. American Marketing Association, www.marketingpower.com (Accessed October 28, 2008).

21. Gordon Wyner, "Sustainability Perspectives," *Marketing Management*, Summer 2010, 45.

22. "Marketing a Green Product," *Business Week Online*, March 5, 2007, 13.

23. "Its Not Easy Being Green," July–August 2008, 14–15, www.usbusiness-review.com.

24. "Easy but Green, Rider," *Marketing Magazine*, July 14, 2008, 29.

25. "Consumers Doubt Green Efforts," *Marketing Management*, July/August 2009, 5.

26. "Sustainability Marketing Has Legs," *Marketing Management*, July/August 2009, 4.

27. Xueming Luo and C. B. Battacharya, "The Debate over Doing Good: Corporate Social Performance, Strategic Marketing Levers, and Firm-Idiosyncratic Risk," *Journal of Marketing*, November 2009, 198–213.

4

1. James Hagerty, "Zippo Preps for a Post-Smoker World," *Wall Street Journal,* March 8, 2011, http://online.wsj.com/article/SB10001424052748704076804576180411173921454.html.

2. This is a partial list of trends projected by the Natural Marketing Institute, "Healthy, Green, Simple—Trends to Watch in the Next Ten Years," *Quirk's Marketing Research Review*, May 2010, 6.

3. "Quick Stats of Women Workers," www.dol.gov (Accessed June 17, 2010).

4. Shushannah Walshe, "Ladies Lock and Load: American Women Buying More Guns," *Daily Beast,* March 11, 2011, www.thedailybeast.com/blogs-and-stories/2011-03-11/number-of-us-women-buying-guns-for-hunting-and-personal-defense-spikes-sharply.

5. "American Time Use Survey—2009 Results," Bureau of Labor Statistics, June 22, 2010, www.bls.gov/news.release/pdf/atus.pdf.

6. Marjorie Connelly, "More Americans Sense a Downside to an Always Plugged-In Existence," *New York Times,* June 6, 2010, www.nytimes.com/2010/06/07/technology/07brainpoll.html?ref=technology.

7. "Welcome to the Weisure Lifestyle," *CNN,* May 11, 2009, http://articles.cnn.com/2009-05-11/living/weisure_1_creative-class-richard-florida-leisure-time.

8. Matt Richtel, "Attached to Technology and Paying a Price," *New York Times,* June 6, 2010, www.nytimes.com/2010/06/07/technology/07/brain.html.

9. David Glenn, "Divided Attention," *Chronicle Review,* February 28, 2010, http://chronicle.com/article/Scholars-Turn-Their-Attention/63746.

10. Population Projections, "Key Facts & Trends," Population Resource Center, www.prcdc.org/300million/Population_Projections (Accessed March 24, 2011).

11. "Cities Grow at Suburbs' Expense during Recession," *Wall Street Journal*, July 1, 2009, A5.

12. "Marketing and Tweens," *Branding*, June 16, 2010.

13. Kathy Grannis, "Back to School Sales Up As Parents Replenish Children's Needs, According to NRF," *National Retailing Federation,* July 15, 2010, www.nrf.com/modules.php?name=News&op=viewlive&sp_id=966.

14. Anjali Athavaley, "Make Room for Junior Decorators," *Wall Street Journal,* December 1, 2010, http://online.wsj.com/article/SB10001424052748704679204575646671354210974.html.

15. "Pew Survey: Teens Love Facebook, Hate Blogging, Are Always Online, and Don't Use Twitter," *Fast Company*, February 3, 2010, www.fastcompany.com/blog/zachary-wilson/and-how/pew-survey-finds-increase-social-media-internet-time-decrese-blogging-te.

16. "Teens Slowly Increase Online Shopping," *emarketer,* April 26, 2011, www.emarketer.com/Article.aspx?R=1008359.

17. Susan Lipston, "Teenage Spending Habits," January 26, 2011, http://susanlipston.com/wordpress/2011/01/26/teenage-spending-habits.

18. "Teens Slowly Increase Online Shopping."

19. "Teen Marketing Techniques," www.ehow.com (Accessed June 18, 2010); Brian Theriot, "Teen Marketing Tips," *Suite101.com,* April 22, 2010, www.suite101.com/content/teen-marketing-tips-a228866.

20. Todd Stone, "Serious GE Lightens Up for YouTube Campaign," *Advertising Age,* October 28, 2010, http://adage.com/article/viral-video-charts/viral-video-ge-lightens-youtube-campaign/146729.

21. "Boomers and GenX the Most Spend-Happy; Millennials Buy More Per Trip," *Quirk's Marketing Research Review*, May 2010, 10.

22. Lynne Lancaster and David Stillman, "The M Factor," *Delta Sky Magazine*, May 2010, 70–73, 100–105.

23. Miles O'Brien, "This Is Your Teen's Brain on Technology and Multitasking," *PBS Newshour,* January 5, 2011, www.pbs.org/newshour/rundown/2011/01/miles-obrien-teen-brains-on-technology.html.

24. Scott Galloway, "Gen Y Affluents: Media Survey," *L2,* December 16, 2010, www.slideshare.net/L2ThinkTank/l2-gen-y-affluents-media-survey.

25. Demographic Profile: America's GENX, MetLife Mature Market Institute, 2009.

26. "Gen X, Y Will Lead Economic Recovery," PriceWaterhouseCoopers, April 5, 2010, www.marketingcharts.com/direct/gen-xy-will-lead-economic-recovery-12482.

27. Todd Hale, "Marketing across the Generations," Nielsen, March 4, 2010, http://blog.nielsen.com/nielsenwire/consumer/mining-the-u-s-generation-gaps.

28. Ibid.

29. Amy Chozick, "Television's Senior Moment," *Wall Street Journal,* March 9, 2011, http://online.wsj.com/article/SB1000142405274870355960457617498327266 5032.

30. Beth Bulik, "Boom in Multigenerational Households Has Wide Implications for Ad Industry," *Advertising Age*, August 23, 2010, http://adage.com/article/news/multigenerational-households-implications-marketers/145506.

31. Chozick, "Television's Senior Moment."
32. Brian Steinberg, "Nielsen; This Isn't Your Grandfather's Baby Boomer," *Advertising Age,* July 19, 2010, http://adage.com/article/mediaworks /nielsen-grandfather-s-baby-boomer/144939.
33. Jennifer Wang, "Reboot Sonny," *Entrepreneur,* June 2010, 68.
34. Sam Fahmy, "Despite Recession, Hispanic and Asian Buying Power Expected to Surge in U.S. According to Annual UGA Selig Center Muliticultural Economy Study," Terry College of Business, November 4, 2010, www.terry.uga .edu/news/releases/2010/minority-buying-power -report.html.
35. Conor Dougherty, "U.S. Nears Racial Milestone," *Wall Street Journal,* June 11, 2010, http://online.wsj.com/article/SB10001424052748 7043121045752985120006681060.html.
36. Sean Callebs, "Whites Become Minority in Kansas," *CNN,* May 22, 2009, http://articles .cnn.com/2009-05-22/living/garden.city.kansas .minorities_1_meatpacking-minority-majority.
37. Pete Born, "Beauty in the Age of Multiplicity," *WWD Beauty Inc.,* March 11, 2011, 8.
38. Ibid.
39. Lisa Lockwood, "Hispanics: A Growing Force," *Women's Wear Daily,* March 23, 2011, 2.
40. Jessica Gray, "Young Latino Americans Drive Population Growth," *Hispanic Market Info,* February 16, 2011, www.hispanicmarketinfo .com/2011/02/16/young-latino-americans-drive -population-growth.
41. Born, "Beauty in the Age of Multiplicity," 8.
42. "Report Shows a Shifting African-American Population," *Brandweek,* January 11, 2009, 6.
43. Bobbi Bowman, "A Portrait of Black America on the Eve of the 2010 Census," *The Root,* February 10, 2010, www.theroot.com/views /portrait-black-america-eve-2010-census.
44. Authors' projections based upon U.S. Census.
45. "Facts for Features: Asian/Pacific American Heritage Month—May 2011," U.S. Census Bureau, March 8, 2011, www.census.gov /newsroom/releases/archives/facts_for_features _special_editions/cb11-ff06.html; "2005–2009 American Community Survey 5-year Estimates," U.S. Census Bureau, http://factfinder.census.gov /servlet/ACSSAFFFacts?_submenuId=factsheet_1& _sse=on (Accessed April 27, 2011).
46. Christine Huang, "GlobalHue Presents: The New Asian American Market," May 2010, www .slideshare.net/christinewhuang/asian-american -market-ad-tech-sf.
47. U.S. News Staff, "Median U.S. Household Income by State," *US News and World Report,* October 5, 2010, www.usnews.com/opinion /articles/2010/10/05/median-us-household -income-by-state.
48. Daniel Gross, "You're Rich. Get Over It," *Slate Magazine,* February 3, 2010, www.slate .com/id/2243529.
49. Robert Longley, "Lifetime Earnings Soar with Education," *About.com,* February 13, 2010, http://usgovinfo.about.com/od/moneymatters/a /edandearnings.htm.
50. David Wessel, "Did 'Great Recession' Live Up to Its Name?" *Wall Street Journal,* April 8, 2010, http://online.wsj.com/article/SB10001424052702 3035912045751696931663552882.html.
51. Monica Garske, "Affordable Store-Brand Products Score with Customers," *AOLNews,* January 21, 2011, www.aolnews.com/2011/01/21 /affordable-store-brand-products-score-with -consumers.
52. "Food Firms Cook Up Ways to Combat Rare Sales Slump," *Wall Street Journal,* April 21, 2010, A1, A18.
53. "Ben Franklin, Where Are You?" *Bloomberg Businessweek,* January 4, 2010, 29.
54. Cate Corcoran, "New App Encourages Users to Strike a Pose," *Women's Wear Daily,* January 11, 2011, 10.
55. "The 50 Most Innovative Companies 2010," *Bloomberg Businessweek,* April 15, 2010, www.businessweek.com/interactive_reports /innovative_companies_2010.html.
56. Partially adopted from John Bessant, Kathrin Moslein, and Bettina Von Stamm, "In Search of Innovation," *Wall Street Journal,* June 22, 2009, R4.
57. Ashlee Vance, "Intel's Bet on Innovation Pays of in Faster Chips," *New York Times,* January 14, 2010, www.nytimes.com/2010/01/15/technology /companies/15chip.html.
58. "FTC Bureau of Competition," www.ftc.gov /bc (Accessed March 25, 2011).
59. "Pretexting," www.ftc.gov/bsp/edu/microsites /idtheft/consumers/pretexting.html (Accessed March 25, 2011).
60. Julie Jargon, "Starbucks in Pod Pact," *Wall Street Journal,* March 11, 2011, http://online.wsj .com/article/SB1000142405274870482300457619 2191958964006.html.
61. Emily Steel and Justin Scheck, "Smartphone Trackers Raise Privacy Worries," *Wall Street Journal,* June 14, 2010, http://online.wsj.com /article/SB10001424052748704067504575304643 134531922.html.

5

1. World Trade Organization, "Trade to Expand by 9.5 Percent in 2010 after a Dismal 2009, WTO Reports," International Trade Statistics, March 26, 2010, www.wto.org/english/news_e/pres10 _e/pr598_e.htm.
2. "How We Win," www.cat.com (Accessed June 14, 2010).
3. "SBA Export Express—A Fact Sheet for Small Businesses," http://SBA.gov/content/sba-export- express-fact-sheet-small-businesses (Accessed March 25, 2011).
4. Gary Locke and Francisco Sanchez, "Exports Support American Jobs," International Trade Administration, April 2010, http://trade.gov /publications/pdfs/exports-support-american-jobs .pdf, 1–2.
5. Locke and Sanchez, "Exports Support American Jobs," 2.
6. "Globalization's Gains Come with a Price," *Wall Street Journal,* May 24, 2007, A1, A12.
7. Martin Neil Baily, Matthew Slaughter, and Laura Tyson, "The Global Jobs Competition Heats Up," *Wall Street Journal,* July 1, 2010, A19.
8. Andrea Nagel and Rachel Brown, "Gains Expected for Makeup," *Women's Wear Daily,* February 4, 2011, 3.
9. Theodore Levitt, "The Globalization of Markets," *Harvard Business Review,* May/June 1983, 92–100.
10. "Ford Chief Bets on One Global Car," *International Herald Tribune,* January 22, 2010, 1, 16.
11. Ellen Gamerman, "Exporting Broadway," *Wall Street Journal,* July 16, 2010, W1–W2.
12. The World Bank, "GNI, Atlas Method (Current US$)," http://data.worldbank.org /indicator/NY.GNP.ATLS.CD/countries (Accessed January 26, 2011).
13. Ibid.
14. "Trop Cher?" *Economist,* March 10, 2010, www.economist.com/node/15659589.
15. Laurie Burkitt, "Burberry Dresses Up China Stores with Digital Strategy," *Wall Street Journal,* April 14, 2011, B9.
16. Ibid.
17. Paul Beckett, Vibhuti Agarwal, and Julie Jargon, "Starbucks Brews Plan to Enter India," *Wall Street Journal,* January 14, 2011, http:// online.wsj.com/article/SB1000142405274870358 3404576079593558838756.html.
18. Peter Coy, "Five Ways Forward with China," *Bloomberg Businessweek,* June 28–July 4, 2010, 4–5; Arnold J. Karr, "Study: China Top Market for Retail Development," *Women's Wear Daily,* June 23, 2010, 2.
19. "Economy Rankings," *Doing Business,* www.doingbusiness.org/rankings (Accessed January 26, 2011).
20. Bruce Einhorn, "Vietnam: An Asian-Tiger Wannabe (Again)," *Bloomberg Businessweek,* June 21–June 27, 2010, 12–13.
21. Larry Elliott and Heather Stewart, "Doha Trade Round Faces Risk of Collapse after 10 Years of Talks," *The Observer,* April 24, 2011, www.guardian.co.uk/business/2011/apr/24 /doha-trade-talks-threat-of-collapse-geneva-wto.
22. Loretta Chao, "Huawei Blames Revenue Slowdown on Protectionism," *Wall Street Journal,* April 27, 2011, http://online.wsj.com/article/SB1 0001424052748703956904576288082357233172.html.
23. Tom Barkley, "U.S. Chamber Kicks Up Campaign for Free Trade," *Wall Street Journal,* May 14, 2010, http://online.wsj.com/article/SB1 0001424052748703464040457524417096173857 4.html.
24. "NAFTA at a Glance," North American Free Trade Agreement, www.naftanow.org/facts (Accessed January 26, 2011).
25. "U.S. Central America-Dominican Republic Free Trade Agreement (CAFTA-DR) Analysis," (Washington, DC: International Trade Association, Summer 2008), 12.
26. "About Us," www.eurunion.org (Accessed April 27, 2011).
27. Natascha Gewaltig, "Greece's Painful Choice," *Bloomberg Businessweek,* February 19, 2010, www.businessweek.com/investor/content /feb2010/pi20100218_722508.htm; Stephen Fidler and Charles Forelle, "World Races to Avert Crisis in Europe," *Wall Street Journal,* May 10, 2010, http://online.wsj.com/article/SB100014 2405274870388030457523563261 8569478 .html; Katie Martin, "Emergency Lenders Play It Straight," *Wall Street Journal,* July 19, 2010, http://blogs.wsj.com/source/2010/07/19 /emergency-lenders-play-it-straight.
28. Gabriele Steinhauser, "EU Fines Procter & Gamble, Unilever over Laundry Detergent Cartel," *Huffington Post,* April 13, 2011, www .huffingtonpost.com/2011/04/13/eu-fines-proctor -gamble-u_n_848508.html.
29. Jonathan Bensky, "World's Biggest Market: European Union Offers Great Opportunities for

U.S. Companies, but There Are Also Plenty of Challenges," *Shipping Digest*, July 30, 2007.

30. Gamerman, "Exporting Broadway," W1–W2.

31. www.franchise.org (Accessed July 20, 2010).

32. Liza Algar, "Abrams & Chronicle Books Announce Sales, Marketing and Distribution Joint Venture to Serve the United Kingdom and Europe Export Markets," June 22, 2010, www .chroniclebooks.com/Chronicle/pressroom /A_CB_mediaRelease.pdf.

33. "Korean Dunkin' Donuts," *EatyourKimchi*, March 13, 2011, www.eatyourkimchi.com /korean-dunkin-donuts.

34. Beckett, Agarwal, and Jargon, "Starbucks Brews Plan to Enter India."

35. Nidhi Dutt, "Mobile Tech Brings Big Retail Brands to Rural India," *BBC News*, March 27, 2011, www.bbc.co.uk/news/business-1284199.

36. 'Will Connors and Sarah Childress, "Africa's Local Champions Begin to Spread Out," *Wall Street Journal*, May 26, 2010, B8.

6

1. "New Tax on Indoor Tanning Goes into Effect," *CBS*, June 30, 2010, www.cbsnews.com/ stories/2010/06/30/eveningnews/main6635131.shtml

2. Lance A. Bettencourt and Anthony W. Ulwich, "The Customer-Centered Innovation Map," *Harvard Business Review*, May 2008, 1–8; also see Anthony W. Ulwich and Lance A. Bettencourt, "Giving Customers a Fair Hearing," *Sloan Management Review*, Spring 2008, 62–68.

3. "LG Electronics: Rural Is the Future," *Wall Street Journal*, May 6, 2010, http://online.wsj .com/article/SB127313731105787137.html.

4. Elisabeth Sullivan, "Virtually Satisfied," *Marketing News*, October 15, 2008, 26.

5. "By the Numbers," *Next*, May 17, 2010, 24.

6. Hui Chen, "The Impact Mechanism of Consumer-Generated Comments of Shopping Sites on Consumer Trust," *Journal of Computers*, 6, no. 1 (January 2011): 43–50, doi:10.4304 /jcp.6.1.43-50.

7. Wendy Moe and Michael Trusov, "The Value of Social Dynamics in Online Ratings Forums," *Journal of Marketing Research*, 48, no. 3 (June 2011): 444–456, www.marketingpower.com /AboutAMA/Documents/JMR_Forthcoming /value_of_social_dynamics.pdf.

8. Barbara Thau, "A J.Crew Wedding Dress? How Far Can Brands Stretch?" *CNBC*, June 24, 2010, www.cnbc.com/id/37820458/A_J_Crew _Wedding_Dress_How_Far_Can_Brands_Stretch.

9. Jeffrey Inman and Russell Winer, "Impulse Buys," *Wall Street Journal*, April 15, 1999, A1; David Silvera, Anne Lavack, and Fredric Kropp, "Impulse Buying: The Role of Affect, Social Influence, and Subjective Well-Being," *Journal of Consumer Research*, 25, no. 1, 2008, 23–33.

10. "2010 Post-Recession Consumer Study," Ogilvy & Mather, March 15, 2010, www.ogilvy .com/News/Press-Releases/March-2010-Eyes -Wide-Open.aspx.

11. Karin Stilley, Jeffrey Inman, and Kirk Wakefield, "Spending on the Fly: Mental Budgets, Promotions, and Spending Behavior," *Journal of Marketing*, May 2010, 34–47.

12. The material on "types of involvement" was adapted from Barry Babin and Eric Harris, *CB²* (Mason: Ohio: South-Western Cengage Learning) 2011, 88–89.

13. "How It Works," Pepsi Refresh Project, July 22, 2010, www.refresheverything.com; "Trading TV Commercials for Cause Marketing," *The Anatomy of Wow*, January 8, 2010, http:// theanatomyofwow.com/index.php/2010/01/08 /trading-tv-commercials-for-cause-marketing/.

14. Joe Piazza, "Booking Spontaneity, at a Price," *Wall Street Journal*, June 7, 2011, http://online .wsj.com/article/SB10001424052702304432304576369792412879516.html.

15. Alice Truong, "Q&A: A Social Network Built on Mobile Phones," *Wall Street Journal*, July 14, 2010, http://blogs.wsj.com/digits/2010/07/14 /mocospace/.

16. Alexandria Alter, "Luxury Lit: A Book for $75,000," *Wall Street Journal*, July 16, 2010, W4.

17. Christina Binkley, "Post-Recession, the Rich Are Different," *Wall Street Journal,* May 12, 2011, http://online.wsj.com/article/SB10001424052748 7037308045763172002215630540.html.

18. Ibid.

19. Ulrich Orth and Lynn Kahle, "Intrapersonal Variation in Consumer Susceptibility to Normative Influence: Toward a Better Understanding of Brand Choice Decisions," *Journal of Social Psychology*, August 8, 2008, 423–448.

20. Gwendolyn Bounds, "In the New Dream Home, Majestic Boilers and Designer Pipes," *Wall Street Journal*, July 15, 2010, A1, A14.

21. Orth and Kahle, "Intrapersonal Variation in Consumer Susceptibility to Normative Influence: Toward a Better Understanding of Brand Choice Decisions," 429.

22. Peter van Eck, Wander Jager, and Peter Leeflang, "Opinion Leaders' Role in Innovation Diffusion: A Simulation Study," *Journal of Product Innovation Management*, vol. 28, no. 2 (March 2011): 187–203.

23. Rama Rao, "Concept Measuring Influence of Spouse Decisions in Purchasing," *Cite Man Network*, March 11, 2010, www.citeman .com/9161-concept-measuring-influence-of -spouse-decisions-in-purchasing.

24. A. Valarmathi, "Children's Influences on Family Decision Making," *Children Blog*, May 14, 2011, http://children.dailydevotional word.com/2011/05/14/childrens-influences-on -family-decision-making.

25. Ira Mayer, "New Report: Teen Spending and Influence," Publicity e-mail, June 16, 2010.

26. Anita Manning, "Teach Your Tech-Challenged Parents, Grandparents Well," *USA Today*, March 10, 2011, http://yourlife.usatoday.com /parenting-family/caregiving/story/2011/03 /Teaching-elderly-to-come-to-grips-with-gadgets -technology/44700622/1.

27. Tamara Schweitzer, "Chris Easter and Bob Horner, Founders of The Man Registry," *Inc.*, July 19, 2010, www.inc.com/30under30/2010/profile -chris-easter-bob-horner-man-registry.html.

28. Sue Shellenbarger, "Daunting Task for Mr. Mom: Get a Job," *Wall Street Journal*, May 19, 2010, http://online.wsj.com/article/SB100 01424052748703957904575252270698575294 .html.

29. Nanette Byrnes, "Secrets of the Male Shopper," *BusinessWeek*, www.businessweek.com /magazine/content/06_36/b3999001.htm (Accessed August 17, 2007); also see Xin He, Jeffrey Inman, and Vikas Mittal, "Gender Jeopardy in Financial Risk-Taking," *Journal of Marketing Research*, August 2008, 414–424.

30. Erik Sherman, "Marketing Tech by Gender? Sure, Why Not? It Works," *Bnet*, May 24, 2011, www.bnet.com/blog/technology-business /marketing-tech-by-gender-sure-why-not-it-works /10826.

31. Steve McClellan, "Are Demographics Dead?" *AdWeek*, February 23, 2010, www.adweek.com.

32. www.ampacet.com, June 1, 2011.

33. Karyn Monget, "Does Sex Sell?" *Women's Wear Daily*, June 21, 2010, 1, 12.

34. "Oh Snap! Baby Carrot Campaign Mimics Junk Food," *CBSNews*, September 2, 2010, www.cbsnews.com/stories/2010/09/02/health /main6829423.shtml.

35. Elizabeth J. Wilson, "Using the Dollar-metric Scale to Establish the Just Meaningful Difference in Price," in 1987 AMA *Educators' Proceedings*, ed. Susan Douglas et al. (Chicago: American Marketing Association, 1987), 107.

36. Sarah Nagle, "Four Keys to Creating Products for the Lady Gaga Generation," *Fast Company Design*, June 1, 2011, www.fastcodesign.com /1663954/four-keys-to-creating-products-for -the-lady-gaga-generation.

37. Katherine Boehret, "Making Hotmail Hot Again," *Wall Street Journal*, June 9, 2010, http:// online.wsj.com/article/SB1000142405274870330 2604575294700105749996.html.

38. Judith Aquino, "The 10 Most Successful Rebranding Campaigns Ever," *Business Insider*, February 10, 2011, www.businessinsider.com/10 -most-successful-rebranding-campaigns-2011-2.

39. Ibid.

40. Jyothi Datta, "Aspartame: Bitter Truth in Artificial Sweeteners?" *Business Line*, www .thehindubusinessline.com/2005/10/04/stories /2005100404220300.htm (Accessed September 14, 2007).

7

1. Murray Sye, "What Do Most Business Marketers Want from Their Online Marketing Plan?" *WhiteSpace*, December 10, 2010, www .whitespace.on.ca/Blog/bid/56260/What-do -most-business-marketers-want-from-their-online -marketing-plan.

2. Michael D. Hutt and Thomas W. Speh, *Business Marketing Management: B2B, 10e.* (Cincinnati: Thomson, 2010), p. 4.

3. Ibid.

4. Sean Callahan, "Interactive Spending Continues to Climb," *BtoB*, March 8, 2010, www.btobonline.com/apps/pbcs.dll/article?AID =/20100308/FREE/303049998/1445/FREE.

5. "B2B Marketers Gain Ground with Social," *eMarketer*, May 27, 2010, www.emarketer.com.

6. "B2B Spending on Social Media to Explode," *eMarketer*, June 1, 2010, www3.emarketer.com /Article.aspx?R=1007725.

7. Karen Bannan, "YouTube for B-to-B: How to Use the Popular Video Site to Expand Your Branding," *BtoB*, May 5, 2010, www.btobonline .com/apps/pbcs.dll/article?AID=/20100503 /FREE/305039965/1445/FREE; Paul Gillin, "B-to-B Firmly in Social Media," *BtoB*, April 12, 2010, www.btobonline.com/article/20100412 /FREE/304129965/b-to-b-firmly-in-social-media.

8. Karen J. Bannan, "10 Great b2b Sites," *BtoB*, September 13, 2010, www.btobonline.com /article/20100913/FREE/309139988/10-great -b-to-b-sites.

9. Gabriel Perna, "WWDC: 'Stickiness' Factor Building iCloud Excitement," *International Business Times,* June 7, 2011, www.ibtimes.com/articles/159025/20110607/apple-steve-jobs-icloud-stickiness-iphone-5.htm.

10. Sasthi Sarma, "Measuring Stickiness with Basic Google Analytics' Key Performance Indicators," *Position²,* June 3, 2010, http://blogs.position2.com/measuring-stickiness-with-basic-google-analytics-key-performance-indicators.

11. Ellis Booker, "B-to-B Marketers Apply Analytics to Social Media," *BtoB,* April 12, 2010, www.btobonline.com/apps/pbcs.dll/article?AID=/20100412/FREE/304089975/1445/FREE.

12. Brian Hook, "Climbing the B2B Social Media Ladder," *E-Commerce Times,* May 27, 2010, www.ecommercetimes.com/rsstory/70081.html?wlc=1296574575.

13. Jean Gianfagna, "Four Lessons Big Direct Marketers Can Learn from Small Mailers," *Smart Marketing Strategy,* May 24, 2011, www.gianfagnamarketing.com/blog/2011/05/24/4-lessons-big-direct-marketers-can-learn-from-small-mailers.

14. "Disintermediation," *marketingterms.com,* www.marketingterms.com/dictionary/disintermediation.

15. "Emerging Trends in B-to-B Social Media Marketing: Insights from the Field," *BtoB,* April 2011, 6–9.

16. Roger Cheng and Don Clark, "Cisco Flips Consumer Strategy," *Wall Street Journal,* April 13, 2011, B3.

17. Christopher Hosford, "'BtoB' Leading Edge Attendees Urged to 'Flip the Funnel' Towards Retention," *BtoB,* June 23, 2010, www.btobonline.com/apps/pbcs.dll/article?AID=/20100623/FREE/100629964.

18. Seth Goldman, "The Big Brewer" *Inc.*, April 21, 2010, www.inc.com/seth-goldman/the-big-brewer.html.

19. Karon Snowdon, "Singapore-Virgin Airline Deal Expands NEtwork," ABC Radio Australia, June 8, 2011, www.radioaustralia.net.au/connectasia/stories/201106/s3238843.htm.

20. "MasterCard and Avis Budget Group Announce New Strategic Marketing Alliance," *Financial,* June 8, 2011, http://finchannel.com/news_flash/Banks/88466_MasterCard_and_Avis_Budget_Group_Announce_New_Strategic_Marketing_Alliance.

21. Robert M. Morgan and Shelby D. Hunt, "The Commitment-Trust Theory of Relationship Marketing," *Journal of Marketing,* 58, no. 3, 1994, 23.

22. Ibid.

23. "Suzuki-VW Alliance to Include Hybrids, Management," *Bloomberg Businessweek,* January 15, 2010, www.businessweek.com/news/2010-01-15/suzuki-vw-alliance-to-include-hybrids-management-update1-.html.

24. Mary Morrison, "Getting in with Government," *BtoB,* May 3, 2010, 13.

25. Ibid.

26. Rebecca Smith and Mike Ramsey, "Rent a Leaf: Enterprise Buys a Fleet," *Wall Street Journal,* July 27, 2010, http://online.wsj.com/article/SB10001424052748704700404575391602609091276.html.

27. Daniel Michaels, "Rivals Race for Tanker Deal," *Wall Street Journal,* July 23, 2010, http://online.wsj.com/article/SB10001424052748704421304575383132903915038.html.

28. "Exostar's Global Customer Base," Exostar, www.exostar.com/Exostar_Customers.aspx.

29. Peter Sanders, "Boeing 787 Lands in Farnborough," *Wall Street Journal,* July 19, 2010, http://online.wsj.com/article/SB10001424052748704196404575374693695488042.html.

30. Marshall Lager, "Listen Up," *Customer Relationship Management,* March 2007, 24–27.

31. "Right-Channeling: Making Sure Your Best Customers Get Your Best Service," Right Now Technologies, June 3, 2009, http://jobfunctions.bnet.com/abstract.aspx?docid=132740.

8

1. Goran Mijuk, "Nestlé Bets on Emerging Markets," *Wall Street Journal,* June 22 2010, http://online.wsj.com/article/SB10001424052748704853404575322382547240528.html.

2. Tim Feran, "Macy's Trying a Local Approach," *Columbus Dispatch,* September 21, 2009, www.dispatch.com/live/content/business/stories/2009/09/21/MY_MACYS.ART_ART_09-21-09_A8_NQF4DB5.html.

3. Veronica Dagher, "Macy's Tailored Merchandise Pays Off," *Wall Street Journal,* August 12, 2010, B3.

4. Lynn Finch, "Danger ahead for Free-Spending Teens," *Walnut Row,* May 26, 2011, www.walnutrow.com/2011/05/26/danger-free-spending-teens/.

5. "JCPenney's, 'New Look. New Year. Who Knew!' Back-to-School Campaign Features Cutting Edge, Creative Marketing Aimed at Teens," *Business Wire,* July 14, 2010, www.businesswire.com/smp/jcpenney-back-to-school.

6. "College Students Annoyed by Mobile Ads," *emarketer,* July 1, 2010, www.emarketer.tv/Article.aspx?R=1007771.

7. Tricia Romano, "Look What I Bought (or Got Free)," *New York Times,* May 5, 2010, www.nytimes.com/2010/05/06/fashion/06skin.html.

8. Cathy Yan, "Can Shopping Be Fun Again?" *Wall Street Journal,* May 6, 2010, http://online.wsj.com/article/SB10001424052748704342604575221543926318602.html.

9. Toni Whitt, "Boomers Rewrite Rules for Marketing," *Herald Tribune,* June 25, 2007, www.heraldtribune.com.

10. Hallmark Corporate Information, "New Hallmark Card Line Helps Women Celebrate Good Times and Convey Support in Tough Times," *Hallmark,* June 22, 2010, http://corporate.hallmark.com/Current-News/New-Hallmark-Card-Line-Helps-Women-Celebrate-Good-Times-and-Convey-Support-in-Tough-Times.

11. Michael Silverstein, "Ten Mistakes Male Executives Make with Female Customers," *Wall Street Journal,* January 15, 2010, http://online.wsj.com/article/SB10001424052748704281204575002992691739142.html; Rachel Brown, "Fashion Gets in the Game: $20 Billion Video Industry Aiming for Female Fans," *Women's Wear Daily,* January 12, 2010, 12.

12. Brown, "Fashion Gets in the Game."

13. Napolean Perdis, "Who's Grooming Who: Makeup and the Modern Male," *Huffington Post,* July 30, 2010, www.huffingtonpost.com/napolean-perdis/whos-grooming-who-makeup-b_665156.html; Paul Casciato, "Fear of Aging Drives Men's Cosmetic Sales," *Reuters,* March 8, 2010, www.reuters.com/article/idUSTRE6273CI20100308.

14. E. J. Schultz, "Weight Watchers Picks a New Target: Men," *Crain's New York Business,* April 22, 2011, www.crainsnewyork.com/article/20110422/FREE/110429947.

15. Christina Binkley, "Post-Recession, the Rich Are a Bit Different," *Wall Street Journal,* May 12, 2011, http://online.wsj.com/article/SB10001424052748703730804576317200215630540.html.

16. Rachel Lamb, "Affluent Consumers Demand Top-Quality Customer Service: Experts," *Luxury Daily,* January 12, 2011, www.luxurydaily.com/affluent-consumers-demand-top-quality-customer-service-experts.

17. Ian Sherr, "Wal-Mart Plans Expansion of Low-Income Money Services," *Reuters,* March 16, 2010, www.reuters.com/article/2010/03/16/walmart-bank-idUSN1516867520100316.

18. "The New Mainstream: How the Buying Habits of Ethnic Groups Are Creating a New American Identity," November 15, 2005, http://knowledge.wharton.upenn.edu/article.cfm?articleid=1270 (Accessed June 9, 2008).

19. Lisa Lockwood, "Hispanics: A Growing Force," *Women's Wear Daily,* March 23, 2011, 2.

20. Doug Anderson and Laurel Kennedy, "Baby Boomer Segmentation: Eight Is Enough," *ACNielsen,* Fall/Winter 2006, 4.

21. Andrew Adam Newman, "The Power of One," *Fortune,* April 19, 2010, 15–16.

22. Thomas Catan, "To Understand Washington Ads, You've Got to Be a Code Breaker," *Wall Street Journal,* March 7, 2011, http://online.wsj.com/article/SB10001424052748704637704576082212342743824.html.

23. Emily Steel, "Exploring Ways to Build a Better Consumer Profile," *Wall Street Journal,* March 15, 2010, http://online.wsj.com/article/SB10001424052748703447104575117972284656374.html.

24. Lowell D'Souza, "Applying the 80-20 Rule to Marketing," *Marketing Bones,* November 28, 2010, http://marketingbones.com/applying-the-80-20-rule-to-marketing.

25. Kasey Wehrum, "Comic Books for Entrepreneurs," *Inc.,* May 2011, www.inc.com/magazine/20110501/comic-books-for-entrepreneurs.html.

26. Anne Riley-Katz, "An Age of Specialization: Reworking Retail's Model to Get Smaller, Fresher," *Women's Wear Daily,* July 14, 2010, 8.

27. Jeff Green and Alan Ohnsman, "At Subaru, Sharing the Love Is a Market Strategy," *Bloomberg Businessweek,* May 24–May 30, 2010, 18–19.

28. "Targeting Wal-Mart's Core Customer Segments," *retailwire.com,* April 2, 2008.

29. Jennifer Valentino-DeVries, "Is the iPad Cannibalizing Other Apple Products?" *Wall Street Journal,* May 17, 2010, http://blogs.wsj.com/digits/2010/05/17/is-the-ipad-cannibalizing-other-apple-products.

30. Adam Baer, "Packaging Designed by Customers," *Inc.,* July 1, 2010, www.inc.com/magazine/20100701/packaging-designed-by-customers.html.

31. "The Birth of SuperJam," SuperJam, www.superjam.co.uk/about.html.

32. "Our Brands," Gap Inc., www.gapinc.com/public/OurBrands/brands.shtml.

33. John Pavlus, "'Bumpy Road' Flips Touchscreen Game Mechanics on Their Head," *Fast Company Design,* June 9, 2011, www

.fastcodesign.com/1664013/bumpy-road-flips
-touchscreen-game-mechanics-on-their-head.
34. Suzanne Vranica, "Grape Nuts Takes Aim at
Men," *Wall Street Journal,* March 26, 2009, B5.

9

1. Ellen Byron, "Wash Away Bad Hair Days,"
Wall Street Journal, June 30, 2010, D1.
2. Ibid.
3. Martin Lindstrom, "Want to Sell Product? Sleep
with Your Customers," *Fast Company,* June 8,
2011, www.fastcompany.com/1758288/familiar
-microscopic-consumer-insights-yet-to-be-discovered.
4. "Second Half of '09 Could Set Research in
Motion," *Quirk's Marketing Research Review,*
July 2009, 80–81.
5. "Marketers Watch as Friends Interact
Online," *Wall Street Journal,* April 15, 2010, B5.
6. Suzanne Vranica, "Tallying Up Viewers," *Wall
Street Journal,* July 26, 2010, http://online.wsj
.com/article/SB100014240527487042490045753
85680793742048.html.
7. Raymond R. Burke, "Virtual Shopping:
Breakthrough in Marketing Research," *Harvard
Business Review,* March/April 1996, 120–131;
Valla Roth, "Winning at Retail with Virtual
Shopping Research," *Quirk's Marketing Research
Review,* June 2011, 46.
8. Roxanne Salen and Susan Stickling, "How
the Shopper Is Changing the Retail and Research
Landscape," *Quirk's Marketing Research Review,*
June 2011, 32.
9. Greg Gates, "Sustainable Compliance within
Reach," *Retail-Merchandiser,* June 6, 2011, www
.retail-merchandiser.com/current-news/1595
-sustainable-compliance-within-reach.html.
10. "US Internet Users," www.emarketer.com,
June 4, 2010.
11. Kira Signer and Andy Korman, "One Billion
and Growing," *Quirk's Marketing Research
Review,* July/August 2006, 62–67.
12. Conversation with Roger Gates, President of
DSS Marketing Research, June 2, 2010.
13. "Research in a Petri Dish: Learning from
Communities," *Marketing News,* September 3,
2009, 22.
14. Andrew Cutler, "Use These Five Web-Based
Approaches to Shrink Your Research Timelines,
Costs," *Quirk's Marketing Research Review,*
January 2011, 28.
15. "About Consumer-Generated Media (CGM),"
Nielsen, www.nielsen-online.com/resources
.jsp?section=about_cgm (Accessed October 25,
2010).
16. "BuzzMetrics," Nielsen, http://en-us.nielsen.
com/content/nielsen/en_us/product_families/nielsen
_buzzmetrics.html (Accessed October 25, 2010).
17. "Products and Solutions: InfoScan Tracking
Service," Information Resources, Inc., www.usa
.infores.com/ProductsSolutions/AllProducts
/AllProductsDetail/tabid/159/productid/83
/Default.aspx (Accessed December 1, 2008).
18. Robert Lee Hotz, "Songs Stick in Teens'
Heads," *Wall Street Journal,* June 13, 2011, http://
online.wsj.com/article/SB1000142405270230384
8104576381823644333598.html.

10

1. Darren Murph, "LG Debuts Optimus
Smartphone Series, Froyo-Powered 'One' and

'Chic' Arriving First," *Engadget,* July 5, 2010,
www.engadget.com/2010/07/05/lg-debuts-optimus
-smartphone-series-froyo-powered-one-and-ch.
2. Roger Cheng, "Apartments Get TV Focus,"
Wall Street Journal, July 4, 2010, B5.
3. Stuart Elliot, "Laundry Soaps Try a
Hint of Horror and Some Tough-Guy Talk,"
New York Times, June 15, 2011, www.nytimes
.com/2011/06/16/business/media/16adco.html.
4. Ethan Smith, "Disney Invites 'Goths' to the
Party," *Wall Street Journal,* February 19, 2010,
http://online.wsj.com/article/SB10001424052748
7042690004575073580675774138.html.
5. Gren Manuel, "Scrabble Rules Are Not Being
Changed," *Wall Street Journal,* April 7, 2010,
http://blogs.wsj.com/source/2010/04/07
/scrabble-rules-are-not-being-changed/.
6. Ellen Byron, "Wash Away Bad Hair Days,"
Wall Street Journal, June 30, 2010, http://online
.wsj.com/article/SB10001424052748704911704575327141935381092.html.
7. Susan Berfield, "Marketing Lessons from
Brand Oprah," *Bloomberg Businessweek,* May
23–May 29, 2011, 20–22.
8. Tanzina Vega, "Walgreens Launches
Campaign to Push Store-Brand Products," *New
York Times,* February 10, 2011, www.nytimes
.com/2011/02/11/business/media/11adco.html.
9. Jenn Abelson, "Seeking Savings, Some Ditch
Brand Loyalty," *Boston Globe,* January 29, 2010,
www.boston.com/news/local/massachusetts
/articles/2010/01/29/shoppers_are_ditching
_name_brands_for_store_brands.
10. "Kroger Brand Products Play a Central Role
in Our Merchandizing Strategy," Kroger Corporate
Web site, www.thekrogerco.com/operations
/operations_manufacturing.htm (Accessed June
15, 2011).
11. Ellen Byron, "Febreze Joins P&G's $1 Billion
Club," *Wall Street Journal,* March 9, 2011, http://
online.wsj.com/article/SB1000142405274870407
6804576180683371307932.html.
12. Sarah Nassauer, "Gee, Your Trash Smells
Terrific," *Wall Street Journal,* June 9, 2011, http://
online.wsj.com/article/SB1000142405270230443
2304576369991322977166.html.
13. "Section 1(a) Timeline: Application Based on
Use in Commerce," United States Patent and
Trademark Office, www.uspto.gov/trademarks
/process/tm_sec1atimeline.jsp (Accessed June 15
2011).
14. Deborah Vence, "Product Enhancement,"
Marketing News, May 1, 2005, 19.
15. Nathan Olivarez-Giles, "Apple Sued Over Its
Use of iCloud Name by iCloud Communications,"
L.A. Times, June 14, 2011, http://latimesblogs
.latimes.com/technology/2011/06/apple-is-sued
-by-phoenix-based-icloud-communications-for
-use-of-icloud-name.html.
16. David Kesmodel, "U.S. Judge Rules in
Bacardi's Favor in Rum Dispute," *Wall Street
Journal,* April 7, 2010, http://online.wsj.com
/article/SB10001424052702303591204575169911818091240.html.
17. "Golfers Beware Those Pings May
Be Pangs," *Holtville Tribune,* June 16,
2011, http://tribwekchron.com/2011/06
/golfers-beware-of-those-pings-may-be-pangs.
18. Emily York, "Miracle Whip Ad Campaign to
Spread 'Boring' Mayo Message," *Advertising Age,*
March 22, 2010, http://adage.com/article?article
_id=142914.
19. "P&G to Build Brands with Packaging and
Design Focus," *Store Brands Decisions,* April 13,

2010, www.storebrandsdecisions.com/news
/2010/04/13/pandg-to-build-brands-with
-packaging-and-design-focus.
20. Stephanie Clifford, "Devilish Packaging,
Tamed," *New York Times,* June 1, 2011, www
.nytimes.com/2011/06/02/business/energy
-environment/02packaging.html.
21. Andrew Newman, "A Sharp Focus on
Design When the Package Is Part of the Product,"
New York Times, July 8, 2010, www.nytimes
.com/2010/07/09/business/media/09adco.html.
22. Susan Carpenter, "Wasteful Packaging:
Do Consumers Care?" *L.A. Times,* April 20,
2011, http://latimesblogs.latimes.com/green
space/2011/04/recycling-packaging-products.html.
23. Kate Galbraith, "A Compostable Chips
Bag Hits the Shelves," *New York Times,*
March 16, 2010, http://green.blogs.nytimes
.com/2010/03/16/a-compostable-chips-bag
-hits-the-shelves; "The Compostable Label,"
Biodegradable Products Institute, www.bpiworld
.org/BPI-Public/Program.html.
24. Dan Alaimo, "CPG Matters: Nutritional
Labeling Provides CPGs, Retailers with Unique
Competitive Edge," *Retailwire,* March 22, 2010,
www.retailwire.com/discussions/sngl_discussion
.cfm/14384.
25. Ariel Schwartz, "The FTC's New Marketing
Rules to Squash Greenwashing," *Fast Company,*
June 10, 2011, www.fastcompany.com/1758615
/what-will-the-ftcs-new-marketing-rules-mean-for
-inauthentic-green-products.
26. Sherry F. Colb, "'Not Milk?': Dairy Petitions
the FDA to Block Labels Like 'Soy Milk' on
Non-Dairy Products," *Findlaw,* May 12, 2010,
http://writ.news.findlaw.com/colb/20100512
.html; Betsy Friauf, "Not Milk?" *Star-Telegram,*
July 24, 2010, D1.

11

1. Reena Jana, "In Data," *BusinessWeek,*
September 22, 2008, 48.
2. "The 50 Most Innovative Companies 2010,"
Bloomberg Businessweek, August 11, 2010,
www.businessweek.com/interactive_reports
/innovative_companies_2010.html.
3. Ibid.
4. Neal Ungerleider, "'Virtual Cane' Lets
Visually Impaired Navigate via Sonar," *Fast
Company,* June 30, 2011, www.fastcompany
.com/1764307/new-virtual-cane-lets-visually
-impaired-navigate-via-sound.
5. "Moleskine World," Moleskine, www
.moleskine.com/moleskine_world (Accessed July
1, 2011).
6. "Procter and Gamble Plans Product
Enhancements," *Business Courier,* February 18,
2010, www.bizjournals.com/cincinnati
/stories/2010/02/15/daily45.html.
7. Ray Smith and Christina Passariello, "The
Anti 'It' Handbag," *Wall Street Journal,* August 6,
2010, http://online.wsj.com/article/SB100014240
52748703545604575407311457877890.html.
8. Elizabeth Holmes, "Talbots Politely Shows
Granny the Door," *Wall Street Journal,* April 12,
2010, http://online.wsj.com/article/SB100014240
52702304703104575174601462751456.html.
9. Joel Rubinson, "Innovating Innovation: The
Best Ideas Can Come from Anywhere," *Fast
Company,* June 17, 2009, www.fastcompany.com
/blog/joel-rubinson/brave-new-marketing/innovating
-innovation-best-ideas-can-come-anywhere.

10. "Women's Financial Style," *Adweek Media*, February 16, 2009, 14; Jack Neff, "Package-Good Players Plan New-Product Surge for 2010," *Advertising Age*, December 7, 2009, http://adage.com/article/news/brands-package-good-players-plan-product-surge-2010/140906/

11. "Focus Groups Take on New Format," *retailwire*, January 25, 2010, online.

12. Nadine Heintz, "Managing: Unleashing Employee Creativity," *Inc.*, June 1, 2009, www.inc.com/magazine/20090601/managing-unleashing-employee-creativity.html.

13. Michael Arndt and Brice Einhorn, "The 50 Most Innovative Companies," *Bloomberg Businessweek*, April 15, 2010, www.businessweek.com/magazine/content/10_17/b4175034779697.htm.

14. Spence Ante and Nathan Becker, "IBM to Open Research Lab in Brazil," *Wall Street Journal*, June 9, 2010, http://online.wsj.com/article/SB10001424052748703302604575294820196514024.html.

15. Chris Newmarker, "General Mills Looks Online for Food Innovators," *Minneapolis/St. Paul Business Journal*, November 4, 2009, www.bizjournals.com/twincities/stories/2009/11/02/daily31.html.

16. Andrew Marton, "2006: A Face Odyssey," *Fort Worth Star-Telegram*, February 16, 2006, E1, E8.

17. Pete Engardio, "Scouring the Planet for Brainiacs," *BusinessWeek*, October 11, 2004, 106.

18. "About Ryz," www.ryz.com/about (Accessed July 1, 2011); Threadless Web Site, www.threadless.com (Accessed July 1, 2011).

19. Hanah Cho, "Baltimore a Valuable Test Market for Chick-fil-A," *Baltimore Sun*, July 25, 2010, http://articles.baltimoresun.com/2010-07-25/business/bs-bz-interview-dan-cathy-20100725_1_chick-fil-a-spicy-chicken-sandwich-market.

20. "Think Big with a Gig: Our Experimental Fiber Network," The Official Google Blog, February 2, 2010, http://googleblog.blogspot.com/2010/02/think-big-with-gig-our-experimental.html; Nancy Gohring, "Majority of US States Request Google Broadband Fibre Network," *Tech World*, July 15, 2010, http://news.techworld.com/networking/3232059/majority-of-us-states-request-google-broadband-fibre-network/; John Sutter, "Topeka 'Renames' Itself, 'Google, Kansas,'" *CNN*, March 2, 2010, www.cnn.com/2010/TECH/03/02/google.kansas.topeka/index.html.

21. David Kesmodel, "Smokeless Products Are Tough Test for Reynolds," *Wall Street Journal*, March 26, 2010, http://online.wsj.com/article/SB10001424052748703523204575129633103406778.html.

22. "Everyday Solutions," P&G, http://pgeverydaysolutions.com/pgeds/index.jsp (Accessed July 5, 2011).

23. Erika Kinetz, "iPad? No—IndiaPad," *Fort Worth Star-Telegram*, July 24, 2010, 9B.

24. Robert Scoble, "PassionPlay," *Fast Company*, November 2008, 90.

25. Kevin J. Clancy and Peter C. Krieg, "Product Life Cycle: A Dangerous Idea," *Brandweek*, March 1, 2004, 26.

26. "Surviving Silly Bandz: Prolonging the Shelf Life of Fads," *Knowledge@Wharton*, July 22, 2010, http://knowledge.wharton.upenn.edu/article.cfm?articleid=2551.

27. Ross Tucker, "Stretch Jeans Expand Appeal," *Women's Wear Daily*, May 20, 2010, 32.

28. Arik Hesseldahl, "The Home Phone's Last Gasp," *Bloomberg Businessweek*, July 26–August 1, 2010, 72.

29. Ronald J. Baker, *Pricing on Purpose: Creating and Capturing Value* (Hoboken, NJ: John Wiley & Sons, 2006), 338.

12

1. "Overview of the 2008–2018 Projections," Bureau of Labor Statistics, December 3, 2010, www.bls.gov/oco/oco2003.htm#employment, percentage based on authors' calculations.

2. Spence Morgan, "Scent Branding Sweeps the Fragrance Industry," *Bloomberg Businessweek*, June 21–27, 2010, 86–87.

3. Alexandra Berzon, "Independent Hotels Sign On with Marriott," *Wall Street Journal*, January 24, 2010, http://online.wsj.com/article/SB10001424052748703415804575023274246886214.html.

4. Valarie Zeithaml, Mary Jo Bitner, and Dwayne Gremler, *Services Marketing* (New York: McGraw-Hill, 2006).

5. Ibid.

6. Bo Burlingham, "Lessons from a Blue-Collar Millionaire," *Inc.*, February 2010, 57–63.

7. Jena McGregor, "USAA's Battle Plan," *Bloomberg Businessweek*, February 18, 2010, http://www.businessweek.com/magazine/content/10_09/b4168040782858.htm.

8. Much of the material in this section is based on Christopher H. Lovelock and Jochen Wirtz, *Services Marketing*, 5th ed. (Upper Saddle River, NJ: Prentice Hall, 2004); Christian Gronroos, *Service Management and Marketing: Customer Management in Service Competition*, 3rd ed. (Hoboken, NJ: John Wiley & Sons, 2007).

9. "Old Spice Voicemail Generator," http://oldspicevoicemail.com.

10. Larry Magid, "Control Facebook Instant Personalization and Other Privacy Settings," *Huffington Post*, May 17, 2010, www.huffingtonpost.com/larry-magid/new-video-control-faceboo_b_578148.html.

11. Lovelock and Wirtz, *Services Marketing*; Gronroos, *Service Management and Marketing*.

12. Ibid.

13. Much of the material in this section is based on Leonard L. Berry and A. Parasuraman, *Marketing Services* (New York: Free Press, 1991), 132–150.

14. Sandra Kofler, "'Psych' Fans Encouraged to Play for USA Character Rewards," *Wall Street Journal*, July 12, 2010, http://blogs.wsj.com/speakeasy/2010/07/12/psych-fans-encouraged-to-play-for-usa-character-rewards/.

15. Andrea Petersen, "Hotels Encourage Guests to Throw Away Their Keys," *Wall Street Journal*, June 9, 2011, http://online.wsj.com/article/SB10001424052702304778304576373773065546978.html

16. "Top Small Company Workplaces," *Inc.*, June 2011, www.inc.com/top-workplaces/2010/profile/biomark-dean-park.html.

13

1. Robert Guth, "New Child-Friendly Malaria Drug Presents Distribution Challenge," *Wall Street Journal*, January 27, 2009, http://online.wsj.com/article/SB123301610361717737.html.

2. Nick Wingfield, "Microsoft to Open New Stores, Hires Retail Hand," *Wall Street Journal*, February 13, 2009, B1.

3. Daisuke Wakabayashi and Jung-Ah Lee, "Gadget Appetite Strains Suppliers," *Wall Street Journal*, July 14, 2010, http://online.wsj.com/article/SB10001424052748703379270457536700 3265429096.html.

4. www.redbox.com (Accessed August 5, 2010).

5. Matthew Futterman, "Verizon Will Carry NFL's RedZone Channel," *Wall Street Journal*, March 9, 2010, http://online.wsj.com/article/SB10001424052748704869304575110180782484198.html.

6. Anjali Cardeiro, "After Buying Its Bottlers, Pepsi Cozies Up to Stores," *Wall Street Journal*, June 21, 2010, B6.

7. "It's HBO," Time Warner, May 9, 2011, www.timewarner.com/our-content/home-box-office.

8. Pete Born, "Celebrity Fragrance 3.0," *Women's Wear Daily*, February 11, 2011, 8.

9. Dana Cimilluca, Betsy McCay, and Jeffrey McCraken, "Coke Near Deal for Bottler," *Wall Street Journal*, February 25, 2010, http://online.wsj.com/article/SB10001424052748704240004575085871950146304.html.

10. Yukari Iwatani Kane and Russell Adams, "Apple Opens a Door, Keeps Keys," *Wall Street Journal*, February 16, 2011, B1.

11. Matt Kinsman, "Popular Science Offers a Peek behind the Apple, Google Subscription Plans," *Folio*, March 2011, 10–11.

12. Molly Prior, "CVS Comes Calling," *Women's Wear Daily*, June 11, 2010, 6.

13. Carol Matlack, "Handbags at the Barricades," *Bloomberg Businessweek*, March 28–April 3, 2011, 80–83.

14. Matthias Williams, "India to Levy 10 Pct Import Tax on Power Gear," *Reuters*, August 12, 2010, http://in.reuters.com/article/2010/08/12/idINIndia-50795020100812.

14

1. "2011 Ford Fiesta Build Your Own," http://bp2.forddirect.fordvehicles.com/2011-Ford-Fiesta.

2. Goodyear Newsroom, "New CEO Kramer Confident in Goodyear's Ability to Grow," April 13, 2010, www.goodyear.com/cfmx/web/corporate/media/news/story.cfm?a_id=156.

3. Much of this section is based on material adapted from Donald J. Bowersox, David J. Closs, and Theodore P. Stank, *21st Century Logistics: Making Supply Chain Integration a Reality* (Oak Brook, IL: Council of Logistics Management).

4. Much of this and the following sections is based on material adapted from the edited volume, Douglas M. Lambert, ed., *Supply Chain Management: Processes, Partnerships, Performance* (Sarasota, FL: Supply Chain Management Institute, 2004).

5. Steve Banker, "General Mills and Tesco: How Supply Chain Boosts Profits," February 3, 2010, http://logisticsviewpoint.com/2010/02/03/general-mills-and-tesco-how-supply-chain-boosts-profits.

6. A. Ellinger, S. Keller, and A. Elmadağ Bas, "The Empowerment of Frontline Service Staff in 3PL Companies," *Journal of Business Logistics*, 31, No. 1 (2010): 79–98.

7. Anjali Cordeiro, "After Buying Its Bottlers, Pepsi Cozies Up to Stores," *Wall Street Journal*, June 21, 2010, B6.

8. "BMW to Push Build-to-Order for X3," Autoweek.com, May 14, 2010, www.autoweek.com/article/20100514/CARNEWS/100519923.

9. Thomas Black, Susanna Ray, Aaron Ricadela, Cliff Edwards, Craig Trudell, Keith Naughton,

and Shruti Date Singh, "Downside of Just-in-Time Inventory," *Bloomberg Businessweek*, March 28–April 3, 2011, 17–18.

10. Elizabeth Holmes, "Tug-of-War in Apparel World," *Wall Street Journal*, July 16, 2010, http://online.wsj.com/article/SB1000142405274870372 28045753693929834597552.html.

11. Geoffrey A. Fowler and Rachel Dodes, "Retailers Tap Stores to Speed Online Orders," *Wall Street Journal*, May 20, 2010, http://online.wsj.com/article/SB1000142405274870356580457 5523854292580710.html.

12. John Miller, "Maersk Orders 10 Huge Container Ships," *Wall Street Journal*, February 22, 2011, B3.

13. Robert Hardman, "Santa's Not So Little Helper," *Mail Online*, December 8, 2009, www.dailymail.co.uk/news/article-1233766/Santas-little-helper-Todays-busiest-online-shopping-day-year-So-ready-biggest-grotto-Lapland.html.

14. Miguel Bustillo, "Wal-Mart Radio Tags to Track Clothing," *Wall Street Journal*, July 23, 2010, http://online.wsj.com/article/SB1000142405274870442130457538321306119809.html.

15. John Wasik, "The Surprising Success of the Green Supply Chain," *Fortune*, August 13, 2010, http://money.cnn.com/2010/08/13/news/companies/corporate_sustainability.fortune/index.htm.

15

1. *Retail Industry Indicators 2010,* National Retail Federation, www.nrf.com (Accessed August 10, 2010).

2. Bureau of Labor Statistics, "Industry at a Glance: NAICS 42–45, Wholesale and Retail Trade," www.bls.gov (Accessed August 10, 2010).

3. *Retail Industry Indicators 2010.*

4. Stores.org 2010 Retail Report (Accessed August 12, 2010).

5. Rachel Dodes, "Saks Makes Shift to Priciest Items," *Wall Street Journal,* May 18, 2011, B3.

6. Elizabeth Holmes, "OMG, These Bags Cost a Lot!" *Wall Street Journal,* May 27, 2010, D1.

7. Simon Zekaria, "Burberry Has Reasons to Be Bullish," *Wall Street Journal,* July 13, 2010, http://blogs.wsj.com/source/2010/07/13/why-burberry-has-reasons-to-be-bullish.

8. "Supermarket Sales," www.fmi.org, (Accessed August 21, 2010).

9. "Walmart Corporate Fact Sheet," March 2010, walmartstores.com/download/2230.pdf.

10. "Restaurant Industry Facts at a Glance," National Restaurant Association, www.restaurant.org/research/facts (Accessed August 12, 2010).

11. Paulina Reso, "Future Vending Machines Will Link Retina Scans to Credit Cards," *New York Daily News,* August 11, 2010, www.nydailynews.com/lifestyle/2010/08/11/2010-08-11_next_generation_of_vending_machines_may_use_thumprint_retinal_scan_to_pay_with_c.html.

12. Leslie Patton, "House Parties with a Commercial Twist," *Bloomberg Businessweek,* February 7–13, 2011, 30–31.

13. www.the-dma.org (Accessed October 30, 2007); http://camcouncil.org/statistics (Accessed August 10, 2010).

14. "Telemarketing: A US and Japanese Market Report," www.streetinsider.com, August 10, 2010.

15. Daniel R. Shiman, "An Economic Approach to the Regulation of Direct Marketing," April 6, 2006, http://www.law.indiana.edu/fclj/pubs/v58/no2/Shiman.pdf.

16. "Worldwide Spending on Direct Mail Expected to Grow," *Marketing News,* August 24, 2010; Teri Evans, "Firms Hold Fast to Snail Mail Marketing," *Wall Street Journal,* January 12, 2010, http://online.wsj.com/article/SB100014240 5274870348100457464690423486041 2.html.

17. Jennifer Valentino-DeVries, "With Catalogs, Opt-Out Policies Vary," *Wall Street Journal,* April 13, 2011, B7.

18. "PC Maker Good Despite Economic Recession," *Electronic Times* (Accessed August 12, 2010).

19. Kris Hudson, "Malls Test Apps to Aid Shoppers," *Wall Street Journal,* April 26, 2011, B6.

20. "Easy Exotic by Padma Lakshmi," HSN, http://kitchen-dining.hsn.com/easy-exotic-by-padma-lakshmi_c-qc_a-7056_xc.aspx?sz=5&cm_re=LN*Brand*EasyExotic&prev=hp!sf&lastbc=!7056&ccm=qc (Accessed July 6, 2011).

21. McDonald's Corporation, "Inside the U.S. Franchising Fact Sheet," www.mcdonalds.com/corp/franchise (Accessed August 21, 2010).

22. Olga Galacho, "Fashionable Touch—Phone Apps Take Clothes Shopping out of the Store," *Daily Telegraph,* August 9, 2010.

23. Janet Adamy, "Why Wendy's Finds Vanilla So Exciting," *Wall Street Journal,* April 6, 2007, B1–B2.

24. Hudson, "Malls Test Apps to Aid Shoppers."

25. Rachel Dodes, "Penney Weaves New Fast-Fashion Line," *Wall Street Journal,* August 11 2010, http://online.wsj.com/article/SB100014240 5274870343510457542158033439667 8.html.

26. Matt Townsend, "The Staying Power of Pop-Ups," *Bloomberg Businessweek,* November 15–21, 2010, 26–27.

27. "USA Technologies: ePort," USA Technologies, www.usatech.com/eport/index.php; "VeriSign Enables Coca-Cola Vending Machine Purchases via Mobile Phones," VeriSign, http://press.verisign.com/easyir/customrel.do?easyirid=AFC0FF0DB5C560D3&version=live&prid=181452&releasejsp=custom_97.

28. Yukari Iwatani Kane and Ian Sherr, "Secrets from Apple's Genius Bar: Full Loyalty, No Negativity," *Wall Street Journal,* June 15, 2011, http://online.wsj.com/article/SB10001424052702304563104576364071955678908.htm.

29. Kaila Krayewski, "The M-Commerce Revolution Begins: Consumers Use Their Mobile Phones for Online Shopping," ISEdb.com, January 21, 2010, http://isedb.com/20100121-2947.php.

30. Chris Foresman, "Wireless Survey: 91% of Americans Use Cell Phones," *Ars Technica,* March 2010, http://arstechnica.com/telecom/news/2010/03/wireless-survey-91-of-americans-have-cell-phones.ars.

16

1. Eric Clemons, Paul Nunes, and Matt Reilly, "Six Strategies for Successful Niche Marketing," *Wall Street Journal,* May 24, 2010, http://online.wsj.com/article/SB10001424052748704130904576464084205858424.html.

2. T. L. Stanley, "Domino's Cooks Up New Pizza, TV Spot," *Brandweek,* October 18, 2010, www.brandweek.com; Todd Wasserman, "As

Domino's Gets Real, Its Sales Get Really Good," *Brandweek,* July 11, 2010, www.brandweek.com; T. L. Stanley, "Marketer of the Year 2010: Russell Weiner, Domino's," *Brandweek,* September 13, 2010, www.brandweek.com.

3. Valerie Bauerlein and Robb Stewart, "Coca-Cola Hopes to Score with World Cup Campaign," *Wall Street Journal,* June 29, 2010, http://online.wsj.com/article/SB100014240527487045692045 75328983721865268.html.

4. Ibid.

5. Ibid.; News Release, "The Coca-Cola Company Reports 2010 Second Quarter and Year-to-Date Results," Coca-Cola Company, July 21, 2010, www.thecoca-colacompany.com/presscenter/nr_20100721_corporate_second_qtr_earnings.html.

6. Jeffrey A. Trachtenberg, "Title + Twitter and YouTube Take Unfinished Book to No.1," *Wall Street Journal,* July 1, 2011, B1, B5.

7. Joseph De Avila, "Who Could Eat All This?" *Wall Street Journal,* March 17, 2010, D1–D2.

8. Ellen Byron, "An Old Dice Game Catches on Again, Pushed by P&G," *Wall Street Journal,* January 30, 2007, A1, A13.

9. Luisa Zargani, "Della Valle Hopes Colosseum Just First Italian Restoration," *Women's Wear Daily,* June 24, 2011, 3.

10. The AIDA concept is based on the classic research of E. K. Strong, Jr., as theorized in *The Psychology of Selling and Advertising* (New York: McGraw-Hill, 1925) and "Theories of Selling," *Journal of Applied Psychology,* 9, 1925, 75–86.

11. Caroline Waxler, "What You Need to Know about the iPad," *Advertising Age Insights,* August 9, 2010, www.adage.com.

12. Thomas E. Barry and Daniel J. Howard, "A Review and Critique of the Hierarchy of Effects in Advertising," *International Journal of Advertising,* 9, 1990, 121–135.

13. Jack Neff, "Cracking the Viral Code: Look at Your Ads. Now Look at Old Spice," *Advertising Age,* September 27, 2010, www.adage.com; Jack Neff, "How Much Old Spice Body Wash Has the Old Spice Guy Sold?" *Advertising Age,* July 26, 2010, www.adage.com; Michael Learmonth, "Viral Old Spice 'Responses' Crush Original Ads in Online Views," *Advertising Age,* July 22, 2010, www.adage.com; Jessica Shambora, "The Adman behind Old Spice's New Life," *Fortune,* October 18, 2010, 39.

14. Anjali Cordeiro, "Promotions Boost Sales for Food and Beverage Makers," *Wall Street Journal,* July 14, 2010, B5.

17

1. "100 Leading National Advertisers 2009," www.adage.com, June 21, 2010.

2. Bradley Johnson, "Global Marketers," *Ad Industry Jobs: Advertising Age Data Center,* www.adage.com (Accessed February 2009); Bradley Johnson, "New Source: Media Work Force Sinks to 15-Year Low," www.adage.com, February 18, 2008.

3. "Global Marketers 2009," *Advertising Age,* http://adage.com/globalmarketers09.

4. Michael R. Solomon, *Consumer Behavior,* 6th ed. (Upper Saddle River, NJ: Prentice Hall, 2004), 275.

5. Tom Duncan, *Integrated Marketing Communications* (Burr Ridge, IL: McGraw-Hill, 2002), 257.

6. Alissa Walker, "Nature's Path Leads Consumers through Complicated Grocery Shelves," *Fast Company*, February 12, 2010, www.fastcompany.com/1548994/natures-path -leads-consumers-through-complicated-grocery -shelves.

7. Suzanne Vranica, "BP Rolling Out New Ads Aimed at Repairing Image," *Wall Street Journal*, June 7, 2010, http://online.wsj.com/article/NA _WSJ_PUB:SB1000142405274870400210457529 0993225476092.html.

8. "Small Army Marketing Campaign Helps Boston Gym Have a Strong Opening," *PRWeb*, May 31, 2011, www.prweb.com/releases /prwebsmallarmystorytelling/gymitmarketing /prweb8507560.htm.

9. Suzanne Vranica, "Barnes & Noble Returns to TV to Tout Nook," *Wall Street Journal*, April 22, 2010, http://online.wsj.com/article/NA_WSJ _PUB:SB100014240527487034040045751983003 33039616.html.

10. 21st Century, "'Door Dings' Commercial— 21st Century Auto Insurance: Same Great Coverage for Less," *YouTube.com*, November 16, 2010, www.youtube.com/watch?v=I0V-hm2EK -M&feature=relmfu.

11. Ibid.

12. "Active Women Say Their Lifestyle Makes Them More Confident, Sexy and Ready to Say 'Yes!'" *PR Newswire*, August 19, 2010, www .prnewswire.com/news-releases/active-women -say-their-lifestyle-makes-them-more-confident -sexy-and-ready-to-say-yes-101083819.html.

13. kswissinc, "CEO Kenny Powers," *YouTube .com*, July 8, 2011, www.youtube.com/user /kswissinc#p/a/u/0/hgGud5gsbIA.

14. Teressa Iezzi, "Kenny Powers Returns for Second K-Swiss Campaign," *Fast Company*, July 11, 2011, www.fastcompany.com/1766322 /kenny-powers-returns-for-second-k-swiss -campaign.

15. Laura Q. Hughes and Wendy Davis, "Revival of the Fittest," *Advertising Age*, March 12, 2001, 18–19.

16. Geoffrey Fowler, "For P&G in China, It's Wash, Rinse, Don't Repeat," *Wall Street Journal*, April 7, 2006.

17. Press release, "TNS Media Intelligence Forecasts 4.2 Percent Increase in U.S. Advertising Spending for 2008," www.tns-mi.com/news /01072008 (Accessed February 20, 2008).

18. PricewaterhouseCoopers, "IAB Internet Advertising Revenue Report," Interactive Advertising Bureau, April 2010, www.pwc.com /us/en/industry/entertainment-media/assets /IAB-Ad-Revenue-Full-Year-2009.pdf; Teddy Wayne, "A Milestone for Internet Ad Revenue," *New York Times*, April 25, 2010, www.nytimes .com/2010/04/26/business/media/26drill.html.

19. Brian Steinberg, "Super Bowl Ads Sold Out Three Months before the Game," *Advertising Age*, October 29, 2010, http://adage.com/article /mediaworks/advertising-super-bowl-ads-sold /146788/.

20. Suzanne Vranica, "Tallying Up Viewers," *Wall Street Journal*, July 26, 2010, http://online .wsj.com/article/SB1000142405274870424900457 5385680793742048.html.

21. Associated Press, "TV's New Attempt at Keeping Viewers Tuned In," *New Jersey Business*, October 5, 2009, www.nj.com/business/index.ssf /2009/10/post_10.html.

22. PricewaterhouseCoopers, "IAB Internet Advertising Revenue Report"; Wayne, "A Milestone for Internet Ad Revenue."

23. "Google Talks about Android, Personalized Ads and New Hires," *Wall Street Journal*, July 15, 2010, http://blogs.wsj.com/digits/2010/07/15/live -blogging-google-on-its-earnings.

24. PricewaterhouseCoopers, "IAB Internet Advertising Revenue Report."

25. Douglas MacMillan, "Farmville? Meet Cheech & Chong," *Bloomberg Businessweek*, June 27–July 3, 2011, 39–40.

26. Ibid.

27. Andrew LaValle, "Start-Ups Find Revenue Source on Hold," *Wall Street Journal*, June 11, 2008, B9.

28. "Massive Incorporated: Video Game Advertising," www.massiveincorporated.com; "Massive Inc. and comScore Prove In-Game Advertising ROI for Bing," Microsoft News Center, May 20, 2010, www.microsoft.com /presspass/press/2010/may10/05-20ingameadroipr .mspx.

29. Suzanne Vranica and Emily Steel, "iPad to Launch with Payload of Ads," *Wall Street Journal*, April 1, 2010, http://online.wsj.com /article/SB1000142405270230333830457515607 3394630854.html.

30. Ryan Singel, "Mobile Phone Companies Get Ad System to Bypass Apps," *Wired*, April 13, 2010, www.wired.com/epicenter/2010/04 /mobile-ads-bypass-apps.

31. Shira Ovide and Marcelo Prince, "Digits Live Show: Hulu Loses Stewart, Colbert," *Wall Street Journal*, March 3, 2010, http://blogs.wsj .com/digits/2010/03/03/digits-live-show-hulu -loses-stewart-colbert/.

32. Andrew Hampp, "Cross-Platform Ads: What's Working?" *Advertising Age*, June 26, 2008, http://adage.com/mediaworks/article ?article_id=128029.

33. Brian Morrisey, "YouTube Stars Brands Love," *Advertising Age*, November 7, 2010, www.adweek.com/news/technology/meet-you tube-stars-brands-love-103733; Irene Slutsky, "Meet YouTube's Most In-Demand Brand Stars," *Advertising Age*, September 13, 2010, http:// adage.com/article/digital/meet-youtube-s-demand -brand-stars/145844.

34. "New PQ Media Report Finds U.S. Branded Entertainment Spending on Consumer Events & Product Placement Dipped Only 1.3% to $24.63 Billion in 2009 & on Pace to Grow 5.3% in 2010, Exceeding Most Advertising & Marketing Segments," *Product Placement News*, July 7, 2010, www.productplacement.biz/201007072619 /product-placement-research/new-pq-media-report -finds-u-s-branded-entertainment-spending-on -consumer-events-product-placement-dipped-only -1-3-to-24-63-billion-in-2009-on-pace-to-grow -5-3-in-2010-exceeding-most-advertising.html.

35. Patricia Odell, "Sponsorship Spending Struggles to Recover," *Promo*, January 28, 2010, http://promomagazine.com/news /sponsorship-spending-struggles-0128/.

36. www.sponsorship.com; www.dominos.com; www.hiltonworldwide.com; www.anheuser-busch .com (Accessed January 2010).

37. Dana Rubenstein, "You Barf, You Lose," *Bloomberg Businessweek*, June 30, 2011, www.businessweek.com/magazine/the-worldclass -eaters-are-getting-full-pockets-07012011.html.

38. "PlayStation®—PS3™, PS2™, PSP® & PSP®go Systems, Games, & PlayStation®Network," Sony Computer Entertainment America, www.playstation.com.

39. Geoffrey Fowler, Ian Sherr, and Niraj Sheth, "A Defiant Steve Jobs Confronts 'Antennagate,'" *Wall Street Journal*, July 16, 2010, http://online .wsj.com/article/SB10001424052748704913304 575371131458273498.html.

18

1. http://promomagazine.com, October 2008 report.

2. Kunur Patel, "Suddenly, Everyone Wants to Be Groupon" *Advertising Age*, November 1, 2010, www.adage.com.

3. Jack Neff, "Coupon Clipping Stages a Comeback," *Advertising Age*, November 1, 2010, www.adage.com.

4. Ian Sherr, "Online Coupons Get Smarter," *Wall Street Journal*, August 25, 2010, http: //online.wsj.com/article/SB100014240527487034 47004575449453225928136.html.

5. Ibid.

6. Bruce Mohl, "Retailers Simplify the Rebate Process," *Boston Globe*, November 7, 2004; FTC Consumer Alert, "Taking the 'Bait' out of Rebates," www.ftc.gov/bcp/edu/pubs/consumer /alerts/alt059.shtm.

7. Convenience Store News Staff, "Loyalty Rewards Membership on the Rise," *Brandweek*, April 17 2009, www.brandweek.com/bw /content_display/news-and-features/direct /e3i76c769b73ce851586daedf100023fcf1.

8. Alaric Dearment, "Rite Aid Trims Losses as Loyalty Program, New Formats Drive Same-Store Sales," *Drug Store News*, June 23, 2011, www .drugstorenews.com/article/rite-aid-trims-losses -loyalty-program-new-formats-drive-same-store -sales.

9. Barbara De Lollis, "Loyalty Programs: Study Reveals Top Complaints; Spam Tops List," *USA Today*, February 8, 2010, http://travel.usatoday .com/hotels/legacy/2010/02/marriott-rewards -hilton-hhonors-intercontinental-priority-club -rewards-choice-wyndham-loyalty/1.

10. Ryan Kim, "Foursquare Looks to AmEx to Further Loyalty Program Ambitions," *GigaOM*, June 23, 2011, http://gigaom.com/2011/06/23 /foursquare-looks-to-amex-to-further-loyalty -program-ambitions.

11. John Wu, "Effects of In-Store Sampling on Retail Sales: Case Study of a Warehouse Store," *FindArticles.com*, Spring 2010, http://find articles.com/p/articles/mi_hb6054/is_201004 /ai_n53928748/.

12. Brian Quinton, "V-8 Fusion Opts for Facebook as Sampling Channel," *PROMO Magazine*, July 22, 2010, http://promomagazine .com/socialmedia/facebook/0722-v8-fusion -facebook-sampling/index.html.

13. Brie Cadman, "Parents Tell Supermarket: No TV Ads on Grocery Store Shelves," *Change.org*, November 5, 2010, http://news.change.org /stories/parents-tell-supermarket-no-tv-ads-on -grocery-store-shelves.

14. "Point-of-Purchase: $17 Billion," *PROMO Magazine*, October 29, 2001, 3; "In Praise of Promotion," *PROMO Xtra*, http://promo magazine.com.

15. Anne Hollard, "MarketingSherpa: Search Marketing and At-Work Coupon Campaigns: Redemption Rate Data and Four Useful Hotlinks," *MarketingSherpa*, www.marketing sherpa.com/article.html?ident=29788.

16. "Internet," CMS, www.couponinfonow.com/Couponing/Internet.cfm.

17. Peter King, "Personal Shoppers Find Clothes to Make the Man," *Wall Street Journal*, August 12, 2010, http://online.wsj.com/article/SB1000142405274870416490457542137362272530 4.html.

18. Michael Beverland, "Contextual Influences and the Adoption and Practice of Relationship Selling in a Business-to-Business Setting: An Exploratory Study," *Journal of Personal Selling & Sales Management*, 21, no. 3, Summer 2001, 207; Gabriel R. Gonzalez, K. Douglas Hoffman, and Thomas N. Ingram, "Improving Relationship Selling through Failure Analysis and Recovery Efforts: A Framework and Call to Action," *Journal of Personal Selling & Sales Management*, 25, no. 1, Winter 2005, 57.

19. Catherine Seda, "The Meet Market," *Entrepreneur*, August 2004, 68; Jim Dickie, "Is Social Networking an Overhyped Fad or a Useful Tool?" *Destination CRM*, January 21, 2005; Kristina Dell, "What Are Friends For?" *Time*, September 21, 2004; Media Releases, www.linkedin.com, December 3, 2007; "About Us," www.linkedin.com/static?key=company_info.

20. Barton Weitz, Stephen Castleberry, and John Tanner, *Selling: Building Partnerships* (Burr Ridge, IL: McGraw-Hill/Irwin, 2004), 198–201.

21. Eileen P. Gunn, "How Twitter Became My Secret Weapon," *Inc.*, June 14, 2011, www.inc.com/eileen-p-gunn/how-twitter-became-my-secret-weapon.html.

22. "Effective Business Presentation—Sales Presentation—Effective Presentation Skill," *Nielsen Business Media*, www.presentations.com.

23. Jennifer Alsever, "Turning Customers into Salespeople," *Inc.*, July/August 2011, www.inc.com/magazine/201107/turning-customers-into-salespeople.html.

19

1. Walter Baker, Michael Marn, and Craig Zawada, "Building a Better Price Structure," *McKinsey Quarterly*, August 2010, www.mckinseyquarterly.com/Building_a_better_pricing_structure_2652 (Accessed August 13, 2010).

2. Franziska Volckner, "The Dual Role of Price: Decomposing Consumers' Reactions to Price," *Journal of the Academy of Marketing Science*, 36, no. 3, Fall 2008, 359–377.

3. Ibid.

4. Timothy W. Martin, "Kroger: No Fears on Price," *Wall Street Journal*, September 30, 2010, B8.

5. "A Natural Experiment in Demand Elasticity: Metered vs Unmetered Electricity," *Ed Dolan's Econ Blog*, http://dolanecon.blogspot.com, August 17, 2010.

6. Edward Lotterman, "Why a Great Crop Year Like 2010 Can Be Bad News for U.S. Farmers," *Idaho Statesman*, August 15, 2010, www.idahostatesman.com/2010/08/15/1302125/ed-lotterman-why-a-great-crop.html.

7. Tammo H. A. Bijmolt, Harald J. Van Heerde, and Rik G. M. Pieters, "New Empirical Generalizations on the Determinants of Price Elasticity," *Journal of Marketing Research*, 42, May 2005, 141–156; Christian Homburg, Wayne Hoyer, and Nicole Koschate, "Customers' Reactions to Price Increases: Do Customer Satisfaction and Perceived Motive Fairness Matter?" *Journal of the Academy of Marketing Science*, 33, no. 1, Winter 2005, 35–49; Gadi Fibich, Arieh Gavious, and Oded Lowengart, "The Dynamics of Price Elasticity of Demand in the Presence of Reference Price Effects," *Journal of the Academy of Marketing Science*, 33, no. 1, Winter 2005, 66–78.

8. "Executives Zero In on Pricing," *Wall Street Journal*, September 27, 2010, B7.

9. "What the Traffic Will Bear," *Forbes*, July 3, 2008, 69.

10. Miguel Bustillo and Jeffrey A. Trachtenberg, "Amazon, Wal-Mart Cut Deeper in Book Duel," *Wall Street Journal*, October 17, 2009, B1.

11. Joseph Cannon and Christian Homburg, "Buyer–Supplier Relationships and Customer Firm Costs," *Journal of Marketing*, 65, January 2001, 29–43.

12. Yun Wan and Nan Hu, "Comparison Shopping Channel Selection by Small Online Vendors: An Exploratory Study (Abstract)," *IGI Global*, 2009, www.igi-global.com/bookstore/Chapter.aspx?TitleId=6735.

13. "How Shopping Bots Really Work," *MSN Money*, July 11, 2005, http://moneycentral.msn.com.

14. The Associated Press, "Sporting a Mullet Pays Off at Pittsburgh Zoo," *Boston Herald*, July 6, 2010, www.bostonherald.com/news/offbeat/.

15. "Wal-Mart Puts the Squeeze on Food Costs," *Fortune*, June 9, 2008, 16.

16. Vicki Young, "Cautions for Luxury: Survey Finds Wealthy Less Keen on Category," *Women's Wear Daily*, September 22, 2009, 20.

17. Katherine Lemon and Stephen Nowlis, "Developing Synergies between Promotions and Brands in Different Price-Quality Tiers," *Journal of Marketing Research*, 39, May 2002, 171–185; also see Valerie Taylor and William Bearden, "The Effects of Price on Brand Extension Evaluations: The Moderating Role of Extension Similarity," *Journal of the Academy of Marketing Science*, 30, no. 2, Spring 2002, 131–140; and Raj Sethuraman and V. Srinivasan, "The Asymmetric Share Effect: An Empirical Generalization on Cross-Price Effects," *Journal of Marketing Research*, 39, no. 3, August 2002, 379–386.

18. Volckner, "The Dual Role of Price."

19. Ibid.

20. Elizabeth Holmes, "The Finer Art of Faking It," *Wall Street Journal*, June 30, 2011, http://online.wsj.com/article/SB100014240527023047912045764015314146929212.html.

21. Merrie Brucks, Valarie Zeithaml, and Gillian Naylor, "Price and Brand Name as Indicators of Quality Dimensions for Consumer Durables," *Journal of the Academy of Marketing Science*, 28, no. 3, Summer 2000, 359–374; Wilford Amaldoss and Sanjay Jain, "Pricing of Conspicuous Goods: A Competitive Analysis of Social Effects," *Journal of Marketing Research*, 42, February 2005, 30–42; also see Margaret Campbell, "Says Who?! How the Source of Price Information and Affect Influence Perceived Price (UN)fairness," *Journal of Marketing Research*, 44, no. 2, May 2007, 261–271.

20

1. Keith Chrzan, "An Overview of Pricing Research," *Quirk's Marketing Research Review*, July/August 2006, 24–29.

2. Kent Monroe and Jennifer Cox, "Pricing Practices That Endanger Profits," *Marketing Management*, September/October 2001, 42–46.

3. Ibid.

4. Carl Baugh, "Dealers Attempt to Fleece GM Volt Buyers; AutoNation Clamps Down on Price Mark-up," *International Business Times*, August 16, 2010, www.ibtimes.com/articles/43638/20100816/gm-volt-nissan-leaf-autonation.htm; "Chevy Volt: Overview," Chevrolet Product Site, http://www.chevrolet.com/volt-electric-car (Accessed October 19, 2011); "Nissan LEAF," Nissan Product Site, http://www.nissanusa.com/leaf-electric-car/index#/leaf-electric-car/index (Accessed October 19, 2011).

5. "Why the Price Is Rarely Right," *Bloomberg Businessweek*, February 18, 2010, 77–78.

6. Julie Jargon and Gina Chon, "Burger King's Latest Pickle," *Wall Street Journal*, September 1, 2010, http://online.wsj.com/article/SB10001424052748704791004575465961922888040.html.

7. Christina Binkley, "Fashion's Elite Wage a War on Discounts," *Wall Street Journal*, August 13, 2009, D6; Andria Cheng, "Shoppers Show Their Staying Power in August," *Market Watch*, September 2, 2010, www.marketwatch.com/story/same-store-sales-top-expectations-in-august-2010-09-02.

8. "Gillette's Latest Innovation in Razors: The 11-Cent Blade," *Wall Street Journal*, October 1, 2010, B1.

9. Vivian Pereira, "Brazilians Embracing New Free-Sample Outlets," *International Herald Tribune*, July 10–11, 2010, 14.

10. Paul Sonne and Laurence Norman, "EU Fines Unilever, P&G over Pricing," *Wall Street Journal*, April 14, 2011, B1.

11. Liam Baldwin, "Freight Price Fixing Cartel Charged," *National Business Review*, September 2, 2010, www.nbr.co.nz/article/freight-price-fixing-cartel-charged-129366.

12. Kevin Scarpati, "Freight Forwarders Fined Millions for Price-Fixing," *Supply Chain Digital*, June 14, 2011, www.supplychaindigital.com/global_logistics/freight-forwarders-fined-millions-for-price-fixing.

13. "How Driving Prices Lower Can Violate Antitrust Statutes," *Wall Street Journal*, January 24, 2004, A1, A11.

14. Evan Clark and Kristi Ellis, "Price-Fixing Plays Out in Supreme Court," *Women's Wear Daily*, June 19, 2008.

15. Bruce Alford and Abhijit Biswas, "The Effects of Discount Level, Price Consciousness, and Sale Proneness on Consumers' Price Perception and Behavioral Intention," *Journal of Business Research*, 55, no. 9, September 2002, 775–778; also see V. Kumar, Vibhas Madan, and Srinin Srinivasan, "Price Discounts or Coupon Promotions: Does It Matter?" *Journal of Business Research*, 57, no. 9, September 2004, 933–941.

16. "How Driving Prices Lower Can Violate Antitrust Statutes."

17. "Safeway Takes Bullet in Grocery Price War," *Wall Street Journal*, October 16, 2009, B1, B5; "Safeway Says 2010 Profit Could Miss Expectations," www.reuters.com, March 3, 2010.

18. Timothy Aeppel, "Guitar Maker Revives No-Frills Act from '30's," *Wall Street Journal*, July 6, 2009, B1, B2; "How to Reach the New Customer," *Marketing News*, February 28, 2010, 19–22.

19. Timothy Aeppel, "Seeking Perfect Prices, CEO Tears Up the Rules," *Wall Street Journal*, March 27, 2007, A1, A16.

20. Ibid.

21. Ragnhild Kjetland and Pavel Alpeyev, "Sony Challenges Apple in Streaming of Videos, Music," *Bloomberg,* September 2, 2010, www.bloomberg .com/news/2010-09-02/sony-challenges-apple -with-video-and-music-streaming-service.html.

22. "Seven Mistakes of Poor Pricers," *Wall Street Journal,* May 24, 2010, R8.

23. Rui (Juliet) Zhu, Xinlei (Jack) Chen, and Srabana Dasgupta, "Can Trade-Ins Hurt You? Exploring the Effect of a Trade-In on Consumers' Willingness to Pay for a Product," *Journal of Marketing Research,* 45, no. 2, April 2008, 159–170.

24. Ibid.

25. Ibid.

26. To learn more about pricing fairness, see Lan Xia, Kent Monroe, and Jennifer Cox, "The Price Is Unfair! A Conceptual Framework of Price Fairness Perceptions," *Journal of Marketing,* 68, no. 4, October 2004, 1–15.

27. "AT&T Adopts Tiered Wireless Broadband Pricing," www.broadcastingcable.com, June 2, 2010.

28. "Sprint, T-Mobile Keep Prices Low on Wireless Broadband," http://news.cnet.com, May 4, 2010.

29. Christopher Heine, "How Gap's 'Groupon' Went Crazy Viral," *ClickZ,* August 25, 2010, www.clickz.com/clickz/news/1729509/how -gaps-groupon-went-crazy-viral.

30. Sam Diaz, "Groupon's $11 Million Gap Day: A Business Winner or Loser?" *ZDNet,* August 23, 2010, www.zdnet.com/blog/btl/groupons -11-million-gap-day-a-business-winner-or -loser/38259.

31. Dilip Soman and John Gourville, "Transaction Decoupling: The Effects of Price Bundling on the Decision to Consume," *MSI Report,* 2002, 98–131; Stefan Stremersch and Gerard J. Tellis, "Strategic Bundling of Products and Prices: A New Synthesis for Marketing," *Journal of Marketing,* 66, no. 1, January 2002, 55–71; "Forget Prices and Get People to Use the Stuff," *Wall Street Journal,* June 3, 2004, A2.

32. Susan Carey, "Airlines to Load on More Fees," *Wall Street Journal,* March 7, 2011, B1.

33. Rebecca Hamilton and Joydeep Srivastava, "When 2+2 Is Not the Same as 1+3: Variations in Price Sensitivity across Components of Partitioned Prices," *Journal of Marketing Research,* 45, no. 4, August 2008, 450–461.

34. Sean Cole, "Less Product, Same Price," *American Public Media,* January 8, 2009, http://marketplace.publicradio.org/display /web/2009/01/08/pm_deceptive_packaging/.

35. Paul Hunt and Greg Thomas, "Scoring Birdies Instead of Bogies," *Pricing Solutions Newsletter,* 2, no. 2, Winter 2009, www .pricingsolutions.com.

21

1. Joseph Hair, Robert Bush, and David Ortinau, *Marketing Research: Within a Changing Information Environment,* 3rd ed. (Burr Ridge, IL: McGraw-Hill/Irwin, 2006), 114.

2. "IBM Helps Construction Firm Boost Number of Clients by 40% through Mobile Real-Time Trends Analysis," *PRNewswire,* September 1, 2010, www.prnewswire.com /news-releases/ibm-helps-construction-firm-boost -number-of-clients-by-40-through-mobile-real -time-trends-analysis-101965838.html.

3. Ibid.

4. Kasey Wehrum, "Learning from the Customer," *Inc.,* March 1, 2011, www.inc.com /magazine/20110301/customer-service-case -studies-crutchfield.html.

5. "My Starbucks Idea," Starbucks, http://mystarbucksidea.force.com/.

6. Terry Maxon, "For Southwest Airlines Team, Work Means Always Having to Say You're Sorry," *Dallas Morning News,* August 15, 2010, www .dallasnews.com/sharedcontent/dws/bus/stories /DN-swapology_15bus.ART0.State.Edition1 .26cd7a0.html.

7. Organic, Inc., "CRM Moves from Elite to Everyman: Four Elements for Creating a Social CRM Strategy," March 16, 2010, www.organic .com/Assets/whitepaper_social_crm_20100312 123657.pdf.

8. Rebecca Reisner, "Comcast's Twitter Man," *BusinessWeek,* January 13, 2009, www .businessweek.com/managing/content/jan2009 /ca20090113_373506.htm.

9. Steve Stecklow and Paul Sonne, "Shunned Profiling Method on the Verge of Comeback," *Wall Street Journal,* November 14, 2010, A1, A14.

10. Neil Savage, "Data Mining Your Digital Footprints," CNNMoney.com, June 14, 2010, http://money.cnn.com/2010/06/14/smallbusiness /sensenetworks/index.htm.

11. Donna Fenn, "10 Ways to Get More Sales from Existing Customers," *Inc.,* August 31, 2010, www.inc.com/guides/2010/08/get-more-sales -from-existing-customers.html.

12. Barton Weitz, Stephen Castleberry, and John Tanner, *Selling: Building Partnerships* (Burr Ridge, IL: McGraw-Hill/Irwin, 2004), 184–185.

13. Brian Rice, "Redbox Proves Creating Customer Loyalty Is as Easy as Saying 'Happy Birthday,'" *Business 2 Community,* July 14, 2011, www.business2community.com/loyalty-marketing /redbox-proves-creating-customer-loyalty-is-as -easy-as-saying-"happy-birthday"-044184.

14. Fenn, "10 Ways to Get More Sales from Existing Customers."

15. Savage, "Data Mining Your Digital Footprints."

16. Chris Shunk, "Subaru Letting Owners Show Loyalty, Hobbies with Free Badge Program," *Autoblog,* May 28, 2010, www.autoblog.com /2010/05/28/subaru-letting-owners-show-loyalty -hobbies-with-free-badge-prog.

17. Miguel Bustillo, "Wal-Mart Radio Tags to Track Clothing," *Wall Street Journal,* July 23, 2010, http://online.wsj.com/article/SB100014240 52748704421304575383213061198090.html.

22

1. Brian Solis, *Engage: The Complete Guide for Brands and Businesses to Build, Cultivate and Measure Success in the New Web* (Hoboken, NJ: John Wiley & Sons, 2010), 37.

2. Teressa Iezzi, *The Idea Writers,* (Basingstroke, England: Palgrave McMillan, 2010).

3. "Social Media for Non Profits," *Primalmedia,* February 18, 2009, www.primalmedia.com/blog /social-media-non-profits.

4. Salma Jafri, "Lady Gaga's Social Media Success and Strategy," Suite101.com, June 5, 2010, http://marketingpr.suite101.com/article .cfm/lady-gagas-social-media-success-and-strategy; Dorothy Pomerantz, "Lady Gaga Leads List of Celeb 100 Newcomers," *Forbes,* June 28, 2010, www.forbes.com/2010/06/22/lady-gaga-kristin -stewart-business-entertainment-celeb-100-10 -newcomers.html.

5. Andrew Hampp, "Gaga, Oooh La La: Why the Lady Is the Ultimate Social Climber," *Advertising Age,* February 22, 2010, http://adage .com/digitalalist10/article?article_id=142210.

6. Solis, *Engage.*

7. Ibid.

8. Universal McCann, "Power to the People— Wave3 Study on Social Media Trends," March 2008, www.slideshare.net/mickstravellin /universal-mccann-international-social-media -research-wave-3.

9. Felix Gillette, "The Rise and Inglorious Fall of Myspace," *Bloomberg Businessweek,* June 27–July 3, 2011, 54–59; Brian Stelter, "News Corporation Sells Myspace for $35 Million," *New York Times,* June 29, 2011, http://mediadecoder .blogs.nytimes.com/2011/06/29/news-corp-sells -myspace-to-specific-media-for-35-million.

10. Aaron Smith, "Mobile Access 2010," Pew Internet & American Life Project, July 7, 2010, www.pewinternet.org/Reports/2010/Mobile -Access-2010.aspx.

11. Yukari Iwatani Kane and Ian Sherr, "iPhone Powers Apple Sales," *Wall Street Journal,* July 20, 2011, http://online.wsj.com/article/SB100014240 52702303661904576456411590795754.html.

12. Shane Snow, "iPad by the Numbers," *Mashable,* July 2010, http://mashable .com/2010/06/07/ipad-infographic-2.

13. Paul Marsden, "Simple Definition of Social Commerce," *Social Commerce Today,* June 2010, http://socialcommercetoday.com/social-commerce -definition-word-cloud-definitive-definition-list.

14. Shar VanBoskirk, "U.S. Interactive Marketing Forecast 2009 to 2014," *Forrester Research,* July 6, 2009, www.forrester.com/rb/Research/us _interactive_marketing_forecast,_2009_to _2014/q/id/47730/t/2.

15. "About CafeMom," www.cafemom.com /about/index.php (Accessed July 21, 2011).

16. *Marketing News* Staff, "Digital Dozen: Step Up to the Bar," *Marketing News,* March 15, 2010, www.marketingpower.com/Resource Library/Publications/MarketingNews/2010/3 _15_10/DigitalDozen.pdf.

17. Jeff Howe, *Crowdsourcing: Why the Power of the Crowd Is Driving the Future of Business* (New York: Three Rivers Press, 2009), 32.

18. Timothy Lloyd, "Beatles Great Paul McCartney Plunges into Crowd Sourcing," *Wall Street Journal,* July 6, 2011, http://blogs.wsj .com/speakeasy/2011/07/06/beatles-great -paul-mccartney-plunges-into-crowd-sourcing.

19. Sean Corcoran, "Defining Earned, Owned and Paid Media," *Forrester Blogs,* December 16, 2009, http://blogs.forrester.com/interactive _marketing/2009/12/defining-earned-owned-and -paid-media.html; Brian Solis, "Why Brands Are Becoming Media," *Mashable,* February 11, 2010.

20. Ibid.

21. Erik Bratt, "Social Media ROI Success Stories," *MarketingProfs,* 2009, www .marketingprofs.com/store/product/27/social -media-roi-success-stories.

22. David Berkowitz, "100 Ways to Measure Social Media," *Inside the Marketers Studio,* November 17, 2009, www.marketersstudio

.com/2009/11/100-ways-to-measure-social
-media-.html.

23. Mike Laurie, "How Social Media Has
Changed Us," *Mashable*, January 7, 2010,
http://mashable.com/2010/01/07/social
-media-changed-us.

24. Charlene Li and Josh Bernoff, *"Groundswell":
Winning in a World Transformed by Social
Technologies,* (Boston: Harvard Business Press,
2009).

25. *North American Technographics Interactive
Marketing Online Survey*, Forrester Research,
June 2009, www.forrester.com/ER/Research
/Survey/Excerpt/1,10198,726,00.html.

26. Juan Carlos Perez, "Forrester Notes Social
Media Contributor Slowdown," *Computerworld*,
September 28, 2010, www.computerworld.com
/s/article/9188538/Forrester_notes_social_media
_contributor_slowdown.

27. Dan Zarella, *The Social Media Marketing
Book* (Beijing, China: O'Reilly, 2010).

28. Rolfe Winkler, "Google+Gaga = Tweet Deal,"
Wall Street Journal, July 15, 2011, C10.

29. Nisha Chittal, "Mark Coatney: *Newsweek*'s
Secret Weapon Is Tumblr's Newest Acquisition,"
Mediaite, July 12, 2010, www.mediaite.com

/online/mark-coatney-newsweeks-secret-weapon
-is-tumblrs-newest-acquisition.

30. Marketing Profs, "Adobe Systems," *Facebook
Success Stories*, 2009, www.marketingprofs.com
/store/product/35/facebook-success-stories.

31. Marketing Profs, *LinkedIn Success Stories,*
2009, www.marketingprofs.com/store/product
/37/linkedin-success-stories.

32. Solis, *Engage*, 64.

33. Ramya Raghavan, "Using Video to Connect
with Your Donors and Prospects," International
Fundraising eConference, May 12–14, 2009.

34. Zarella, *The Social Media Marketing Book*.

35. Solis, *Engage*, 54.

36. Solis, *Engage*, 97.

37. David Sax, "Yelp's Online Reviewing Mafia,"
Bloomberg Businessweek, June 2, 2011, www
.businessweek.com/magazine/content/11_24/b42
32083260194.htm.

38. Solis, *Engage*, 51.

39. Irina Slutsky, "Nothing Casual about This
Game Obsession," *Advertising Age*, January 10,
2011, 2.

40. "Social Gaming Integral to Social
Networking," *Marketing Profs*, February 19,
2010, www.marketingprofs.com/charts/2010

/3425/social-gaming-integral-to-social
-networking.

41. Lon Safko and David K. Brake, *The Social
Media Bible: Tactics, Tools & Strategies for
Business Success* (Hoboken, NJ: John Wiley &
Sons, 2009).

42. Emily Glazer, "Target: Customers on the Go,"
Wall Street Journal, May 16, 2011, http://online
.wsj.com/article/SB1000142405274870413220457
6285631212564952.html.

43. John Kennedy, "NFC Mobile Marketing
Kicks Off with VH-1's 'Basketball
Wives,'" *Silicon Republic,* July 21, 2011,
www.siliconrepublic.com/new-media/
item/22787-nfc-mobile-marketing-kicks.

44. *Marketing News* Staff, "Digital Dozen:
Benjamin Moore Paints App Success," *Marketing
News*, March 15, 2010, www.marketingpower
.com/ResourceLibrary/Publications/Marketing
News/2010/3_15_10/Digital Dozen.pdf.

45. Beth Kanter, "Screencast: Using Widgets to
Build Community on Blogs Featured on NTEN
Blog," *Beth's Blog*, March 20, 2007, http://beth
.typepad.com/beths_blog/2007/03/screncast
_using.html.

Index

Boldface indicates key term.

KEY TERMS

 LO 1 **marketing** the activity, set of institutions, and processes for creating, communicating, delivering, and exchanging offerings that have value for customers, clients, partners, and society at large

exchange people giving up something in order to receive something they would rather have

 LO 2 **production orientation** a philosophy that focuses on the internal capabilities of the firm rather than on the desires and needs of the marketplace

sales orientation the ideas that people will buy more goods and services if aggressive sales techniques are used and that high sales result in high profits

marketing concept the idea that the social and economic justification for an organization's existence is the satisfaction of customer wants and needs while meeting organizational objectives

market orientation a philosophy that assumes that a sale does not depend on an aggressive sales force but rather on a customer's decision to purchase a product; it is synonymous with the marketing concept

societal marketing orientation the idea that an organization exists not only to satisfy customer wants and needs and to meet organizational objectives but also to preserve or enhance individuals' and society's long-term best interests

KEY CONCEPTS

LO 1 **Define the term *marketing*.** Marketing is the activity, set of institutions, and processes for creating, communicating, delivering, and exchanging offerings that have value for customers, clients, partners, and society at large. Marketing also requires all facets of a company to work together to pool ideas and resources. One major goal of marketing is to create an exchange. An exchange has five conditions, as listed below. Even if all five conditions are met, an exchange might not occur. People engage in marketing whether or not an exchange happens.

Five conditions of exchange

1. There must be at least two parties.
2. Each party has something that might be of value to the other party.
3. Each party is capable of communication and delivery.
4. Each party is free to accept or reject the exchange offer.
5. Each party believes it is appropriate or desirable to deal with the other party.

LO 2 **Describe four marketing management philosophies.** The role of marketing and the character of marketing activities within an organization are strongly influenced by its philosophy and orientation. A production-oriented organization focuses on the internal capabilities of the firm rather than on the desires and needs of the marketplace. A sales orientation is based on the beliefs that people will buy more products if aggressive sales techniques are used and that high sales volumes produce high profits. A market-oriented organization focuses on satisfying customer wants and needs while meeting organizational objectives. A societal marketing orientation goes beyond a market orientation to include the preservation or enhancement of individuals' and society's long-term best interests.

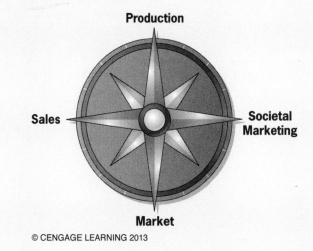

© CENGAGE LEARNING 2013

© 2013 Cengage Learning. All Rights Reserved. May not be scanned, copied or duplicated, or posted to a publicly accessible website, in whole or in part.

LO 3   **customer value** the relationship between benefits and the sacrifice necessary to obtain those benefits

customer satisfaction customers' evaluation of a good or service in terms of whether it has met their needs and expectations

relationship marketing a strategy that focuses on keeping and improving relationships with current customers

empowerment delegation of authority to solve customers' problems quickly—usually by the first person the customer notifies regarding a problem

teamwork collaborative efforts of people to accomplish common objectives

LO 3   **Discuss the differences between sales and market orientations.** First, sales-oriented firms focus on their own needs; market-oriented firms focus on customers' needs and preferences. Second, sales-oriented companies consider themselves to be deliverers of goods and services, whereas market-oriented companies view themselves as satisfiers of customers. Third, sales-oriented firms direct their products to everyone; market-oriented firms aim at specific segments of the population. Fourth, although the primary goal of both types of firms is profit, sales-oriented businesses pursue maximum sales volume through intensive promotion, whereas market-oriented businesses pursue customer satisfaction through coordinated activities.

	What is the organization's focus?	What business are you in?	To whom is the product directed?	What is your primary goal?	How do you seek to achieve your goal?
Sales Orientation	Inward, on the organization's needs	Selling goods and services	Everybody	Profit through maximum sales volume	Primarily through intensive promotion
Market Orientation	Outward on the wants and needs of customers	Satisfying customer wants and needs and delivering superior value	Specific groups of people	Profit through customer satisfaction	Through coordinated marketing and inter-functional activities

© CENGAGE LEARNING 2013

LO 4   **Describe several reasons for studying marketing.** First, marketing affects the allocation of goods and services that influence a nation's economy and standard of living. Second, an understanding of marketing is crucial to understanding most businesses. Third, career opportunities in marketing are diverse, profitable, and expected to increase significantly during the coming decade. Fourth, understanding marketing makes consumers more informed.

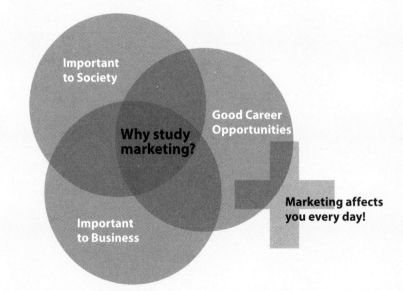

© CENGAGE LEARNING 2013

KEY TERMS

 strategic planning the managerial process of creating and maintaining a fit between the organization's objectives and resources and the evolving market opportunities

 strategic business unit (SBU) a subgroup of a single business or collection of related businesses within the larger organization

 market penetration a marketing strategy that tries to increase market share among existing customers

market development a marketing strategy that entails attracting new customers to existing products

product development a marketing strategy that entails the creation of new products for present markets

diversification a strategy of increasing sales by introducing new products into new markets

portfolio matrix a tool for allocating resources among products or strategic business units on the basis of relative market share and market growth rate

star in the portfolio matrix, a business unit that is a fast-growing market leader

cash cow in the portfolio matrix, a business unit that generates more cash than it needs to maintain its market share

problem child (question mark) in the portfolio matrix, a business unit that shows rapid growth but poor profit margins

dog in the portfolio matrix, a business unit that has low growth potential and a small market share

planning the process of anticipating future events and determining strategies to achieve organizational objectives in the future

marketing planning designing activities relating to marketing objectives and the changing marketing environment

marketing plan a written document that acts as a guidebook of marketing activities for the marketing manager

KEY CONCEPTS

 Understand the importance of strategic planning. Strategic planning is the basis for all marketing strategies and decisions. These decisions affect the allocation of resources and ultimately the financial success of the company.

 Define strategic business units (SBUs). Each SBU should have these characteristics: a distinct mission and a specific target market; control over resources; its own competitors; a single business; plans independent from other SBUs in the organization. Each SBU has its own rate of return on investment, growth potential, and associated risks, and requires its own strategies and funding.

 Identify strategic alternatives and know a basic outline for a marketing plan. Ansoff's opportunity matrix presents four options to help management develop strategic alternatives: market penetration, market development, product development, and diversification. In selecting a strategic alternative, managers may use a portfolio matrix, which classifies strategic business units as stars, cash cows, problem children (or question marks), and dogs, depending on their present or projected growth and market share. Alternatively, the GE model suggests that companies determine strategic alternatives based on the comparisons between business position and market attractiveness.

A marketing plan should define the business mission, perform a situation analysis, define objectives, delineate a target market, and establish components of the marketing mix. Other elements that may be included in a plan are budgets, implementation timetables, required marketing research efforts, or elements of advanced strategic planning.

 Develop an appropriate business mission statement. The firm's mission statement establishes boundaries for all subsequent decisions, objectives, and strategies. A mission statement should focus on the market(s) the organization is attempting to serve rather than on the good or service offered.

 Describe the components of a situation analysis. In the situation (or SWOT) analysis, the firm should identify its internal strengths (S) and weaknesses (W) and also examine external opportunities (O) and threats (T). When examining external opportunities and threats, marketing managers must analyze aspects of the marketing environment in a process called environmental scanning. The six macroenvironmental forces studied most often are social, demographic, economic, technological, political and legal, and competitive.

 Identify sources of competitive advantage. There are three types of competitive advantage: cost, product/service differentiation, and niche. Sources of cost competitive advantage include experience curves, efficient labor, no frills goods and services, government subsidies, product design, reengineering, production innovations, and new methods of service delivery. A product/service differentiation competitive advantage exists when a firm provides something unique that is valuable to buyers beyond just low price. Niche competitive advantages come from targeting unique segments with specific needs and wants. The goal of all these sources of competitive advantage is to be sustainable.

© 2013 Cengage Learning. All Rights Reserved. May not be scanned, copied or duplicated, or posted to a publicly accessible website, in whole or in part.

mission statement a statement of the firm's business based on a careful analysis of benefits sought by present and potential customers and an analysis of existing and anticipated environmental conditions

marketing myopia defining a business in terms of goods and services rather than in terms of the benefits customers seek

 SWOT analysis identifying internal strengths (S) and weaknesses (W) and also examining external opportunities (O) and threats (T)

environmental scanning collection and interpretation of information about forces, events, and relationships in the external environment that may affect the future of the organization or the implementation of the marketing plan

 competitive advantage a set of unique features of a company and its products that are perceived by the target market as significant and superior to those of the competition

cost competitive advantage being the low-cost competitor in an industry while maintaining satisfactory profit margins

experience curves curves that show costs declining at a predictable rate as experience with a product increases

product/service differentiation competitive advantage the provision of something that is unique and valuable to buyers beyond simply offering a lower price than that of the competition

niche competitive advantage the advantage achieved when a firm seeks to target and effectively serve a small segment of the market

sustainable competitive advantage an advantage that cannot be copied by the competition

 marketing objective a statement of what is to be accomplished through marketing activities

 marketing strategy the activities of selecting and describing one or more target markets and developing and maintaining a marketing mix that will produce mutually satisfying exchanges with target markets

 Explain the criteria for stating good marketing objectives. Objectives should be realistic, measurable, time specific, and compared to a benchmark. They must also be consistent and indicate the priorities of the organization. Good marketing objectives communicate marketing management philosophies, provide management direction, motivate employees, force executives to think clearly, and form a basis for control.

 Discuss target market strategies. Targeting markets begins with a market opportunity analysis (MOA), which describes and estimates the size and sales potential of market segments that are of interest to the firm. In addition, an assessment of key competitors in these market segments is performed. After the market segments are described, one or more may be targeted by the firm.

 Describe the elements of the marketing mix. The marketing mix is a blend of product, place, promotion, and pricing strategies (the four Ps) designed to produce mutually satisfying exchanges with a target market. The starting point of the marketing mix is the product offering—tangible goods, ideas, or services. Place (distribution) strategies are concerned with making products available when and where customers want them. Promotion includes advertising, public relations, sales promotion, and personal selling. Price is what a buyer must give up in order to obtain a product and is often the most flexible of the four marketing mix elements.

 Explain why implementation, evaluation, and control of the marketing plan are necessary. Before a marketing plan can work, it must be implemented—that is, people must perform the actions in the plan. The plan should also be evaluated to see if it has achieved its objectives. Poor implementation can be a major factor in a plan's failure, but working to gain acceptance can be accomplished with task forces. Once implemented, one major aspect of control is the marketing audit, and ultimately continuing to apply what the audit uncovered through postaudit tasks.

 Identify several techniques that help make strategic planning effective. First, management must realize that strategic planning is an ongoing process and not a once-a-year exercise. Second, good strategic planning involves a high level of creativity. The last requirement is top management's support and participation.

market opportunity analysis (MOA) the description and estimation of the size and sales potential of market segments that are of interest to the firm and the assessment of key competitors in these market segments

 marketing mix a unique blend of product, place (distribution), promotion, and pricing strategies designed to produce mutually satisfying exchanges with a target market

four Ps product, place, promotion, and price, which together make up the marketing mix

 implementation the process that turns a marketing plan

into action assignments and ensures that these assignments are executed in a way that accomplishes the plan's objectives

evaluation gauging the extent to which the marketing objectives have been achieved during the specified time period

control provides the mechanisms for evaluating marketing results in light of the plan's objectives and for correcting actions that do not help the organization reach those objectives within budget guidelines

marketing audit a thorough, systematic, periodic evaluation of the objectives, strategies, structure, and performance of the marketing organization

KEY TERMS

 LO 1

ethics the moral principles or values that generally govern the conduct of an individual or a group

 LO 2

morals the rules people develop as a result of cultural values and norms

code of ethics a guideline to help marketing managers and other employees make better decisions

Foreign Corrupt Practices Act (FCPA) a law that prohibits U.S. corporations from making illegal payments to public officials of foreign governments to obtain business rights or to enhance their business dealings in those countries

 LO 3

corporate social responsibility (CSR) a business's concern for society's welfare

pyramid of corporate social responsibility a model that suggests corporate social responsibility is composed of economic, legal, ethical, and philanthropic responsibilities and that the firm's economic performance supports the entire structure

sustainability the idea that socially responsible companies will outperform their peers by focusing on the world's social problems and viewing them as opportunities to build profits and help the world at the same time

green marketing the development and marketing of products designed to minimize negative effects on the physical environment or to improve the environment

KEY CONCEPTS

 LO 1

Explain the concept of ethical behavior. Ethics are the moral principles or values that generally govern the conduct of an individual or group. They are standards of behavior by which conduct is judged. Standards that are legal may not always be ethical. An ethics violation offends a person's sense of justice or fairness. Ethics basically constitute the unwritten rules developed to guide interactions. Many ethical questions arise from balancing a business's need to produce profit for shareholders against its desire to operate honestly and with concern for environmental and social issues.

LO 2

Describe ethical behavior in business. Business ethics may be viewed as a subset of the values of society as a whole, with a foundation based on the cultural values and norms that constitute a culture's morals. The ethical conduct of businesspeople is shaped by societal elements, including family, education, and religious institutions. As members of society, businesspeople are morally obligated to consider the ethical implications of their decisions. Ethical decision making can be grouped into three basic approaches. The first approach examines the consequences of decisions. The second approach relies on rules and laws to guide decision making. The third approach is based on a theory of moral development that places individuals or groups in one of three developmental stages: preconventional morality, conventional morality, or postconventional morality.

In addition to personal influences, there are many business influences on ethical decision making. Some of the most influential include the extent of ethical problems within the organization, top management's actions on ethics, potential magnitude of the consequences, social consensus, probability of a harmful outcome, length of time between the decision and the onset of consequences, and the number of people affected.

Many companies develop a code of ethics to help their employees make ethical decisions. A code of ethics can help employees identify acceptable business practices, be an effective internal control on behavior, help employees avoid confusion when determining whether decisions are ethical, and facilitate discussion about what is right and wrong.

Studies show that ethical beliefs vary little from country to country. However, there are enough cultural differences, such as the practice of bribery or gift giving, that laws such as the Foreign Corrupt Practices Act (FCPA) have been put in place to discourage and attempt to modify the current acceptance of such practices.

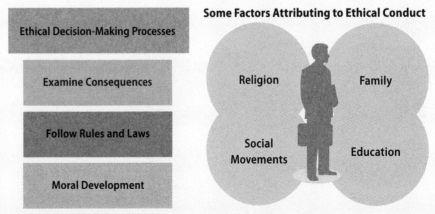

Ethical Decision-Making Processes

Examine Consequences

Follow Rules and Laws

Moral Development

Some Factors Attributing to Ethical Conduct

Religion

Family

Social Movements

Education

© CENGAGE LEARNING 2013

© 2013 Cengage Learning. All Rights Reserved. May not be scanned, copied or duplicated, or posted to a publicly accessible website, in whole or in part.

4 **cause-related marketing** the cooperative marketing efforts between a for-profit firm and a nonprofit organization

 3 **Discuss corporate social responsibility.** Responsibility in business refers to a firm's concern for the way its decisions affect society. Social responsibility has four components: economic, legal, ethical, and philanthropic. These are intertwined, yet the most fundamental is earning a profit. If a firm does not earn a profit, the other three responsibilities are moot. Most businesspeople believe they should do more than pursue profits. Although a company must consider its economic needs first, it must also operate within the law, do what is ethical and fair, and be a good corporate citizen. *Sustainability* is the concept that socially responsible companies will outperform their peers by focusing on the world's social problems and viewing them as an opportunity to earn profits and help the world at the same time. Social responsibility is growing, but it can be costly and the benefits are not always immediate. In addition, some surveys report that consumer desire to purchase responsible products does not always translate to actually purchasing those products. One branch of social responsibility is green marketing, which aids the environment and often the bottom line of a business.

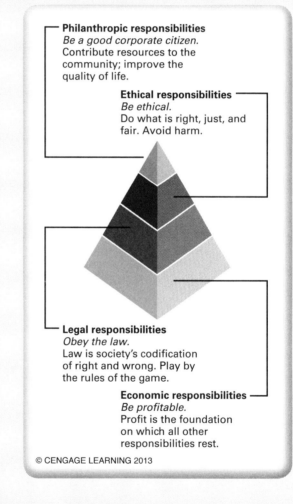

Philanthropic responsibilities
Be a good corporate citizen.
Contribute resources to the community; improve the quality of life.

Ethical responsibilities
Be ethical.
Do what is right, just, and fair. Avoid harm.

Legal responsibilities
Obey the law.
Law is society's codification of right and wrong. Play by the rules of the game.

Economic responsibilities
Be profitable.
Profit is the foundation on which all other responsibilities rest.

© CENGAGE LEARNING 2013

 4 **Explain cause-related marketing.** Cause-related marketing is the cooperative effort between a for-profit firm and a nonprofit organization. It is different from philanthropy, which is a specific, tax-deductible donation. Cause-related marketing is very popular because it can enhance the reputation of the corporation and also make additional profit for the company. However, consumers sometimes feel that every company is tied to a cause, resulting in consumer cause fatigue.

KEY TERMS

target market a group of people or organizations for which an organization designs, implements, and maintains a marketing mix intended to meet the need of that group, resulting in mutually satisfying exchanges

environmental management when a company implements strategies that attempt to shape the external environment within which it operates

component lifestyles the practice of choosing goods and services that meet one's diverse needs and interests rather than conforming to a single, traditional lifestyle

demography the study of people's vital statistics, such as age, race and ethnicity, and location

Generation Y people born between 1979 and 1994

Generation X people born between 1965 and 1978

baby boomers people born between 1946 and 1964

purchasing power a comparison of income versus the relative cost of a standard set of goods and services in different geographic areas

inflation a measure of the decrease in the value of money, expressed as the percentage reduction in value since the previous year

recession a period of economic activity characterized by negative growth, which reduces demand for goods and services

KEY CONCEPTS

Discuss the external environment of marketing and explain how it affects a firm. The external marketing environment consists of social, demographic, economic, technological, political and legal, and competitive variables. Marketers generally cannot control the elements of the external environment. Instead, they must understand how the external environment is changing and the impact of that change on the target market. Then marketing managers can create a marketing mix to effectively meet the needs of target customers.

Describe the social factors that affect marketing. Within the external environment, social factors are perhaps the most difficult for marketers to anticipate. Several major social trends are currently shaping marketing strategies. First, people of all ages have a broader range of interests, defying traditional consumer profiles. Second, changing gender roles are bringing more women into the workforce and increasing the number of men who shop. Third, a greater number of dual-career families has created demand for time-saving goods and services.

Explain the importance to marketing managers of current demographic trends. Today, several basic demographic patterns are influencing marketing mixes. Because the U.S. population is growing at a slower rate, marketers can no longer rely on profits from generally expanding markets. Marketers are also faced with increasingly experienced consumers among the younger generations such as tweens and teens. And because the population is also growing older, marketers are offering more products that appeal to middle-aged and older consumers.

Explain the importance to marketing managers of growing ethnic markets. Growing minority populations make the marketer's task more challenging. Hispanics are the fastest growing segment of the population, followed by African Americans. Many companies are now creating departments and product lines to effectively target multicultural market segments. Companies have quickly found that ethnic markets are not homogeneous.

Identify consumer and marketer reactions to the state of the economy. In recent years, U.S. incomes have risen at a slow pace. At the same time, the financial power of women has increased, and they are making the purchasing decisions for many products in traditionally male-dominated areas. During a time of inflation, marketers generally attempt to maintain level pricing to avoid losing customer brand loyalty. During times of recession, many marketers maintain or reduce prices to counter the effects of decreased demand; they also concentrate on increasing production efficiency and improving customer service.

© 2013 Cengage Learning. All Rights Reserved. May not be scanned, copied or duplicated, or posted to a publicly accessible website, in whole or in part.

basic research pure research that aims to confirm an existing theory or to learn more about a concept or phenomenon

applied research research that attempts to develop new or improved products

Consumer Product Safety Commission (CPSC) a federal agency established to protect the health and safety of consumers in and around their homes

Food and Drug Administration (FDA) a federal agency charged with enforcing regulations against selling and distributing adulterated, misbranded, or hazardous food and drug products

Federal Trade Commission (FTC) a federal agency empowered to prevent persons or corporations from using unfair methods of competition in commerce

Identify the impact of technology on a firm. Monitoring new technology and encouraging research and development (R&D) of new technology are essential to keeping up with competitors in today's marketing environment. Innovation through R&D needs to be stimulated by upper management and fostered in creative environments. Innovation is increasingly becoming a global process, with more patents being awarded to non-U.S. citizens. Without innovation, U.S. companies can't compete in global markets. Companies that are innovators have stronger performance in their respective markets.

Discuss the political and legal environment of marketing. All marketing activities are subject to state and federal laws and the rulings of regulatory agencies. Marketers are responsible for remaining aware of and abiding by such regulations. Some key federal laws that affect marketing are the Sherman Act, Clayton Act, Federal Trade Commission Act, Robinson-Patman Act, Wheeler-Lea Amendments to the Federal Trade Commission Act, Lanham Act, Celler-Kefauver Antimerger Act, and Hart-Scott-Rodino Act. Many laws, including privacy laws, have been passed to protect the consumer as well. The Consumer Product Safety Commission, the Federal Trade Commission, and the Food and Drug Administration are the three federal agencies most involved in regulating marketing activities.

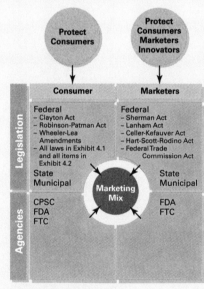

© CENGAGE LEARNING 2013

Explain the basics of foreign and domestic competition. The competitive environment encompasses the number of competitors a firm must face, the relative size of the competitors, and the degree of interdependence within the industry. Declining population growth, rising costs, and shortages of resources have heightened domestic competition.

KEY TERMS

 global marketing marketing that targets markets throughout the world

global vision recognizing and reacting to international marketing opportunities, using effective global marketing strategies, and being aware of threats from foreign competitors in all markets

gross domestic product (GDP) the total market value of all final goods and services produced in a country for a given time period

job outsourcing sending U.S. jobs abroad

 multinational corporation a company that is heavily engaged in international trade, beyond exporting and importing

capital intensive using more capital than labor in the production process

global marketing standardization production of uniform products that can be sold the same way all over the world

multidomestic strategy when multinational firms enable individual subsidiaries to compete independently in domestic markets

 Mercosur the largest Latin American trade agreement; includes Argentina, Bolivia, Brazil, Chile, Colombia, Ecuador, Paraguay, Peru, and Uruguay

Uruguay Round an agreement to dramatically lower trade barriers worldwide; created the World Trade Organization

World Trade Organization (WTO) a trade organization that replaced the old General Agreement on Tariffs and Trade (GATT)

KEY CONCEPTS

 Discuss the importance of global marketing. Businesspeople who adopt a global vision are better able to identify global marketing opportunities, understand the nature of global networks, create effective global marketing strategies, and compete against foreign competition in domestic markets. Large corporations have traditionally been the major global competitors, but more and more small businesses are entering the global marketplace. Despite fears of job losses to other countries with cheaper labor, there are many benefits to globalization, including the reduction of poverty and increased standards of living.

 Discuss the impact of multinational firms on the world economy. Multinational corporations are international traders that regularly operate across national borders. Because of their vast size and financial, technological, and material resources, multinational corporations have great influence on the world economy. They have the ability to overcome trade problems, save on labor costs, and tap new technology. There are critics and supporters of multinational corporations, and the critics question the actual benefits of bringing capital-intensive technology to impoverished nations. Many countries block foreign investment in factories, land, and companies to protect their economies.

Some companies presume that markets throughout the world are more and more similar, so some global products can be standardized across global markets.

 Describe the external environment facing global marketers. Global marketers face the same environmental factors as they do domestically: culture, economic and technological development, political structure and actions, demography, and natural resources. Cultural considerations include societal values, attitudes and beliefs, language, and customary business practices. A country's economic and technological status depends on its stage of industrial development, which, in turn, affects average family incomes. The political structure is shaped by political ideology and such policies as tariffs, quotas, boycotts, exchange controls, trade agreements, and market groupings. Demographic variables include the size of a population and its age and geographic distribution. A shortage of natural resources also effects the external environment by dictating what is available and at what price.

 Identify the various ways of entering the global marketplace. Firms use the following strategies to enter global markets, in descending order of risk and profit: direct investment, joint venture, contract manufacturing, licensing and franchising, and exporting.

Risk Levels for Five Methods of Entering the Global Marketplace

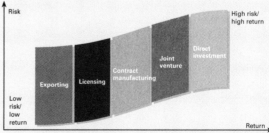

© CENGAGE LEARNING 2013

© 2013 Cengage Learning. All Rights Reserved. May not be scanned, copied or duplicated, or posted to a publicly accessible website, in whole or in part.

General Agreement on Tariffs and Trade (GATT) a trade agreement that contained loopholes enabling countries to avoid trade-barrier reduction agreements

North American Free Trade Agreement (NAFTA) an agreement between Canada, the United States, and Mexico that created the world's then-largest free trade zone

Central America Free Trade Agreement (CAFTA) a trade agreement, instituted in 2005, that includes Costa Rica, the Dominican Republic, El Salvador, Guatemala, Honduras, Nicaragua, and the United States

European Union (EU) a free trade zone encompassing 27 European countries

World Bank an international bank that offers low-interest loans, advice, and information to developing nations

International Monetary Fund (IMF) an international organization that acts as a lender of last resort, providing loans to troubled nations, and also works to promote trade through financial cooperation

Group of Twenty (G-20) a forum for international economic development that promotes discussion between industrial and emerging-market countries on key issues related to global economic stability

 LO 4 **exporting** selling domestically produced products to buyers in other countries

buyer for export an intermediary in the global market who assumes all ownership risks and sells globally for its own account

export broker an intermediary who plays the traditional broker's role by bringing buyer and seller together

export agent an intermediary who acts like a manufacturer's agent for the exporter; the export agent lives in the foreign market

 LO 5 **List the basic elements involved in developing a global marketing mix.** A firm's major consideration is how much it will adjust the four Ps—product, promotion, place (distribution), and price—within each country. One strategy is to use one product and one promotion message worldwide. A second strategy is to create new products for global markets. A third strategy is to keep the product basically the same but alter the promotional message. A fourth strategy is to slightly alter the product to meet local conditions.

Global Marketing Mix

Product + Promotion	Place (Distribution)	Price
One Product, One Message	Channel Choice	Dumping
Product Invention	Channel Structure	Countertrade
Product Adaptation	Country Infrastructure	Exchange Rates
Message Adaptation		Purchasing Power

© CENGAGE LEARNING 2013

 LO 6 **Discover how the Internet is affecting global marketing.** Simply opening an e-commerce site can open the door for international sales. International carriers, such as UPS, can help solve logistics problems. Language translation software can help an e-commerce business become multilingual. Yet cultural differences and old-line rules, regulations, and taxes hinder rapid development of e-commerce in many countries.

Opening an e-commerce site on the Internet . . .

. . . immediately puts a company in the international marketplace.

licensing the legal process whereby a licensor allows another firm to use its manufacturing process, trademarks, patents, trade secrets, or other proprietary knowledge

contract manufacturing private label manufacturing by a foreign company

joint venture when a domestic firm buys part of a foreign company or joins with a foreign company to create a new entity

direct foreign investment active ownership of a foreign company or of overseas manufacturing or marketing facilities

 LO 5 **floating exchange rates** a system in which prices of different currencies move up and down based on the demand for and the supply of each currency

dumping the sale of an exported product at a price lower than that charged for the same or a like product in the "home" market of the exporter

countertrade a form of trade in which all or part of the payment for goods or services is in the form of other goods or services

© ISTOCKPHOTO.COM/BRANDON ALMS / © ISTOCKPHOTO.COM/ANDREA KRAUSE

6 Consumer Decision Making

KEY TERMS

 consumer behavior processes a consumer uses to make purchase decisions, as well as to use and dispose of purchased goods or services; also includes factors that influence purchase decisions and product use

 consumer decision-making process a five-step process used by consumers when buying goods or services

need recognition result of an imbalance between actual and desired states

want recognition of an unfulfilled need and a product that will satisfy it

stimulus any unit of input affecting one or more of the five senses: sight, smell, taste, touch, hearing

internal information search the process of recalling past information stored in the memory

external information search the process of seeking information in the outside environment

nonmarketing-controlled information source a product information source that is not associated with advertising or promotion

marketing-controlled information source a product information source that originates with marketers promoting the product

evoked set (consideration set) a group of brands, resulting from an information search, from which a buyer can choose

 cognitive dissonance inner tension that a consumer experiences after recognizing an inconsistency between behavior and values or opinions

 involvement the amount of time and effort a buyer invests in the search, evaluation, and decision processes of consumer behavior

KEY CONCEPTS

 Explain why marketing managers should understand consumer behavior. An understanding of consumer behavior reduces marketing managers' uncertainty when they are defining a target market and designing a marketing mix.

 Analyze the components of the consumer decision-making process. The consumer decision-making process begins with need recognition, when stimuli trigger awareness of an unfulfilled want. If additional information is required to make a purchase decision, the consumer may engage in an internal or external information search. The consumer then evaluates the additional information and establishes purchase guidelines. Finally, a purchase decision is made.

 Explain the consumer's postpurchase evaluation process. Consumer postpurchase evaluation is influenced by prepurchase expectations, the prepurchase information search, and the consumer's general level of self-confidence. When a purchase creates cognitive dissonance, consumers tend to react by seeking positive reinforcement for the purchase decision, avoiding negative information about the purchase decision, or revoking the purchase decision by returning the product.

 Identify the types of consumer buying decisions and discuss the significance of consumer involvement. Consumer decision making falls into three broad categories: routine response behavior, limited decision making, and extensive decision making. High-involvement decisions usually include an extensive information search and a thorough evaluation of alternatives. In contrast, low-involvement decisions are characterized by brand loyalty and a lack of personal identification with the product. The main factors affecting the level of consumer involvement are previous experience, interest, perceived risk of negative consequences (financial, social, and psychological), and social visibility.

 Identify and understand the cultural factors that affect consumer buying decisions. Cultural influences on consumer buying decisions include culture and values, subculture, and social class. Culture is the essential character of a society that distinguishes it from other cultural groups. The underlying elements of every culture are the values, language, myths, customs, rituals, laws, and the artifacts, or products, that are transmitted from one generation to the next. The most defining element of a culture is its values. A culture can be divided into subcultures on the basis of demographic characteristics, geographic regions, national and ethnic background, political beliefs, and religious beliefs.

 Identify and understand the social factors that affect consumer buying decisions. Social factors include such external influences as reference groups, opinion leaders, and family. Consumers seek out others' opinions for guidance on new products or services and products with image-related attributes or because attribute information is lacking or uninformative. Consumers may use products or brands to identify with or become a member of a reference group, or to follow an opinion leader. Family members also influence purchase decisions; children tend to shop in similar patterns as their parents.

© 2013 Cengage Learning. All Rights Reserved. May not be scanned, copied or duplicated, or posted to a publicly accessible website, in whole or in part.

routine response behavior the type of decision making exhibited by consumers buying frequently purchased, low-cost goods and services; requires little search and decision time

limited decision making the type of decision making that requires a moderate amount of time for gathering information and deliberating about an unfamiliar brand in a familiar product category

extensive decision making the most complex type of consumer decision making, used when buying an unfamiliar, expensive product or an infrequently bought item; requires use of several criteria for evaluating options and much time for seeking information

 culture the set of values, norms, attitudes, and other meaningful symbols that shape human behavior and the artifacts, or products, of that behavior as they are transmitted from one generation to the next

value the enduring belief that a specific mode of conduct is personally or socially preferable to another mode of conduct

subculture a homogeneous group of people who share elements of the overall culture as well as unique elements of their own group

social class a group of people in a society who are considered nearly equal in status or community esteem, who regularly socialize among themselves both formally and informally, and who share behavioral norms

 reference group a group in society that influences an individual's purchasing behavior

primary membership group a reference group with which people interact regularly in an informal, face-to-face manner, such as family, friends, and co-workers

secondary membership group a reference group with which people associate less consistently and more formally than a primary membership group, such as a club, professional group, or religious group

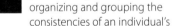 **Identify and understand the individual factors that affect consumer buying decisions.** Individual factors that affect consumer buying decisions include gender; age and family life cycle stage; and personality, self-concept, and lifestyle. Beyond obvious physiological differences, men and women differ in their social and economic roles, and that affects consumer buying decisions. A consumer's age generally indicates what products he or she may be interested in purchasing. Marketers often define their target markets in terms of consumers' life cycle stage, following changes in consumers' attitudes and behavioral tendencies as they mature. Finally, certain products and brands reflect consumers' personality, self-concept, and lifestyle.

 Identify and understand the psychological factors that affect consumer buying decisions. Psychological factors include perception, motivation, learning, values, beliefs, and attitudes. These factors allow consumers to interact with the world around them, recognize their feelings, gather and analyze information, formulate thoughts and opinions, and take action. Perception allows consumers to recognize their consumption problems. Motivation is what drives consumers to take action to satisfy specific consumption needs. Almost all consumer behavior results from learning, which is the process that creates changes in behavior through experience. Consumers with similar beliefs and attitudes tend to react alike to marketing-related inducements.

aspirational reference group a group that someone would like to join

norm a value or attitude deemed acceptable by a group

nonaspirational reference group a group with which an individual does not want to associate

opinion leader an individual who influences the opinions of others

socialization process how cultural values and norms are passed down to children

 personality a way of organizing and grouping the consistencies of an individual's reactions to situations

self-concept how consumers perceive themselves in terms of attitudes, perceptions, beliefs, and self-evaluations

ideal self-image the way an individual would like to be perceived

real self-image the way an individual actually perceives himself or herself

 perception the process by which people select, organize, and interpret stimuli into a meaningful and coherent picture

selective exposure the process whereby a consumer notices certain stimuli and ignores others

selective distortion a process whereby a consumer changes or distorts information that conflicts with his or her feelings or beliefs

selective retention a process whereby a consumer remembers only that information that supports his or her personal beliefs

motive a driving force that causes a person to take action to satisfy specific needs

Maslow's hierarchy of needs a method of classifying human needs and motivations into five categories in ascending order of importance: physiological, safety, social, esteem, and self-actualization

learning a process that creates changes in behavior, immediate or expected, through experience and practice

stimulus generalization a form of learning that occurs when one response is extended to a second stimulus similar to the first

stimulus discrimination a learned ability to differentiate among similar products

belief an organized pattern of knowledge that an individual holds as true about his or her world

attitude a learned tendency to respond consistently toward a given object

CHAPTER REVIEW

Business Marketing

KEY TERMS

 business marketing (industrial marketing) the marketing of goods and services to individuals and organizations for purposes other than personal consumption

 business-to-business electronic commerce the use of the Internet to facilitate the exchange of goods, services, and information between organizations

stickiness a measure of a Web site's effectiveness; calculated by multiplying the frequency of visits by the duration of a visit by the number of pages viewed during each visit (site reach)

disintermediation the elimination of intermediaries such as wholesalers or distributers from a marketing channel

reintermediation the reintroduction of an intermediary between producers and users

 strategic alliance (strategic partnership) a cooperative agreement between business firms

relationship commitment a firm's belief that an ongoing relationship with another firm is so important that the relationship warrants maximum efforts at maintaining it indefinitely

trust the condition that exists when one party has confidence in an exchange partner's reliability and integrity

keiretsu a network of interlocking corporate affiliates

 original equipment manufacturers (OEMs) individuals and organizations that buy business goods and incorporate them into the products they produce for eventual sale to other producers or to consumers

KEY CONCEPTS

 Describe business marketing. Business marketing provides goods and services that are bought for use in business rather than for personal consumption. Intended use, not physical characteristics, distinguishes a business product from a consumer product.

 Describe the role of the Internet in business marketing. The rapid expansion and adoption of the Internet have made business markets more competitive than ever before. The number of business buyers and sellers using the Internet is rapidly increasing. Firms are seeking new and better ways to expand markets and sources of supply, increase sales and decrease costs, and better serve customers. With the Internet, every business in the world is potentially a local competitor.

 Discuss the role of relationship marketing and strategic alliances in business marketing. Relationship marketing entails seeking and establishing long-term alliances or partnerships with customers. A strategic alliance is a cooperative agreement between business firms. Firms form alliances to leverage what they do well by partnering with others that have complementary skills.

 Identify the four major categories of business market customers. Producer markets consist of for-profit individuals and organizations that buy products to use in producing other products, as components of other products, or in facilitating business operations. Reseller markets consist of wholesalers and retailers that buy finished products to resell for profit. Government markets include federal, state, county, and city governments that buy goods and services to support their own operations and serve the needs of citizens. Institutional markets consist of very diverse nonbusiness institutions whose main goals do not include profit.

 Explain the North American Industry Classification System. NAICS provides a way to identify, analyze, segment, and target business and government markets. Organizations can be identified and compared by a numeric code indicating business sector, subsector, industry group, industry, and industry subdivision. NAICS is a valuable tool for analyzing, segmenting, and targeting business markets.

 Explain the major differences between business and consumer markets. In business markets, demand is derived, inelastic, joint, and fluctuating. Purchase volume is much larger than in consumer markets, customers are fewer in number and more geographically concentrated, and distribution channels are more direct. Buying is approached more formally using professional purchasing agents, more people are involved in the buying process, negotiation is more complex, and reciprocity and leasing are more common. And, finally, selling strategy in business markets normally focuses on personal contact rather than on advertising.

© 2013 Cengage Learning. All Rights Reserved. May not be scanned, copied or duplicated, or posted to a publicly accessible website, in whole or in part.

LO 5 **North American Industry Classification System (NAICS)** a detailed numbering system developed by the United States, Canada, and Mexico to classify North American business establishments by their main production processes

LO 6 **derived demand** the demand for business products

joint demand the demand for two or more items used together in a final product

multiplier effect (accelerator principle) phenomenon in which a small increase or decrease in consumer demand can produce a much larger change in demand for the facilities and equipment needed to make the consumer product

business-to-business online exchange an electronic trading floor that provides companies with integrated links to their customers and suppliers

reciprocity a practice whereby business purchasers choose to buy from their own customers

LO 7 **major equipment (installations)** capital goods such as large or expensive machines, mainframe computers, blast furnaces, generators, airplanes, and buildings

accessory equipment goods, such as portable tools and office equipment, that are less expensive and shorter-lived than major equipment

raw materials unprocessed extractive or agricultural products, such as mineral ore, lumber, wheat, corn, fruits, vegetables, and fish

component parts either finished items ready for assembly or products that need very little processing before becoming part of some other product

processed materials products used directly in manufacturing other products

supplies consumable items that do not become part of the final product

business services expense items that do not become part of a final product

Characteristic	Business Market	Consumer Market
Demand	Organizational	Individual
Purchase volume	Larger	Smaller
Number of customers	Fewer	Many
Location of buyers	Geographically concentrated	Dispersed
Distribution structure	More direct	More indirect
Nature of buying	More professional	More personal
Nature of buying influence	Multiple	Single
Type of negotiations	More complex	Simpler
Use of reciprocity	Yes	No
Use of leasing	Greater	Lesser
Primary promotional method	Personal selling	Advertising

© CENGAGE LEARNING 2013

LO 7 **Describe the seven types of business goods and services.** Major equipment includes capital goods, such as heavy machinery. Accessory equipment is typically less expensive and shorter-lived than major equipment. Raw materials are extractive or agricultural products that have not been processed. Component parts are finished or near-finished items to be used as parts of other products. Processed materials are used to manufacture other products. Supplies are consumable and not used as part of a final product. Business services are intangible products that many companies use in their operations.

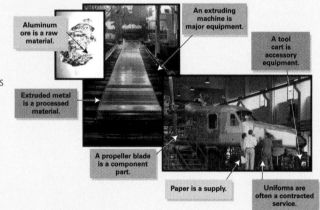

Aluminum ore is a raw material.

An extruding machine is major equipment.

A tool cart is accessory equipment.

Extruded metal is a processed material.

A propeller blade is a component part.

Paper is a supply.

Uniforms are often a contracted service.

PHOTOS COURTESY OF CHAPEL HOUSE PHOTOGRAPHY

LO 8 **Discuss the unique aspects of business buying behavior.** Business buying behavior is distinguished by five fundamental characteristics. First, buying is normally undertaken by a buying center consisting of many people who range widely in authority level. Second, business buyers typically evaluate alternative products and suppliers based on quality, service, and price—in that order. Third, business buying falls into three general categories: new buys, modified rebuys, and straight rebuys. Fourth, the ethics of business buyers and sellers are often scrutinized. Fifth, customer service before, during, and after the sale plays a big role in business purchase decisions.

LO 8 **buying center** all those people in an organization who become involved in the purchase decision

new buy a situation requiring the purchase of a product for the first time

modified rebuy a situation in which the purchaser wants some change in the original good or service

straight rebuy a situation in which the purchaser reorders the same goods or services without looking for new information or investigating other suppliers

8 Segmenting and Targeting Markets

KEY TERMS

LO 1 **market** people or organizations with needs or wants and the ability and willingness to buy

market segment a subgroup of people or organizations sharing one or more characteristics that cause them to have similar product needs

market segmentation the process of dividing a market into meaningful, relatively similar, and identifiable segments or groups

LO 4 **segmentation bases (variables)** characteristics of individuals, groups, or organizations

geographic segmentation segmenting markets by region of a country or the world, market size, market density, or climate

demographic segmentation segmenting markets by age, gender, income, ethnic background, and family life cycle

family life cycle (FLC) a series of stages determined by a combination of age, marital status, and the presence or absence of children

psychographic segmentation segmenting markets on the basis of personality, motives, lifestyles, and geodemographics

geodemographic segmentation segmenting potential customers into neighborhood lifestyle categories

benefit segmentation the process of grouping customers into market segments according to the benefits they seek from the product

usage-rate segmentation dividing a market by the amount of product bought or consumed

80/20 principle a principle holding that 20 percent of all customers generate 80 percent of the demand

KEY CONCEPTS

LO 1 **Describe the characteristics of markets and market segments.** A market is composed of individuals or organizations with the ability and willingness to make purchases to fulfill their needs or wants. A market segment is a group of individuals or organizations with similar product needs as a result of one or more common characteristics.

LO 2 **Explain the importance of market segmentation.** Before the 1960s, few businesses targeted specific market segments. Today, segmentation is a crucial marketing strategy for nearly all successful organizations. Market segmentation enables marketers to tailor marketing mixes to meet the needs of particular population segments. Segmentation helps marketers identify consumer needs and preferences, areas of declining demand, and new marketing opportunities.

LO 3 **Discuss the criteria for successful market segmentation.** Successful market segmentation depends on four basic criteria: (1) a market segment must be substantial and have enough potential customers to be viable; (2) a market segment must be identifiable and measurable; (3) members of a market segment must be accessible to marketing efforts; and (4) a market segment must respond to particular marketing efforts in a way that distinguishes it from other segments.

LO 4 **Describe the bases commonly used to segment consumer markets.** Five bases are commonly used for segmenting consumer markets. Geographic segmentation is based on region, size, density, and climate characteristics. Demographic segmentation is based on age, gender, income level, ethnicity, and family life cycle characteristics. Psychographic segmentation includes personality, motives, and lifestyle characteristics. Benefits sought is a type of segmentation that identifies customers according to the benefits they seek in a product. Finally, usage segmentation divides a market by the amount of product purchased or consumed.

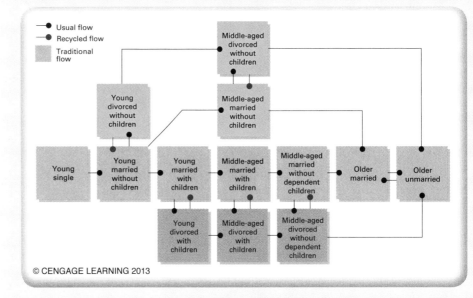

© CENGAGE LEARNING 2013

© 2013 Cengage Learning. All Rights Reserved. May not be scanned, copied or duplicated, or posted to a publicly accessible website, in whole or in part.

LO 5 **satisficers** business customers who place an order with the first familiar supplier to satisfy product and delivery requirements

optimizers business customers who consider numerous suppliers (both familiar and unfamiliar), solicit bids, and study all proposals carefully before selecting one

 LO 7 **target market** a group of people or organizations for which an organization designs, implements, and maintains a marketing mix intended to meet the needs of that group, resulting in mutually satisfying exchanges

undifferentiated targeting strategy a marketing approach that views the market as one big market with no individual segments and thus uses a single marketing mix

concentrated targeting strategy a strategy used to select one segment of a market for targeting marketing efforts

niche one segment of a market

multisegment targeting strategy a strategy that chooses two or more well-defined market segments and develops a distinct marketing mix for each

cannibalization a situation that occurs when sales of a new product cut into sales of a firm's existing products

 LO 8 **one-to-one marketing** an individualized marketing method that utilizes customer information to build long-term, personalized, and profitable relationships with each customer

 LO 9 **positioning** developing a specific marketing mix to influence potential customers' overall perception of a brand, product line, or organization in general

position the place a product, brand, or group of products occupies in consumers' minds relative to competing offerings

product differentiation a positioning strategy that some firms use to distinguish their products from those of competitors

 LO 5 **Describe the bases for segmenting business markets.** Business markets can be segmented on two general bases. First, businesses may segment markets based on company characteristics, such as customers' geographic location, type of company, company size, and product use. Second, companies may segment customers based on the buying processes those customers use.

 LO 6 **List the steps involved in segmenting markets.** Six steps are involved when segmenting markets: (1) selecting a market or product category for study; (2) choosing a basis or bases for segmenting the market; (3) selecting segmentation descriptors; (4) profiling and evaluating segments; (5) selecting target markets; and (6) designing, implementing, and maintaining appropriate marketing mixes.

 LO 7 **Discuss alternative strategies for selecting target markets.** Marketers select target markets using three different strategies: undifferentiated targeting, concentrated targeting, and multisegment targeting. An undifferentiated targeting strategy assumes that all members of a market have similar needs that can be met with a single marketing mix. A concentrated targeting strategy focuses all marketing efforts on a single market segment. Multisegment targeting is a strategy that uses two or more marketing mixes to target two or more market segments.

Targeting Strategy	Advantages	Disadvantages
Undifferentiated Targeting	• Potential savings on production/marketing costs	• Unimaginative product offerings • Company more susceptible to competition
Concentrated Targeting	• Concentration of resources • Can better meet the needs of a narrowly defined segment • Allows some small firms to better compete with larger firms • Strong positioning	• Segments too small or changing • Large competitors may more effectively market to niche segment
Multisegment Targeting	• Greater financial success • Economies of scale in producing/marketing	• High costs • Cannibalization

© CENGAGE LEARNING 2013

 LO 8 **Explain one-to-one marketing.** One-to-one marketing is an individualized marketing method that utilizes customer information to build long-term, personalized, and profitable relationships with each customer. Successful one-to-one marketing comes from understanding customers and collaborating with them rather than using them as targets for generic messages. Database technology makes it possible for companies to interact with customers on a personal, one-to-one basis.

 LO 9 **Explain how and why firms implement positioning strategies and how product differentiation plays a role.** Positioning is used to influence consumer perceptions of a particular brand, product line, or organization in relation to competitors. The term *position* refers to the place that the offering occupies in consumers' minds. To establish a unique position, many firms use product differentiation, emphasizing the real or perceived differences between competing offerings. Products may be differentiated on the basis of attribute, price and quality, use or application, product user, product class, or competitor.

perceptual mapping a means of displaying or graphing, in two or more dimensions, the location of products, brands, or groups of products in customers' minds

repositioning changing consumers' perceptions of a brand in relation to competing brands

CHAPTER REVIEW 9
Decision Support Systems and Marketing Research

KEY TERMS

 marketing information everyday information about developments in the marketing environment that managers use to prepare and adjust marketing plans

decision support system (DSS) an interactive, flexible, computerized information system that enables managers to obtain and manipulate information as they are making decisions

database marketing the creation of a large computerized file of customers' and potential customers' profiles and purchase patterns

 marketing research the process of planning, collecting, and analyzing data relevant to a marketing decision

 marketing research problem determining what information is needed and how that information can be obtained efficiently and effectively

marketing research objective the specific information needed to solve a marketing research problem; the objective should be to provide insightful decision-making information

management decision problem a broad-based problem that uses marketing research in order for managers to take proper actions

secondary data data previously collected for any purpose other than the one at hand

marketing research aggregator a company that acquires, catalogs, reformats, segments, and resells reports already published by marketing research firms

research design specifies which research questions must be answered, how and when the data will be gathered, and how the data will be analyzed

KEY CONCEPTS

 Explain the concept and purpose of a marketing decision support system. A decision support system (DSS) makes data instantly available to marketing managers and allows them to manipulate the data themselves to make marketing decisions. Four characteristics make a DSS especially useful to marketing managers: They are interactive, flexible, discovery oriented, and accessible. Decision support systems give managers access to information immediately and without outside assistance. They allow users to manipulate data in a variety of ways and to answer "what if" questions. And, finally, they are accessible to novice computer users.

 Define marketing research and explain its importance to marketing decision making. Marketing research is a process of collecting and analyzing data for the purpose of solving specific marketing problems. Marketers use marketing research to explore the profitability of marketing strategies. They can examine why particular strategies failed and analyze characteristics of specific market segments. Managers can use research findings to help keep current customers. Moreover, marketing research allows management to behave proactively, rather than reactively, by identifying newly emerging patterns in society and the economy.

LO 3 Describe the steps involved in conducting a marketing research project. The marketing research process involves several basic steps. First, the researcher and the decision maker must agree on a problem statement or set of research objectives. The researcher then creates an overall research design to specify how primary data will be gathered and analyzed. Before collecting data, the researcher decides whether the group to be interviewed will be a probability or nonprobability sample. Field service firms are often hired to carry out data collection. Once data have been collected, the researcher analyzes them using statistical analysis. The researcher then prepares and presents oral and written reports, with conclusions and recommendations, to management. As a final step, the researcher determines whether the recommendations were implemented and what could have been done to make the project more successful.

LO 4 Discuss the profound impact of the Internet on marketing research. The Internet has simplified the secondary data search process. Internet survey research is surging in popularity. Internet surveys can be created rapidly, are reported in real time, are relatively inexpensive, and are easily personalized. Often researchers use the Internet to contact respondents who are difficult to reach by other means. The Internet can also be used to conduct focus groups, to distribute research proposals and reports, and to facilitate collaboration between the client and the research supplier. Text-message-based research and giving consumers blogging assignments are new trends that give marketers quick feedback (text-messaging) or in-depth information over time (blogging).

 Discuss the growing importance of scanner-based research. A scanner-based research system enables marketers to monitor a market panel's exposure and reaction to such variables as advertising, coupons, store displays, packaging, and price. By analyzing these variables in relation to the panel's subsequent buying behavior, marketers gain useful insight into sales and marketing strategies.

© 2013 Cengage Learning. All Rights Reserved. May not be scanned, copied or duplicated, or posted to a publicly accessible website, in whole or in part.

primary data information that is collected for the first time; used for solving the particular problem under investigation

survey research the most popular technique for gathering primary data, in which a researcher interacts with people to obtain facts, opinions, and attitudes

mall intercept interview a survey research method that involves interviewing people in the common areas of shopping malls

computer-assisted personal interviewing an interviewing method in which the interviewer reads questions from a computer screen and enters the respondent's data directly into the computer

computer-assisted self-interviewing an interviewing method in which a mall interviewer intercepts and directs willing respondents to nearby computers where each respondent reads questions off a computer screen and directly keys his or her answers into a computer

central-location telephone (CLT) facility a specially designed phone room used to conduct telephone interviewing

executive interview a type of survey that involves interviewing businesspeople at their offices concerning industrial products or services

focus group seven to ten people who participate in a group discussion led by a moderator

open-ended question an interview question that encourages an answer phrased in the respondent's own words

closed-ended question an interview question that asks the respondent to make a selection from a limited list of responses

scaled-response question a closed-ended question designed to measure the intensity of a respondent's answer

observation research a research method that relies on four types of observation: people watching people, people watching an activity, machines watching people, and machines watching an activity

mystery shoppers researchers posing as customers who gather observational data about a store

Explain when marketing research should be conducted. Because acquiring marketing information can be time-consuming and costly, deciding to acquire additional decision-making information depends on managers' perceptions of its quality, price, and timing. Research, therefore, should be undertaken only when the expected value of the information is greater than the cost of obtaining it.

Explain the concept of competitive intelligence. Intelligence is analyzed information, and it becomes decision-making intelligence when it has implications for the organization. By helping managers assess their competition and vendors, CI leads to fewer surprises. CI is part of a sound marketing strategy, helps companies respond to competitive threats, and helps reduce unnecessary costs.

behavioral targeting (BT) a form of observation marketing research that combines a consumer's online activity with psychographic and demographic profiles compiled in databases

ethnographic research the study of human behavior in its natural context; involves observation of behavior and physical setting

experiment a method of gathering primary data in which the researcher alters one or more variables while observing the effects of those alterations on another variable

sample a subset from a larger population

universe the population from which a sample will be drawn

probability sample a sample in which every element in the population has a known statistical likelihood of being selected

random sample a sample arranged in such a way that every element of the population has an equal chance of being selected as part of the sample

nonprobability sample any sample in which little or no attempt is made to get a representative cross section of the population

convenience sample a form of nonprobability sample using respondents who are convenient or readily accessible to the researcher—for example, employees, friends, or relatives

measurement error an error that occurs when there is a difference between the information desired by the researcher and the information provided by the measurement process

sampling error an error that occurs when a sample somehow does not represent the target population

frame error an error that occurs when a sample drawn from a population differs from the target population

random error an error that occurs when the selected sample is an imperfect representation of the overall population

field service firm a firm that specializes in interviewing respondents on a subcontracted basis

cross-tabulation a method of analyzing data that lets the analyst look at the responses to one question in relation to the responses to one or more other questions

consumer-generated media (CGM) media that consumers generate and share among themselves

scanner-based research a system for gathering information from a single group of respondents by continuously monitoring the advertising, promotion, and pricing they are exposed to and the things they buy

BehaviorScan a scanner-based research program that tracks the purchases of 3,000 households through store scanners in each research market

InfoScan a scanner-based sales-tracking service for the consumer packaged-goods industry

neuromarketing a field of marketing that studies the body's responses to marketing stimuli

competitive intelligence (CI) an intelligence system that helps managers assess their competition and vendors in order to become more efficient and effective competitors

KEY TERMS

 LO 1   **product** everything, both favorable and unfavorable, that a person receives in an exchange

 LO 2   **business product (industrial product)** a product used to manufacture other goods or services, to facilitate an organization's operations, or to resell to other customers

consumer product a product bought to satisfy an individual's personal wants

convenience product a relatively inexpensive item that merits little shopping effort

shopping product a product that requires comparison shopping because it is usually more expensive than a convenience product and is found in fewer stores

specialty product a particular item for which consumers search extensively and are very reluctant to accept substitutes

unsought product a product unknown to the potential buyer or a known product that the buyer does not actively seek

 LO 3   **product item** a specific version of a product that can be designated as a distinct offering among an organization's products

product line a group of closely related product items

product mix all products that an organization sells

product mix width the number of product lines an organization offers

product line depth the number of product items in a product line

product modification changing one or more of a product's characteristics

KEY CONCEPTS

 LO 1   **Define the term *product*.** A product is anything, desired or not, that a person or organization receives in an exchange. The basic goal of purchasing decisions is to receive the tangible and intangible benefits associated with a product. Tangible aspects include packaging, style, color, size, and features. Intangible qualities include service, the retailer's image, the manufacturer's reputation, and the social status associated with a product. An organization's product offering is the crucial element in any marketing mix.

 LO 2   **Classify consumer products.** Consumer products are classified into four categories: convenience products, shopping products, specialty products, and unsought products. Convenience products are relatively inexpensive and require limited shopping effort. Shopping products are of two types: homogeneous and heterogeneous. Because of the similarity of homogeneous products, they are differentiated mainly by price and features. In contrast, heterogeneous products appeal to consumers because of their distinct characteristics. Specialty products possess unique benefits that are highly desirable to certain customers. Finally, unsought products are either new products or products that require aggressive selling because they are generally avoided or overlooked by consumers.

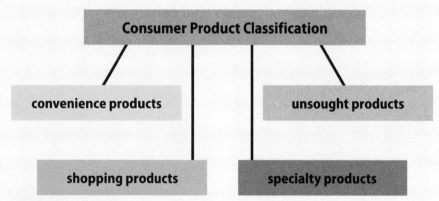

© CENGAGE LEARNING 2013

 LO 3   **Define the terms *product item*, *product line*, and *product mix*.** A product item is a specific version of a product that can be designated as a distinct offering among an organization's products. A product line is a group of closely related products offered by an organization. An organization's product mix includes all the products it sells. Product mix width refers to the number of product lines an organization offers. Product line depth is the number of product items in a product line. Firms modify existing products by changing their quality, functional characteristics, or style. Product line extension occurs when a firm adds new products to existing product lines.

 LO 4   **Describe marketing uses of branding.** A brand is a name, term, or symbol that identifies and differentiates a firm's products. Established brands encourage customer loyalty and help new products succeed. Branding strategies require decisions about individual, family, manufacturers', and private brands. The table on the next page compares manufacturers' and private brands.

© 2013 Cengage Learning. All Rights Reserved. May not be scanned, copied or duplicated, or posted to a publicly accessible website, in whole or in part.

planned obsolescence the practice of modifying products so those that have already been sold become obsolete before they actually need replacement

product line extension adding additional products to an existing product line in order to compete more broadly in the industry

 brand a name, term, symbol, design, or combination thereof that identifies a seller's products and differentiates them from competitors' products

brand name that part of a brand that can be spoken, including letters, words, and numbers

brand mark the elements of a brand that cannot be spoken

brand equity the value of company and brand names

global brand a brand that obtains at least a third of its earnings from outside its home country, is recognizable outside its home base of customers, and has publicly available marketing and financial data

brand loyalty consistent preference for one brand over all others

manufacturer's brand the brand name of a manufacturer

private brand a brand name owned by a wholesaler or a retailer

captive brand a brand manufactured by a third party for an exclusive retailer, without evidence of that retailer's affiliation

individual branding using different brand names for different products

family branding marketing several different products under the same brand name

co-branding placing two or more brand names on a product or its package

trademark the exclusive right to use a brand or part of a brand

service mark a trademark for a service

generic product name identifies a product by class or type and cannot be trademarked

Comparing Manufacturers' and Private Brands from the Reseller's Perspective

Key Advantages of Carrying Manufacturers' Brands	Key Advantages of Carrying Private Brands
• Heavy advertising to the consumer by manufacturers such as Procter & Gamble helps develop strong consumer loyalties.	• A wholesaler or retailer can usually earn higher profits on its own brand. In addition, because the private brand is exclusive, there is less pressure to mark down the price to meet competition.
• Well-known manufacturers' brands, such as Kodak and Fisher-Price, can attract new customers and enhance the dealer's (wholesaler's or retailer's) prestige.	• A manufacturer can decide to drop a brand or a reseller at any time or even become a direct competitor to its dealers.
• Many manufacturers offer rapid delivery, enabling the dealer to carry less inventory.	• A private brand ties the customer to the wholesaler or retailer. A person who wants a DieHard battery must go to Sears.
• If a dealer happens to sell a manufacturer's brand of poor quality, the customer may simply switch brands and remain loyal to the dealer.	• Wholesalers and retailers have no control over the intensity of distribution of manufacturers' brands. Walmart store managers don't have to worry about competing with other sellers of Sam's American Choice products or Ol' Roy dog food. They know that these brands are sold only in Walmart and Sam's Club stores.

© CENGAGE LEARNING 2013

 Describe marketing uses of packaging and labeling. Packaging has four functions: containing and protecting products; promoting products; facilitating product storage, use, and convenience; and facilitating recycling and reducing environmental damage. As a tool for promotion, packaging identifies the brand and its features. It also serves the critical function of differentiating a product from competing products and linking it with related products from the same manufacturer. The label is an integral part of the package, with persuasive and informational functions. In essence, the package is the marketer's last chance to influence buyers before they make a purchase decision.

 Discuss global issues in branding and packaging. In addition to brand piracy, international marketers must address a variety of concerns regarding branding and packaging, including choosing a brand name policy, translating labels and meeting host-country labeling requirements, making packages aesthetically compatible with host-country cultures, and offering the sizes of packages preferred in host countries.

 Describe how and why product warranties are important marketing tools. Product warranties are important tools because they offer consumers protection and help them gauge product quality.

Express warranty = written guarantee

Implied warranty = unwritten guarantee

 persuasive labeling a type of package labeling that focuses on a promotional theme or logo, and consumer information is secondary

informational labeling a type of package labeling designed to help consumers make proper product selections and lower their cognitive dissonance after the purchase

universal product codes (UPCs) a series of thick and thin vertical lines (bar codes), readable by computerized optical scanners, that represent numbers used to track products

 warranty a confirmation of the quality or performance of a good or service

express warranty a written guarantee

implied warranty an unwritten guarantee that the good or service is fit for the purpose for which it was sold

Developing and Managing Products

KEY TERMS

 LO 1

new product a product new to the world, the market, the producer, the seller, or some combination of these

 LO 2

new-product strategy a plan that links the new-product development process with the objectives of the marketing department, the business unit, and the corporation

product development a marketing strategy that entails the creation of marketable new products; the process of converting applications for new technologies into marketable products

brainstorming the process of getting a group to think of unlimited ways to vary a product or solve a problem

screening the first filter in the product development process, which eliminates ideas that are inconsistent with the organization's new-product strategy or are obviously inappropriate for some other reason

concept test a test to evaluate a new-product idea, usually before any prototype has been created

business analysis the second stage of the screening process where preliminary figures for demand, cost, sales, and profitability are calculated

development the stage in the product development process in which a prototype is developed and a marketing strategy is outlined

simultaneous product development a team-oriented approach to new-product development

test marketing the limited introduction of a product and a marketing program to determine the reactions of potential customers in a market situation

KEY CONCEPTS

 LO 1

Explain the importance of developing new products and describe the six categories of new products. New products are important to sustain growth and profits and to replace obsolete items. New products can be classified as new-to-the-world products (discontinuous innovations), new product lines, additions to existing product lines, improvements or revisions of existing products, repositioned products, or lower-priced products. To sustain or increase profits, a firm must innovate.

 LO 2

Explain the steps in the new-product development process. First, a firm forms a new-product strategy by outlining the characteristics and roles of future products. Then new-product ideas are generated by customers, employees, distributors, competitors, vendors, and internal research and development

1	New-product strategy
2	Idea generation
3	Idea screening
4	Business analysis
5	Development
6	Test marketing
7	Commercialization
	New product

© CENGAGE LEARNING 2013

personnel. Once a product idea has survived initial screening by an appointed screening group, it undergoes business analysis to determine its potential profitability. If a product concept seems viable, it progresses into the development phase, in which the technical and economic feasibility of the manufacturing process is evaluated. The development phase also includes laboratory and use testing of a product for performance and safety. Following initial testing and refinement, most products are introduced in a test market to evaluate consumer response and marketing strategies. Finally, test market successes are propelled into full commercialization. The commercialization process involves starting up production, building inventories, shipping to distributors, training a sales force, announcing the product to the trade, and advertising to consumers.

 LO 3

Discuss global issues in new-product development. A marketer with global vision seeks to develop products that can easily be adapted to suit local needs. The goal is not simply to develop a standard product that can be sold worldwide. Smart global marketers also look for good product ideas worldwide.

 LO 4

Explain the diffusion process through which new products are adopted. The diffusion process is the spread of a new product from its producer to ultimate adopters. Adopters in the diffusion process belong to five categories: innovators, early adopters, the early majority, the late majority, and laggards. Product characteristics that affect the rate of adoption include product complexity, compatibility with existing social values, relative advantage over existing

© 2013 Cengage Learning. All Rights Reserved. May not be scanned, copied or duplicated, or posted to a publicly accessible website, in whole or in part.

simulated (laboratory) market testing the presentation of advertising and other promotional materials for several products, including a test product, to members of the product's target market

commercialization the decision to market a product

 innovation a product perceived as new by a potential adopter

diffusion the process by which the adoption of an innovation spreads

 product life cycle (PLC) a concept that provides a way to trace the stages of a product's acceptance, from its introduction (birth) to its decline (death)

product category all brands that satisfy a particular type of need

introductory stage the full-scale launch of a new product into the marketplace

growth stage the second stage of the product life cycle when sales typically grow at an increasing rate, many competitors enter the market, large companies may start to acquire small pioneering firms, and profits are healthy

maturity stage a period during which sales increase at a decreasing rate

decline stage a long-run drop in sales

substitutes, visibility, and "trialability." The diffusion process is facilitated by word-of-mouth communication and communication from marketers to consumers.

 Explain the concept of product life cycles. All brands and product categories undergo a life cycle with four stages: introduction, growth, maturity, and decline. The rate at which products move through these stages varies dramatically. Marketing managers use the product life cycle concept as an analytical tool to forecast a product's future and devise effective marketing strategies.

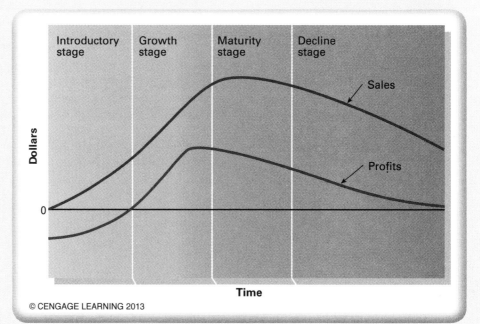

© CENGAGE LEARNING 2013

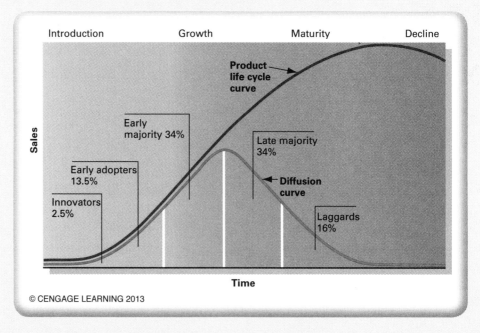

© CENGAGE LEARNING 2013

CHAPTER REVIEW

CHAPTER REVIEW

12 Services and Nonprofit Organization Marketing

KEY TERMS

 LO 1 **service** the result of applying human or mechanical efforts to people or objects

 LO 2 **intangibility** the inability of services to be touched, seen, tasted, heard, or felt in the same manner that goods can be sensed

search quality a characteristic that can be easily assessed before purchase

experience quality a characteristic that can be assessed only after use

credence quality a characteristic that consumers may have difficulty assessing even after purchase because they do not have the necessary knowledge or experience

inseparability the inability of the production and consumption of a service to be separated; consumers must be present during the production

heterogeneity the variability of the inputs and outputs of services, which causes services to tend to be less standardized and uniform than goods

perishability the inability of services to be stored, warehoused, or inventoried

 LO 3 **reliability** the ability to perform a service dependably, accurately, and consistently

responsiveness the ability to provide prompt service

assurance the knowledge and courtesy of employees and their ability to convey trust

empathy caring, individualized attention to customers

tangibles the physical evidence of a service, including the physical facilities, tools, and equipment used to provide the service

KEY CONCEPTS

 LO 1 **Discuss the importance of services to the economy.** The service sector plays a crucial role in the U.S. economy, employing nearly 80 percent of the workforce.

 LO 2 **Discuss the differences between services and goods.** Services are distinguished by four characteristics. Services are intangible performances in that they lack clearly identifiable physical characteristics, making it difficult for marketers to communicate their specific benefits to potential customers. The production and consumption of services occurs simultaneously. Services are heterogeneous because their quality depends on such elements as the service provider, individual consumer, location, and the like. Finally, services are perishable in the sense that they cannot be stored or saved. As a result, synchronizing supply with demand is particularly challenging in the service industry.

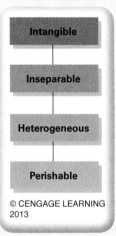

© CENGAGE LEARNING 2013

LO 3 **Describe the components of service quality and the gap model of service quality.** Service quality has five components: reliability (ability to perform the service dependably, accurately, and consistently), responsiveness (providing prompt service), assurance (knowledge and courtesy of employees and their ability to convey trust), empathy (caring, individualized attention), and tangibles (physical evidence of the service).

The gap model identifies five key discrepancies that can influence customer evaluations of service quality. When the gaps are large, service quality is low. As the gaps shrink, service quality improves. Gap 1 is found between customers' expectations and management's perceptions of those expectations. Gap 2 is found between management's perception of what the customer wants and specifications for service quality. Gap 3 is found between service quality specifications and delivery of the service. Gap 4 is found between service delivery and what the company promises to the customer through external communication. Gap 5 is found between customers' service expectations and their perceptions of service performance.

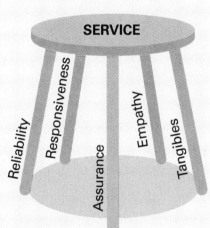

© CENGAGE LEARNING 2013

© 2013 Cengage Learning. All Rights Reserved. May not be scanned, copied or duplicated, or posted to a publicly accessible website, in whole or in part.

gap model a model identifying five gaps that can cause problems in service delivery and influence customer evaluations of service quality

 core service the most basic benefit the consumer is buying

supplementary services a group of services that support or enhance the core service

mass customization a strategy that uses technology to deliver customized services on a mass basis

 internal marketing treating employees as customers and developing systems and benefits that satisfy their needs

 nonprofit organization an organization that exists to achieve some goal other than the usual business goals of profit, market share, or return on investment

nonprofit organization marketing the effort by nonprofit organizations to bring about mutually satisfying exchanges with target markets

public service advertisement (PSA) an announcement that promotes a program of a federal, state, or local government or of a nonprofit organization

© CENGAGE LEARNING 2013

LO 4 Develop marketing mixes for services. "Product" (service) strategy issues include what is being processed (people, possessions, mental stimulus, information), core and supplementary services, customization versus standardization, and the service mix. Distribution (place) decisions involve convenience, number of outlets, direct versus indirect distribution, and scheduling. Stressing tangible cues, using personal sources of information, creating strong organizational images, and engaging in postpurchase communication are effective promotion strategies. Pricing objectives for services can be revenue oriented, operations oriented, patronage oriented, or any combination of the three.

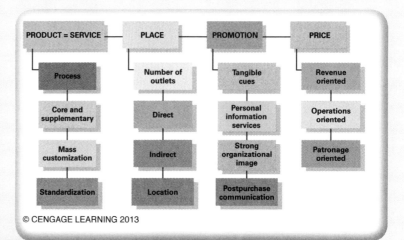

© CENGAGE LEARNING 2013

LO 5 Discuss relationship marketing in services. Relationship marketing in services involves attracting, developing, and retaining customer relationships. There are three levels of relationship marketing: Level 1 focuses on pricing incentives; level 2 uses pricing incentives and social bonds with customers; and level 3 uses pricing, social bonds, and structural bonds to build long-term relationships.

LO 6 Explain internal marketing in services. Internal marketing means treating employees as customers and developing systems and benefits that satisfy their needs. Employees who like their jobs and are happy with the firm they work for are more likely to deliver good service.

LO 7 Discuss global issues in services marketing. The United States has become the world's largest exporter of services. Although competition is keen, the United States has a competitive advantage because of its vast experience in many service industries. To be successful globally, service firms must adjust their marketing mix for the environment of each target country.

LO 8 Describe nonprofit organization marketing. Nonprofit organizations pursue goals other than profit, market share, and return on investment. Nonprofit organization marketing facilitates mutually satisfying exchanges between nonprofit organizations and their target markets. Several unique characteristics distinguish nonbusiness marketing strategy, including a concern with services and social behaviors rather than manufactured goods and profit; a difficult, undifferentiated, and in some ways marginal target market; a complex product that may have only indirect benefits and elicit very low involvement; distribution that may or may not require special facilities depending on the service provided; a relative lack of resources for promotion; and prices only indirectly related to the exchange between the producer and the consumer of services.

KEY TERMS

 LO 1

marketing channel (channel of distribution) a set of interdependent organizations that eases the transfer of ownership as products move from producer to business user or consumer

channel members all parties in the marketing channel who negotiate with one another, buy and sell products, and facilitate the change of ownership between buyer and seller in the course of moving the product from the manufacturer into the hands of the final consumer

discrepancy of quantity the difference between the amount of product produced and the amount an end user wants to buy

discrepancy of assortment the lack of all the items a customer needs to receive full satisfaction from a product or products

temporal discrepancy a situation that occurs when a product is produced but a customer is not ready to buy it

spatial discrepancy the difference between the location of a producer and the location of widely scattered markets

 LO 2

retailer a channel intermediary that sells mainly to consumers

merchant wholesaler an institution that buys goods from manufacturers and resells them to businesses, government agencies, and other wholesalers or retailers and that receives and takes title to goods, stores them in its own warehouses, and later ships them

agents and brokers wholesaling intermediaries who do not take title to a product but facilitate its sale from producer to end user by representing retailers, wholesalers, or manufacturers

KEY CONCEPTS

 LO 1

Explain what a marketing channel is and why intermediaries are needed. A marketing channel is a business structure of interdependent organizations that reach from the point of product origin to the consumer. Its purpose is to physically move products to their final consumption destination, representing "place" or "distribution" in the marketing mix. A marketing channel gets the right product to the right place at the right time. Members of a marketing channel create a continuous and seamless supply chain that performs or supports the marketing channel functions. Channel members provide economies to the distribution process in the form of specialization and division of labor; overcoming discrepancies in quantity, assortment, time, and space; and providing contact efficiency.

LO 2

Define the types of channel intermediaries and describe their functions and activities. The most prominent difference separating intermediaries is whether they take title to the product. Retailers and merchant wholesalers take title, but agents and brokers do not. Retailers are firms that sell mainly to consumers. Merchant wholesalers are those organizations that facilitate the movement of products and services from the manufacturer to producers, resellers, governments, institutions, and retailers. Agents and brokers facilitate the exchange of ownership between sellers and buyers. Channel intermediaries perform three basic types of functions. Transactional functions include contacting and promoting, negotiating, and risk taking. Logistical functions performed by channel members include physical distribution, storing, and sorting functions. Finally, channel members may perform facilitating functions, such as researching and financing.

LO 3

Describe the channel structures for consumer and business products and discuss alternative channel arrangements. Marketing channels for consumer and business products vary in degree of complexity.

 LO 4

Discuss the issues that influence channel strategy. When determining marketing channel strategy, the supply chain manager must determine what market, product, and producer factors will influence the choice of channel. The manager must also determine the appropriate level of distribution intensity. Intensive distribution is distribution aimed at maximum market coverage. Selective distribution is achieved by screening dealers to eliminate all but a few in any single area. The most restrictive form of market coverage is exclusive distribution, which entails only one or a few dealers within a given area.

 LO 5

Describe the different channel relationship types and their unique costs and benefits. Channel relationships can be plotted on a continuum ranging from arm's length to integrated, with cooperative relationships somewhere in between. Arm's-length relationships generally consist of unique transactions that are intended to occur once or very infrequently and are pursued when closer relationships are undesirable or impractical. A major weakness of arm's-length relationships is the potential for opportunistic behavior, which may occur when the members lack a common goal, when one company is more dependent on the other than vice versa, or when there is uncertainty in the relationship or the market. Integrated relationships, on

© 2013 Cengage Learning. All Rights Reserved. May not be scanned, copied or duplicated, or posted to a publicly accessible website, in whole or in part.

logistics the efficient and cost-effective forward and reverse flow and storage of goods, services, and related information into, through, and out of channel member companies

 direct channel a distribution channel in which producers sell directly to consumers

dual distribution (multiple distribution) the use of two or more channels to distribute the same product to target markets

strategic channel alliance a cooperative agreement between business firms to use the other's already established distribution channel

 intensive distribution a form of distribution aimed at having a product available in every outlet where target customers might want to buy it

selective distribution a form of distribution achieved by screening dealers to eliminate all but a few in any single area

exclusive distribution a form of distribution that establishes one or a few dealers within a given area

 arm's-length relationship a relationship between companies that is loose, characterized by low relational investment and trust, and usually taking the form of a series of discrete transactions with no or low expectation of future interaction or service

cooperative relationshi a relationship between companies that takes the form of informal partnership with moderate levels of trust and information sharing as needed to further each company's goals

integrated relationship a relationship between companies that is tightly connected, with linked processes across and between firm boundaries and high levels of trust and interfirm commitment

the opposite end of the spectrum, are very close relationships that are backed by formal agreements and can result in great efficiency and effectiveness. However, given that integrated relationships tend either to involve high levels of expense (in the case of vertical integration), many companies prefer cooperative relationships in some settings. Cooperative relationships are a hybrid form of relationship that are governed by formal contract, are temporary, and are enforced by the agreement itself.

 Explain channel leadership, conflict, and partnering. Power, control, leadership, conflict, and partnering are the main social dimensions of marketing channel relationships. Channel power refers to the capacity of one channel member to control or influence other channel members. Channel control occurs when one channel member intentionally affects another member's behavior. Channel leadership is the exercise of authority and power. Channel conflict occurs when there is a clash of goals and methods among the members of a distribution channel. Channel conflict can be either horizontal, between channel members at the same level, or vertical, between channel members at different levels of the channel. Channel partnering is the joint effort of all channel members to create a supply chain that serves customers and creates a competitive advantage. Collaborating channel partners meet the needs of consumers more effectively by ensuring that the right products reach shelves at the right time and at a lower cost, boosting sales and profits.

 Discuss channels and distribution decisions in global markets. Global marketing channels are becoming more important to U.S. companies seeking growth abroad. Manufacturers introducing products in foreign countries must decide what type of channel structure to use—in particular, whether the product should be marketed through direct channels or through foreign intermediaries. Marketers should be aware that channel structures in foreign markets may be very different from those they are accustomed to in the United States. Global distribution expertise is also emerging as an important skill for channel managers, as many countries are removing trade barriers.

Identify the special problems and opportunities associated with distribution in service organizations. Managers in service industries use the same skills, techniques, and strategies to manage logistics functions as managers in goods-producing industries. The distribution of services focuses on four main areas: minimizing wait times, managing service capacity, improving service delivery, and establishing channel-wide network coherence.

 channel power the capacity of a particular marketing channel member to control or influence the behavior of other channel members

channel control a situation that occurs when one marketing channel member intentionally affects another member's behavior

channel leader (channel captain) a member of a marketing channel that exercises authority and power over the activities of other channel members

channel conflict a clash of goals and methods between distribution channel members

horizontal conflict a channel conflict that occurs among channel members on the same level

vertical conflict a channel conflict that occurs between different levels in a marketing channel, most typically between the manufacturer and wholesaler or between the manufacturer and retailer

channel partnering (channel cooperation) the joint effort of all channel members to create a channel that serves customers and creates a competitive advantage

KEY TERMS

 LO 1 **supply chain** the connected chain of all of the business entities, both internal and external to the company, that perform or support the logistics function

supply chain management a management system that coordinates and integrates all of the activities performed by supply chain members into a seamless process, from the source to the point of consumption, resulting in enhanced customer and economic value

 LO 2 **supply chain integration** when multiple firms in a supply chain coordinate their activities and processes so that they are seamlessly linked to one another in an effort to satisfy the customer

 LO 3 **business processes** bundles of interconnected activities that stretch across firms in the supply chain

customer relationship management (CRM) process allows companies to prioritize their marketing focus on different customer groups according to each group's long-term value to the company or supply chain

customer service management process presents a multi-company, unified response system to the customer whenever complaints, concerns, questions, or comments are voiced

demand management process seeks to align supply and demand throughout the supply chain by anticipating customer requirements at each level and creating demand-related plans of action prior to actual customer purchasing behavior

KEY CONCEPTS

 LO 1 **Define the terms *supply chain* and *supply chain management*, and discuss the benefits of supply chain management.** Management coordinates and integrates all of the activities performed by supply chain members into a seamless process from the source to the point of consumption. The benefits of supply chain management include reduced costs in inventory management, transportation, warehousing, and packaging; improved service; and enhanced revenues.

 LO 2 **Discuss the concept of supply chain integration, and explain why each of the six types of integration is important.** The six types of integration are as follows: (1) Relationship integration is the ability of two or more firms to develop tight social connections among their employees, resulting in smoother personal interactions. (2) Measurement integration is the idea that performance assessments should be transparent and similar across all the supply chain members. (3) Technology and planning integration refers to the creation and maintenance of information technology systems that connect managers throughout the supply chain. (4) Material and service supplier integration reflects a focus on integrating processes and functions with those who provide the company with the goods and services it needs to execute its core functions. (5) Internal operations integration is the development of capabilities for the firm's internal functional areas to communicate and work together on processes and projects. (6) Customer integration implies that firms evaluate their own capabilities and use them to offer long-lasting, distinctive, value-added offerings in ways that best serve their customers.

 LO 3 **Identify the eight key processes of excellent supply chain management, and discuss how each of these processes affects the end customer.** The key processes that leading supply chain companies focus on are (1) customer relationship management, (2) customer service management, (3) demand management, (4) order fulfillment, (5) manufacturing flow management, (6) supplier relationship management, (7) product development and commercialization, and (8) returns management. When firms practice excellent supply chain management, each of these processes is integrated from end to end in the supply chain. These processes are made up of bundles of interconnected activities that supply chain partners are constantly focused on when delivering value to the customer.

 LO 4 **Discuss the key strategic decisions supply chain managers must make when designing their companies' supply chains.** The logistics supply chain consists of several interrelated and integrated logistical components: (1) sourcing and procurement of raw materials and supplies, (2) production scheduling, (3) order processing, (4) inventory control, (5) warehousing and materials handling, and (6) transportation. The logistics information system integrates and links all of the logistics functions of the supply chain. The supply chain team, in concert with the logistics information system, orchestrates the movement of goods, services, and information from the source to the consumer. Supply chain teams typically cut across organizational boundaries, embracing all parties who participate in moving product to market. Procurement is the purchase of raw materials, supplies, and components according

© 2013 Cengage Learning. All Rights Reserved. May not be scanned, copied or duplicated, or posted to a publicly accessible website, in whole or in part.

order fulfillment process a highly integrated process, often requiring persons from multiple companies and multiple functions to come together and coordinate to create customer satisfaction at a given place and time

manufacturing flow management process concerned with ensuring that firms in the supply chain have the needed resources to manufacture with flexibility and to move products through a multi-stage production process

supplier relationship management process supports manufacturing flow by identifying and maintaining relationships with highly valued suppliers

product development and commercialization process includes the group of activities that facilitates the joint development and marketing of new offerings among a group of supply chain partner firms

returns management process enables firms to manage volumes of returned product efficiently while minimizing returns-related costs and maximizing the value of the returned assets to the firms in the supply chain

 logistics the process of strategically managing the efficient flow and storage of raw materials, in-process inventory, and finished goods from point of origin to point of consumption

logistics information system the link that connects all the logistics functions of the supply chain

supply chain team an entire group of individuals who orchestrate the movement of goods, services, and information from the source to the consumer

mass customization (build-to-order) a production method whereby products are not made until an order is placed by the customer; products are made according to customer specifications

to production scheduling. Order processing monitors the flow of goods, and inventory control systems regulate when and how much to buy. Warehousing provides storage of goods until needed by the customer, while the materials-handling system moves inventory into, within, and out of the warehouse. Finally, the major modes of transportation include railroads, motor carriers, pipelines, waterways, and airways.

LO 5 Discuss new technology and emerging trends in supply chain management. Several emerging trends are changing the job of today's supply chain manager. Technology and automation are bringing up-to-date distribution information to the decision-maker's desk. Technology is also linking suppliers, buyers, and carriers for joint decision making, and it has created a new electronic distribution channel. Many companies are saving money and time by outsourcing to third-party carriers to handle some or all aspects of the distribution process.

just-in-time production (JIT) a process that redefines and simplifies manufacturing by reducing inventory levels and delivering raw materials at the precise time they are needed on the production line

order processing system a system whereby orders are entered into the supply chain and filled

electronic data interchange (EDI) information technology that replaces the paper documents that usually accompany business transactions, such as purchase orders and invoices, with electronic transmission of the needed information to reduce inventory levels, improve cash flow, streamline operations, and increase the speed and accuracy of information transmission

inventory control system a method of developing and maintaining an adequate assortment of materials or products to meet a manufacturer's or a customer's demand

materials requirement planning (MRP; materials management) an inventory control system that manages the replenishment of raw materials, supplies, and components from the supplier to the manufacturer

distribution resource planning (DRP) an inventory control system that manages the replenishment of goods from the manufacturer to the final consumer

automatic replenishment program a real-time inventory system that triggers shipments only when a good is sold to the end user

materials-handling system a method of moving inventory into, within, and out of the warehouse

 outsourcing (contract logistics) a manufacturer's or supplier's use of an independent third party to manage an entire function of the logistics system, such as transportation, warehousing, or order processing

electronic distribution a distribution technique that includes any kind of product or service that can be distributed electronically, whether over traditional forms such as fiber-optic cable or through satellite transmission of electronic signals

15 CHAPTER REV
Retailing

KEY TERMS

 retailing all the activities directly related to the sale of goods and services to the ultimate consumer for personal, nonbusiness use

 independent retailer a retailer owned by a single person or partnership and not operated as part of a larger retail institution

chain store a store that is part of a group of the same stores owned and operated by a single organization

franchise the right to operate a business or to sell a product

gross margin the amount of money the retailer makes as a percentage of sales after the cost of goods sold is subtracted

 department store a store housing several departments under one roof

buyer a department head who selects the merchandise for his or her department and may also be responsible for promotion and personnel

specialty store a retail store specializing in a given type of merchandise

supermarket a large, departmentalized, self-service retailer that specializes in food and some nonfood items

scrambled merchandising the tendency to offer a wide variety of nontraditional goods and services under one roof

drugstore a retail store that stocks pharmacy-related products and services as its main draw

convenience store a miniature supermarket, carrying only a limited line of high-turnover convenience goods

KEY CONCEPTS

 Discuss the importance of retailing in the U.S. economy. Retailing plays a vital role in the U.S. economy for two main reasons. First, retail businesses

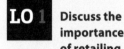

contribute to our high standard of living by providing a vast and diverse number of goods and services. Second, retailing employs a large part of the U.S. working population—more than 15 million people.

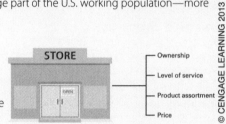 **Explain the dimensions by which retailers can be classified.** Many different kinds of retailers exist. A retail establishment can be classified according to its ownership, level of service, product assortment, and price. On the basis of ownership, retailers can be broadly differentiated as independent retailers, chain stores, or franchise outlets. The level of service retailers provide can be classified along a continuum from high to low. Retailers also classify themselves by the breadth and depth of their product assortments; some retailers have concentrated product assortments, whereas others have extensive product assortments. Finally, stores are also classified by general price levels from discounters offering low prices to exclusive specialty stores where high prices are the norm. Retailers use the latter three variables to position themselves in the marketplace.

 Describe the major types of retail operations. The major types of retail stores are department stores, specialty stores, supermarkets, drugstores, convenience stores, discount stores, and restaurants. *Department stores* carry a wide assortment of shopping and specialty goods, are organized into relatively independent departments, and offset higher prices by emphasizing customer service and decor. *Specialty stores* typically carry a narrower but deeper assortment of merchandise, emphasizing distinctive products and a high level of customer service. *Supermarkets* are large self-service retailers that offer a wide variety of food products and some nonfood items. *Drugstores* are retail formats that sell mostly prescription and over-the-counter medications, health and beauty aids, cosmetics, and specialty items. *Convenience stores* carry a limited line of high-turnover convenience goods. *Discount stores* offer low-priced general merchandise and consist of four types: full-line discounters, specialty discount retailers, warehouse clubs, and off-price retailers. Finally, *restaurants* straddle the line between the retailing and services industries; although restaurants sell a product—food and drink—to final consumers, they can also be considered service marketers because they provide consumers with the service of preparing food and providing table service.

© 2013 Cengage Learning. All Rights Reserved. May not be scanned, copied or duplicated, or posted to a publicly accessible website, in whole or in part.

© CENGAGE LEARNING 2013

discount store a retailer that competes on the basis of low prices, high turnover, and high volume

full-line discount store a retailer that offers consumers very limited service and carries a broad assortment of well-known, nationally branded "hard goods"

mass merchandising a retailing strategy using moderate to low prices on large quantities of merchandise and lower levels of service to stimulate high turnover of products

supercenter a retail store that combines groceries and general merchandise goods with a wide range of services

specialty discount store a retail store that offers a nearly complete selection of single-line merchandise and uses self-service, discount prices, high volume, and high turnover

category killer a specialty discount store that heavily dominates its narrow merchandise segment

warehouse membership club a limited-service merchant wholesaler that sells a limited selection of brand name appliances, household items, and groceries on a cash-and-carry basis to members, usually small businesses and groups

off-price retailer a retailer that sells at prices 25 percent or more below traditional department store prices because it pays cash for its stock and usually doesn't ask for return privileges

factory outlet an off-price retailer that is owned and operated by a manufacturer

 nonstore retailing shopping without visiting a store

automatic vending the use of machines to offer goods for sale

direct retailing the selling of products by representatives who work door-to-door, office-to-office, or at home sales parties

direct marketing (direct response marketing) techniques used to get consumers to make a purchase from their home, office, or other nonretail setting

 Discuss nonstore retailing techniques. Nonstore retailing, which is shopping outside a store setting, has four major categories. *Automatic vending* uses machines to offer products for sale. In *direct retailing*, the sales transaction occurs in a home setting, typically through door-to-door sales or party plan selling. *Direct marketing* refers to the techniques used to get consumers to buy from their homes or place of business. Those techniques include telemarketing, direct mail, and catalogs and mail order. *Electronic retailing* includes online retailing and 24-hour, shop-at-home television networks.

LO 5 Define *franchising* and describe its two basic forms. Franchising is a continuing relationship in which a franchiser grants to a franchisee the business rights to operate or to sell a product. Modern franchising takes two basic forms. In *product and trade name franchising*, a dealer agrees to buy or sell certain products or product lines from a particular manufacturer or wholesaler. *Business format franchising* is an ongoing business relationship in which a franchisee uses a franchiser's name, format, or method of business in return for several types of fees.

LO 6 List the major tasks involved in developing a retail marketing strategy. Retail management begins with defining the target market, typically on the basis of demographic, geographic, or psychographic characteristics. After determining the target market, retail managers must develop the six variables of the retailing mix: product, place, promotion, price, presentation, and personnel.

LO 7 Describe new developments in retailing. Two major trends are evident in retailing today. First, adding *interactivity* to the retail environment is one of the most popular strategies in retailing in recent years. Small retailers as well as national chains are using interactivity to involve customers and set themselves apart from the competition. Second, *m-commerce* (mobile e-commerce) is gaining in popularity. M-commerce enables consumers to purchase goods and services using wireless mobile devices, such as mobile telephones, pagers, PDAs, and handheld computers.

PRODUCT Width and depth of product assortment
PLACE Location and hours
PROMOTION Advertising, publicity, public relations
PRICE
PRESENTATION Layout and atmosphere
PERSONNEL Customer service and personal selling
TARGET
© CENGAGE LEARNING 2013

telemarketing the use of the telephone to sell directly to consumers

online retailing a type of shopping available to consumers with personal computers and access to the Internet

 franchisor the originator of a trade name, product, methods of operation, and the like that grants operating rights to another party to sell its product

franchisee an individual or business that is granted the right to sell another party's product

 retailing mix a combination of the six Ps—product, place, promotion, price, presentation, and personnel—to sell goods and services to the ultimate consumer

product offering the mix of products offered to the consumer by the retailer; also called the *product assortment* or *merchandise mix*

destination store a store that consumers purposely plan to visit

atmosphere the overall impression conveyed by a store's physical layout, decor, and surroundings

KEY TERMS

 LO 1

promotion communication by marketers that informs, persuades, and reminds potential buyers of a product in order to influence an opinion or elicit a response

promotional strategy a plan for the optimal use of the elements of promotion: advertising, public relations, personal selling, sales promotion, and social media

competitive advantage one or more unique aspects of an organization that cause target consumers to patronize that firm rather than competitors

 LO 2

communication the process by which we exchange or share meaning through a common set of symbols

interpersonal communication direct, face-to-face communication between two or more people

mass communication the communication of a concept or message to large audiences

sender the originator of the message in the communication process

encoding the conversion of a sender's ideas and thoughts into a message, usually in the form of words or signs

channel a medium of communication—such as a voice, radio, or newspaper—for transmitting a message

noise anything that interferes with, distorts, or slows down the transmission of information

receiver the person who decodes a message

decoding interpretation of the language and symbols sent by the source through a channel

feedback the receiver's response to a message

KEY CONCEPTS

 LO 1

Discuss the role of promotion in the marketing mix. Promotional strategy is the plan for using the elements of promotion—advertising, public relations, sales promotion, personal selling, and social media—to meet the firm's overall objectives and marketing goals. Based on these objectives, the elements of the promotional strategy become a coordinated promotion plan. The promotion plan then becomes an integral part of the total marketing strategy for reaching the target market along with product, distribution, and price.

 LO 2

Describe the communication process. The communication process has several steps. When an individual or organization has a message it wishes to convey to a target audience, it encodes that message using language and symbols familiar to the intended receiver and sends the message through a channel of communication. Noise in the transmission channel distorts the source's intended message. Reception occurs if the message falls within the receiver's frame of reference. The receiver decodes the message and usually provides feedback to the source. Normally, feedback is direct for interpersonal communication and indirect for mass communication.

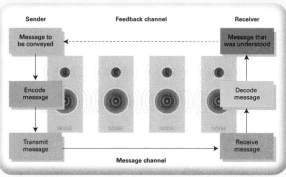

© CENGAGE LEARNING 2013

 LO 3

Explain the goals and tasks of promotion. The fundamental goals of promotion are to induce, modify, or reinforce behavior by informing, persuading, and reminding. *Informative promotion* explains a good's or service's purpose and benefits. Promotion that informs the consumer is typically used to increase demand for a general product category or to introduce a new good or service. *Persuasive promotion* is designed to stimulate a purchase or an action. Promotion that persuades the consumer to buy is essential during the growth stage of the product life cycle, when competition becomes fierce. *Reminder promotion* is used to keep the product and brand name in the public's mind. Promotions that remind are generally used during the maturity stage of the product life cycle.

LO 4

Discuss the elements of the promotional mix. The elements of the promotional mix include advertising, public relations, sales promotion, personal selling, and social media. *Advertising* is a form of impersonal, one-way mass communication paid for by the source. *Public relations* is the function of promotion concerned with a firm's public image. *Sales promotion* is typically used to back up other components of the promotional mix by stimulating immediate demand. *Personal selling* typically involves direct communication, in person or by telephone; the seller tries to initiate a purchase by informing and persuading one or more potential buyers. Finally, *social media* are promotion tools used to facilitate conversations among people online.

© 2013 Cengage Learning. All Rights Reserved. May not be scanned, copied or duplicated, or posted to a publicly accessible website, in whole or in part.

LO 4 **promotional mix** the combination of promotional tools—including advertising, public relations, personal selling, sales promotion, and social media—used to reach the target market and fulfill the organization's overall goals

advertising impersonal, one-way mass communication about a product or organization that is paid for by a marketer

public relations the marketing function that evaluates public attitudes, identifies areas within the organization the public may be interested in, and executes a program of action to earn public understanding and acceptance

publicity public information about a company, product, service, or issue appearing in the mass media as a news item

sales promotion marketing activities—other than personal selling, advertising, and public relations—that stimulate consumer buying and dealer effectiveness

personal selling a purchase situation involving a personal, paid-for communication between two people in an attempt to influence each other

LO 5 **AIDA concept** a model that outlines the process for achieving promotional goals in terms of stages of consumer involvement with the message; the acronym stands for attention, interest, desire, and action

 integrated marketing communications (IMC) the careful coordination of all promotional messages for a product or a service to ensure the consistency of messages at every contact point at which a company meets the consumer

 push strategy a marketing strategy that uses aggressive personal selling and trade advertising to convince a wholesaler or a retailer to carry and sell particular merchandise

pull strategy a marketing strategy that stimulates consumer demand to obtain product distribution

LO 5 **Discuss the AIDA concept and its relationship to the promotional mix.** The AIDA model outlines the four basic stages in the purchase decision-making process, which are initiated and propelled by promotional activities: (1) attention, (2) interest, (3) desire, and (4) action. The components of the promotional mix have varying levels of influence at each stage of the AIDA model. Advertising is a good tool for increasing awareness and knowledge of a good or service. Sales promotion is effective when consumers are at the purchase stage of the decision-making process. Personal selling is most effective in developing customer interest and desire.

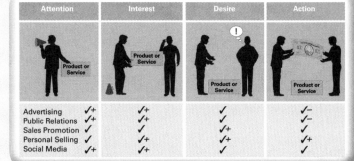

© CENGAGE LEARNING 2013

LO 6 **Discuss the concept of integrated marketing communications.** Integrated marketing communications is the careful coordination of all promotional messages for a product or service to ensure the consistency of messages at every contact point where a company meets the consumer—advertising, sales promotion, personal selling, public relations, and social media, as well as direct marketing, packaging, and other forms of communication. Marketing managers carefully coordinate all promotional activities to ensure that consumers see and hear one message. Integrated marketing communications has received more attention in recent years due to the proliferation of media choices, the fragmentation of mass markets into more segmented niches, and the decrease in advertising spending in favor of promotional techniques that generate an immediate sales response.

LO 7 **Describe the factors that affect the promotional mix.** Promotion managers consider many factors when creating promotional mixes. These factors include the nature of the product, product life-cycle stage, target market characteristics, the type of buying decision involved, availability of funds, and feasibility of push or pull strategies. As products move through different stages of the product life cycle, marketers will choose to use different promotional elements. Characteristics of the target market, such as geographic location of potential buyers and brand loyalty, influence the promotional mix as does whether the buying decision is complex or routine. The amount of funds a firm has to allocate to promotion may also help determine the promotional mix. Last, if a firm uses a push strategy to promote the product or service, the marketing manager might choose to use aggressive advertising and personal selling to wholesalers and retailers. If a pull strategy is chosen, then the manager often relies on aggressive mass promotion, such as advertising and sales promotion, to stimulate consumer demand.

© CENGAGE LEARNING 2013

Advertising and Public Relations

KEY TERMS

LO 1

advertising response function a phenomenon in which spending for advertising and sales promotion increases sales or market share up to a certain level but then produces diminishing returns

LO 2

institutional advertising a form of advertising designed to enhance a company's image rather than promote a particular product

product advertising a form of advertising that touts the benefits of a specific good or service

advocacy advertising a form of advertising in which an organization expresses its views on controversial issues or responds to media attacks

pioneering advertising a form of advertising designed to stimulate primary demand for a new product or product category

competitive advertising a form of advertising designed to influence demand for a specific brand

comparative advertising a form of advertising that compares two or more specifically named or shown competing brands on one or more specific attributes

LO 3

advertising campaign a series of related advertisements focusing on a common theme, slogan, and set of advertising appeals

advertising objective a specific communication task that a campaign should accomplish for a specified target audience during a specified period

advertising appeal a reason for a person to buy a product

unique selling proposition a desirable, exclusive, and believable advertising appeal selected as the theme for a campaign

KEY CONCEPTS

LO 1

Discuss the effects of advertising on market share and consumers. Advertising helps marketers increase or maintain brand awareness and, subsequently, market share. Typically, more is spent to advertise new brands with a small market share than to advertise older brands. Brands with a large market share use advertising mainly to maintain their share of the market. Advertising affects consumers' daily lives as well as their purchases. Although advertising can seldom change strongly held consumer attitudes and values, it may transform a consumer's negative attitude toward a product into a positive one. Additionally, when consumers are highly loyal to a brand, they may buy more of that brand when advertising is increased. Finally, advertising can also change the importance of a brand's attributes to consumers. By emphasizing different brand attributes, advertisers can change their appeal in response to consumers' changing needs or try to achieve an advantage over competing brands.

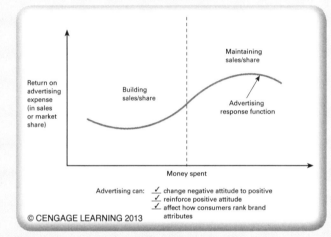

© CENGAGE LEARNING 2013

LO 2

Identify the major types of advertising. Advertising is any form of nonpersonal, paid communication in which the sponsor or company is identified. The two major types of advertising are institutional advertising and product advertising. *Institutional advertising* is not product oriented; rather, its purpose is to foster a positive company image among the general public, investment community, customers, and employees. *Product advertising* is designed mainly to promote goods and services, and it is classified into three main categories: pioneering, competitive, and comparative. A product's place in the product life cycle is a major determinant of the type of advertising used to promote it.

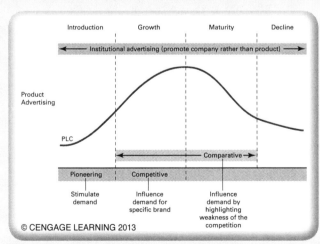

© CENGAGE LEARNING 2013

© 2013 Cengage Learning. All Rights Reserved. May not be scanned, copied or duplicated, or posted to a publicly accessible website, in whole or in part.

medium the channel used to convey a message to a target market

media planning the series of decisions advertisers make regarding the selection and use of media, allowing the marketer to optimally and cost-effectively communicate the message to the target audience

cooperative advertising an arrangement in which the manufacturer and the retailer split the costs of advertising the manufacturer's brand

infomercial a 30-minute or longer advertisement that looks more like a television talk show than a sales pitch

advergaming placing advertising messages in Web-based or video games to advertise or promote a product, service, organization, or issue

media mix the combination of media to be used for a promotional campaign

cost per contact (cost per thousand or CPM) the cost of reaching one member of the target market

cost per click the cost associated with a consumer clicking on a display or banner ad

reach the number of target consumers exposed to a commercial at least once during a specific period, usually four weeks

frequency the number of times an individual is exposed to a given message during a specific period

audience selectivity the ability of an advertising medium to reach a precisely defined market

media schedule designation of the media, the specific publications or programs, and the insertion dates of advertising

continuous media schedule a media scheduling strategy in which advertising is run steadily throughout the advertising period; used for products in the later stages of the product life cycle

flighted media schedule a media scheduling strategy in which ads are run heavily every other month or every two weeks, to achieve a greater impact with an increased frequency and reach at those times

LO 3 Discuss the creative decisions in developing an advertising campaign. Before any creative work can begin on an advertising campaign, it is important to determine what goals or objectives the advertising should achieve. The objectives of a specific advertising campaign often depend on the overall corporate objectives and the product being advertised. Once objectives are defined, creative work can begin (e.g., identifying the product's benefits, developing possible advertising appeals, evaluating and selecting the advertising appeals, executing the advertising message, and evaluating the effectiveness of the campaign).

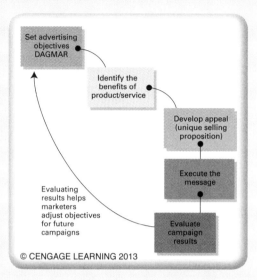

© CENGAGE LEARNING 2013

LO 4 Describe media evaluation and selection techniques. Media evaluation and selection make up a crucial step in the advertising campaign process. Major types of advertising media include newspapers, magazines, radio, television, the Internet, and outdoor media such as billboards and bus panels. Recent trends in advertising media include shopping carts, computer screen savers, DVDs, CDs, interactive kiosks, advertisements run before movies, posters on bathroom stalls, and "advertainments." Promotion managers choose the advertising campaign's media mix on the basis of the following variables: cost per contact, reach, frequency, characteristics of the target audience, flexibility of the medium, noise level, and the life span of the medium. After choosing the media mix, a media schedule designates when the advertisement will appear and the specific vehicles in which it will appear.

LO 5 Discuss the role of public relations in the promotional mix. Public relations is a vital part of a firm's promotional mix. A company fosters good publicity to enhance its image and promote its products. Popular public relations tools include new-product publicity, product placement, consumer education, sponsorship, and company Web sites. An equally important aspect of public relations is managing unfavorable publicity in a way that is least damaging to a firm's image.

pulsing media schedule a media scheduling strategy that uses continuous scheduling throughout the year coupled with a flighted schedule during the best sales periods

seasonal media schedule a media scheduling strategy that runs advertising only during times of the year when the product is most likely to be used

 product placement a public relations strategy that involves getting a product, service, or company name to appear in a movie, television show, radio program, magazine, newspaper, video game, video or audio clip, book, or commercial for another product; on the Internet; or at special events

sponsorship a public relations strategy in which a company spends money to support an issue, cause, or event that is consistent with corporate objectives, such as improving brand awareness or enhancing corporate image

crisis management a coordinated effort to handle all the effects of unfavorable publicity or another unexpected unfavorable event

KEY TERMS

LO 1

consumer sales promotion sales promotion activities targeting the ultimate consumer

trade sales promotion sales promotion activities targeting a marketing channel member, such as a wholesaler or retailer

LO 2

coupon a certificate that entitles consumers to an immediate price reduction when they buy the product

rebate a cash refund given for the purchase of a product during a specific period

premium an extra item offered to the consumer, usually in exchange for some proof of purchase of the promoted product

loyalty marketing program a promotional program designed to build long-term, mutually beneficial relationships between a company and its key customers

frequent buyer program a loyalty program in which loyal consumers are rewarded for making multiple purchases of a particular good or service

sampling a promotional program that allows the consumer the opportunity to try a product or service for free

point-of-purchase (P-O-P) display a promotional display set up at the retailer's location to build traffic, advertise the product, or induce impulse buying

LO 3

trade allowance a price reduction offered by manufacturers to intermediaries, such as wholesalers and retailers

push money money offered to channel intermediaries to encourage them to "push" products—that is, to encourage other members of the channel to sell the products

KEY CONCEPTS

LO 1 **Define and state the objectives of sales promotion.** Sales promotion consists of those marketing communication activities, other than advertising, personal selling, and public relations, in which a short-term incentive motivates consumers or members of the distribution channel to purchase a good or service immediately, either by lowering the price or by adding value. The main objectives of sales promotion are to increase trial purchases, consumer inventories, and repeat purchases. Sales promotion is also used to encourage brand switching and to build brand loyalty. Sales promotion supports advertising activities.

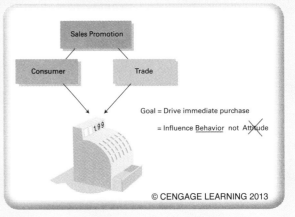

LO 2 **Discuss the most common forms of consumer sales promotion.** Common forms of consumer sales promotion include coupons and rebates, premiums, loyalty marketing programs, contests and sweepstakes, sampling, and point-of-purchase displays. *Coupons* are certificates entitling consumers to an immediate price reduction when they purchase a product or service. Coupons are a particularly good way to encourage product trial and brand switching. Similar to coupons, *rebates* provide purchasers with a price reduction, although it is not immediate. To receive a rebate, consumers generally must mail in a rebate form with a proof of purchase. *Premiums* offer an extra item or incentive to the consumer for buying a product or service. Premiums reinforce the consumer's purchase decision, increase consumption, and persuade nonusers to switch brands. Rewarding loyal customers is the basis of *loyalty marketing programs*. Loyalty programs are extremely effective at building long-term, mutually beneficial relationships between a company and its key customers. Contests and sweepstakes are generally designed to create interest, often to encourage brand switching. Because consumers perceive risk in trying new products, sampling is an effective method for gaining new customers. Finally, *point-of-purchase displays* set up at the retailer's location build traffic, advertise the product, and induce impulse buying.

© 2013 Cengage Learning. All Rights Reserved. May not be scanned, copied or duplicated, or posted to a publicly accessible website, in whole or in part.

relationship selling (consultative selling) a sales practice that involves building, maintaining, and enhancing interactions with customers in order to develop long-term satisfaction through mutually beneficial partnerships

 sales process (sales cycle) the set of steps a salesperson goes through in a particular organization to sell a particular product or service

lead generation (prospecting) identification of those firms and people most likely to buy the seller's offerings

referral a recommendation to a salesperson from a customer or business associate

networking a process of finding out about potential clients from friends, business contacts, coworkers, acquaintances, and fellow members in professional and civic organizations

cold calling a form of lead generation in which the salesperson approaches potential buyers without any prior knowledge of the prospects' needs or financial status

lead qualification determination of a sales prospect's (1) recognized need, (2) buying power, and (3) receptivity and accessibility

preapproach a process that describes the "homework" that must be done by a salesperson before he or she contacts a prospect

needs assessment a determination of the customer's specific needs and wants and the range of options the customer has for satisfying them

sales proposal a formal written document or professional presentation that outlines how the salesperson's product or service will meet or exceed the prospect's needs

sales presentation a formal meeting in which the salesperson presents a sales proposal to a prospective buyer

negotiation the process during which both the salesperson and the prospect offer special concessions in an attempt to arrive at a sales agreement

follow-up the final step of the selling process, in which the salesperson ensures delivery schedules are met, goods or services perform as promised, and the buyers' employees are properly trained to use the products

LO 3 List the most common forms of trade sales promotion. Manufacturers use many of the same sales promotion tools used in consumer promotions, such as sales contests, premiums, and point-of-purchase displays. In addition, manufacturers and channel intermediaries use several unique promotional strategies: trade allowances; push money; training; free merchandise; store demonstrations; and business meetings, conventions, and trade shows.

LO 4 Describe personal selling. Personal selling is direct communication between a sales representative and one or more prospective buyers in an attempt to influence each other in a purchase situation. Broadly speaking, all businesspeople use personal selling to promote themselves and their ideas. Personal selling offers several advantages over other forms of promotion. Personal selling allows salespeople to thoroughly explain and demonstrate a product. Salespeople have the flexibility to tailor a sales proposal to the needs and preferences of individual customers. Personal selling is more efficient than other forms of promotion because salespeople target qualified prospects and avoid wasting efforts on unlikely buyers. Personal selling affords greater managerial control over promotion costs. Finally, personal selling is the most effective method of closing a sale and producing satisfied customers.

© CENGAGE LEARNING 2013

LO 5 Discuss the key differences between relationship selling and traditional selling. *Relationship selling* is the practice of building, maintaining, and enhancing interactions with customers in order to develop long-term satisfaction through mutually beneficial partnerships. *Traditional selling*, on the other hand, is transaction focused. That is, the salesperson is most concerned with making a one-time sale and moving on to the next prospect. Salespeople practicing relationship selling spend more time understanding a prospect's needs and developing solutions to meet those needs.

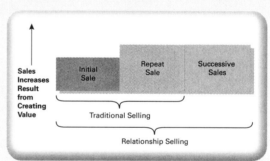

© CENGAGE LEARNING 2013

LO 6 List the steps in the selling process. The selling process is composed of seven basic steps: (1) generating leads, (2) qualifying leads, (3) approaching the customer and probing needs, (4) developing and proposing solutions, (5) handling objections, (6) closing the sale, and (7) following up.

© CENGAGE LEARNING 2013

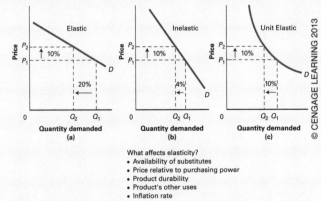

KEY TERMS

price that which is given up in an exchange to acquire a good or service

revenue the price charged to customers multiplied by the number of units sold

profit revenue minus expenses

return on investment (ROI) net profit after taxes divided by total assets

market share a company's product sales as a percentage of total sales for that industry

status quo pricing a pricing objective that maintains existing prices or meets the competition's prices

demand the quantity of a product that will be sold in the market at various prices for a specified period

supply the quantity of a product that will be offered to the market by a supplier at various prices for a specified period

price equilibrium the price at which demand and supply are equal

elasticity of demand consumers' responsiveness or sensitivity to changes in price

elastic demand a situation in which consumer demand is sensitive to changes in price

inelastic demand a situation in which an increase or a decrease in price will not significantly affect demand for the product

unitary elasticity a situation in which total revenue remains the same when prices change

KEY CONCEPTS

Discuss the importance of pricing decisions to the economy and to the individual firm. Pricing plays an integral role in the U.S. economy by allocating goods and services among consumers, governments, and businesses. Pricing is essential in business because it creates revenue, which is the basis of all business activity. In setting prices, marketing managers strive to find a level high enough to produce a satisfactory profit.

$$PRICE \times SALES\ UNITS = REVENUE$$
$$REVENUE - COSTS = PROFIT$$
$$PROFIT\ DRIVES\ GROWTH,\ SALARY\ INCREASES,\ AND\ CORPORATE\ INVESTMENT.$$

List and explain a variety of pricing objectives. Establishing realistic and measurable pricing objectives is a critical part of any firm's marketing strategy. Pricing objectives are commonly classified into three categories: profit oriented, sales oriented, and status quo. Profit-oriented pricing is based on profit maximization, a satisfactory level of profit, or a target *return on investment* (ROI). The goal of profit maximization is to generate as much revenue as possible in relation to cost. Often, a more practical approach than profit maximization is setting prices to produce profits that will satisfy management and stockholders. The most common profit-oriented strategy is pricing for a specific return on investment relative to a firm's assets. The second type of pricing objective is sales oriented, and it focuses on either maintaining a percentage share of the market or maximizing dollar or unit sales. The third type of pricing objective aims to maintain the status quo by matching competitors' prices.

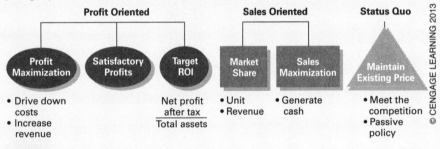

Explain the role of demand in price determination. *Demand* is a key determinant of price. When establishing prices, a firm must first determine demand for its product. A typical demand schedule shows an inverse relationship between quantity demanded and price: When price is lowered, sales increase; and when price is increased, the quantity demanded falls. For prestige products, however, there may be a direct relationship between demand and price: The quantity demanded will increase as price increases.

© 2013 Cengage Learning. All Rights Reserved. May not be scanned, copied or duplicated, or posted to a publicly accessible website, in whole or in part.

 yield management systems (YMS) a technique for adjusting prices that uses complex mathematical software to profitably fill unused capacity by discounting early purchases, limiting early sales at these discounted prices, and overbooking capacity

 variable cost a cost that varies with changes in the level of output

fixed cost a cost that does not change as output is increased or decreased

average variable cost (AVC) total variable costs divided by quantity of output

average total cost (ATC) total costs divided by quantity of output

marginal cost (MC) the change in total costs associated with a one-unit change in output

markup pricing the cost of buying the product from the producer, plus amounts for profit and for expenses not otherwise accounted for

keystoning the practice of marking up prices by 100 percent, or doubling the cost

profit maximization a method of setting prices that occurs when marginal revenue equals marginal cost

marginal revenue (MR) the extra revenue associated with selling an extra unit of output or the change in total revenue with a one-unit change in output

break-even analysis a method of determining what sales volume must be reached before total revenue equals total costs

 selling against the brand stocking well-known branded items at high prices in order to sell store brands at discounted prices

extranet a private electronic network that links a company with its suppliers and customers

prestige pricing charging a high price to help promote a high-quality image

---

Marketing managers must also consider demand elasticity when setting prices. *Elasticity of demand* is the degree to which the quantity demanded fluctuates with changes in price. If consumers are sensitive to changes in price, demand is elastic; if they are insensitive to price changes, demand is inelastic. Thus, an increase in price will result in lower sales for an elastic product and little or no loss in sales for an inelastic product.

 Understand the concept of yield management systems. *Yield management systems* use complex mathematical software to profitably fill unused capacity. The software uses techniques such as discounting early purchases, limiting early sales at these discounted prices, and overbooking capacity. These systems are used in service and retail businesses and are substantially raising revenues.

 Describe cost-oriented pricing strategies. The other major determinant of price is cost. Marketers use several cost-oriented pricing strategies. To cover their own expenses and obtain a profit, wholesalers and retailers commonly use *markup pricing:* They tack an extra amount onto the manufacturer's original price. Another pricing technique is to maximize profits by setting the price where marginal revenue equals marginal cost. Still another pricing strategy determines how much a firm must sell to break even; this amount in turn is used as a reference point for adjusting price.

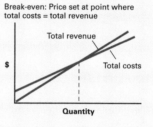
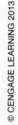

Markup: Cost + x% = Price
Profit maximization: Price set at point where MR = MC

Break-even: Price set at point where total costs = total revenue

© CENGAGE LEARNING 2013

 Demonstrate how the product life cycle, competition, distribution and promotion strategies, customer demands, the Internet and extranets, and perceptions of quality can affect price. The price of a product normally changes as it moves through the life cycle and as demand for the product and competitive conditions change. Management often sets a high price at the introductory stage, and the high price tends to attract competition. The competition usually drives prices down because individual competitors lower prices to gain market share. Adequate distribution for a new product can sometimes be obtained by offering a larger-than-usual profit margin to wholesalers and retailers. The Internet enables consumers to compare products and prices quickly and efficiently. Price is also used as a promotional tool to attract customers. Special low prices often attract new customers and entice existing customers to buy more. Large buyers can extract price concessions from vendors. Such demands can squeeze the profit margins of suppliers. Perceptions of quality can also influence pricing strategies. A firm trying to project a prestigious image often charges a premium price for a product. Consumers tend to equate high prices with high quality.

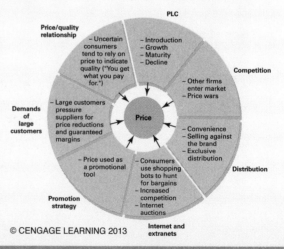

© CENGAGE LEARNING 2013

20 CHAPTER REV
Setting the Right Price

KEY TERMS

LO 1

price strategy a basic, long-term pricing framework that establishes the initial price for a product and the intended direction for price movements over the product life cycle

price skimming a pricing policy whereby a firm charges a high introductory price, often coupled with heavy promotion

penetration pricing a pricing policy whereby a firm charges a relatively low price for a product initially as a way to reach the mass market

status quo pricing charging a price identical to or very close to the competition's price

LO 2

unfair trade practice acts laws that prohibit wholesalers and retailers from selling below cost

price fixing an agreement between two or more firms on the price they will charge for a product

predatory pricing the practice of charging a very low price for a product with the intent of driving competitors out of business or out of a market

LO 3

base price the general price level at which the company expects to sell the good or service

quantity discount a price reduction offered to buyers buying in multiple units or above a specified dollar amount

cumulative quantity discount a deduction from list price that applies to the buyer's total purchases made during a specific period

KEY CONCEPTS

LO 1

Describe the procedure for setting the right price. The process of setting the right price on a product involves four major steps: (1) establishing pricing goals; (2) estimating demand, costs, and profits; (3) choosing a price policy to help determine a base price; and (4) fine-tuning the base price with pricing tactics. A price strategy establishes a long-term pricing framework for a good or service. The three main types of price policies are price skimming, penetration pricing, and status quo pricing.

LO 2

Identify the legal constraints on pricing decisions. Government regulation helps monitor four major areas of pricing: unfair trade practices, price fixing, price discrimination, and predatory pricing. Many states have enacted unfair trade practice acts that protect small businesses from large firms that operate efficiently on extremely thin profit margins; the acts prohibit charging below-cost prices. The Sherman Act and the Federal Trade Commission Act prohibit both price fixing, which is an agreement between two or more firms on a particular price, and predatory pricing, in which a firm undercuts its competitors with extremely low prices to drive them out of business. Finally, the Robinson-Patman Act makes it illegal for firms to discriminate between two or more buyers in terms of price.

LO 3

Explain how discounts, geographic pricing, and other pricing tactics can be used to fine-tune the base price. Several techniques enable marketing managers to adjust prices within a general range in response to changes in competition, government regulation, consumer demand, and promotional and positioning goals. Techniques for fine-tuning a price can be divided into three main categories: discounts, allowances, rebates, and value-based pricing; geographic pricing; and other pricing tactics.

The first type of tactic gives lower prices to those who pay promptly, order a large quantity, or perform some function for the manufacturer. Additional tactics in this category include seasonal discounts, promotion allowances, and rebates (cash refunds).

Geographic pricing tactics—such as FOB origin pricing, uniform delivered pricing, zone pricing, freight absorption pricing, and basing-point pricing—are ways of moderating the impact of shipping costs on distant customers.

A variety of "other" pricing tactics stimulate demand for certain products, increase store patronage, and offer more merchandise at specific prices.

More and more customers are paying price penalties, which are extra fees for violating the terms of a purchase contract. The perceived fairness or unfairness of a penalty may affect some consumers' willingness to patronize a business in the future.

LO 4

Discuss product line pricing. Product line pricing maximizes profits for an entire product line. When setting product line prices, marketing managers determine what type of relationship exists among the products in the line: complementary, substitute, or neutral. Managers also consider joint (shared) costs among products in the same line.

© 2013 Cengage Learning. All Rights Reserved. May not be scanned, copied or duplicated, or posted to a publicly accessible website, in whole or in part.

noncumulative quantity discount a deduction from list price that applies to a single order rather than to the total volume of orders placed during a certain period

cash discount a price reduction offered to a consumer, an industrial user, or a marketing intermediary in return for prompt payment of a bill

functional discount (trade discount) a discount to wholesalers and retailers for performing channel functions

seasonal discount a price reduction for buying merchandise out of season

promotional allowance (trade allowance) a payment to a dealer for promoting the manufacturer's products

rebate a cash refund given for the purchase of a product during a specific period

value-based pricing setting the price at a level that seems to the customer to be a good price compared to the prices of other options

FOB origin pricing a price tactic that requires the buyer to absorb the freight costs from the shipping point ("free on board")

uniform delivered pricing a price tactic in which the seller pays the actual freight charges and bills every purchaser an identical, flat freight charge

zone pricing a modification of uniform delivered pricing that divides the United States (or the total market) into segments or zones and charges a flat freight rate to all customers in a given zone

freight absorption pricing a price tactic in which the seller pays all or part of the actual freight charges and does not pass them on to the buyer

basing-point pricing a price tactic that charges freight from a given (basing) point, regardless of the city from which the goods are shipped

single-price tactic a price tactic that offers all goods and services at the same price (or perhaps two or three prices)

LO 5 Describe the role of pricing during periods of inflation and recession.
Marketing managers employ cost-oriented and demand-oriented tactics during periods of economic inflation. Cost-oriented tactics include dropping products with a low profit margin, using delayed-quotation pricing and escalator pricing, and adding fees. Demand-oriented pricing methods include price shading and increasing demand through cultivating selected customers, creating unique offerings, changing the package size, and heightening buyer dependence.

To stimulate demand during a recession, marketers use value-based pricing, bundling, and unbundling. Recessions are also a good time to prune unprofitable items from product lines. Managers strive to cut costs during recessions in order to maintain profits as revenues decline. Implementing new technology, cutting payrolls, and pressuring suppliers for reduced prices are common techniques used to cut costs.

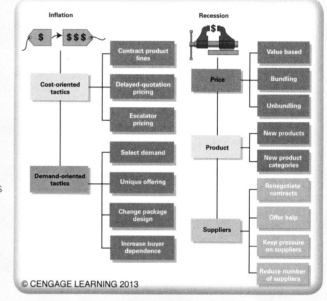

© CENGAGE LEARNING 2013

flexible pricing (variable pricing) a price tactic in which different customers pay different prices for essentially the same merchandise bought in equal quantities

price lining the practice of offering a product line with several items at specific price points

leader pricing (loss-leader pricing) a price tactic in which a product is sold near or even below cost in the hope that shoppers will buy other items once they are in the store

bait pricing a price tactic that tries to get consumers into a store through false or misleading price advertising and then uses high-pressure selling to persuade consumers to buy more expensive merchandise

odd–even pricing (psychological pricing) a price tactic that uses odd-numbered prices to connote bargains and even-numbered prices to imply quality

price bundling marketing two or more products in a single package for a special price

unbundling reducing the bundle of services that comes with the basic product

two-part pricing a price tactic that charges two separate amounts to consume a single good or service

consumer penalty an extra fee paid by the consumer for violating the terms of the purchase agreement

LO 4 product line pricing setting prices for an entire line of products

joint costs costs that are shared in the manufacturing and marketing of several products in a product line

LO 5 delayed-quotation pricing a price tactic used for industrial installations and many accessory items in which a firm price is not set until the item is either finished or delivered

escalator pricing a price tactic in which the final selling price reflects cost increases incurred between the time the order is placed and the time delivery is made

price shading the use of discounts by salespeople to increase demand for one or more products in a line

KEY TERMS

 LO 1 **customer relationship management (CRM)** a company-wide business strategy designed to optimize profitability, revenue, and customer satisfaction by focusing on highly defined and precise customer groups

 LO 2 **customer-centric** a philosophy under which the company customizes its product and service offering based on data generated through interactions between the customer and the company

learning an informal process of collecting customer data through customer comments and feedback on product or service performance

knowledge management the process by which learned information from customers is centralized and shared in order to enhance the relationship between customers and the organization

empowerment delegation of authority to solve customers' problems quickly—usually by the first person the customer notifies regarding the problem

interaction the point at which a customer and a company representative exchange information and develop learning relationships

 LO 3 **touch points** all possible areas of a business where customers communicate with that business

point-of-sale interactions communications between customers and organizations that occur at the point of sale, normally in a store

KEY CONCEPTS

 LO 1 **Define *customer relationship management.*** Customer relationship management (CRM) is a company-wide business strategy designed to optimize profitability, revenue, and customer satisfaction by focusing on highly defined and precise customer groups. This is accomplished by organizing the company around customer segments, encouraging and tracking customer interaction with the company, fostering customer-satisfying behaviors, and linking all processes of a company from its customers through its suppliers.

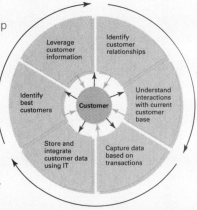

© CENGAGE LEARNING 2013

 LO 2 **Explain how to identify customer relationships with the organization.** Companies that implement a CRM system adhere to a customer-centric focus or model. A customer-centric company focuses on learning the factors that build long-lasting relationships with valuable customers and then builds its system on what satisfies and retains those customers. Building relationships through CRM is a strategic process that focuses on learning, managing customer knowledge, and empowerment.

LO 3 **Understand interactions with the current customer base.** The interaction between the customer and the organization is considered to be the foundation on which a CRM system is built. Only through effective interactions can organizations learn about the expectations of their customers, generate and manage knowledge about them, negotiate mutually satisfying commitments, and build long-term relationships. Because customers provide information to organizations across a wide variety of touch points, consumer-centric organizations are implementing new and unique approaches for establishing interactions specifically for this purpose. They include Web-based interactions, point-of-sale interactions, and social media interaction.

LO 4 **Outline the process of capturing customer data.** Based on the interaction between the organization and its customers, vast amounts of information can be obtained. Effective use of a CRM system depends on what type of data is acquired and how those data can be used effectively for relationship enhancement. The channel, transaction, and product or service consumed all constitute touch points between a customer and the organization. These touch points represent possible areas within a business where customer interactions can take place and, hence, the opportunity for acquiring data from the customer.

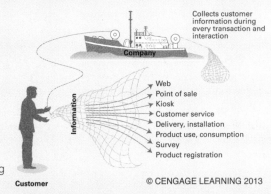

© CENGAGE LEARNING 2013

© 2013 Cengage Learning. All Rights Reserved. May not be scanned, copied or duplicated, or posted to a publicly accessible website, in whole or in part.

LO 5 **data warehouse** a central repository for data from various functional areas of the organization that are stored and inventoried on a centralized computer system so that the information can be shared across all functional departments of the business

database a collection of data, especially one that can be accessed and manipulated by computer software

response list a customer list that includes the names and addresses of individuals who have responded to an offer of some kind, such as by mail, telephone, direct response television, product rebates, contests or sweepstakes, or billing inserts

compiled list a customer list developed by gathering names and addresses from telephone directories and membership rosters, usually enhanced with information from public records, such as census data, auto registrations, birth announcements, business start-ups, or bankruptcies

 LO 6 **lifetime value analysis (LTV)** a data manipulation technique that projects the future value of the customer over a period of years using the assumption that marketing to repeat customers is more profitable than marketing to first-time buyers

predictive modeling a data manipulation technique in which marketers try to determine, based on some past set of occurrences, what the odds are that some other occurrence, such as a response or purchase, will take place in the future

 LO 7 **campaign management** developing product or service offerings customized for the appropriate customer segment and then pricing and communicating these offerings for the purpose of enhancing customer relationships

 LO 5 **Describe the use of technology to store and integrate customer data.** Customer data gathering is complicated because information needed by one unit of the organization (e.g., sales and marketing) is often generated by another area of the business or even a third-party supplier (e.g., an independent marketing research firm). Because of the lack of standard structure and interface, organizations rely on technology to capture, store, and integrate strategically important customer information. The process of centralizing data in a CRM system is referred to as data warehousing. A data warehouse is a central repository of customer information collected by an organization.

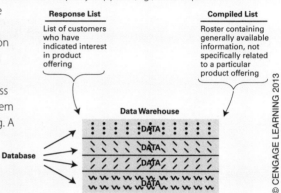

LO 6 **Describe how to identify the best customers.** As a process strategy, CRM attempts to manage the interactions between a company and its customers. To be successful, organizations must identify customers who yield high profitability or high potential profitability. To accomplish this task, significant amounts of information must be gathered from customers, stored and integrated in the data warehouse, and then analyzed for commonalities that can produce segments that are highly similar yet different from other customer segments. A useful approach to identifying the best customers is recency-frequency-monetary (RFM) analysis. Data mining uses RFM, predictive modeling, and other approaches to identify significant relationships among several customer dimensions within vast data warehouses. These significant relationships enable marketers to better define the most profitable customers and prospects.

 LO 7 **Explain the process of leveraging customer information throughout the organization.** One of the benefits of a CRM system is the capacity to share information throughout the organization. This allows an organization to interact with all functional areas to develop programs targeted to its customers. This process is commonly referred to as campaign management. Campaign management involves developing customized product/service offerings for the appropriate customer segment and pricing and communicating these offerings for the purpose of enhancing customer relationships.

Marketing Information

CRM Database

Applications

✓ Campaign management

✓ Retaining loyal customers

✓ Cross-selling other products or services

✓ Designing targeted marketing communications

✓ Reinforcing customer purchase decisions

✓ Inducing product trial by new customers

✓ Increasing effectiveness of distribution channel marketing

✓ Improving customer service

© CENGAGE LEARNING 2013

KEY TERMS

LO 1

social media any tool or service that uses the Internet to facilitate conversations

social commerce a subset of e-commerce that involves the interaction and user contribution aspects of social online media to assist online buying and selling of products and services

crowdsourcing using consumers to develop and market products

LO 2

owned media online content that an organization creates and controls

earned media a public relations term connoting free media such as mainstream media coverage

paid media content paid for by a company to be placed online

LO 5

blog a publicly accessible Web page that functions as an interactive journal, whereby readers can post comments on the author's entries

corporate blogs blogs that are sponsored by a company or one of its brands and maintained by one or more of the company's employees

noncorporate blogs independent blogs that are not associated with the marketing efforts of any particular company or brand

microblogs blogs with strict post length limits

social networking sites Web sites that allow individuals to connect—or network—with friends, peers, and business associates

media sharing sites Web sites that allow users to upload and distribute multimedia content like videos and photos

KEY CONCEPTS

LO 1

Describe social media, how they are used, and their relation to integrated marketing communications. Social media, commonly thought of as digital technology, offer a way for marketers to communicate one-on-one with consumers and measure the effects of those interactions. Social media include social networks, microblogs, and media sharing sites, all of which are used by the majority of adults. Smartphones and tablet computers have given consumers greater freedom to access social media on the go, which is likely to increase usage of social media sites. Many advertising budgets are allotting more money to online marketing, including social media, mobile marketing, and search marketing.

LO 2

Explain how to create a social media campaign. A social media campaign should take advantage of the three media categories: *owned media*, *earned media*, and *paid media*. To use these types of media in a social media campaign, first implement an effective listening system. Marketers can interact with negative feedback, make changes, and effectively manage their online presence. Paying attention to the ways that competing brands attract and engage with their customers can be particularly enlightening for both small businesses and global brands. Second, develop a list of objectives that reflects how social media dynamically communicate with customers and build relationships.

LO 3

Evaluate the various methods of measurement for social media. Hundreds of metrics have been developed to measure social media's value, but these metrics are meaningless unless they are tied to key performance indicators.

LO 4

Explain consumer behavior on social media. To effectively leverage social media, marketers must understand who uses social media and how they use it. If a brand's target market does not use social media, a social media campaign might not be useful. There are six categories of social media users: creators, critics, collectors, joiners, spectators, and inactives. A new category is emerging called "conversationalists," who post status updates on social networking sites or microblogs.

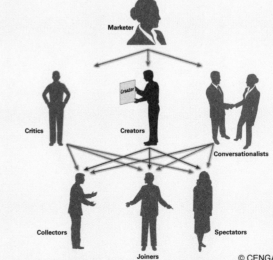

© CENGAGE LEARNING 2013

© 2013 Cengage Learning. All Rights Reserved. May not be scanned, copied or duplicated, or posted to a publicly accessible website, in whole or in part.

social news sites Web sites that allow users to decide which content is promoted on a given Web site by voting that content up or down

location-based social networking sites Web sites that combine the fun of social networking with the utility of location-based GPS technology

review sites Web sites that allow consumers to post, read, rate, and comment on opinions regarding all kinds of products and services

LO 5 Describe the social media tools in a marketer's toolbox and how they are useful. A marketer has many tools to implement a social media campaign. However, new tools emerge daily, so these resources will change rapidly. Some of the strongest social media platforms are blogs, microblogs, social networks, media creation and sharing sites, social news sites, location-based social networking sites, and virtual worlds and online gaming. Blogs allows marketers to create content in the form of posts, which ideally build trust and a sense of authenticity in customers. Microblogs, like Twitter, allow brands to follow, retweet, respond to potential customers' tweets, and tweet content that inspires customers to engage the brand, laying a foundation for meaningful two-way conversation. Social networks allow marketers to increase awareness, target audiences, promote products, forge relationships, attract event participants, perform research, and generate new business. Media sharing sites give brands an interactive channel to disseminate content. Social news sites are useful to marketers to promote campaigns, create conversations, and build Web site traffic. Location-based social networking sites can forge lasting relationships and loyalty in customers. Review sites allow marketers to respond to customer reviews and comments about their brand. Virtual worlds are fertile ground for branded content, and online gaming allows marketers to integrate their message onto a game platform.

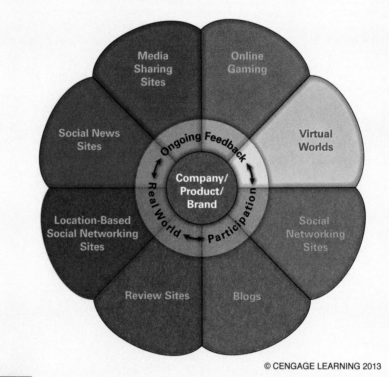

© CENGAGE LEARNING 2013

LO 6 Describe the impact of mobile technology on social media. There are five reasons for the popularity of mobile marketing: (1) mobile platforms are standardized, (2) fewer consumers are concerned about privacy and pricing policies, (3) advertising can be done in real time, (4) mobile marketing is measurable, and (5) there is a higher response rate than with traditional advertising. Because of the rapid growth of Smartphones, well-branded, integrated apps allow marketers to create buzz and generate customer engagement. Widgets allow customers to post a company's information to its site, are less expensive than apps, and broaden that company's exposure.

FEATURES, ADVANTAGES, BENEFITS

One of the most important decisions in your life is choosing a career. Not only will your career choice affect your income and lifestyle, but it also will have a major impact on your happiness and self-fulfillment.

You can use many of the basic concepts of marketing introduced in this book to get the career you want by marketing yourself. The purpose of marketing is to create exchanges that satisfy individual as well as organizational objectives, and a career is certainly an exchange situation for both you and an organization. The purpose of this appendix is to help you market yourself to prospective employers by providing some helpful tools and information.

It is important to understand what type of job will be beneficial to you in the long run. One way to look objectively at what type of job to undertake is to perform a self-analysis. These two cards contain some exercises, resources, and other guidance to performing self-analysis, and there are many other resources available to professionals.

One way to begin looking objectively at career decisions is to develop a Feature-Advantage-Benefit matrix, such as the one below.

Need of Employer	Feature of Job Applicant	Advantage of Feature	Benefit to Employer
This job requires:	I have:	This feature means that:	You will:
• Frequent sales presentations to individuals and groups.	• Taken 10 classes that required presentations.	• I require limited or no training in making presentations.	• Save on the cost of training and have an employee with the ability and confidence to be productive early.
• Knowledge of personal computers, software, and applications.	• Taken a personal computer course and used Lotus in most upper-level classes.	• I can already use Word, Excel, dBase, SAS, SPSS, and other software.	• Save time and money on training.
• A person with management potential.	• Been president of a student marketing group and social fraternity president for two years.	• I have experience leading people.	• Save time because I am capable of stepping into a leadership position as needed.

INTERVIEW SELF-ASSESSMENT

How assertive are you (or will you be) as you interview for a position? The questions in the assessment below will help you to evaluate your assertiveness.

Answer yes or no to the questions, being honest with yourself. If you have five or fewer yes answers, you still have some work to do. A good score is seven or more yes answers.

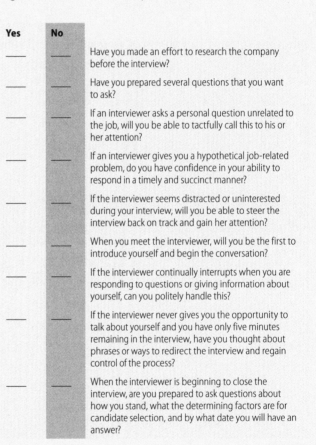

Yes	No	
___	___	Have you made an effort to research the company before the interview?
___	___	Have you prepared several questions that you want to ask?
___	___	If an interviewer asks a personal question unrelated to the job, will you be able to tactfully call this to his or her attention?
___	___	If an interviewer gives you a hypothetical job-related problem, do you have confidence in your ability to respond in a timely and succinct manner?
___	___	If the interviewer seems distracted or uninterested during your interview, will you be able to steer the interview back on track and gain her attention?
___	___	When you meet the interviewer, will you be the first to introduce yourself and begin the conversation?
___	___	If the interviewer continually interrupts when you are responding to questions or giving information about yourself, can you politely handle this?
___	___	If the interviewer never gives you the opportunity to talk about yourself and you have only five minutes remaining in the interview, have you thought about phrases or ways to redirect the interview and regain control of the process?
___	___	When the interviewer is beginning to close the interview, are you prepared to ask questions about how you stand, what the determining factors are for candidate selection, and by what date you will have an answer?

(continued)

© 2013 Cengage Learning. All Rights Reserved. May not be scanned, copied or duplicated, or posted to a publicly accessible website, in whole or in part.

SAMPLE INTERVIEW QUESTIONS

At an interview, potential employers appreciate candidates who have taken the time to consider what they would like in a position, or what they need to know about jobs that may not come up without a question. Some questions that are appropriate for job candidates to ask at an interview are:

- Where is the organization going?
- What plans or projects are being developed to maintain or increase its market share?
- Have many new product lines been decided upon recently?
- Is the sales growth in the new product line sustainable?
- Who are the people with whom I will be working? May I speak with some of them?
- May I have a copy of the job description?
- What might be a typical first assignment?
- Do you have a performance appraisal system? How is it structured?
- How frequently will I be evaluated?
- What is the potential for promotion in the organization?
- In promotions, are employees ever transferred between functional fields?
- What is the average time to get to _____ level in the career path?
- Is your policy to promote from within, or are many senior jobs filled by experienced people from outside? Do you have a job posting system?
- What type of training will I receive? When does the training program begin? Is it possible to move through your program faster?
- About how many individuals go through your internship program?
- What is the normal routine of a (an) _____ like? Can I progress at my own pace, or is it structured?
- Do employees normally work overtime?
- How much travel is normally expected? Is a car provided to traveling personnel?
- How much freedom is given to new people? How much discipline is required?
- How much input does a new person have?
- How much decision-making authority is given to new personnel?
- How frequently do you relocate employees? Is it possible to transfer from one division to another?
- What is the housing market for a single person in _____ (city)? Is public transportation adequate?
- How much contact with and exposure to management is there?
- How soon should I expect to report to work?

SOME AVAILABLE MARKETING CAREERS

- Sales
- Public Relations
- Retailing
- Advertising
- Marketing Management
- Marketing Research
- Product Management
- Product Development
- Brand Management
- Event Planning
- Customer Service
- Social Media Marketing

HELPFUL WEB SITES FOR JOB SEARCHES AND RÉSUMÉ WRITING

- www.monster.com
- DirectEmployer.com
- www.careerbuilder.com
- www.provenresumes.com
- www.careerjournal.com

© ISTOCKPHOTO.COM/DAN WILTON

FREQUENTLY ASKED INTERVIEW QUESTIONS

Thinking of the questions a potential employer may ask at an interview is a great way to prepare. By evaluating questions based on skills, your mind will be able to easily recall and adjust to questions in an interview. Showing a potential employer the ability to quickly respond to questions demonstrates calm under pressure and the time taken to prepare. This card has an extensive list of frequently asked questions at interviews.

- Of the jobs you've had to date, which one did you like best? Why?
- Why do you want to work for our company?
- Tell me what you know about our company.
- Do any of your relatives or friends work for our company? If so, in what jobs?
- Tell me about yourself, your strengths, weaknesses, career goals, and so forth.
- Is any member of your family a professional marketer? If so, what area of marketing?
- Why do you want to start your career in marketing?
- Persuade me that we should hire you.
- In what extracurricular activities did you participate in at college? What leadership positions did you have in any of these activities?
- What benefits have you derived from participation in extracurricular activities that will help you in your career?
- Where do you see yourself within our company in five years? In ten years? Twenty years?
- What is your ultimate career goal?
- What do you consider your greatest achievement to date?
- What is your biggest failure to date?
- What is (was) your favorite subject in school? Why?
- Are you willing to travel and possibly relocate?
- How would the people who know you describe you?
- How would you describe yourself?
- What do you like most about marketing?
- What do you like least about marketing?
- If we hire you, how soon could you start work?
- What is the minimum we would have to offer you to work with us?
- What goals have you set for yourself? How are you planning to achieve them?
- Who or what has had the greatest influence on the development of your career interests?
- What factors did you consider in choosing your major?
- Why are you interested in our organization?
- What can you tell me about yourself?
- What two or three things are most important to you in a position?
- What kind of work do you want to do?
- What can you tell me about a project you initiated?
- What are your expectations of your future employer?
- What is your GPA? How do you feel about it? Does it reflect your ability?
- How do you resolve conflicts?

- What do you feel are your strengths? Your weaknesses? How do you evaluate yourself?
- What work experience has been the most valuable to you and why?
- What was the most useful criticism you ever received, and who was it from?
- Can you give an example of a problem you have solved and the process you used?
- Can you describe the project or situation that best demonstrates your analytical skills?
- What has been your greatest challenge?
- Can you describe a situation where you had a conflict with another individual and explain how you dealt with it?
- What are the biggest problems you encountered in college? How did you handle them? What did you learn from them?
- What are your team-player qualities? Give examples.
- Can you describe your leadership style?
- What interests or concerns you about the position or the company?
- In a particular leadership role you had, what was the greatest challenge?
- What idea have you developed and implemented that was particularly creative or innovative?
- What characteristics do you think are important for this position?
- How have your educational and work experiences prepared you for this position?
- Can you take me through a project where you demonstrated skills?
- How do you think you have changed personally since you started college?
- Can you tell me about a team project that you are particularly proud of and discuss your contribution?
- How do you motivate people?
- Why did you choose the extracurricular activities you did? What did you gain? What did you contribute?
- What types of situations put you under pressure, and how do you deal with the pressure?
- Can you tell me about a difficult decision you have made?
- Can you give an example of a situation in which you failed and explain how you handled it?
- Can you tell me about a situation when you had to persuade another person of your point of view?
- What frustrates you the most?
- Knowing what you know now about your college experience, would you make the same decisions?
- What can you contribute to this company?
- How would you react to having your credibility questioned?
- What characteristics are important in a good manager? How have you displayed one of these characteristics?
- What challenges are you looking for in a position?
- What two or three accomplishments have given you the most satisfaction?
- Can you describe a leadership role of yours and tell why you committed your time to it?
- How are you conducting your job search, and how will you make your decision?
- What is the most important lesson you have learned in or out of school?
- Can you describe a situation where you had to work with someone who was difficult? How was the person difficult, and how did you handle it?

(continued)

© 2013 Cengage Learning. All Rights Reserved. May not be scanned, copied or duplicated, or posted to a publicly accessible website, in whole or in part.

- We are looking at a lot of great candidates; why are you the best person for this position?
- How would your friends describe you? Your professors?
- What else should I know about you?

HOW TO ACT DURING AN INTERVIEW

- Think positive. Be enthusiastic, interested, knowledgeable, and confident.
- Take few notes. It is acceptable to take notes during the interview, but limit them to things that are essential to remember. You want to focus more on listening and observing rather than writing.
- Relate to the interviewer. Build positive rapport with the interviewer. Listen and observe; relate yourself to the employer or position.
- Watch your body language. Be aware of nervousness (fidgeting, shaking leg, tapping, etc.). Project confidence (eye contact, firm handshake, upright posture).
- Be aware of the questions the employer asks. Answer with information relevant to the position. Provide a direct answer; avoid being long-winded.
- Think about the questions you ask. They should indicate that you know something about the job. Avoid questions that could easily be answered elsewhere through research. Obtain information you need to know to be satisfied with the job (interviewing is a two-way process). Salary and benefit questions should be asked after the job is offered.
- Achieve effective closure. Ask when the employer expects to make a decision. Restate your interest and ability to perform the job. Show confidence and enthusiasm (smile, end with a firm handshake). Obtain the employer's business card, if possible (it may be useful when writing a thank-you letter).

RECAP: Preparing for an Interview

- PRACTICE
  - Questions you may be asked
  - Questions you want to ask about the position and organization
  - Role-playing an interview
- SELF-ASSESSMENT
  - Goals
  - Skills, abilities, accomplishments
  - Work values (important factors you look for in a job)
  - Experiences
  - Personality
- RESEARCH
  - Obtain company literature
  - Write or visit the organization
  - Talk to people familiar with the organization
- OBTAIN REFERENCES
- PLAN AHEAD
  - Attire to be worn to the interview
  - Directions to the interview site
  - Time of arrival (get there with at least 5–10 minutes to spare)

© THINKSTOCK IMAGES/JUPITERIMAGES